The Voices of the Consul

The Rhetorics of Cicero's de lege agraria I *and* II

BRIAN A. KROSTENKO

OXFORD
UNIVERSITY PRESS

OXFORD
UNIVERSITY PRESS

Oxford University Press is a department of the University of Oxford. It furthers
the University's objective of excellence in research, scholarship, and education
by publishing worldwide. Oxford is a registered trade mark of Oxford University
Press in the UK and certain other countries.

Published in the United States of America by Oxford University Press
198 Madison Avenue, New York, NY 10016, United States of America.

© Oxford University Press 2023

All rights reserved. No part of this publication may be reproduced, stored in
a retrieval system, or transmitted, in any form or by any means, without the
prior permission in writing of Oxford University Press, or as expressly permitted
by law, by license, or under terms agreed with the appropriate reproduction
rights organization. Inquiries concerning reproduction outside the scope of the
above should be sent to the Rights Department, Oxford University Press, at the
address above.

You must not circulate this work in any other form
and you must impose this same condition on any acquirer.

Library of Congress Cataloging-in-Publication Data
Names: Krostenko, Brian A., author.
Title: The voices of the consul : the rhetorics of Cicero's De lege agraria
I and II / B.A. Krostenko.
Description: New York, NY : Oxford University Press, 2023. | Includes
bibliographical references and index.
Identifiers: LCCN 2023007378 (print) | LCCN 2023007379 (ebook) |
ISBN 9780199734207 (hardback) | ISBN 9780197695265 (epub) |
ISBN 9780197695272 | ISBN 9780199838134
Subjects: LCSH: Cicero, Marcus Tullius. De lege agraria. |
Rhetoric, Ancient.
Classification: LCC PA6279.A8 K76 2018 (print) | LCC PA6279.A8 (ebook) |
DDC 875/.01—dc23/eng/20230506
LC record available at https://lccn.loc.gov/2023007378
LC ebook record available at https://lccn.loc.gov/2023007379

DOI: 10.1093/oso/9780199734207.001.0001

Printed by Integrated Books International, United States of America

*Aleksandrze i Anastazji
ukochanym córkom*

Contents

Acknowledgments — ix

Foreword — xi

Abbreviations — xix

1. The Rhetoric and Politics of *de lege agraria I & II* — 1
2. Anxiety and Responsibility — 38
3. Responsibility and Anxiety — 65
4. *Libertas* and the Duty of Oversight — 98
5. *Commodum* and the Fear of Exclusion — 141
6. Ideologies of Identity: Cicero and Rullus — 179
7. Images of Identity: Pompey, Rullus, and Cicero — 212
8. *Dignitas* — 246
9. Two Views of Capua and the *ager Campanus* — 287

Appendix 1. Table of Major Divisions — 319

Appendix 2. The Rhetorical Structure of the Treatments of Capua and the ager Campanus — 323

Appendix 3. The Rhetorical Structure of the Treatment of the Placement of Colonies — 345

Works Cited — 349

Index — 369

Acknowledgments

IT IS A pleasure to acknowledge the many debts I have incurred in the writing of this book. The first and foremost are to the National Endowment for the Humanities, which sponsored a year of leave in 2001–2002, and to the National Humanities Center (NHC), where I spent that leave and where the work that became this book was begun. At the NHC I gratefully acknowledge the unflagging support, assistance, and interest of the then-director, W. R. Connor, and all the staff, especially Joel Elliott, Jean Houston, Kent Mullikin, Lynwood Parish, Eliza Robertson, and above all Corbett Capps.

In a field with a small and well-worked canon, the judgment and interest of others are important. I am also indebted to the faculties and students at universities at which I delivered talks that later became sections of this book: the University of North Carolina at Greensboro; the University of Tennessee, Knoxville; Harvard University; the State University of New York at Buffalo; the University of Washington; the University of Texas at Austin; Hillsdale College; Vanderbilt University; Wabash College; the Institute of History at the University of Warsaw; and John Paul II Catholic University of Lublin. At all of these schools I enjoyed receptive and interested audiences, each of which enabled me to learn something different and helpful about the project. I am especially grateful for conversations on several of those occasions with Christopher Craig, John Dugan, and Andrew Riggsby. It was an enriching experience to present part of the work at a conference in Kraków on the linguistic representations of identity in rhetorics ancient and modern, and I thank the organizers, Peter Agocs, Joanna Janik, and especially Jakub Filonik.

I owe a particular debt of gratitude to colleagues in Poland during two years spent there as a visiting scholar. Łukasz Niesiołowski-Spanò and Marek Węcowski of the Zakład Historii Starożytnej in the Instytut Historycyzny at the University of Warsaw and Jacek Soszyński of the Instytut Historii Nauki Polskiej Akademii Nauk, im. Ludwika i Aleksandra Birkenmajerów, Warsaw, provided invaluable aid of every kind and, more than that, camaraderie and friendship, intellectual and otherwise.

At Notre Dame I have many debts. The first are to the colleagues who were members of writing groups and reviewed chapters or portions of chapters and talked through outlines and approaches—Christopher Baron, Hildegund Müller, Denis Robichaud, Robert Goulding, and especially Margaret Meserve. The book took its final shape in independent studies with two students, Jim Wismer and Brendan Coyne, whose keen insights into matters of language, power, politics, and rhetoric are important to that shape. The book benefited from many conversations with Martin Bloomer about time, memory, and the construction of persona in Roman rhetorical culture and with Sarah Stroup about the poetics of prose and the cultural moment of the late Republic. Last and most important, I owe a debt to my research assistant, Hannah VanSyckel, whose keen eye and mind greatly improved the format and content of every chapter. None of these students and colleagues is to be charged with the flights of fancy or errors of fact that doubtless remain.

It has been a pleasure to work with the staff at Oxford University Press. I gratefully acknowledge the support, interest—and patience—of Stefan Vranka and the careful attention of Chelsea Hogue, Bala Subramanian, and Bríd Nowlan. I am grateful to Jack Oster for assistance in compiling the index.

These have not been years when it was pleasant to contemplate rhetoric, populism, republicanism, and citizenship. The path was made easier by lively conversations with my family—my wife Joan and our daughters Aleksandra and Anastazja—and, more important, by their support, patience, understanding, and love.

Foreword

ζητεῖ γὰρ [ἡ ῥητορικὴ] οὐ περὶ αὐτοῦ τοῦ δικαίου, ἀλλὰ τῶν ἐπὶ μέρους δικαίων.

[Rhetoric] isn't concerned with justice in the abstract but with what counts as just in particular cases.

—Diogenes Laertius, *Lives of Eminent Philosophers*, 3.1.55

Cicero's speeches "On the Agrarian Law" (*de lege agraria*) I and II, one to the senate and one to the people, were the first two that he gave as consul, a momentous occasion for him and, as he believed, for the Roman Republic. The animating concern of these pages is, how does the rhetoric of those two speeches work? There has been no book-length critical study addressing that question. The rhetoric has oftenest been laid to one side. Scholarly interest in the speeches, which record some features of a complex land law, has concerned mostly historical details, reading through the rhetoric or past it.[1] When the rhetoric of the speeches has been treated directly, that has typically been in the course of studies broader in one way or another. The speeches are rich in ethical and programmatic vocabulary, duly recognized in studies devoted to those topics.[2] Other, closer analyses of the rhetoric of the speeches have had broader or at least not strictly rhetorical

---

[1] "Surprisingly, in view of the potential of the second speech on the Agrarian Law for revealing something of Cicero's career-strategy, it has received *per se* very little scholarly attention.... Most comment has come from historians of the late Roman Republic and biographers of Cicero," Hopwood 2007: 73.

[2] Hellegouarc'h 1963 remains an indispensable source for the vocabulary of political groupings. Achard 1981 examines the "optimate" speeches, among which he includes *LA* 1, for their core concepts and the ideology of their programmatic vocabulary, in which *optimi cives* take a stand against *improbi*.

concerns—the intellectual debates, political practices, or economics of the time.[3] Studies which take as their point of departure the rhetoric of the speeches as such have also had broader frames of reference in view—the canons of classical rhetoric or other paired speeches of Cicero.[4]

All these approaches, by beginning from outside a speech, tend to foreground commonalities and continuities (like lexical entries describing overall groupings and trends). This book, by contrast, begins from within, from the form of these two texts themselves, and thus (like a note or commentary pointing out a distinctive usage) looks first to particularities. It doesn't plot a long arc but describes, if you like, the tangent to the curve at a certain moment. In that approach the book has two emphases—first, on allusion and not on explicitness. Any rhetor appeals to the values and sensibilities of his audience. But the appeal need not depend on naming a value or even invoking its common features directly. Rather, images and phrases and words may bring out—and manipulate and modify—an unnamed value or other such points of reference no less clearly. Such allusions provide a better lens for reading explicitly programmatic passages than the reverse; the allusions are, as it were, the practice rather than the theory. Second, this book emphasizes form over argument. That is, it looks first not at the historical accuracy or strict logical coherence of any given stretch of a speech. These criteria are not always helpful since, reliant as they are upon some notional truth external to the text (what is extrinsically true or what extrinsically "makes sense"), they draw attention away from the internal workings of the text itself, which may be powerful or suggestive even if they are unhistorical or unsound. Instead this book looks first to what the formal details of any given stretch of the speeches contribute to its meaning. Sometimes those details are easy enough to isolate as being known devices of classical rhetoric. But classical rhetorical theory has quite limited explanatory power for many aspects of language,[5] and oftener the book

---

[3]. Arena 2012 reconstructs the intellectual and philosophical background of debates on *libertas* in the late Republic, in which the second speech looms large. Morstein-Marx 2004 makes use chiefly of the second speech in a "thick description" of the practice of the open assembly or *contio*. The main focus of Jonkers 1963, a running commentary on all three speeches, is Cicero's appeals to the two audiences in light of the political economy as Jonkers envisions it. Cf. also the works cited in ch. 1 n. 76.

[4]. Classen 1985 analyzes paired passages from the agrarian speeches chiefly in terms of the figures of classical rhetoric and their communicative effect. Mack 1937 reads various paired speeches of Cicero together, arguing that the differences have chiefly to do with the different social positions of the audiences. His views are adjusted and developed in Thompson 1978.

[5]. In particular allusion, implicature, and tone of voice are under- or untheorized; the accent is on analyzable figures and effects, larger structural features, and types of argument. That is not to say that classically trained rhetoricians or poets did not appreciate implicature and the rest; their force, presumably, is one of the things they learned by rewriting the same content with

rests on uncovering, through their linguistic traces, allusions to various concepts and practices, and on recovering the implicit and shifting roles Cicero constantly scripts for himself, his opponent, and his audiences. In short the book reflects (some of) the method and emphases of functionalist approaches to language. The form of the speeches—they have almost exactly the same outline—invites exactly that kind of analysis, since corresponding passages can be set beside each other to draw out, in detail, the particularities of each, and that will be a chief feature of every chapter where such comparison is possible.

The book, in short, privileges the local over the global and the particular over the general. From such close readings will emerge, I dare to hope, not so much a map of the whole Roman psychic imaginary as a detailed snapshot of Cicero's attempt to hierarchize and arrange various of its elements at a particular moment—a Cicero not deploying tokens of fixed meaning but almost constantly renegotiating the meanings of tokens and concepts and even the basic constituents of discourse ("we" "you" "Rome") in accord with his view of the situation. That brings us from the internal dynamic of the speeches to the world without. The snapshot has something to contribute to understanding Cicero's own political life. The deep coherence of the imagery and ideas—a coherence hitherto poorly plumbed—in speeches given at the moment of Cicero's supreme political triumph, suggests, to me at any rate, someone with fairly particular hopes for (one version of) good government before the hardening conservatism that came with exile, or the urgent republicanism that came with the lapse of the state into autocracy (which makes his later speeches and writings an imperfect guide to where he stood before). He makes an agrarian law—an unusual focus for the first addresses of a newly elected consul—into a kind of allegory for what the state should not be and what he professed to hope it could be. He probes the clauses of the law, not from the point of view of the agrarian economy, but through the lens of power relations and as a way of understanding them.

And the snapshot also has something to contribute to understanding Roman political life. That life was a distinctive one, with a peculiar fusion of oligarchy and democracy and great importance placed on cultural memory, public place, and shared ritual, and its forms were being reshaped in the late Republic, signally in the increasing importance of the *contio* or open assembly. *LA* 1 and 2 engage closely with practically every major aspect of that life as few other speeches of

---

different form, in the required exercises, even if they lacked a precise framework for labeling what they had learned (though cf. Quint. *Inst.* 8.4.1 on the effects of substituting one word for another). Within ancient studies the limits of classical rhetoric have been contemplated first and most often by scholars of the New Testament, with its generically distinctive set of texts, for example in the work of Richard Horsley or Vernon Robbins.

Cicero do; for that reason a study of their rhetoric that opens up rhetorical form itself as a record of the lived reality of a political moment may hope to contribute to broader discussions of Roman political life, which has been a rich topic of discussion in recent years.[6] There is another aspect of that life that *LA* 1 and 2 also reveal. Their deep coherence and their idealisms do not mean that they do not sometimes fall into distortion and even, at times, extremism, and in that sense they reflect, in my view, not Cicero's simple resistance to populist politics and policies, as has sometimes been supposed, but the anxieties and distrust that characterize the fraught politics of the late Republic. And the agrarian law in question, in its unusual mechanisms—an unusualness often overlooked—has a certain boldness driven, in part, by that same distrust. On that view Cicero's rhetoric exposes the political difficulties of a moment at the price of feeding the political difficulties of a moment. That is not the cardinal theme of the following pages, which in accord with the book's method, concentrate on the internal dynamics of the speeches; but those difficulties will often come into view when the objectives of the proposers of the bill in a particular passage under discussion are imagined.

The chapters proceed as follows. Chapter 1, "The Rhetoric and Politics of *de lege agraria* I & II," after an introduction to the circumstances of the speech, offers a preview of the thesis, that Cicero is aiming not simply to reflect back his audiences' prejudices but to create distinctive visions of *libertas* and *dignitas*, and a preview of the method, the kind of comparison of formal details just described, which in this study relies on breaking up parallel passages into their several components, the better to isolate distinctive elements. The chapter closes with a sketch of the agrarian law that is the topic of the speeches in its political and economic context. The bill was in points creative and bold and might very well have attracted skepticism from, and prompted anxieties in, those concerned with power relations.

The next two chapters are of the same character: they illustrate chief points of method by the close comparison of corresponding passages, and they offer readings of those passages that lay the foundation for the interpretations developed by the study's end. Chapter 2, "Anxiety and Responsibility," compares, point by point, two passages that imagine abusive land commissioners abroad. The passages show how Cicero positions the senate and the people "up high" and "down low" respectively—a difference that I argue is not a simple reflection of each audience's "natural" position but a deliberate act of repositioning: a view of abuse "from above" is a reminder of how innovations can disrupt the competitive balance of the elite—a counter to the opportunism (or indifference) of (some of)

---

6. See the references in ch. 1 nn. 23 and 31.

the senate; and a troubling tableau, only visible from "down low," is a reminder of how sovereignty can be misused—a counter to the materialism of the people, eager, in hard times, to authorize a land bill for its own succor.

The passages of Chapter 2 are easy to compare point by point, since their structure is obviously identical. Chapter 3, "Responsibility and Anxiety," illustrates how passages that look quite different may also be built on identical templates—a mark of the workings of Cicero's compositional technique and an important model for subsequent chapters, where detecting shared templates makes detailed comparison possible. The passages in question, which develop the image of an auction in quite different ways, also show the importance of unlabeled allusions to cultural institutions and practices and even to the physical environment of both speeches. If the senate and people of Chapter 2 were prompted to anxiety and responsibility respectively, the two tableaux of an auction take them in opposite directions— the people to the anxiety of losing state property that the bill will wrest onto the block, the senate to the responsibility of restraining profligacy as if of a wayward child who would sell off the family patrimony. The chapter also illustrates that Cicero often inverts, rather than invokes, cardinal values, and that, too, will be an important point for remaining chapters. Thus do Chapters 2 and 3 together aim to give a picture of both of Cicero's chief techniques in the two speeches and of his cardinal objectives before each audience, which the emotional postures into which he presses them, positioning them constantly between responsibility and anxiety—that is, between what should be and what might be—capture perfectly.

The picture of the people that emerges is of a people prompted to use their *libertas* responsibly. That idea is probed in the next two chapters. Chapter 4, "*Libertas* and the Duty of Oversight," considers the appeal to *libertas* in the popular speech. Such appeals must have been common in public assemblies, but this chapter illustrates how the popular speech specially emphasizes only certain aspects of the idea: failures of procedure and breaches of what might be called the constitutional principles that underlie them. That is a narrowing of the idea of *libertas* to focus on means, and a rather small set of them, and not on the larger ends to which the exercise of liberty might lead (such as agrarian reform; the bill's proponents must also have invoked *libertas*, but focusing on objectives and not methods). The chapter lays out the workings of several passages that illustrate the corruption made possible by bad procedure. Consonant with Cicero's appeal to the principles that underlie (his view of) *libertas* is his concomitant appeal to the people's duties—and that includes, in a kind of rebuff of the most aggressive version of populist politics, cooperation with responsible magistrates. The chapter also incidentally illustrates the depth of the people's procedural knowledge and historical memory. Cicero might sometimes position the people "down low," but he does not talk down to them.

Chapter 4 raises two questions—first, what about those in the audience who didn't care about means and only cared about ends, Cicero's objections be damned? Wouldn't they acquire farmland as the bill promised? Cicero's anticipation of that response is treated in Chapter 5, "*Commodum* and the Fear of Exclusion." *Commodum*, that is, material benefit or emolument, was a chief aspect of the popular understanding of *libertas*. But the hope for benefits, by way of a kind of zero-sum logic, also came with the fear of exclusion, and Cicero stokes that fear. Pompey, the people's champion, as many of them thought, will be hampered (the agrarian bill thus does not add a new provider but instead threatens one the people already have); and above all the mechanisms of the bill, which envisaged purchase from private owners—Cicero makes the point in part through an echo of the colonization ritual—guarantee that the plots of land will be poor. Both arguments have their exaggerations, but neither is without foundation, an important point for understanding the symbolic economy of the speeches.

Chapter 4 raises another question: what is a responsible magistrate? Whom shall the people trust? Cicero's attempt to deal with that concern in the popular speech is treated in Chapter 6, "Ideologies of Identity: Cicero and Rullus." Cicero, recounting the details of his own election, does not simply draw on, but redraws the significance of, some cardinal political terms—*nobilis, popularis, otium*—in order to make himself the true embodiment of the people's will. The ideology thus created allows him to turn the unusual electoral mechanism for the land commission into proof that Rullus, the tribune who proposed the bill, is Cicero's opposite, a schemer interested in his own profit and a would-be tyrant interested in his own power—*nobilis* in the bad sense, one might say, not only a counterpoint to Cicero but a contradiction in an officer who was supposed to have the people's interests at heart. The polarity thus developed between consul and tribune is also used to assign Pompey his place in the political world: the tribune fears him, and he is a principled populist like the consul himself. These interpretations would not have been fully possible without the analysis of earlier chapters, which reveals Cicero's techniques and priorities and thus allows apparently conventional or sophistic expressions to be raised to their full significance—especially important for the early sections of the speeches, where the senate version is not extant. Chapter 7, "Images of Identity: Pompey, Rullus, and Cicero," continues the exploration of identity, not so much ideologically as in terms of rhetorical technique. The images of the three figures created in the early sections of the popular speech govern, and likewise reveal the import of, Cicero's rich allusions—to legal debates, to historical memory, even to folk religion— and, above all, deepen those pictures memorably. And that is ultimately Cicero's objective: to leave his audience with templates to understand the chief political figures of their day, like a memorable image on a coin.

Chapter 8, "*Dignitas*," turns to the senate speech. The picture that emerges from Chapters 2 and 3 is of a senate being prompted to understand its *dignitas* as a communal responsibility, not a personal glory. As the popular speech modulates the idea of *libertas* to mean procedure and responsibility, so does the senate speech modulate the idea of *dignitas* to mean not pride of place but civic duty. In one sense that is unsurprising. But the details of Cicero's treatments show that he is reflecting, and even openly acknowledging, the calculus of the political classes: the wish to accumulate as much power as one could for oneself was measured against the wish to minimize opportunities for one's opponents. Cicero accents the latter to move senators away from the former; the moment, on his view, requires not jockeying for position but banding together. His discourse of unity is not flattery but encouragement, meant to contain the enemy within. The political ideology thus revealed opens up the *peroratio* of the senate speech: there Cicero, drawing on the putatively shared philosophical sensibilities of the governing class, promises that a disciplined senate unified behind himself will mean a return to the senatorial glory of days past.

The last chapter, Chapter 9, "Capua and the *ager Campanus*, or the *ager Campanus* and Capua," offers close readings of the last of the arguments of the speeches, the plan to colonize Capua and the Campania. The chapter, as did Chapter 2, illustrates how very deeply Cicero's governing idea in each speech guides his selection of almost every detail. All of the techniques revealed in previous chapters—allusion to other genres and practices, manipulation of templates and sequence of topics, appeals to the surrounding space, rewriting of historical memory, the ideologies inscribed onto Cicero and Rullus—are needed to read the passages accurately. Inasmuch as the passages represent the chief promise of the bill—fine land and political sway—they are, in their way, more important than the obviously programmatic *exordium* and *perorationes* that are treated in earlier chapters. But both Capua passages also illustrate a kind of undertheme of the previous chapters: that while Cicero's visions apprehend genuine flaws in the law, they also treat worst-case scenarios as the likeliest outcome. That, I briefly suggest, is the consequence of a political culture that depended so heavily on formal rhetoric. Cicero's idealistic vision, inasmuch as it is defended with polarities and distortions, paradoxically replicates the very political problems that the idealisms are designed to solve.

For the text of the speech, I have, except where noted (and not always in matters of spelling and punctuation), followed the recent text of Manuwald. Translations unless indicated are my own. All dates are BCE except where noted. I have aimed in the first instance to express in contemporary English my sense for the communicative thrust of the original, rather than to remain strictly faithful to its syntactic forms; the latter practice, in my view, often produces a dry rendering ("Latinese," one might say) that obscures the force of Cicero's speech and even the sequence of his thoughts. Elements of the translations that don't have a clear correspondent in the Latin are enclosed in brackets.

The many topics that converge in Cicero's speeches *de lege agraria* I and II could each be treated at length, even only to the extent of the mark they leave on those speeches. There is Roman land law (the Rullan bill depends on earlier laws, underlies important later ones, and is entangled with the vexed question of *Sullani possessores*); the Roman political economy (the measures of the Rullan bill reflect the proposers' assessment of capital flow and their ideas of economic stability); Roman political decisions in the East (some of the property to be sold under the bill owed its status to decisions, not always clear, of Sulla and Pompey); the maneuvering of the *populares* in 64 and 63 (either they or another group of the same name are manifestly behind the bill); the rhetorical and political sophistication of the people at a *contio* (it has often been regarded as low, but there are many indications that that view is incorrect); the nature of the Roman state itself (it is an oligarchy but also clearly dependent on the ebbs and flows of popular support, with obvious consequences for assessing rhetoric); the political moods in 64 and 63 of distinctly different, and not homogeneous, groups (the people as a body must have been feeling both anxiety and energy, some senators must have been worried, others excited); Cicero's political career (these were the first speeches he gave as consul, a major occasion for him, and the first evidence, for some, of an increased conservatism); rhetorical theory (Cicero's treatises have some useful remarks on the different approaches to be used before senate and people); Cicero's rhetorical practice (the categories of Greek theory, which undergird Cicero's, do not always much account for what Cicero actually does, especially in small matters of style); stylistics (the two speeches have distinctly different styles); semantics (some of the differences between the two speeches have to do with apparently simple choices of word or phrase); the nature of political slogans and stereotypes (Cicero uses many in these speeches but seemingly not in their standard form, if there is such a thing); the intellectual life of the late Republic (the senate speech alludes to philosophical categories); and cultural semiotics (the language of law, of poetry, of procedure and even folk religion and regional pronunciations play roles in the speeches). This study does not aim to provide exhaustive treatments of these topics (and could not, given my own limitations as a scholar and as a person). Its more modest aim is to unpack Cicero's discourse in order to show how he created internally consistent and integrated visions (I do not say "persuasive"; that is another matter) of a complex and multifaceted issue during a challenging political time at a moment of personal triumph. My modest hope is that the study, for all its limitations, will contribute to the view that a full appreciation of Cicero's rhetoric should begin with an openness to the many cultural competencies of the man himself.

Abbreviations

L&S	Charlton T. Lewis and Charles Short, *A Latin Dictionary*
LSJ	Henry George Liddell, Robert Scott, and Henry Stuart Jones, *A Greek-English Lexicon*, 9th edn.
RE	August Pauly, Georg Wissowa, et al., eds. *Paulys Real-encyclopädie der classischen Altertumswissenschaft*
OLD	*Oxford Latin Dictionary*
RS[3]	T. Mommsen, *Römisches Staatsrecht*, 3rd edn. (1887–1888)
TLL	*Thesaurus Linguae Latinae*

Classical authors and works are generally abbreviated according to the conventions of the *OLD* and *LSJ*, with the exception of *de lege agraria*, which is abbreviated *LA*.

I
The Rhetoric and Politics of *de lege agraria I & II*

1.1. INTRODUCTION

Qua re qui possum non esse popularis, cum videam haec omnia, Quirites, pacem externam, libertatem propriam generis ac nominis vestri, otium domesticum, denique omnia quae vobis cara atque ampla sunt in fidem et quodam modo in patrocinium mei consulatus esse collata?

Since I see that all of these things, citizens—peace abroad, the liberty that belongs your nation and name, tranquility at home—in a word, everything you hold important and valuable—has been, as it were, deposited for protection into my consulship, how I could possibly not be "a man of the people"?

—Cicero, *de lege agraria* 2.9

On January 1, 63, Marcus Tullius Cicero assumed the Roman Republic's highest regular elected office, the consulship. It was a rare moment. The consulship was the virtual preserve of noble families; Cicero's family was not noble, making him, in Roman political parlance, a "new man."[1] Rare, too, was the character of his first addresses to the senate and the people that same month, the speeches that have come down to us as *de lege agraria* I and II and the subject of this study. Newly installed consuls, it seems, customarily devoted those occasions,

---

1. Cicero was the first in thirty years (C. Caelius Calvus had been elected in 94; before him T. Didius in 98 and C. Marius in 107). On *novi homines*, see refs. in ch. 6 n. 7; on Cicero as *novus homo*, see Van der Blom 2010.

before the people at least, to thanking the electorate and praising their famous forebears.[2]

But Cicero mounted a fierce assault. A few weeks before his consulship began, a tribune of the *plebs* or commons, Publius Servilius Rullus, had proposed an agrarian bill.[3] Such laws had a long history at Rome: the state appointed commissioners to settle colonists on plots of land.[4] But for Cicero this particular bill was a Trojan horse: outwardly a land law; covertly a bid for power.[5] In his address to the people, gathered in the Forum in an open assembly he had called, Cicero attacked the bill in detail.[6] Scrutinizing select measures of the bill in the order of their appearance,[7] he argued that the mechanisms and innovations of the bill amounted to an assault, largely covert, on that cherished Roman ideal, *libertas*—at root, the right of a free people to govern itself. A few days before, in a very different venue—in the temple of Jupiter Capitolinus, the symbolic heart of the Roman state, where the senate had assembled to see him take his oath of

---

2. Or so Cicero suggests; cf. *LA* 2.1 (cited in Table 6.2.1.A), *Fin.* 2.74 (on the occasion of taking the praetorship), Suet. *Tib.* 32.1, Plu. *Aem.* 11.1; Morstein-Marx 2004: 10 ("Sallust's speech of Marius (*Iug.* 85) is to be set against this background"); Laser 1997: 145–6.

3. *RE* II A (Servilius 80), Sumner 1966: 571–72, Ward 1972: 252–53. Rullus held a *contio* on Dec. 12 (*contionem in pridie Idus advocari iubet*, *LA* 2.13), two days after taking office, to present the bill (if Madvig's correction to *in pridie Idus* from the transmitted *in primis* is correct; for discussion and bibliography, see Manuwald 2018: 214–15). The bill was promulgated sometime before January 1, when Cicero formally took office (*aliquando tandem me designato lex in publicum proponitur*, *LA* 2.13), and only then, says Cicero, did he acquire its full text (2.13), though he was aware an agrarian bill was being planned (2.11). Apparently no further tribunician *contiones* followed before Cicero gave his speech in the senate on January 1 (cf. n. 8).

4. For an overview of the bill in the context of agrarian legislation, see Flach 1990: 71–76.

5. "Examining the law from its first clause to its last, my fellow citizens, I can only find in it a single intention, a single objective, a single purpose: to use the pretense of an 'agrarian law' to install ten kings as masters over the treasury, tax-properties, all the provinces, the whole government, kingdoms, free peoples—the whole world!" (*atque ego a primo capite legis usque ad extremum reperio, Quirites, nihil aliud cogitatum, nihil aliud susceptum, nihil aliud actum nisi uti decem reges aerari, vectigalium, provinciarum omnium, totius rei publicae, regnorum, liberorum populorum, orbis denique terrarum domini constituerentur legis agrariae simulatione atque nomine*, *LA* 2.15). The introduction of the senate speech is missing, but the tenor of the remainder suggests it must have offered a comparable argument at the outset.

6. For the occasion, cf. Mouritsen 2001: 55.

7. Cicero's discussion follows a logical order: first, the election of a commission with appropriate authority (*LA* 2.16 *primum*–19); then the gathering of funds (1.1–13 *cogitare*, 2.38–57 *liberare*); then the acquisition of land (1.14–15, 62 *parta*–72); then the settlement of colonists (1.16–17, 73–75), including one in Capua (1.18–22 *occuparint*, 2.76–97). *Contra* Vasaly 1993: 221.

office—Cicero had also assailed the bill,[8] using different language but attacking the very same measures, in the very same order, often with the same structures of argument and even rhetorical figures, and making the same basic claim: the political order is under threat!

The claims of these two speeches were broad and bold, so much the more on two such important inaugural occasions. Cicero was veritably staking his consulship on defeating the measure.[9] That was no small risk: the bill was perfectly in step with its times. First, it was economically attractive. In those days, economic distress was acute. Sallust describes "massive debt through the whole world,"[10] and Cicero's own speeches suggest troubled financial markets.[11] Rullus's bill promised some relief. The chosen settlers would of course acquire land. But large landowners saddled with unprofitable tracts—evidently a group of some size in those days—would also benefit: special measures of the bill would let those tracts be sold off.[12]

Second, the bill had political support and could surely count on more. Its design was fiscally intelligent. It surveyed all possible sources of public property to find funding without placing a burden on the treasury, suggesting backers who were politically shrewd and financially sophisticated. The bill was also

---

8. *prima illa mea oratione Kalendis Ianuariis*, *LA* 2.6; *Pis.* 4; *in senatu Kalendis Ianuariis*, *Att.* 2.1.3; Gell. *NA* 13.25.4. Cicero was exercising his privilege to address the senate on a topic of concern to him without calling for any formal action (Mommsen *RS*³ III.2: 948). After the popular speech a few days later, a tribunician *contio* followed (*LA* 3.1, with Morstein-Marx 2004: 192 n. 133; cf. Harvey 1972: 186; Gelzer 1968: 71–72); Cicero was excluded. To that meeting (or meetings) the brief third speech (which is not considered in this study, cf. n. 42) is probably the response; it concerns primarily the issue of *Sullani possessores* (to translate expansively, "landowners who held property thanks to the events of the time of Sulla," on whom see Drummond 2000). *Att.* 2.1.3, a list of Cicero's published consular orations, mentions a fourth speech, likely delivered after yet another *contio*. Plutarch records that the tribunes summoned the consuls to appear before the people and that Cicero did so but also bade the whole senate follow him, leading to the bill's defeat (*Cic.* 12.6; cf. ch. 8.5 *fin.*): these circumstances do not obviously fit the third speech, still less the second (cf. Morstein-Marx 2004: 192 n. 130). Harvey 1972: 190 suggests the possibility that the fourth was a literary production.

9. If it was usually the case that "by the time a vote actually took place the fate of a bill had almost always already been determined by its reception in prior mass meetings" (Morstein-Marx 2004: 124; cf. Laser 1997: 66–69, 138), then Cicero, who had not addressed the crowd on this topic before, was taking a risk.

10. On debt as historical cause in Sallust's narrative, see Shaw 1979.

11. . . . *aes alienum per omnis terras ingens erat* (Sall. *Cat.* 16.4); *fidem de foro . . . . sustulistis* (*LA* 1.23; ch. 6, Table 6.2.2.P); *sublata erat de foro fides . . .* (*LA* 2.8; ch. 6, Table 6.2.2.P); *revocavi fidem* (*LA* 2.103; cf. ch. 7 nn. 79 and 80). See further ch. 1.3 Economic Anxieties. On the problem of debt in the late Republic, see Kühnert 1991: 57–60.

12. See ch. 5.3.

constitutionally astute. It reflected what might be called the constitutional theory of the *populares* or "men of the people," according to which the people exercised directly the full sovereignty that in the Roman constitution really was theirs.[13] To take one example, the bill let the people, solely by their own vote and without the other usual formalities, invest the decemvirs with *imperium* or 'the right of command,' the highest form of executive power in the Roman state (*LA* 2.29).[14] This intelligent bill could surely have counted on wide popular support. High debt must have led to calls for reform and redistribution; these would take a revolutionary form at the end of Cicero's consular year, in the movement of Catiline, but in 64 reformers and their supporters must still have been looking to ordinary means, of which an agrarian bill was one. Hence Cicero's remark, at the end of the second speech, "Has there ever been an assembly where someone has argued so successfully for an agrarian bill as I have argued against one?" (*quis enim umquam tam secunda contione legem agrariam suasit quam ego dissuasi? LA* 2.101).[15]

Last, the bill had an eye to political circumstances. The great general Pompey, who, thanks to bills passed by the people, had recently brought peace and order to the long troubled east—yet another in a long string of military accomplishments—was at that time at the peak of his popularity.[16] Never again would his political capital be so high. Rullus's bill prudently took him into account. It exempted him by name from certain burdens that the bill would impose on military commanders (*LA* 1.13, 2.60), and it created in the Rullan commission a body that would have control over Italian land—which Pompey would presumably soon need to settle his returning army, after the practice of the time.

There was, then, much to commend the bill both to the ordinary voter in the popular assembly and to those with sharper eyes for political and financial advantages (discussed further in Chapter 1.3). The Rullan bill was a bill for its times. But it failed, and Cicero's opposition, boldly displayed at the outset of his

---

13. Cf. n. 76.

14. See ch. 1.4 Mechanisms.

15. The remark is part of the *peroratio*, on which see ch. 7.4.

16. Hence the attempts, in his absence, to use the courts to attack his friends and keep him in his place: the tribune Cornelius (on whom cf. n. 71) was tried in 67; the tribune Manilius in 66; and Cornelius again that same year. Cicero defended Cornelius on the second occasion successfully (*Vat.* 5–6) to popular acclaim, in speeches that survive fragmentarily (see Crawford 1994: 67–148; Griffin 1973; Ward 1970). Pompey's popularity at this time also leaves a mark in the *Commentariolum Petitionis*, where the candidate is advised to claim to the *optimates* that any support of his for popular causes was only intended to curry favor with Pompey; cf. ch. 6 n. 76; Seager 2002: 63–74.

term of office, seems to have been the chief instrument of its defeat.[17] How Cicero successfully resisted such a well-aimed and well-timed bill, and why he wanted to resist it, are important questions both for the history of Roman rhetoric and for late Republican politics. *De lege agraria I* and *II* give invaluable insight into those questions. This book sets out an approach to the speeches, partly adapted, often novel, and thereby makes clear in detail the tactics and objectives of the two orations, objectives and tactics that have been only partly appreciated and sometimes quite misunderstood.

Cicero's master tactic rests not on a claim but on a counterclaim. *Libertas*, typically for the major keywords of a society, had various shades of meaning.[18] When populist politicians adopted *libertas* as a watchword, they linked it to the sovereignty of the popular assemblies and to material benefit.[19] That inflection of *libertas* fit this bill perfectly: the people would be creating powerful commissioners as of right; and it was exactly material benefit that agrarian bills provided by transferring state property to private hands. Those must have been the aspects of *libertas* that Rullus stressed. Cicero's appeal to *libertas* before the people thus becomes not sycophancy or not only sycophancy, as has sometimes been assumed,[20] but a counteroffensive, denying *libertas* to Rullus's bill by pointing to other aspects of that value. Cicero is less trying to claim than to reclaim—and even remold—*libertas*. The epigraph to this section is not a sophistry, as if Cicero was only claiming to be *popularis* because he loved the *populus*,[21] but emblematic of Cicero's actual tactics. In one clause of the law after the next, Cicero professes to detect those aspects or corollaries of *libertas* that Rullus's bill does not embody but violates: transparency, correct procedure, equity, physical security. In *de lege agraria II*, Cicero's *libertas* is almost theoretical and governmental, rather than material and partisan. Cicero upholds a purer version of *libertas*.

---

17. L. Caecilius Rufus had promised his veto (Cic. *Sull.* 65), perhaps, as Harvey 1972: 206 surmises, in return for Cicero's support of a bill lightening the penalties of the *lex Calpurnia de ambitu*, which had caught up a kinsman of Rufus's; but the issue was dropped. Carcopino 2013: 150 apparently believed the veto was actually interposed.

18. The theoretical issues are incisively laid out in Skinner 1980; for the nuances of *libertas* as I understand their relevance to the second speech, cf. ch. 4.1. For a reconstruction of the debates around *libertas*, see Arena 2012 with refs., Wirszubski 1960.

19. Hellegouarc'h 1963: 555–58; Wirszubski 1960: 46, who stresses the link between the ideal of *aequitas* and *leges agrariae* and *frumentariae*; ch. 5.1.

20. Signally by Jonkers 1963 (who also imagines that in the senate speech Cicero means merely to flatter the "capitalists"); on the inadequacy of that treatment, see Blänsdorf 2002: 41–42, Veyne 1964.

21. On this trope, and Cicero's invocation of *otium*, see ch. 6.2 (Re)reading Cicero's Election.

Cicero, then, takes a populist slogan and gives it a not quite populist twist.[22] That is not wholly surprising; in an open assembly or *contio*, where Cicero delivered his second speech, *libertas* was the coin of the realm, and Cicero almost had to appeal to it in some way.[23] But it was Cicero's genius to see that, appropriately adjusted, the very same tactic could be used in the senate speech. The political class, the smallish, generally wealthy circle from which magistrates were elected, also cherished *libertas*—but, so to speak, as seen from above. For the highest offices in particular, the people's exercise of its liberty almost always turned to that class as the only suitable leaders of the community (hence the relative rarity of *novi homines*).[24] For the political class, *libertas* thus shaded into other values, namely *dignitas* 'stature' and *auctoritas* 'influence,' which the people invested or recognized in them by the act of election.[25] In the upper classes *libertas* meant pride in rank and stature. But class privilege did not, of course, mean class unity. Within that group, competition for prestige, position, and power was fierce. In the upper classes *libertas* thus also meant jealous rivalry, a regular feature of Roman aristocratic life.[26] Rullus's bill must have stimulated that rivalry: the bill offered the prospect of a post that was politically useful (it was able to help—or hurt—Pompey), was constitutionally significant (it came with *imperium*), and was fiscally important (it oversaw many financial transactions and land transfers). Before the senate, Cicero does exactly what he does before the people: drawing on the same set of clauses, he detects those aspects or corollaries of the relevant

---

22. For the idea that thereby Cicero means to assimilate *libertas* to the values of the *optimates*, cf. Yakobson 2010: 297–300.

23. "*Libertas* was the common ideal invoked by all Romans who aspired to power, no matter what their political views and methods might have been," Mouritsen 2001: 11; cf. Morstein-Marx 2004: 205–207, Arena 2012: 14–72. On the *contio* and its ideology, see Arena 2012, especially 231–41, Tan 2008, Morstein-Marx 2004, Hölkeskamp 2000 and 1995; on the definition of a *contio*, Frolov 2013.

24. For these data, see Badian 1990.

25. Cf. Wirszubski 1960: 36: "In the Late Republic . . . *dignitas* often denotes not only the respect freely inspired by a person's merit, but also—and in the first place—a title to be given, through office, the allegedly deserved opportunity of exercising one's *auctoritas* in the State." The relationship of *dignitas* to *libertas* thus varied: they were seen as opposites (cf. 15–17); complements (*SPQR*); or nested, with *dignitas* inside of *libertas*. The last configuration appears in *LA* 1 (*non modo dignitatis retinendae, verum ne libertatis quidem recuperandae spes, LA* 1.17; ch. 8.4 Dignitas; J9 in Appendix 3). The corresponding phrase in the popular speech has only *facultas recuperandae vestrae libertatis* (*LA* 2.75).

26. The paradox, and essentially military character of the notion, is captured by Earl 1967: 21, speaking of a different value: "*Virtus*, for the Republican noble, consisted in the winning of personal preeminence and glory by the commission of great deeds in the service of the Roman state."

version of *libertas* that the Rullan bill does not embody but threatens: fair competition, limits on exceptional stature, clarity of intention, beneficent paternalism. In *de lege agraria I*, Cicero's *libertas* stresses not personal advantage but shared governance, and it invests *dignitas* not in persons but in a whole body. Cicero's *dignitas* takes an aristocratic sensibility and prunes back its individualism in favor of collectivism. He upholds a purer version of *dignitas*.

That, in brief, is what this book argues, by way of the method and principles discussed in the next section. If that vision of the speeches is at all correct, then Cicero's approach has an impressive effect. On the one hand, he projects a consistent persona. Before both bodies he offers what is on the gross level the same argument, based on the same clauses of the law. The senators who attended the open assembly would have seen Cicero dissecting, in the exact same order, the exact same clauses as he had in the senate; tribunes present at the first meeting of the senate could not truthfully claim in a later assembly of their own that Cicero had taken a wholly different approach before the whole people. (Rullus, as it appears, made that very mistake, saying in the senate that his bill would 'drain off' the plebs—like so much swamp water).[27] Thereby, I venture to suggest, Cicero was representing—in the first instance to the political class, who are the only ones who would have seen both speeches—the sort of consul he hoped to be: equitable, principled, consistent.

On the other hand, within each group, Cicero also projects a distinctive persona—distinctive regardless of either group's knowledge of the other speech. He positions himself within the ambit of a cardinal value of each of his audiences but also redirects and rarefies those values. Like the people, he cherishes *libertas*—but only if rightly understood. Like the senate, he respects *dignitas*—but only if rightly understood. He is of each audience but also, in a sense, above them. In that way, too, Cicero was representing the sort of consul he hoped to be—alert, but not beholden, to the values of the various tiers of society and able to speak to each in its own terms so as to draw it beyond itself and put it in mind of good governance and societal balance.

That consistent and distinctive persona has a striking effect. It makes Cicero himself the resolution of ideological differences and political categories. Perhaps the approach especially suited a "new man"? "New men" owed their position not to inherited rank but, in the slogan of the times, to their *virtus et industria*.[28] That kind of hard work is something Cicero refers to at critical points in both speeches,[29] and the audiences of Cicero's agrarian speeches would both have

---

27. *LA* 2.70; Table 7.3.5 and attendant discussion in ch. 7.3 *fin*.

28. Krostenko 2004a: 252–5.

29. *LA* 1.27, the *peroratio* (cf. ch. 8.5, quotation E); *LA* 2.2, the *exordium* (Table 6.2.1.C and D).

seen just those values: a critic reading closely, clause by clause (*industria* or 'hard work'), with high moral ideals in mind (*virtus*, once 'courage' and then also 'uprightness'). Be that as it may, Rullus's bill had prompted Cicero not only to refine the ideologies of senate and people but also to do so in a way that scripted a special role for himself—which makes his attacks on that bill a new consul's manifesto after all.[30] That raises a point—not another principle but an artifice of my own. I will speak of Cicero's rhetoric in the following pages for the most part in terms of the dynamic between himself and his audiences, that is, as if he meant to appeal to them, as he manifestly did. But in his refittings of *libertas* and *dignitas*—to put it more expansively, in his hierarchizing of various elements of the Roman social imaginary in order to reclaim two cardinal values on his own terms—it is fair, I think, to see a certain degree of wish fulfillment. Cicero is writing a kind of script for his audiences—but also for himself.

1.2. READING THE SPEECHES
Logos

etsi sine re nulla vis verbi est, tamen eadem res saepe aut probatur aut reicitur alio atque alio elata verbo.

A word has no meaning unless it corresponds to some actual thing; even so, the very same thing may meet with acceptance or rejection, according as it is expressed with one word or another.

—Cicero, *Orator* 72

That view of the speeches, which it is the purpose of this book to develop and explore, may, I imagine, seem as bold as Cicero's orations that January. The speeches, when not overlooked, have not typically been seen as creative, much less principled.[31] But my view of the speeches draws directly from an analysis of

---

30. Cf. "Doch indem er sich sowohl vor dem Senat wie auch vor dem Volk einer geschickten Auswahl passender und wirkungsvoller Argumente und Illustrationen bedient und diese in Formulierungen kleidet, die die so verschiedenen Hörergruppen unmittelbar anzusprechen geeignet sind, vermag er diese nicht nur für eine Ablehnung des Gesetzesvorschlages zu gewinnen, sondern ihnen auch sein politisches Programm gleich bein seinem Amtsantritt nahezubringen," Classen 1985: 309 (on his approach, see further n. 34).

31. For a brief descriptive survey of critical responses, see Manuwald 2018: x–xi. The most skeptical reading is that of Jonkers 1963. Seeing the popular speech as articulating a meaningful ideal presupposes their importance in the political process. The impetus for that view was the work of Fergus Millar, especially Millar 1998, which has spurred a lively and ongoing debate about the acuity and involvement of the popular audience. The main lines of reinterpretation and response are represented by Morstein-Marx 2004: 13–23; Hölkeskamp 2000, 2010; and

their form.[32] While, as I have noted, the structure of the two speeches is almost identical, dissecting the same clauses of Rullus's bill in the same order, the word choice and figures of speech of corresponding passages are different. To restate that point in the terms of classical rhetoric, the topics (*inventio*) and their sequential arrangement (*dispositio*) are virtually identical: Cicero plainly had one template in mind.[33] But the choices of word, image, and figures of speech in each oration (various aspects of *elocutio*) typically differ, sometimes markedly: Cicero plainly had two distinct audiences in mind. In effect we have two drafts of the same speech tailored to two different audiences—the same piece of music, if you like, with different orchestrations. Each version throws the particulars of the other into relief, which provides a rare chance to probe Cicero's language very closely.[34] The chief task of interpreting Cicero's agrarian speeches is deciding what the differences between the versions mean.

My view, sketched in the previous section, is that they point to two deeply consistent, distinctive, and nuanced views of *libertas* and *dignitas*. Let me begin to defend it here by a sample of some of the chief techniques of this book. Rullus's

---

Mouritsen 2001. The debate has been deepened by the essays in Steel and van der Blom 2013. The debate has had the effect of making partly or wholly obsolete earlier studies of the agrarian speeches that, like this study, use point-by-point comparison, viz. Mack 1937, Jonkers 1963, and Classen 1985, which depend on the now untenable idea that the people were wholly ignorant (not to say that they were equal partners either).

32. The text of Cicero's speeches is not a stenographic record; on the relation between transmitted texts and the delivered original, cf. Craig 1993: 257–58, who, drawing on Cicero's avowed purpose in publishing speeches—to educate aspiring orators—points out, "[Cicero's] speeches only serve as exemplars to educate only insofar as they depict what he would need to say to persuade a particular listening audience in a given set of circumstances. He may publish a speech with some changes, or even a speech that he never delivered . . . but it will still represent what would work in a given set of circumstances. We must admit that we can never know verbatim what Cicero actually said. Nonetheless, the proper way to appreciate one of his speeches as oratory is precisely to treat it as a transcript." For a defense that the language of *LA* 2, at least, is a fair representation of the type of rhetoric used in a *contio*, cf. Morstein-Marx 2004: 25–31. In my view the two speeches so precisely and consistently capture two guiding ideas that the transmitted versions must faithfully represent the force and general form of the delivered speeches, even if some details vary.

33. For an outline of the speeches by corresponding sections (and the location of their treatment in this study), cf. Appendix 1.

34. That is the method of Mack 1937, but his chief focus is on paired speeches other than *de lege agraria*. The most detailed rhetorical comparison is that of Classen 1985. Classen relies primarily on topic, section and sentence length, and sentence type (e.g. questions) as indices of Cicero's attempts to control mood and as a direct index of each audience's interests, perceptions, and capacities; the underlying model is for the most part that an orator simply responds to the more or less fixed dispositions of his audience. For his general assessment of the rhetorical differences between the two speeches, see 361–66.

bill would have allowed state properties to be sold on the spot and not, as then usual, at Rome and in public view. Cicero criticizes the lack of transparency before both audiences at exactly corresponding places in each speech (tables throughout are numbered by the section in which they appear):[35]

Table 1.2. Absence of constraint on decemviral sales (*LA* 1.7, 2.56)

in senatu	*ad populum*
hic permittit sua lege decemviris ut in quibus commodum sit tenebris, ut in qua velint solitudine, bona populi Romani possint divendere.	decemviri vestra vectigalia non modo non vobis, Quirites, arbitris sed ne praecone quidem publico teste vendent?
"But Rullus ('this one') with his law grants the decemvirs the power to liquidate the property of the Roman people in whatever dark corner suits them, in any desolate spot they choose!"	"Shall the decemvirs then sell your tax properties[i] not only out of your sight, citizens, but without even a herald to serve as a public witness?"

[i] Strictly speaking *vectigalia vendent* is "sell taxes," that is, "sell contracts to collect taxes," but the section discusses a measure to sell rented properties, not merely the contracts to collect that rent (*in omnibus his agris aedificiisque vendendis permittitur decemviris ut vendant 'quibuscumque in locis' videatur, LA* 2.55).

The basic idea is the same, but the differing *elocutio* creates different perspectives. The popular version foregrounds vision: not only will the people not be observers (*arbitri* in its original meaning, still common later), but neither will there even be a lowly public official as a witness (*testis*). That is especially regrettable: the transactions are for the Roman people's property; the land, as the passage rightly points out, is "theirs." The senate version, by contrast, foregrounds license. The decemvirs do not merely "sell," as in the popular speech; rather Rullus "permits" (*permittit*) them the "capacity" (*ut . . . possint*, lit. "that they be able") to sell in whatever darkness "suits them" (*commodum sit*) or whatever desolate spot "they choose" (*velint*). The image is enhanced by the rare *divendere*, found in Cicero in only one other passage—also, as it happens, of an outrageous exercise of executive power.[36] To "sell (*-vendere*) in multiple directions (*di[s]-*)" is quite like

---

35. For more detail on this aspect of the law, and for a fuller treatment of these snippets and the passages from which they come, see ch. 4.2.

36. See ch. 4.2 *Licentia(e)* and n. 35.

"selling as one will."[37] A complementary and overlapping image is legal authority, a warrant which Rullus's bill will have. The law is "his" (*sua lege*): he is, as he was permitted to do, using his tribunician right to propose plebiscites.[38] *Permittere ut possint* denotes permission but is also a pleonasm probably taken from legal language.[39] The lands are named, not *vectigalia*, but *bona populi Romani*, the formal title for state property, historically managed by the senate through censors and consuls.

The configurations of the two audiences differ accordingly. The popular version projects a people that takes its role in the polity seriously by ensuring that transactions be witnessed.[40] The senate version projects a senate coming together to resist a tribune pressing his rights to propose legislation too far. The underlying values also differ. The popular version raises a constitutional or procedural concern; the senate version raises a political and ethical concern. It can almost be said, even from these brief examples, that the underlying values are respectively *libertas* and *dignitas*—and quite particular forms thereof. And yet both speeches ultimately espouse the same idea: the relevant bodies must live up to their duties—philosophers and plowmen, as it were, who each must know his part.

What are the other patterns of imagery in the speeches? How do they work together? Are some of them directed to one audience and not the other? If the same sets are used before both audiences, are there adjustments? What are they? How are they made? Here I have explicated two sentences in terms of simple word choice (*divendere, commodum, arbitri*); what about other features of language—the traditional rhetorical figures, for example, or stylistic tones and colorings, or even syntax? How and what do they contribute? What are the full pictures of *libertas* and *dignitas* that thus emerge? Are they distinctive, as I have been asserting, and if so, how? How do those conceptions relate to Cicero's view of the bill? of the political situation? of his own political role? At a still more abstract level,

---

37. Likewise German *ausverkaufen* as opposed to *verkaufen*; Polish *wyprzedać się* as opposed to *sprzedawać*.

38. *Sua lege* is not sarcastic; cf. ch. 5 n. 26. The phrase also appears at *LA* 1.2 (ch. 3, Table 3.1, row B), 2.43 (ch. 4, Table 4.4, row D), and 2.69 (ch. 7, Table 7.3.3).

39. Cf. *TLL* 10.1.1558.25–32.

40. Cf. Millar 1998 and the articles gathered in Millar 2002, which defend the important role of the crowd and the genuine *contio* in Roman life. Cf. North 1990: 20: "Democracy at Rome should be seen as a very particular form, badly in need of classification and of comparison to similar systems, where high and entrenched élite authority is combined with an arbitrative power retained by popular voting." For a contrary view, see Hölkeskamp 1995; 2000.

what models of Roman society appear? Such are the questions which this book explores, beginning, as here, by attention to details of language. Here, then, is the method of the book—an attempt to describe the cognitive and cultural roots of linguistic expressions (more or less the technique of contemporary discourse analysis).[41] It is an approach that Cicero, in the epigraph to this section, may almost be said to have anticipated: he noted that different forms of expression (*eadem res . . . alio atque alio elata verbo*) create different perceptions (*aut probatur aut reicitur*). Just so in our passages.

Let me draw out here six principles implied in this analysis. They underlie the following chapters but have not been fully recognized in many other treatments of the speeches. First, the particularity of the language and argument of each speech must always be set into relief by examining the language and argument of the other, whenever that is possible (the beginning of the senate speech is mutilated)—call it the Contrastive Principle. That is, of course, a basic principle of discourse analysis and structural linguistics, which, where possible, see the significance of an element in a system in terms of its contrasts to other elements in that system. To take a simple example from within one semantic field, 'croak' is a colloquial word for 'die'; a speaker who uses 'croak' instead of 'die' signals emotional distance of some kind (humor, disrespect, etc.). Distinctions that choose different semantic fields—that is, that substitute one semantic field for another in otherwise comparable stretches of speech—are equally revealing. Attention to such distinctions can expose the implications and entailments of an utterance. A chief benefit of this approach is that it opens up ordinary language—for example, *commodum sit* (wherever it "suits them") in the passage above—and gives that language due weight beside more obvious programmatic claims (like "I am defending liberty").[42]

Not all previous analyses have taken advantage of the possibility of comparison.[43] Perhaps, to speculate, that omission, in some cases at least, has to do with the senate speech. The popular speech is considerably amplified: where sections

---

41. Discourse analysis has many meanings; I use it here in the sense of critical discourse analysis as developed and represented by Norman Fairclough and Michael Halliday, which has certain commonalities with traditional philological close reading. See e.g. Fairclough 1992; 1995; Webster 2015. On "unpacking" the features of language for their cultural significance, see Palmer 1996: 113–69. For an attempt to "to link style and persuasive effect," see Fotheringham 2013, a detailed discourse-analytical treatment of Cicero's *pro Milone*.

42. Hence this study does not consider *LA* 3, which is Cicero's brief response to a *contio* of Rullus (cf. n. 8). The speech is not programmatic in the same way as his first two public orations as consul and not part of a matched set amenable to the method of analysis here proposed.

43. The analysis of Morstein-Marx 2004, which is concerned with contional rhetoric broadly, focuses primarily on the second speech and for the most part does not consider that the bill's mechanisms really were unusual nor that Cicero attacks the same measures of the bill on virtually the same terms in the senate speech.

of the speeches can be compared, the longer version is almost always in the second speech, from one-fifth to up to six times longer than the corresponding section in the senate speech.[44] The second speech also has a few set pieces or addenda with no direct correspondent in the first (the reverse is not true). That gives the senate speech the appearance of a kind of outline for the fuller popular speech. But it is a mistake to think of the senate speech that way. Its rhetoric is just as worthy of close attention. Passages without *amplificatio*—the tactic of producing "fullness"—may be no less rhetorically significant than passages that do have it. The terse, compact, and allusive is not unrhetorical because the full, expansive, and histrionic is. Indeed, the restraint of the senate version is exactly what Cicero says *decorum* toward that "shrewd body" required.[45] I return to the topic of *decorum* later in this chapter.

Other analyses have relied on comparing corresponding sections. But frequently in these analyses the presence or absence of a topic, or the length at which a topic is treated, have been seen as direct signs of the interests or sensibilities of the hearers.[46] That is a mistake, and a species of a broader problem. If the presence, absence, or relative frequency or scope of a feature or topic corresponds to a particular audience, those differences cannot be considered simple and direct reflections of the sensibilities of that audience. That is to confuse correlation with cause. The point is easy to make with an individual word. Cicero uses *divendere* only in the senate speech, but that does not make it a "senatorial" word, somehow inherently appropriate before that body. Rather, the senate speech depicts the decemvirs as having too much freedom of choice, and the word *divendere* is chosen to harmonize with that idea. It is a core metaphor of that particular speech, rather than its venue, that made Cicero choose *divendere*. The same idea applies

---

44. The speech to the people numbers about 10,300 words and the extant portion of the speech to the senate about 2,290. The beginning of the senate speech, however, is not extant; the comparable sections of the popular speech run to about 6,860 words, so that, for those sections, the popular speech is roughly three times fuller. The differences are greatest in the section on Capua; Cicero explicitly notes in the senate version that he intends to be briefer there (cf. C20 in Appendix 2). It is usually the contional speech that is shorter: cf. Manuwald 2018: xl; Piña-Polo 1996: 124; Ramsey 2007: 131.

45. "All of this has to be handled less elaborately in the senate; for one thing, that is a shrewd body, and there also has to be time for many others to speak. Furthermore one has to avoid the appearance of showing off one's talents. An open assembly, by contrast, can absorb all the force that a speech can offer and demands impressiveness and variety" (*Atque haec in senatu minore apparatu agenda sunt; sapiens enim est consilium multisque aliis dicendi relinquendus locus, vitanda etiam ingeni ostentationis suspicio; contio capit omnem vim orationis et gravitatem varietatemque desiderat*, *de Orat.* 2.333–4, Antonius speaking). On *decorum* generally, cf. *Or.* 71–74 and *de Orat.* 3.210–11.

46. Thus Mack 1937; Thompson 1978. On Classen 1985 see n. 34.

to length. Cicero treats the topic of the *silva Scantia*, an otherwise unknown plot of land in Italy that would be sold under the bill, at much greater length in the senatorial speech (a paragraph at *LA* 1.4 but only the word *silvas* at *LA* 2.48; cf. ch. 3, Table 3.1.D). That is surely not because the tract was somehow inherently of greater interest to the senate (unless one wishes to imagine that the tract was illegally occupied, and Cicero took the opportunity to flatter its possessor). Rather Cicero makes the tract a symbol of tribunician interference in the prerogatives of censors and consuls—an instance of overstepping that is a key theme of the senate speech.[47] Of course Cicero is building on what the senate knows better; but he is giving the forest a meaning that suits not their knowledge but his purpose. Call this the Principle of Projected Significance. Marrucinus Asinius knew what a napkin was, but its meaning in Catullus 12 is Catullus's creation.[48]

There is a third principle: the presence of a concept need not be signaled by the name of that concept. The formal features of a text—the details of its words, figures, syntax, and structures—may signal the presence of a concept no less well. No clique of teenagers needs to say "conformity" to enforce conformity, and no Roman orator needed to name *libertas* or *commodum* or *dignitas* on every occasion when those concepts were in play.[49] Even the short analysis here makes that clear enough; call it the Principle of the Unnamed Referent. Natives of a language or a culture know the significant features or allied signifiers of their words, concepts, practices, and institutions, and these features and signifiers are themselves enough to put them in mind of a word, a concept, a practice, or an institution. Such allusive evocation has been recognized as an important part of Cicero's art in some other speeches but has hitherto been almost entirely overlooked in the agrarian speeches and undertheorized as a central component of his rhetoric.[50]

Fourth, and here the analysis of this snippet is merely suggestive, the extrinsic definitions of a concept are not an infallible guide to the workings of a particular speech. The central values of a society—like *libertas* or *clementia* or σωφροσύνη

---

47. The example is not, *pace* Classen 1985: 365, "entirely outlandish" ("ganz ausgefallene"). See ch. 3.3 Going Too Far.

48. Cf. Fitzgerald 1995: 96.

49. Implicitly recognized by Leonhardt 1998, who, beginning from Cicero's theoretical pronouncements, examines the polarity of 'the good' and 'the useful' in *LA* 1 and 2, not every instance of which is signaled by a word for 'good' or 'useful.' For the idea that ideas and concepts need not be lexically founded, see Langacker 1987.

50. Axer 1980 explores the use of comic and theatrical language in Cicero's *pro Sexto Roscio Comoedo*. Leigh 2004 and Geffcken 1973 probe the relationship of the *pro Caelio* to comic performance. Krostenko 2017–2018 explores "deipnosophistry" as an organizing intellectual motif in Cicero's speech for king Deiotarus.

or *liberté* or *gościnność*—escape rigid definition. As well they should: like individual words, they need some flexibility to be used in the shifting and complex real world. Indeed it is that very flexibility that competing parties exploit and even increase, laying claim to values in a way that represents their own understanding and justifies their own interests—and sometimes bends the meaning of a word.[51] The question here, then, should not simply be, to what values do the speeches appeal, but also, *how* do the speeches make the appeal to *their* version of the values seem plausible? That is an especially important question for our speeches. The open assembly or *contio*, as I noted, favored *popularis* rhetoric. During a time of *popularis* ferment, appeals to *libertas* were no doubt positively trite and required special energies to revitalize them.[52] Saying what *libertas* or *dignitas* "is," as if those values were steady and fixed, obscures both the flexibility of concepts and the dynamism of the speeches. Cicero, in these speeches, is not adopting those values; he is adapting them. To put it another way, an idea in a speech is to that idea as a whole as a few passages using a word are to a whole lexical entry for the word—demonstrated related but not fully identical. Call that principle the Primacy of Local Context.

Pathos

Non enim omnis fortuna, non omnis honos, non omnis auctoritas, non omnis aetas nec vero locus aut tempus aut auditor omnis eodem aut verborum genere tractandus est aut sententiarum semperque in omni parte orationis ut vitae quid deceat est considerandum; quod et in re de qua agitur positum est et in personis et eorum qui dicunt et eorum qui audiunt.

Not every social position, every office, every rank, every age—or even every place or time or listener!—can be approached with the same kind of language or idea. Just as propriety must be given due regard in every aspect of life, so in every single part of an oration, which is to say in the topic, in the persona of the speaker, and in the persona of the listener.

—Cicero, *Orator* 71

The four principles just articulated might be called matters of *logos*, to borrow from Aristotle's scheme of rhetoric, which famously divided the rhetorical act

---

51. Cf. Skinner 1980.

52. On the importance of *libertas* in contional rhetoric, see ch. 4.1.

into its medium (*logos*), its effect on the audience (*pathos*), and the character of its speaker (*ethos*). There are two more principles implicit in the analysis here, both issues of *pathos*. It is possible, as I have noted, to regard Cicero's rhetoric as simply reflecting back to his audiences their own orientations. Indeed, his own theoretical pronouncements recommend that the orator adapt himself to his hearers.[53] But the underlying reason for that position is important. Such adaptation is an aspect of *decorum*, and in ancient rhetorical thought *decorum* was not just a matter of courtesy. It was, rather, a matter of due proportion, which, according to Cicero, informed not only orators handling cases but also literary critics analyzing poetry and philosophers describing the nature of duty.[54] In the epigraph to this section, from a discussion of *decorum*, Cicero uses a conceptual *figura etymologica* to draw out that idea. *Decorum* is not simply "beautiful": it really means keeping in mind *quid deceat* "what is fitting"; the aesthetic is really ethical. I have already mentioned an instance of *decorum* so understood, Cicero's advice to speak briefly in the senate: before that body it is fitting not to show off (*vitanda ... ingeni ostentationis suspicio*), to leave time for the many others to speak (*multis ... aliis dicendi relinquendus locus*), and to respect the experience of that shrewd group (*sapiens ... est consilium*, de Orat. 2.333).

Such adaptation—and here is the fifth principle; call it Creative Decorum—should not be equated with fawning or ingratiation. In a culture in which "decorous" exchanges were the rule, adaptation to audience must have been expected and even demanded. The speaker, in a sense, had no choice; the audience set the bar. The burden on a speaker, therefore, was to find a way to make his point within those constraints.[55] In the *pro Marcello* Cicero praises Caesar's fabled *clementia* 'mercy,' but in doing so he turns *clementia* into a *sapientia* 'wisdom' that places demands on Caesar, who (in the world of the speech) becomes subject to *sapientia* in rather the same way as his *clementia* made others subject to him.[56] Thus does epideixis, which Caesar's high position perhaps demanded, become

---

53. *Or.* 71–74, 159.

54. "This deep and broad topic is therefore customarily treated by philosophers in their considerations of duty (not when they are discussing the Good as such; that is its own topic), by literary commentators in their interpretation of poets, and by rhetoricians in their handling of every type and section of an oration" (*itaque hunc locum longe et late patentem philosophi solent in officiis tractare—non cum de recto ipso disputant, nam id quidem unum est—, grammatici in poetis, eloquentes in omni et genere et parte causarum, Or.* 72).

55. This, in a sense, is the rhetorical version of what Ober, in his 1989 study of rhetoric in Athenian democracy, calls "[the audience's] ideological control" (*contra* for Roman contional rhetoric, Morstein-Marx 2004: 16).

56. Krostenko 2005: 279–80.

exhortation. Likewise in a "decorous" speech the speaker may appear sympathetic to his audience's views, may even indulge them, but that does not mean his own purpose cannot be sensible, intelligent, and even honorable. There is nothing surprising about a contional speech appealing to *libertas* and a senate one to *dignitas*; the meaningful question is, what is the *specific content* of those appeals. To push the point farther, to orate "decorously" may also be an intelligent and creative position and need not in and of itself be a compromise of one's own integrity.

But now we have come to an issue of personal ethics beyond my immediate purpose. Let us return to our two sentences (if by now I am not working them too hard). In the senate, that "shrewd body," the implication of *permittit sua lege* was clear: a tribune was altering the law; C. Gracchus had carried a bill which, to thwart corruption, bound the censors to let public contracts in Rome. Thus it might seem like Cicero is indulging his audience, appealing to the conservative strain in the governing class, reluctant to tamper willy-nilly with precedents, even tribunician ones. But Rullus's measure was not an innovation: the *lex agraria* of 111 had a similar provision, allowing state land in Greece and Africa to be sold there.[57] The provision made good sense if the intent was to sell to tenants already renting the land, an obvious market.[58] Doubtless many senators knew that. It would have been obvious to them that Cicero was casting the measure not in legal terms, considering precedent or practicality, but in ethical terms, pointing to the need for restraint. And the senate boasted shrewd judges of policy and politics; some of them are certain to have seen real opportunities of various kinds in Rullus's bill. The ethically restrained and unified senate that Cicero projects was not sitting before him. He is not, or is not only, responding to their fixed dispositions but rather directing them to a particular ideal.

The same is true of the popular variant. *Vestra* attached to *vectigalia* might seem like flattery: the tax contracts are yours! The empire belongs to you! *Est igitur res publica res populi!* And strictly speaking that was true. The people were in theory fully sovereign. But I hazard that Rullus himself, in arguing for his bill, also said *vestra*. The bill was funded largely by reclaiming or liquidating public properties of various kinds. Rullus must have asked, why retain "your" assets in these times of financial distress? The power to solve the problem is in your hands! The question, then, is not what *vestra* denotes but what it connotes: liquidation and profit (as Rullus must have taken it) or oversight and conservatism (as Cicero would have it)? The opinion of the "people" on that issue will have

---

57. The *duumviri* were to sell land in Greece (lines 99–100; Lintott 1992: 281) and rent land in Africa (line 83).

58. Jonkers 1963: 14 ad *LA* 1.4; Jonkers 1963: 21 ad *LA* 1.7.

varied. The crowd for a *contio* was always mixed: (some of) the *plebs Romana* in the strict sense (the four urban tribes); (some) members of the other thirty-one tribes, now peopled partly by Italians dispossessed by Sulla; and, on this particular occasion—the inaugural assembly of a new consul—doubtless members of many census classes who might not otherwise attend many *contiones* but were interested to see and hear Cicero.[59] The willingness of these different groups to overlook real or apparent irregularities in hope of profit must have varied. The "people" interested in good government that Cicero projects were not standing before him.[60] He is not, or is not only, responding to their fixed dispositions but rather trying to direct them to a particular ideal—almost regardless of who was in front of him at that moment. To put that last point another way, *populus Romanus* is itself an ideological value term with multiple connotations, subject to the fourth principle in the previous section, the primacy of the workings of a particular context.

In short, Cicero is not appealing to unified audiences; he is trying to make disparate audiences feel unified. He is not flattering their views; he is trying to rally them to one possible view. That amounts to a sixth principle; call it the Principle of Projected Identity. This is like the Principle of Projected Significance, but where that principle has in mind topics, this one has in mind an audience's ideas about itself. The principle points up a risk: thinking of Cicero's audiences as homogeneous. That has been a feature of some previous analyses. In particular, the audiences have been viewed as socioeconomically uniform: the senate as selfish landowners and the people as simpletons and materialist.[61] A public meeting and a session of the senate were, of course, quite different venues, and there will have been truisms or attitudes generally easier to display in front of one or the other; but regarding an audience as homogeneous—economically, intellectually, or politically—may make those truisms and attitudes appear to be mere reflex or simple obligation or empty flattery and thus obscure their contribution to the specific strategy of a particular speech. A repeated slogan may look the same in isolation but—and here again we come back to the fourth principle—it takes its color from its contexts.

If issues of *logos* and *pathos* have hindered a full analysis of Cicero's agrarian speeches, so, perhaps, has an issue of *ethos*: Cicero himself. Cicero does not seem

---

59. On the composition of the contional crowd, see for example Mouritsen 2017: 73–76; on the importance of the *plebs* therein, Tan 2008.

60. For an exploration of the idea that "audiences had greater powers of resistance to the 'dominant ideology' than often assumed," see Morstein-Marx 2013.

61. This view dominates Jonkers 1963.

like a credible voice in matters of agrarian reform. His theoretical writings of some twenty years after the date of these speeches are one reason. When they treat the political economy, they envision a Roman state rooted in the landed aristocracy and managed chiefly by the senate.[62] His opposition to a land bill and to tribunician initiative in our speeches are consistent with that view, and it is tempting to ascribe his opposition to a deeply held ideological stance. That can make Cicero's position in our speeches seem mendacious or worse, as if he were only defending an unspoken article of faith any way he can.[63] Not far different is assuming Cicero merely wanted to keep the support of the *optimates*, if they are thought to have opposed land reform as a body. But the agrarian speeches can and should also be examined for their links to Cicero's political ideals. The outlines of those ideals are clear enough. The events of the Catilinarian conspiracy later in Cicero's consulship, in which a disgruntled aristocrat rallied the indebted to the banner of revolution, spurred Cicero's articulation of an ideal already to be seen in his earlier life: the *consensus omnium bonorum*, 'agreement among all the good,' that is, the political cooperation of right-minded members of all social ranks.[64] Closely related is Cicero's championing of the *concordia ordinum*, 'harmony of the orders,' by which he meant chiefly cooperation between the senate and the so-called equestrians, the wealthy class whose business interests sometimes put them at odds with the senate. Both *consensus* and *concordia* required members of various social groups to step outside of their own interests to consider the

---

62. On Cicero's general conservatism in matters of land tenure, see Wood 1983; 1988.

63. For Cicero's opposition to land distribution, see *Off.* 2.78. The matter is complicated by *Att.* 1.19 (60) and *Fam.* 13.4 (45), in which, inter alia, Cicero describes himself as a protector the property of the citizens of Volaterrae, in his resistance to Flavius's land law of 60 and to a member of Caesar's land commission, respectively. It is tempting to see these letters as full and factual accounts of his motivations in resisting agrarian legislation, but it seems to me, rather, that the reverse is the case: that to Atticus he purposes to sound more capitalist (let us say) than he was, and to Caesar's land commissioner he foregrounds personal connections, as commonly in letters, as grounds for requesting a favor; not every letter is confessional (nor is every oration misleading). I intend to treat the letters elsewhere.

64. See *Catil.* 4.14–17, where he claims that citizens of all orders and even slaves are united in opposition to Catiline (on which see Wood 1988: 193–94). In a letter some twenty years later Cicero speaks of "the unity of the good which I myself engineered" (*illum consensum bonorum quem ego idem effeceram, Fam.* 5.21.2). The most extensive articulation of the ideal is at *Sest.* 97–98, a speech delivered in 56 after Cicero's exile. For an assessment of the issues there, see Kaster 2006: 31–37. Rawson 1975 [1983]: 13 suggests that Cicero's "lifelong attempts to reconcile classes and parties ... may spring to some extent from his early connections with [M. Aemilius] Scaurus and Lucius Crassus" (who had been engaged with solving two major sources of political conflict in their times, "the Italian allies' desire for citizenship" and the composition of criminal juries).

common good.[65] That ideal is consonant with my suggestion earlier, by way of the Principle of Projected Identity, that Cicero is trying to create consensus within disparate and even fractured groups.[66] Openness to the possibility that Cicero is expressing genuine ideals (and, con comitantly, pointing out genuine flaws in the bill) amounts to a seventh principle of this analysis—call it Idealistic Rhetoric. That openness certainly makes good sense for this moment in Cicero's political life: these were his first speeches as consul, the right place for programmatic idealism; and these speeches were given at and for the moment of his supreme political triumph before exile made him strident and the slide of the republic into tyranny gave him urgency. But this line of thought is easier to probe once the agrarian speeches themselves are analyzed in more detail and their idealisms—and elisions and omissions and failures—become clear; I treat Cicero's persona chiefly in Chapters 6 and 7 and address some of the complications and failures of his idealisms—and all idealisms have their flaws—in Chapter 9. The next section turns to another issue that must be considered before analyzing the speeches: the law itself.

1.3. READING THE CONTEXT

Ego qualem Kalendis Ianuariis acceperim rem publicam, Quirites, intellego, plenam sollicitudinis, plenam timoris.

I well know the condition of the state I inherited on the 1st of January, citizens: wracked with anxiety and with fear.
—Cicero, *de lege agraria* 2.8

Aristotle's scheme of *logos*, *ethos*, and *pathos* provides a convenient scheme for isolating principles to analyze Cicero's first two agrarian speeches and set into relief the deficits of some prior analyses. There is one matter that lies outside that scheme—the *polis* itself, one might say, that is, the context in which Cicero's speeches were given. To wit, the Rullan bill was an innovative measure that had a clear view of political and economic circumstances. That clear view is exactly

---

65. For a history of these ideas, see Lobur 2008.

66. Not quite the same point, but worth quoting here, is Mack 1937: 12—a general claim about Cicero especially clear in the agrarian speeches: "So machte es Cicero sich geschickt zunutze, daß sich Senatsreden und Volksreden geradezu komplementär ergänzten, um auf dem politischen Broschürenmarkt eine möglichst breite und durchschlagende Wirkung zu erzielen. Zugleich kämpfte er so für sein politisches Ziel, den *consensus omnium bonorum*, das Ziel, daß er während seines ganzen Lebens zu verwirklichen bestrebt gewesen ist."

what underlies the innovations—and the innovations, in turn, are what inspires Cicero's resistance.

Political Anxieties

The sixties were indeed days "full of anxiety" and "full of fear,"[67] just as Cicero says in the epigraph to this section. "Fear" registers the real political ferment of those days (from one perspective). As I have mentioned, in the 60s political momentum was with the *populares* or "men of the people," so called not after their class of origin but after their base of power and professed objects of concern and opposed to the political dominance of (certain factions of) the senate.[68] That was a noteworthy reverse. It had not been twenty years since the dictator Sulla, victorious in the civil war of 82, had tilted the constitution heavily in the senate's favor.[69] Above all he had severely curtailed the powers of the people's officers, the tribunes. But these were restored in 70, with the acquiescence and support of the great general Pompey, then consul. Tribunes presently took the lead in bringing measures that aimed severally to undo Sulla's remaining arrangements, exploit popular sovereignty, curb abuses of authority, or serve the good of the commons.

The efforts did not always succeed—but were usually divisive. Thus C. Cornelius, tribune of 67 and a former officer of Pompey, pushed an ambitious program that checked privilege and championed equity. He tried to block profiteering by legates sent overseas, thus limiting the value of legateships as political rewards, and he called for the return of some properties confiscated by Sulla. (Sulla, among other legally dubious and politically ruthless moves, had political opponents "proscribed" or declared public enemies, making their lives forfeit and their property public).[70] For the first century CE historian Asconius, Cornelius was *iusto pertinacior*: he "went too far" or "crossed the line" (lit. was

---

67. Cf. also *LA* 1.23; ch. 6, Table 6.2.2, row M.

68. That much, at least, is safe to ascribe to the *populares*, who, with their "opposite" the *optimates*, continue to be conceptualized in numerous ways; see e.g. Mouritsen 2017: 112–23, Hölkeskamp 2010: 76–97, Robb 2010: 15–33, with bibliography. On the role of Cicero's own political self-justification in bending the meaning of *popularis*, see Tracy 2008–2009.

69. He had barred tribunes from holding further offices; cut (somehow) their *intercessio* or veto power (Cic. *Ver.* 2.1.155); and very likely abolished their right to initiate legislation (Livy *Epit.* 89; cf. Cic. *Leg.* 3.22). For other ancient sources on Sulla's reforms, see Broughton 1952: 39–40, 74–76, 79. On Sulla's treatment of the tribunate, see Kunkel and Witman 1995: 655–59, Sandberg 2001: 36–40. For an assessment of Sulla's effects on the Roman "constitution," see Steel 2014.

70. For details of the proscriptions, see Hinard 1985.

"more stubborn than was proper").[71] His program made the atmosphere tense. Cicero—then running for praetor and thus highly attuned to the mood of the city—complains to his friend and confidant Atticus that the climate had worsened rapidly.[72]

Other tribunes exploited the legal right of the popular assembly to grant military commands—a right Sulla had, in theory, made obsolete.[73] Aulus Gabinius in 67 proposed a law granting a special command with broad authority for Pompey against pirates, then a menace in the Mediterranean. The mechanism, a tribunician law, was populist, as was no small part of the objective: piracy, by hampering trade, drove up grain prices, which hit the poor harder. The next year C. Manilius, also then tribune, proposed that the war against Mithridates, king of Pontus in Asia Minor who had long roiled the Eastern frontier, be entrusted to Pompey, already in the field—replacing the Pontic command of L. Licinius Lucullus, a staunch supporter of senatorial primacy. These measures, too, were divisive: the senate, at least, were divided about the wisdom of the Manilian law and had opposed the Gabinian law almost to a man, having tried to block it by a favorite trick, putting up a tribune to interpose his veto.[74] (The veto, which could block almost any political action, was a powerful tool, and senatorial factions sometimes found a tribune to use it in their interests.) But Gabinius came near to having his colleague voted out of office.[75]

Here were not merely squabbles over power and privilege. Behind the initiatives lay a kind of *popularis* constitutional theory.[76] In championing special

---

71. For a reconstruction of the events and circumstances of Cornelius' tribunate, see Ward 1970; Griffin 1973; Gruen 1974: 213–16.

72. "I'm really excited about them—and completely disgusted with everything else. You can't imagine how much worse you will find things in the short time since you left" (*summum me eorum studium tenet, sicut odium iam ceterarum rerum; quas tu incredibile est quam brevi tempore quanto deteriores offensurus sis quam reliquisti, Att.* 1.11.3, 67, of his library and the delayed elections respectively, cf. Shackleton-Bailey 1965 *ad loc.*).

73. Sulla's arrangements regularized promagistracies and therefore, in principle, fixed the pool of available military commanders.

74. Gabinian Law: Plu. *Pomp.* 25.3–4 depicts a senate fearing broad powers and only Caesar speaking in favor. Manilian Law: Plu. *Pomp.* 30.3 depicts a senate privately anxious but, except for Catulus, afraid to speak out publicly; Cic. *Leg. Man.* gives a more nuanced picture, with four distinguished consulars in favor (68) and Catulus and Hortenius opposed on traditionalist grounds (52–63).

75. Ascon. 72C. The tribune, one L. Trebellius, withdrew his veto only because the voting had begun and was about to ratify Gabinius's bill.

76. Cf. Mackie 1992: 71: "If we want to understand the place in Roman politics of the people called *popularis*, we will have to look beyond their flattery of the populace, beyond the fact that they legislated for the people's benefit, and beyond their motives as well. The missing criterion

commands, Gabinius and Manilius were exploiting the *de iure* sovereignty of the Roman people to bypass a traditional prerogative of the senate. That was how the famous populist reformers, the brothers Gracchi, won passage of their agrarian bills and other legislation in the 120s, and that was how the populist tribune C. Saturninus secured commands for C. Marius in the 100s. In getting a fellow tribune ousted, Gabinius was following the lead of Tiberius Gracchus, who had forced a colleague out of office on the grounds that a tribune who ignored the will of the people thereby voided the authority vested in him.[77] The view struck a blow at the very idea of a magistracy: the elected official became only a kind of mouthpiece with conditional and revocable authority; full authority remained with the people. The idea is like that behind the recall elections of recent US politics: failures, often of ideological purity, are held to warrant removal from office before office-holders complete their terms.

In these measures, then, there is a maximalist understanding of popular sovereignty. There were complementary attempts to limit or remedy arbitrary exercises of authority. Among the reforms of Cornelius was a requirement that praetors, who declared at the beginning of their offices the sorts of cases they would allow, be bound by that declaration—blocking arbitrary deviations that could, say, favor a friend or ally.[78] Other examples are more striking. Julius Caesar, after being elected curule aedile in 65, prosecuted the killers of the proscribed for murder, implicitly rejecting Sulla's legal maneuver of nearly twenty years before. More striking still was a trial later in 63, in which Caesar would revive an old procedure to try one Rabirius, present at the killing of the tribune Saturninus almost forty years before. The target was not the old man but the form of senate decree by which the killing was justified and thus the authority of the senate itself.[79] This was almost an attempt to reclaim history; not only Saturninus in

---

would appear to be their use of *popularis* ideology: the fact that they not only flattered the populace or distributed material benefits, but also encouraged it to seek power, as of right, at the senate's expense." Cf. Wiseman 1994 *passim*; Wiseman 2009; Arena 2012: 6–8. For an overview of tribunes and their programs in 63, see Drummond 1999. On the political culture of ancient Rome more generally, see Hölkeskamp 2010.

77. Plu. *TG* 15, esp. 15.2; App. *BC* 1.12; Arena 2012: 124–25.

78. On this *edictum perpetuum*, see Gruen 1974: 251. Asconius *Corn.* 52.7–8 C observes that the measure "squelched the enthusiasm or favoritism of ambitious praetors who had been in the habit of giving inconsistent rulings" (*studium aut gratiam ambitiosis praetoribus qui varie ius dicere assueverant sustulit*). On that problem, see Lintott 1977.

79. For a summary of the issues in the *pro Rabirio*, cf. Tyrrell 1978. Other such *popularis* measures are the reduction of the penalties of the *lex Calpurnia* and the restoration of the *lex Domitia*. As Mitchell points out, all this is very likely to be "the work of a single, organized,

100 but Tiberius Gracchus in 133, his brother Gaius in 121, and the populist rebel Marcus Aemilius Lepidus in 77 had been pursued under that same decree—the first three killed. Voiding the decree was a symbolic redemption of their deaths. The apologies for past injustice of contemporary political cultures are perhaps not far different.

Economic Anxieties

Cicero's description of the atmosphere of 64 as fearful registers the anxiety of those like himself who dreaded instability. And even on an uncharitable interpretation, instability in some form really was likely to accompany the efforts of the *populares*. But Cicero's "fear" also registers another anxiety—economic anxiety, and there "fear" is no biased description. Debt was a pressing problem. Sallust, as we have seen, mentions "massive (*ingens*) debt" in 63. The problem must have been building. Debt relief had probably been a plank in the losing consular campaign of L. Sergius Catilina, or Catiline, in the summer of 64. The next year, undaunted or desperate or both, he ran again, and the chief feature of his supporters, as Cicero describes them, is debt, cutting across class lines, from holders of large estates to small farmers and businessmen.[80] When after his second rebuff Catiline decided at last on the coup that would be famously suppressed by Cicero, one of the boons he promised to his co-conspirators was *tabulae novae*, literally "new accounts," that is, the abolition of debts.[81]

The immediate cause of debt appears to have been tight credit.[82] That problem in turn is partly linked to Sulla's colonies. Sulla, abusing his post of dictator,

---

and powerfully backed reform movement" (1979: 182)—something very like the platform of a modern political party. For a different view, see Drummond 1999.

80. First class: those unwilling to sell properties despite great debt (2.18); second class: political hopefuls in great debt (2.19); third class: Sullan colonists in debt, along with poor rustics (2.20); fourth class: varied, but long indebted and targets of civil lawsuits (2.21); fifth class: thugs and the like (2.22); sixth class: gamblers, adulterers (2.23).

81. Sall. *Catil.* 21.2. So the apparent meaning of the phrase, which is repeated by Cicero (*Cat.* 2.18) as a possible desideratum of the first class of n. 80; cf. also *Off.* 2.84, where Cicero records that calls for *tabulae novae* were never fiercer than when he was consul. A universal bankruptcy settlement, forcing creditors to take partial payment in satisfaction of debts, would normally be called a *lex de aere alieno* 'debt law.' According to Sallust, Catiline also promised "proscription of the rich, magistracies, priesthoods, looting . . ." (*proscriptionem locupletium, magistratus, sacerdotia, rapinas . . . , Cat.* 21.2).

82. Cicero mentions the issue in both of our speeches, attributing it to tribunician disruption: cf. ch. 6, Table 6.2.2, row P. His attribution of the collapse solely to political causes need not, of course, be correct.

had forcibly carved out settlements for his veterans and confiscated land from political enemies. Some of the dispossessed drifted to the city. They were among the new voters probably enrolled by the censors of 70.[83] That made political campaigns more expensive, not least because elections commonly featured bribery, and the pool of voters was now larger and, perhaps, poorer. A spate of measures against bribery in these years show that money was indeed being spent that way.[84] Furthermore recent administrative decisions had widened the pool of political competitors. With these changes, more money per person was now needed by more people, and that, by normal market forces, would have driven up the cost of borrowing.

Second, the rural real estate market—a very important market in an economy not fully monetized and dependent on land as a store of value—must have been stagnant. Here again Sulla's new colonies also played a role. They had not flourished. The story can be glimpsed in the sources. The land was not always good;[85] some colonists, for that or other reasons, failed,[86] and then sold, transferred, or abandoned their property.[87] Large landowners came into possession of some of

---

83. Voters: "The censors of 70, the first since the early 80s, had perhaps inscribed on the rolls of the centuriate assembly for the first time a mass of Italian voters, including well-off men full of goodwill to friends of Pompey and often to Cicero himself; the increase in bribery in elections from this period may indicate that the old noble houses had less control than before" (Rawson 1975: 51); cf. Wiseman 1969: 65–67. Competitors: Among the arrangements imposed by Sulla in 82–81 was a senate doubled in size, from 300 to 600, and guaranteed entry into it for all twenty quaestors. As of 70, tribunes, ten each year, were no longer blocked from pursuing other offices.

84. The *lex Acilia et Calpurnia de ambitu* was passed in 67 (Dio 36.38.1–40.1). The excesses of the campaign of 64 prompted Cicero as consul to propose a law on bribery the next year, which expanded previous legislation by adding the extra penalty of ten years' exile (Dio 37.29.1, *Vat.* 37), extending culpability under the law over those bribed to meet or attend the candidates and over those who gave seats at shows or dinners to particular tribes (*Mur.* 67) and preventing anyone within two years of an election from giving a gladiatorial show (*Sest.* 133). On all these efforts, see Lintott 1990: 1–16; Riggsby 1999: 21–49.

85. See Brunt 1971: 310–11, who points out that Sallust has M. Aemilius Lepidus complain that veterans have been "relegated to swamps and forests" (*relegati in paludes et silvas*, Sal. *Or. Lep.* (*Hist.* 1.49M) 23). Cicero also describes Sullan colonial land as swampy (*pestilens*, *LA* 1.15, 2.70, 2.71, 2.98) and also sterile (*vastus*, *LA* 2.70; *sterilis*, *LA* 2.70 bis); see further discussion in chs. 5.3, 7.3.

86. The very fact that it is difficult to determine where all of them were is one sign of their failure. For a list of settlement areas, see Keaveney 1982a: 515–33; for the failures of the colonies, Keaveney 1982b: 153–54.

87. That is suggested in particular by the apparent mechanics of Rullus' bill; see ch. 7.3 The Voices of the (Un-)Tribune.

that land[88] but must not have always been able to profit. Poorer land, as we know from agricultural writers, needed close on-site management and was thus hard to work profitably with slaves.[89] Furthermore, not only were the original Sullan colonists forbidden to alienate in the first place,[90] but restitution of confiscated land was now in the air.[91] In short, some poorer and unprofitable Sullan colonial land was now held under insecure title. That made the land hard to profit from, sell,[92] or borrow against, producing both a need for borrowing (to meet maintenance costs or service debt) and a smaller pool of good collateral against which to borrow.

The prospect of Pompey's return must have made the problem worse. In the span of a few years, Pompey, thanks to the tribunician bills already mentioned, had stabilized the East, defeating the pirates and dislodging Mithridates. Now, exceeding the limits of his brief, he was reorganizing Asia Minor. No major commands were on the horizon; his return to Rome must have seemed imminent. And that prospect must have bent the credit market. Indeed, Pompey's quick victories had probably already had an effect.[93] With the famously profitable East at long last secure, lenders would be calling in loans to shift capital there.[94] That was almost certainly the destination of the hard currency whose export Cicero

---

88. *at videmus, ut longinqua mittamus, agrum Praenestinum a paucis possideri* (*LA* 2.78; C6 in Appendix 2). Praeneste had harbored Marius and was punished by Sulla with the foundation of a military colony.

89. Cf. Havas 1976 and ch. 7 n. 43.

90. The only evidence is Cicero: *nam si dicent per legem id* [= expansion of personal holdings by acquisition of colonial plots] *non licere, ne per Corneliam quidem licet* (*LA* 2.78; C6 in Appendix 2). On the complexities of *Sullani possessores*, see Drummond 2000; on their treatment in these speeches through the person of Rullus's father-in-law, see ch. 7.3 The Voices of the (Un-)Tribune.

91. The tribune Cornelius (n. 71) had proposed such restitution in 67 and the issue was possibly still alive in 64. See the references in ch. 6 n. 41.

92. Cicero's first class of Catilinarian supporters are those so in love with their properties they cannot bear to sell them, despite their debts (*eorum, qui magno in aere alieno maiores etiam possessiones habent, quarum amore adducti dissolvi nullo modo possunt, Catil.* 2.18), but their reluctance makes sense if they were hoping for prices to rise.

93. Pompey made short work of the pirates and by the summer of 65 had driven Mithridates to the Cimmerian Bosporus. Rather than follow him, Pompey—plainly not considering him a threat—had chosen to push east and south, busying himself with affairs in Syria and beyond. For a summary of Pompey's career, see Seager 2002 [1979].

94. Gruen 1974: 427. After the defeat of Mithridates Roman Asia was the site of rapid reinvestment; cf. Frank 1933: 278, 342–46, 387–89, 392.

would block later in 63.[95] Once it seemed Pompey was returning, credit must have tightened all the more. Some creditors will have wished to square accounts in advance of possible instability and disruption, in case Pompey followed the precedent of Sulla and returned from the East to extract a dictatorship, as many thought he would.[96] Caesar seems to have had a similar effect on finance in 49.[97] The agricultural economy must have been affected in particular. Some nursed the hope that Pompey would undo Sulla's dispossessions.[98] Would he? Furthermore, it was now the practice that generals disbanding their troops found them farm plots. Sulla's colonies had settled tens of thousands of men. Would Pompey do the same? The questions must have further slowed sales of land, investment in it, or its use as collateral.[99] In effect secure title to much agricultural property was held in suspension.

1.4. THE RULLAN BILL

Audacia duplicem frontem habet.

There are two sides to 'boldness.'

—Marius Victorinus, *Explanationes in Ciceronis Rhetoricam* 1.3: 167, 20 Halm

It was this complex of problems—a stagnant agricultural economy, along with the likely needs of a returning Pompey—that the Rullan bill was designed to attack, using the constitutional theory of the *populares*, the principles of which are clear enough in the attested measures of the bill. The measures are aimed at a set of problems that really come down to one thing: *ager publicus*. *Ager publicus*, or formally *ager publicus populi Romani* "public land of the Roman people," was land that Rome confiscated from defeated enemies. That land was managed in a

---

95. *Vat.* 12, *Flac.* 67.

96. Cf. Vell. 2.40.2 (*quippe plerique non sine exercitu venturum in urbem adfirmarunt et libertati publicae statuturum arbitrio suo modum*), Dio 37.44.3, Plu. *Pomp.* 43.1, App. *Mith.* 116, and see Gruen 1970: 239.

97. Frederiksen 1966: 132; for an account of Caesar's measures to check the problem, as bold and creative as the problem of debt was wide, cf. 133–41.

98. Gruen 1970.

99. Valerius Maximus describes a comparable problem following the rebellion of Catiline: "at a time when the state was so roiled by Catiline's fury that, on account of the unrest, not even the wealthy could pay their creditors the money they owed by selling off property" (*Catilinae furore ita consternata re publica, ut ne a locupletibus quidem debitae pecuniae propter tumultum pretiis possessionum deminutis solvi creditoribus possent*, 4.8.3).

variety of ways, including permitting private exploitation: untenanted land could be occupied if there was no contrary directive.[100] Such occupied and exploited, but formally still public, land was the target of the famous Gracchan legislation: the legislation limited the amount of such land that large holders could occupy. That was an obvious source of land and required little legal maneuvering to make it available for settlement: it already belonged to the state.[101] But by Cicero's time almost all of the *ager publicus* acquired by land confiscation after the Second Punic War and held under *possessio* (or 'possession,' in its narrow sense of physical control) by wealthy landowners at the time of the Gracchan legislation was now held under maximally private ownership (*dominium*, in later agrimensorial jargon): that was the effect of an agrarian law of 111, five years before Cicero's birth.[102]

Sources of Land

The Rullan bill therefore had to be creative—not only in finding land but also in devising the constitutional and other mechanisms to acquire or control it. And that it did, with the creativity and constitutional theory typical of the *populares*. The framers' basic line of thought can be read off the details of the bill. There was only one major tract of *ager publicus* left in Italy, the fertile *ager Campanus* around Capua, with the nearby *ager Stellas*. They were already occupied by tenants, but the Rullan bill would colonize them, probably by subdividing the land further, as resettlement schemes sometimes did.[103] But how to subdivide it? That task would

---

100. For a full history of *ager publicus*, see Roselaar 2010.

101. On Cicero's engagement with that idea, see ch. 7, Table 7.3.4, row K with discussion.

102. That much is clear despite the difficulties of interpretation of this law. On the law, see Roselaar 2010; Sacchi 2005; de Ligt 2001; Lintott 1993, with C. Mackay's review; Johannsen 1971. What public land remained thereafter was given over to Sulla's veterans ("The remaining *ager occupatorius* was privatized during the period of Sulla, when large areas of land were needed for distributions to veteran soldiers. After this period we never hear of it again," Roselaar 2010: 297). Sulla created some fresh *ager publicus* by punitive sequestrations, and some of it, as at Volaterrae (cf. n. 63) and Arretium, had not been wholly distributed, but such land appears not to have been extensive. The chief remaining public land was thus the *ager Campanus* (Roselaar 2010: 286, 297), which neither the Gracchi nor Sulla had touched (*LA* 1.21, 2.18 = C17 in Appendix 2); For a full list of locations of *ager publicus*, see Roselaar 2010: 298–325. There is indirect testimony to the relative lack of *ager publicus* in Italy in *LA* 2. Cicero sneers at Rullus for having dredged up Italian territories to sell by, as it were, poring over the plat-books at the county courthouse (*LA* 1.2, 1.4; see further ch. 3.3 The Wastrel). Rullus's method implies available properties were not easy to find.

103. For the example of Arretium, cf. Plin. *NH* 3.52, which names three groups of settlers there (*Veteres, Fidentiores, Iulienses*); Brunt 1971: 306.

be complicated. Surveying and settling properties was time-consuming. The decemvirs would need help and would need time. Each was thus assigned twenty *finitores* or surveyors, with, it seems, some powers of independent judgment—a considerable staff;[104] and the decemvirs would be in office for five years, an unattested term for agrarian commissioners.[105]

But the *ager Campanus* was slated to absorb only 5,000 new settlers.[106] If a higher number of settlers were to be given land, for example (some of) Pompey's returning army, more land was needed. From where? Abroad? Overseas colonies, such as earlier legislation had sometimes proposed,[107] seem to have been ruled out in the first instance (left as an option, it may be, for future legislation, perhaps after consulting a returned Pompey). In Italy, then? Where? Some of Sulla's colonies had been abandoned; these could be repeopled. But that land was, one may hazard, likely to be poorer, which, as we have seen, was at least part of why it had been abandoned in the first place.[108] The better land was in private hands, and that included possessors of other Sullan land no longer in the hands of the original colonists.

But using that land posed five major problems. First, as noted earlier, there was a problem of title, since the original Sullan assignations forbade alienation. The bill solved the problem by granting title to secondary possessors, freeing them to sell.[109] Second, there was a constitutional issue. The Rullan decemvirate would

---

104. For the complexities of colonizing land created by the lack of verifiable platting, see Roselaar 2010, esp. 86–145.

105. The Gracchan commissioners were elected yearly; other commissions seem to have dissolved when their business was done. When fixed terms are attested, they are three years (Liv. 32.29.4, 197, to found five colonies, cf. 34.45.2; 34.53.2, 194, to found two colonies). It is only after the Rullan bill that five-year terms appear, in Pompey's superintendence of the grain supply in 62 and in governorships. For a survey of special commands, see Boak 1918, Baldson 1939. For a list of military *imperia extra ordinem*, see Gruen 1974: 534–43.

106. *LA* 2.76, 77, 96; C4 and C5 in Appendix 2.

107. Junonia was founded on the site of Carthage by Gaius Gracchus (122); Narbo Martius was established in Transalpine Gaul (118); and Saturninus and C. Marius aimed to provide allotments there and establish colonies in Achaea, Macedonia, and Sicily, among other places (sources for the last in Scullard 1982: 400). For a history of Roman colonization under the Republic, see Salmon 1969.

108. Cicero cites as possible settlement sites under the Rullan bill two Apulian coastal towns where colonies had been abandoned—the one arid and the other swampy (*in Sipontina siccitate, in Salpinorum pestilentiae, LA* 2.71). See further ch. 5.3 Home Sweet Home.

109. The clause read *qui post Marium et Carbonem consules agri, aedificia, lacus, stagna, loca, publice data adsignata, vendita, concessa sunt, ea omnia eo iure sint, ut quae optimo iure privata sunt* (*LA* 3.7); Drummond 2000.

have reclaimed or transferred land across the empire, sometimes in provinces formally under the control of a governor. To ensure the validity of the decisions, the bill granted the commissioners *praetoria potestas*, or the rank of praetor, the second-highest regular officer. That rank brought *imperium*, the "right of command," in which the necessary civil jurisdiction was entailed.[110]

Third, there was a problem of labor. Some of the Sullan land was not ideal, and the experience of his colonists had suggested that veterans did not always make the best farmers or farm managers. The bill saw that problem. Pompey's veterans could be assigned to the fine land in the Campania—perhaps even leaving the land in the hands of the current possessors and accepting rent from them, as was sometimes done by new possessors. But less good land would need experienced hands at the plow, and the bill planned to put them there. The Roman populace was divided into tribes. The first four were the so-called "urban tribes," originally residents of the city, and the remaining thirty-one were "rural tribes." The distribution of allotments was to begin with the first of rural tribes, omitting the four urban tribes, apparently a breach of (some now unknown) conventional order.[111] By the 60s, the rural tribes included citizens from (now non-contiguous) geographical districts from all over Italy—and thus included citizens dispossessed or disrupted by the Sullan colonial schemes or debt problems, some of whom now lived in Rome, as noted earlier.[112] A resettlement scheme would have found support among such immigrants, as also among the old urban plebs proper, with whom the new arrivals competed for doles, housing, and day labor.[113] Was there a further, purely political motive behind the measure? Were some *populares* glad

---

110. Lintott 1999: 96–97. The *lex agraria* of 111 (24, 33–6) shows adjudications of the status of land reserved to consuls, praetors, and sometimes censors.

111. *LA* 2.79, C7 in Appendix 2. Cicero implies that the four urban tribes usually came first; see ch. 9.2.

112. "Probably men registered in the urban tribes were predominantly freedmen, while peasants who had drifted into Rome remained in their old rural tribes; certainly, those who had migrated since the last census in 69 will have done so," Brunt 1971: 313. If Rullus really did remark in the senate that some of the *plebs urbana* had to be "drained off" (cf. n. 27), it is these tribesmen he had in mind, which is to say *plebs urbana* in the loose, and not the technical, sense; the four urban tribes were not immediate beneficiaries of the bill. Cicero in *Att.* 1.19.4 must have had the same population in mind (cf. *Italiae solitudinem frequentari posse*, cf. ch. 7 n. 71). For the different political aims of the *plebs urbana* and the *rustici*, see Meier 1980: 95–100.

113. Grain distributions had been reintroduced in 73, but the number was restricted to 40,000, excluding some four-fifths of the urban poor (Brunt 1971: 119–20). It is not clearly known how the doles were administered. But, if the dole was not confined to the urban tribes, more poor in the city in and of itself meant more competition. Caesar's reduction of the number may work hand in glove with his colonization of the *ager Campanus*.

to see a reduction in the number of Italians, with their apparent fondness for conservative and moderate characters like Cicero, thus tipping the balance of urban voters in favor of an urban proletariat that was or was becoming, as it were, predictably volatile? Was the measure also a kind of redistricting?

There was a fourth problem, not confined to Sullan land: purchasing land required money. That was not a purely financial problem. It had a political aspect. If the senate, which traditionally oversaw state finances, controlled the funding source, or could gain access to funds once gathered, the project could be starved. Similar things had happened to agrarian projects before.[114] The framers of the bill, doubtless to forestall such interference, decided to create a dedicated revenue stream—as it were, a declaration of fiscal independence. But such a stream posed a topographical problem. Without known funding, it was hard to know in advance how many colonies could be founded or how much land could be bought. The bill's solution was to allow the decemvirs free choice about where to found colonies (*LA* 1.16, 2.73–4). That was in marked distinction to most agrarian bills, which envisioned particular colonies in advance.[115] The broad, untargeted authority made the Rullan decemvir less like a commissioner and more like a magistrate able to exercise wide personal discretion.

Sources of Funds

And, to come to the fifth problem, there was, of course, the purely financial question: Where would the independent revenue stream come from? The Rullan bill turned chiefly to sales of various kinds of public property of various kinds (*LA* 1.1–13 *deferat*, 2.38–59). That was a thoughtful solution. The public, in theory, already had a right to the value of that property, and the bill was merely acting on that right (rather as the Gracchan land legislation was merely taking possession of what was already public). But of the particular kinds of public property available, each posed obstacles of its own. One source of funds was to be spoils of war (*LA* 1.11–13, 2.59), which formally belonged to the state. That presented a political problem. The richest pending source of spoils was Pompey, who had just pacified Asia Minor. But in 63, a bill was less likely to pass a popular assembly if it appeared to harm Pompey's interests. The rhetoric of Cicero's second speech

---

114. The senate had allowed Tiberius's commission an insultingly paltry sum (Plu. *TG* 13) for expenses. Plotius's scheme of 70 (Cic. *Att.* 1.18.6, Dio 38.5.1–2, Plu. *Luc.* 34.3–4; Gabba 1950; Smith 1957; Marshall 1972) also failed for lack of cash, but that would have been capital expenditure, not operating costs.

115. Cf. Flach 1990.

alone, which cites him constantly (*LA* 2.23–5, 46, 49, 52–4, 60–62, 99), makes that clear. Hence the bill excepted Pompey by name (*LA* 1.13, 2.60). Not only would he thus benefit, but an enemy of his would suffer. Surely one source of war spoils the framers had in mind was Pompey's predecessor Lucullus, who had returned from the East laden with wealth (Plu. *Luc.* 36.6) and was still awaiting a triumph outside the city. On this point, then, the bill was more or less openly partisan.

A second source of funds was various properties in Italy and Sicily (*LA* 1.2–6, 2.46–55). In some cases, at least, these had already been slated for sale.[116] The bill had shrewdly identified another unexploited source of revenue already belonging to the public and asked the public to authorize the sale as of right. But here the problem was constitutional practice. Selling off such property was not normally a job for agrarian commissioners; finances were generally under the superintendence of the senate, and selling off properties was, ultimately, the role of censors or, if no censors were in office, of consuls.[117] The Rullan bill would be transferring to an irregular officer the duty of a regular officer. That was also true, more boldly so, of another category of public property, which was a third source of funds. There were various properties in the provinces, some already being rented, others probably simply occupied. Some of these properties, which were sometimes specifically named in the bill and sometimes not, would also be sold (*LA* 1.5, 2.50–51); here, too, an untapped source of revenue had astutely been found. Cicero's complaints that the decemvirs would gather funds from every available source is not naked exaggeration.[118] But here, too, there was a problem. In the

---

116. *datur igitur eis primum ut liceat vendere omnia DE QVIBVS VENDENDIS SENATVS CONSVLTA FACTA SVNT M. TVLLIO CN. CORNELIO CONSVLIBUS POST<VE> EA*; Ferrary 1988: 149–50 and n. 41. The properties were slated for sale, according to Cicero, to remedy revenue shortfalls (*propter angustias aerarii, LA* 2.36). Cicero names some of the properties (*LA* 2.36): generically, *loca publica urbis* "public urban spaces" and *sacella* "consecrated plots" (*LA* 2.36); specifically, the *mons Gaurus* (now Monte Barbaro) in the Campania, well-watered, rich in vines, and producing a decent wine (Col. 1.5.2, Plin. *Nat.* 14.64; other references in Manuwald 2018: 274; Harvey 1972: 43 speculates that by *mons Gaurus* Cicero is referring generally to the southeast portion of the *ager Campanus*, which had been under Capua's control until it became *ager publicus* in 211); willow groves near Minturnae (for speculation as to their precise location, see Harvey 1972: 45–46 with references); and the *via Herculanea* that ran between Puteoli and Baiae (Diod. Sic. 4.22.1–2; Prop. 1.11.1–2; 3.18.1–4). Of all these Cicero says only *vendere*: doubtless only their use rights were for sale.

117. For censors selling state property, see Livy 32.7.1–3; for the details of the censorship, see Suolahti 1963.

118. At the beginning of the section of on the purchase of land, Cicero summarizes the previous sections, on the gathering of funds, thus: "So it's now plain to you, conscript fathers, how the decemviral fund is built up and heaped up from every source by all possible means" (*videtis iam, patres conscripti, omnibus rebus et modis constructam et coacervatam pecuniam decemviralem, LA*

provinces all forms of jurisdiction normally belonged to provincial governors. How could a decemvir work there? Legitimate authority was needed. This, then, is another reason—and perhaps the chief one—for the grant, not merely of *imperium*, but of *praetoria potestas* specifically, which would create an authority functionally parallel to a provincial governor. Here the constitutional precedent was the special military commands of recent years.[119] Those commands had also created overlapping spheres of authority, sending out a commander elected by the popular assembly into provinces that were in the hands of governors whom the senate had chosen.[120]

The bill was thus creative in its attempt to build an independent revenue stream to allow the purchase of land. Rullan decemvirs would have a wide writ. They would have been able to work both in Italy and in the provinces, probably cooperatively in the former and singly in the latter, though some provincial tasks might also have required joint effort (for example, determining land tenancy in Asia Minor). Hence another problem: jurisdiction. *Imperium* was usually linked to a specific geographical region. But not so that of the decemvirs. According to Cicero, the bill did not limit their *imperium*, formally (*iure*) or geographically (*regionibus . . . certis*, *LA* 2.35),[121] and decemvirs could visit any province at all (*omnis provincias obeundi . . . summa potestas datur*, *LA* 2.34) and even return to

---

1.14); "But imagine, citizens, that the decemvirs have acquired their money—as much as there is on earth! Imagine they've omitted nothing: that they've sold every city, field, and kingdom, and even your tax-properties, and on top of that they have the war spoils of your commanders" (*parta sit pecunia, Quirites, decemviris tanta quanta sit in terris, nihil praetermissum sit, omnes urbes, agri, regna denique, postremo etiam vectigalia vestra venierint, accesserint in cumulum manubiae vestrorum imperatorum, LA* 2.62).

119. For a survey of special commands, see Boak 1918; for a list of military *imperia extra ordinem*, see Gruen 1974: 534–43. The constitutional particulars are not always clear. For discussions of the precise relation of the *imperium* of Pompey's commands, *maius* or not, to that of governors, see Ehrenberg 1953; Jameson 1970.

120. Signally, a piece of tribunician legislation, the *lex Manilia*, passed by the tribal assembly, gave Pompey the command over Mithridates, taking it from Lucullus, who had secured Asia as his proconsular province in the ordinary way, by a drawing of lots, after his term of office.

121. "There's never even been a kingdom that was not limited, if not by some law as such, at least by certain physical boundaries. But this one has no boundaries at all! It contains, according to the terms of the bill, every kingdom, and your empire in all its breadth, and districts that you do not control ('are free of you') or sometimes have never even heard of" (*nullum enim regnum fuit umquam quod non se, <si> minus iure aliquo, at regionibus tamen certis contineret. Hoc vero infinitum est, quo et regna omnia et vestrum imperium, quod latissime patet, et ea quae partim libera a vobis, partim etiam ignorata vobis sunt, permissu legis continentur, LA* 2.35). *Infinitum*, also applied by Cicero to M. Antonius's special command against the pirates in 74 (*Ver.* 2.2.8, 2.3.213), is, at least in part, literally meant ("without a physical boundary"); *contra* Brennan 2000: 427–8, Jameson 1970: 542.

Italy (*cum velint, Romae esse*, ibid.). According to Cicero, this was the old privilege only of a consul.[122] Here, too, the special military commands of recent years were the immediate model: they had permitted crossing provincial boundaries. But in the Rullan bill such special authority, for the first time, is meant for a non-military purpose.[123]

Mechanisms

In short in 64 boldness and ingenuity were required to find and arrange for control of land and still more to pay for it. Resistance, already predictable in the case of an agrarian bill, was all the more predictable; and so measures, some of dubious integrity, were included to ensure the bill's success and block any arbitrary exercise of authority against it (such exercises, as we have seen, being a target of *popularis* activity). One such measure concerned the procedure normally required to grant praetorian *imperium*, the *lex curiata*.[124] The passage of that law was a mere formality, carried out by lictors representing a now long obsolete form of assembly. Rullus's bill specified that a particular praetor sponsor the bill for that *lex*: the first praetor elected or, if necessary, the last.[125] Roman laws did sometimes designate officers by order of election. But it was now January. The election for that year's praetors had been held the previous summer. The bill therefore had particular men in mind—men who could evidently be counted on to carry the job through.[126] But, second, even if the *lex curiata* failed to pass, the decemvirs would still have their authority (*LA* 2.29)—as it were, still assume their duties, even if a judge refused to administer the oath of office; the popular will was thus implicitly sufficient to create the power. Third, the electoral mechanism was both populist

---

122. Cic. *Att.* 8.15.3, cf. *Phil.* 4.9; "Senators (and C. evidently has only Senators in view) other than the Consuls or those charged with an office or mission outside of Italy had to obtain special permission to go overseas," Shackleton-Bailey 1968: 355 (ad *Att.* 3.6).

123. There is also a kind of non-military forerunner in the mission of P. Cornelius Lentulus Marcellinus to the then brand-new province of Cyrene in 75 (Sall. *Hist.* 2.43M), probably to collect monies in the wake of the grain shortages of that year; see Badian 1965: 120; Brennan 2000: 408–9. Lentulus did not, however, hold *imperium* or work outside of Cyrene.

124. Mommsen, *RS*³ I:99, 609–15; Lintott 1991: 49; other references in Manuwald 2018: 246.

125. *iubet enim, qui primus sit praetor factus, eum legem curiatam ferre; sin is ferre non possit, qui postremus sit* (*LA* 2.28). A law could designate a magistrate by his election order: for such designations, see Ferrary 1977: 647–51; the Greek translations of the *lex de piratis* contain the phrases ὕ]πατος ὃς ἂν πρῶτος γένητ[αι "whichever consul is elected first" and ὕπατος ὁ πρῶτος γενόμενος "the first consul elected."

126. Cf. "The provisions for the appointments of the commissioners openly sought as far as possible to ensure the election of particular persons," Gelzer 1968: 44.

in feel and easy to manipulate. The Roman constitution had various electoral procedures. To elect the chief priest, seventeen of the thirty-five tribes of the one of the assemblies, the *Comitia Tributa* or tribal assembly, were chosen by lot; the victorious candidate thus had to carry only nine tribes (*LA* 2.16). The mechanism originated as a legal nicety. Through it the people had a share in electing a priesthood, properly a privilege of the very oldest noble families, the patricians; but at the same time a majority would not have voted, satisfying the religious scruple against the popular election of priests. Rullus—most unusually, for no religious scruples were involved—proposed to use the same mechanism to elect the decemvirs.[127] (Perhaps there was also the matter of convenience. Metellus Pius, the most recent *pontifex maximus*, had probably died in 64, so that the *comitia pontificis maximi* were soon to be called.)[128] When Caesar as consul in 59 pushed through Campanian legislation which adapted Rullus's bill, he discarded this mechanism (though perhaps less out of punctiliousness than because he did not need it).[129] Fourth, Rullus would preside at the election, a duty which allowed him to draw the lots for the elector tribes (*LA* 2.20).[130] All told, skullduggery seems very likely. Rigged lots and targeted bribery could ensure the right candidates. And even if the lots were not rigged and the electoral tribes were thus truly not known until the last moment, bribery was nonetheless still possible—but only for the truly wealthy, who could hedge their bets across all tribes.[131] That, it seems, is exactly

---

127. 'Item,' inquit, 'eodemque modo,' capite altero, 'ut comitiis pontificis maximi' (*LA* 2.18). On the electoral mechanism, see also chs. 5.1 and 6.3.

128. The suggestion is that of Ross-Taylor 1942: 422. Manuwald 2018: 225 speculates that "[t]he scheme could also be interpreted as endowing the election with a semi-sacred significance."

129. For further details of Caesar's bill, see Flach 1990: 78–81. For Cicero's attitude toward laws affecting the *ager Campanus* after our speeches, see Stockton 1962.

130. As Manuwald 2018: 244 notes, "There does not seem to be another example of a Tribune of the People proposing [an agrarian] law and assigning chairing the elections to the committee to himself (Mommsen *RS*² 629)." Cicero also criticizes the measure by saying the drawing of lots will be performed *nullo custode*, lit. "with no guard." In electoral contests *custodes*—roughly, 'election judges'—ensured fairness by observing the voting and tallies, both in a private capacity on behalf of individual candidates and in a public capacity in tribes other than their own. But sortitions apparently required no such safeguards; so suggests the *Lex Flavia Malacitana*, which specifies *custodes* for the election (ch. 55) but not for the lots to select the *praerogativa*, the first unit to vote (ch. 53). There is, then, nothing unusual about the absence of *custodes* for Rullus' drawing, as Zumpt pointed out (1861: 51). On lots in Roman political life, cf. Rosenstein 1995; on cheating, on the whole probably rare, 70–72.

131. Mitchell 1979: 191. Some commentators have seen the use of the mechanism in the Rullan bill as an attempt to thwart bribery: in theory bribery was more difficult when the electoral tribes could not be known in advance (Hardy 1913: 244; Afzelius 1943: 224–26; acknowledged as a possibility by Gabba 1966: 771). If the lots were rigged, this difficulty is overcome. But even if they were not, bribery was not impossible. As Mitchell points out, successful bribery

how Caesar was elected *pontifex maximus* later in 63; the bribery was notorious, doubtless financed by the very rich Crassus.[132]

Crisis without Alternative

While 64 was thus a time that called for social welfare measures, like agrarian bills, it was also a challenging time to craft an agrarian bill. Not only was it not possible to find and arrange for the control and purchase of land without boldness and ingenuity, but that ingenuity required still further ingenuity to get the measure passed. Even if the ends of the bill were sensible and even laudable, its means and mechanisms were not wholly free of suspicion. There are two sides to boldness. Viewing the Rullan bill as an unalloyed good that a newly ennobled Cicero disingenuously resisted in order to defend the wealthy landowners whose political support he craved oversimplifies things considerably. The picture, as I hope to have shown, is more complicated. At the same time the broad situation is also quite familiar to students of late Republican history. Crises could not be solved without a boldness that bent the system—and thereby generated crises.[133] That is the "crisis without alternative," in Christian Meier's memorable phrase. Cicero understood the dangers of such boldness, and his appeal to *libertas* in its senatorial and popular inflections is precisely an attempt to keep the system from being bent and thereby precipitating a crisis—exactly as Caesar would do four years later, when he forced his version of the Rullan bill upon the Roman state. This last section has revealed another issue: the importance of land. It served as a store of wealth; it served as collateral for notes of debt, which were themselves a form of currency; it was coveted by magnates and ordinary soldiers alike. That

---

in an ordinary election required bribing only eighteen tribes (of thirty-five); successful bribery in this election required wider bribery, to ensure the electoral nine were bought. That simply required very deep pockets—which Crassus had. In 63 Crassus, Caesar's creditor (Plu. *Caes.* 11.1–2), succeeded in getting him elected as *pontifex maximus* under precisely this mechanism. On Caesar's election, cf. Suet. *Div. Jul.* 13, a passage that may give a hint of how the election could be rigged: Suetonius notes that Caesar won more votes in the tribes of the other two candidates, Isauricus and Catulus, than they received in all the tribes together. That suggests targeted bribery, intended to overcome points of strong resistance. With sufficient knowledge of who intended to run for decemvir, Crassus might have been able to do the same thing for the decemviral election. Plutarch *Caes.* 7.2 mentions Caesar's borrowing as well as his popularity. Flattery is the chief factor advanced by Dio 37.37.1–3.

132. Cf. n. 131.

133. Of *sine populi Romani notione, sine iudicio senatus* (*LA* 2.57, on which cf. ch. 4, Table 4.3.1, row J with discussion), Jonkers 1963: 28 aptly remarks "in order to prevent chicanery, Rullus's measures had to be carried out dictatorially." That is exactly the problem.

makes control of land a constant flashpoint. Debating a law about land is therefore not just debating policy; it is debating something more fundamental, as fundamental as Meliboeus's grief and Tityrus's joy. If the values upon which Cicero draws have very deep roots, so too do his anxieties about the means and ends of redistributing land. That he found a land law a suitable vehicle to reflect on fundamental values makes excellent sense.

2

Anxiety and Responsibility

2.1. THE RULLAN DECEMVIRATE AND LIBERAE LEGATIONES

iam illud apertum est profecto, nihil esse turpius quam quemquam legari nisi rei publicae causa.

Plainly nothing is more disgraceful than for anyone to be appointed an ambassador except on official business.

—Cicero, *de Legibus* 3.18

THIS CHAPTER, LIKE the next, has two concurrent purposes, one methodological and the other interpretive. To begin from method: Cicero's speeches *de lege agraria* I and II, as I have noted, are formally remarkable; they are almost identical in outline but vary in expression.[1] That invites the approach to reading them sketched in Chapter 1: the close comparison of corresponding sections, on what I called the Contrastive Principle (ch. 1.2 *Logos*). This chapter illustrates that method and its value in detail. Two whole corresponding sections are set against each other. Their differences of word choice, rhetorical figures, imagery, and like effects are examined for their entailments—not just what they say but what they imply. The entailments and implications show up the deep coherence of the passages, virtually every detail of form serving distinct guiding ideas.

---

1. For an overall section-by-section comparison, see Appendix 1.

This approach also yields particular readings of the two passages. The second purpose of this chapter is to present those readings. The passages each configure their audiences in ways that do not merely reflect back their social positions, as it were passively, but actively press the audiences to see themselves in a particular way—Projected Identity, as I called it in Chapter 1. Those identities allude to *dignitas* and *libertas*—the Unnamed Referents—and that in distinctive inflections. Those inflections are given point by another unnamed referent—the abusive overseas governor, which, seen from two distinct angles, underlies both passages. The passages here examined, in short, both exemplify the method of this study and lay the foundations for the interpretation it will offer.

Understanding the two passages requires some background. A distinguishing feature of the Rullan bill, as I have noted, was its many means of raising money, which all exploited or reclaimed public properties of various kinds (*LA* 1.1–13 *deferat*, 2.38–59). Among these were various categories of state land across the empire—in Asia Minor, in Africa, in Spain, in Greece (*LA* 1.1, 5, *fr.* 3; 2.38–9, 50–51)—some already under lease, some occupied and held as private.[2] The bill proposed the powers necessary to assess and extract their value or use-value. The commissioners, traveling at state expense (*LA* 2.32), would be able to sell certain tax-properties (*LA* 1.1–6, 2.47–55); to determine the boundaries of public lands (*LA* 1.10, 2.56–57); and to sell or rent land on the spot (*LA* 1.7, 2.55–56), even in a province governed by a promagistrate, with whom such authority would otherwise lie. Their decisions would be made valid by *imperium*, the "right of command" of higher magistrates (*LA* 2.26). Thus could a Rullan decemvir travel widely, make binding decisions abroad, determine the status and value of land, and sell to current tenants—an obvious, and probably often the intended, market. Such powers were needed to extract the value of the targeted assets, which were widely separated, varied in legal status, and in some cases had doubtless not even been properly surveyed. It was a big toolkit for a complicated job.

But Cicero would have it that the ends do not justify the means. He uses a particular figure to draw out that point: the *libera legatio*. Roman ambassadorships, or *legationes*, to foreign nations were significant posts. They were vested with *imperium*, and their expenses were paid by the state or, abroad, by provincials. The rank was also granted to senators traveling on private business—the

---

2. For more detail on the properties, see ch. 8 n. 2.

"free ambassadorship" (that is, "free" of official duties). The post was doubtless meant to protect the dignity of a senator outside of Rome (and keep him responsible).[3] But the benefits to "free ambassadors" (*liberi legati*) were considerable: latitude of movement (the movements of senators were otherwise restricted)[4] and subsidized travel (local communities were obliged to host them as if their business were official). Thus the post became a political reward and an instrument of abuse.[5] Cicero tried to limit such *legationes* later in 63 but managed only to shorten the previously open-ended term.[6] In his treatise on laws of 45, quoted in the epigraph to this section, he called the practice "disgraceful" (*turpe*).[7]

The position was evidently well enough known, and in bad enough odor, that Cicero could make it into a symbol for a particular kind of danger: an irregular post with *imperium* that enjoyed liberties outside of Rome. If *liberi legati* are bad, he argues, Rullan decemvirs will be that much worse, with their greater power to require services, with their authority to alienate property, with the opportunity to extract bribes! In both speeches the basic structure of that comparison, laid out here, is identical: the argument *a fortiori* ("from the stronger"), which sets a lesser against a greater term.[8]

---

3. Mommsen *RS*[3] II: 690–2.

4. Mommsen *RS*[3] III: 912–13.

5. Gruen 1974: 253.

6. Rotondi 1912: 419–20.

7. *Leg.* 3.18; on the sense of *turpis*, cf. ch. 5,3 Bad Land and n. 54. The passage goes on to say: "I won't go into instances of the past and present behavior of persons who use a *legatio* to take up inheritances or pursue debts—I suppose it comes down to a basic human flaw. But, honestly, what is more disgraceful than a senator serving as a legate without a particular charge, without orders, without any genuine political function?" (*omitto quem ad modum isti se gerant atque gesserint, qui legatione hereditates aut syngraphas suas persecuntur. In hominibus est hoc fortasse vitium. Sed quaero quid reapse sit turpius, quam sine procuratione senator legatus, sine mandatis, sine ullo rei publicae munere?*). Elsewhere Cicero professes not to object while acknowledging the moral difficulty (*Flac.* 86). But under the threat of Clodius's tribunate, Cicero considered accepting a *legatio* from Caesar in 59 (*Att.* 2.18.3; a *legatio*, as being an official rank, offered immunity during the year of office) and was granted one by Dolabella in 44 (*Att.* 15.11.4); cf. also *Fam.* 11.1.2, 12.21.

8. The argument *a fortiori* is one version of what Aristotle calls ἐκ τοῦ μᾶλλον καὶ ἧττον "[argument] from the greater and lesser" or loosely "argument from relative degree" (*Rhet.* 2.23.4 = 1397b); the *Rhet. Her.*'s term is *contrarium* (4.25), which has in mind ἐναντιότης (cf. Quint. *Inst.* 9.2.106 and see 9.3.90).

Table 2.1. Rhetorical Structure of the Treatment of *Liberae Legationes* (*LA* 1.8–9, 2.45–6)[i]

in senatu	*ad populum*
\multicolumn{2}{c}{A. Introduction}
Iam illa omnibus in provinciis, regnis, liberis populis quam acerba, quam formidolosa, quam quaestuosa concursatio decemviralis futura sit, non videtis?	Atque illud circumspicite vestris mentibus una, Quirites.
"Surely you can see how harsh, how terrifying, how profitable the decemviral tour will be in every province and kingdom and free people?"	"And this next point, citizens, you should think about together, long and hard."
\multicolumn{2}{c}{B. Lesser Term: *liberi legati* are bad}
Hereditatum obeundarum causa quibus vos legationes dedistis, qui et privati et privatum ad negotium exierunt, non maximis opibus neque summa auctoritate praediti, tamen auditis profecto quam graves eorum adventus sociis nostris esse soleant.	Legatos nostros, homines auctoritate tenui, qui rerum privatarum causa legationes liberas obeunt, tamen exterae nationes ferre vix possunt.
"The men on whom you bestow ambassadorships so they can attend to inheritances are private citizens traveling on private business without a grant of extensive resources or supreme authority; but I'm sure you've heard how grievous for our allies their arrivals usually are."	"Our ambassadors, men of slight authority who take up free ambassadorships for private business, are [already] almost more than foreign nations can bear."
\multicolumn{2}{c}{C. Corrobation of Lesser Term: the weight of *imperium*}
Ø	Grave est enim nomen imperi atque id etiam in levi persona pertimescitur, propterea quod vestro, non suo nomine, cum hinc egressi sunt, abutuntur.
	"For the very title 'office-holder'[ii] is a serious one and anxiously respected even in insignificant persons—for it is your name, not their own, that they abuse once they've left here."

(*continued*)

Table 2.1. Continued

in senatu	*ad populum*

D. Greater Term: decemvirs will be worse

Quam ob rem quid putatis impendere hac lege omnibus gentibus terroris et mali, cum immittantur in orbem terrarum decemviri summo cum imperio, summa cum avaritia infinitaque omnium rerum cupiditate?	Quid censetis, cum isti decemviri cum imperio, cum fascibus, cum illa delecta finitorum iuventute per totum orbem terrarum vagabuntur, quo tandem animo, quo metu, quo periculo miseras nationes futuras?
"So what terror and evil do you think are in store, under this law, for all the nations, when decemvirs with a full measure of *imperium*—and of greed—and with a boundless desire for everything are sent out upon the world?"	"What do you think will happen, when these decemvirs—with *imperium*, and *fasces*, and their select band of youthful surveyors—will be wandering the whole world over? What do you think those poor nations will feel? will fear? will be in danger of?"

E. Corroboration of Greater Term (1): imposition of *munera*

quorum cum adventus graves, cum fasces formidolosi...	Est in imperio terror; patientur. Est in adventu sumptus; ferent. Imperabitur aliquid muneris; non recusabunt.
"Not only will their arrivals be grievous, their *fasces* fearful..."	"*Imperium* means fear: they'll endure it. Arrival means expense: they'll bear it. Some service will be commanded; they will not refuse."

F. Corroboration of Greater Term (2): right to alienate property

...tum vero iudicium ac potestas erit non ferenda; licebit enim quod videbitur publicum iudicare, quod iudicarint vendere.	Illud vero quantum est, Quirites, cum is decemvir, qui aliquam in urbem aut exspectatus ut hospes aut repente ut dominus venerit, illum ipsum locum quo venerit, illam ipsam sedem hospitalem in quam erit deductus publicam populi Romani esse dicet! At quanta calamitas populi, si dixerit...

Table 2.1. Continued

in senatu	*ad populum*
"... but, what is more, their actual power of judgment and authority will be unbearable: they will be allowed to adjudge whatever they please as public property and to sell what they have so adjudged."	"But another power is even greater, citizens! When the decemvir who has come upon some city, expected like a guest or suddenly like a master, can declare that the very place he has come to, the very seat of hospitality to which he has been escorted, is now the public property of the Roman people! What a disaster for the locals, if he does so..."

G. Corroboration of Greater Term (3): opportunity to extract bribes; other profiteering

Etiam illud quod homines sancti non facient, ut pecuniam accipiant ne vendant, tamen id iis ipsum per legem licebit. Hinc vos quas spoliationes, quas pactiones, quam denique in omnibus locis nundinationem iuris ac fortunarum fore putatis?	... quantus ipsi quaestus, si negarit!
"And the very thing that [these] scrupulous men wouldn't do—take money *not* to sell—will nonetheless be for them *legally* permissible. What kind of plundering, what kind of deal-making, what kind of trafficking in titles and properties[ii] do you think this provision will make possible—everywhere?"	"... what a profit for himself, if he does not!"

H. Comparandum of the *lex Gabinia* and the *lex Manilia*

Ø	Atque idem qui haec appetunt queri nonnumquam solent omnis terras Cn. Pompeio atque omnia maria esse permissa. Simile vero est multa committi et condonari omnia, labori et negotio praeponi an praedae et quaestui, mitti ad socios liberandos an ad opprimendos!

(continued)

Table 2.1. Continued

in senatu	*ad populum*
	"And the same people who hanker after all these powers occasionally complain that Cn. Pompey was given authority over 'all the lands and all the seas.' As if it were the same to be entrusted with much and to be gifted with everything, to be put in charge of toil and labor or loot and profit, to be sent to liberate allies or crush them!"
	I. Deceptive Character of Rullus's Law
Ø	Denique, si qui est honos singularis, nihilne interest, utrum populus Romanus eum cui velit deferat, an is impudenter populo Romano per legis fraudem surripiatur?
	"And if there is any extraordinary political office, does it make no difference whether the Roman people grants it to the man of their choice, or it is shamelessly stolen from the Roman people by a deceptive law?"

[i] A remark about formatting: I will, here and throughout, break up passages into corresponding segments for ease of comparison. I will letter the segments and, if needed for clarity, I will also add 's' = 'senate version' and 'p' = 'popular version' after and the chapter section number before. Thus, for example, 'Table 2.1.B-s' will mean: "The senate version of the second element of the passage in the comparative table in Chapter 2, section 2.1, with attendant discussion in that section." Tables will be numbered not continuously but according to the section in which they appear.

[ii] For this sense of *nomen*, cf. *haec pompa lictorum meorum nomenque imperi quo appellor* "my parade of lictors and the title of 'office-holder' I go by" (*Fam.* 2.16.2); so also *LA* 1.2 (= Table 3.1.C-s), also in reference to the powers of the decemvirs.

[iii] "In this context *ius* refers to title rights of properties (*OLD s.v. ius*² 10b) and *fortunae* to property (*OLD s.v. fortuna* 12)," Manuwald 2018: 140.

Cicero exaggerates. "Every nation" (D-s, D-p) was not at risk of having land seized; rather, as the passage itself makes clear enough, only possessors of Roman public lands. But the passages aren't meant to be taken literally, as if they were the briefs of constitutional lawyers; they are meant to be reflections—or rather two distinct reflections—on the risks and responsibilities of creating irregular offices.

2.2. INSIDE AND OUTSIDE, FAR AND NEAR

Σκοπεῖν δὲ καὶ ἐν τῇ μεταλλαγῇ τῶν ὀνομάτων εἰ οὐ ταὐτὸν
ἔτι σημαίνει.

*One must also check to see if when the names change there isn't
also a change of meaning.*

—Aristotle, *Topica* 149a (= 6.11), of compound definitions

The distinct perspectives of each passage are opened up by two pairs of words in the greater term of the comparison (D), which describes the nature of the decemvirs. In the senate speech, the decemvirs are "sent out upon the world" (*immittantur in orbem terrarum*); in the popular speech they "will be wandering the whole world over" (*per totum orbem terrarum vagabuntur*). The underlying scheme of the two verbs is different. "Send out upon" (*immittere*) imagines both a point of origin and a destination. It is a common verb for throwing military units into battle.[9] By contrast "wander" (*vagari*) describes randomness. In Cicero's oratory *vagari* typically connotes in particular the "marauding" of uncivilized or dangerous men, for example *passim vagabantur armati* "Armed men coursed freely" (*Tul.* 19).[10] In such instances *vagari* often appears with expressions for the entirety of some domain, like *passim* 'in every direction,' *dispersus* 'scattered; here and there,' or, as in our passage, *totus* 'all (of).' Such words reflect and augment, or perhaps even produce, the connotations of menace: nowhere is safe. The Rullan decemvirs "wander" in two other places in the popular speech—but never in the senate speech.[11]

---

9. "vi adversativa et hostili praep. in i. q. *incitare, iaculari* sim. (refl. i. q. *invehi, irruere sim.*) . . . α homines: **(I)** generatim (fere in re militari, *cf.* Paul. Fest. p. 107, 22 M)," *TLL* 7.1.470.42–4. The word can be used in the sense of 'siccing' or 'letting slip' a hunting dog (Cic. *Verr.* 2.4.47, metaphorically of humans). As Manuwald 2018: 138 observes after *OLD s.v.* 2.d, it is also a word for 'send to make a seizure of property' (cf. *TLL* 7.1.470.73).

10. Likewise *hi contra* (in distinction to those who are *animo demisso atque humili*) *vagantur laeti atque erecti passim toto foro cum quibusdam minis et barbaro atque immani terrore verborum* (*Font.* 33), *praedones . . . qui . . . toto mari dispersi vagabantur* (*Flac.* 30), *homines nondum neque naturali neque civili iure descripto fusi per agros ac dispersi vagarentur . . .* (*Sest.* 91), *et nunc tota Asia vagatur, volitat ut rex* (*Phil.* 11.6). The only passage where *vagari* appears to lack hostile connotations is in the *pro Marcello*, where Caesar's name can no more than "wander far and wide" (*vagabitur modo tuum nomen longe atque late*, 29) if he does not stabilize Rome.

11. *cum velint, Romae esse, cum commodum sit, quacumque velint summo cum imperio iudicioque rerum omnium vagari ut liceat conceditur* ("They are granted permission to be at Rome when it suits them and to wander wherever they please with full right of command and authority over everything," *LA* 2.34, in a list of the bill's powers), *cum imperio, cum iudicio omnium rerum,*

The two verbs thus do not frame the scene in the same way. The cameras, so to speak, are aimed differently. The senate sees the decemvirs unleashed; the people see them arrive. The senate sees the scene from above; the people see it from below. (Here is an instance of what I meant by 'entailment' above.) Thus the senate has a high and distant perspective, but the people have the victims' perspective. That is the very implication of a second pair of words, *terror* and *metus*—which describe the 'fear' of foreign nations in D:

LA 1	LA 2
quid … impendere … terroris et mali	*quo … animo, quo metu, quo periculo*
"What terror and evil … are in store"	"What feelings, what fear, what danger"

Terror properly describes the quality of an external cause of fear; *metus* properly describes the internal response to a frightening stimulus.[12] A Vergilian commentator defines *terror* as "strictly, what is brought upon another party" but *metus* as "what people who are afraid feel."[13] The distinction is nicely captured by a line of Plautus; Jupiter had arrived suddenly, making everyone collapse in fear, and he commands them to get back up: *exsurgite, inquit, qui terrore meo occidistis prae metu* (*Am.* 1066). *Terrore meo* "by way of the terror I inspire" (implying *ego terreo*) is the stimulus; *prae metu* "for fear" (implying *vos metuitis*) is the response.[14] The

---

cum infinita potestate, cum innumerabili pecunia non solum illis in locis vagari verum etiam ad ipsius exercitum pervenire ("not only to wander in those places with *imperium,* and total judicial authority, and unlimited power, and countless monies, but to go right up the commander's army," *LA* 2.54; Table 5.2.G).

12. *Terror* is "the fact or quality of inspiring terror, or an instance of it" (*OLD s.v.* 1), *metus* "fear of what may happen, alarm, apprehension" (*OLD s.v.* 1).

13. "*Terror* is properly what is brought upon another party, for example *ille mihi habet terrorem* 'He frightens me' [lit. "he holds *terror* for me"], that is, 'He is to be feared,' or, to put it another way, is *terribilis* 'to be feared.' *Metus,* by contrast, is what people who are afraid feel" ('*terror*' *est proprie qui aliis infertur, ut si dicas 'ille mihi habet terrorem,' id est, timendus est: unde et 'terribilis' dicitur. 'metus' autem est quem habent timentes,* Serv. Dan. *Aen.* 11.357 *quod si tantus habet mentes et pectora terror*). Because a fearful stimulus and the fearful response are naturally linked, one word could be used for the other, as the commentator *loc. cit.* observes of the Vergilian line: "But Vergil here uses *terror* for *metus* by extension: the meaning is, 'If we fear Turnus that much'" (*sed nunc usurpative 'terrorem' pro 'metu' posuit, nam hoc dicit: 'quod si tantum Turnum timemus'*). The schoolmasterly definitions of the late antique commentary tradition must be regarded with caution, but this distinction seems accurate.

14. For another neat illustration, cf. Liv. 43.19.5: *postquam animadvertit, quantus agminis sui terror esset, undecim alia castella eodem metu in potestatem redigit* "after noticing how much terror his force inspired, he reduced the other eleven forts by exploiting that very fear," where *terror* is the property of the *agmen* and *metus* the response of the intimidated garrisons.

senate thus sees a fear descending from above; the people see one welling up from within.

In short, the pairs *terror* ~ *metus* and *immittere* ~ *vagari* are emblematic of two perspectives: one is close to suffering and the other far from it. Other details deepen and complement those perspectives. Joined to *terroris* in the senate speech is *mali* 'evil,' a broad ethical category; joined to *quo metu* in the popular speech is *quo animo*, a phrase common in Cicero in calls for empathy with someone's state of mind,[15] a call made the stronger by the anaphoric tricolon (***quo** tandem animo*, ***quo** metu*, ***quo** periculo*).[16] The senate are, perhaps, called to ethical reflection; the people are certainly called to empathy. In the senate speech *terror* 'overhangs' (*impendere*, as *terror* elsewhere does, but *metus* never):[17] the senate sees the storm cloud. In the popular speech the victims are 'wretched' (*miseras*): the people see the storm-tossed. *Miser*, like *vagari*, appears nowhere in the senate speech at all, but it does occur in one other place in the popular speech—also a bid for sympathy with the potentially dispossessed. Rullus's law, after the fashion of some agrarian laws, called for the subdivision of an already occupied piece of land, the *ager Campanus*, which Cicero imagines will lead to the ejection of the current tenants: "Those poor souls, born and raised in those fields, practiced in turning its clods, will have nowhere to go on such short notice" (*illi miseri nati in illis agris et educati, glebis subigendis exercitati, quo se subito conferant non habebunt, LA* 2.84 = C18 in App. 2; ch. 9.2 *Vtile*).

In short, the pairs *terror* ~ *metus* and *immittere* ~ *vagari* in D are emblematic of the distinct ways in which each audience is positioned—close to suffering in the popular speech and far from it in the senate speech. The creation of *liberi legati* in B is framed in a reverse and complementary way—one from inside the structures of power, the other from outside them. In the popular speech, the legates simply "undertake" their posts (*legationes liberas obeunt*, B-p); in the senate speech, by

---

15. Cf. *quo me tandem animo fore putatis* (*Ver.* 1.40), *quo tandem igitur animo esse existimatis aut eos qui vectigalia nobis pensitant, aut eos qui exercent atque exigunt* (*Man.* 16), *quo tandem igitur animo fuisse illos arbitramini* (*Clu.* 29). Likewise *Mur.* 4, 89, *Planc.* 78, *Mil.* 35, *Phil.* 5.22. An audience may also be encouraged to think about its own responses: *quo tandem animo sedetis, iudices, aut haec quem ad modum auditis?* (*Ver.* 2.5.123), cf. *Man.* 11, 12, *Catil.* 1.16, all with *tandem* (cf. n. 16).

16. The tricolon is made more emphatic still by *tandem*, which strengthens and dramatizes questions, like formal English 'ever' ('what shall I do?' → 'what ever shall I do?'); cf. *OLD s.v.* 1.b.

17. *licet . . . omnes minae terrores periculaque impendeant* (*S. Rosc.* 31), *quantus rei publicae terror impenderet?* (*Phil.* 5.37), *semper aliqui talis terror impendet* (*Tusc.* 4.35), *cui semper aliqui terror impendeat?* (*Tusc.* 5.62). Cf. *metus opinio impendentis mali, quod intolerabile esse videatur* (*Tusc.* 4.14, cf. 4.80, 5.14): *metus* is the response to the thought that an evil is coming.

contrast, the moment of investiture is depicted: the senate "granted" (*dedistis*, B-s) the ambassadorships, and the commissioners were "vested" (*praediti*, ibid.) with resources and authority. The people see the kings; the senate sees the coronation. In the senate speech, the nature of the free legates' business is given in detail, "private" men on "private business" (*et privati et privatum ad negotium*, B-s; their unofficial purpose is emphasized by the repetition of *privatus*), "attending to inheritances" (*hereditatum obeundarum causa*, ibid.; their personal purpose is emphasized by the fronting of the phrase: *quibus* is the true head of the clause).[18] But the popular speech has them simply acting in unspecified "private business" (*rerum privatarum causa*, B-p). The people see the briefcase; the senate see what's inside.

The modalities of knowledge in B show a comparable distinction. In the senate speech Cicero assumes his hearers know of the abuses (*auditis profecto* "I'm sure you've heard," B-s); they are a knowledgeable circle from inside the Beltway, as it were. Cicero speaks from among them. In the popular speech, by contrast, it is Cicero who instructs or perhaps reminds (*exterae nationes ferre vix possunt*, B-p). He speaks from above them (and, at that moment, literally so—he was on the Rostra). Likewise in the introductions (A). The senate can "do the math": *non videtis?* "Surely you can see?" "Isn't it obvious to you?" The suppression of the interrogative enclitic *-ne* is emphatic: where *nonne* in a question simply expects a positive answer, *non* alone often indicates surprise or indignation.[19] But in the popular speech Cicero is a guide, soberly asking for the audience's full attention (*atque illud circumspicite vestris mentibus una*). The particular phrase here used, lit. "look it all over with your minds," is rare. It lays genuine stress on cognitive analysis (in contrast to the very common *videte* 'see' or *cognoscite* 'know,' which sometimes do no more than signal a new topic).[20] The senate sees already (or

---

18. The phrase itself is also distinctive. *Hereditates obire* is unparalleled (cf. *TLL* 6.3.2635.36–7). *L&S s.v.* II.B.4. invent a meaning 'enter upon, take possession of,' but probably Cicero intends the phrase recall *legationem obire*, the proper phrase for assuming a commissionership (*Font.* 34, *Phil.* 9.8, *Att.* 15.7, Nep. *Di.* 1.4; cf. *Phil.* 9.3 *obirent . . . legationis munus*) and comparable civic duties (cf. *L&S*, ibid.). The *liberi legati* "undertake [a duty]" that is really a personal benefit.

19. See Murphy 1991.

20. The commonest imperative for an intellectual operation in Cicero's speeches is *videte*, used almost 90 times, rarely with special reinforcement (*per deos immortales*, *S. Rosc.* 153, *Ver.* 2.3.218, *Caec.* 40); *videte* is the only imperative to appear in the figures presented in the *Rhet. Her.* (4.20, 4.29, 4.42, 4.63). Next is *cognoscite*, used some 60 times, often associated with the reading of testimony, once paired with *perspicite* (*LA* **2.95**), and reinforced once by *diligenter* (*Cael.* 55), usually by *quaeso* (*S. Rosc.* 25, *Ver.* 1.16, 2.1.106, 2.3.53, 2.3.106, 2.3.167, 2.3.170, 2.5.25, *LA* **2.75**, *Flac.* 20, 46). *Attendite* appears some 30 times, reinforced generally by *diligenter* (*Ver.* 2.2.82, 2.3.72, 2.3.104, 2.4.102, 2.5.42, *Caec.* 86, *Mil.* 23, *orat. deperd.* 2 *fr.* 8), once with an added *animos*

Cicero is vexed that they don't); but the people don't see yet, and Cicero must make them see. Changes of word make changes of perspective—perspectives that, as we will see, represent projected identities.

2.3. REPOSITIONING THE AUDIENCES

non ad veritatem solum sed etiam ad opiniones eorum qui audiunt accommodanda est oratio.

A speech has to take into account not only the truth but also the perspectives of the audience.

—Cicero, *Partitiones Oratoriae* 90

In short, the two passages have two distinct and consistent perspectives. When the *liberi legati* set off, the senate speech shows it from within the structures of power, the popular speech from without. When the decemvirs arrive, the people are shown pain from up close and the senate from afar. It is tempting to think that those differences simply reflect the status and condition of the two audiences: it seems natural for the senate to be somehow "up high" and the people to be somehow "down low." Cicero's language, on that view, is merely responsive: among insiders, he speaks more like an insider; among outsiders, more like an outsider. To some extent and in some details that must be true. As Cicero observes in the epigraph, a speech must take into account not only the truth but also the views of its listeners.

Where the Audiences Were

But that cannot be the whole explanation. There is a general theoretical reason. What an audience was really thinking, about itself or about things generally,

---

(*LA* 2.38). The compounds of **specio* are the rarest. *Perspicite* occurs six times, thrice unreinforced (*LA* 1.15, *LA* 2.33, *Clu.* 168), thrice with reinforcement (*coniectura, Man.* 26; *atque cognoscite*, **LA 2.95**; *etiam atque etiam, Sul.* 76). *Circumspicite* occurs only four times, twice unreinforced (*Clu.* 147, *Catil.* 4.4), twice reinforced (*mentibus vestris*, **LA 2.45**, *Sul.* 70). From the point of view of imperatives for intellectual operations, then, as the boldface is meant to show, the second speech *LA* is unusual, with one instance of the rare *circumspicite vestris mentibus* (2.45), two instances of the rare *perspicite* (2.33, 2.95), and the only instance of the addition of *animos* to *attendite* (2.38). *LA* 2 also has the highest number of instances of *videte* in a single speech, with eight (2.19, 2.20, 2.23, 2.28, 2.30, 2.31, 2.68, 2.89; second is *de domo sua*, with five, 14, 40, 115, 119, 130). The density reflects Cicero's posture as a guardian of the people's true best interests, pointing out that the seemingly attractive bill conceals danger after danger (thus e.g. *legis agrariae simulatione atque nomine, LA* 2.15) and therefore requires close examination. For more on that posture, cf. ch. 5.1 and *LA* 2.9, discussed in ch. 6.2).

cannot be straightforwardly read off what an orator implies that they were thinking (what I called in Chapter 1 the Principle of Projected Significance or Assumed Consent); nor should it be assumed that an audience is homogeneous (the unity of an audience is, as I suggested, also the orator's projection). Adaptations to a particular audience, rather, should themselves be viewed as attempts to persuade and to unify (or, it may be, divide). More importantly, there is a specific historical reason. If Cicero wanted to meet the people and the senate where they were in January 63, then in these passages he is doing it backward. Their positions, or rather the positions of a good many in both audiences, were likely to have been very much the *opposite* of the way Cicero configures them. Whereas he implies a people far from power and sensitive to suffering, in those days some considerable part of the people must have been feeling rather the reverse: close to power and indifferent to the suffering of other groups, or at least to the suffering Cicero depicts here (the dispossession of what were, in effect, squatters).[21] It was, as we have seen, a time of populist ferment. *Popularis* ideology, especially as regards measures to relieve debt, was an important part of public discourse by the summer of 64. If later attestations of Catiline's rhetoric from that summer are any fair indication, the mood was one of righteous anger. Just before the consular election, Catiline remarked that only someone downtrodden (*miser*) could be a faithful defender of the downtrodden and that the downtrodden and wounded should pay no heed to the promises of the lucky and healthy.[22] His remarks (which need not be read as revolutionary, still less mad) are a blunt acknowledgment of a problem—the oppressiveness of debt—and the suggestion of a remedy—populist policies.[23]

In Catiline's mouth the political idea is expressed with bitterness; but in that same strand of thought there must also have been elements of pride. The chief instrument of *popularis* politics, the tribunate, stripped of its powers some dozen years before our speeches, had regained them in 70. Tribunes, using their recovered right to bring legislation before the popular assembly, had created powerful military commands for Pompey against the pirates and against the wily Pontic king Mithridates—the commands mentioned at the end of our passage

---

21. Cf. Classen 1985: 313–14, who notes that before the people Cicero is interested in denouncing "die tyrannischen Gelüste der Dezemvirn," whereas before the senate Cicero wishes to stress "die konkreten Auswirkungen der Gesetzesklauseln für die Provinzen."

22. *Mur.* 50. Interrogated by Cicero in the senate about those remarks, Catiline replied that the state had two bodies: one weak with a weak head, the other strong but without a head—unless he got elected (*ibid.* 51). Sallust has Catiline complain to his co-conspirators that "the government ha[d] become the prerogative and domain of a few powerful people" (*res publica in paucorum potentium ius atque dicionem concessit, Cat.* 20.7). On Catiline against the background of populist politics, see Harrison 2008, who argues he failed where Clodius would succeed.

23. The pitch of Catiline's voice, then, should be seen as that of a reformer: cf. Waters 1970.

(H-p)—and Pompey had succeeded spectacularly. The exercise of popular sovereignty had thus solved real problems; the "democrats," and with them the people, must have been feeling their oats. So why not create powerful officers? Why not seize public property from its possessors to ease the debt crisis? Not everyone will have thought that way, of course; some in the audience for Cicero's public address would have feared disruption (agrarian laws meant changes of possession). But they were not the ones Cicero, if he would defeat the bill, had to speak to.

Nor can the senate have been feeling uniformly "up high," if that means close to power and an advocate of clean government. The energy of the *populares* will have put the senate as an institution on the defensive. In particular some old aristocrats must have been sour, having grudgingly seen the consulship go to a knight[24] and now seeing the leading edge of an aggressive populist program[25] (and they surely knew that the Rullan bill was only the leading edge). But they were not the ones that Cicero, if he would defeat the bill, had to speak to. Some senators will have welcomed the prospect of the decemvirate: for one thing, it would have overseen many transactions and thus presented many financial and political opportunities.[26] Cicero refers with periphrasm (*pronominatio*, *Rhet. Her.* 4.42) to two (not necessarily fully distinct) groups of supporters, those who in 65 had previously supported the annexation of Egypt (*LA* 1.1), a lucrative enterprise, and those hoping for material gain from the Rullan bill (*LA* 2.37, 2.65). (Crassus fits both groups and is probably meant).[27] According to Plutarch, many leading men supported the bill, including Cicero's consular colleague, C. Antonius Hybrida (*Cic.* 12.3).[28] Furthermore, Rullus's bill would have given the commission

---

24. As Sallust puts it, describing the period before Cicero's election, "Earlier the majority of the nobility had been seething with envy in the belief that the consulship would be as it were defiled if it were won by a 'new man,' excellent though he be" (*namque antea pleraque nobilitas invidia aestuabat, et quasi pollui consulatum credebant, si eum quamvis egregius homo novos adeptus foret, Catil.* 23.6); on the hostility of the old nobility, see e.g. Ciaceri 1939: 174–7. According to Sallust, it was fear of Catiline and C. Antonius that softened their pride: "But when danger came, envy and pridefulness stood back" (*sed ubi periculum advenit, invidia atque superbia post fuere*, ibid.). It is, however, a mistake to see that as true for the whole populace or as a sole cause; Cicero was a tireless campaigner who cultivated ties to every social group. Cf. Plut. *Cic.* 7.1–2, Gruen 1974: 138–9, Rawson 1975: 44–59, and especially Mitchell 1979: 93–176.

25. Cf. ch. 1 nn. 76, 79.

26. Cf. Gruen 1974: 350, Wiseman 1994: 350.

27. See further ch. 4.4 (on Crassus and Egypt) and n. 85 there.

28. Plutarch's main source for the discussion of these speeches seems to be the speeches themselves, but this particular fact is not found in any of them; I expect it was stated in, or could be fairly inferred from, the lost beginning of the senate speech, unless Plutarch was extrapolating from the passages just cited.

control of most of the remaining free land in Italy—exactly what was needed for Pompey's returning troops. And there was the further issue of what Pompey might do when he got back with that army. In the event, he would disband it, but no one knew that yet. So why not benefit financially and politically *now*, before a possible realignment—or worse?[29]

Where the Audiences Are Meant to Go

What, then, is the point of Cicero's configurations—which, so to speak, go against the current? His purpose can begin to be seen, I suggest, in his use of certain rhetorical figures: the same rhetorical figure used in different places, and the same topic treated with different figures, draw out different political issues. (That is an implicit claim about how rhetoric works which will inform this study, viz. that rhetorical figures are not "decorations" that are "added" to an idea after its birth but are integral to the very act of conceiving an idea at all.)

The figure used in different places is the triplet, dividing a whole into its parts. It appears in the popular version of E, which describes demanding services from local communities. Both versions have the same basic idea: the exercise of official power will be dreadful. The senate version is brief: *quorum cum adventus graves, cum fasces formidolosi*... ("Not only will their arrivals be grievous, their *fasces* fearful..."). But the popular version amplifies the idea with a three-fold parallelism, as Table 2.3 illustrates.

Table 2.3. (*LA* 2.46 = Table 2.1.D-p, reformatted)

Authority of Decemvirs	*Est in imperio terror; patientur.* "*Imperium* means fear: they'll endure it."
Expenses Imposed	*Est in adventu sumptus; ferent.* "Arrival means expense: they'll bear it."
Services Demanded	*Imperabitur aliquid muneris; non recusabunt.* "Some service will be commanded; they will not refuse."

In the senate speech official power is registered in a single word, *fasces*, the symbol of *imperium*. In the popular speech there is the word *imperium*, echoed in *imperabitur*, and the official demands are named, *munera* sc. *publica* '(public)

---

29. Cf. ch. 1 n. 96.

duties' (a service owed to the state, *OLD s.v.* 2) and *sumptus* 'expenses' or 'liabilities.' In the senate version the fearfulness is a property of the *fasces* (they are *formidolosi*) and the *adventus* (they are *graves*, in a phrase repeated from the lesser argument, B-s); in the popular speech the fearfulness is an experience of the victims, who must endure terror and bear expense and bow to commands, the verbs which end each member of the triplet. The popular version thus foregrounds the official abuse of power more strongly, a grim beast with three faces. In that speech the decemvirs lord it over others, like the Verres who engineered thefts by the weight of his office (*vi metu imperio fascibus . . . eripuisse atque abstulisse*, *Ver.* 2.4.14).

Like E, the popular and senate versions of G also have the same basic idea: the bill will allow decemvirs to extract bribes. Cicero has in mind what seems to have been a real possibility under the law. If the decemvirs found that a property was public, selling it outright was probably not their only option. They could probably also leave it in private hands but redeem its use-value—in effect, collecting rent or taxes that were in arrears.[30] Determining the amount to be paid opened the door to corruption. And out-and-out extortion was also possible, if a decemvir extracted a bribe *not* to declare a particular property public—protection money, as it were. Cicero, then, is here imagining a worst-case, but legitimately possible, scenario (as commonly in the speeches). In the popular version that kind of graft gets a mere half a sentence. *At quanta calamitas populi, si dixerit, quantus ipsi quaestus, si negarit!* ("What a disaster for the locals, if he declares [property public], what a profit for himself, if he does not!, F-G-p). (And the stronger accent is of course in the first half of that sentence: *calamitas* is a word for a sudden disaster;[31] the idea of graft leaves little mark.) But in the senate speech *quaestus* is amplified into a triplet: the law will allow *spoliationes, pactiones*, and *nundinationem iuris ac fortunarum* "plundering, deal-making, trafficking in law and fortunes" (G-s). The nouns all rhyme, or nearly so, and that, just like the parallelisms of E-p, melds many things into one. The three kinds of corrupt profiteering reflect the precisions, veritably legalistic, of those who understand exactly

---

30. "[T]he bill could have meant the reinstatement of public land as genuinely public after it had been appropriated by private individuals, not necessarily entailing a sale in every case" (Manuwald 2018: 146).

31. Used in both speeches for the destruction of Carthage (one of the properties that would be sold; *LA* 1.5, 2.51), it is also applied to severe financial blows, like being cheated out of a legacy (Cic. *Ver.* 2.2.35) or having one's property seized and sold to satisfy debtors (the *bonorum venditio*, Cic. *Quinct.* 49, 94; see ch. 3.2 A Fatal Auction). Other examples include being falsely included on a proscription list (Cic. *S. Rosc.* 7, 13) or being maneuvered into expenditure by the abuse of the terms of a contract (Cic. *Ver.* 2.1.135, 141). Cf. also *sublata erat de foro fides non ictu aliquo novae calamitatis* (*LA* 2.8 = Table 6.2.2.P-p).

how corruption in its various forms works. Cicero certainly did; to say nothing of his extensive research into the misdeeds of the governor Gaius Verres, during his praetorship of 66 Cicero was the chairman of the extortion court (*quaestio de repetundis*), to which the triplet is perhaps a kind of sidewise allusion. Cicero knows whereof he speaks, and the senate knows he knows.

At all events the triplet of G-s is also the keynote of the whole passage: it is precisely prefigured in the introduction, A-s. There the decemvirs' travels are described as a *concursatio* 'going from place to place [in haste]' (on which more presently). The three adjectives in anaphora with *concursatio*—*quam acerba, quam formidolosa, quam quaestuosa*—anticipate *spoliatio, pactio,* and *nundinatio,* in exactly that order:

quam acerba	*spoliatio*	"harsh ... plundering"
quam formidolosa	*pactio*	"terrifying ... deal-making"
quam quaestuosa	*nundinatio*	"profitable ... trafficking"

There is nothing *formidolosa* about a *pactio* in and of itself, but Cicero has in mind *pactiones* made under the threat of the publication of property.[32] The *formidolosa pactio* is "an agreement made under duress"—"an offer you can't refuse," one might say. (That, as it happens, is exactly the connotation in legal texts of *metus*, the term for 'fear' used in the popular speech).[33] The prefiguration in effect elevates a subpoint to the topic sentence: the opportunity to extract bribes is really only a supporting argument, as the chart makes clear (an illustration of the value of the Contrastive Principle), but in the senate version it appears in its own place and at the head of the section. "Harsh ... plundering," "terrifying ... deal-making," and "profitable ... trafficking," in a sense, knit the passage together. These decemvirs aren't lording it over others; these decemvirs are dashing around lining their pockets.

In short, Cicero uses the triplets to lay an accent on different aspects of the abuse of power—in the popular speech, on officially authorized abuse, and in the senate speech, on illicit profits. That distinction is nicely consonant with Cicero's two treatments of the decemvirs' second power, the right to alienate property and sell it on the spot (F). (The provision probably applied to occupied property that was already public and whose value or use-value was simply being reclaimed.)[34] Here the distinct perspectives are drawn out not by the same figure deployed

---

32. For some examples of such *pactiones* made under duress, cf. *Ver.* 2.3.37, 2.3.38, 2.3.69 (potentially, with *condiciones*).

33. Cf. Lübtow 1932 and Berger 1953 *s.v.*

34. See ch. 4.4.

in different places but different figures deployed of the same topic. The senate version of F has a cluster of cognates, the *figura etymologica*: "judging" (*iudic-*) appears thrice: "their actual power of judgment (*iudicium*) and authority will be unbearable; they will be allowed to adjudge public (*iudicare*) whatever they please and to sell what they have so adjudged (*iudicarint*)." Its sameness indexes difference, highlighting distinct competencies folded into the same persons (rather like the echoing "j" of "judge and jury.") Furthermore, these decemvirs will have not merely *iudicium* but specifically *iudicium ac potestas*. The phrase, which here obviously has to do with jurisdiction over property,[35] also seems to be a kind of merism of Cicero's for the full range of an official's powers, and with a particular connotation. Cicero otherwise uses it, not of regular magistrates, but specifically of authorities whose decisions were not subject to any superior authority (*maior potestas*)—jurors in a certain court, the college of priests, a provincial commander.[36] The suggestion of broad power is deepened by references to an absence of limits. The decemvirs "will be permitted" (*licebit*) to control "whatever they please" (*quod videbitur*). Here, then, with the pungency of a jurist or an imperial rescript, is constitutionally precise language—apt for a description of the source of precisely taxonimized profiteering.

The chief figure of F-p, by contrast, is a (concise) *demonstratio* ('clear description'), which brings a scene vividly before the eyes of the audience.[37] The scene is full of pathos. A decemvir is taken, as was the practice, to the house of a locally prominent citizen—a *sedes hospitalis*, "seat of hospitality" (or perhaps "his host's house"; the phrase is unparalleled)[38]—only to sell it out from under his feet. The

---

35. Cf. Manuwald 2018: 139 ad 1.9 *iudicium ac potestas*.

36. Jurors: *Cluent.* 80 (of the *quaestio de sicariis et veneficis*, or murder court, which, after Sulla's reforms, had sole authority to pass a verdict and impose penalties; on the *quaestiones*, see Gruen 1968: 258–64; Rotondi 1912: 352–63). Priests: *Dom.* 1 and 143 (of the college of *pontifices*, who in religious matters were subject to no laws and were not subordinate to the senate or the people; for a description, see Wissowa 1912: 501–23). Military commander: *LA* 2.52 (of Pompey) and probably 2.60 (of the decemvirs who enter Pompey's camps; see Table 7.2.1.B). The connotation of a commander with full sway is probably also meant in *LA* 2.39, where, in a summary of the bill, *dicio* is conjoined to the expression (cited in ch. 4 n. 80).

37. *Demonstratio est cum ita verbis exprimitur ut geri negotium et res ante oculos esse videatur* (*Rhet. Her.* 4.68). Cf. Quint. *Inst.* 8.3.61, 9.2.40 (*evidentia, repraesentatio, sub oculos subiectio*; the Greek is ἐνάργεια 'clearness, distinctness').

38. Manuwald 2018: 292 takes the phrase to refer "not specifically [to] the house in which a *decemvir* is put up and entertained, but more generally the town and its area." That reading, which is possible (whole tracts of *ager publicus* were indeed at risk), to my mind blunts the sharp irony of *hospitalitas* inverted. Suggestive, but not decisive, is that *hospitalis* is typically linked to smaller spaces (*domus*, Cic. *Ver.* 2.4.3, V. Max. 9.12 ext. 4; *cubiculum*, Liv. 1.58.2; *deversorium*, 21.63.10; *mensa*, 23.9.4).

host will never host again; a guest has unseated him. But the point is not mere situational irony, grim as that may be; the point is more precise. The decemvir had been shown respect, "formally escorted" to the residence, doubtless by an honorific delegation (thus the connotations of *deductus* here);[39] but his host is rewarded by having his house declared "state property of the Roman people" (*publicam populi Romani*), a formal phrase for such property (cf. *ager publicus populi Romani*, the full legal name of state-held land). The formal language is the point. Correct deference is trodden under by authorized abuse, accent on the latter. The word *dominus* reflects the idea. An arriving property owner would naturally receive the welcome of his estate foreman—and, if he wished, be perfectly within his rights to have him whipped on the spot.

In short, rhetorical figures show how in each speech Cicero wishes to highlight different problems: authorized abuse in the popular speech and graft in the senate speech. The people see the mailed fist; the senate see sticky fingers. And that is the reason for Cicero's positioning of each audience. A people set low are well positioned to see the law's cruel force; a senate set high, to see its reckless breadth. Cicero has, to recast the epigraph of this section, taken into account *part* of each audience's self-understanding in order to show them the truth as *he* understands it; his Decorum is Creative. Those positionings, in turn, have a particular objective: to reverse a mood and a perception in (some of) each of Cicero's audiences. If (some of) the people were eager to use their sovereignty to ease problems on the domestic front, Cicero prompts them to caution: uncareful creation of powerful irregular officers has real dangers; the vast powers of sovereignty must be used thoughtfully and responsibly. The latter idea in particular leaves clear marks in the popular passage. The basic logical structure of both passages, an *a fortiori* argument, is exactly identical, as the above chart makes clear. But, as the chart also makes clear, the popular version has three added sections (C, H, and I) external to the greater and lesser arguments (the logic works perfectly well without them, as the senate version shows). The addenda share a nature and a purpose: they all point to the proper workings of popular sovereignty. The problem with the sovereignty of the Roman people, as indeed with the sovereignty of any people in a republic, is that officials once installed exercise authority from and through their own persons, regardless of the will of the people. The will of the people is, as it were, displaced

---

39. "de comitatu, potissimum honoris causa" (*TLL* 5.1.273.80–1); examples at 5.1.273.82–274.50. Cf. the legal phrase *deductio in domum mariti* "conducting into the husband's home" and *magnam adfert opinionem, magnam dignitatem cotidiana in deducendo frequentia* "It makes a very favorable impression and enhances your stature if a large crowd escorts you [to the Forum] everyday," [Q. Cic.] *Pet.* 36.

onto and incorporated into the official. That is exactly the problem described in C: the *imperium* of the *liberi legati* is fearful because "it is [the people's] name, not their own, that they abuse once they've left here" (*propterea quod vestro, non suo nomine, cum hinc egressi sunt, abutuntur*). Even an insignificant (*levis* 'light') person, when vested with official authority, becomes formidable (*gravis* 'heavy', the opposite of *levis* and here, if metaphorically 'eminent,' also literally 'burdensome'). A detail of the wording nicely supports the notion. The departure of someone for a province would normally be described with *proficiscor* 'set out [for],' a word which implies a destination.[40] But when the free legates leave Rome, they 'go out' (*egressi sunt*). *Egredi* regularly connotes departure (*-gredi*) from within (*e-*) some defined space—a city, a ship, a military camp.[41] In this case the delimited space is not merely the literal city, whose boundary remained procedurally significant,[42] but, as we will see (*LA* 2.55–56, ch. 4.2), the constraints that public view, as emblematic of proper procedure, imposes on officials. The *liberi legati* have no such constraints; with no one's eyes upon them they are free to act abroad as they will and thus free to misuse (*abutuntur*) their authority. *Egredi* here is thus almost 'be let loose.' The decemvirs will be so much the worse.

What is the solution to that problem? I-p gives one answer: honest legislation is vital. The Rullan decemvirate is an "extraordinary office" (*honos singularis*); the procedures to create it ought therefore to guarantee that the people truly have a free choice and that the position not be 'stolen' (*surripiatur*) from them. If someone will exercise powers "in the name of the people," then the people should know what the powers are. H-p rounds out the solution: when a plebiscite vests authority, it should only be vested, as it was by the Gabinian and Manilian Laws, for honorable and limited purposes. A detail of the wording nicely supports that warning. Much was 'entrusted' (*committi*) to Pompey but to the decemvirs everything will be 'gifted' or 'surrendered' (*condonari*, the preverb echoing against *committi*, and sameness again indexing difference). *Committere* is an act of trust; *condonari* is an act of surrender.

---

40. Hence, e.g., Cicero's frequent use of *proficiscor* with *in provinciam* (e.g., *Ver.* 2.1.34, 2.1.91, 2.2.62, *Phil.* 11.27, *Fam.* 1.9.20, 3.2.1, *Att.* 1.16.14).

41. Ships (and other nautical uses): *TLL* 5.2.284.15–59; military camps: *TLL* 5.2.284.60–63; the city: *TLL* 5.2.279.15–23. The *TLL* assigns the sense "praecipue fines certos transgredi" to the transitive use (5.2.285.54) but the connotation is more broadly present.

42. The city limits were, in the form of the walls, the effective limit of a tribune's authority, which only extended to a mile outside them (Liv. 3.20.7; D.H. *Ant. Rom.* 8.87) and, in the (not identical) form of the *pomerium*, marked out a line that a returning commander in possession of *imperium* could not cross without forfeiting that power (see Drogula 2007).

The three addenda, then, are almost a kind of user's guide to popular sovereignty (a point explored in greater detail in ch. 4.1): if the people would create powerful officials, then they must take care that the powers are correctly crafted. That idea suits the context of the passage exactly. The *liberae legationes* passages are the only major sections placed differently in the two speeches (cf. Appendix 1). The popular version appears in the middle of Cicero's treatment of the bill's proposals to raise money by selling various properties. Cicero's attacks on all those proposals depend, in one way or another, on their (alleged) failures of procedure and process—in other words, on their disregard of and disrespect for the sovereignty of the people. (Not that all the people were particular about process; I take up that point next, in section 2.4.)

Cicero's positioning of the senate also aims to reverse a mood and a perception. If some of them were eager for the decemvirate as being lucrative and politically useful, Cicero prompts them to caution: uncareful creation of irregular officers has dangers; enriching oneself is one thing, but this bill would create outsized opportunities for graft. That idea is the very point of beginning from the triply evil *concursatio*. And that idea lies behind the *sancti* of G-s: the bill will authorize what a 'scrupulous' person would of course never dare to do. *Sanctus*, originally 'sacrosanct,' and then 'ratified,' as of documents or legal acts, came to mean also 'upright, scrupulous, moral';[43] and the phrase *homo* (or *vir*) *sanctus* is used *causa pro effectu* especially of someone who treats his obligations with care. His word is his bond. An instance from the *pro Caelio* captures the flavor of the phrase. Cicero calls L. Lucceius a *sanctissimus homo* "an entirely scrupulous man" and a *gravissimus testis* "very credible witness" whom jurors would gladly have as a "partner in [their] sworn obligations" (*socium vestrae religionis iurisque iurandi*, 54).[44] The adjectives joined to *vir* or *homo sanctus* show neighboring or partly synonymous concepts. The *vir* or *homo sanctus* is also commonly *diligens* 'careful,' *integer* 'upright,' or *religiosus* 'scrupulous.'[45] He is moderate and prudent,[46]

---

43. Cf. *OLD s.v.* 4 "(in a moral sense) scrupulous, upright, blameless, virtuous, etc."; *L&S s.v. sancio* II.B.2 "Of character, *morally pure, good, innocent, pious, holy, just*, etc. (freq. and class.)."

44. For the link of the phrase to scrupulous behavior, cf. *habemus hominem in fetialium manibus educatum, unum praeter ceteros in publicis religionibus foederum sanctum ac diligentem* (*Ver.* 2.5.49); *ab utroque tantummodo fidi interpretes adhibentur, praeterea Dabar internuntius, sanctus vir et ex sententia ambobus* (Sal. *Iug.* 109.4); *tam circumspecte quam religiosus homo sanctusque solet tueri fidei commissa* (Sen. *Dial.* 9.11.2). Cf. n. 45.

45. *diligens* (*homo*, *Clu.* 91, 107, 133), *integer* (*homo*, *Cael.* 52; *vir*, *Phil.* 2.103), *innocens* (*homo*, *Ver.* 2.3.182), *modestus* (*homo*, *Arch.* 9; parallel to *summa religione ac modestia*, *Balb.* 50), *religiosus* (*homo*, *Ver.* 2.5.49, *Pis.* 28, Sen. *Dial.* 9.11.2; *vir*, *Q. Rosc.* 43; cf. *Balb.* 50).

46. *frugalis* (*homo*, *Flac.* 71), *prudens* (*vir*, *Dom.* 21), *sapiens* (*vir*, *Flac.* 15, *Planc.* 12, *Flor.* 1.6), *temperans* (*homo*, *Font.* 38; *vir*, *Ver.* 2.4.83).

and above all *gravis* 'serious,' 'estimable,' 'eminent.'[47] The point of *sancti* is therefore sharp: Rullus's law would legitimate an abuse that the important—but informal—ethical standards of the ruling class supposedly otherwise barred. The law in effect tears up the gentlemen's agreement that keeps things in balance. A concern with imbalance suits the context of the passage exactly. The *liberae legationes* passages are the only major sections placed differently in the two speeches. The senate version is framed by images of graft unchecked: Rullus selling wherever he will (*LA* 1.7 = Table 4.2-s) and the decemvirs taxing as much as they will (*LA* 1.10 = Table 8.4.1-s). Not that all the senate were gentlemen, still less statesmen; that is a point I take up in the next section.

2.4. WHAT IS(N'T) THERE

pleraque significare melius putamus quam dicere.

And we very often think it better to hint at something than to say it outright.

Quintilian, *Institutio Oratoria* 8.pr.24

In a word, Cicero's implicit warning of pending imbalance and his implicit prompt to use sovereignty responsibly aim to reverse the moods and perceptions of (some of) the senate and (some of) the people respectively. That tactic is, as it were, under the radar; it does not depend on overt statements ("change your mood"), and it does not use programmatic slogans ("use sovereignty responsibly"); rather, it rests on the entailments and implications of the language of the texts. The force of the argument is in its language, figures, and imagery, not in its dictates or its logical claims; the *elocutio*, one might say, *is* the *argumentatio*, at least in part.

Idealized Audiences

But there is more to that argument than a rhetorical tactic or an attempt at emotional readjustment. If the people are to think less eagerly and more responsibly, and the senate are to think less selfishly and more systemically, then they are also being called to particular civic identities. In Cicero's appeals to *pathos* there are, as it were, projected ideals of the *polis*. Those ideals, which the rest of this study will make clearer in detail, are clear enough even here. The "people" that Cicero projects are called to be sober, careful, mindful of precedent, chary of unintended

---

47. *homo*, *Deiot.* 20, Plin. *Ep.* 1.22.1, 5.3.3; *vir*, *Pis.* 47, Plin. *Ep.* 3.3.1, 4.17.4, Quint. *Inst.* 5.12.21, Gel. 9.5.8, Apul. *Apol.* 101.

consequences. That is obviously an idealized vision, and there is a bold mark of that call. In Cicero's version of the Gabinian and Manilian laws in H-p, Pompey was entrusted with a broad, but not boundless, authority in order to accomplish a task that was needful and toilsome, not personally profitable, for an honorable, not abusive, purpose. This sketch of the law is of course tendentious. Popular support for the bills was not, or not solely, motivated by the statesmanlike wish to liberate allies. It also had in mind the damage done to the grain supply by the pirates and to tax revenues in an Asia roiled by Mithridates (as Cicero himself stresses in his speech in support of the Manilian law).[48] Factionalism must also have played a role: Lucullus, whom Pompey replaced in the war against Mithridates (and whom Cicero is careful to praise in that same speech),[49] had served as Sulla's right-hand man for many years and was closely identified with the *optimates* or senatorial conservatives; Pompey, who had restored the tribunate, was beloved of the *populares*. At work, then, were materialism and triumphalism—the very engines of the Rullan bill, and the very motives that leave no trace in this passage. Pointedly projected onto the people is a corrective, and even distinctive, version of *libertas*. Materialism and triumphalism must be set aside.

The senate as projected in this excerpt—scrupulous, exercising oversight, self-disciplined—is obviously also idealized. Leaving aside broader questions of senatorial rhetoric and its moral idealisms,[50] the senate of this passage is the very same senate that has been sending out abusive *liberi legati* in the first place. The *liberi legati* are already something of a *terror*, and the senate know it (*auditis*, B-s). That collective responsibility leaves a mark in *quibus vos legationes dedistis* "[The men] to whom you grant ambassadorships" (B-s). The *vos* "you" is unnecessary: like English phrase accent or cleft sentences, its purpose is to emphasize, here the agency of the senate ("to whom *you* grant ...," "to whom it is *you* who grant ..."), and of the whole senate at that. No subset is recognized; collective responsibility is not lessened (as it might have been by something like "the men to whom you, persuaded by certain persons, have sometimes decided to grant ambassadorships..."). To send out decemvirs to line their pockets would imbalance the system—but it would also extend their current unfortunate practice. Many (most?) senators coveted wealth and power. But that is paradoxically exactly why Cicero's imputations about graft must have had teeth. A thief knows a thief, as the Greek proverb goes, and a wolf a wolf (ἔγνω δὲ φώρ τε φῶρα, καὶ λύκος λύκον), and graft in all its variety was a senatorial art. The image of a rapacious *concursatio* is not in the

---

48. *Man.* 4–7, 14–19. See further ch. 4.1 *fin*.

49. *Man.* 20–21.

50. The lexical and conceptual set is collected and thoroughly probed by Achard 1981.

first instance a pathetic appeal to the senate's tender-hearted concern for provincials (before it, after all, Cicero does not acknowledge their *metus*), but, somewhat more coldly, an illustration of exactly what people practiced in the ways and means of corruption—like some senators—can and will do with new modes of authority. Cicero's appeal to the ideals that do or can knit the ruling class together is also a kind of acknowledgment of the passions that can divide them, as if claiming collective virtue as a bulwark against corruption also meant mastering individual vice (a theme revisited in the *peroratio*, explored in Chapter 8.5). Pointedly projected onto the senate is a corrective, and even distinctive, version of *dignitas*.

The Specter(s) of the Governor

What Quintilian, in a later rhetorical age, considers a fault—"hinting" rather than "saying"—is constitutive of Cicero's whole technique: *libertas* and *dignitas* are the unnamed ideals of the passages, and that in distinct inflections. The hidden force of those ideals accounts for another feature of the passages: the invocation of a figure that can be repelled only by the embrace of the very values projected onto each audience. If the Rullan decemvirs are overtly *liberi legati* writ large, covertly they are corrupt governors by another name. Many of the details of the senate speech recall governors—so the very word *concursatio* (a word that, as I have suggested, is a kind of keynote for the whole senate version). *Concursatio* did not only mean 'going from place to place [in haste]'; it was also the word used specifically for the 'circuit,' 'tour,' or 'assizes' of a promagistrate through his province. One of the derelictions of Verres, the corrupt governor of Sicily, was that he was at his leisure "at the height of summer—the time when other praetors inspect their provinces and make their circuits" (*aestate summa, quo tempore ceteri praetores obire provinciam et concursare consuerunt, Ver.* 2.5.80).[51] Senators would have recognized that as the relevant, quasi-technical sense of the word here.[52] The very

---

51. Cf. *Ver.* 2.5.29 (*cum concursant ceteri praetores*); that passage also describes why summer, when grain is being threshed, is the right time for an assize tour. Manuwald 2018: 137 *ad loc.* interprets differently, seeing *concursatio* as the action of a "band of robbers roaming around." Yonge 1912 renders "invasion," having in mind the later military sense of 'skirmish' first attested in Livy (30.34.2, cf. *TLL* 4.0.113.77–84).

52. The word also described door-to-door electioneering: "The fashion now is that practically everyone visits everybody else's house" (*hoc novo more omnes fere domos omnium concurs[a]nt,* Cic. *Mur.* 44). For comparable instances, cf. *concursare circum tabernas* (Cic. *Catil.* 4.17), *ut nostras villas obire et mecum simul lecticula concursare possis* (Cic. *Fam.* 7.1.5). By way of ridiculing the veracity of dreams, Cic. *Div.* 2.129 uses the verb to suggest the gods would have to go from house to house to deliver them. A more literal sense of the word ('running together') appears in the popular speech, of the people who rush to find out the doings of the Capuan duumvir (*LA* 2.94, C31 in Appendix 3).

fact of profiteering also recalls governors. Extortion was their signature crime, tried regularly in the "extortion court" (*quaestio de repetundis*)—the court over which Cicero as praetor had presided in 65. The cumulated competencies recalled in the *figura etymologica* of *iudic-* (F-s) also recall governors, who had very wide authority in their own spheres.

And these quasi-governors would have some advantages over the ordinary type. The senate version continually draws attention to the geographical breadth of the decemvirs' power (*omnibus in provinciis, regnis, liberis populis* "in every province and kingdom and free people," A-s; *omnibus gentibus* "for all the nations," D-s; *in omnibus locis* "everywhere," G-s). Here lurks a comparison—or rather a contrast—to provincial governors: the *imperium* of the latter was closely bound to precise geographical limits. Not so that of the decemvirs: the bill would have granted them the old consular privilege of crossing provincial boundaries without loss of authority (*LA* 2.34). Perhaps *sanctus*, too, has governors in mind. Limitations on the broad authority of provincial governors were relatively few.[53] A sense of fair play and a scrupulous regard for their obligations were therefore necessary—to Cicero's mind, at least (his posture here is consonant with his professed regard for provincials).[54] But for a Rullan decemvir on his *concursatio*, moving from town to town inspecting properties, conscientiousness would be quite irrelevant: what the scruples of a *vir sanctus* might otherwise have forbidden, the terms of this law would openly sanction. An Unnamed Referent of the senate version of the *liberae legationes* passage is a governor unchecked, here a symbol of boundless graft and competitive imbalance—and a prompt to anxiety about the Rullan bill.

Before the people, too, Cicero alludes to rampant governors. For one thing hospitality violated and demands imposed were, I hazard, incidents many of the

---

53. On this topic, see Drogula 2011.

54. For example, advising his brother on how to govern Asia, Cicero warns against *gratia*, here, 'personal political favors': *sed vis iuris eiusmodi est quibusdam in rebus, ut nihil sit loci gratiae* (*Q. fr.* 1.2.10), . . . *sit summa in iure dicendo severitas, dummodo ea ne varietur gratia, sed conservetur aequabilis* (1.1.20), *constantia est adhibenda et gravitas, quae resistat non solum gratiae, verum etiam suspicioni* (1.1.20). Cicero's position in my view should not be dismissed as posturing or rhetorical convenience (per the possibility of Idealist Rhetoric, the seventh principle; ch. 1.2 *Pathos, fin.*). Much of Cicero's early career was a defense of Sicilians abused by the governor Verres. He took pride in his own scruples, once declaring that "My arrival [*sc.* in Sicily to investigate Verres's crimes] required no one's labor and no one's expense, either officially or privately" (*nemini meus adventus labori aut sumptui neque publice neque privatim fuit, Ver.* 2.1.16). Later Cicero championed such scruples in theory, for example in his treatise on laws already mentioned (*sociis parcunto, Leg.* 3.9, cf. also *Man.* 6, 13), and in practice, for example suspending delegations that were to be sent from Cilicia to Rome at the expense of the locals to praise the previous governor, Appius Claudius (*Fam.* 3.8.2), ostensibly out of concern for their finances; cf. also *Fam.* 3.10.6.

people knew of chiefly from hearing extortion trials pled in the Forum. But the allusions are very clear in D-p and H-p, the segments that frame the enumeration of powers. Segment D in both speeches describes decemvirs equipped with *imperium*, and both versions stress the importance of that right by means of the same figure of speech, a triplet with anaphora (again, a mark of Cicero's mental mapping of his speeches?). But *imperium* is the only shared element:

LA 1	*LA 2*
summo cum imperio	*cum imperio*
"with a full measure of *imperium*"	"with *imperium*"
summa cum avaritia	*cum fascibus*
"and a full measure of greed"	"and *fasces*"
infinita omnium rerum cupiditate	*cum illa delecta finitorum iuventute*
"and a boundless desire for everything"	"and their select band of youthful surveyors"

In the now familiar pattern, the senate version sees inside and the popular version, looking from afar, sees the outward signs of power. They see the *fasces* on proud display.[55] The "band of youthful surveyors" alludes to a provision of the bill, mentioned earlier in the speech (*LA* 2.32), that allowed the decemvirs to choose for their support staff twenty surveyors of equestrian rank each.[56] Cicero imagines that they will be chosen on the basis of youthful beauty. Cicero elsewhere (*LA* 2.53 = Table 5.2.F-p) calls them *formosus*, 'handsome' or 'comely,' which, if said of males, is otherwise always applied to the attractive slaves or retainers of rich households. And gathering lovely attendants was, it seems, a vice of Roman governors abroad.[57]

An allusion to governorships is also clear in H-p, where, as we have seen, Cicero compares the Rullan bill to the Gabinian and Manilian laws, which gave Pompey

---

55. For the "showmanship" of the *fasces*, see Marshall 1984: 135, Hölkeskamp 2011: 169.

56. The *finitores* would very likely have been young: Nicolet 1970 argues that *ex equestri loco* means specifically the son or grandson of an equestrian, suggesting that the Rullan bill meant not only to insure surveyors of high status but also to react to the failures of the census since 70 (Crassus and Q. Lutatius Catulus abdicated the censorship in 65, leaving the census incomplete) and the vagaries of equestrian status generally. As Manuwald 2018: 292 *ad loc.* observes, "The final item [of this triplet] . . . stresses the point that will have the most immediate effect on the peoples visited, namely the presence of land-surveyors."

57. See ch. 5.2 and n. 40.

the command against the pirates and Mithridates respectively. Some backers of the Rullan bill had apparently complained that the laws granted powers that were too broad.[58] Cicero tries to reverse their claim: it is rather the Rullan bill that is worse. The contrast is not very convincing on its face: wide-ranging military campaigns permitted far greater abuse and far greater enrichment than this or any agrarian commission could. But Cicero is not aiming to be realistic; he is using the clauses of the law as a point of departure for reflecting on governmental relations. Cicero makes the Rullan bill sound like a provincial governorship: Roman governors really did have wide control, really did sometimes mistreat allies, and really did often profit. And thus Cicero is being paradoxical: the Gabinian and Manilian laws, however broad, were rightly crafted; but the ostensibly populist Rullan bill is really an excuse to pillage abroad—and therefore it is exactly like the provincial commands that high officials maneuvered into the hands of their friends. The Unnamed Referent of the popular version of the *liberae legationes* passage is a governor unchecked, here a symbol of power unbridled—and a prompt to caution in the matter of the Rullan bill.

* * *

I have spoken of these passages as if the chief emotional prompt was to anxiety in the senate and to responsibility in the people, respectively; that is how, taken in isolation, they seem to me. But of course each emotion is, or can be, linked to the other: anxiety can be a spur to responsible caution, and a sense of responsibility can be a spur to anxiety. In the speeches as whole, Cicero certainly does hold his listeners, to coin a phrase, *spemque metumque inter dubios*. The other side of the picture developed in this chapter—where, again through the working of Unnamed Referents, it is the senate that is presented with a clear model of responsibility and the people with a dreadful picture of power awry—is explored in Chapter 3.

---

58. Cf. *Man.* 59–60; the broad set of powers Pompey was granted against the pirates doubtless spurred similar complaints.

3

Responsibility and Anxiety

3.1. SALES OF PROPERTIES IN ITALY AND SICILY

> sed in hoc, quod postremum dixi, amplificatio potest plurimum, eaque una laus oratoris est et propria maxime.
>
> But as to my last point—the power of Embellishment is considerable: that above all else is the orator's skill.
>
> —Cicero, *de Oratore* 3.105

This chapter, like Chapter 2, has two purposes: it illustrates a method and offers interpretations of particular passages. The chief points of method are two. One concerns templates. The *liberae legationes* passages, equal in length and clear in structure, are obviously built on the same template, making their segments easy to compare. This chapter shows that two corresponding passages that differ markedly in length, tone, and theme may also rest on an identical template—a clear mark of how Cicero structured his composition and a warrant for the Contrastive Principle. Subsequent chapters will also arrange corresponding passages by their not always obvious shared templates, which, there as here, makes possible more precise comparisons. The other point of method also builds on Chapter 2. There the idea of the provincial governor lay behind the passages; the passages in this chapter are likewise allusive—to cardinal values, to cultural practices, even to the environs—so much so that they reveal the Unnamed Referent as central to Cicero's technique. That idea will also be important for later chapters; the consistent presence of such referents is a mark of Cicero's sense for the acuity of his audiences and for the features of the Roman psychic imaginary in the late 60s.

This method, as before, yields particular readings of two passages. Both are adaptations of the same conceit, that certain of the bill's proposed sales are like an auction; and both passages incorporate the same technique, playacting. But the adaptations and the characters Cicero plays are very different and aim at different effects. The senate, prompted to think in ethical and constitutional categories, is urged to resist a threat to themselves arising from within; if the *liberae legationes* passage was pitched to make them anxious, here they are shown the antidote, the modes of their responsibilities. The people, prompted to think in legal categories, is urged to forestall a threat to themselves that will bear down from above; if the *liberae legationes* passage showed them the means and modes of their responsibilities, here they are show grounds for anxiety, a spur to caution. In short, the emotional accents of the *liberae legationes* passages are reversed. Taken together, then, the passages considered in this chapter and in Chapter 2 are emblematic of the positions between hopes and fears where Cicero sets each audience—a tension to which, as we will see in later chapters, he is himself the resolution.

Among the bill's sources of funding were various *agri vectigales* or "tax properties" across the empire; they or their use rights were to be sold. The properties seem to have been largely overlooked or underproducing, and it was well to extract their value.[1] Some of the properties were in Italy and Sicily; Cicero's treatment of them is depicted in Table 3.1 (as before, parts are lettered for ease of reference):

Table 3.1. Rhetorical Structure of the Treatments of the Sale of Italian and Sicilian Properties (*LA* 1.2–4, 2.17–9)

in senatu	*ad populum*
A. Allegation of Disruption	
Videte nunc proximo capite ut impurus helluo turbet rem publicam, ut a maioribus nostris possessiones relictas disperdat ac dissipet, ut sit non minus in populi Romani patrimonio nepos quam in suo.	Intellexistis quot res et quantas decemviri legis permissu venditori sint. Non est satis. Cum se sociorum, cum exterarum nationum, cum regum sanguine impleverint, incidant nervos populi Romani, adhibeant manus vectigalibus vestris, irrumpant in aerarium.
"Look how in the next article [of the bill] the impudent glutton roils the state! how he squanders and scatters the possessions our ancestors left us! how he wastes the patrimony of the Roman people just the way he wastes his own!"	"You've heard [*sc.* in the discussion of previous articles] the full extent of the property the decemvirs will sell under the law. But that's not enough [for them]. First they get to glut themselves on the blood of allies and of foreign nations and of kings, and now they get to cut the hamstrings of the Roman people, lay their hands on your tax properties, burst into the treasury!"[i]

---

1. For more detail on the properties, cf. chs. 5.2, 8.2 with n. 2.

Table 3.1. Continued

in senatu	*ad populum*

B. Summary of Sales Provision

	Sequitur enim caput, quo capite ne permittit quidem, si forte desit pecunia, quae tanta ex superioribus recipi potest ut deesse non debeat, sed plane, quasi ea res vobis saluti futura sit, ita cogit atque imperat ut decemviri vestra vectigalia vendant nominatim, Quirites.
Perscribit in sua lege vectigalia quae decemviri vendant,	
"In his law he sets out the tax properties the decemvirs are to sell;"	"How so? If funds turn out to be insufficient—which shouldn't happen, with the very large sums that can be raised under previous articles of the law—in the next article he does not merely *permit*, but openly, as if the measure were guaranteed to preserve you, *positively compels* that the decemvirs sell off specifically named tax-bearing properties of yours, fellow citizens."

C. Sale as Auction

hoc est, proscribit auctionem publicorum bonorum. Agros emi volt qui dividantur; quaerit pecuniam. Videlicet excogitabit aliquid atque adferet. Nam superioribus capitibus dignitas populi Romani violabatur, nomen imperi in commune odium orbis terrae vocabatur,[ii] urbes pacatae, agri sociorum, regum status decemviris donabantur; nunc praesens certa pecunia {numerata} quaeritur. Exspecto quid tribunus plebis vigilans et acutus excogitet.

Eam tu mihi ex ordine recita de legis scripto populi Romani auctionem, quam me hercule ego praeconi huic ipsi luctuosam et acerbam praedicationem futuram puto.

(continued)

Table 3.1. Continued

in senatu	*ad populum*
"... that is, he sets up an auction of public properties. [That's because] he wants to buy fields and divide them up, [and] he needs money. And what will he do? Think something up and bring it [before us] of course! Why not? In previous articles [of the bill] the dignity of the Roman people was ravaged; the word *imperium* made a world-wide object of hatred; pacified cities, the territory of allies, and kings in their might were handed over to the decemvirs; [and] now the goal is ready cash, a fixed sum, {counted out}. I can't wait to hear what the alert and clever tribune of the plebs has thought up!"	(*To the clerk*) "Read you me the aforesaid auction of the Roman people, following the text of the law as it is written—(*to the people*) a proclamation that I swear I think will rouse feelings of bitterness and grief even in this clerk here."[iii]

D. Italian Properties, Especially Forests

'Veneat,' inquit, 'silva Scantia.' Vtrum tandem hanc silvam in relictis possessionibus, an in censorum pascuis invenisti? Si quid est quod indagaris, inveneris, ex tenebris erueris, quamquam iniquum est, tamen consume sane, quod commodum est, quoniam quidem tu attulisti; silvam vero tu Scantiam vendas nobis consulibus atque hoc senatu? tu ullum vectigal attingas, tu populo Romano subsidia belli, tu ornamenta pacis eripias? Tum vero hoc me inertiorem consulem iudicabo quam illos fortissimos viros qui apud maiores nostros fuerunt, quod, quae vectigalia illis consulibus populo Romano parta sunt, ea me consule ne retineri quidem potuisse iudicabuntur. Vendit Italiae possessiones ex ordine omnis. Sane est in eo diligens; nullam enim praetermittit.	*Auctio*—Vt in suis rebus, ita in re publica luxuriosus nepos, qui prius silvas vendat quam vineas! Italiam percensuisti; perge in Siciliam.

Table 3.1. Continued

in senatu	*ad populum*
"'Sell the Scantian wood!' he says. (*to Rullus*) Wait a minute! Where did you find this wood? Listed in Odd Properties? Or in the Censors' Pastures? If you've sniffed something out, discovered it, dug it out of the shadows, unfair though it is, go ahead, eat up what 'suits' [you]! And it would, wouldn't it? It's *your* proposal, after all. But how dare you try to sell the Scantian wood when *I* am consul and *these* men are senators! How dare you touch *any* revenue-bearing property! How dare you take from the Roman people the aids of war and the ornaments of peace! I shall judge myself a very ineffective consul indeed, in comparison to the most brave men who served our ancestors [in that office], if people come to judge that the revenue properties which were won for the Roman people during their consulships could not even be *preserved* during mine! [*to the senate*] He sells the properties of Italy in detail. And he's really very thorough there; he doesn't skip a one."	(*Reading of Italian properties*) "He's exactly the same kind of high-living wastrel with public property as he is with his own, selling off forest property before vineyards! (*To the clerk*) That completes the survey of Italy; now, on to Sicily." [iv]

E. Sicilian Properties

Persequitur in tabulis censoriis totam Siciliam; nullum aedificium, nullos agros relinquit. Audistis auctionem populi Romani proscriptam a tribuno plebis, constitutam in mensem Ianuarium, et, credo, non dubitatis quin idcirco haec aerari causa non vendiderint ii qui armis et virtute pepererunt, ut esset quod nos largitionis causa venderemus.	*Auctio*—Nihil est in hac provincia quod aut in oppidis aut in agris maiores nostri proprium nobis reliquerint quin id venire iubeat. Quod partum recenti victoria maiores vobis in sociorum urbibus ac finibus et vinculum pacis et monumentum belli reliquerunt, id vos ab illis acceptum hoc auctore vendetis?

(*continued*)

Table 3.1. Continued

in senatu	*ad populum*
"He goes through all of Sicily in the Censorial Registers; there's not a building, not a field he leaves off. You've heard an auction of [the property of] the Roman people declared by the tribune of the plebs, scheduled for the month of January, and I'm sure you agree that the men who won these properties in courageous campaigns decided not to sell them to replenish the treasury in order that we could have something to sell to finance handouts!"	(*Reading of Sicilian properties*) [v] "There is nothing in this province that our ancestors left us to have as ours, not in the towns and not in the fields, that he does not order to be sold. What our ancestors gained, what, when their victory was fresh, they left in the cities and territories of allies in order to anchor the peace and commemorate war, what you received from them—will you sell [all] that at the suggestion of this man here?" [vi] [vi]

[i] The subjunctives describe an imagined possibility: thus Jonkers 1963: 90 ("I am inclined to think this might be a sarcastic application of the potential subjunctive; 'Then [after that] they will' etc."); Manuwald 2018: 294 *ad loc.* ("a cautiously worded prediction"). Canter 1936: 462 sees the verbs as ironic concessions. English 'get to' ("to secure an opportunity, manage, or be permitted (to be or do something)," *OED s.v.* 'get' 28b) seems to me to capture the meaning and tone.

[ii] The phrases recapitulate specific sections of the bill, as the popular speech makes clear. *Dignitas . . . violabatur* refers to the unusual election mechanism (= *LA* 2.16 *primum*–22), with *dignitas* in a sense something like 'sovereignty'; *nomen . . . vocabatur*, to the powers of the decemvirs (= *LA* 2.26–35 *continentur*); *urbes . . . donabantur*, to the sales of various public property (= *LA* 2.35 *datur*–44); and *nunc praesens* etc., to the sale of *vectigalia* (= *LA* 2.46 *intellexistis*–55 *cogitarent*). For the range of meanings of *imperium*, cf. Richardson 2008: 66–79.

[iii] *Contra* Manuwald 2018: 296, who considers a switch of addressees in the same sentence unlikely; but there obviously is such a switch, since *recita* is directed to the *praeco* and *huic ipsi praeconi* spoken of him. Cicero "breaks the fourth wall" of his own brief performance (which is what this is; see 3.2 A Fatal Auction).

[iv] It is better to take *perge* as directed to the *praeco* (D'Amore 1938: 65), a part of the continuing performance, than to Rullus (a possibility noted by Manuwald 2018: 297 *ad loc.*).

[v] That the properties were read at this point is suggested by Marek 1983, followed by Manuwald 2018: 297, in my view rightly, since it adds to the drama that Cicero is here staging.

[vi] For Jonkers (1963: 92–93), this sentence serves not to cap the discussion of Sicily but to introduce the subsequent discussion of Asian territories; he refers *recenti victoria* to Sulla's actions against Mithridates (88–84)—a date rather too close to justify saying *maiores*. Freese 1930, by contrast, refers the sentence to Sicily, applying *recenti victoria* to the defeat of Athenion's Sicilian slave revolt in 101 by Manius Aquilius—a date too remote for *recenti*. Zumpt 1861: 86 n. 49 had interpreted correctly: *recenti* is relative not to Cicero's own time but to that of the *maiores*: they arranged Sicily when their own victories were, to them, still "fresh." That is consonant with a theme of the popular speech, respecting the arrangements of the *maiores*, which is especially important in the treatment of Capua; see the passages gathered in section C9 of Appendix 2.

The passages have the same template: the underlying structure, despite appearances, is exactly identical. And the passages draw from the same *inventio*. Two images are shared. In both speeches Rullus is a "wastrel" (*nepos*, A-s, D-p). And in both speeches a bulk auction is imagined, the *populi Romani auctio* (E-s, C-p; with *auctio* a genitive describes the owner whose property is being liquidated—for example, *Sexti auctio facta est* lit. "An auction of Sextius took place" = "Sextius's property was sold off at auction").[2] The chart makes clear that the passages are, in the terms of classical rhetoric, "amplified"—the orator's special skill—by two figures designed to evoke indignation: the senate version signally by an *exclamatio* directed to Rullus (D-s), and the popular version, as I will argue, by a kind of *descriptio* or vivid depiction which displays the consequences of an act—by way of an Unnamed Referent.[3] In each speech only one or the other of the shared images is the guiding motif, the hook on which Cicero hung his *amplificatio*.

3.2. THE POPULAR VERSION
A Fatal Auction

bona ... voci acerbissimae subiecta praeconis.

*The property ... was turned over to that most bitter of voices—
the auctioneer's.*

—Cicero, *Philippic* 2.64

---

2. E.g. *Culleonis auctio facta est* (*Q. fr.* 2.2.2), *Sexti [Peducaei] auctioni operam [dare]* (*Att.* 12.50.1), *auctio Peducaei* (*Att.* 13.2.3 = 2b), *P. Deci* (*Phil.* 11.13, to cover insolvency), cf. *de Brinniana auctione* (*Att.* 13.12.4); Jonkers 1963:15, apparently unaware of this idiom, remarks of 1.4, where the phrase *auctio Romani populi* is also used (cf. Table 3.1.E-s), "Noteworthy is the invidious expression 'the sale of Roman people.' It is not the property of the Roman people that is to be sold, but the Roman people themselves will be betrayed and sold!" A genitive with *auctio* can of course describe what is being sold (*auctio publicorum bonorum, LA* 1.2; *quarum rerum, Att.* 7.3.9; *rerum supervacuarum*, Petr. 38), but, as in the examples here, the Roman people are in the first instance owners.

3. "If we use Direct Address appropriately—rarely, and when the importance of the situation demands—we can bring the mind of the listener to outrage on the topic of our choice" (*Hac exclamatione* (= ἀποστροφή) *si loco utemur, raro, et cum rei magnitudo postulare videbitur, ad quam volemus indignationem animum auditoris adducemus, Rhet. Her.* 4.22), "[Vivid Description], in giving concise and clear expression to all the consequences of an action, stirs up outrage or sympathy" (*hoc genere exornationis* (= *descriptione*) *vel indignatio vel misericordia potest commoveri, cum res consequentes conprehensae universae perspicua breviter exprimuntur oratione, Rhet. Her.* 4.51).

The leading image in the popular version is the auction.[4] The key to Cicero's development of the image there is his address to *praeco* 'crier' or 'clerk' (C-p): it is unusually full.[5] In most such addresses, Cicero says simply *recita* 'Read.'[6] He adds 'to me' (*mihi*) only once elsewhere;[7] 'you' (*tu*), never. Most instances of *recita* have no overt object;[8] of the dozen or so that do, like this one (*eam . . . populi Romani auctionem*), only two have deictics like *eam*,[9] but neither with the deictic separated from its noun as here. A very few other commands specify source or manner but never, as here, both together (*ex legis scripto, ex ordine*).[10] In only one other place does Cicero add an aside, as here (*quam . . . futuram puto*).[11]

The added details have a purpose: to turn the language of the law into the text of an auction. The aside calls the clerk's reading not a *recitatio*, the normal word for 'reading out' a text in court, but a *praedicatio*, the word for the '[formal] announcement' of the details of an auction.[12] More important, a *praedicatio* is

---

4. On the mechanisms and semiotics of auctions, see García Morcillo 2008, 2016; on this passage as reflective of them, García Morcillo 2016: 121–25.

5. Classen 1985: 321 notes the "theatralische Aufforderung" (without further explication).

6. *Ver.* 2.1.37 (2x, once with *denuo*), 2.1.57, 2.1.84, 2.1.96, 2.1.106, 2.1.128 (3x), 2.1.143 (2x), 2.1.150, 2.2.24, 2.3.26, 2.3.45, 2.3.74, 2.3.83, 2.3.89, 2.3.124 (2x), 2.3.154, 2.3.175, 2.4.12, 2.4.53, 2.4.143, 2.5.54, 2.5.61, *Clu.* 148, *Flac.* 78, *Cael.* 55. These citations alone illustrate the importance of documentation in the *Verrines*, on which see Butler 2002.

7. *Recita mihi, quaeso, hunc primum libellum, deinde illum alterum* (*Ver.* 2.2.183).

8. Cf. n. 6. Objects without indication of source or manner appear in: *Quinct.* 60 (*edictum*), *Ver.* 2.1.83 (*quas ad Neronem litteras misit*), 2.1.94 (*omnium testimonia*), 2.2.183 (n. 7), 2.3.85 (*testimonium publicum Liparensium, deinde quem ad modum nummi Valentio sint dati*), 2.3.120 (*tandem quot acceperit aratores agri Leontini Verres*), 2.3.123 (*litteras L. Metelli, quas ad Cn. Pompeium et M.Crassum consules, quas ad M. Mummium praetorem, quas ad quaestores urbanos misit*), 2.3.126 (*cetera*), 2.3.168 (*reliqua*), *Q. Rosc.* 43 (*testimonium T. Manili et C. Lusci Ocreae, duorum senatorum, hominum ornatissimorum qui ex Cluvio audierunt*), *Clu.* 168 (*quod* [=*testimonium*]), cf. *Ver.* 2.5.50 (*recitentur foedera*).

9. *Q. Rosc.* 37 (*istam restipulationem clarius*), *Ver.* 2.2.183 (n. 7). The reading of *LA* here followed, *Quirites eam*, is that of Clark, for the *quam* of the manuscripts, which Manuwald 2018 daggers.

10. Source: *Ver.* 2.3.102 (*sationes et pactiones ex litteris publicis*), 2.3.124 (*de epistula reliqua*), *Ver.* 2.4.12 (*ex tabulis*), cf. 2.3.26 (*da, quaeso, scribae, recitet ex codice professionem*); manner: *Q. Rosc.* 37 (*istam restipulationem clarius*). Other adverbs are *Ver.* 2.1.37 (*denuo*), *Ver.* 2.3.120 (*tandem quot acceperit aratores agri Leontini Verres*).

11. *Sest.* 10, addressed not to the *praeco* but to the defendant's son: "Kindly read the decurional decrees from Capua, [L.] Sestius—that will allow your still young voice to give some sign to your enemies of what exactly it will be able to do when it matures" (*recita, quaeso, [L.] Sesti, quid decrerint Capuae decuriones, ut iam puerilis tua vox possit aliquid significare inimicis vestris, quidnam, cum se conroborarit, effectura esse videatur*).

12. For *praedicare* and *praedicatio* of *praecones*, cf. *TLL* 10.2.552.48–63, 10.2.543.63–75. Zumpt 1861: 48 notes the unusualness of the word here: "*Praedicatio*, i.e. recitatio (notabilisque ea est significatio, quae apud Ciceronem quidem uno hoc loco reperiatur)."

acted out. *Ex ordine* is, in effect, a stage direction. The law contained long lists first of Italian, then of Sicilian properties (cf. *nominatim* "specifically named," B-p); reading them out "in [complete] order, one after another" would have made the text of the law sound like an auction lot.[13] *Ex legis scripto* is not only the guarantor of that lot; it, too, is surely also a stage direction: the herald must have made a show of holding up a copy of the law.[14] In short, Cicero switches, or rather fuses, modes of speech; the court clerk becomes an auctioneer. The Latin facilitates that recasting: *praeco* described both roles; that is doubtless why Cicero made a point of using the word.[15] And Cicero plays a role of his own. The extra pronouns (*eam tu mihi*) form a cluster at sentence head. Such an apparently unremarkable grouping is in fact infrequent.[16] But that sort of cluster is commoner in the precise language of the law;[17] that is what Cicero here affects. He becomes, for a moment, not a consul holding a *contio* but a magistrate formally opening an auction, intoning binding commands in full and formulaic legal Latin, from the very place where public auctions were often held.[18]

Cicero has a certain procedure in mind. Especially grievous among auctions was the *bonorum venditio*, lit. simply "sale of goods," when assets were completely

---

13. For this sense of *ex ordine* and like expressions, cf. *TLL* 9.2.951.50–81. For another instance of the sense 'one after another', cf. *LA* 1.4 = Table 3.1 D-s.

14. Cicero makes a point earlier in the speech of saying he sent secretaries out to copy out the text of the law, which Rullus had allegedly refused to share (*concurrunt iussu meo plures uno tempore librarii, descriptam legem ad me adferunt*, *LA* 2.13).

15. On Roman civil service grades, of which the *praeco* is one, see Jones 1949; Mommsen *RS*³ I: 63–366. The ambiguity of *praeco* here is noted by Harvey 1972: 65.

16. Manipulating and searching text files and databases, I count about thirty comparable collations in all of Cicero's oratory; about a dozen of these involve preposed or postposed relative clauses, where one of the pronouns recapitulates or previews that clause (e.g. **qua vociferatione** in *ceteris iudiciis accusatores uti consuerunt*, **ea** *nos hoc tempore utimur qui causam dicimus*, *S. Rosc.* 12). The pragmatics and phrase structure of the remaining examples vary. The closest parallel is perhaps **huic** ego me **bello** *ducem profiteor*, *Quirites* "I pronounce myself commander of this war, fellow citizens" (Cic. *Catil.* 2.11)—notably also a formal declaration (and also with hyberbaton, noted in bold). For *eam* Manuwald 2018: 296 *ad loc.* prints †quam†, noting "the wide hyperbaton of *eam* and *auctionem* would be odd," but on my view that is a deliberate stylistic affect.

17. For example, a formula used to challenge title to property evidently ran: "The property which is in the field which is called the Sabine [Field], **that** [property] **I** claim to be mine by the right of the Quirites. **Thence I thee** summon, **there** to contest ownership according to the law" (*fundus qui est in agro qui Sabinus vocatur,* **eum ego** *ex iure Quiritium meum esse aio.* **inde ibi ego te** *ex iure manum consertum voco, Mur.* 26; Cicero is mocking the verbosity of legal language). On the two styles of Latin legal language, the one parsimonious ("laconique, elliptique jusqu'à l'obscurité"), the other (as here) full ("phraséologie redondante"), see Marouzeau 1959.

18. Cic. *Ver.* 2.3.40; *LA* 2.55–56 (= Table 4.2.C–D); Manuwald 2018: 123; Gargola 2009: 116–119. The formality probably echoes the language of the *lex venditionis* promulgated by the presiding official; see Magdelain 1978: 32–46.

liquidated to satisfy creditors (roughly the sheriff's sale of US jurisdictions).[19] The experience was living death, or so Cicero depicts it in *pro Quinctio*:[20]

> When your property is seized by the praetor's edict, not only is your property seized: so is your good name and your reputation. You're not even allowed to die in quiet obscurity: notices about you are posted in the most public places. Receivers and trustees are appointed over you to declare the rules and terms of your destruction; the crier's voice calls and fixes your price; and thus you are sentenced to a bitter funeral while you're still alive and able to see it—if it can even be called a funeral. It's not a gathering of friends paying their last respects—it's a gathering of property buyers ripping to pieces what's left of a life, like so many butchers. (*Quinct.* 50)[21]

This particular procedure is the Unnamed Referent of the passage; so suggest two details. Cicero ascribes to the crier the emotion of *luctus* or 'grief' (*quam . . . ego praeconi huic ipsi luctuosam et acerbam praedicationem futuram puto*, "a proclamation that I swear I think will rouse feelings of bitterness and grief even in this clerk here," C-p). *Luctus* is the *vox propria* for the 'grief,' 'sorrow,' or 'lamentation' that follows irrevocable loss.[22] That is precisely the right emotion for the *bonorum venditio*, which, as the quoted passage shows, was a kind of legal death. It is the word Cicero uses elsewhere in the *pro Quinctio*: *luctuosum est tradi alteri cum bonis, luctuosius inimicis* ("To be handed over to somebody else together with one's property is grievous enough—to one's enemies, that much more grievous," *Quinct.* 95). The irony is that in our speech that emotion is felt by the crier; the crier is experiencing what he usually causes (thus *luctuosam* is surely also another

---

19. Worse, the creditors, via the *missio in possessionem*, will already have had *possessio* of the assets. On this law, see Cic. *Quinct.* 30; Gaius 4.102; Kinsey 1971; Solazzi 1901; Greenidge 1901: 281–86.

20. Cf. "[The *bonorum emtio*] was in effect, as to a debtor, an execution," Long 1875: 208. (The *emptio* is same process as the *bonorum venditio*, viewed from the other side).

21. *Ergo hercule, cuius bona ex edicto possidentur, huius omnis fama et existimatio cum bonis simul possidetur; de quo libelli in celeberrimis locis proponuntur, huic ne perire quidem tacite obscureque conceditur; cui magistri fiunt et domini constituuntur, qui qua lege et qua condicione pereat pronuntient, de quo homine praeconis vox praedicat et pretium conficit, huic acerbissimum vivo videntique funus indicitur, si funus id habendum est quo non amici conveniunt ad exsequias cohonestandas, sed bonorum emptores ut carnifices ad reliquias vitae lacerandas et distrahendas* (*Quinct.* 50). Thirty days after a creditor took possession of the property, *infamia* attached to the debtor (Greenidge 1901: 285)—a kind of social death. On auctions in the *pro Quinctio*, see García Morcillo 2016: 117–21.

22. *TLL* 7.2.1737.62 "causa [luct]us plerumque est mors propinquorum."

stage direction: to read dolefully, like the *lacrimoso* of musical expression). His voice, so often bitter to others, is now bitter to himself. And that fits: the crier, a civil servant, is here calling out a kind of death warrant for his own polity.

Second, the grimness of the *bonorum venditio* explains precisely Cicero's choice of introductory imagery in Table 3.1.A-p. The decemvirs have drained the "blood" of non-Romans, a reference to the sale of extra-Italian lands (*LA* 2.38–44), with a common metaphor for the 'health' or 'vigor' of an institution;[23] now, in selling off *vectigalia*, they would "cut the hamstrings" (*incidant nervos*) of the Roman people. *Nervi* is a common metaphor for 'strength' and elsewhere associated specifically with *vectigalia*.[24] Here cutting nerves is tantamount to "bursting into" (*inrumpant*) the *aerarium* "state treasury"—which is elsewhere sometimes metaphorized as *viscera* 'innards.'[25] There is thus an ascending scale of violence: draining blood, cutting muscle, penetrating the guts. This is the only place in either speech with concatenated images of bodily violence.[26] The metaphors are not mere decoration. Rather, images of violence very precisely—and very memorably—symbolize Cicero's representation of the economics of the Rullan bill in the popular speech: it is a zero-sum transaction, in which the decemvirs prosper only when somebody else bleeds—just as in a *bonorum venditio*, when so many butchers gather "to rip the leavings of a life to pieces."[27] The logic of the image of violence is the same as the logic of the image of the auction. Nobody gains unless somebody else loses (as we will see further in ch 5)

---

23. On *sanguen*, *L&S* s.v. II, *OLD* s.v. 5. Cf. *quae cum... de sanguine detraxisset aerarii* (Cic. *Ver.* 2.3.83), where, as *L&S* note, the image is from blood-letting; *rei publicae sanguine saginantur* (Cic. *Sest.* 78). For the text of *LA* 2.38–9, see ch. 4 n. 80.

24. *de populi Romani victu, de vectigalium nervis, de sanguine detraxisset aerari* (Cic. *Ver.* 2.3.83), *si vectigalia nervos esse rei publicae semper duximus* (*Man.* 17).

25. *pecuniam ad emendos agros constitutam, ereptam ex visceribus aerari* (*Dom.* 23), *exstruit villam in Tusculano visceribus aerari* (*Dom.* 124). When the *aerarium* is tapped, the usual verb is *exhaurire* 'drain' (e.g. *Sest.* 103 [cited in n. 27], *Vat.* 5, *Pis.* 37, 57, *Off.* 2.72).

26. There are a few single images: the settlement of a colony in Capua, which Cicero, with a memory of Sullan colonies, claims will be settled by thugs ready to kill (*LA* 2.77, 81 = C5 in Appendix 2); the debilitation of Capua by the *maiores*, who "cut every sinew of the city" (*nervis urbis omnibus exsectis, LA* 2.91 = C30-p in Appendix 2); and, perhaps, the imagined settlement of a colony on the Janiculum "right on our heads and necks" (*in capite atque cervicibus nostris, LA* 2.74 = Table 8.4.3-p = J5-p in Appendix 3).

27. Cicero here thus anchors and vivifies what was evidently a standard argument against agrarian bills: *cum Lucius Saturninus legem frumentariam de semissibus et trientibus laturus esset, Q. Caepio, qui per id temporis quaestor urbanus erat, docuit senatum aerarium pati non posse largitionem tantam* (*Rhet. Her.* 1.21; on the bill, see Mattingly 1969), *frumentariam legem C. Gracchus ferebat: iucunda res plebei, victus enim suppeditabatur large sine labore; repugnabant boni, quod et ab industria plebem ad desidiam avocari putabant et aerarium exhauriri videbant* (*Sest.* 103).

The Power of the Law

... quod quidem perquam durum est, sed ita lex scripta est.

... which, to be sure, is quite harsh—but that is how the law is written.

—Ulpian, *Digesta* 40.9.12.1

All this imagery is meant to reverse a particular perception and a particular mood. This measure of the Rullan bill must have looked sensible enough. The Italian and Sicilian properties seem to have been overlooked or underused. So suggest Cicero's own treatments. He says almost nothing of the fiscal value of any particular tract (as he does for some other categories of property).[28] The senate speech implies the properties had to be ferreted out of obscure records (Table 3.1.D-s). In the popular speech Cicero's interjection to the herald (*Italiam percensuisti; perge in Siciliam* "That completes the survey of Italy; now, on to Sicily") conveniently marks a break in the list, perhaps a sign that the locations were otherwise obscure. The proposed sales thus well illustrate the Rullan bill's keen nose for untapped sources of cash. The bill in effect called on the decemvirs to do what the censors, who were charged with exploiting state property,[29] evidently had not. Selling such properties would by definition not harm current tax revenues. But raising significant cash from such parcels evidently required a fair number of them, if the apparently longish lists are any indication.[30] In any case the lands would find a ready market. The bill waived the usual requirement that public properties be sold or let in Rome (*LA* 1.7, 2.55 *atque*–2.56 *vendent*) and thereby opened sales to current leaseholders or occupiers ready to buy but not able to travel.[31] No auctioneer would have called out the whole lot at Rome.

In short, resources lay untapped: why not authorize a tribune to exploit them? But that view implies a conception of the law: it is an expression of the popular will. "The law is what the people authoritatively establish," as the jurist Gaius puts it (*lex est quod populus iubet et constituit, Inst.* 1.3). A formulation in the *Rhetorica ad Herennium* is similar: "Legislation is that form of law which is ratified by popular vote" (*lege ius est id quod populi iussu sanctum est*, 2.19). Rullus doubtless touted his legislation with that idea in mind, as a rightful use of popular

---

28. Cf. *LA* 2.50–1 = Table 8.2.A–B-p; and C13 in Appendix 3.

29. Polybius 6.17.2; Mommsen *RS*³ 2.1.426–64; Lintott 1999: 119–20.

30. See further ch. 5.2 *init.*, *LA* 1.5–6, 2.50–51 = Table 8.2.

31. See further ch. 4 n. 24.

sovereignty. And that is the perception Cicero here is trying to reverse. A law could be thought of differently. Once enacted, it was a force unto itself, its words binding. That, as Cicero notes in a theoretical work, is what the common people understand by *lex*: a written text that ordains what it wills (*sancit quod vult, Leg.* 1.19).[32] In that view a law's point of origin, popular will or otherwise, no longer matters; authority transfers upward: a magistrate is a law that can talk, and a law is a magistrate that can't (*Leg.* 3.2).[33] And fair results might not matter either, which is what Ulpian observes of a particular law in the epigraph to this section.

It is exactly that side of a law's power, impersonal and binding, that the playlet of the *bonorum venditio* is meant to dramatize. Cicero's command enacts that power: a magistrate pronounces formulas; the crier obeys. The crier's recitation illustrates that power in its source, in its effect, and in his reaction. The source of his recitation is the written—that is to say, impersonal—text of the law (*ex legis scripto*). The effect of his recitation is, in the phrase, a speech act: saying the words alters legal reality (as when a police officer says, "You're under arrest"; the words cause the condition).[34] Common ownership of the properties is dissolved with a word. Onto the block they go, one after another, and the people can only watch. Last, the recitation brings the crier himself to bitter grief—an emotion of helplessness. The auction is harsh—but that's what's in the text.

As the violent, zero-sum imagery of Table 3.1.A-p prepares for the idea of liquidation, so the language of B-p prepares for precisely this conception of the law. The form of the text is stressed: it is an "article ... in which article" (*caput ... quo capite*); the repeated and incorporated antecedent is frequent in legal and official documents.[35] The power of naming is stressed: the measure sells tax properties *nominatim* 'by name, expressly.' Indifference to circumstances is stressed: this measure operates regardless of how much money is raised by other measures. And above all the authority of the law is stressed: it is a binding command. Rullus does

---

32. "But since our discussion here concerns the popular understanding of things, it will sometimes be necessary to speak in the popular fashion and use 'law' to mean, as the common people do, a written text that issues a binding command or prohibition as it sees fit" (*sed quoniam in populari ratione omnis nostra versatur oratio, populariter interdum loqui necesse erit et appellare eam legem, quae scripta sancit, quod vult, aut iubendo aut prohibendo, ut vulgus appellat, Leg.* 1.19, part of a discussion for the terms for "law"); "In this 'popular' version of *lex* there is emphasis on the written form rather than the relation to reason," Dyck 2004: 113.

33. *Vt enim magistratibus leges, ita populo praesunt magistratus, vereque dici potest magistratum legem esse loquentem, legem autem mutum magistratum* (*Leg.* 3.2). On the idea of the law as a "mute magistrate," see Dyck 2004: 432–33, with *Off.* 1.89.

34. Cf. Searle 1975.

35. Cf. Manuwald 2018: 295 *ad loc.* who cites as an example *ex[t]ra eum agrum, quei ager ex lege* from the *Lex Agraria* of III, *cap.* 4.

not merely "permit" (*permittit*) but "positively compels" (*cogit atque imperat*, lit. "compels and commands") the sale. The antithesis is not contrived: it contrasts a law that grants a right (*lex permissiva*, in later terminology) to one which imposes an obligation (*lex praeceptiva*).[36] *Cogit atque imperat* lays special stress on compulsion. A *lex praeceptiva* often 'bids' (*iubet*, as later in the passage in Table 3.1.E-p), sometimes 'commands' (*imperat*),[37] but is said to 'compel and command' only here. Cicero otherwise pairs the verbs only once, to express the force of "onerous lusts that have overmastered the use of reason."[38]

Here, then, is a bitter irony. As we saw, the decemvirs strike fear (*metus*) into the hearts of locals and divert gain to themselves (*quaestus, illa delecta finitorum iuventus*) because their lawful authority (*cum fascibus*) lets them wander where they will (*vagabuntur*) in the name of the Roman people (*vestro non suo nomine*, 2.45–6 = Table 2.1-p). That idea is magnified here—in the immediately subsequent passage. The decemvirs, selling off the people, would owe their power to a plebiscite: they use "the Roman people's, not their own, name" against the very Roman people. The people saw residents of the provinces bleed; now they see their own wealth hacked up and their own hamstrings cut. They were positioned to see *metus*, but now, like the *praeco*, they are positioned to feel *luctus*. Their own command (*populi iussus*, in the phrase) gave force to the law that now sternly commands them (*cogit atque imperat*). This people is like the Sorcerer's Apprentice: they will have summoned spirits they cannot control.[39] If in the

---

36. Cf. "Laws may enjoin, forbid, allow, or punish," in Modestinus's famous formulation (*legis virtus haec est imperare vetare permittere punire, Dig.* 1.3.7).

37. *imperare*: *TLL* 7.1.587.13–16 (e.g. Cic. *Phil.* 11.28); *iubere*: e.g. Ter. *Ph.* 124, 293, 407, 413, Cic. *Caec.* 54, *Rab. Post.* 8, *Inv.* 2.79, 145, *Leg.* 2.24, etc. (the *TLL* article is organized chiefly by syntax, not animacy).

38. *graves enim dominae cogitationum lubidines infinita quaedam cogunt atque imperant, quae quia nec expleri nec satiari ullo modo possunt, ad omne facinus inpellunt eos, quos inlecebris suis incenderunt* "Onerous lusts that have overmastered the use of reason insistently force (*cogunt atque imperant*) upon one virtually boundless appetites, which, because they can never be sated or fulfilled, impel those inflamed by their temptations into every sort of crime" (*Rep.* 6.1, fr. 5 = Non. 424.28M). There is one *imperet vique cogat* (Cic. *Ver.* 2.2.43; the subject is *praetor*). The verbs are also paired once in Terence, with *cogo atque impero* outranking *iubeo* in imperative force (PARMENO: *iubesne?* CHAREA: *iubeam? cogo atque impero*; P: "Is that what you want me to do?" C: "*Want* you to do? That's what I'm absolutely *telling* you to do!" *Eu.* 389). Manuwald 2018 prints *cogitat atque imperat* (*cogit* is an emendation), partly on the grounds that *ita* here is strange; *ita* pointing forward to the content of an indirect command is rare, to be sure, but not unattested (*etsi Dexippo quoque ita imperavi, statim ut recurreret* "Though I have also given Dexippus specific orders to return immediately," Cic. *Fam.* 14.3.4) and in my view has the effect here, coupled with the force of the conjoined verbs, of emphasizing the specific form of the sale.

39. *Die ich rief, die Geister,* | *werd' ich nun nicht los* (Goethe, *Der Zauberlehrling*, ll. 91–92).

liberae legationes passage the accent was on responsibility, here it is on anxiety. The *metus* has become the audience's.

3.3. THE SENATE VERSION
The Wastrel

parum expatravit an parum helluatus est?

"What, he hasn't plowed through enough? hasn't squandered enough?"

—Catullus 29.16, of Caesar's protégé, Mamurra

The passages share the image of a wastrel. In the popular speech the image is only a quick gibe tucked into the long lists of properties (Table 3.1.D-p). The last of the Italian tracts was apparently a forest, prompting Cicero to liken Rullus to a wastrel who sold off forest land before vineyards—a known type, apparently.[40] But in the senate speech the organizing motif is not the auction but the wastrel, which in that version appears in the first segment of the template (Table 3.1.A-s). The image is fully developed and is the keynote of the passage. Rullus is not only a *nepos*. He is also an *impurus helluo* 'filthy glutton.' That epithet is used instead of his name, as if filthy gluttony is his essence; the figure is *pronominatio* or ἀντονομασία 'alternate naming.'[41] *Helluo* and its derivatives have a precise use: reckless spending, especially of an inheritance, on drink, fine food, and high living.[42] Virtually every element of that meaning of the word is here individually

---

40. Vineyards were, other things being equal, more profitable than forestland. Cato, ranking nine kinds of land, puts vineyards first (*vinea est prima, vel si vino multo est*) and *glandariae silvae* last (*Agr.* 1). A *nepos* who sold off *silvae* before *vineae* would thus not be attacking debt but preserving cash flow—for continued indulgence, the implication appears to be. Perhaps a *nepos* might value a personal stock of wine (note Cato's *vino multo*) over a personal stock of timber (on the economic realities behind this passage, see Aymard 1947). The Forum crowd had ample reason to know typical kinds of sellers and sales; the auction rooms of the *atria Licinia* were just north of the Forum, at the entrance to the *Macellum* or Marketplace (Cic. *Quinct.* 12, 25; Serv. *Aen.* 1.726). On the *LA* passage, see Aymard 1947.

41. *Rhet. Her.* 4.42, citing *Africani nepotes = Gracci*. Cf. Quint. *Inst.* 8.6.29–30, who observes that, as poets commonly say *Pelides* for *Achilles* or *divum pater atque hominum rex* for *Iuppiter*, so orators occasionally call someone *impius* or *parricida* in lieu of a name.

42. *qui per luxuriam . . . bona sua consumit, nepos*, ἄσωτος (*TLL* 6.3.2597.20–23). For a clear example of the element of expenditure, cf. *et helluato sera patrimonio | in fratre parsimonia* ("and the parsimony in your brother's case that came too late—the inheritance already squandered," Verg. *Cat.* 13.11–12). For a clear example of the element of consumption, cf. *helluatus . . . rei publicae sanguine* ("having glutted on the blood of the republic," Cic. *Dom.* 124). The word was

reinforced. The idea of appetite is drawn out—and worsened—by *impurus*, with its overtones of sexual hunger.[43] Catullus did the same, in the epigraph to the section: lampooning the profligacy of the notoriously profligate Mamurra, Caesar's *praefectus fabrum*, he worsens *helluatus est* with *expatravit* and its probable sexual meaning.[44]

The element of recklessness is brought out by *disperdat ac dissipet* "squanders away and scatters" (Table 3.1.A-s; the figure is *interpretatio* or συνωνυμία, in which near-synonymic words or phrases are strung together).[45] This particular *interpretatio* seems especially forceful. *Disperdo*, only here in Cicero, was on its own apparently a dramatic word for the 'complete dissipation' of an inheritance or the 'utter ruination' of a person.[46] At all events *dis- dis-* is a verbal icon for what the wastrel does—"scatter and scatter." The effect is quite like that of Vergil's Juno goading Aeolus to kill the Trojans: *age **di**versos et **di**sice corpora ponto* "Drive them asunder and scatter their bodies over the sea" (*Aen*. 1.70). The element of wasting patrimony is drawn out in several ways. There is the very word *patrimonium*. There is also unusual word order (*trangressio* or ὑπερβατόν).[47] The usual

---

indelicate: Cicero uses it for Cato's "gobbling up" Stoic philosophy but apologizes (*si hoc verbo in tam clara re utendum est, Fin.* 3.7, Cicero's only non-invective use).

43. The original sense is 'tainted,' and thus generically 'disgusting, foul' (*TLL* 7.726.6–52) and specifically 'lecherous, sexually unrestrained' (*TLL* 7.726.53–727.27), in Cicero's oratory often with overtones of religious transgression. *Impurus helluo* appears only here (Manuwald 2018: 121 *ad loc.*; Classen 1985: 320 n. 51). Opelt 1965: 157–58 gathers instances of *helluo* along with those of *ganeo* and *ebrius*.

44. For Mamurra's extravagances, cf. Cic. *Att*. 7.7.6; Catullus 114. On the sense of the rare *expatravit*, 'consume energetically and completely,' and its possibly sexual overtones, see Thomson 1997 ad Cat. 29.16; cf. *TLL* 5.2.1600.30 ("i. confecit, consumpsit; an patrando i. futuendo?"); cf. Kroll 1923: 55 n.: "Doch kann auch die erotische Bedeutung von *patrare* (Pers. 1.18) darin liegen; 'verhurt.'" Rullus is the first of Cicero's political opponents to be called a *helluo* and the only one in any speech before Cicero's exile. The term later connotes someone who misuses government power to enrich himself (not the immediate idea here), in particular Aulus Gabinius, who illegally arranged a lucrative province for himself (*Sest.* 26, 55, *Dom.* 124), reveled in the dubiously authorized plundering of Cicero's property (*Pis.* 22); and siphoned to himself the profits of the *publicani* in Syria (*Prov.* 11, *Pis.* 14). Cf. Achard 1981: 330–31.

45. The examples in the *Rhet. Her.* are phrases rather than words: *rem publicam radicitus evertisti, civitatem funditus deiecisti* and *patrem nefarie verberasti, parenti manus scelerate attulisti* (4.38).

46. Property: *TLL* 5.1.1404.15–32; persons: 1404.49–83. The dramatic tone may be due to the double preverbs, a rare combination (*dispereo*, mostly ante-classical; *dispercutio*, once in Plautus) and not very common before late Latin (cf. Cooper 1895: 289–94), when marked emphatic forms become ever more rapidly generalized as unmarked forms.

47. *Rhet. Her.* 4.44. In particular, this example is not *transiectio*, where one element of a constituency is "thrown over" to another place in sentence, breaking another constituent (**instabilis**

way of saying 'properties left by our forebears' would be *possessiones a maioribus nostris relictas,* lit. "properties by our elders left" (where the arrangement of the participial phrase parallels the common Subj-*x*-Vb order of Latin sentences); but in *a maioribus nostris possessiones relictas,* lit. "by our elders properties left," where the order is *x*-Subj-Vb, weight is thrown onto the left-displaced *maioribus.*[48] Last, there is the word *nepos.* If *nepos* had passed from its proper meaning 'grandson' (cf. Skt. *nápāt* 'descendant; grandson') to 'profligate' by way of 'youth handling inheritance foolishly' (as it were, 'trust fund baby'), and if those connotations still clung to the word, this context would have drawn them out.[49] And the imputation may have been accurate: Rullus's father was apparently wealthy.[50]

A very full picture of the prodigal is thus developed. The image is meant to reverse a mood and a perception.[51] Cicero wants to change the look of a particular feature of the bill: the thoroughness of its lists. That is a feature the senate passage constantly emphasizes. Rullus "wrote up in full" (*perscribit,* Table 3.1.B-s) the properties he intends to sell. The fullness appears in the same three ways for both the Italian and the Sicilian properties; Rullus examined official records diligently to produce a complete list (Table 3.3.1).

---

in istum plurimum fortuna valuit, instead of *instabilis fortuna*), but *perversio,* where elements of a constituency are "flipped around" out of their usual order (**hoc vobis deos inmortales arbitror** *dedisse* **virtute pro vestra**, instead of *arbitror deos immortales hoc vobis dedisse* and *pro vestra virtute*). On hyperbaton in Latin, see Powell 2010.

48. Laughton 1964: 46–50, arguing that exceptions to the principle that the predicative participle follows its noun are generally motivated by emphasis or by syntactic attraction (for example, a relative clause beginning with an agent or relative), observes that clauses with expressions of agent in which the noun precedes the participle are "quite exceptional," citing this very instance and very aptly surmising that "Cicero may have wished to enhance by juxtaposition the contrast of ideas between *relictas* and *disperdat.*"

49. There is no agreement on how the sense developed from 'grandson' to 'profligate.' Festus 162 L. speculates that the meaning arises because those who are heedless of property are like grandsons whose parents and grandparents are still alive and thus also spend recklessly. Walde-Hofmann *s.v.* see a development from 'grandson' > 'Liebling' > 'mißratener, verzogener Liebling.' Ernout-Meillet *s.v.* entertain the possibility that there were two words, one of them Etruscan (*nepos luxuriosus a Tuscis dicitur,* Festus 162 L). For further details, see Heller 1962. *Nepos* was perhaps piquant in the sense 'profligate' at Cicero's time; at any rate that meaning is not attested before him (the first instance seems to be *quis tam perditus ac profusus nepos non adesa iam sed abundanti etiam pecunia sic dissolutus fuisset ut fuit Sex. Naevius? Quinct.* 40).

50. Or at any rate extravagant: Rullus's father was the first to serve whole boars at banquets (Plin. *Nat.* 8.210); cf. Manuwald 2018: 121.

51. I thus disagree with Classen (1985: 322; cf. Manuwald 2018: xliv), who sees the image merely as a "personal attack" ("persönlicher Angriff") that does not enlighten the audience about the problems of the law; on the contrary the *specific* form of those attacks *is* a critique of a *particular aspect* of the law. The image of the *helluo* is not a simple broadside but a very precise metaphor.

Table 3.3.1. Official Thoroughness in *LA* 1.3–4

Official Records	Italy	*relictae possessiones, censorum pascua* (D-s)
	Sicily	*tabulae censoriae* (E-s)
Diligence	Italy	*diligens* (D-s)
	Sicily	*persequitur*, lit. 'runs through the whole series' (E-s)
Complete List	Italy	*nullam [possessionem]... praetermittit* (D-s)
	Sicily	*nullum aedificium, nullos agros relinquit* (E-s)

In the popular speech only the very last phrase has a correspondent: Rullus left nothing untouched in Sicilian towns or fields (*nihil est... quod aut in oppidis aut in agris...*, Table 3.1.E-p).

Such thoroughness was surely a selling point to some in the senate: why not exploit all these things that can be exploited? (The sentiment need not have been statesmanlike: many sales meant many chances to profit, according to who possessed what where and who became a decemvir; and support for an agrarian bill was a way to burnish one's *popularis* credentials). But Cicero saw in the thoroughness an opening to assign the law a different meaning. That is exactly what the vivid picture of the prodigal does: it reverses the polarity of drawing up lists. When the prodigal compiles lists of ancestral properties to sell, it is a reprehensible, and not an admirable or acceptable, act; it is gathering up only so as to scatter away. It is *diligentia* not in service of *utilitas*, still less *honestas*, but in the thrall of *helluatio*. There is a sly conceptual paradox here: *diligens* was, or could be, the antonym of *luxuriosus*, a usage which dates to the late Republic.[52] Cicero instead makes *diligentia* not the opposite of *luxuria* but proof of it. (The very idea, and the very word, appear in the last of the *argumenta*, Cicero's treatment of the plan to colonize the *ager Campanus*: "What a difference," he exclaims, "there is between your (pl.) kind of diligence and the diligence of private owners!" *LA* 2.82 = C15 in Appendix 2).

Hence the imagery for research in D-s. The properties in his bill that Rullus has "tracked down, found, rooted out of the darkness" (*indagaris, inveneris, ex tenebris erueris*—another *interpretatio*). *Eruo* 'dig up = recover obscure *or* forgotten information' and *indago* 'hunt down, track down' can be used metaphorically

---

52. Cf. *TLL* 5.1.1183.23 "i. q. parcus, frugi, tenax (*opp.* prodigus, profusus)." The *Rhet. Her.*, as an example of the figure of speech *permutatio* (ἀλληγορία), which "says one thing but means another" (*aliud verbis, aliud sententia demonstra[t]*), gives *homo parcus et diligens* for a man who is *prodigus et luxuriosus* (4.46).

for thorough research, which might otherwise have been admirable.[53] But in the context of prodigality, the literal overtones of the words seep through—*eruo*, what a pig's snout does, and *indago*, what a dog on scent does.[54] The ambiguities give Rullus the cast of a hound or hungry swine.[55] Rullus "dug up" the properties? Well of course! He's a "pig"![56] Catullus's *uncta devorare patrimonia* of Mamurra (29.22) makes exactly the same kind of joke. *Vnctus*, quite like English 'rich,' is both 'flavorful [from fat]' (as in 'rich foods') and 'luxurious' or the like (as in 'richly appointed'). Of course Mamurra "gobbles up" inheritances—they're "rich"![57] And the idea of diligence awry also explains the phrase *praesens certa pecunia {numerata}*. The intended effect is not hyperbole.[58] The point, rather, is that Rullus is looking for money 'guaranteed' (*certa*), 'in cash' (*praesens*) and perhaps 'counted out' (*numerata*).[59] The idea does not make much sense applied specifically to this

---

53. *Eruo* of thorough research: *TLL* 7.1.1105.22–3, "aliquid (quasi) obrutum vel reconditum eximere, extrahere . . . , scrutando proferre; retegere"; *indago* of investigation: *TLL* 5.2.844.73–5, "de rebus magis incorporeis vel animo cognoscendis (saepius vi originaria ex contextu apparente . . .)." For Cicero's own thoroughness in the prosecution of Verres, see Butler 2002.

54. Snout: Ov. *Met.* 15.113, Col. 7.9.7 (cf. of a mattock or plow, Var. *L.* 5.136, *Log.* fr. 40; Col. *Arb.* 6.2); cf. *TLL* 5.2.843.78–9, "i. q. foras educere, proferre, eximere quibuslibet modis (plerumque sive fodiendo sive sursum deorsum dando)." Dog on scent: cf. *TLL* 7.1.1104.63 ("proprie de venatione, i. q. feras investigare"); *ut ad cursum equum . . . , ad indagandum canem, sic hominem . . . ad intellegendum et agendum esse natum* (Cic. *Fin.* 2.40).

55. The expressions are thus not "fast synonymen Wiederholungen" (Classen 1985: 320).

56. It is worth passing on Cicero's remarks about ambiguities: "An ambiguous remark is quite acceptable in and of itself, as I've mentioned already; that's because it takes a clever person to turn the meaning of a word into something other than the way others understand it; but the effect is impressive rather than amusing" (*ambiguum per se ipsum probatur id quidem, ut ante dixi, vel maxime; ingeniosi enim videtur vim verbi in aliud, atque ceteri accipiant, posse ducere; sed admirationem magis quam risum movet, de Orat.* 2.254).

57. Quinn 1973: 179–80; cf. Ellis 1876: 80, "*uncta* and *devorare* are in relation to each other, the *patrimonia* being regarded as so many morsels successively swallowed."

58. Apparently the view of Classen (1985: 320), who observes merely that this sentence is a "hateful" (gehässig) conclusion to the paragraph's line of thought.

59. *Pecunia certa* is usually a 'fixed amount,' often used of legal judgments or disputed or legateed sums; cf. *TLL* 3.900.3–27. Zumpt 1861: 3 therefore rightly suggested that *certa* here does not have this technical meaning, because no known amount was at issue; rather, Rullus wanted 'guaranteed' money. *Pecunia praesens* is 'in cash' (as opposed to by charge or in kind); the text of a law recounted at *Ver.* 2.1.146 has *pecunia praesens solvetur*, cf. Ulp. *Dig.* 14.3.5.15, 42.1.15.7, Pomp. *Dig.* 40.4.41.1. *Numerata* is also 'in cash' and has some overlap with *praesens* (cf. *pecuniam sibi esse in nominibus, numeratam in praesentia non habere, Ver.* 2.5.17; cf. *Phil.* 3.10, *Top.* 13). *Numerata* does not appear in all branches (it is bracketed by Manuwald and deleted by Wunder) and might have arisen as an intrusive gloss on *praesens*. On the other hand, *certa pecunia numerata quaeritur* gives a very unusual rhythm (Zieliński 1904: 200), and that in my view is a possible argument, not for excision (so Manuwald 2018: 124), but for retention, as if Cicero here affects staccato speech.

measure of the bill: there is no reason why the Italian and Sicilian properties, as opposed to any of the other sources of revenue in the bill, should be the ones to yield "cash on the barrelhead." But the phrase very much suits the image of the misplaced diligence of a prodigal, counting up coin after coin from the sale of tract after tract—and refusing to extend credit.[60] Rullus becomes the *dominus auctionis*, standing at the elbow of the *argentarius* ('banker'), who handled the financial details of an auction.[61]

Does the image of the reckless wastrel also script a role for the senate? Corresponding sections of these excerpts, despite often quite different appearances, have comparable rhetorical functions. The introductory sections (Table 3.1.A-s and -p), for example, establish the major motifs—the shamelessness of the wastrel and the brutality of a zero-sum transaction. That raises the question whether the correspondence runs deeper: if the popular version simulates a *bonorum venditio*, the senate version might also simulate or recall some formal process. There is a relevant one. A law of the Twelve Tables (V.7) provided for conservatorship (*cura*) for the mentally incompetent (*furiosi*; the legal meaning is broader than 'mad, raging'). The principle extended to wastrels (*prodigi*).[62] Relatives applied to a magistrate to be appointed *curatores* 'caretakers' or 'conservators.' Thereupon the incompetent or prodigal could not undertake any financial act (for example, alienating property) without their consent.[63] The mechanism was not moribund: the three relevant categories, *furiosus*, *prodigus*, and *cura*, underlie the humor of Catullus 41, where the girl is mentally incompetent, her lover is a spendthrift, and the girl is a ward of her relatives.[64] The language of the relevant interdict is preserved: *quando tibi bona paterna avitaque nequitia tua disperdis, liberosque tuos ad egestatem perducis, ob eam rem tibi ea re commercioque interdico* ("Since by thy prodigality thou misdispendest the goods of thy father and

---

60. On cash vs. credit at estate sales, see Rauh 1989.

61. For *praesenti pecunia* used of an auction, cf. *venibunt quiqui licebunt, praesenti pecunia* "They'll be sold for the hammer price, cash on the barrelhead!" (Pl. *Men.* 1159).

62. *lex duodecim tabularum furiosum itemque prodigum, cui bonis interdictum est, in curatione iubet esse agnatorum* (Ulp. *Lib. Sing. Regularum* 12.2); *furiosi quoque et prodigi, licet maiores viginti quinque annis sint, tamen in curatione sunt adgnatorum ex lege duodecim tabularum; sed solent Romae praefectus urbi vel praetor et in provinciis praesides ex inquisitione eis curatores dare* (Just. *Inst.* 1.23.3).

63. Sohm 1901: 228, 231, 513, 515.

64. Sanity: *non est sana puella*, "The girl isn't sane" (3); spendthrift: *decoctoris*, "bankrupt," lit. "boiler-over" (4); ward: *propinqui, quibus est puellae cura | amicos medicosque convocate*, "You relatives of the girl who have care of her—call in friends and physicians!" (5–6). Cf. Ellis 1876: 114–16 ("There seems to be a legal allusion running through the whole of this poem," 114).

grandfathers, and bringest unto hard need thine own children, on that account I on thee lay a ban therefrom and from commerce," *Pauli Sententiae* 3.4a.7).[65]

Cicero appears to have this procedure and its underlying principles in mind. That certainly explains the projected roles of both the senate and Cicero. As Cicero was the *magister auctionis* before the people, here he becomes a would-be *curator* who will protect the commonwealth, and the senate are like magistrates at an *inquisitio* being asked to block the transactions of a *prodigus*. What is more, Cicero seems to invoke the very language of the relevant edict. *Impurus helluo* recalls *nequitia tua* (in the edict *nequitia* has its older sense 'prodigality').[66] *Bona paterna avitaque* is recalled by *populi Romani patrimonio* (which is a striking metaphor: *patrimonium* is properly not the public *fiscus* or the *aerarium* but the private estate of a *paterfamilias*).[67] *Paterna avitaque* finds a parallel in *a maioribus nostris* (which, as noted earlier, is unusually left-displaced, underscoring it). And above all, the edict contains the rare word *disperdo*, which Cicero uses only once—here. Cicero is, as before, displaying his *ethos*: as the former chairman of the *repetundae* court taxonomized extortion (*LA* 1.8 = Table 2.1.A-s), here the former *praetor urbanus* alludes to an interdict. It is certainly an apt interdict: it calls for checking the wayward and preserving wealth. If the *liberae legationes* passage showed the risk—a disequilibrating *concursatio*—this passage shows the antidote: collective responsibility and a firm hand against the *furiosi* in their ranks. Is that more than a metaphor? Is that also an implicit reconfiguration? The image makes *patres conscripti* into *patres familiarum*.

---

65. The interdict may not have existed at the time of the Twelve Tables, making this a later addition; see Jolowicz and Nicholas 1972: 122 n. 4. On the concept of *commercium* here, see Roselaar 2012.

66. Cf. *OLD s.v.* 1. Gellius, gathering passages to prove that *nequitia* formerly did not mean, as in his day, 'cunning' (*sollertia astutiaque*, 6.11.1), cites older authors with this sense: Q. Claudius Quadrigarius (fr. 15 Peter, of which Gellius remarks *Q. . . . Claudius in primo annalium 'nequitiam' appellavit luxum vitae prodigum effusumque* "Quintus Claudius in the first book of his *Annals* uses *nequitia* for a wasteful and profligate life of luxury," 6.11.7) and Scipio Aemilianus (*ORF* 21.19 = 6.11.9), who attributes all human misdeeds to "wickedness and profligacy" (*malitia atque nequitia*; the latter in context clearly means 'profligate').

67. The *OLD* and *L&S s.v.* rightly see this use of *patrimonium* as figurative. The *TLL* (10.1.754.14) sees here the first instance of *patrimonium* used not "privatorum" but "rei publicae." (The *OLD* records one earlier but not comparable instance, *Caec.* 75: *quapropter non minus diligenter ea quae a maioribus accepistis, publica patrimonia iuris quam privatae rei vestrae retinere debetis*, "Accordingly you should preserve with equal energy what you inherited from your ancestors: not only the patrimonies of your private property but the public patrimony of the law"). That *patrimonium* applied to the *fiscus* was a living metaphor is suggested by its two other appearances in the agrarian speeches, in dramatic passages concerning the *ager Campanus* (*LA* 1.21, C10 in Appendix 2; *LA* 2.80, C9 in Appendix 2, Manuwald 2018: 121).

Going Too Far

Non omne quod licet honestum est.

Not everything legal is respectable.

—Paulus, *Digesta* 50.17.144

Thus does Cicero aim to reverse a mood and a perception. The image of the wastrel's auction turns the apparent *diligentia* of the bill into *luxuria* and *helluatio* and, what is more, of a kind that demands intervention. That image implies not only a role for the senate but also an underlying principle: duty to the "family's" property. And the passage also appeals to another principle, also implicit in the image of the auction. *Curatio* barred a wastrel from selling off inherited assets. But absent that remedy, such sales were of course not illegal—but neither were they held in high regard. That is, as Paulus puts it, they were "permitted" (*licet*) but not "respectable" (*honestum*). And that was also a fair way of thinking about the bill, or these proposed sales, at least. There was no legal bar to proposing to the people that they sell some of their own assets. At the same time, the Rullan bill, on this as on other points, seems to have overstepped recent informal limits (the tribunate had only been restored to full strength a half-dozen years before).[68] The senate version makes Rullus's impropriety clear: his proposal interferes in the duties of the regular magistrates. A tribune's proposal very well could (*licet*), but—or so Cicero would have the senate think—it's not quite right (*honestum*).

That tension between the possible and the seemly appears very strikingly in Table 3.1.D-s. The section refers to two kinds of property. *Relictae possessiones* 'odd properties' were lands not assigned for occupation,[69] and *pascua censorum*, lit. 'the censors' pastures,' came to be used *species pro genere* for all revenue-bearing property.[70] Cicero imagines Rullus has found the Italian and Sicilian properties

---

68. It is possible to think of the Rullan bill as a first attempt to test the full powers of a restored tribunate—a test which was a precursor for the ambitious tribunician career of P. Clodius Pulcher. On that career, see Tatum 1999. For an account of the events of 70, see Santangelo 2014.

69. Mommsen *RS*³ 2.1.439 n. 4; Kunkel and Wittmann 1995: 447 n. 190. Cf. Fron. *contr. agr.* p. 21.7–22.8 Lachmann: *relicta autem loca sunt quae sive locorum iniquitate sive arbitrio conditoris {relicta} limites non acceperunt* 'Excluded places' are those that were never formally centuriated (lit. 'did not receive boundaries') because of the unevenness of the terrain or the decision of the founder."

70. "Even now the censors tablets call any property that generates public revenue 'pasture land,' because for a long time that was the only kind of revenue" (*etiam nunc in tabulis censoriis pascua dicuntur omnia, ex quibus populus reditus habet, quia diu hoc solum vectigal fuerat*, Plin. *Nat.* 18.11). Cf. also Mommsen *RS*³ 2.1434 n. 3. In the popular speech, the technical names are not used: as in the *liberae legationes* passages, the people see only the briefcase, but the senate sees what's inside.

in those two places; he then affects to let him sell from the first set but not from the second (Table 3.3.2).[71]

Table 3.3.2. Kinds of Property in *LA* 1.3 (= Table 3.1.D-s, reformatted)

Source of Property	Cicero's Response
1a. *utrum tandem hanc silvam in relictis possessionibus . . .*	1b. *Si quid est quod indagaris, inveneris, ex tenebris erueris, quamquam iniquum est, tamen consume sane, quod commodum est, quoniam quidem tu attulisti.*
"Where did you find this wood? Listed in Odd Properties?"	"If you've sniffed something out, discovered it, dug it out of the shadows, unfair though it is, go ahead, eat up what 'suits' [you]! And it would, wouldn't it? It's *your* proposal, after all!"
2a. . . . *an in censorum pascuis invenisti?*	2b. *silvam vero tu Scantiam vendas nobis consulibus atque hoc senatu? tu ullum vectigal attingas, tu populo Romano subsidia belli, tu ornamenta pacis eripias?*
"Or in the Censors' Pastures?"	"But how dare you try to sell the Scantian wood when *I* am consul and *these* men are senators! How dare you touch *any* revenue-bearing property! How dare you take from the Roman people the aids of war and the ornaments of peace!"

Cicero doubtless concedes some sales (1b) because they were legitimate (and also shrewd: *relictae possessiones* were by definition unused). But he never admits to that legality. Instead he treats even that half of the proposal as offensive, attacking as he retreats. That is manifest in his choice of tone and word. The tone is sarcastic or condescending. So suggests the pairing *tamen . . . sane*, only here in Cicero's speeches and evidently colloquial (whence my colloquial translation "Go ahead and . . .").[72] The half-image of Rullus as a dog or pig (Table 3.1.D-s; Table 3.3.21-b)

---

71. Cf. Jonkers 1963:13, Hardy 1924:78.

72. *Tamen . . . sane* is otherwise in Cicero only at *Att.* 9.9.4 (*Trebatium nostrum, etsi, ut scribis, nihil bene sperat, tamen videre sane velim*, "Even if our Trebatius has lost all hope, as you write,

contributes to that tone. Other word choices also make Rullus's proposal offensive. It is *iniquum*—that is, not *aequum* 'fair' or 'reasonable' or, as probably here, 'equitable [in distinction to the strict letter of the law]', as often in Roman jurisprudence and legal thought.[73] That is, Rullus has the right to sell the land—but it isn't the way things are done. *Iniquum* here is something of an equivalent to Paulus' implicit *inhonestum*. What is 'inequitable' is clear: Rullus is a political partisan. His proposal is "beneficial" (*commodum*) because "[he's] the one who brought it in" (*tu attulisti*). *Commodum* 'advantage(ous)' was a *popularis* keyword, typically implying material benefit to the people. But here it is sarcastically meant: the beneficiary is Rullus.[74] And Rullus did not 'bring his proposal forward' (*referre*), the normal word for proposals to the senate; he "brought it in" (*attuli[t]*) as if it were something from "out there"[75]—the roil of tribunician *contiones*, perhaps, or secret conferences with fellow tribunes. *Attulisti* here is not far from "dropped it on our desks."

In short, in 1b what might have been a question of policy ("Shall we sell certain lands?") is turned into a question of politics ("Shall we accept this *populist* idea?"). In Table 3.3.2-2b, where Cicero fulminates against the sale of any *pascua censorum*, his strategy is comparable but distinct. The issue of legality is again sidestepped (doubtless because that part of the proposal was also perfectly legal). But his chief objections draw on a different idea: not partisan politics but constitutional irregularity. As everyone in the senate knew, managing the sale of

---

I still would like to see him anyway"), *Att.* 16.11.6 (*is tamen egit sane strenue et agit* "But you can't say he wasn't and isn't energetic," of Octavian), and *Tusc.* 1.49 (*nec tamen mihi sane quicquam occurrit, cur non Pythagorae sit et Platonis vera sententia* "But still I, anyway, can't see why Pythogoras and Plato's view can't be right"). The apparently colloquial tone is possibly because the pairing is redundant (*tamen* marks a concession, and with imperatives so does *sane*, cf. *L&S* s.v. II.B.2.b.(γ.) with *OLD* s.v. 8).

73. For this sense, cf. *multaque pro aequitate contra ius dicere* (Cic. *de Orat.* 1.240, of a speech of Ser. Galba). *Caec.* 84 contains a fine metaphor for capturing the distinction: there Cicero contrasts the *campus aequitatis* to the *angustiae verborum*—"the broad field of justice" to "the narrow straits of literalism." That is not the only shade of *aequitas* in jurisprudential thought; sometimes *aequitas* and *ius* are conceived of as complementary. Cf. ch. 4.3 and n. 64.

74. *Commodum* is used twice sarcastically even in the popular speech: "It will be 'suitable' to claim that Pergamum, Smyrna, Tralles, Ephesus, Miletus, Cyzicus—indeed all of Asia that was recovered after 88!—are Roman public property" (*commodum erit Pergamum, Smyrnam, Trallis, Ephesum, Miletum, Cyzicum, totam denique Asiam quae post L. Sullam Q. Pompeium consules recuperata sit populi Romani factam esse dicere*, *LA* 2.49; on the measure here at issue, cf. ch. 4.4); and, in a summary of the measures of the bill at the end of the speech (recalling *LA* 2.51–55 = Table 5.2-p), Cicero accuses Rullus and his fellow tribunes of planning to march into Pompey's camp and sell the very camp out from under him "if it's advantageous to [them]" (*ut veniretis in castra Cn. Pompei atque ipsa castra, si commodum vobis esset, venderetis*, *LA* 2.99).

75. Hence for "gaudium, verba, nuntius" (*TLL* 1.1196.7–55); "auxilium" sim. (56–68); commands brought by a legate (68–85); *consilium* (Cic. *Off.* 3.49, *Att.* 15.1a.5, Liv. 4.48.6, 23.8.9).

vectigalia was the job of the censor;[76] but if no censors were in office, as was the case in January 63,[77] those duties fell to the consuls—which is to say, to Cicero. That is why Cicero angrily invokes his office (*nobis consulibus*).[78] And that is also why Cicero amplifies the idea of *vectigal*, using conventional phrases for their value (*subsidia belli, ornamenta pacis*), which it is his duty to guard.[79] Rullus, in a word, is interfering in the duty of regular magistrates—another imbalance, like the threat of too many resources in decemviral hands.

That interference is a theme of the passage, brought out in figures and words. Two plays on words stress the point. The first, in Table 3.1.E-s, recalls the reading of the bill before senate debate began: *audistis auctionem **populi** Romani proscriptam a tribuno **plebis*** "You've heard an auction of [the property of] the Roman people declared by the tribune of the plebs."[80] Calling Rullus not by name but by his office lets *plebis* stand against *populi*: the property of the whole community, the *populus Romanus*, is threatened by a representative of the *plebs* alone.[81] He is an errant member of the group whose spending plan is mad. Another play on words highlights another breach. Two successive clauses begin with echoing words (Table 3.1.B-s and C-s):

perscribit *in sua lege vectigalia quae decemviri vendant,*
hoc est, **proscribit** *auctionem publicorum bonorum.*

"In his law **he sets out** the tax properties the decemvirs are to sell; that is, **he sets up** an auction of public properties."

---

76. *Vrbis templa, vias, aquas, aerarium, vectigalia tuento* (Cic. *Leg.* 3.7); for further details, see Suolahti 1963, Strong 1968.

77. Lucius Aurelius Cotta (*RE* 103) and (perhaps) Manius Acilius Glabrio (*RE* 38) were elected in 64 but resigned without even having completed the *lectio senatus*. See Broughton 1986 3.3.

78. Surely here meaning only Cicero himself; cf. Manuwald 2018: 126.

79. *Subsidium belli* and *ornamentum pacis* or variants are stock phrases; cf. *Ver.* 2.3.14 (*subsidium belli atque pacis*, of Sicily), *Ver.* 2.5.124 (*et belli adiumenta et pacis ornamenta*, of the ministrations of the Tyndaritani, a Sicilian people), *Man.* 6 (*pacis ornamenta et subsidia belli*, of *vectigalia*), *LA* 2.80 = Appendix 2, C10-p (*pacis ornamentum, subsidium belli*, of the *ager Campanus*). Notable here is *de Orat.* 2.171: *si aerari copiis et ad belli adiumenta et ad ornamenta pacis utimur, vectigalibus serviamus* "If we use the resources of the treasury to aid war and ornament peace, then we have to protect tax revenue" (cited as an example of argument *ex eis quae sunt orta de causis* "the effects of causes").

80. Zumpt 1861: 4; Classen 1985: 321 n. 55.

81. The same pun is used in the popular speech (*LA* 2.17)—but to a different effect, highlighting infringements of that cardinal popular value, *libertas*. For the text, ch. 5.1, and for discussion, see ch. 6.3.

(Using the same root with different preverbs was considered a form of wordplay; I have tried to capture the effect with two versions of 'set.'[82]) The second sentence is not simply a restatement of the first but draws out its constitutional implication. *Perscribit*, lit. "writes out in full," represents the thoroughness that Cicero otherwise discredits. But *proscribere* is a technical word, 'post notice,' regularly used of auctions.[83] It appears one more time in this passage (*proscriptam*, Table 3.1.E-s)—but nowhere in the popular speech, despite its reenactment of an auction. As everyone in the senate knew, "posting notice" of sales of public property was the job of the quaestor.[84] Cicero's gloss turns Rullus's lawcraft (*perscribit*) into usurpation of another magistrate's prerogative (*proscribit*). What is worse, it's also a rush job: the sale was slated for January—and it was already January.[85]

Choices of word highlight other breaches. Earlier measures of the bill, by Cicero's lights, injured various constituencies in the empire.[86] In the popular speech they are attached to *sanguine* "blood," but the comparable senate list adds extra details.

LA 1.2 (= Table 3.1.C-s)	*LA* 2.46 (= Table 3.1.A-p)
agri sociorum "the territory of allies"	*cum ... sociorum* "the blood of allies"
urbes pacatae "pacified cities"	*cum exterarum nationum* "and of foreign nations"
regum status "kings in their high rank"	*cum regum sanguine* "and of kings"

---

82. Cf. *Rhet. Her.* 4.29–30, where one example is *demus operam, Quirites, ne omnino patres <conscripti> circumscripti putentur* "Let us strive, fellow citizens, that no one think the conscript fathers have been completely deceived" (*conscripti* fell out by a *lapsus oculi* to the subsequent *circumscripti*). Cicero makes the same kind of pun in several other places in the senate speech: *perscribit ~ proscribit* (2), *praefinitum ~ infinitum* (10 = Table 8.4.1.A-B-s); *praeponitur ~ opponitur* (20, cf. ch. 9.3 Honestum); *amissis ~ intermissis* (21). The corresponding passages in the popular speech contain no such figure. Cf. also Harvey 1972: 22.

83. "technice in iure et in vita publica," *TLL* 10.2.2174.51; 10.2.2175.10–21 for auctions. *Proscribere* does appear in the third speech (3.14, 15).

84. Kunkel and Wittmann 1995: 517–18.

85. Cf. Manuwald 2018: 128.

86. Here listed, apparently, in a conventional order: cf. *omitto socios exteras nationes reges tetrarchas* (*Mil.* 76).

Responsibility and Anxiety

The added details remind the senate of its role. *Regum status* and not *regna* recalls a rank that the senate granted (the unparalleled phrase is not a simple metonymy for 'kingdoms').[87] "Pacified" (*pacatae*) is a formal status that the senate determined through its legates. In this context, *agri* recalls that a senatorial commission set the limits and status of some allied territories. In short, the decemvirs' victims are described in ways that recall the senate's purview in foreign policy.[88] If the people see blood, as if in news clips, the senate hear of political interference, as if in a diplomatic cable. In their environs these details doubtless had an extra semiotic charge. The senate's leading role in foreign policy was exercised not least in the wake of military victory, and Cicero and the senate were at that very moment in a shrine to Roman military supremacy: the temple of Jupiter Optimus Maximus (or Jupiter Capitolinus), where Cicero had just taken his oath of office. It was there that victorious military commanders ended their triumphal processions by offering sacrifice and depositing tokens of their victory. Cicero names those tokens clearly in the immediately subsequent passage (*insignia atque infulae imperi* "symbols and garlands of empire," *LA* 1.6 = Table 8.2.D-s) and elsewhere makes that temple a symbol of the very idea of empire, "[the] citadel of all nations."[89] Cicero thus links the senate's role to Roman military tradition.

He invokes that tradition much more dramatically in the two *a fortiori* arguments of the passage. One, in Table 3.1.E-s, concerns the senate:

> I'm sure you agree that the men who won these properties in courageous campaigns (*armis et virtute*, lit. "by arms and courage") decided not to sell them to replenish the treasury in order that we could have something to sell to finance handouts (lit. *largitionis causa* 'for the sake of largesse')!

That is, the elders did not forego a better purpose at the time to finance a lesser purpose in the future (the irony makes the logic of the argument the reverse of its surface form). The elders are not named but described (another *pronominatio*) as those who won *armis et virtute*. The phrase, only here in Cicero's oratory, is uncommon elsewhere, and there highly patriotic. In Livy Marcus Curtius, on the verge of plunging into the sinkhole in the Forum that would later bear his name, declares that the Romans know no greater blessing than "arms and courage"

---

87. "The term *status* insinuates that Rullus's measures will not only affect the possessions of these kings, but also their political status," Manuwald 2018: 124.

88. Similarly, *LA* 1.11 (Table 8.3.1.A-s) uses the formal designations *civitates liberae, amici reges*, and *vectigalia populi Romani*, and not merely *exterae nationes, reges*, and *vectigalia vestra*.

89. *LA* 1.18 = C1 in Appendix 2; ch. 9.3 *Honestum*.

(7.6.3).[90] Elsewhere in Livy the phrase connotes "fighting with might and main," especially as against relying on defensive structures.[91] The worth of what the elders gained is stressed by how they gained it; their *arma et virtus* put a kind of permanent lien on the property. Like Cicero's concessions to Rullus (Table 3.1.D-s), the whole image has a partisan political side. *Largitio* 'largesse' alludes to bribery and is here made to include populist policies that provide material benefits.[92] The corresponding *a fortiori* argument of the popular speech in E-p also uses military imagery—but the accent is on the practical and the material: a single inheritance bequeathed undivided (*quod . . . id*) and so to be maintained.

The other *a fortiori* argument of the senate version (Table 3.1.D-s) concerns Cicero himself. He will consider himself an ineffective consul (*iners*) if he cannot even keep (*retinere*) territories that the bravest (*fortissimi*) of the elders won; he would be failing at the easier task. The comparison hinges on double meanings. *Fortis* and *iners* are opposites in two senses. Sometimes the opposition is military: the 'brave' or 'strong' versus the 'tentative' or 'sluggish.' Thus in a note of Servius: in olden times painted shields were only for the valiant (*fortes*); hesitant soldiers (*inertes*) and raw recruits (*tirones*) had plain.[93] Other times the opposition is civic: the 'energetic,' 'dedicated,' or 'upstanding' citizen versus the 'indolent' or 'useless' one.[94] Thus in a list of antonyms, Cicero characterizes the

---

90. *an ullum magis Romanum bonum quam arma virtusque esset*, cf. 34.13.9, *Curtius . . . interpretatus urbem nostram virtute armisque praecipue excellere* (V. Max. 5.6.2), *cuius [belli] pars magna, eiusdem Metelli Macedonici virtute armisque fracta erat* (Vell. 1.12.1). Cf. also *ut armis | ac virtute velint patriam defendere terram | praesidioque parent decorique parentibus esse* (Lucr. 2.641–3, of the armed escorts of Magna Mater).

91. Thus the Roman troops fleeing from Eretum after a battle against the Sabines, "nowhere offering a fair fight, defended themselves by the terrain and entrenchment, not the strength of their arms" (*nusquam se aequo certamine committentes, natura loci ac vallo, non virtute aut armis tutabantur*, 3.42.4)—which Livy considers a "disgrace" (*dedecus*, 3.42.2). Cf. 3.60.8, 27.18.8, 32.17.7, 37.32.5. Porphyrio explicates Regulus's lament in Horace (*hic unde vitam sumeret inscius | pacem duello miscuit, Carm.* 3.5.37–38) thus: "What [Horace] means is that [Regulus] turned himself over to the enemy when he should have saved his life by the force of his arms" (*cum deberet, inquit, vitam virtute atque armis quaerere, commisit se hostibus*).

92. Likewise Cicero attributes the word to the tribunes who won't admit him to their drafting sessions: *negabant me adduci posse ut ullam largitionem probarem* (*LA* 2.12). On the two kinds of *largitio*, cf. Cic. *Off.* 2.52–64, which distinguishes *liberales* from *prodigi*, with Dyck 1996: 156. On the danger *largitio* posed to *fides*, see Yakobson 1992.

93. *nam apud maiores virorum fortium picta erant scuta, e contra inertium et tironum pura erant* (Serv. *Aen.* 7.796, cf. 11.409). Cf. *quis, pro deum fidem, ita comparatus, vel iners atque inbellis, fortissimum virum <non> vicerit?* (Liv. 44.38.10). For other examples of the sense "sine virtute bellica," cf. *TLL* 7.1.1309.1–30, *OLD s.v. iners* 3.

94. For further examples of the sense "sine quavis virtute, nihili, nullius pretii," cf. *TLL* 7.1.1312.9–62.

supporters of the insurrectionist Catiline as *inertes* and the good citizens who oppose them as *fortes*.[95] *Iners* of this latter kind may describe 'ineffective' or 'lazy' magistrates: Verres was an "ineffective and worthless praetor" (*praetoris inertissimi nequissimique, Ver.* 2.5.100)—and Cicero would later accuse himself of being ineffective and worthless for failing to act against Catiline (*sed iam me ipse inertiae nequitiaeque condemno, Catil.* 1.4).[96]

Iners and *fortis*, then, form an antonymic pair in both the civic and military senses (Table 3.3.3).

Table 3.3.3. *Antonyms in LA 1.4* (= Table 3.1.D-s)

	Military	Civic
fortis	'brave, strong'	'energetic'
iners	'shirker'	'ineffective'

But in this passage, as the shading is meant to suggest, the opposition crosses spheres of activity: the *viri fortissimi* of times past were military men, whereas Cicero's *inertia* would be civic. The crossing makes the conceptual spheres overlap. The civic is militarized and vice-versa. From one direction, Cicero, whose career was unmilitary, links himself to military values. Cicero's civic *fortitudo* will be worthy of the ancestors' military *fortitudo*.[97] From the other direction, military values inform fiscal policy, just as in the *armis et virtute* of Table 3.1.E-s.

---

95. "Who can abide a sneak attack by the useless upon the energetic, the foolish upon the sensible, the drunken upon the sober, the sluggish upon the wakeful?" (*hoc vero quis possit ferre, inertis homines fortissimis viris insidiari, stultissimos prudentissimis, ebrios sobriis, dormientis vigilantibus? Catil.* 2.10). Cf. also *vicissent improbos boni, fortes inertis* (*Sest.* 43), cf. *Balb.* 51, *Parad.* 2.19, *Off.* 3.31. *Inertia* is, of course, also opposed to *labor* (e.g. Plin. *Pan.* 3.5).

96. Cf. *sed si quis est invidiae metus, non est vehementius severitatis ac fortitudinis invidia quam inertiae ac nequitiae pertimescenda* "If ill will is any cause for anxiety, the ill will that comes from severity and courage is no more acutely to be feared that the ill-will that comes from ineffectiveness and incompetence" (*Catil.* 1.29). For another association of *inertia* with ineffective magistrates, cf. *Carbo graviter ferebat sibi quaestorem obtigisse hominem singulari luxuria atque inertia* (*Ver.* 2.1.34). For another contrast of laziness vs. "courage," cf. *hoc statu quem habetis vestra non ignavia quaesitum sed virtute partum* (*LA* 2.103, cf. ch. 7.4 with n. 82).

97. My guess is that this theme figured importantly in the lost *exordium* of the senate speech (for the missing sections and topics, cf. Appendix 1). Here, at all events, is already the line of thinking that led Cicero to equate his saving of the city from Catiline's conspiracy with military victory—to Pompey's irritation (*Schol. Bob.* 167 Stangl, cf. *Fam.* 5.7.2, *Sul.* 67, *Planc.* 85).

The key is the idea of gain and loss. In the financial world, they may be fluid: an expenditure does not mean a net loss for all time; and expenses of capital may yield other sorts of gain. That was the idea behind the Rullan bill: sold properties would finance new colonies or revitalize old ones. Militarily, by contrast, gain and loss are starker affairs, measured in land surrendered or secured. By that standard, property must be preserved—and Cicero, like a commander, will see to exactly that. *Retineri* 'to be preserved' (Table 3.1.D-s *fin.*), coming shortly after *fortissimos*, probably has military overtones.[98] Cicero, and with him the senate, must, not only politically but also quite literally, hold their ground. Such an exercise of duty—collective duty—is the antidote to Rullus's selfish imbalancings and disruptions. That is exactly the idea Cicero has in mind in the very last sentence of the senate speech: the republic sorely needs a senate with the authority it had in the days of old—which Cicero can restore, if only they will join him in "defending the common dignity" (*ad communem dignitatem defendendam*, LA 1.27, cf. ch. 8.5, citation F).

3.4. CONCLUSION

Significatio est res quae plus in suspicione relinquit quam positum est in oratione.

The figure of Suggestion leaves more to the imagination than is actually expressed in the oration.

—Rhetorica ad Herennium 4.67

The passages analyzed in this and the preceding chapter allow a working hermeneutic for the speeches to be posited. The speeches, as I hope to have made clear, are informed by a precise ideology that is thoroughgoingly reflected in the selection of formal features, which give expression to that ideology for the most part allusively and indirectly. Several corollaries and principles emerge. First, the deep coherence of the formal features, plainly a mark of Cicero's careful craftsmanship, justify examining them—or rather continuing to examine them—for their ideological import. What might look like stray details, as we will see, often prove to be weighty. The coherence also suggests semiotically alert audiences used to seeing meaning in (apparently) small gestures—a reasonable thing in a highly rhetorical culture and a culture so dependent on display and symbol.

That brings us to the matter of allusion and indirection. That technique perfectly suits a semiotically alert audience. And perhaps that is how rhetoric usually

---

98. *OLD* s.v. 8.

works—not so much persuasion in any strictly rational sense as a display and redirection of known tokens of shared meaning. In that case reliance on indirection, implication, allusion, and symbol is the very nature of the beast. Much of rhetoric, on that view, is dog-whistle politics. At all events a certain indirection suited this occasion. These were Cicero's first consular speeches, and both audiences, doubtless expecting that they would be programmatic, must have been ready to detect in their details and images Cicero's calling cards and political parables. Cicero, one might say, now knew (or wished!) that he had now himself become one of the high-ranking persons he mentions in *pro S. Roscio Amerino*, whose comments about politics are read for deeper meanings.[99] He was himself able to make such gestures now, knowing full well they would be read into. His gestures had gained semiotic weight.

And that, in turn, sheds light on an aspect of Cicero's technique in these speeches. The vignettes analyzed in this chapter and in Chapter 2 cannot have been meant to be realistic. State properties would never have been sold off one by one in the Forum. Neither was the *silva Scantia* some crown jewel of state finances, demanding a wroth defense. Nor would every decemvir have seized his host's property from under his feet or bled hapless provincial townsmen dry by extortion in its various forms and shapes. But Cicero was not aiming to be realistic—or even reasonable. The tableaux are icons meant to vividly and memorably symbolize power relations. The speeches, one might say, are an extended version of the subcategory of *significatio* called *exsuperatio* ('hyperbole'), in which the bounds of truth are exceeded in order to rouse suspicions (*Rhet. Her.* 4.67). To put that idea in its strongest form, Cicero uses the details of the bill less to critique the bill itself than to reflect on the nature of power. The clauses and features of the bill become so many pegs on which to hang political reflections; the bill becomes a kind of excuse to put forward a political vision, almost as if another bill might have served just as well ("any stick to beat a dog," in the phrase). To put the idea more mildly: the details of this particular bill imply, or can with some justification be read to imply, certain kinds of power relations, and Cicero's main purpose is to expose them ("where there's smoke, there's fire," one might say). But in either case Cicero reads the bill not narrowly, as a legislative proposal aimed at a particular set of problems (which it was), but broadly, as a kind of charter for government (which, in part, it also was). He reads the details of the law not as a

---

99. *siqui istorum . . . in quibus summa auctoritas est atque amplitudo, si verbum de re publica fecisset, id quod in hac causa fieri necesse est, multo plura dixisse, quam dixisset, putaretur* (*S. Rosc.* 2). Cicero has in mind specifically "reading between the lines" to deduce his opinion about Sulla (on which issue, see Buchheit 1975), but his observation about discourse applies more broadly, of course.

sober policy expert, carefully and accurately mapping out all probable benefits and costs, but as a (deeply suspicious) op-ed or think-tank writer, energetically probing, by the standard of his own vision, the political ideas that seem to lie behind the details.

And that raises the question, what is the nature of that vision? Does Cicero mean any of what he says? To my mind he does, at least in part. The ideal of a sober populace and a responsible senate that informs almost every detail of the passages we have thus far seen is a version of the concord and harmony across groups of society that Cicero later overtly championed.[100] And its constitutional analysis (which, it should not be forgotten, is the same in both speeches: they both attack the same provisions of the law, commonly for the same defects) not only seems to have identified flaws that Caesar avoided in his later version of the bill,[101] but, in seeing the danger of the popular assembly unleashed and the need for a unified and principled senate, foresees exactly the dangers and challenges of half a decade thence, when the tribune Clodius would upset the political order.[102] Cicero's solution may be a fantasy, but the problem is real.[103]

In this connection a consistent aspect of the tableaux that we have seen deserves notice. They frequently depend not merely on allusion but also on one kind of inversion or another: a land commissioner who is paradoxically worse than an abusive governor; diligence that paradoxically turns out to be greed; power as a reason not for confidence but for caution; people that are active superintendents and not passive beneficiaries; a civil magistrate with military values; and so on. Those inversions can be seen as so many clever rhetorical ploys—the sophist's delight in perversion and reversal. But they can also be seen as reflecting closely, on the levels of concept and of metaphor, the very reversals of the audiences' perceptions and attitudes, both of themselves and of Cicero's role, that, as I have been suggesting, it is Cicero's purpose to effect. That is, the *inventio* and *elocutio* exactly reflect Cicero's objectives with *pathos* and *ethos*; figure and form suit purpose. Is that, too, ultimately a piece of political analysis? that the conventional categories by which the collective life was governed were in need of

---

100. Cf. ch. 1.2 *Pathos, fin.*

101. Cf. ch. 1.4 Mechanisms and ch. 6.3 with n. 57.

102. See ch. 9.4 and n. 55.

103. This analysis thus steers a kind of a middle course between Williamson 2005, who takes the second agrarian speech as a typical instance of presenting a law (which it was not), and Morstein-Marx 2004, who reads the second speech chiefly in terms of the conventions of contional rhetoric and less as a seriously meant piece of constitutional analysis (which on my view it is).

reconfiguration, recombination, and repurposing (precisely as Augustus would do)? At all events here is one last piece of the hermeneutic that will guide the rest of this study: the close analysis of passages will be open to the possibility that Cicero's imagery and ideology depends upon reversals, inversions, and recastings. In that vein the next chapters explore a *libertas* that isn't populist, a consul who is a tribune, a tribune who is a tyrant, and an equestrian by birth who is a true noble.

4

Libertas *and the Duty of Oversight*

4.1. INTRODUCTION

Est igitur . . . res publica res populi.

What 'republic' means, then, is 'the people's enterprise.'
—Africanus in Cicero, *de Republica*, 1.39

The images of the *liberae legationes*, the wastrel, and the auction are tableaux meant to probe power relations. Together they position their listeners between anxiety and responsibility: the tableaux dramatize to each audience certain dangers inherent (in Cicero's view) in the bill's proposals, and they project onto each audience ideal roles and identities that (in Cicero's view) are checks on those perils. Thus the senate are shown the dangers of an imbalanced competitive system but likewise prompted to exercise collective guidance, taking seriously the ideology of their high station; the people are shown the dangers of the broad powers that only they can create but likewise prompted to keep possible consequences in mind, regarding their sovereignty seriously.

The dynamic that thus emerges from those pairs of passages is, in my view, a fair symbol for and summary of the import of both whole speeches (which is why I began with them). It is, at any rate, clear enough that they project on each audience two coherent sensibilities. Those sensibilities, I submit, rest in each case on a single valuing standard. The chief purpose of this chapter is to probe the standard of the popular speech directly, guided by the method—close comparison, the expectation of inversion, etc.—developed inductively in the preceding chapters. The popular speech, as I have been suggesting, rests ultimately on the idea of *libertas*. That is certainly the value that Cicero invokes overtly. The idea grows in prominence through the opening sections. He begins his speech by describing his successful consular campaign, in particular his election by acclamation. There *libertas* is a grace note; there was not even a need, says Cicero, to count votes, that "silent protector of the people's liberty" (Cicero means the secret ballot, *LA* 2.4).[1] By the time the *exordium* ends, *libertas* has emerged as an important theme. Forecasting the difficulties that will face him as consul, Cicero lays claim to the word *popularis*. He can do no other than be "a man of the people" because "the people" have entrusted to him what is dearest to them: peace abroad, domestic tranquility, and the "liberty proper to [their] nation and name" (*libertatem propriam generis ac nominis vestri*, *LA* 2.9).[2] In the next section, the *propositio* (*LA* 2.10 *nam*—16 *defendere*), where Cicero, per the canons of classical rhetoric, lays out "what he intends to prove," *libertas* has become the keynote.[3] There the note is sounded thrice. Rullus's bill dangles plots in front of the Roman people even as it robs them of their liberty; in Rullus's bill the tribunate, meant to be the bulwark of liberty, becomes instead the vanguard of tyranny; the bill is a secret attack on the liberty won by the elders' hard toil (*LA* 2.15-16).[4]

The invocation of *libertas* is no surprise. That value was a populist watchword, and the open public assembly, or *contio*, favored populist rhetoric.[5] Many of Cicero's previous public appearances had conformed to that expectation.[6] But what *libertas* means, here or elsewhere, isn't a simple question. There are three reasons for that. There is first a semantic reason. Important concepts do not have the same nuances, or even meanings, in every source. For one thing, cognitive categories, of which semantic fields are one kind, are inherently flexible, typically comprising a "family" of related elements.[7] Membership in the category does not require possessing all the elements—does not require every box to be checked, as it were. In the case of culturally important concepts, their very importance encourages different parties to lay claim to them for their own ends, which not only exploits that flexibility but may even stretch the meaning of the concept—a

---

1. The full passage appears in Table 6.2.1.F.

2. For the full passage, see pp. 196–97 and cf. Table 6.2.2.S-p.

3. *Propositio est per quam ostendimus summatim quid sit quod probari volumus* (*Rhet. Her.* 2.28, cf. *de Orat.* 3.203, *Or.* 137; Manuwald 2018: 220). The definition of a *divisio* may be compared: *(divisio) dividit per enumerationem aut per expositionem, quibus de rebus in totam orationem disputatio futura sit* (*Rhet. Her.* 4.52). Cf. 1.4, Cic. *Inv.* 1.31.

4. For the full passage, with more analysis, cf. ch. 7.3 The Voices of the (Un-)Tribune.

5. Cf. ch. 1 n. 23.

6. On the *popularis* cast of Cicero's early career, cf. Morstein-Marx 2004: 207–209; ch. 5.1.

7. For a theory of "radial categories" as explicative of this phenomenon, see Lakoff 1987, with Rosch 1983.

kind of conceptual "mission creep," so to speak.[8] The briefest of reflections on the uses and meanings of "freedom" in US political discourse is enough to show that. One must thus be alert to the possibility that a given text might not simply have adopted the core values it cites but might have adapted and even contested their meaning—and perhaps inconsistently at that. Second, there is a generic reason. A speech, other things being equal, is not a treatise for the ages but a temporary arrangement, for a particular purpose, of the ideas, signs, and images of a culture (as I began to suggest at the end of ch. 3). Third, there is the reason of Cicero's technique. As we have just seen (ch. 3.4), central to his technique in these speeches is inversion and reversal. It is thus well to expect that Cicero's versions of core values will be distinctive.

Libertas had acquired several distinct strands of meaning by the late Republic. The heart of its meaning, its ideological core, one might say, had long been a legal one, the right of self-governance. That meaning was typically conceived of antithetically: the status of a free nation, as opposed to that of a subject people.[9] That aspect of the meaning loomed large in the civic myths of a polity that dated its second birth to the ouster of kings.[10] *Libertas* could also denote the particular constitutional forms by which self-government was expressed and exercised, what might be called the procedural side of the idea (or, to put it more abstractly, the actualizing of the condition). That side of the idea could be a point of contention. The Roman body politic assembled in different forms for different purposes with different operating procedures, and a particular party might see, or claim to see, one or another body or procedure as embodying *libertas* better—for example, the secret ballot to which Cicero alludes in *LA* 2.4. In the late Republic *libertas* commonly connoted in particular the centrality of the *concilium plebis*—which, of course, is not a necessary entailment of the idea of self-governance.[11] The idea of *libertas* also came to have what might be called an operational side: an elected official might be expected to remain in close conformity to the will of the body

---

8. On that notion, see Skinner 1980. Cf. also Laser 1997: 155–56: "Libertas war trotz ihren doppelten Bedeutung und ihres Schlagwortartigen Charakters ein Begriff, auf dessen Beachtung die Masse fixiert war und für dessen Bewahrung sie sich engagierte."

9. See Schofield 2021: 27–32, Wirszubski 1960: 1–3.

10. A signal example is Livy 2.1, in which the years of regal rule at Rome had allowed a community to coalesce, the better to enjoy the liberty Brutus won them. On Livy's construction of Brutus there, see Robbins 1972.

11. See Arena 2012: 117–26; "Whilst Polybius inserts the role of the tribune of the plebs within a complex web of institutional checks and balances, which act as one of the guarantors of the commonwealth's liberty, Tiberius Gracchus presents the tribune as an institutional enabler of the people's political power, power which resided solely in their hands—that is, ultimately, in the popular assembly" (126).

that elected him—which is not a necessary entailment of the idea of the centrality of one or another electoral body. A striking instance of that idea is Tiberius Gracchus's call for the ouster of Octavius, a colleague who had vetoed his agrarian measure.[12] Last, *libertas* had practical connotations that varied by social stature. For the aristocracy *libertas* connoted the opportunity to compete for the distinctions that confirmed their worth.[13] (That is not without paradox: the liberty of the masses thereby reinforced the privilege of the few.) For the people *libertas* often connoted material benefits or *commoda*. The idea is a version of *clientela*, in which officeholders owed supporters for their support, and is a result of Roman imperialism, which exploited provinces.[14] (That aspect of *libertas* is also not without paradox: the people who were notionally masters of the world—so Cicero calls them once in this speech[15]—were the dependents of potentates.)

The complex of ideas is a coherent one, linked by various contiguities, a "family" in the way I suggested earlier.[16] But, as I have already tried to indicate, the coherence of the set does not mean that an individual feature is or must be exactly consistent with all the others. Foregrounding one feature over another can give the concept a different force and flavor. Accenting *commodum* acknowledges dependence (the people must wait for benefits); accenting procedure acknowledges sovereignty (the people have oversight). Likewise, a given matter can be made to appear congruent with *libertas* or discordant with it, according to which

---

12. Plut. *TG* 15.3. A tribune's sacrosanctity, argued Tiberius, depended on his being consecrated to the people; therefore if he injured the people, *ipso facto* he had resigned his office. Tiberius's example was followed in 67 by Gabinius when Trebellius threatened to veto his measure awarding the command against the pirates to Pompey. Perhaps, as Arena 2012: 128, suggests, Cicero echoes Gabinius's arguments in his own defense of Cornelius, who had acted in contravention of a veto: *neque . . . passus est plus unius collegae sui quam universae civitatis vocem valere et voluntatem* (*Corn.* 1.31 Crawford, *q.v. ad loc.*). For a depiction of the tense political scene underlying Octavius' deposition, see Morgan and Walsh 1978.

13. Cf. ch. 8.2 with its epigraph.

14. For the view that that is a post-Gracchan development in Roman imperial attitudes, see Badian 1968: 76–92.

15. Of a Rullus who brought the law, gave a minority electoral power, oversaw the election, drew the lots for the tribes he wanted, and got elected the candidates he wanted, Cicero remarks, "Good Lord, I don't think he could convince his own slaves that this is fair, let alone you, the masters of all nations!" (*vix me hercule servus hoc eum suis, non vobis omnium gentium dominis probaturum arbitror*, *LA* 2.22; for the context of this quote, see ch. 6.3).

16. Not the identical idea, but well worth noting here, is Arena's (2012: 7) invocation of "family resemblances" as a criterion for understanding styles of political reasoning, which she defines as "neither the ideologies of the nineteenth century nor Freeden's morphological complex around a given core of concepts, but rather systems of thought, more or less coherent in themselves, that displayed distinct orientations on questions relating to fundamental evaluative terms such as liberty, justice and sovereignty."

aspect of *libertas* is stressed. A profitable scheme that also bypasses established public procedure may be said to serve *libertas* (its practical end is satisfied) or violate it (its procedural aspect is disregarded). It may seem a consequence of this perspective that a core concept ultimately has no meaning at all. But that is wrong. Rather, the related, but not identical, elements embraced by a concept are manipulated and fought over precisely because those elements *really do* belong to the concept. Those elements should be thought of not as canceling each other out but as vying for position and priority.

This brief overview sets into relief and draws out the significance of the elements in a passage we have seen. The popular version of the *liberae legationes* passage has three "extra" sections not required by the logic of the argument and absent from the senate version. One addendum reflects on the risks of granting *imperium*: "*liberi legati* abroad abuse [the Roman people's], not their own, name" (*vestro, non suo, nomine*, Table 2.1.C-p). Another uses the *lex Gabinia* and *lex Manilia*, which gave Pompey the commands against the pirates and Mithridates respectively, to suggest that a grant of broad power must have limited objectives and a worthy purpose: whereas Pompey was entrusted with much (*multa committi*) in order to free allies (*ad socios liberandos*), the decemvirs would be handed everything (*condonari omnia*) in order to crush them (*opprimendos*, Table 2.1.H-p). The last addendum implies that if an outsized honor is to be granted, the Roman people should grant it knowingly "to the man of their choice" and not have it "stolen" (*surripiatur*) from them by a deceptive law (*per legis fraudem*, Table 2.1.I-p).

The three addenda are not flattery and are not frippery. As I already suggested (ch. 2.3 Where the Audiences are Meant to Go), the addenda together form a kind of "user's guide" to sovereignty. That claim can now be broadened and contextualized: the "user's guide" is Cicero's very particular adaptation of the idea of *libertas*; the guide has in mind not the stock version of *libertas* but a custom version of Cicero's. So with the constitutional aspect of *libertas*. Broadly, Table 2.1.H and I are conventional: in acknowledging the right of the people to create special powers, they implicitly defer to the authority of the *concilium plebis*. But the expression of the idea in H deserves notice: the Roman people risk having a special office "stolen" from them (*surripiatur*; the verb implies not merely theft but sly or stealthy theft).[17] The semantics and schema of "sly theft"—and the word *surripiatur* is specially emphasized[18]—reverses the emotional coloring of sovereignty. Sovereignty becomes not a point of pride but a source of worry; it

---

17. "To snatch or take away secretly, to withdraw privily, to steal, pilfer, purloin," *L&S s.v.*, cf. *OLD s.v.* 2.

18. The word forms a heroic clausula (that is, the ending of a hexameter, *sūrrĭpĭātŭr*), very rare in Cicero (cf. Manuwald 2018: 294).

prompts not confidence but skepticism about legislators and anxiety about procedure. Another metaphor perhaps supports the idea of skepticism: if *per legis fraudem* is an allusion to contract law, then legislators were parties to an agreement bound to avoid *fraus* 'dishonest conduct.'[19] But these legislators are cheaters.

Other features of *libertas* are drawn into this reversal and remolding. The oppositional connotations of *libertas*, which are ultimately a question of legal status, are transferred to the political level: it is not that a free people stand against kings and their subjects, but that public assemblies stand against populist politicians (a paradoxical idea that also receives stronger expression in the *exordium*, a topic of ch. 6). The operational side of *libertas* becomes not a question of obedience (a magistrate failing to heed the people's will) but a problem of displacement (a decemvir will abuse "the people's name"). The practical side of *libertas* is also reversed. The people expected *commoda* as the fruits of their liberty. That was ultimately part of an exchange: the people granted offices (which are thus sometimes called *beneficia*) and in return they received benefactions. The metaphor of threatened theft recasts that notion. The people are still benefactors, in possession of something valuable; but now it is something to guard jealously and dispense prudently, not invest hopefully. The question now is not return on investment but duty of care.

That last reversal has wider implications. If the people have a duty of care, they are in a position of responsibility. They are, in that sense, themselves like magistrates. And it is exactly that idea of responsibility that is projected onto them in Table 2.1.H-p: they supported the Gabinian and Manilian Laws, it is implied, because the bills had honorable and limited purposes. That, too, is an inversion, or rather a revision. Those pieces of tribunician legislation must have been a source of pride in some, perhaps many, quarters of the populace, as if yet again—as before with the Gracchan land bills, say, or Saturninus's *quaestio de maiestate*—the exercise of popular sovereignty had made right what the aristocracy could not.[20] Hard problems had been solved: the bills had led to safe seas and stable Asian revenues.

---

19. For the implications of *fraus* in contract law, see Zimmerman 1990: 702–703; Berger 1953 s.v. Is the later technical sense of *in fraudem legis* or *fraus legi facta* already here? That is an act in which the letter of the law is fulfilled but its spirit violated (cf. *contra legem facit, qui id facit, quod lex prohibet; in fraudem vero legis, qui salvis verbis legis sententiam eius circumvenit* "A person acts against the law who does what the law forbids; a person acts in evasion of the law who respects the wording of the law but circumvents its intention," Paulus *Dig.* 1.3.29; *fraus enim legi fit, ubi quod fieri noluit, fieri autem non vetuit, id fit*, Ulp. *Dig.* 1.3.30). That fits to a tee Cicero's critique of Rullus' bill, in which the powers the bill grants will be used but not for the benefit of the people; *fraus legis* is also used in the senate speech of what Cicero intends to prove in his *contio* (*LA* 1.25).

20. Cicero's remarks in his speech on the Manilian Law surely reflect a real current of thought: "If you [passed the Gabinian Law] rashly and without due political thought, [the

Benefits had been won: great returns to the treasury were in the offing. On that view, the objections made at the time—such as that the Manilian law was too broad[21]—were misbegotten, and the results retroactively justified the authorizing actions. So why not use another plebiscite to secure other benefits? That is what (some of) the people must have wondered and what Rullus surely argued (and perhaps even believed). But a concern for benefits leaves no overt mark in Table 2.1.H-p. Cicero's handling of the law implies something quite different: it is not that results justify methods; still less that any piece of tribunician legislation is somehow automatically good; rather, it is that a law must be properly crafted and must have a high purpose. Cicero has recast the meaning of the laws into something rather different from what many of their supporters likely felt them to mean at the time. He has assigned to the laws a particular ethical implication after the fact—exactly the intellectual method of the *exemplum*, the Roman moral parable.[22]

In short, behind the addenda to the popular version of the *liberae legationes* passage stands the idea of *libertas*, not "out of the box," but modified into a particular, and rather narrow, set of features: skepticism toward populist legislators, responsible and foresightful governance, and proper procedure. That is obviously something of a fantasy, given the way Roman assemblies worked in the tumultuous late Republic, and no little part of it, perhaps especially skepticism toward populist legislators, plainly reflects Cicero's own political views. But that is precisely the kind of *libertas* that—not invoked by name but palpable, an Unnamed Referent—recurs consistently through the middle sections of *de lege agraria* II. This chapter explicates three passage that nicely illustrate that *libertas* and, what is more, each leave the people with memorable images for aspects of the concept—a populist Sulla, a long-haired Numidian king, the centumviral court and pirates in the night. Presupposed throughout is an audience familiar with the stakes and the terms of debate and semiotically astute.

---

opponents of the Manilian Law] are right to try to guide your enthusiasms with their advice. But if you were the ones who were more politically astute at the time, if you were the ones who on your own authority, despite their resistance, brought dignity to this empire and safety to the world, then at some point these leading men should admit that they, and everybody else, have to obey the authority of the full Roman people" (*hoc si vos temere fecistis, et rei publicae parum consuluistis, recte isti studia vestra suis consiliis regere conantur. Sin autem vos plus tum in re publica vidistis, vos eis repugnantibus per vosmet ipsos dignitatem huic imperio, salutem orbi terrarum attulistis, aliquando isti principes et sibi et ceteris populi Romani universi auctoritati parendum esse fateantur, Leg.* 64). On the dramatic struggles to get this bill passed, cf. D.C. 36.30.4–36a, with Morstein-Marx 2004: 179–83.

21. *Leg.* 52–56 recounts (and refutes) that argument of Hortensius against the bill (cf. *Quid igitur ait Hortensius? Si uni omnia tribuenda sint, dignissimum esse Pompeium, sed ad unum tamen omnia deferri non oportere*, 52).

22. On the nature and function of the *exemplum*, see Langlands 2013.

4.2. OUT OF SIGHT

Locis remotis qui latet, lex est sibi.

Whoever lies hidden in faraway places is his own law.

—Publilius Syrus, *Sententiae* L15

One passage lays special stress on procedure failed and the bill's implicit disrespect for the role of the people. A chief source of cash for the Rullan bill was the sale of properties: those recensed by the senate after 81 (*LA* 2.35–37); public property acquired after 88 (*LA* 1.1, 2.38–44); and *vectigalia* from Italy (*LA* 1.4, 2.48), Sicily (*LA* 1.4, 2.48–9), south-central and northwest Asia Minor (*LA* 1.5, 2.50), land around Corinth, Carthage, and New Carthage (*LA* 1.5, 2.51), and Pompey's recent gains (*LA* 1.6, 2.51–52).[23] Cicero caps his discussion of these sales by treating another measure, the free location of sale. The Rullan bill would have permitted state properties to be sold on the spot. That was not an innovation: the *lex agraria* of 111 had a similar provision, allowing sales of state land in Greece and Africa to take place there.[24] But the measure did violate the spirit of a law of C. Gracchus, which, to thwart corruption, bound the censors, who oversaw public contracts, to lease them at Rome.[25]

In both speeches Cicero impugns the measure with an argument *a fortiori*—or rather two such arguments, the one appealing to the law (why should these decemvirs have a right that the censors do not?) and the other to sensibility (why should this law actually condone what other sellers of property have the decency not to do?).[26] (Within this section, the elements will be referenced only by letters; elsewhere, as Table 4.2.A, etc.)

---

23. For more detail on the last three sets, cf. ch. 8.2 and n. 2.

24. The *duumviri* were to sell land in Greece (lines 99–100; Lintott 1992: 281) and rent land in Africa (line 83); cf. Hardy 1924: 80. Sale on the spot was also the practice for Sicilian tithes, save for wine, oil, and vegetables (Cic. *Ver.* 2.3.13–15), and in 210 Q. Fulvius Flaccus had liquidated Campanian lands in Capua (Livy 27.3.1).

25. Mommsen, *RS*³ 2.1.430.

26. Cicero perhaps had in mind two elements of a conventional descending hierarchy of *ius* preserved in the *Rhetorica ad Herennium* (2.19): *lege ius est quod populi iussu sanctum est* ("a principle ratified by a public vote," cf. "A law is a formally declared command of the people," *lex est quod populus iubet atque constituit*, Gaius *Inst.* 1.3; ch. 3.2 The Power of the Law) and *consuetudo ius est quod sine lege aeque ac si legitimum sit usitatum est* ("a regularly observed principle effectively, if not actually, law"). From Table 4.2. E come the snippets examined in the introduction (ch. 1.2 *Logos*).

Table 4.2. Rhetorical Structure of the Treatment of the Provision Permitting Sales Abroad (*LA* 1.7, 2.55–56)

in senatu	*ad populum*

A. Introduction

Hoc vero cuius modi est, quod eius auctionis quam constituunt locum sibi nullum definiunt? Nam decemviris quibus in locis ipsis videatur vendendi potestas lege permittitur.	Atque in omnibus his agris aedificiisque vendendis permittitur decemviris ut vendant 'quibuscumque in locis videatur.' O perturbatam rationem, o libidinem refrenandam, o consilia dissoluta atque perdita!
"And what is this supposed to be? [The decemvirs] do not limit themselves to holding this auction they propose in a specific place. The law grants them the power of sale in any places that seem suitable to them."	"And in selling all these fields and buildings the decemvirs are permitted to sell 'in whatever places seem suitable.' [I can't believe] the twisted reasoning! the haughtiness that must be stopped! the dissolute and ruinous designs!"

B. Lesser Term (1): Censors obligated to sell at Rome

Censoribus vectigalia locare nisi in conspectu populi Romani non licet;	Vectigalia locare nusquam licet nisi in hac urbe, hoc aut illo ex loco, hac vestrum frequentia.
"Censors are not permitted to let tax-contracts except in full view of the Roman people—"	"Tax-contracts may be let nowhere except in this city, from this place here or that one there,[i] with you all gathered as you are now!"

C. Greater Term (1): Decemvirs will be able to sell in remote locations

his vendere vel in ultimis terris licebit?	Venire nostras res proprias et in perpetuum a nobis abalienari in Paphlagoniae tenebris atque in Cappadociae solitudine licebit?
"but these [decemvirs] will be permitted to sell [them] on the very ends of the earth?"	"Will it be possible for our personal properties to be sold in the shadows of Paphlagonia and the desolation of Cappadocia and forever pass out of our control?"

D. Lesser Term (2): Compunction to sell at public auctions

At hoc etiam nequissimi homines consumptis patrimoniis faciunt, ut in atriis auctionariis potius quam in triviis aut in compitis auctionentur;	L. Sulla cum bona indemnatorum civium funesta illa auctione sua venderet et se praedam suam diceret vendere, tamen ex hoc loco vendidit nec, quorum oculos offendebat, eorum ipsorum conspectum fugere ausus est;

Table 4.2. Continued

in senatu	*ad populum*
"Even the worst sort of men, once they've gone through their patrimonies, regularly hold their auctions in auction halls and not out in the street or at crossroads."	"When L. Sulla was selling off the property of uncondemned citizens in that murderous auction of his, claiming that he was selling his war spoils, even so he sold it from this place, and did not dare to flee from the sight of the very people who could not bear to look at him;"
E. Greater Term (2): Absence of constraint on decemviral sales	
hic permittit sua lege decemviris ut in quibus commodum sit tenebris, ut in qua velint solitudine, bona populi Romani possint divendere.	decemviri vestra vectigalia non modo non vobis, Quirites, arbitris sed ne praecone quidem publico teste vendent?
"But Rullus ('this one') with his law grants the decemvirs the power to liquidate the property of the Roman people in whatever dark corner suits them, in any desolate spot they choose!"	"Shall the decemvirs then sell your tax-properties not only out of your sight, Quirites, but without even a herald to serve as a public witness?"

[i] Manuwald 2018: 311 *ad loc.* obelizes *aut illo*; Zumpt 1861: 94 n. prints it, arguing that, despite the corruptions of the transmitted texts, there very likely were two places where sales customarily took place, one for censors, one for consuls and praetors if no censors were in office, namely the Rostra and, perhaps, the Temple of Castor or a basilica. Not decisive, but worth noting here, is Cicero's fine use of the physical surroundings of his speeches (e.g. *LA* 2.65–67 = Table 5.3.1, where Cicero uses the city gates; *LA* 2.74 = J5 in Appendix 3, where Cicero surely gestured toward the Janiculum).

Both passages draw on the same idea (that is, their *inventio* is the same): to allow sales out of public view is to grant permission too broad. Cicero thus imposes his own meaning on the feature: what the bill needed to permit he converts into what the bill should by no means permit. But where the accent lies in each version—on "public view" before the people and on "permission too broad" before the senate—is very different.[27]

---

[27]. Classen's treatment of this passage (1985: 310–14) is difficult to compare directly. It does not analyze the double *a fortiori* argument and its points of comparison, and it depends on a different sectioning of the text. In the senate speech, the *liberae legationes* segment (1.8–9) comes between the free location of sale (1.7) and the imposition of taxes on certain public lands

Licentia(e)

The senate speech, as usual, makes a valuable contrast. There the accent is on "permission too broad." Cicero achieves that effect in part by pleonasms. Where the popular speech has simply "the decemvirs are permitted to sell . . ." (*permittitur xviris ut vendant*, A-p), the senate speech has *vendendi potestas lege permittitur*, lit. "they are legally granted the capacity to sell" (A-s). Where the popular speech has simply "shall sell" (*vendent*, E-p), the senate speech has *permittit sua lege . . . ut possint divendere*, lit. "he grants with his law that they be able to sell off" (E-s). The pleonasms probably echo legal language[28] and perhaps the language of the bill itself. But Cicero also pushes the idea of broad permission (what the law allows) into the idea of unrestricted choice (what the decemvirs want). Where the popular speech has "in whatever place seems suitable" (*quibuscumque in locis videatur*, A-p), the senate speech has "they do not limit themselves *etc.*" (*eius auctionis . . . locum sibi nullum definiunt*, B-p); that is, it stresses that the design is deliberate and self-serving (NB *sibi*). The popular speech links "darkness" and "desolation" to particular districts (*in Paphlagoniae tenebris atque in Cappadociae solitudine*, C-p)[29]; but the senate speech links them to choice ("in whatever dark corner suits them, in any desolate spot they choose," *ut in quibus commodum sit tenebris, ut in qua velint solitudine*, E-s).

In short, the accent in the senate version is on broad permission. The *nequissimi homines* of its second lesser term give that issue an ethical cast. The phrase does not express general disapprobation but has a specific connotation. Elsewhere in Cicero the phrase is commonest in relation to the profligates C. Verres and Marc Antony and their hangers-on.[30] As the logic of an *a fortiori* argument

---

(1.10); in the popular speech it comes after the sale of public property outside of Italy (38–44; cf. Appendix 1). Classen, noting the different placement of the *liberae legationes* in the popular speech only in passing (314), compares the entire complex 1.7–10 of the senate speech only to 2.55–57 of the popular speech, thus arriving at a conclusion grounded chiefly in their disparate lengths: he argues that the greater detail of the senate treatment is a compliment to their knowledge and interest in the provinces, whereas the popular treatment, before an ignorant and uninterested audience, relies on emotion.

28. Cf. *TLL* 10.1.1558.25–32 ("pleonastice, sc. enunt. secund. praebet verbum facultatem indicans"), where most of the examples of *permittere ut possint* vel sim. are laws or similar binding declarations, e.g. *quae lex permittit, ut furem noctu liceat occidere*, lit. "A law that permits that it is allowed to kill a thief at night," Cic. *Tul.* 52; on pleonasm in legal language, cf. ch. 3 n. 2317.

29. Cicero's descriptions are accurate: Cappadocia was, in its west, a virtually treeless plateau, a "desolation"; the mountainous and wooded Paphlagonia was full of "shadows."

30. Of Verres or his cohort: *Ver.* 2.1.63, 2.2.71, 2.2.192, 2.3.30, 2.3.33, 2.5.100; of Antony or his cohort: *Phil.* 2.7, 2.56, 2.58, 2.67, 2.70, 5.14, 13.33. A tawdry tableau from the second *Philippic* captures the type: *apothecae totae nequissimis hominibus condonabantur; alia mimi rapiebant,*

demands, the *nequissimi homines* are both like and unlike the decemvirs. On the one hand, they are fellow prodigals. As the one has burnt through (*consumptis*) inheritances, so the other would sell off state properties (*bona divendere*). 'Broad permission,' stretched into 'unrestricted choice,' is thus folded by the figure of *nequissimi homines* into outright 'caprice' or 'indulgence.' On the other hand, spendthrifts though they are, unlike the decemvirs they are at least in the regular habit (that is the meaning of *hoc faciunt ut* here)[31] of selling in a proper auction-house and not just "out in the streets" (*in triviis aut in compitis*).[32] That is, they bow to convention *in spite of* their own lack of self-discipline. Even such lack of discipline sets itself limits.

The framers' lawcraft thus appears in a poor light. If 'broad permission' means 'unrestricted choice,' which in turn means 'whim,' then, by a kind of transitivity, signs of 'broad permission' are proof of 'whim.' Cicero has thus imposed a new meaning on the law: his pleonastic restatements of the law—or even paraphrases of the law itself—become proof of ethical failure.[33] The effect is captured in *divendere*, which denotes 'selling' [*vendere*] 'in multiple directions' [*dis-*]. It is a normal word for 'selling off' booty or the like.[34] But in this context, its denotation acquires overtones of waste and whim.[35] It is almost as if Cicero has melded

---

alia mimae; domus erat aleatoribus referta, plena ebriorum ("Entire storehouses were turned over to the lowest sort; mime-actors made off with some things, mime-actresses others; the house was stuffed with gamblers, full of drunks," 2.67).

31. *Hoc faciunt ut auctionentur*, lit. "This they do, that they auction" is not a mere periphrasis for *auctionantur* "They auction," but foregrounds the idea of a regular practice (e.g. *at id ne ferae quidem faciunt, ut ita ruant itaque turbent, ut earum motus et impetus quo pertineant non intellegamus* "Not even wild animals generally rush and roil to the extent that we cannot understand the intent of their motion and energy," Cic. *Fin.* 1.34). Perhaps there are also overtones of 'making a special effort' or 'making the decision to' (e.g. *fecit, ut filiam bonis suis heredem institueret*, Cic. *Ver.* 2.1.104, which Greenwood 1935: 233 aptly renders "had taken the step of making his daughter his heir").

32. *Pace* Manuwald 2018: 136, the point of these places is not that they are more visible than auction houses, but that they are not the proper and regular place.

33. At *LA* 2.22, Cicero similarly repurposes the head (*index*) of Rullus's law in exactly the same way; ch. 6.3.

34. Livy 1.53.3, 10.17.7, 21.21,1, 37.5.3 (*praeda*); 3.13.10 (*bona*).

35. The other appearance of *divendere* in Cicero, as it happens, also describes outrageous exercises of executive power: ... *scelera urbani consulatus, in quo pecuniam publicam maximam dissipavit, exsules sine lege restituit, vectigalia divendidit, provincias de populi Romani imperio sustulit, regna addixit pecunia, leges civitati per vim imposuit, armis aut obsedit aut exclusit senatum* ("... the crimes while he was consul in the city: the waste of vast public funds, the unauthorized restoration of exiles, the liquidation of tax revenues, the removal of provinces from the empire of the Roman people, taking bribes to award kingships, the imposition of laws on the state by force, the violent siege or lockout of the senate," *Phil.* 7.15, of Marc Antony), cf.

the two meanings of *licentia*, both a 'legal capacity' and 'wantonness' (English 'license' is very similar).[36] The bill is a license for license.

Libido and *Libertas*

In sum, the senate speech refracts the law through ethical concerns. Ethics is not a chief concern of the popular version; there the accent is on "public view." Where the senate speech has simply "in full view of the Roman people" (*in conspectu populi Romani*, B-s), the popular speech has an ascending (and narrowing) tricolon: "in this city, from this place here or that one there, with you all gathered as you are now!" (*in hac urbe, hoc aut illo ex loco, hac vestrum frequentia*, B-p)— that is, not in distant places that are out of sight (*tenebrae* 'darkness,' in effect the opposite of *hoc . . . ex loco*, C-p) with nobody there (*solitudo* 'desolation,' the opposite of *frequentia*, C-p).[37] Where the senate speech sees broad permission as sanctioning caprice (E-s), the popular speech points to a formal flaw, the lack of witnesses: "not only out of your sight, Quirites, but without even a herald to serve as a public witness!" (*non modo vobis, Quirites, arbitris, sed ne praecone quidem publico teste*, E-p, where *arbiter* has its meaning 'spectator, eye-witness').[38] Most Roman political procedures were conducted out of doors in the full view of witnesses. And witnessing procedures was the public's role. In short, visibility is symbolic of correct procedure.[39] The decemvirs in remote places would be their own law.

The figure of Sulla in the second lesser term gives this issue of visibility a distinct political cast. He, as the structure of the *a fortiori* argument requires, is both like and unlike the decemvirs. Their scheme for selling is like his: they, too, want

---

vastata provincia, correptis vectigalibus, praecipue civibus Romanis omnibus crudelissime denudatis ac divenditis (*Fam.* 12.15.1, P. Lentulus, in a dispatch about the outrages of Dolabella). See also ch. 1.2 *Logos*.

36. Legal capacity: *TLL* 7.2.1354.55–6 "significatur alicui aliquid licere (cf. licet), fere i.q. potestas, facultas, permissio, sim."; examples 1354.58–1355.11. Wantonness: *TLL* 7.2.1355.29–30 "praevalente notione status liberi (cf. licens), fere i.q. effrenatio, intemperantia, libertas sim."

37. The idea is specifically lack of visibility, not just generally "Fremdheit" (*pace* Classen 1985: 311, who asks, "Sind diese fernen Gegenden dem Volke geläufig?"; the issue is not familiarity but procedure).

38. *TLL* 2.0.404.23–76.

39. For the importance of the "public gaze" in Roman political life, see Millar 1984 and 1986; Laser 1997: 186–88; Bell 1997, esp. 3–5; cf. "The legislative, electoral, and somewhat vestigial judicial powers of the People presupposed continuous direct observation by the citizenry of their present and potential leaders," Morstein-Marx 2004: 9, Hölkeskamp 2010: 100–101.

to hold an irregular auction, as he did (the *praeda* of D-p is the seized property of civil opponents, which by a cruel legal fiction he declared "war booty" and sold off).[40] But unlike the decemvirs, he felt bound to sell from the very Rostra (*ex hoc . . . loco*, D-p) in full view of the people. The implication is important. Sulla was no populist. Much of his domestic political program aimed to curtail the popular role sharply.[41] That is why here the people "could not bear to look at him" (lit. "he offended [their] eyes," *quorum oculos offendebat*, D-p). But they also conferred legitimacy, even informally. And for Sulla, as Cicero would have it, such was the power of correct form that, despite his leanings, he still felt bound to observe it (he "did not dare to flee"). That puts the framers' lawcraft in a poor light. If an optimate who scorned the public still stood before them, someone who does not must scorn them all the more (Caesar, at the outbreak of the civil war, would make a comparable argument to his troops).[42]

Hence a feature of the opening tricolon: "[I can't believe] the twisted reasoning! the haughtiness that must be stopped! the dissolute and ruinous designs!" (*o perturbatam rationem, o libidinem refrenandam, o consilia dissoluta atque perdita*). The rebuke is not simply ethical. *Libido* here means not 'sensual desire' but the 'inordinate desire' of an abusive public official.[43] The sense is close to 'haughtiness,' 'high-handedness,' or 'arbitrariness.' But in Cicero such capricious officials are almost always *iudices* or regular holders of *imperium*.[44] In the *pro Milone*, for

---

40. Cf. *tantum animi habuit ad audaciam ut dicere in contione non dubitaret, bona civium Romanorum cum venderet, se praedam suam vendere* (Cic. *Ver.* 2.3.81); cf. *S. Rosc.* 124–28, Sal. *Or. Lep.* (*Hist.* 1.49M) 18, Vell. 2.28.4; Plut. *Sull.* 33.2.

41. He had limited the tribune's right of veto (Cic. *Leg.* 3.22, Caes. *Civ.* 1.5, 7), barred tribunician legislation not approved by the senate (Liv. *per.* 89), eliminated tribunician legislation, barred tribunes from further political careers (App. *BC* 1.100), limited *contiones* (Cic. *Clu.* 110), eliminated popular election of priests (D.C. 37.37), abolished grain doles (Sall. *Hist.* 1.55 11 M), and restored certain jury pools to the senate alone (Cic. *Ver.* 1.37, Tac. *Ann.* 11.22). On Sulla, see Keaveney 1982b.

42. "Sulla, who had completely gutted the powers of the tribunate, at least left it in possession of the veto; but Pompey, who might seem to have restored the lost privileges, took away even what they had before" (*Sullam nudata omnibus rebus tribunicia potestate tamen intercessionem liberam reliquisse; Pompeium, qui amissa restituisse videatur bona, etiam quae ante habuerint ademisse, Civ.* 7.3).

43. *TLL* 7.2.1334.80 "spectat potius ad licentiam, superbiam sim.: α magistratuum aliorumve hominum publica potestate praeditorum"; examples through 7.2.1335.42. The idea, like that of lust, is the failure to impose limits on oneself. Cf. Hellegouarc'h 1963: 259, for whom *libido* is the opposite of *continentia* = σωφροσύνη, and Dunkle 1967: 19: "In reference to the despot *libido* can mean either lust for unchecked sexual fulfillment and political power or political caprice, i.e., government by the whim of one."

44. Cf. the examples in the *TLL* (citation in n. 43).

example, Cicero imagines that the *libido* of a Clodius with *imperium* would have threatened foreign and domestic property alike.[45] Earlier in the popular speech, Cicero, as if defending the idea of checks and balances, observes that "tribunician influence has from time to time impeded arbitrary action on the part of consuls" (... *vis tribunicia non numquam libidini restitit consulari*, 2.14).[46] But here at issue is *libido tribunicia*, which must be "reined in" (*refrenanda*). Here, as in Table 2.1.I-p, where Rullus's bill "pinches" an honor, it is again the tribunes who incongruously injure the people.

The paradox is acute: the patrician's patrician respects the people; the people's officer, the tribune, and his decemvirs do not. The image of Sulla may on its face seem "far-fetched," as one commentator calls it;[47] Sulla's bloody confiscations and cruel legal fictions were not very much like an authorized sale of already public properties. But the comparison is meant, not to be plausible, but—like the image of the *bonorum venditio*—to memorably symbolize power relations. And the image is all the more memorable in this case because it is strikingly convenient. Cicero was not pulling a comparison out of thin air; he was taking advantage of a nearby prop. On the speaker's platform where Cicero was standing there was a gilt equestrian statue of Sulla, looking out toward the people, his hand stretched out in a gesture of address (*adlocutio*).[48] And the prop was convenient in another way: popular hatred for Sulla ran deep (the statue itself would fall victim to that very hatred).[49] Cicero (another inversion) inscribes his own meaning onto

---

45. "If he had once obtained real power,—I say nothing of our allies, of foreign nations, and kings, and tetrarchs; for you would have prayed that he might direct himself against them rather than against your possessions, your houses, and your money: money do I say? your children, rather, and your wives! I have no doubt whatever that he would never have kept his unrestrained lusts away from them" (*imperium ille si nactus esset—omitto socios exteras nationes reges tetrarchas; vota enim faceretis ut in eos se potius inmitteret, quam in vestras possessiones, vestra tecta, vestras pecunias—pecunias dico? a liberis me dius fidius et a coniugibus vestris numquam ille effrenatas suas libidines cohibuisset, Mil.* 76). There is a play on both senses of *libido* here; Clodius would have exhibited 'haughtiness' in seizing property but 'lust' in attacking children and wives.

46. For *vis* as "ability to control affairs, political weight, power, influence," cf. *OLD s.v.* 11. The idea of checks and balances as such did not exist expressly but was certainly an operative principle of Roman governance, as Polybius observed (6.11–13); cf. Wirszubski 1960: 17–27.

47. Jonkers 1963: 99.

48. Cic. *Phil.* 9.13, App. *BC* 1.97, Suet. *Jul.* 75.4, D.C. 42.18.2, 43.49.1; an image of the statue appears on coins (Crawford 1974: no. 381).

49. Suet. *Jul.* 75.4. The statue was re-erected on Caesar's orders (Suet. *Jul.* 75.4 and D.C. 43.49.1–2).

the statue: not the paternal restorer of order, as Sulla doubtless meant it,[50] but respect, however grudging, for the collective. That is a fine mnemonic for his interpretation of this part of the law's mechanism—a lasting prompt to skepticism toward populist politics for any listener who thereafter cast a glance at Sulla as he passed through the Forum. As the image of *nequissimi homines* turned *licentia* from law to ethics, so a repurposed Sulla turns the meaning of *popularis* from ends to means, as if nothing can be called *popularis* that does not have due regard for the constitutional role of the people, to whom he stretches out his arm. Even he knew *libertas* really comes down to correct procedure.

4.3. PROFITABLE EXCEPTIONS

superioribus annis taciti indignabamini . . . reges et populos
liberos paucis nobilibus vectigal pendere . . .

In earlier years you were in quiet rage . . . that kings and free
peoples pay taxes directly to a few nobles!

—from a speech of the tribune Gaius Memmius, Sallust, Bellum
Iugurthinum 31.9

Another passage also emphasizes failures of procedure but lays equal stress on respect for proper governance—and that of a particular kind. Rullus's law had two exemptions. The *Ager Recentoricus* in Sicily would have been exempt from a "huge tax" (*pergrande vectigal, LA* 1.10, 2.56) that was one source of funding for the bill;[51] and some North African lands then in the possession of the Numidian king Hiempsal would have been excluded from the sale of other North African *agri vectigales* (*LA* 1.10–11, 2.58–9).[52] There is nothing wrong with named exemptions

---

50. On the image Sulla wished to project, see Mackay 2000 and Sumi 2002; on his conversion into a symbol of cruelty and of clemency, see Dowling 2000.

51. The *ager Recentoricus*, in an island whose toponyms are reasonably well attested, is otherwise unknown, which has attracted attempts at emendation, including to generic names like *ager censorius* (so Zumpt 1861: 96–97). But that would make the bill exempt an entire category of property. That seems unlikely: Cicero suggests that the exception is the result of bribery (*LA* 1.10–11, 2.57)—the act of a single interested party, not of a single party by way of class action, still less of every single party who happened to be living on the same kind of territory. For the details of Sicilian land, see Marek 1997. For the argument that the name refers to a special kind of *ager publicus*, see Kunkel and Wittmann 1995: 340 n. 148.

52. Hiempsal II, king of Numidia, was in possession of some African coastal territory that was *ager publicus populi Romani*. Scipio Aemilianus had allowed Masinissa (or Micipsa?) *possessio* over some land to the west of the original Roman province; that land appears in the *lex agraria* of 111 (see Lintott 1992: 267–68 with refs.). Hiempsal must have inherited control (so Gsell

as such, which some Roman laws had.[53] And there were good legal and probably political reasons for these particular exceptions. The status of the lands was ambiguous, as Cicero's discussion makes clear; and Pompey, whom the bill ostensibly favors, may have preferred the current arrangements.[54] Furthermore, the ambiguous legal status of the properties surely played a role in the framers' thinking; it was prudent to exempt them to bar objections (whether pretended or sincere).

But in a bill otherwise apparently so detailed, that there should be only two exceptions was curious. Cicero imposes his own meaning. He blames bribery: the exemptions must have been bought. The clauses of Rullus's law had been up for sale, like the vote of a corrupt juror or the rulings of a corrupt governor.[55] In both speeches Cicero couches this objection in the form of a *complexio*. In that figure of thought, each of two alternatives is disproved or otherwise questioned—for example, "Why should I accuse you of anything now? If you're respectable, you haven't deserved it—but if you're not, you won't care!"[56] The elements of the *complexiones* are ordered differently in each speech; their sequence in each is indicated here by small Roman numerals. (Within this section, the elements will be referenced only by capital letters; elsewhere, as "Table 4.3.1.A," etc.):

1928: 80) and was, it seems, confirmed in his occupation of (at least part of) the coastal portion of that territory in a senatorial treaty concluded by C. Aurelius Cotta, *cos.* 75—a treaty which, however, had never been confirmed by the people (Cic. *LA* 1.10, 2.58) and was therefore not valid (on the senate's inability to validate a treaty on its own, see Brunt 1988: 140–41).

53. See ch. 7.2 and n. 2.

54. In 82 and 81 it was Pompey who had arranged matters in Sicily (App. *BC* 1.56.247, Vell. 2.18.6, Liv. *per.* 77, Plut. *Pomp.* 10) with an eye to enlarging his *clientelae* (Badian 1984: 270–71). In 81 it was Pompey who reinstated Hiempsal to the throne; he had been ousted by his brother (H)iarbas (Sal. *Hist.* 1.53M, App. *BC* 1.368, Plut. *Pomp.* 12, Liv. *per.* 89; Badian 1984: 271–72; there, too, he increased his *clientela*, cf. Cic. *Balb.* 51). Jonkers (1963: 27–28) reasonably surmises the African territories had become a political football (cf. Cicero's *sed ab aliis agitari saepe in senatu, non numquam ex hoc loco,* D-p).

55. A regular vice of Verres: *quae ipse semper habuit venalia, fidem, ius iurandum, veritatem, officium, religionem* (*Ver.* 2.3.144), *fidem cum proposuisses venalem in provincia, valuit apud te plus is qui pecuniam maiorem dedit* (*Ver.* 2.2.78), *venalem . . . iurisdictionem habu[it]* (*Ver.* 2.2.119).

56. The example is from the *Rhetorica ad Herennium*, which calls the figure a *divisio* (= διαίρεσις) (*cur ego nunc tibi quicquam obiciam? si probus es, non meruisti; si improbus, non commovere,* 4.52) and the related logical structure a *duplex conclusio* (2.39). Cicero's example is similar: *complexio est, in qua, utrum concesseris, reprehenditur, ad hunc modum: 'Si inprobus est, cur uteris? Si probus, cur accusas?'* (*Inv.* 1.45).

Table 4.3.1. Rhetorical Structure of the Treatments of Exempted Territories (*LA* 1.10–11, 2.57–59)

INTRODUCTION
A. Two Exemptions

(i.) Sunt tamen in tota lege exceptiones duae non tam iniquae quam suspiciosae.

ø

"In the entire law, there are [only] two exemptions—not unreasonable ones but suspicious."

B. *Ager Recentoricus* exempted from the tax

(ii.) Excipit enim in vectigali imponendo agrum Recentoricum Siciliensem,

(i.) Excipitur hoc capite ager \<in\> Sicilia Recentoricus;

"[The law] exempts from the tax the *ager Recentoricus* in Sicily..."

"In this section the *ager Recentoricus* \<in\> Sicily is exempted..."

C. Special circumstances of *Ager Recentoricus*

ø

(ii.) quem ego excipi et propter hominum necessitudinem et propter \<rei\> [ii] aequitatem, Quirites, ipse vehementer gaudeo. Sed quae \<est\> haec impudentia! Qui agrum Recentoricum possident, vetustate possessionis se, non iure, misericordia senatus, non agri condicione defendunt. Nam illum agrum publicum esse fatentur; se moveri possessionibus, antiquissimis sedibus, ac dis penatibus negant oportere.

"... which I personally, fellow citizens, am very glad to see exempted: I know the people and \<the cause\> is just. But what impudence this \<is\>! The possessors of the *ager Recentoricus* base their claims on the antiquity of their possession, not on the law; and on the mercy of the senate, not the status of the territory. They freely admit that it's public land—but they argue that they should not be dislodged from their possessions, their ancient abodes, and their household gods."

(*continued*)

Table 4.3.1. Continued

D. Treaty Lands exempted from sale

(iii.) in vendendis agris eos agros de quibus cautum sit foedere. Hi sunt in Africa, qui ab Hiempsale possidentur.

(vii.) 58. Atque etiam est alia superiore capite quo omnia veneunt quaestuosa exceptio, quae teget eos agros de quibus foedere cautum est. Audivit hanc rem non a me, sed ab aliis agitari saepe in senatu, non numquam ex hoc loco, possidere agros in ora maritima regem Hiempsalem quos P. Africanus populo Romano adiudicarit; ei tamen postea per C. Cottam consulem cautum esse foedere.

"... and from sale such lands as are protected by treaty. These are in Africa in the possession of Hiempsal."

"In the previous section (the one where everything is sold off!), there's also another profitable exemption, which exempts territories which are protected by treaty. [Rullus] heard it argued, often in the senate, and sometimes from the Rostra here—and not by me, but by others—that king Hiempsal possessed territory on the African coast that P. Africanus had adjudged to the Roman people, but that C. Cotta as consul had secured [Hiempsal that territory] by treaty."

COMPLEXIO, PART I (EXEMPTION UNNECESSARY)

E. If the treaty is sufficient to protect Hiempsal...

(iv.) Hic quaero, si Hiempsali satis est cautum foedere...

ø

"So my question is, if Hiempsal is adequately protected by treaty..."

F. ... and the *Ager Recentoricus* is private...

(v.) et Recentoricus ager privatus est,

(iii.) Ac, si est privatus ager Recentoricus,

"and the *ager Recentoricus* is private..."

"And besides, if the *ager Recentoricus* is private..."

G. ... the exemption is unnecessary

(vi.) quid attinuerit excipi?

(iv.) quid eum excipis?

"... what was the point of exempting them?"

"... why are you excepting it?"

Table 4.3.1. Continued

COMPLEXIO, PART II (REASON IS BRIBERY)
H. But if the treaty is insufficient to protect Hiempsal . . .

(vii.) sin et foedus illud habet aliquam dubitationem . . .	(viii.) Hoc quia vos foedus non iusseritis, veretur Hiempsal ut satis firmum sit et ratum. Cuicuimodi est illud, tollitur vestrum iudicium, foedus totum accipitur, comprobatur.
"But if there is some doubt about the treaty . . ."	"Since this is not a treaty that you ratified, Hiempsal is afraid that the treaty is not quite fixed and firm. However that may be, *your* right to decide is cast to one side and the whole treaty is accepted, no questions asked."

I. . . . and the *Ager Recentoricus* is public . . .

(viii.) . . . et ager Recentoricus dicitur non numquam esse publicus,	(v.) Sin autem publicus,
"and, as is sometimes alleged, the *ager Recentoricus* is public . . ."	"But if it *is* public . . ."

J. . . . then the cause for the exemptions is bribery

(ix.) quem putet existimaturum duas causas in orbe terrarum repertas quibus gratis parceret? Num quisnam tam abstrusus usquam nummus videtur quem non architecti huiusce legis olfecerint? [iii]	(vi.) *[Ager Recentoricus]* quae est ista aequitas ceteros, etiam si privati sint, permittere ut publici iudicentur, hunc excipere nominatim quem publicum esse fatentur? Ergo eorum ager excipitur qui apud Rullum aliqua ratione valuerunt, ceteri agri omnes qui ubique sunt sine ullo dilectu, sine populi Romani notione, sine iudicio senatus decemviris addicentur?
"who, I want to know, did Rullus imagine would think that, in the whole wide world, he only managed to find *two* parties to spare—for free? Is there any coin so well hidden that the masterminds of this law haven't sniffed it out?"	" . . . how can it possibly be fair to allow other territories to be judged public, even if they are private, while excepting this territory by name—which [the possessors] *admit* is public? So it must be that exceptions are being granted to possessors who have secured influence with Rullus . . . somehow or other! And all the other territories, anywhere in the world, will be given over to the decemvirs—without any distinction, without an examination by the Roman people, without the judgment of the senate!"

(continued)

Table 4.3.1. Continued

(ix.) *[Hiempsal]* Quod minuit auctionem decemviralem laudo, quod regi amico cavet non reprehendo, quod non gratis fit indico. 59. Volitat enim ante oculos istorum Iuba, regis filius, adulescens non minus bene nummatus quam bene capillatus.

"Now that does make the decemvirs' auction smaller—of that I approve. And it protects a client king—I have no objection there. But it can't be happening for free—and that's my point. They have a vision dancing in their heads: Juba, the king's son, a young man with a wallet as fat as his hair is thick!"

---

ii The supplement is Pluygers', to balance the preceding *hominum*.
iii The last sentence also serves as a transition to the next section; cf. Table 8.3.1.A.-s.

Table 4.3.2 makes clear that in the senate speech, the premises of both halves of the *complexio* are bundled in pairs (E and F; H and I) with shared apodoses (G and J), but in the popular speech, each exception is treated separately (for the *Ager Recentoricus*, F, G; I, J; for the African territories, H and J, with only the second half of the *complexio* fully expressed):

Table 4.3.2. The *Complexiones* of *LA* 1.10–11, 2.57–59

Senate Version	Popular Version	
If the treaty protects Hiempsal ... (E.)		
... and the *Ager Recentoricus* is private (F.),	If the *Ager Recentoricus* is private (F.),	
what's the point of the exemptions? (G.)	what's the point of the exemption? (G.)	
But if the treaty does not protect Hiempsal ... (H.)		H. The treaty may not protect Hiempsal, so ... (H.)
... and the *Ager Recentoricus* is public (I.),	But if the *Ager Recentoricus* is public (I.),	

Table 4.3.2. Continued

Senate Version	Popular Version	
... the reason for the exemption must be bribery (J.).	the reason for the exemption must be bribery (J.).	... the reason for the exemption must be bribery (J.).

The compressed senate version keeps the focus narrow, on strictly legal issues and the curiosity of a mere two exemptions (J-s).[57] The split structure of the popular speech gives Cicero room to amplify. That he does in precisely the same ways for both exceptions. He attaches the same three points to the Recentorici and to Hiempsal, turning their cases into two parables, one might say, of the same import, which thus become mutually reinforcing.

Their first shared feature is the same as in the treatment of the free location of sale: the oversight of the people has been bypassed. The Recentorici are an obscure exception; but it implies a still broader, and graver, obscurity: that "all other territories, wherever they are, without any distinction, will be given over to the decemvirs without an examination (*notio*) by the Roman people, without the judgment of senate!" (J-p). Cicero makes the same point when he first mentions the tax: the decemvirs will be able to change the status of properties "without any debate and without any advisory counsel" (*nulla disceptatione, nullo consilio,* 2.57), where *disceptatio* implies debate before the people in a *contio* or the like.[58] The measure about Hiempsal's land also bypasses the people. The senate speech simply says there were some doubts about the treaty's validity (*habet aliquam dubitationem*, H-s). The popular speech gives a reason: the people had not ratified it (*vos ... non iuss[istis]*, H-p), but Rullus's bill acts as if they had, thereby doing away with their judgment, accepting and sanctioning the treaty entire (*tollitur*

---

57. Classen 1985: 328.

58. For *disceptatio* linked to the Roman people, cf. *Ver.* 2.5.138, *Flac.* 97, *LA* 1.23 (*lacesso vos [tribunos], in contionem voco, populo Romano disceptatore uti volo*, cf. Table 6.2.2.R-s), and especially *LA* 3.1: "The tribunes of the plebs would have done better, fellow citizens, to say in my presence what they have been representing to you about me; in that way they would have shown respect for ("kept") your ability to judge a debate fairly, for the established practice of their predecessors, and for the rights that come with their position of authority" (*commodius fecissent tribuni plebis, Quirites, si, quae apud vos de me deferunt, ea coram potius me praesente dixissent; nam et aequitatem vestrae disceptationis et consuetudinem superiorum et ius suae potestatis retinuissent*). *Consilium* is common for the deliberation of the senate (*TLL* 3.459.49 ff.). The *Rhet. Her.* preserves a similar pair: *in contione aut in consilio* (3.4).

vestrum iudicium, foedus totum accipitur, comprobatur).[59] There is another gesture to popular oversight. Rullus, who bypasses the people, had paradoxically learned of the treaty precisely because it was discussed not only in the senate but sometimes in front of the people (*saepe in senatu, non numquam ex hoc loco*, D-p).

But the "parables" suggest a vision that goes beyond simple oversight. There is also the idea of active responsibility. The *notio* 'examination' of J-p typically means an inquiry by a judge or magistrate; Cicero otherwise uses the word mostly of censors.[60] The technical term projects a people carefully sifting through the details of a complex law (as the *disceptatio* of *LA* 2.57 = Table 8.4.1.E, where Cicero first mentions the tax). The *iudicium* of H-p implies a people denied the chance to think through a treaty. *Notio* and *iudicium* are something of a stretch here, if complex treaties were approved more or less routinely.[61] In short, not only is Cicero projecting responsibility onto the people, he is also recasting actual political practice. There is another recasting, too. Treaties were approved by the *comitia centuriata* or "centuriate assembly," which was weighted heavily in favor of the monied classes. The focus and instrument of populist politics were not that assembly but the *comitia tributa* and the related *concilium plebis*. Cicero blurs the lines.[62]

A *libertas* distinctly different from its most *popularis* inflection is thus implicit. That accounts for a third feature both "parables" share. In both halves of the *complexiones* the defects of procedure also include the senate. In the matter of the tax, not only was the *notio* of the people bypassed, so was the senate's "judgment" (*iudicium*, J-p). In the matter of the treaties, Rullus not only sidesteps the people (*tollitur vestrum iudicium*, H-p) but he also disregards a senate that had often

---

59. Perhaps the effect is sharpened by *comprobare*, if the word implied some deliberative body ('approve [*probare*]-together [*com*]'), as in the examples from the *OLD*, which cites Cic. *Dom.* 58 (*tribus proscriptionem*), Caes. *Civ.* 2.20.5 (*cives Romani factum*), Nep. *Han.* 3.1 (*id ... delatum publice*), Liv. 37.45.14 (*senatus populusque Romanus pacem*). The *TLL* recognizes the technical use ("fere i. q. 'probum habere, putare', i. verba vel actionem alicuius pro bene vel recte factis **agnoscere**, ea **accipere**, **approbare**, speciatim decreta vel consulta alicuius ordinis vel imperii," 3.0.2163.29–31) but does not list examples separately.

60. Censors: *Prov.* 46, *Pis.* 10, *Sest.* 55, *Off.* 3.111. Praetor: *Caec.* 35. Pontifices: *Dom.* 34. Cf. *OLD* s.v. 2.

61. Cf. *Sest.* 109 with Morstein-Marx 2004: 189.

62. Cf. Morstein-Marx 2004: 15–16 "speakers in the assembly typically addressed whatever crowd stood in front of them as the acutal embodiment of the *populus Romanus*, with all that the august title entailed—sometimes with paradoxical consequences, as when Cicero calls upon his audience for the *Pro lege Manilia* (*In Support of the Manilian Law*), probably a heterogeneous crowd of largely foreign, partly even Hellenic, descent, not to abandon the Imperial traditions of '*our* ancestors' who had destroyed the city of Corinth, defeated the great Hellenistic kings, and crushed Carthage."

debated the issue (D-p). It was appropriate to include the senate, of course: it customarily oversaw the two issues here, disposing provinces and formulating treaties. But its inclusion has another aspect, made clear in Cicero's account of the Recentorici. Their land claim (C-p) rested not on dispositive right (cf. *iure*), nor on clear title or affirmative easement (cf. *agri condicio*), but on antiquity of possession (*vetustate possessionis*); thence the senate's mercy (*misericordia*). The word "mercy" is well chosen. The senate had, in effect, generously chosen to treat the foreign Recentorici as if they were Roman citizens with the right of *usucapio* (acquisition by uninterrupted possession for a fixed period).[63] And that merciful arrangement is, by Cicero's lights, also "just" (cf. *aequitatem <rei>*). Cicero means something specific by that. *Aequitas*, at root 'fairness,' was an animating principle of Roman legal thought, manifest in *ius* or positive law but not necessarily coextensive with it. In the latter case, if a law strictly interpreted would lead to an "unfair" result, a magistrate might look instead to a "level," that is, a "balanced," outcome, whatever the letter of the law.[64] That is precisely the situation here: *ius* well justifies expulsion; *aequitas*, with *vetustas possessionis* in view, urges the opposite. Presupposed in Cicero's rhetoric is an audience that appreciates at least some of the niceties of legal debates.[65]

The senate, in short, is here imagined as an equitable magistrate: they use their power fairly. That is also exactly Cicero's own posture: he supports the exemptions in theory because he is a fair and responsible magistrate himself. He is very glad for the Recentorici not only because the arrangement is equitable but also because he has personal ties (*necessitudo*) to them. That is a reminder of Cicero's service as quaestor in western Sicily; his integrity there was well known. Nor does Cicero object (*non reprehendo*) to exempting Hiempsal; that protects a client king (*regi amico cavet*, J-p). Here is also a Cicero concerned for diplomacy

---

63. For the details of *usucapio*, see Watson 1968: 21–62. Strictly speaking *usucapio* was not possible over provincial land (or for a foreigner possessor); the equivalent principle in provinces is the *praescriptio longi temporis*. The prerequisites for such forms of possession were acquisition *bona fide* ("in good faith") and *iusta causa* ("for a just reason"), conditions met here by the senate's grant of tenure.

64. See Schiller 1978: 552–555; Berger 1953 *s.v.* with refs. The difference is that between formalist and realist approaches in US jurisprudence. For Cicero's conception of the relation between *ius (civile)*, *aequitas*, and *mos*, with a corresponding complication of legal definitions, see Harries 2006: 51–74.

65. It is worth quoting here Crook 1967: 8: "legal talk and terminology seem rather more frequent and more at home in Roman literature than in ours. Legal terms of art could be used for literary metaphor, could be the foundation of stage jokes or furnish analogy in philosophical discussion. And a corollary of this is that many a passage of Latin *belles lettres* needs a knowledge of the law for its comprehension."

and geopolitical order. More important, Cicero evokes the memory of C. Aurelius Cotta (not mentioned in the senate speech). Cotta was no doubt held in high regard by the people generally. Though from the heart of the nobility, he had worked to overturn Sulla's law barring tribunes from holding other offices.[66] By implication Cotta's arrangement with Hiempsal also had the common good in mind, even if (*tamen*, D-p) the land might really have been Roman property. Of course Scipio Aemilianus, who claimed the land for the Roman people in the first place, will also have had the common good in mind.[67] Aemilianus and Cotta are, as it were, in an argument about the status of Hiempsal's lands that only the people can resolve—another reflection of the idea of their active responsibility.

In both "parables," then, is a distinctive version of *libertas*, so consistent that Cicero must have had it in mind as he selected details to add. His *amplificatio* depends on a particular *inventio*. In that vision, as with the free location of sale, *libertas* is narrowed to procedure and process. So important is procedure here, in fact, that the results almost don't matter: Cicero has no objection to either exemption in principle; his objection is to the process and to the alleged bribery. Concomitantly, Cicero has reworked the practical side of *libertas*: the people have a duty of care. And he has reworked the operational side of *libertas*, too: it is not that higher magistrates are to conform to the popular will; it is that the people are to cooperate with, and even defer, to them. That is a striking inversion: beneath the reworked tropes of popular rule here lies the model of the "mixed constitution." In that model, as a definition in the *Rhetorica ad Herennium* tidily expresses it, the "dignity of the state" (*civitatis amplitudo*) consists in popular suffrage and the counsel of magistrates together (*suffragia populi et magistratus consilium*).[68]

---

66. On the law, cf. Asconius in Cic. *Corn.* 67.1–5C.

67. That side of Aemilianus is also brought out in the popular treatment of Carthage, which the bill proposed to sell (Table 8.2.C). In the senate speech Scipio consecrated the site simply "in response to a religious scruple that he received" (*oblata aliqua religione*), whereas in the popular speech he might have done so "on the advice of his council, because of a religious scruple that attached to that site and its antiquity" (*propter religionem sedum illarum ac vetustatis de consili sententia*). The people's Aemilianus acts, not on what appears to him, but on objective and communalist principles; *de consili sententia* is regular for the advisers of magistrates (cf. ch. 8 n. 9).

68. The author illustrates the figure of speech *definitio* by a definition of *maiestas deminuta*: " 'Sovereignty offended' is a charge that attaches to damaging those features of the state that give it dignity. And what are those, Q. Caepio? The vote of the people and the advisory capacity of the magistracy. And what did you do when you destroyed the voting bridges? Strip the people of its vote and the magistracy of its advisory capacity!" (*maiestatem is minuit qui ea tollit ex quibus rebus civitatis amplitudo constat. Quae sunt ea, Q. Caepio? Suffragia populi et magistratus consilium. Nempe igitur tu et populum suffragio et magistratum consilio privasti cum pontes disturbasti,* 2.17). For a discussion of the idea, see Arena 2012: 81–117; a central idea,

The principles of that "counsel" have a particular form here. Cicero projects a governing class ruling not by martial values and their analogues (*virtus*),[69] but by values like *aequitas* and *misericordia*: the people are to trust them—and they must deserve to be trusted.

If all this is one very particular model of *libertas*, it is also a standard that Rullus falls short of. His guiding principle is certainly not equity and mercy. That emerges from the descriptions of the two exempted parties. The Recentorici are anxious. That is brought out by pathos. They fear ouster not from 'fields' or 'homes' but from their *antiquissimae sedes* and *di penates* (the words, in *oratio obliqua*, represent their thoughts, not Cicero's). The phrases are affecting. The *di penates*, gods of hearth and home, capture the poignancy of dislocation, just as elsewhere in Cicero.[70] *Sedes antiqua(e)* is a phrase, evidently rather grand in tone (whence my "ancient abodes"), that Cicero otherwise reserves for temples as the dwelling places of gods. This phrase, too, is elsewhere used in contexts of dislocation or its reverse.[71] As for Hiempsal, he is rich. That is brought out by humor. On

---

for Cicero certainly, is that a mix of senatorial *consilium*, magisterial *imperium*, and popular *libertas* does not mean that the senate should not be in charge (97, quoting Lintott 1999: 223).

69. That was a watchword of optimate rhetoric; see Achard 1981: 402–408. For examples of the praise of *virtus*—Pompey's—in a popular context, cf. *Leg. Man.* 3, 10, 29–30, where Pompey's virtue is accompanied by *innocentia* 'integrity,' *temperantia* 'moderation, restraint,' *fides* 'trustworthiness, good faith,' *ingenium* 'intelligence,' *facilitas* 'accessibility, readiness to be approached' and *humanitas* 'being civilized, humane.' *Facilitas* in particular was perhaps the opposite of Lucullus, who was a notorious martinet.

70. Thus, for example: "But, by way of the order you sent, he would have already been expelled from his farm, already turned out headlong from his household gods, already—the worst part of it!—beaten up at the hands of his own slaves" (*at hic quidem iam de fundo expulsus, iam a suis dis penatibus praeceps eiectus, iam, quod indignissimum est, suorum servorum manibus nuntio atque imperio tuo violatus esset, Quinct.* 83). Cf. also: *nudum eicit domo atque focis patriis disque penatibus praecipitem* (*S. Rosc.* 23), *ista tua pulchra Libertas deos penatis et familiaris meos lares expulit, ut se ipsa tamquam in captivis sedibus conlocaret?* (*Dom.* 108), *Dom.* 109, *Sest.* 30, *Sest.* 145, *Lig.* 33, *Phil.* 12.14.

71. *in suis antiquis sedibus summa cum gratulatione civium et laetitia reponitur* (*Ver.* 2.4.74, of a statue stolen by Verres); *teque, Latona et Apollo et Diana, quorum iste Deli non fanum, sed, ut hominum opinio et religio fert, sedem antiquam divinumque domicilium nocturno latrocinio atque impetu compilavit* (*Ver.* 2.5.185). The same "kinesis" is present when the phrase is used in Livy and Lucretius: *tum vero ad hoc retracti ex distantibus locis in sedem antiquam videbamur ut iterum periremus et alterum excidium patriae videremus...* (Liv. 28.39.7), *hostes montem, antiquam sedem maiorum suorum, ceperunt* (Liv. 39.32.3), *rursus in antiquas redeunt primordia sedes* (Lucr. 6.871). There is a "static" variant in Pliny: *antiqua Laestrygonum sedes* (*Nat* 3.59). Jonkers (1963: 26) surmises that *di penates* means some religious scruple inhered in the site, perhaps because purported descendants of Aeneas lived there, and Rullus wished to "void his plans being upset on religious grounds, as C. Gracchus's had been when he endeavored to found the *colonia* of Junonia."

a visit to Rome, Hiempsal's son, Juba, with his full coiffure and deep pockets, had evidently made a lasting impression.[72] Cicero recalls the scene with a memorable rhyme (*nummatus ~ capillatus*) and, in *nummatus*, lit. 'having coins,' a jocular neologism (the suffix *-atus* 'wearing, having' is usually used for clothing or bodily features; the effect might be captured by "long-haired . . . and fat-walleted").[73]

Cicero's descriptions draw out what Sicilian peasants and a king with his princeling have in common: dependence on the good will of the senate. That is obvious for the Recentorici, who need their mercy (*misericordia senatus*). And it is also quite clear for Hiempsal. He is a *rex amicus*, literally "friend king" (J-p); the title *amicus*, granted by the senate to certain monarchs, was a tactful label for a quite unequal relationship.[74] He, too, depended on Rome's good will, which is what Juba had apparently gone to solicit—or rather purchase. Cicero is thus not just accusing Rullus of bribery; he is also implying what Rullus's guiding principle is: choose your victims well. The one would have had no real trouble paying, and the others would have had no real choice except to pay. The one, in hope, could absorb the loss; the others, in fear, would have had to. Rullus is cast in the mold of the extortionate Verres, inspiring fear where needed and holding out hope when useful.[75]

In short, the memorable images of rich princeling and ousted peasants make Rullus into an artful extortionist. And there, in the now familiar pattern, is a rewriting, or rather an extension, of a known concept. The corrupt aristocrat could and did exploit high office and high connections. Sallust's Memmius, in a populist invective, complains of exactly that: "Kings and free peoples pay a tax directly to a few nobles!" (*reges et populos liberos paucis nobilibus vectigal pendere*,

---

72. Juba must have come to Rome on some recent occasion as an emissary of his father (not to lobby Pompey to restore his father to the throne; that had happened in 81, when Juba was only five or so). Juba would visit Rome again in 62, to plead his father's side against a Numidian named Masintha, when Caesar notoriously yanked his beard (Suet. *Jul.* 71). In 109 the tribune C. Mamilius Limetanus proposed a *quaestio* for those "on whose advice Jugurtha had ignored the decrees of the senate and who while holding a *legatio* or *imperium* had received monies from him," etc. (Sal. *Jug.* 40.1).

73. There is another, also jocular, instance in Cicero: *Balbus mihi confirmavit te divitem futurum: id utrum Romano more locutus sit, bene nummatum te futurum, an, quomodo Stoici dicunt, omnes esse divites, qui caelo et terra frui possint, postea videro* ("Balbus assures me that you're going to be rich. I guess I'll find out eventually if he was talking like a Roman and meant your pockets would be stuffed—or the way the Stoics do and meant everyone who lives and breathes is rich!", *Fam.* 7.16.3, 54 BCE). The Numidians wore their beards long and their hair thick; cf. Manuwald 2018: 317 ad 2.59 *Iuba . . . bene capillatus*. Perhaps the neologism also anchors a hidden pun (*Iuba ~ iuba* 'flowing hair, mane'); so Classen 1985: 327 n. 65.

74. *Amici reges* were kings of nations allied to Rome; see Lintott 1993: 32–36.

75. *quibus opus esset, metum offerre, quibus expediret, spem ostendere* (*Ver.* 2.2.135).

Iug. 31.9, the epigraph to this section).[76] By *vectigal*, which might as it were be printed in scare quotes, Memmius doesn't mean a "tax" literally (taxes were paid to the treasury). Rather, in the case of free peoples, *vectigal* means exactions imposed by a governor, in order to finance games, for example, or fund parting gifts for himself (Cicero uses the word *vectigal* in that same way);[77] in the case of kings, *vectigal* probably means gifts sent by client kings to leading senators to ensure they remained in good standing (hence Juba and all his cash).[78] Rullus, who likewise targets susceptible kings and vulnerable free people, apes the style of that kind of aristocrat. He is no literal *nobilis*, despite his claims to the contrary,[79] but he knows how to achieve the same results as the worst of them by using the chief tool available to him—a plebiscite with discreet privileges. Just as the golden Sulla paradoxically respects the people more than the tribune does, so in this passage the tribune paradoxically profits more than the equitable senate. If the Rullan bill ignores established procedure, it also exploits established procedure. The implicit check is oversight and a responsible governance, and that includes prudent cooperation with regular magistrates.

4.4. EGYPT

Non enim simpliciter solum quaeritur quid honestum sit, quid utile, quid aequum, sed etiam ex comparatione, quid honestius, quid utilius, quid aequius, atque etiam, quid honestissimum, quid utilissimum, quid aequissimum.

---

76. Cf. *nam postquam res publica in paucorum potentium ius atque dicionem concessit, semper illis reges, tetrarchae vectigales esse, populi, nationes stipendia pendere; ceteri omnes, strenui, boni, nobiles atque ignobiles, vulgus fuimus, sine gratia, sine auctoritate, iis obnoxii, quibus, si res publica valeret, formidini essemus* (Sal. *Cat.* 20.7, from a speech of Catiline).

77. *minus esse aliquanto in Scapti nomine quam in vectigali praetorio* "the amount owed to Scaptius was somewhat less than the governor's exaction" (Cic. *Att.* 5.21.11), *quod iniquo et gravi vectigali aedilicio... Asiam liberasti* (*Q. fr.* 1.1.26); Shackleton Bailey 1980: 124 notes re *vectigali aedilicio*, "This seems to be the only source of information on the subject. Evidently it was a 'voluntary' contribution by provincial communities to the expenses of Roman shows."

78. "[N]atürlich zahlen die Könige und freien Völker den Römern kein *vectigal*, aber die hier gemeinten Geschenke der Klienten an ihre privaten Patrone werden mit diesem Wort als Anmaßung einer an sich dem Staat zustehenden Leistung gebrandmarkt" (Timpe 1962: 355 n. 3); "The taxes paid by the subject peoples (*populi liberi*), it is alleged, are employed only for the maintenance of the Roman nobles who govern them; an exaggeration, but see Cic. *Imp. Pomp.* 14. What *vectigal* did kings pay? Perhaps the reference is to the lavish gifts sent to Roman *nobiles* by kings who were their clients... [cf.] Badian 1984: 161–2. In S.'s own day, vast sums were paid by foreign kings to *principes* to procure their recognition by the senate" (Paul 1984: 79). Comber and Balmaceda 2009 *ad loc.* capture the idea with the translation 'tribute.'

79. See ch. 6.3 (Re)reading the Decemviral Election.

> *Questions [of the character of an issue] are not absolute questions of uprightness or utility or equity; they are relative questions of what has a greater, or even the greatest, degree of uprightness or utility or equity.*
>
> —Cicero, *Partitiones Oratoriae* 66

The three chief features of Cicero's reconfigured *libertas*—skepticism about populist legislators, responsible governance, and proper procedure—appear distinctly in a last passage. One of the three major categories of public land to be sold under the Rullan bill were lands outside of Italy that had become public property after 88 (*LA* 1.1, 2.38–44). Which properties exactly is not clear. The bill did not list them in detail (as it did for the *agri vectigales* discussed earlier). Instead it named categories of property (Cicero quotes the phrase *qui agri quae loca aedificia aliudve quid*, *LA* 2.38).[80] The bill had in mind lands in Asia Minor that Sulla had punitively declared public property but that had in the meantime, at least in part, fallen under the control of private landowners.[81] The Rullan bill would have allowed reclamation or recovery of their use-value (that is the business of the decemvir we have seen, seizing land from under his host's feet). One clear sign of that intention is the date: 88 was the year cited in various senate decrees confirming Sulla's decisions after the fact.[82]

---

80. Cicero takes issue with the vagueness of the language: "The law reads 'Lands, locations, buildings' ... but there are things besides that. There're slaves, flocks, gold, silver, ivory, clothing, furniture, and so on. All valuable assets ... so how do we figure this? Did he think people would take it wrong if he named them all? [That can't be it:] he doesn't care what people think. So what *was* he thinking? He thought [listing everything] would take too long, and he was afraid of leaving something out! So he added, 'And anything else'! Short and to the point, as you can see: *nothing* is left out! And as a result whatever became public property of the Roman people outside of Italy during the consulship of L. Sulla and Q. Pompeius or thereafter, he orders the decemvirs to sell. What that means, fellow citizens, is that under this clause every race and nation and province and kingdom has been handed over on a silver platter to the power, authority, and discretion of the decemvirs (*'Qui agri, quae loca, aedificia.' Quid est praeterea? Multa in mancipiis, in pecore, auro, argento, ebore, veste, supellectili, ceteris rebus. Quid dicam? invidiosum putasse hoc fore, si omnia nominasset? Non metuit invidiam. Quid ergo? Longum putavit et timuit ne quid praeteriret; ascripsit 'aliudve quid,' qua brevitate rem nullam esse exceptam videtis. Quicquid igitur sit extra Italiam quod publicum populi Romani factum sit L. Sulla Q. Pompeio consulibus aut postea, id decemviros iubet vendere. Hoc capite, Quirites, omnis gentis, nationes, provincias, regna decemvirum dicioni, iudicio potestatique permissa et condonata esse dico*, *LA* 2.38–9). On the quoted clause *qui agri* etc. Ferrary 1988: 150–51.

81. The details are complicated and cannot be discussed fully here; I intend to explore the point elsewhere.

82. "Everything Sulla had done as consul or proconsul they voted to confirm and ratify in perpetuity" (οἱ καὶ πάντα, ὅσα διῴκησεν ὁ Σύλλας ὑπατεύων τε καὶ ἀνθυπατεύων, βέβαια καὶ ἀνεύθυνα ἐψηφίζοντο εἶναι, App. *BC* 1.97); Gabba 1966: 774.

In both speeches Cicero dramatizes the breadth of the measure. It will, he says, lead to the sale of whole districts or their famous cities up and down the Asian coast,[83] all recovered from Mithridates after that date. Cicero does not mean to describe the force of the law literally but to draw out the imprecision, and therefore danger, of the law (and land tenure must really have been sorely disrupted by Mithridates's advances). Cicero closes the lists with the greatest danger: the measure, he alleges, aims at gaining control of Egypt (*LA* 1.1, 2.41). In theory the date of 88 allowed that, too. That was the year Ptolemy X Alexander I was ousted from the throne by his elder brother and, in order to finance a fleet to regain his position, pledged his kingdom to Rome as surety. But, probably in late 87 or early 86, he died without having achieved his purpose, thereby forfeiting the kingdom.[84] His son, Ptolemy XI Alexander II, was installed by Sulla in 80, only to be murdered by the Alexandrians shortly thereafter. The Egyptian throne had since been occupied by Ptolemy XII Auletes, the son of Ptolemy IX by a mistress. The matter of the bequest was still unresolved in 65, when Crassus and Caesar tried to gain control of Egypt in different ways.[85] The legal complexities gave the senate pause, and the attempts failed.[86] In both of our speeches, Cicero makes that failure a chief feature of his argument: those who could not gain control of Egypt openly are now trying to do so covertly; other elements vary (Roman numerals indicate their sequence):

---

83. The places listed in a fragment of the senate speech (fr. 3) probably referring to the same measure of law coincide with those of the popular speech at 2.39–40. The list here takes the form of [District]: location in *LA* 1 fr. 3 ~ location in *LA* 2.39–40. [Bithynia]: ø ~ *Bithynia*; [Propontis]: *tota Propontis atque Hellespontus* ~ *Cyzicus*; [Mysia]: *Mysia* ~ *Pergamum*; [Lesbos]: ø ~ *Mitylene*; [Lydia]: ø ~ *Smyrna, Ephesus, Tralles*; [Caria]: ø ~ *Miletus*; [Phrygia]: *Phrygia* ~ ø; [Lycia, Cilicia]: *omnis ora Lyciorum atque Cilicum* ~ ø. These cities and districts had all cooperated with Mithridates, and most can be shown to have been suffering from indemnities after 88. For a list of Asian cities and their treatment by Sulla, see Santangelo 2007: 122–23. On the reasons for the cities selected here, see Gabba 1966: 772–75.

84. For identification of the testator as Ptolemy X Alexander I (*RE* Ptolemaios 31) and the date of his will as late 87 or early 86, see Badian 1967: 178–92. Some have argued that the testator was his son, Ptolemy XI Alexander II (*RE* Ptolemaios 32; see references in Manuwald 2018: 1 n.). The many other complications of this period of Egyptian history must be left aside here; for a concise account, see Brennan 2000: 414–416.

85. "In 65 BCE the censor M. Licinius Crassus (*RE* Licinius 68; cos. 70, 55) tried to turn Egypt into a tributary province, but was prevented by his colleague Q. Lutatius Catulus (Plut. *Crass.* 13.1). C. Iulius Caesar (curule aedile 65, cos. 59 BCE) also made attempts to be assigned Egypt as a province by a People's plebiscite via the Tribunes, but failed because of the opposition of the nobility (Suet. *Iul.* 11). It is debated whether Crassus and Caesar were working together (Ward 1972; see also Marshall 1976: 65–67, 75–76; Ward 1977: 152–53, 161). Because they each acted in official roles, their activities could be described as happening in the 'open,' in contrast to the current initiative," Manuwald 2018: 117.

86. Badian 1967: 185.

Table 4.4. Rhetorical Structure of the Treatment of the Possible Sale of Egypt (*LA* 1.1, 2.41–44)

A. Bill Covertly Permits Seizure of Egypt

[*not extant*]   (i.) Quid? Alexandrea cunctaque Aegyptus ut occulte latet, ut recondita est, ut furtim tota decemviris traditur!

"And that's not all! There's something hiding beneath the surface, tucked away, handed over to the decemvirs on the sly: Alexandria and all of Egypt!"

B. Egypt Bequeathed to the Roman people

(ii.) Dicent enim decemviri, id quod et dicitur a multis et saepe dictum est, post eosdem consules regis Alexandrini testamento regnum illud populi Romani esse factum.

(ii.) Quis enim vestrum hoc ignorat, dici illud regnum testamento regis Alexae populi Romani esse factum?

"For the decemvirs will repeat the claim that many make and have made, that in 87 Egypt became the Roman people's by the testament of the king of Alexandria."

"Of course you all know what they say—that in his will king Alexas left that kingdom to the Roman people."

C. Complications of the Will

ø

(iii.) Hic ego consul populi Romani non modo nihil iudico sed ne quid sentiam quidem profero. Magna enim mihi res non modo ad statuendum sed etiam ad dicendum videtur esse. Video qui testamentum factum esse confirmet; auctoritatem senatus exstare hereditatis aditae sentio tum quom Alexa mortuo nos legatos Tyrum misimus, qui ab illo pecuniam depositam nostris recuperarent. Haec L. Philippum saepe in senatu confirmasse memoria teneo; eum qui regnum illud teneat hoc tempore neque genere neque animo regio esse inter omnis fere video convenire. Dicitur contra nullum esse testamentum, non oportere populum Romanum omnium regnorum <ap>pententem videri, demigraturos in illa loca nostros homines propter agrorum bonitatem et omnium rerum copiam.

Table 4.4. Continued

"But on this occasion I, a consul of the Roman people, have no official position on this matter, and I am not even going to say what I think. It seems to me a consequential matter to even talk about, let alone decide. I see that there is a party who can confirm the execution of a will; and I understand that the senate expressed its willingness to accept the terms of the will when, on the occasion of Alexas's death, we sent legates to Tyre to retrieve for our citizens the money that had been deposited with him.[i] I recall that L. Philippus confirmed these details on many occasions in [meetings of] the senate; and I see almost everyone agrees that the current occupier of the throne has neither the blood nor the disposition of a royal. There are also arguments on the other side: that no [valid] will exists; that the Roman people shouldn't seem like they covet kingdoms; that our men will migrate to Egypt with its fertile fields and boundless resources."

D. Alexandria at risk

(iii.) Dabitis igitur Alexandream clam petentibus iis quibus apertissime pugnantibus restitistis?

(iv.) Hac tanta de re P. Rullus cum ceteris decemviris conlegis suis iudicabit, et utrum iudicabit? Nam utrumque ita magnum est ut nullo modo neque concedendum neque ferendum sit. Volet esse popularis; populo Romano adiudicabit. Ergo idem ex sua lege vendet Alexandream, vendet Aegyptum, urbis copiosissimae pulcherrimorumque agrorum iudex, arbiter, dominus, rex denique opulentissimi regni reperietur. Non sumet sibi tantum, non appetet; iudicabit Alexandream regis esse, a populo Romano abiudicabit. Primum cur populi Romani hereditatem decemviri iudicent, cum vos volueritis de privatis hereditatibus centumviros iudicare? Deinde quis aget causam populi Romani? ubi res ista agetur? qui sunt isti decemviri, quos prospiciamus regnum Alexandream Ptolomaeo gratis adiudicaturos?

(continued)

Table 4.4. Continued

"Are you willing to hand Alexandria over to the secret designs of people whose open assault you resisted?"	"And so Rullus here with his other colleagues in the decemvirate will be able to rule on this consequential matter? [ii] So which way will he rule? Not that we should let him rule or accept his ruling either way—it's too important a matter. But suppose he chooses to play the populist and rules for the Roman people. What would that mean? That by the terms of his own law he can sell Alexandria, that he can sell Egypt, that he will turn out to be judge, arbitrator, and master of a very rich city and very splendid territory—the king of a very wealthy kingdom! But suppose he decides not to be greedy and not to appropriate that much? Suppose he says Alexandria belongs to the king and denies the claim of the Roman people? First, what business do decemvirs have judging an inheritance of the *Roman people*, when your policy has been to have the centumviral court decide about *private* inheritances? And who would represent the side of the Roman people? Where would this process of theirs be held? Are there decemvirs who we can imagine will grant the kingdom of Alexandria to Ptolemy for nothing? Show me them!"
	E. Secret Attempt Replaces Open Attempt
(i.) Quae res aperte petebatur, ea nunc occulte cuniculis oppugnatur.	(v.) Quod si Alexandrea petebatur, cur non eosdem cursus hoc tempore quos L. Cotta L. Torquato consulibus cucurrerunt? cur non aperte ut antea, cur non item ut tum, derecto et palam regionem illam petierunt? an qui etesiis, qui per cursum rectum regnum tenere non potuerunt, nunc caecis [iii] tenebris et caligine se Alexandream perventuros arbitrati sunt?

Table 4.4. Continued

"They're digging secret tunnels to the same objective that they once made for openly."	"And if they were aiming for Alexandria, why didn't they follow the same paths this time that they did when L. Cotta and L. Torquatus were consuls (65 BCE)? Why didn't they aim for that region openly—the way they did before? Heading straight there, out in the open—the way they did then? Or did they think that, after they couldn't make it to the kingdom sailing straight with the wind behind them, they could get to Alexandria in the pitch black in the fog?"
	F. Plans are Mad
(iv.) Haec, per deos immortalis! utrum esse vobis consilia siccorum an vinulentorum somnia, et utrum cogitata sapientium an optata furiosorum videntur?	[cf. (v.), on night sailing]
"Good Lord! What do you think? Are these sober plans, or drunken dreams? Are these prudent plans, or mad hopes?"	

---

i On *auctoritas senatus,* which refers to a senate resolution vetoed by a tribune, cf. *OLD s.v. auctoritas* 4a, Cic. *Fam.* 1.7.4, Manuwald 2018: 285.
ii "P. Rullus" is deliberately formal, hence my "Rullus here"; cf. Manuwald 2018: 167.
iii On the reading here, see n. 116.

The tableaux are not malicious fantasies. It was not out of the question that a decemvir, who would be in office for five years, might, whether on his own or at the behest of someone else—like Crassus—try to find some way to profit from the unclarities and opportunities of the Egyptian situation. Gabinius would shortly do that very thing.[87] Still, Rullus's bill did not in the first instance attach Egypt. Cicero himself admits as much, after a fashion: he alleges that Egypt is a *hidden* target of the bill (D and E-s, A- and E-p), drawing, in the case of the popular speech, on its theme of secrecy (the drafters kept Cicero out, *LA* 2.12;

---

87. In 55, while governor of Syria, induced by a bribe of 10,000 talents, he invaded Egypt and restored Ptolemy Auletes to the throne (Cic. *Pis.* 48–50).

unscrupulous lawmakers are sneak thieves, *LA* 2.46; the bill is a power grab in the guise of agrarian legislation, *LA* 2.15, 16). But the tenuous link shows up Cicero's technique clearly. His objective in both speeches, as I have been arguing, is to create memorable symbols of power relations: though the link of the Egyptian situation to the bill is slight, it makes a fine—and already well known—symbol for the difficulties of governance. In the realm of complex legal and financial questions, Egypt is, in the phrase, good to think with. In particular, C-p, which treats the complications of the inheritance of Egypt, and D-p, which treats the possible sale of Alexandria, each leave the audience on the horns of dilemma (again the figure of *complexio*).[88] In those dilemmas, and the framing passages A-p and E-p, Cicero's distinctive version of *libertas* leaves clear marks, in the form of very different roles for him, for Rullus, and for the Roman people.[89]

A Complicated Inheritance

C-p sketches two possibilities: Egypt belongs to the Roman people or it doesn't. Cicero lays out the arguments on each side of the debate. They are, at root, arguments drawn from stasis theory, a standard method in classical rhetoric for determining the point at issue in a case. The argument *pro* frames the issue as one of definition: the statutory definition of accepting an inheritance has been satisfied. The argument *contra* frames the issue as a question of competing goods, here that material benefits and practical concerns are outweighed by decency.[90] But Cicero works out those arguments in a way that imposes roles on him and on the people. His own role he depicts pointedly: he takes no position on the matter of Egypt. The recusal is striking. First, he rejects the prerogative of his office, which he explicitly underscores (*hic ego consul populi Romani . . .*). The consul, this time (*hic* "on this occasion," lit. "here," suggests a departure from the expected; the effect is not far from "consul though I may be"), will issue neither a binding declaration (*iudico*) nor a considered opinion (*quid sentiam*). Since legal complexities are at issue, those specific words probably have a technical

---

88. This reflects very exactly the configuration of Egypt in Greco-Roman thought: cf. "In many [Greek] texts, Egypt becomes a place to experiment with conflicting poles of dichotomies and explore in-between places" (Mazurek 2022: 61).

89. Classen's treatment of the popular version asserts only the communicative effect of sentence forms (an exclamation calls for attention; a piling up of figures creates a dramatic picture of dangers) without reference to their semantics or cultural or political allusions (1985: 317–18).

90. The broad categories in stasis theory are *definitio* (ὅρος) and *qualitas* (ποιότης). The argument *contra* actually begins with a question of *coniectura* (στοχασμός), which considers the issue of whether something happened or not (*Rhet. Her.* 1.18). See Calboli 1969: 218–21.

air: *iudico* recalls the *iurisdictio* of a magistrate with *imperium* and *sentio* the *sententia* of a juror or jurist.[91] Second, Cicero is stepping back from his previous position. Two years earlier, in response to Crassus's efforts, he had strongly opposed accepting the will. The sentiments of the (mostly lost) speech he delivered in the senate on the topic, the *de rege Alexandrino*, were presumably known beyond the senate.[92] In short, Cicero is not doing what he might, and he is not saying what he did before.

That throws a burden onto the people. The argument *pro* casts the history of the will in terms of Cicero's perception. He sees (*video*) and has been given to understand (*sentio*) and remembers (*memoria teneo*) and sees (*video*). This is a distinct voice: the voice of the witness, whose "duty it is to say what he knows or has heard."[93] The audience become a kind of jury, to whom Cicero is witnessing. The argument *contra* invokes an ethical category, "being greedy for kingdoms" (*appetentem . . . regnorum*). Now the audience becomes a magistrate whom Cicero is advising. Two details draw that out. *Appetens* and like phrases are otherwise used of individuals with tyrannical aspirations.[94] Here it is the people, expressly so named, that risk looking like a covetous politician. Second, accepting the will will cause the resettlement of "our men" into rich fields: willy-nilly the people themselves become like sponsors of an agrarian bill ousting tenants; the politics of *commodum* are thus wholly reversed. Here, then, is a miniature dramatization of the same issue we saw with the Recentorici: the argument *pro*, with the people as jury, rests on *ius* 'the letter of the law,' whereas the argument *contra*, with the people as a magistrate, rests on *aequum* 'an equitable outcome.' The choices are clear: embrace the law, and allow damage to Rome's reputation; or protect Rome's reputation, and bypass a rich inheritance. Such the difficulties of foreign policy and imperial finance.

---

91. The scope of *iurisdictio* included granting possession; cf. *ius dicentis officium latissimum est: nam bonorum possessionem dare potest, et in possessionem mittere, pupillis non habentibus tutores constituere, iudices litigantibus dare* (Ulp. *Dig.* 2.1.1). In principle granting possession was part of a consul's powers, though effectively dormant by the late Republic.

92. For the political background of this speech and surviving fragments with commentary, see Crawford 1994: 43–57.

93. *officium est . . . testis dicere, quae sciat aut audierit* (*Rhet. Her.* 4.47, part of the illustration of the figure of *distributio*).

94. Classen 1965: 394, 398–99; "The intentions of the Roman People are described by wording reminiscent of that typically applied to individuals unconstitutionally seeking 'regal' power (e.g. Cic. *Dom.* 101; *Mil.* 72; *Phil.* 2.114)," Manuwald 2018: 287. In distinction to *peto*, the neutral term, and to *expeto* 'seek (from some source),' *appeto* is 'seek (with some object in mind)' and hence often 'grasp after' (*L&S* I) or 'be greedy for' (*L&S* II.A), especially of money (*L&S* II.B); the *TLL* recognizes a subset of greed for others' property (2.0.287.53–63).

Alexandria

The horns of the dilemma of C-p are sharp. But whether the whole people appreciated the problem is doubtful: some, perhaps many, must have thought: Take the large sum, take the rich lands, procedural and ethical niceties be damned. (Cicero's pitch to that part of the demographic is the topic of Chapter 5). But Cicero's objective in C-p is not only to draw out the difficulties of governance; it is also to prepare for a contrast between himself and Rullus, who is the chief figure of D-p. Whereas in C-p Cicero does not pull rank, implicitly deferring to the people, or at least making a show of recognizing the limits of power, in the tableau of E-p Rullus abuses his authority flagrantly and ignores the people utterly.

The section rests on the premise that Rullus has been duly elected and is now in a position to decide the fate of Alexandria; like the auction of Chapter 3, it is a fevered vision of the future. If Rullus judges Alexandria Roman, then there is a failure of responsible governance; if he leaves it free, then there will have been a grave failure of procedure. Rullus may declare Alexandria Roman. Then the terms of his law are a problem: they will make him a "king." Cicero is drawing upon—and refitting—a political smear. Accusations of kingly aspiration were a regular feature of Republican political invective. The image implied arrogance, arbitrariness, and excess ambition.[95] But in Egypt Rullus would hold sway in an *actual* kingdom (*rex . . . regni*). The metaphor of *rex*, just like *eruo* and *indago* (ch. 3.3 The Wastrel), is partly reliteralized. And that ascent is permitted by the terms of Rullus's own law (*ex sua lege*). That is the point of the triplet of nouns (*iudex, arbiter, dominus* "judge, arbitrator, master"), which here have their technical senses. A decemvir could decide whether a given property is public or private: that is like a *iudex*, who usually had a delimited task (he ruled on an issue). A decemvir could set boundaries between parcels in the field: that was one role of an *arbiter*, who had wider discretionary powers (he solved a problem). A decemvir could sell at will: that is like a *dominus*, who had maximally allowable discretion over his property ("quiritary ownership"). The technical senses are thus arranged in an ascending tricolon by breadth of authority, and the culmination is kingship. And there is the people's problem of responsible governance: is the benefit of a

---

95. Tiberius Gracchus was famously accused of coveting *regnum* (Cic. *Amic.* 41, Sal. *Jug.* 31.7, Flor. *Epit.* 2.2.18), as was Saturninus later (Flor. *Epit.* 2.4.18). Cicero accused Verres of being a *rex* and *tyrannus* (e.g. 2.1.82, 2.3.71, 76–77, 2.4.123, 2.5.103). For other instances, see Hellegouarc'h 1963: 560–61. For the relation of the trope to Hellenistic monarchy, see Erskine 1991 and Dunkle 1967. Erskine 1991:114 points out that "with the exception of the *De Lege Agraria* the examples of this charge being used in Cicero's speeches are in fact less frequent than we might expect (or indeed than is often suggested)"; besides *de lege agraria* the accusation occurs not surprisingly oftenest in the *Philippics*.

decemvirate with wide powers that might provide *commoda*—and that is Rullus's imagined posture for this half of the dilemma; he would "choose to play the populist" (*volet esse popularis*)[96]—worth the risk of financing someone up the ladder of authority into tyranny?

But what if Rullus awards Egypt to the sitting king? Then the problem will have been not responsible governance but procedure. Cicero probes that issue through the template of the centumviral court, which adjudicated private inheritances.[97] The failed procedure has two aspects. There is first (*primum*) a question of jurisdiction, posed *a fortiori*: if there is a duly authorized court for private inheritances (which are less important), why should the decemvirs act as an unauthorized court for a public bequest (which is more important)? The popular role is highlighted: the centumviral court exists because *vos voluistis* "thus you resolved" (or "ordered" or "consented").[98] Just as the "you" above (Table 4.3.1.H-s) referred to the *comitia centuriata*, the "you" here refers to a public assembly from well before living memory: the court was in existence, at the latest, by the mid-140s.[99] The people then gathered before Cicero are heirs and embodiments of a tradition; and that tradition, as they know, had designed a representative court, with three members from each tribe—not a hand-picked crew of ten (*P. Rullus cum ceteris decemviris conlegis*, D-p).

Besides a jurisdictional failure, there is also a procedural failure in a stricter sense, which is Cicero's next topic (*deinde*), expressed in three questions, with an accent on the value of formal, agonistic proceedings and on the people and their role. An agonistic procedure needs agonists. But under Rullus's procedure authority will rest with him alone. No one will be there to argue against him—or, as Cicero puts it, to argue the side of the people (*causam populi Romani*). Second, there is a problem of venue. Agonistic procedures, like most others, should be held publicly. But "this process of theirs" (*ista res*), like the sale of *vectigalia*, could

---

96. For that sense of *volo*, cf. *OLD* s.v. 5b 'to be disposed, care (to),' 5c 'to take voluntary action (to).'

97. Cic. *de Orat.* 1.173 describes their many competencies, which, besides wills, included, among others, cases involving acquisition by length of possession (*usucapio*), changes in the shape of land by the effect of water (*adluvio, circumluvio*), air rights (as we might call them; *lumina* "sources of light"), and guardianships (*tutelae*). As Greenidge 1901: 41 points out, the various aspects of this jurisdiction all concern ratable property, that is, goods taken account of in the census.

98. *L&S* s.v. B.1.b(b) 4–6.

99. The first known case before the court was around 145 (Cic. *de Orat.* 1.181, 238). The court had 105 members, three from each of the thirty-five tribes, implying that the late Republican form of the court took shape after 241, when the tribes reached that number. For the nature, arrangement, and history of the court, see Kelly 1976; for its competences, Greenidge 1901: 182–95.

take place anywhere (*ubi . . . agetur?*). In that way the splendors of Alexandria are really no better than the shadows of Cappadocia. And an agonistic procedure needs fair judges.[100] But any process without oversight invites corruption, the implication of *gratis* "for free" (D-p *fin.*), and with "the decemvirs created by this law" (the implication of *isti decemviri*), it's impossible to imagine (*prospiciamus*, lit. "foresee") a different result. The imputation is not rhetorical malice. Egypt was indeed rich. Auletes would later do exactly what Cicero claims is possible: pay a bribe to secure the throne.[101] The centumviral court was a suggestive symbol of all these aspects of jurisdiction and process. Its proceedings were familiar, visible from the Forum.[102] Anyone passing a session of the court—the court "they" established—might think of decemvirs footloose in luxurious Alexandria, "forgetting the rigorous habits of the Roman people."[103] Here, as with the image of Sulla facing the people, Cicero uses a feature of the Forum as a mnemonic. And again the people confront the problem of responsible governance: is the benefit of creating a position with wide-ranging authority worth the risk that its holder will enrich himself through bribery? Such are the difficulties of foreign policy and imperial finance, determining not just what is useful or respectable but also the relative degrees thereof.

Bonnie Princes and Night Raids

In short, in the popular speech Cicero handles Egypt and Alexandria the same way: he uses the ambiguity of their status (Roman or not?) to craft two *complexiones* that dramatize the problems of responsible governance, bowing to the people's role, duties, and traditions—and casting Rullus in a bad light. Does a peculiar detail enhance the effect? For the king the manuscripts of the senate speech have either a local adjective (*regis Alexandrini*, B-s) or a name

---

100. This issue was a standard part of rhetorical instruction: *ex translatione controversia nascitur cum aut tempus differendum aut accusatorem mutandum aut iudices mutandos reus dicit* (*Rhet. Her.* 1.22). As Caplan 1954: 40 notes, this particular *status* does not really suit Roman procedure, which allowed objections not at trial but at a preliminary hearing before the magistrate.

101. He paid almost 6,000 talents to Caesar, according to Suetonius (*Jul.* 54.3).

102. Where precisely the court met in Republican times is not attested, but no doubt it was in one of the four basilicas. Under the Empire it met in the *Basilica Iulia* (cf. Plin. *Ep.* 5.9).

103. Like Gabinius's soldiers (cf. n. 87): they, adopting the loose habits of Alexandrine life, had forgotten "the name and the rigorous habits of the Roman people" (*. . . iam in consuetudinem Alexandrinae vitae ac licentiae venerant et nomen disciplinamque populi Romani dedidicerant . . .*, Caesar, *Civ.* 3.109).

(*regis Alexandri, ibid.*).[104] But the popular speech has a genitive *Alexae* (B-p) and an ablative *Alexa* (C-p). These are familiar forms, the Latinized versions of Ἀλεξᾶς, the hypocoristic of Ἀλέξανδρος (like Ἀντιπᾶς for Ἀντίπατρος, Ἱππᾶς for Ἱππομέδων, etc.).[105] In the first instance the hypocoristic gives a certain air of familiarity, as if of a person long discussed and well known, so especially in C, where the royal title is not used (*Alexa mortuo*, not *rege Alexa mortuo*). But perhaps Cicero also had another effect in mind. If some remembered Juba—and it is clear from these speeches alone that the people had a very deep and detailed memory[106]—, then some also remembered Ptolemy XI Alexander II, the haughty princeling whom Sulla brought back to Rome and sent off to assume the Egyptian throne.[107] The boy doubtless cut a figure as Sulla's courtier[108] and in town talk might well have been dubbed *Alexa(s)*, perhaps first by Sulla himself.[109] The name, in that form, was thus in itself an icon for Egyptian dynasts—wealthy, arrogant, and a source of political trouble. And Rullus will either be their patron or join their ranks.

The popular passage ends where it began, with a prompt to skepticism: the Rullan bill is a secret attempt where an open attempt failed (E-p). The idea appears in both speeches, but the metaphors differ. In the senate speech, the supporters of the bill are digging "tunnels" (*cuniculi*)—a careful and laborious approach by land, apt, perhaps, to represent the "long game" of sly lawcraft and

---

104. *Rex Alexandrinus* is usual for Ptolemaic kings (Cic. *Fam.* 1.7.4; 8.4.5 [Caelius]; *Att.* 2.16.2; *Q. fr.* 2.2.3; *Dom.* 20; *Pis.* 49) and is thus read by Manuwald 2018.

105. Klotz's edition prints *Alexae* in the senate speech, too, on the grounds of consistency. The name is also used in the *Scholia Bobensia* (p. 92.18–20 Stangl) and is the name of a citizen of Heraclea in Cic. *Balb.* 50. On this form of the hypocoristic, see Petersen 1937; the forms seem to be originally Ionic and don't appear in Attic inscriptions until the time of Augustus.

106. On the issue of the contional audience's "civic knowledge," see Morstein-Marx 2004: 72–77; on "cultural memory" at Rome in an earlier period, see Hölkeskamp 2006; on popular memory, Wiseman 2014. For an analogous case, the workings of social memory in Athenian culture, see Steinbock 2013.

107. He had been turned over to Mithridates by the Coans but escaped and fled to Sulla, whose "close acquaintance" (συνήθης) he became (App. *BC* 1.102). Sulla sent him back to Egypt in 80 to take over the throne but, aping the brutality of his mentor, he was shortly killed by the locals. See refs. in Manuwald 2018: 118.

108. On the second day of his triumph, 30 January 81, Sulla had paraded citizens that Cinna had exiled but he had now restored, who hailed him as "savior" and "father" (Plu. *Sull.* 34.1); was the young Egyptian king part of such a display? There were in any case many magnificent shows at which the young king might have been seen. On Sulla's propaganda, see Ramage 1991.

109. Cicero would then be using the son's nickname for the father, unless the son was the testator; see n. 84.

political maneuvering. In the popular speech, the bill is like an attack by sea. Nautical imagery, otherwise absent from both speeches, here provides a precise metaphor (like the images of bodily violence in *LA* 2.47 = Table 3.1.A-p). These sailors do not now have following winds (*etesiae*);[110] thus it is winter (the Etesian winds die down between September and May). And they are sailing in the pitch-black night (*caecis tenebris*) in "obscuring mists" or a "blinding storm" (*caligo*).[111] In part that is another image for invisibility; the dark conceals their movements. But the image as worked out here has another effect. The seamanship of the ancients was cautious. Sailing in a winter storm at night, with no stars and no moon, was risky—unless the sailors were recklessly bold. The metaphor (hinting at the boldness of pirates?) is not of sly lawcraft but of runaway greed—the very fault of *appetitio regni* which the Roman people are to avoid. But, if the people are skeptical about the bill and probe it for hidden objectives, they will notice its failures of procedure, which can only be a sign of the dangerous ambition of the legislators, whom they must therefore not empower, so as to forestall that abuse. That, as I argued, was also the point of the image of arbitrary sales in the *liberae legationes* passage from which we began—and which follows immediately upon this image of a reckless voyage. The decemvirs are cruel on land and crazed at sea, their vices exposed by (Cicero's version) of *libertas*.

4.5. CONCLUSION

ἐπειδὴ λόγου δύναμις τυγχάνει ψυχαγωγία οὖσα, τὸν μέλλοντα ῥητορικὸν ἔσεσθαι ἀνάγκη εἰδέναι ψυχὴ ὅσα εἴδη ἔχει. ἔστιν οὖν τόσα καὶ τόσα, καὶ τοῖα καὶ τοῖα, ὅθεν οἱ μὲν τοιοίδε, οἱ δὲ τοιοίδε γίγνονται.

Since rhetoric is, in effect, the art of influencing the soul, the aspiring rhetorician will have to know how many types of soul

---

110. The correct winds to make Alexandria: *quibus rebus animadversis legiones sibi alias ex Asia adduci iussit, quas ex Pompeianis militibus confecerat. Ipse enim necessario etesiis tenebatur, qui navigantibus Alexandria flant adversissimi venti,* Caes. *Civ.* 3.107.1, cf. Cic. *Fam.* 12.25.3, 15.11.2, Lucr. 6.716.

111. *Caligo*, with (probably) the root of Sanskrit *kāla* 'black' and the Hesychian gloss κηλήνη = μέλαινα 'black,' refers to 'mists,' 'storms,' etc. not qua atmospheric phenomena but in respect of their effect on vision; cf. *TLL* 3.0.158.41 "vapor nebulae vel fumi, obscuritas, nox, tenebrae." Since the accent of the passage is on obscurity rather than repugnance, I prefer the reading *caecis* to the *taetris* 'foul' of many codices. *Caecus* is normal "de eo quod lumen non habet" (*TLL* 3.0.44.70–45.44; cf. *OLD* s.v. 5 "(of night, clouds, etc.) Opaque, dark, black, impenetrable... (w. spec. active force) blinding" and occasionally modifies *tenebrae* elsewhere (e.g. Cic. *Dom.* 24 [metaphorically], Lucr. 2.746, 6.35–36).

> *there are. There aren't that many or that many kinds, which*
> *gives this group or that such and so a character.*
> —Plato, *Phaedrus*, 271d

Attention to Local Context reveals an Unnamed Referent in the passages considered in this chapter—*libertas*, and that of a particular kind, narrowed and remolded to three particular elements: skepticism toward legislators, proper procedure, and responsible governance. That remolding and narrowing is a very precisely aimed stroke. Rullus's bill was in general outline an ordinary agrarian bill: it seated commissioners; it distributed land; it established or re-established colonies. But it is precisely in its constitutional innovations and adaptations, rather than its broad purposes, that the Rullan bill was unusual; it fell short of *libertas*— or, more precisely, could be claimed to have fallen short of it—not in its ends but in some of its means and methods and their probable or possible consequences. Seeing those failures takes a skeptical eye, a respect for proper governance, and a constitutionalist's sense for the implications of procedure. It takes respect for principle, precedent, and process.

It is exactly that identity that the passages of this chapter are intended to project onto the audience. Each passage, with its memorable imagery, draws out a somewhat different face of that identity. Sales on the spot were probably meant to ensure efficiency; Cicero makes them appear to bypass popular oversight. He makes a Sulla that he converts from lordliness to deference into a symbol of that issue—and a prompt to look past partisan polarities. The exceptions for the Recentorici and Hiempsal were probably the prudent bracketing of difficult issues; Cicero makes them recall the abuse of legislative and administrative practices. He sketches household gods left behind and the long locks of foreign royals as tokens and reminders of the cruelty and cronyism of which the ruling class was indeed capable—and a prompt to trust responsible magistrates. Egypt was probably not targeted by the bill in the first instance; but its richness was already a convenient symbol for the sore temptation to conceal true intentions and ignore principles. Cicero makes a brazen night raid symbolize such veiled avarice and invokes the centumviral court as a bulwark of the relevant principles—and a reminder of "your" inherited identity.

Here, in short, is not only Projected Identity but also Creative Decorum: Cicero turns deference to the people's authority, obligatory in a contional speech, into something like a political manifesto. He takes what they respect and turns it into what he wants to them to respect. There are three further points to note. First, as I suggested earlier, beginning from parallel passages and working through their details "opens up ordinary language ... and gives that language due weight beside more obvious programmatic claims." This chapter, I hope, which probes the ideology behind passages that are not obviously programmatic, illustrates that claim. Second, this chapter supports the claim crystallized in Chapter 3.4: Cicero's distinct ideological vision guides his selection of almost every detail and depends on an audience alert to symbol and suggestion.

Those points are points of *logos*; there is also an issue of *pathos*. Was any of this vision compelling to Cicero's audience? Did anyone really think of Sulla's statue differently, for example? Or did they scoff at Cicero's semiotic gambit? Did anyone really worry about (allegedly) bogus exemptions? Or did they keep their eyes on the prize of a plot of land? The answers depend entirely on how the audience is imagined. If it is thought of as heterogeneous—the impression of unity, as I have argued, is a projection—then, whatever the Overton Window at a given Republican *contio* looked like exactly, there will have been some groups that were attracted by the principles and ideals that Cicero points to and made anxious by the prospect of their failure. It is at them, I suggest, and perhaps mostly at them—the persuadable middle, neither dead set against nor rabidly for—at whom Cicero aims the passages considered in this chapter, each of them, like a Roman coin recalling the moneyer's family, stamped with one clear and memorable image. Those in the audience fervently for the measure, who thought that the ends justified the means, who thrilled to the extremes of populist rhetoric, who took the *res* of *res publica* to mean not so much "the people's enterprise" as "the people's wealth," who were ready to countenance abuse, skullduggery, and even tyranny if it meant a chicken in their pot—those, one might say, whose souls were of a different type—could never be persuaded. But those just next to them on the opinion curve, whatever shape that had, perhaps could be persuaded, if their hopes for *commodum* could be dashed. Those hopes—and Cicero's efforts to dash them, too—are the subject of Chapter 5.

5

Commodum *and the Fear of Exclusion*

5.1. INTRODUCTION

lucrum sine damno alterius fieri non potest.

Nobody gains unless somebody else loses.
—Publilius Syrus, *Sententiae* L6

Libertas, like many important concepts, comprised a cluster of related ideas, not a single notion. Chapter 4 explored Cicero's treatment of the constitutional and operational branches of the idea. That treatment, as attention to the Local Context showed, narrowed and elevated those branches to an ideal—even a kind of manifesto—of responsible governance, proper procedure, and skepticism toward legislators. But *libertas* had other branches, too. Above all, it had a practical component: the fruits of liberty were to be *commoda*: tangible material benefits for the electorate.[1] That branch is the chief focus of this chapter. Hope for *commoda* loomed large in popular and populist thought. Whatever the origins of the notion as a populist "plank," it doubtless grew in prominence in response to the economic crises of the late second and early first century. There is a striking illustration of the place of the concept in the *Commentariolum Petitionis*, a booklet of election advice supposedly addressed to Cicero.[2] He should have three goals: to make the senate see him as a defender of their influence (*auctoritas*); to

---

1. Cf. ch. 1.1 and n. 19.

2. For the place of the ideas of this booklet in Roman electoral practice, see Yakobson 1999. The authorship of the booklet is ascribed to Cicero's brother, Quintus. For the view that the booklet is anachronistic, see Henderson 1950 and Nisbet 1970; for the contrary view, Balsdon

make the *equites* and wealthy conservatives see him as a champion of peace and domestic tranquility; and to make the people see him as "not ill-disposed to their advantages" (*a suis commodis non alienum*) because he had stood up for popular causes.[3] The last bit of advice speaks to the centrality of *commodum*—and astutely points out what was a real gap in Cicero's portfolio: while, especially early in his career, Cicero had broken with the aristocracy, signally in defense of the Sicilians abused by Verres, neither was he ever a robust champion of material outlay to the people; that is, his populism did not extend to social welfare, which is a gap that his campaign is prudently advised to bridge.

If the importance of *commodum* was a problem for Cicero's consular campaign, it was also a problem if he would oppose the Rullan bill: the bill was expressly designed to provide material benefits. While Cicero argues consistently and precisely that the bill's methods and means were corrupt and not consonant with the ideal—or rather an ideal—of *libertas*, those who thought the ends justified the means—that is, those who placed *commodum* before due process—will have regarded these objections as mere technicalities, so long as the bill delivered the goods. Thus Cicero lays down another line of defense: the bill won't deliver the goods, either. As the bill's mechanisms are an abuse of sovereignty, so are the bill's promised benefits a sham and an illusion. If—to allude to a common polarity of ancient rhetorical thought—the bill falls short of *honestas*, treating the people's powers with disrespect, it also falls short of *utilitas*, promising what it cannot deliver.[4]

To make the practical argument, Cicero draws on a hope and a fear that doubtless really did attach to *commodum*. A stretch of the *LA* 2 captures that hope and that fear. In the very first of the arguments proper Cicero treats the mechanism for electing the decemvirs. We have seen a sketch of that mechanism already (ch. 1.4); here is the beginning of Cicero's full treatment of it, in

---

1963. The writer is at all events an astute observer. On the importance of popular support as a concept in the text, see Morstein-Marx 1998.

3. *sed haec tibi sunt retinenda: ut senatus te existimet ex eo quod ita vixeris defensorem auctoritatis suae fore, equites et viri boni ac locupletes ex vita acta te studiosum oti ac rerum tranquillarum, multitudo ex eo quod dumtaxat oratione in contionibus ac iudicio popularis fuisti, te a suis commodis non alienum futurum* (53). Cf. also *largitio et spes commodi propositi* "[official] outlay and the hope of a promised advantage" as a *popularis* rhetorical strategy for *contiones* (*Sest.* 105).

4. Sometimes Cicero uses another line of defense, attempting to coopt or overwrite *commodum*. Thus he makes it out that support for the Manilian bill meant support for liberating allies rather than stabilizing Asian revenues (Table 2.1.H-p); and in the *exordium* and *peroratio* he attempts to convert *otium* into a form of *commodum* (ch. 6.2 and ch. 7.4). But mostly he does not attempt to reconfigure or challenge or invert the value; rather he claims, straightforwardly, that despite appearances the bill simply does not serve *commodum*.

which he claims the very mechanism represents a reduction or appropriation of *libertas*:[5]

> The first section of the agrarian bill is designed in their minds to subtly probe your willingness to tolerate the curtailment of your liberty. The law orders the tribune of the plebs who has proposed the law to oversee the election of decemvirs[6] by seventeen tribes—which means that a man returned by nine tribes becomes a decemvir. What I want to know is: why did [Rullus] lay the foundation of his enterprise and his [proposed] laws on depriving the Roman people of their vote? Agrarian laws have often established commissioners in panels of three, or five, or ten; but when did that ever happen except by a vote of the [full] thirty-five tribes? That's what I want to know from this "popular" tribune of the plebs. It's well understood that all power, commands, and commissions derive from the [will of] the entire Roman people, and in particular those [powers] which are established for some advantage and benefit of the people—in that case the whole body politic chooses the man they think will most have the interests of Roman people at heart, and each individual citizen can, by his support and his vote, pave the way for himself to secure some benefit. And yet a tribune of the plebs, of all people, has come up with a plan that deprives the Roman people of their voting power and invites a few tribes, not according to a clear legal requirement,[7] but by the random kindness of lots, to usurp [your] liberty.

> *Primum caput est legis agrariae quo, ut illi putant, temptamini leviter quo animo libertatis vestrae deminutionem ferre possitis. iubet enim tribunum plebis qui eam legem tulerit creare decemviros per tribus xvii, ut, quem viiii tribus fecerint, is decemvir sit. Hic quaero quam ob causam initium rerum ac legum suarum hinc duxerit ut populus Romanus suffragio privaretur. Totiens legibus agrariis curatores constituti sunt iiiviri, vviri, xviri; quaero a populari tribuno plebis ecquando nisi per xxxv tribus creati sint. Etenim cum omnis potestates, imperia, curationes ab universo populo Romano proficisci*

---

5. For the historical details that lie behind the mechanism, see ch. 6.3.

6. *Creare* is idiomatic of magistrates presiding over elective assemblies (cf. *TLL* 4.1164.59–84 "de magistratu qui comitia habet") as well as of electoral bodies voting someone into office.

7. If the distinction of the later legal tradition already existed and Cicero has that sense in mind, *condicio iuris* is specifically a "requirement imposed by law for the validity of a legal transaction" (Berger 1953, *s.v.*). In Cicero the phrase also means "the principles of civil procedure" or the like (*Q. Rosc.* 37) and "principles of justice" or the like (*Rep.* 3.19).

convenit, tum eas profecto maxime quae constituuntur ad populi fructum aliquem et commodum, in quo et universi deligant quem populo Romano maxime consulturum putent, et unus quisque studio et suffragio suo viam sibi ad beneficium impetrandum munire possit. Hoc tribuno plebis potissimum venit in mentem, populum Romanum universum privare suffragiis, paucas tribus non certa condicione iuris sed sortis beneficio fortuito ad usurpandam libertatem vocare. (*LA* 2.16–17)

There are two features to notice—first, Cicero's handling of constitutional law. His main point is correct. Special commissioners normally were elected by the full thirty-five tribes,[8] and the authority of various forms of office (listed here, as often, in a descending hierarchy)[9] did derive from the will of the people. But another point is not quite right. *Tum eas profecto maxime* etc. "and in particular those" seems to suggest that, as a point of law, there are kinds of measures, agrarian laws among them, where the people were somehow especially sovereign. Cicero has here transposed onto constitutional theory the people's own political practice: they did tend to defer to the senate—as, for example, in the matter of treaties (cf. ch. 4.3)—but were more keenly attentive when their own material interests, here expressly named (*fructus et commodum*, "benefit and advantage"), seemed to be directly at stake. They show up when entitlements are on the ballot, as it were, but not for school board elections. The *libertas* that is here at risk is really *commodum*.

Second, Cicero lays out the rationale for the people's practice. The body politic chooses an official who "will most have the interests of the Roman people at heart" (*populo Romano maxime consul[et]*), where *consulo* doubtless implies material benefits;[10] and each voter paves the way for himself to "secure a benefit" (*ad beneficium impetrandum*), where *beneficium* certainly connotes material benefits

---

8. Cf. Cic. *Leg.* 3.10. For Jonkers 1963: 66 the claim is misleading because Cicero is comparing the decemviral commission to *tres-* or *quinqueviri agris dandis assignandis*, chosen by the *comitia tributa*, but that is exactly the point.

9. Cf. e.g. *magistratus curationes sacerdotia* (Cic. *Ver.* 2.3.126), *magistratum potestatem imperium curationemve cuius rei* (*CIL* 6.930.10, the *lex de imperio Vespasiani*), *in magistratu potestate curatione legatione vel quo alio officio munere ministeriove publico* (Maecian. *Dig.* 48.11.1.pr).

10. Cf. *LA* 2.22 *etenim si populo consulis, remove te a suspicione alicuius tui commodi, fac fidem te nihil nisi populi utilitatem et fructum quaerere, sine ad alios potestatem, ad te gratiam benefici tui pervenire* ("If you really have the people's interests at heart, get rid of the suspicion that you will benefit personally, give proof that you seek only the people's advantage and profit, let others do the job while you get the credit for your good deed"), where *consulis* clearly means material benefits.

(the idea is precisely analogous to that of *clientela*, the Roman social institution which bound together the lesser and the greater by exchanges of favors).[11] The two clauses represent a calculus of materialist politics. The clauses have different orientations. The first looks to the whole: the collective (*universi*) chooses the best man. The second looks to the individual: each single voter (*quisque*) pledges his support and his vote (*studium et suffragium suum*) in hopes of a path to gain for himself (*viam sibi ad beneficium*...). The implicit idea is that the aggregate of individual calculations of maximal personal advantage leads to maximal communal advantage. Through the choices of each the collective finds a grand benefactor for all. The clauses amount to a justification of materialist politics, as if individual acts of naked self-interest always combined to redound to the best collective good.

The passage is meant to raise anxieties. There is perhaps the anxiety of distortion. If the aggregate of individual calculations of advantage leads to the maximum collective good, then reducing the size of the input group, as Rullus's bill demands, reduces the chances of the most broadly useful result. A smaller group leads to a distorted outcome. But there is certainly the anxiety of being excluded. Cicero stokes that anxiety by using *quisque*. Elections in the *comitia tributa* were not decided by a majority of voters but a majority of tribes. But saying *quisque* instead of *singulae tribus* makes everyone look over his shoulder, as it were, including at his own tribesmen, and wonder. What if a particular tribe backed the losing candidate? What if, to press Cicero's *viam munire*, a tribe that thought it was paving a sure path found it had only built a bridge to nowhere? Wouldn't that keep them from "securing benefits"? Wouldn't *universi* turn out to mean just the partisans of the victor?

That is the very issue that Cicero shortly brings to the fore:

> The men that the nine tribes, selected by Rullus himself, will choose as decemvirs will become our lords and masters in every respect, as I will presently show. And in return, the decemvirs, in order to show they are grateful for and mindful of the benefit, will acknowledge that they are indebted to the known men of the nine tribes—but as for the remaining twenty-six tribes, there will be nothing which the decemvirs will not feel it is perfectly within their rights to deny them.
>
> *quos viiii tribus decemviros fecerint ab eodem Rullo eductae, hos omnium rerum, ut iam ostendam, dominos habebimus. Atque hi, ut grati ac memores benefici esse videantur, aliquid se viiii tribuum notis hominibus debere*

---

11. For overviews of *clientela*, see Deniaux 1993, Wallace-Hadrill 1989; for a socioliterary assessment of the mutual exchange of gifts, see Griffin 2003.

confitebuntur, reliquis vero vi et xx tribubus nihil erit quod non putent posse suo iure se denegare. (*LA* 2.21)

Cicero here has another feature of the electoral process in mind: not only would the decemvirs be elected by a minority of tribes, but Rullus would oversee the drawing of lots for the electoral tribes and thus be able choose the ones that he prefers.[12] The outcome would not be universally good; here there is no *quisque* writ large that somehow becomes *universi*. Rather, the body politic would be cleft in two. The two resulting groups are marked out by the idioms of social exchange. The decemvirs will be *grati ac memores benefici* to the electoral tribes. The three lexemes, which frequently occur together, stress ties between giver and receiver—again, the idea of *clientela*.[13] The particular form of that "grateful memory" here is implied by the phrase *noti homines*: they are probably *divisores* or "bribery agents" (lit. "dividers," that is, 'distributors [of cash]') in the relevant tribes.[14] To the victors go the spoils. The excluded tribes face a different future. The decemvirs will "deny" (*denegare*) any and every petition of theirs: the word specifically denotes refusing a request for a favor.[15] Here, very precisely, is the zero-sum vision of the epigraph: somebody gains only because somebody else loses.

The cultural and political underpinnings of Cicero's rhetoric thus become clear. *Libertas* in its practical aspect included a hope for *commodum*; but that must have come with the fear of exclusion. The flipside, and even consequence, of the cheering prospect of a patron and a protector was anxiety about a lack of patronage and protection. To draw out those anxieties, Cicero uses the procedures of the bill itself, which, unusual as they were, lent themselves to being so used. But the linkage between procedural points and economic anxiety doubtless already

---

12. *LA* 2.21.

13. In *de Legibus*, using the same lexemes, Cicero elevates the principle to a cultural universal: *quae autem natio non comitatem, non benignitatem, non gratum animum et beneficii memorem diligit?* ("Does not every nation value agreeability, kindness, and the grateful memory of good turns?" 1.32). For two other instances of the occurrence of all three lexemes together, cf. *O ingratifici Argivi, inmoenes Grai, inmemores benefici,* | *exulare sinitis, sistis pelli, pulsum patimini* (Acc. *trag.* 364–5 Ribbeck), *Hagesaretus Larisaeus magnis meis beneficiis ornatus in consulatu meo memor et gratus fuit meque postea diligentissime coluit* (Cic. *Fam.* 13.25.1).

14. On distributing bribes through *divisores*, see Lintott 1990: 7–8, Vanderbroeck 1987: 62–64. Cf. Zumpt 1861: 50: "*Noti* autem *homines* sunt, quos in sua quemque tribu plurimum posse notum est, quorum opera ad tribus conficiendas expetitur atque emitur"; Manuwald 2018: 234, "it apparently was not unusual in election campaigns to rely on well-connected and opinion-forming men in each tribe," citing *Comm. Pet.* 30, 32. (That would be the precinct captain, for you older Chicagoans.)

15. *TLL* 5.1.524.29 "de voluntate, actione i. q. recusare, vetare, non admittere," *L&S s.v.* II, *OLD s.v.* 2.

existed. Granting powers to officials is an act of trust, both in the eventual efficacy of the proposed powers and in the good will of the empowered officers. Any such an act of trust, almost by its very nature, can arouse anxiety. What if the powers didn't work as advertised—what if they *couldn't*? What if the chosen officers did not really have good will? Those anxieties must have been all the deeper in late 64 and early 63. Debt, as we have seen, was crushing; Catiline's populist indignation had real roots. And the very form of the bill, Cicero's attacks on particular measures aside, must have already brought some anxiety in tandem with the hopes it stirred: the commission, in office for five years, would be distributing fixed and finite resources and deciding land questions not readily reversible. Procedure in these passages thus has a different valence than it did in Chapter 4: it does not connote the pride of oversight that represents sovereignty; rather, it is emblematic of the fairness—or unfairness—of a proposition. Procedure has a different valence if you think of it as something you control or as something somebody else does.

Here, then, is a supplement and parallel to the argument of Chapter 4. Rullus had doubtless invoked *libertas* in defense of his bill and appealed to the economic anxieties that were then acute. But just as Cicero flipped the import of *libertas*, making it a reason to oppose rather than support the bill, so in the passage just quoted, and in the passages considered elsewhere in this chapter, he flips the import of anxiety. If (some of) the people, excited by Pompey's successes, thought they knew how to choose protectors and providers, Cicero insinuates that—himself excepted— they do not; that is exactly what the procedures of Rullus's bill show. *Studium* for Rullus is not an extension or complement of their *studium* for Pompey but a contradiction to it. And if (some of) the people, excited by Pompey's success, thought that, if a tribunician bill that bent constitutional norms had achieved a beneficial military result, they could achieve an economic result the same way, paving themselves a path to securing land (or a like benefit), Cicero argues that good land won't be there either: that is exactly what the procedures of Rullus's bill show. *Studium* for Rullus is not a sure road to securing a *beneficium* but a dangerous path to disappointment.

5.2. SELLING POMPEY'S CONQUESTS

Dwóch orłów razem się nie gnieździ.

You can't have two eagles in the same nest.

—Maciej Dobrzyński in Adam Mickiewicz, *Pan Tadeusz*, 12.378

One of the sources of funds for the Rullan bill, as we have seen several times, was the sale of tax properties (*agri vectigales*) or their tax contracts (*vectigalia*). The parcels can be sorted into three groups: (1) those in Italy and Sicily (*LA* 1.3–4,

2.48–49, the topic of the auction considered in ch. 3); (2) those in Western Asia Minor, Greece, Spain, and Africa (*LA* 1.5, 2.50–51); and (3) those in Paphlagonia, Pontus, and Cappadocia recently secured from Mithridates by Pompey (*LA* 1.6, 2.52–55). On the whole the selection reflects the bill's thoughtful design. Some of the properties seem not to have been uncommonly fertile;[16] others seem to have been overlooked or underused. It is thus unlikely that the sales would have harmed current tax revenues. Raising significant cash from such lots required a goodly number to be sold or let. Hence their wide geographical distribution: the bill's framers had obviously surveyed state holdings from across the empire.[17] These often far-flung lands could count on a ready market: the bill waived the usual requirement that public properties be sold or let in Rome (1.7, 2.55 *atque*–2.56 *vendent*; cf. Table 4.2), as we have seen, and thus opened sales to current lease-holders or occupiers ready to buy but not able to travel.

Cicero structures his treatment of the sales the same way in both speeches: he nests the second set into the third; that is, the treatment of Pompey's gains is made into a frame for other items. This section discusses the end of that frame. The deep template, as close comparison reveals, is ultimately the same but augmented and amplified considerably in the popular version (Roman numerals give the sequence of elements in each speech; one element is also treated elsewhere, as indicated in Table 5.2.)

Table 5.2. Rhetorical Stucture of the Treatments of the Sales of Pompey's Gains (*LA* 1.6, 2.51–55)

in senatu	*ad populum*
A. Sale of Pompey's Conquests (= Table 8.2.D)	
(i.) 6. His insignibus atque infulis imperi venditis quibus ornatam nobis maiores nostri rem publicam tradiderunt, iubent eos agros venire quos rex Mithridates in Paphlagonia, Ponto Cappadociaque possederit.	(i.) 51. . . . Verum inter hos agros captos veteribus bellis virtute summorum imperatorum adiungit regios agros Mithridatis, qui in Paphlagonia, qui in Ponto, qui in Cappadocia fuerunt, ut eos decemviri vendant.

---

16. Cicero mentions the fertility only of the *ager Corinthius* (1.5, 2.52); for the passage see Table 8.2.B. Its wine and olives are mentioned by Livy (27.31.1), Vergil (*G.* 2.519), and Pliny (*Nat.* 14.74), among others. If any of the others were as fertile, he surely would have made something of it.

17. Cicero attests to that thoroughness sarcastically: he mocks Rullus's *diligentia* (*LA* 2.51, Table 8.2.C.-p), cf. *LA* 1.3–4 (Table 3.3.1).

Table 5.2. Continued

in senatu	ad populum
"Having sold off these symbols and garlands of empire that adorned the state that our elders passed on to us, they order the sale of the territories which king Mithridates possessed in Paphlagonia, Pontus, and Cappadocia."	"But among these territories captured in ancient wars by the courage of the highest commanders he adds the former royal territories of Mithridates ¹—territory in Paphlagonia and in Pontus and in Cappadocia—with orders that the decemvirs sell them."
B. Incomplete Procedures	
ø	(ii.) 52. Itane vero? non legibus datis, non auditis verbis imperatoris ...
ø	"Is that so? No laws have been passed; the commander has given no report ... "
C. State of War Continues	
(iii.) ... eos ipsos agros in quibus ille etiam nunc bellum gerat atque versetur?	(iii.) ... nondum denique bello confecto, cum rex Mithridates amisso exercitu regno expulsus tamen in ultimis terris aliquid etiam nunc moliatur atque ab invicta Cn. Pompei manu Maeote et illis paludibus et itinerum angustiis atque altitudine montium defendatur, cum imperator in bello versetur, in locis autem illis etiam nunc belli nomen reliquum sit ...,
"... of the very territory in which he is even now waging war and engaged?"	"... in fact the war is not even finished yet: Mithridates, despite a lost army and ejection from his kingdom, nonetheless, defended from the unbeaten force of Gnaeus Pompey by Maeotis and its swamps, narrow passes, and high mountains, is, there on the ends of the earth, hard at work on something even now; the commander is still engaged in war; and that district is still officially in a state of war."
D. Territory still in Pompey's Control	
ø	(iv.) ... eos agros quorum adhuc penes Cn. Pompeium omne iudicium et potestas more maiorum debet esse decemviri vendent?
	"Shall the decemviri therefore sell territories which by tradition should still be under the authority and jurisdiction of Gnaeus Pompey alone?"

(continued)

Table 5.2. Continued

in senatu	*ad populum*
	E. Selling Territory in Sinope
∅	(v.) Et, credo, P. Rullus—is enim sic se gerit ut sibi iam decemvir designatus esse videatur—ad eam auctionem potissimum proficiscetur! Is videlicet, antequam veniat in Pontum, litteras ad Cn. Pompeium mittet, quarum ego iam exemplum ab istis compositum esse arbitror: 'P. Servilius Rullus tribunus plebis xvir s. d. <Cn.> Pompeio Cn. f.' (Non credo ascripturum esse 'Magno,' non enim videtur id quod imminuere lege conatur concessurus verbo.) 'Te volo curare ut mihi Sinopae praesto sis auxiliumque adducas, dum eos agros quos <tu> tuo labore cepisti ego mea lege vendam.' ii
	"And doubtless Publius Rullus will be the one to take charge of that particular auction—he's already acting as if he thinks he is decemvir-elect. I can see it now: before he arrives in Pontus, he will send a letter to Gnaeus Pompey; I bet they have already composed a draft: "Publius Servilius Rullus, tribune of the plebs, decemvir, sends greetings to <Gnaeus> Pompey, son of Gnaeus. (I don't think he'll add 'the Great'—I doubt he'll grant in words what he's trying to ruin with a law). 'I want to you to make yourself available to me at Sinope and bring me help there, when I shall be selling under my law the territory which you secured by your labor.'"
	F. Selling Territory near Pompey's Camp
(ii.) Num obscure videntur prope hasta praeconis insectari Cn. Pompei exercitum, qui venire iubeant...	(vi.) An Pompeium non adhibebit? in eius provincia vendet manubias imperatoris? Ponite ante oculos vobis Rullum in Ponto inter nostra atque hostium castra hasta posita cum suis formosis finitoribus auctionantem. Neque in hoc solum inest contumelia, quae vehementer et insignis est et nova, ut ulla res parta bello nondum legibus datis, etiam tum imperatore bellum administrante, non modo venierit verum locata sit.

Table 5.2. Continued

in senatu	*ad populum*
"How much more obvious could they be? They're practically chasing down Cn. Pompey's army with a herald's spear in hand, ordering the sale . . ."	"But maybe he won't summon Pompey? Maybe he'll sell a commander's spoils right in his province? [iii] Imagine it! Rullus, in Pontus, holding an auction in the company of his handsome surveyors, the spear posted right between our camp and the enemy's! The fact that any property gained in war is even rented out—say nothing of sold!—when no laws have yet been passed and when the commander is still managing the war is not the only insult—although it is a quite remarkable and novel kind of insult!"
	G. Motives of the Legislators
∅	(vii.) Plus spectant homines certe quam contumeliam; sperant, si concessum sit inimicis Cn. Pompei cum imperio, cum iudicio omnium rerum, cum infinita potestate, cum innumerabili pecunia non solum illis in locis vagari, verum etiam ad ipsius exercitum pervenire, aliquid illi insidiarum fieri, aliquid de eius exercitu, copiis, gloria detrahi posse. Putant, si quam spem in Cn. Pompeio exercitus habeat aut agrorum aut aliorum commodorum, hanc non habiturum, cum viderit earum rerum omnium potestatem ad decemviros esse translatam. Patior non moleste tam stultos esse qui haec sperent, tam impudentis qui conentur; illud queror, tam me ab eis esse contemptum ut haec portenta me consule potissimum cogitarent.

(continued)

Table 5.2. Continued

in senatu	ad populum
	"But [these] men aim at more than insult; they hope that, if Gnaeus Pompey's enemies are allowed not only to move freely in that territory but even to come right up to his army, with *imperium*, with universal jurisdiction, with unlimited power, with limitless cash, they can launch a kind of ambush on him and take away some of his army, of his resources, and of his glory. They think that, if Gnaeius Pompey's army has any hope of getting land or other benefits from him, they will lose that hope, once they see that authority over all such resources has been transferred to the decemvirs. I am not really surprised to find that there are people foolish enough to entertain these hopes or shameless enough to try them; my complaint is that they think so little of me that they devised these monstrous plans when I, of all people, was consul!"

[i] For the meaning here, see Broughton 1934: 212 (and cf. "The term *agri regii* in Cicero's list of public lands probably does not mean crown land, since the Macedonian properties mentioned in the same passage include only the former private holdings of the kings of Macedon," Broughton 1934: 212); Fletcher 1939: 27; Magie 1950: 1047–48 (who, while accepting Broughton's distinction, prudently does not believe that former private estates were the only source of all later *ager publicus*).

[ii] On the formality of *P. Rullus*, cf. Manuwald 2018: 167.

[iii] That is, in distinction to Sinope, which was not a part of the *provincia* proper; Lucullus established it as a free town after its capture (App. *Mith.* 83; cf. Plu. *Luc.* 23.2–5; Magie 1950: 342).

The amplifications and additions of the popular version (as in the popular version of the *liberae legationes* passage) are carefully calibrated to serve one broad idea. The idea is signaled, in part, by programmatic words (*virtus*, A; *mos maiorum*, D; *commoda, gloria*, G); but the extrinsic definitions or conceptions of those notions fail to capture the real thrust of the passage. That appears in smaller, not obviously programmatic details.

Two common elements cast the particularity of the popular version into relief. Both versions share a chief argument (C) and an image (F). Both speeches (correctly) make the technical argument that no disposition of territory should begin before an official end to hostilities. The senate version (C-s) has "is even now waging war and engaged" (*ille etiam nunc bellum gerat atque versetur*). The fuller popular version is more formal: it names Pompey's official role, *imperator* (that is, the duly authorized holder of *imperium*), and it makes war a matter of official labeling (the "name of war," *belli nomen*, remains—the notion is not far from "technically still in a state of war," C-p). Furthermore, the popular version is framed with extra elements that also look to formalities. Formal control is stressed in D: where the land in question in the senate speech is simply *agros* (in C-s), the popular speech has "territories which by tradition should still be under the authority and jurisdiction of Gnaeus Pompey alone" (*eos agros quorum adhuc penes Cn. Pompeium omne iudicium et potestas more maiorum debet esse*). Several elements of Pompey's legal authority are highlighted. Its breadth is highlighted: *iudicium ac potestas*, as we have seen,[18] appears to be a technical merism of Cicero's for the full range of the powers of an official not subject to collegial *imperium*. The origin of his authority is highlighted: it is settled practice (*mos maiorum*). And the validity of the authority is highlighted: *penes Cn. Pompeium* describes not simple possession but possession in a legal or technical sense; the phrase means something like "duly vested in Gnaeus Pompey."[19] In B-p it is violated procedure that is stressed: the formalities that marked the end of a war have not yet taken place. *Non legibus datis* refers to the laws a commander issued in a pacified province on the advice of ten legates sent out by the senate; those laws, after formal ratification, would become the *lex* or *formula* of a province.[20] *Non auditis verbis imperatoris* refers to the dispatches that commanders sent back to Rome, here no doubt chiefly the request that the senate send out the ten legates.[21] Both speeches also illustrate the overreach with the same image,

---

18. See ch. 2.3 and n. 36.

19. For similar examples, cf. *cum penes te praetorium imperium ac nomen esset* "when you were vested with the title and powers of a praetor" (Cic. *Ver.* 2.5.40), *cum iudicia penes equestrem ordinem essent* "when the courts were in the hands of the equestrian order" (*Scaur*. fr. d. Clark = Asc. 19.8 Clark). In Caesar *penes* is only used of formal control of persons or property (*Civ.* 1.76.4, 1.87.1, 2.20.8). Cf. Paul. Fest.'s distinction: "The difference between *apud* and *penes* is that *apud* signifies what a party in a particular place has, and *penes*, what a party has full rights over and may dispose of as he will" (*'apud' et 'penes' in hoc differunt, quod alterum personam cum loco significat, alterum personam et dominium ac potestatem*, 20.19 Lindsay).

20. *Lex*: Mommsen *RS*³ 2.1: 685, 692; Lintott 1993: 28–32; ten-man commissions: Cic. *Ver.* 2.2.32, 2.2.39–40, *Att.* 13.6a.

21. Cic. *Fam.* 5.7, *Pis.* 40; cf. Zumpt 1861: 91, Mommsen *RS*³ 3.2: 1107. There is no evidence that Pompey sent the request, and he ignored the commission that had been working with his predecessor, Lucullus (Plu. *Luc.* 35.5, 36.1; Mommsen *RS*³ 2.1: 692–93 n. 9).

imagining an auction near Pompey's army (F). But the tableaux are different. The senate version makes the decemvirs aggressive camp followers, "chasing down" (*insectari*) Pompey's army with a spear—a symbol of the sale of war booty here reliteralized.[22] The popular version, by contrast, again stresses formalities. Again the relevant laws have not been issued (*nondum legibus datis*); again the official commander is still running a war (*etiam tum imperatore bellum administrante*). And a technical term for "loot" is used (*manubiae*, on which more presently).

In short, the popular version sketches a Pompey in lawful possession of the Mithridatic territories. That sets the decemvirs into relief: they will not be skirting the law; they will be invoking an alternate—and superior—law. That is the point of E-p. That element, only in popular speech, imagines another possible point of sale besides the camps, Sinope. That Pontic city, a free city and the site of royal residences,[23] was in territory that Rullus intended to sell, along with Paphlagonia to the east and Cappadocia to the south,[24] and it was a convenient point from which to oversee sales in Pontus and Cappadocia. Cicero imagines a letter in Rullus's voice—the figure is προσωποποιία, lit. "mask-making," a standard vehicle for animating a character, theme, or idea[25]—serving notice on Pompey to appear in that city. The message of the letter is in its mixed tone. On the one hand, it signals that Rullus, too, will have legitimate authority. He appends "decemvir" to his name, as magistrates and officials rightfully could. He is acting under a law, "my law." (*Mea lege* is not in and of itself sarcastic or pompous: when the sponsor of a bill appeared in the immediate context, it was common to use, not the usual adjective taken from the *nomen* of the sponsor, like *Tullia*, *Manilia*, or *Servilia*, but a possessive adjective.)[26]

---

22. For the *hasta* as symbol of an auction, cf. *Phil.* 2.64, *Off.* 2.27. *Insectari* is an aggressive verb, used by Cicero of the Furies (*Leg.* 1.40) and of hunting animals in hot pursuit (*N.D.* 2.127, *Div.* 2.144). Its other appearance with *hasta*, in Plautus, describes a madman attacking his family (*nam istic hastis insectatus est domi matrem et patrem*, *Capt.* 549).

23. *Sinopen atque Amisum, quibus in oppidis erant domicilia regis, omnibus rebus ornata ac referta* (*Man.* 21).

24. Within a year and half Pompey would fold Paphlagonia into the province of Bithynia and Pontus.

25. The *Rher. Her.* calls the figure *conformatio* (4.66); cf. also Cic. *de Orat.* 3.205, *Top.* 45, and for further terminological and definitional variation, see Calboli 1969: 427–28 and cf. Hopwood 2007: 87.

26. So *vendet eos mea lege quanti volet* ("Under my law he will be able to sell them for as much as he wants," *LA* 3.14, Rullus speaking), *quo minus reus mea lege fias* ("to keep you from being prosecuted under my legislation," *Vat.* 37, Cicero speaking), cf. also e.g. *Planc.* 83 (*mea*), *Dom.* 25, 82, 128 (*tua*), *Vat.* 35 (*tua*), *Phil.* 2.110 (*tua*), *LA* 1.2, 7, 2.22, 43, 69, 3.3 (*sua*), *Red. Sen.* 26 (*sua*), *Sest.* 135 (*sua*), *Phil.* 7.16 (*sua*), *Leg.* 3.22 (*sua*).

But Rullus wields his legitimate authority with arrogance. He requests that Pompey be *praesto* "on hand" to meet him: the word commonly connotes being available for a superior person or purpose.[27] He is apparently brusque: *volo te curare*, lit. "I want you to see to it," seems blunt; in letters Cicero usually says *velim cures* "I would like you to make sure,"[28] and he does not use *volo* + *te* + infinitive to deliver imperatives.[29] Is *s[alutem] d[icit]* "sends greetings," as opposed to *s[alutem] p[lurimam] d[icit]* "sends warm greetings," also on the cool side? Certainly cool is *auxilium adducas*: Rullus would probably have been within his rights to ask for soldiers to keep order at auctions (or maybe tamp down trouble with the dispossessed); but telling Pompey, of all people, to "bring aid" or "bring up troops,"[30] in those words, is to address him as a junior commander or client king.

Cicero is trying to reverse a perception: this bill isn't for Pompey but against him. And here, as in Chapter 3.2 The Power of the Law, the instrument is authorized abuse. Nicely emblematic of this mix of the arrogant and the officially sanctioned is Rullus's imagined unwillingness to address Pompey with his *cognomen*, *Magnus* 'the Great.' The omission is not simply hostile. It has a certain technical correctness. Pompey did not win *Magnus* 'Great' as a *cognomen ex virtute* linked to a triumph, the usual source of *cognomina*, but was first so dubbed by Sulla (with some sarcasm perhaps, as if "Pompey, the Legend"?).[31] *Magnus* was more

---

27. Cicero, for example, writes to Appius Claudius, *a.d. XI Kal. Iun. Brundisium cum venissem, Q. Fabi<us Vergili>anus, legatus tuus, mihi praesto fuit* ("When I arrived at Brundisium on May 20, your deputy, Q. Fabius Vergilianus, was on hand to meet me," *Fam.* 3.3.1). Cf. *negat umquam se a te in Deiotari tetrarchia pedem discessisse; in primis finibus tibi praesto se fuisse dicit, usque ad ultimos prosecutum* (of Deiotarus and Caesar, *Deiot.* 42), *Att.* 3.8.2, 4.1.4, 4.13.1, 5.13.1, 13.46.1, Liv. 31.14.3, 38.15.10, 45.13.12.

28. *Velim cures* or *cures velim*: *Fam.* 13.56.2, 14.5.2, 14.19.1, 16.21.8, *Att.* 1.5.7, 3.12.2, 8.5.2, 11.4a.1, 11.6.7, 13.8.1, 13.48.2, 14.16.4, 15.15.4, *Q. fr.* 3.6.2; cf. also *Quinct.* 19. The parallels are not wholly decisive, since a proper analysis of the question would require assessing, in every case, the relative status of the communicants and the particular request at hand, as well as the use of alternate expressions—a task beyond the limits of this study.

29. *Volo* + *te* + infinitive in Cicero is most commonly used with *scire* (*Fam.* 3.8.5, 9.10.3, 9.24.1, 12.11.2, 13.41.1, *Att.* 1.18.6, 2.23.2, 7.1.5, 12.19.2, *Q. fr.* 3.3.1) or other intellectual operations (*suspicari*, *Fam.* 5.2.3; *existimare*, *Fam.* 10.1.4; 13.9.2, 13.18.2, *Att.* 13.21a.2; *intellegere*, *Att.* 1.10.2; *tibi persuadere*, *Att.* 10.8a.1) and also expresses strong advice or sincere hope (*neque tamen non te cautum esse volo et insidias vitantem* "Still it's not at all the case that I don't want you to be careful and avoid traps," *Fam.* 11.20.2; cf. *Fam.* 11.22.1, 12.13.4, 14.3.5, 16.4.3, *Att.* 13.33a.2). As Zumpt 1861: 92 n. 53 aptly notes, "notanda verba *te volo curare* et *praesto sis*, imperantium et parentium propria."

30. Elsewhere *auxilia adducere* is only military: cf. e.g. *B. Afr.* 1.1, *B. Alex.* 51.3, Hirt. *Gal.* 8.7.5, Liv. 28.13.5, 29.30.8. For the singular of *auxilium* as 'auxiliary forces' in lieu of the commoner plural, cf. *TLL* 2.1627.27–49.

31. Cf. Plu. *Pomp.* 11–13.1–3; Sulla may only have confirmed what the army itself had granted. According to Plu. *Pomp.* 13.4–5, Pompey did not start using the epithet until he went to Spain in 77.

nickname than title. Cicero means to show a Rullus doing what he technically can—in some formal contexts even Cicero himself omits *Magnus*[32]—but for the wrong reason: the technical correctness is an expression of contempt. The pointed parallelism <*tu*> *tuo labore cepisti* ~ *ego mea lege vendam* ("You secured by your labor" ~ "I shall be selling under my law") captures the thrust of the whole letter: legitimate authority plucks the fruits of another's toil. The letter is closely reminiscent of the *bonorum venditio* of Chapter 3, not only in *inventio* (there, too, a law is harshly applied) but in *actio* or "delivery, performance." There a long list of properties was a script for Cicero and his weeping herald; here the letter is a script for making Rullus sound brusque or arrogant or imperious, perhaps comically so, as Cicero no doubt did, whatever form that took in the Latin of his day.

E-p, then, uses the proprieties of language to depict the wielding of a legitimate, superior authority. F-p does precisely the same thing but using the proprieties of space. Rullus is imagined as exercising his legal right to sell the territories (or their tax contracts), and not just sell them but sell them on the spot. Cicero's image is striking. Rullus is depicted not simply nearby somewhere, nor, as in F-s, in pursuit of Pompey's army, but with the auction block positioned between Pompey's camp and the enemy's. The image is not meant to be realistic; as Cicero himself makes clear enough (C-p), Mithridates, having suffered grave reverses (*amisso exercitu, regno expulsus*), was now holed up in Panticapaeum on the other side of the Black Sea (Cicero enumerates the geographical features as if from Mithridates's point of view looking toward Pompey: the *Maeotis* or Sea of Azov, with its marshy terrain, and the narrow passage up the coast of Colchis, where the mountains come close to the sea). There was no camp where Pompey and Mithridates were faced off. The point of the image is its symbolism: Rullus has intruded on a space that the commander controlled access to; Rullus has set up shop on Pompey's "turf." Cicero's instruction to create a mental picture (*ponite ante oculos*, lit. "set before [your] eyes") vivifies that idea: it makes the audience look from the front of Pompey's camp across no man's land to the enemy camp.[33] The audience are, as it were, briefly arrayed before the *porta praetoria* beside Pompey's soldiers and see Rullus's auction right in their line of sight.

---

32. A formal letter would have used all three names and, in Pompey's case, *imperatori*, too; so Cicero addresses him (*Fam.* 5.7.1.sa.). On naming conventions, see Adams 1978.

33. The idiom *ponere ante oculos* is common enough (e.g. *Marc.* 21, *Deiot.* 20, *Phil.* 2.115, 11.7, 12.14, 13.4, *de Orat.* 2.264), though often calling for recollection, rather than (as here) fictive imagination; in effect Cicero has asked the audience to participate actively in building the *demonstratio* (on that figure, see ch. 2.3 and n. 37).

Two details support the image. Rullus is selling Pompey's *manubiae*. *Manubiae* normally means mobile property in the personal control of the commander.[34] But here Cicero applies the word to the lands conquered by Pompey—the only time in classical Latin the word describes real estate and not goods and chattels. Cicero is making a compendious analogy: Rullus is taking lands from Pompey as if they were *res mobiles* and selling them off to traders on the spot along with the army's other wins.[35] Pompey has had to turn over his booty to the real commander like Plautus's Chrysalus: "Now I must submit all this loot to the quaestor!" (*nunc hanc praedam omnem iam ad quaestorem deferam, Bac.* 1075).[36] And that commander is corrupt, as another detail makes clear, also compendiously. The bill allowed the decemvirs to engage twenty surveyors (*finitores*) each (*LA* 2.32). But Rullus's are *formosi*. There is the sting. In Cicero's oratory *formosus* as a physical quality of males is not 'handsome' but 'beautiful' or even 'pretty'—a not quite respectable quality.[37] In other speeches Cicero applies the adjective only to the attractive slaves or retainers of wealthy households. Thus C. Malleolus left behind him "a great mass of silver plate, a large number of slaves, many artisans, and many beautiful individuals" (*grande pondus argenti, familiam magnam, multos artifices, multos formosos homines, Ver.* 2.1.91).[38] The quality is proper to young men.[39] Vergil's Alexis has the very features: twice called *formose puer* (*Ecl.* 2.17, 45), he is part of a household retinue, "his master's darling" (*formosum . . . Alexin | delicias domini*, 2.1–2). Rullus will have a lovely young retinue, using a right of his position to live large. He will exercise a usual vice of Roman governors abroad—but facilitated, in

---

34. For details on kinds of booty, see ch. 8.3; on *manubiae*, ch. 8.3.

35. For *mercatores* following armies, see *B. Afr.* 75, Liv. 28.22.3. For the commercial activity of the camp followers called *lixae*, who appear e.g. in Liv. 23.16.8, 14, 40.28.3, see Silver 2016.

36. On that practice, see the references in ch. 8 nn. 22 and 23.

37. *Formos-*, of course, has an entirely different flavor as a philosophical and rhetorical term, where it renders, and absorbs the connotations of, Greek καλόν, e.g. *Off.* 1.126, *decorum illud in omnibus factis, dictis, in corporis denique motu et statu cernitur idque positum est in tribus rebus, formositate, ordine, ornatu ad actionem apto*; *Fin.* 4.74, *Fam.* 9.14.4; so with sarcastic ambiguity at *Mur.* 61.

38. Likewise, Piso travels with his "slender dancers" (*cum [suis] teneris saltatoribus*) and the three "beautiful brothers" (*formosis fratribus*) Autobolus, Athamas, and Timocles (*Pis.* 89, the example Nicolet 1970: 87 uses to assign *formosus* "a distinct polemical quality"). Cf. *Ver.* 2.1.92, 2.5.63, 73, *Fin.* 2.23. Nepos applies the adjective only to Alcibiades (*Alc.* 1.2) and the young Hasbrudal (*Ham.* 3.2), Lucilius only to Q. Opimius (senior), who *formosus homo fuit et famosus* "a man who had good looks . . . and a reputation to go with it" (11.419 Marx).

39. Hence Cicero's stereotypes: *cur neque deformem adulescentem quisquam amat neque formosum senem?* "Why doesn't anybody find ugly youths or handsome old men attractive?" (*Tusc.* 4.70).

this case, by a clause of his own bill.[40] The law lets him make Pompey's *manubiae* into simple *praeda*, and he will spend the gains on things like precious acolytes—paraded in front of Pompey's stout soldiers. The corrupt governor is again the Unnamed Referent, as in Chapter 2; and the unnamed frame of reference is the semiotics of space.[41]

G-p, which has no correspondent in the senate speech, is ostensibly different in topic: it moves from the *contumelia* of selling Pompey's properties right in front of him to a more serious matter, an assault on his *gratia*. But G-p is really just a gloss on the semiotics of E-p and F-p. These decemvirs are exercising their granted authority: they can, under the terms of the bill, travel freely (*illis in locis vagari*), including in Pompey's own province (*verum etiam ad ipsius exercitum pervenire*), with wide authority over property (*cum imperio, cum iudicio omnium rerum, cum infinita potestate*), and many resources (*cum innumerabili pecunia*; the *cum* phrases are virtually a summary of Cicero's view of the bill). And the decemvirs use that authority aggressively: they weaken Pompey, in effect setting themselves up as alternate patrons, with his resources. Their dimming of Pompey's glory is the political result of the letter that Pompey will read and the display of power and patronage that Pompey's soldiers would see. In short, E-, F- and G-p together have a specific purpose: to dramatize and then gloss the idea of competing legal authorities. To dismiss "the picture of Rullus summoning Pompey by letter, and conducting his auction midway between the two camps" as "too silly and far-fetched to have imposed even upon a Roman mob"[42] is to miss the very precise reflection on the use of power that the two vignettes both contain and to underestimate the ability of a Roman audience to appreciate the semiotics and symbolism of language and of ritual.

G-p, with its talk of *copiae* and *commoda*, and E-p, with its mention of sales, thus make obvious what is in any case implicit, that procedural discourse here

---

40. Gaius Gracchus, on returning from Sardinia, claimed before the people that "no beautiful boys waited [on us]" (*versatus sum in provincia, quomodo ex usu vestro existimabam esse, non quomodo ambitioni meae conducere arbitrabar. Nulla apud me fuit popina neque pueri eximia facie stabant et in convivio liberi vestri modestius erant quam apud principia*, ORF 48.26 = Gel. 15.12.2; the speech is *ad populum cum ex Sardinia rediit*, 124 BCE). Apparently his audience needed reassurance on the point. The senate speech might have made the same imputation: the fragment *imberba iuventute* "beardless youth" (*LA* 1. fr. 1; Charisius p. 95.18–21 Keil) probably also refers to the *finitores*, as Nicolet 1970: 73–74 n. 1 suggested; cf. Manuwald 2018: 292.

41. For the expression of culture through spatial relations, broadly analogous to animal territoriality, see the work of Edward Hall (e.g. 1963, 1969), who coined the term "proxemics."

42. Hardy 1924: 80. Likewise, the details of the letter show that they are not, *pace* Classen 1985: 325, "völlig aus der Luft gegriffenen Einzelheiten" meant to create a dramatic perspective on an otherwise sober list.

reflects anxieties about *commodum*. Supporters of the bill among the people hoped they were creating another patron and protector, as they, on one view, had created Pompey. Cicero wants to reverse that perception. The measures of the bill, on his analysis, reveal that they are creating a rival to Pompey. They are not creating another font of support but simply dividing up a fund they already have. The imagery of the opening of the whole topic should be seen in this light. Cicero there professes to be exercising the duty imposed on him by the people when he was elected praetor: that "[he], together with [the people], protect [Pompey's] dignity in his absence by whatever means [he] could" (*ut, quibuscumque rebus possem, illius absentis dignitatem vobiscum una tuerer*).[43] He concludes the opening thus:

> Accordingly, since I perceive that virtually this entire law is being readied to throw over [Pompey's] resources like a siege engine, I shall resist the plans of these men and I shall certainly make sure that every single one of you can not only see but grasp what I see.
>
> *Quam ob rem, cum intellegam totam hanc fere legem ad illius opes evertendas tamquam machinam comparari, et resistam consiliis hominum et perfuium profecto, quod ego video, ut id vos universi non solum videre verum etiam tenere possitis* (*LA* 2.50).

The bill wants to to "throw over" his resources utterly; the same verb is used for "destroying" cities.[44] The phrase is evidently vivid: *opes evertere*, found nowhere else in Cicero, is used by Vergil only in a forceful line: not the judgment of Paris but "the gods' cruelty, the gods', casts down this prosperity, tears Troy utterly down!" (*divum inclementia, divum, | has evertit opes sternitque a culmine Troiam, Aen.* 2.603). And the image is ironic: what Pompey should be doing literally to Panticapaeum—bringing its walls down with a battering ram—is what the decemvirs will be doing metaphorically to him. But above all the image represents an economic idea: a zero-sum transaction, in which the conquering

---

43. For the immediately preceding passage and the corresponding senate section (*LA* 1.5), see Table 7.2.3.

44. *L&S* s.v. I.B.1.b. cite *urbes* (Cic. *Off.* 1.82), *Carthago* (*Rep.* 6.11), *castellum* (Hor. *Ep.* 2.2.34), *Troia* (Ov. *Met.* 13.169). The phrase does not reappear until the work of later historians: *eversas Assyriorum opes* (Amp. *Lib. Mem.* 12.1), *regum, quorum opes saepius adsentatio quam hostis evertit* (Curt. 8.5.6). *TLL* assigns these instances to those that reflect not "merus sensus vertendi" but "delendi, perdendi, tollendi notio," cf. 5.1031.60–1032.16. For other instances of *evertere* applied to monetary resources, cf. *TLL* 5.1032.42–49; 5.1025.36–41 (*s.v. eversio*).

decemvirs take and the overthrown Pompey gives. Nobody gains unless somebody else loses. That is the frame of reference Cicero meant his listeners to bring to this passage.

The idea of a Pompey diminished is of course not very realistic (perhaps for that reason the argument is located right in the middle of the *argumenta*, where Cicero says the weakest arguments should be housed).[45] He would remain quite able to enrich the treasury, even if the Mithridatic lands came under the control of the decemvirs: the bill excepted Pompey by name from surrendering war spoils to the Rullan project (*LA* 1.13, 2.60–62; Tables 7.2.1 and 7.2.2), and that was no small benefit, as the vast wealth of his triumph two years later would show. But neither is Cicero's image simply unrealistic. If the decemvirs established the terms of exploiting what Pompey had won or recovered, that really would diminish his *copiae*. If the decemvirs were eventually authorized to create colonies abroad (it is not obvious that the Rullan bill itself granted that authority), they might well have settled Pompey's discharged soldiers on that same Asian land; and that really would reduce his *exercitus*. And if Pompey wanted to settle his returning soldiers in Italy, the path to those *commoda* lay through the Rullan commission, which would have control over that land: that would lessen his *gratia*. The intention of the framers was almost certainly to anticipate Pompey's needs; but Cicero makes them out to be snatching an initiative that otherwise lay with Pompey. If they were preparing the way for him, they were also riding his coattails and even stealing credit—and more—and that, in line with the zero-sum vision of the section, is what Cicero draws out.

In short, Cicero turns Pompey himself into a symbol of the bill's empty promises of *commodum*. He uses Pompey to think with. Strikingly and paradoxically, he focalizes the fear of exclusion with tableaux of a diminished Pompey. That conversion is also, or so it seems to me, an inversion, and of a very pointed kind. When the *lex Manilia* transferred the Mithridatic command to Pompey from Lucullus, Pompey, upon arriving in Asia Minor, set about undoing many of his decisions as a show of supremacy (Plu. *Pomp.* 31.1). After an unpleasant meeting with Lucullus in Galatia (31.4),[46] Pompey pitched camp near him, took over as many of his soldiers as he could, and worked to undermine his authority

---

45. "If there are any middling arguments (not flawed arguments; those belong nowhere), it's best to set them somewhere right in the middle of the crowd" (*si quae erunt mediocria, nam vitiosis nusquam esse oportet locum, in mediam turbam atque in gregem coniciantur, de Orat.* 2.314).

46. For an account of the interchange according to the rules of Roman politeness, see Hall 2009: 21–22.

(31.5). Lucullus accused him of being a vulture who fed on bodies others had killed (31.6) and usurping their glory (31.7).[47] Such the clashes of two eagles in the same nest. In the tableaux of Rullus boldly (or rashly) setting up shop near Pompey's camp, his own surveyors in tow; in his imperious letter demanding troops and boasting of selling what Pompey's labor had won; forced to turn over his booty like a common soldier; and enduring a display of power by a greater magistrate, there are distinct echoes of the propaganda war between Pompey and Lucullus.[48] The complaints of the kind that Lucullans laid against Pompey are hung, appropriately adjusted, upon Rullus—but the roles, with no little irony, are reversed: Pompey is the establishment figure and Rullus the disrupter. The template that many in the audience must have already had about the relations between Lucullus and Pompey is refitted to express the relations between Pompey and Rullus—what Quintilian might have called a *mutua accusatio* (*Inst.* 3.10.4 = ἀντικατηγορία).

5.3. THE PURCHASE OF LAND

*multa fidem promissa levant, ubi plenius aequo
laudat venalis qui vult extrudere merces.*

*Too many promises break down trust, when a seller
tries to push his wares with unfair praise.*

—Horace, *Epistles* 2.2.10–12

Cicero draws on the nexus of anxieties about process and providers in another part of the argument. Agrarian bills commonly reclaimed *ager publicus* for settlement. But by Cicero's time there was not much *ager publicus* left, thanks to the agrarian law of 111.[49] The one large parcel remaining, the rich and already occupied *ager Campanus*, along with the neighboring *ager Stellas*, would have been colonized by the bill, probably by subdividing parcels held by current tenants.[50] But it was evidently felt that still more land was needed. The bill thus authorized the purchase of land from private owners. The logic of Cicero's arguments against the idea fall into three sets. The first set is a kind of preliminary

---

47. On Plutarch's narrative priorities in this account, see Wet 1981.

48. Cf. Plu. *Luc.* 35.7.

49. Cf. ch. 1.4 The Rullan Bill.

50. Brunt 1971: 306–309.

argument; the decemvirs' juridical rights and ability to amass money are out of all proportion:

(A) The decemvirs, having gathered a great deal of money (*LA* 1.14, 2.62–3)…
(B) …will use it to purchase land (*LA* 1.14, 2.63).
(C) That means the decemvirs will have broad rights to buy and sell properties (*LA* 1.14, 2.63–64).

(A) is partly summary and not relevant only to the purchase of the land; the set describes a general problem exacerbating the specific problems of the land purchase provisions. The second set of arguments is procedural and legislative: purchasing land from private parties is not a well-established practice, and neither the location nor the quality of the plots is properly specified:

(D) Purchase from Private Owners Violates Tradition (*LA* 2.65)
(E) Location of Properties Unspecified (*LA* 2.66)
(F) Law Permits Uncultivable Property to be Bought (*LA* 2.67)

The third set of arguments, G–L (*LA* 2.68–70), engages with the land purchase provision itself, claiming it creates perverse incentives; these arguments give a particularly clear picture of the persona Cicero crafts for Rullus, and for that reason are treated in Chapter 6, whose theme is the personae of the chief personalities of the speech. This chapter focuses on arguments D–F, which appear only in the popular speech. These addenda, just like the treatment of Pompey (ch. 5.2), draw on the nexus between procedure, profit, and a protector. Like Cicero's treatment of Pompey, the arguments aimed to show that *studium* for ostensibly populist measures is no guarantee of *commoda*. In particular, just as certain procedures of the bill show the decemvirs will challenge, and not supplement, Pompey, so do certain other procedures show that Rullus's bill is selling a bill of goods.

Bad Land

Arguments D–F are found in Table 5.3.1.

Table 5.3.1. Part of the Rhetorical Stucture of the Treatment of the Purchase of Land (*LA* 2.65–67)

ad populum

D. Purchase from Private Owners Violates Tradition

65. . . . Hic ego iam illud quod expeditissimum est ne disputo quidem, Quirites, non esse hanc nobis a maioribus relictam consuetudinem ut emantur agri a privatis quo plebes publice deducatur; omnibus legibus agris publicis privatos esse deductos. Huiusce modi me aliquid ab hoc horrido ac truce tribuno plebis fateor exspectasse; hanc vero emendi et vendendi quaestuosissimam ac turpissimam mercaturam alienam actione tribunicia, alienam dignitate populi Romani semper putavi.

"And I'm not even going to press here a point that would be very easy to make, fellow citizens: that our forefathers did not pass on to us any custom of leading out the plebs to settlements purchased from private persons at public expense; that, instead, under every agrarian law private persons have been led *off* public land! [i] I figured this tribune of the plebs would do something along these lines, fierce and ragged as he is; but I have always thought this kind of lucrative and unethical buying and selling operation was inappropriate for the action of a tribune and beneath the dignity of the Roman people." [ii]

E. Location of Properties Unspecified

Iubet agros emi. 66. Primum quaero, quos agros et quibus in locis? Nolo suspensam et incertam plebem Romanam obscura spe et caeca exspectatione pendere. Albanus ager est, Setinus, Privernas, Fundanus, Vescinus, Falernus, Literninus, Cumanus, † ancasianas †. Audio. Ab alia porta Capenas, Faliscus, Sabinus ager, Reatinus; <ab alia> Venafranus, Allifanus, Trebulanus. Habes tantam pecuniam qua hosce omnis agros et ceteros horum similis non modo emere verum etiam coacervare possis; cur eos non definis neque nominas, ut saltem deliberare plebes Romana possit quid intersit sua, quid expediat, quantum tibi in emendis et in vendendis rebus committendum putet? 'Definio,' inquit, 'Italiam.' Satis certa regio! Etenim quantulum interest utrum in Massici radices, an in Silam silvam aliove deducamini?

(continued)

Table 5.3.1. Continued

"He wants fields to be purchased. My first question is, which fields? In which locations? I don't want the Roman plebs hanging in suspense, unsure, in blind hope and groundless anticipation! (*Pointing south*) [iii] [Look at all] these fields—around Alba, Setia, Privernum, Fundi, Vescia, Mount Falernus, Liternum, Cumae, ... Yes, yes, I know! (*Pointing northwest*) [iv] Out this other gate are the fields around Capena, Falerii, and Reate, and in Sabine country; (*pointing east*) [v] <and out *that* other gate> the fields around Venafrum, Allifae, and Trebula. [Well, Rullus?] You have enough money that you could buy every one of those fields and others like them—and all at once, in a big heap! [vi] So why don't you specify them by name, so the Roman people can at least have a chance to decide what's in their interest, and what suits their purposes, and how much power to buy and sell they think they should entrust you with? "I specify Italy." Oh yes! That's a very specific district! [*to the people*] After all, it doesn't make the slightest bit of difference if you're being settled in the foothills of Massicum, or in the Sila forest or somewhere!"

F. Law Permits Uncultivable Property to be Bought

67. Age, non definis locum; quid? naturam agri? 'Vero,' inquit, 'qui arari aut coli possit.' 'Qui possit arari,' inquit, 'aut coli,' non 'qui aratus aut cultus sit.' Vtrum haec lex est, an tabula Veratianae auctionis? in qua scriptum fuisse aiunt. 'Iugera cc in quibus olivetum fieri potest, iugera ccc ubi institui vineae possunt.' Hoc tu emes ista innumerabili pecunia quod arari aut coli possit? Quod solum tam exile et macrum est quod aratro perstringi non possit? Aut quod est tam asperum saxetum in quo agricolarum cultus non elaboret?

[*to Rullus*] "Okay, so you don't specify the location. What do you specify? The type of land? [*to the people*] 'Quite so,' he says: 'Land that can be plowed and cultivated.' Did you catch that? "That *can* be plowed or cultivated"—not 'that *has been* plowed or cultivated." [*to Rullus or to the people*] What is this—a law, or a notice for one of Veratius's auctions? Supposedly one of the items was: '200 acres, suitable for an olive grove; 300 acres, able to be planted with vines.' [*to Rullus*] So your plan, with all that countless money, is to buy what *can* be plowed or cultivated? [*to Rullus or to the people*] What soil is so thin and poor that it can't be scraped with a plow? What grove of rocks is so rough that the work of farmers can't eke something out of it?"

---

[i] Following Zumpt 1861: 106, who takes *agris publicis* as indicating separation, not destination; *contra* Manuwald 2018: 328, who regards the change in the sense of *deduco* ('to lead to a destination' vs. 'to lead away from a place') as harsh. But the pun, I think, is exactly the point: good agrarian bills 'lead out' colonies to public land (*TLL* 5.1.273.27–80) by 'leading off,' that is, 'formally ejecting' (*OLD* s.v. 1.c, *TLL* 5.1.273.22–26 "de possessore expellendo") private persons that have occupied *ager publicus*. The latter sense of *deduco* also occurs at *LA* 2.68 (Table 7.3.2.H-p.). Cicero has in mind Gracchan-style legislation, in which possessors of *ager publicus* were ejected.

Table 5.3.1. Continued

[ii] Lit. 'foreign to tribunician activity, foreign to the dignity of the Roman people.'

[iii] Pointing toward the *Porta Capena* and the *Via Appia*; the first six locations are all along that road. The road turned east at Sinuessa, but Cicero's *Liternum* shows that in his mind he is continuing south, down what would later be the *via Domitiana*, on which Cumae also lies. The name of the last *ager* in the list is garbled. Zumpt's conjecture *Acerranus* and Clark's *Nucerinus* reference two towns, Acerrae and Nuceria, that would require the path traced by the towns to turn sharply inland or leap to the other side of the bay of Naples, respectively.

[iv] Pointing toward the *Porta Fontinalis* in the Servian wall and the *Via Flaminia*; *Capena* (now La Civitucola) lay between that road and the Tiber, and *Falerii* lay right on the road. Not far past Falerii the road passed into Sabine territory (*ager Sabinus*). Reate was reached most directly by the *via Salaria* but is mentioned here because it was in that territory (Zumpt 1861: 107).

[v] Pointing toward the *Porta Esquilina* and the *Via Labicana*, which joins up with the *via Latina* not far outside of Rome (so Gell 1846: 5–6). Venafrum and Allifae lay on the *via Latina*, and Trebula in a mountain tract which abutted it. The second *ab alia* is thus a reasonable restoration. The *via Labicana*, unlike the *via Latina*, skirted the Alban Hills and so was a less strenuous route leaving Rome (cf. Smith 1854 *s.v. via Labicana*; for a survey of ancient sources and some problems of the topography of the junction, see Thein 2005). As Zumpt 1861: 107 notes, with the three lists of territories "... optimum agrum Italiae urbem Romam situm complectitur." For Vasaly 1993: 227–31 these lists leave Capua as an unnamed endpoint, foreshadowing its prominence in the last of the *argumenta* (treated in ch. 9).

[vi] This is the only instance listed in the *TLL* of *coacervo* in the apparent sense 'heap up' ("in cumulum cogere") used of immobile items ("res immobiles," 3.0.1367.4–6), the *OLD* assigns the use to the sense 'amass' (*s.v.* b). The literal form of the phrase, "not only *emere* but also *coacervare*," shows that *coacervare* must mean something above and beyond ordinary purchasing. 'Purchase all at once'—as it were 'purchase on a single bill of sale'—seems to me to suit the passage. The image is of heaping everything indiscriminately onto one of the plates of a weighing scale, part of the language of the marketplace.

The three addenda are, as it were, all built from the same kit: they each have exactly the same three features. They allege a defect of process; imply that Rullus is a poor guardian or Cicero a good one; and anchor the point by appeal to the semiotics of known points of reference. And the whole set is knitted together by a single governing notion.

The claim of the first addendum, D, is fair enough. Purchasing land from private owners seems to date only to the late 80s,[51] and it had probably also been

---

51. Cf. *CAH*² IX 621, which points out that the first attested distribution of private land follows the civil wars of 83–80 and "even of that the origins often lay in *occupatio*"; Manuwald 2018: 328.

a part of the (failed) *lex Plotia agraria*, a law of 70 or 69 which had Pompey's Spanish veterans in mind.[52] Cicero's moral inference depends on what precedes. He had just pointed out (*LA* 2.64) that the upstanding leaders of the past—men like Luscinus or Calatinus, or more recently Cato and Laelius, whom the people know[53]—had never proposed bills with such a wide array of powers; and they were men of wisdom and restraint (*sapientia, temperantia*), privately and publicly (*in publicis privatisque, forensibus domesticisque rebus*), even to the point of poverty (*paupertas*). That is, Cicero links personal restraint to modest laws; conversely, a law with wide powers must *ipso facto* have self-enrichment in mind. If, in the phrase, *stilus virum arguit*, then so does *lex legislatorem*. That is the idea expressed very precisely in *quaestuosissimam ac turpissimam mercaturam*. This is a trade agreement, not a colonial plan; it is meant not for the good of the people but for personal profit; and it authorizes illegality (that is the apparent sense of *turpis* here, which may describe an action that is legally invalid because it is illicit or immoral; hence my translation 'unethical').[54]

The issue of purchase from private persons is thus a shibboleth for proper guardianship of the people. Cicero is not just against the "trafficking"; rather, it is that "he has always thought" it wrong (*semper putavi*), probably referring to his earlier opposition to the *lex Plotia* (and as if he had resisted it out of respect for the people's rights—a rewriting, as he did with the significance of popular support for the *lex Manilia*). Rullus, by contrast, is true neither to his office nor to the "dignity" of his charges (the not particularly common phrase *dignitas*

---

52. Flach 1990: 71. If Dio 38.5.2, which attributes the failure of a previous land bill to shortfalls in the treasury, refers to Plotius's bill, then that bill would also have authorized purchase from private owners; *ager publicus* was already state property and could probably be transferred with less expense. On Plotius's bill, see Marshall 1972; Smith 1957; Gabba 1950.

53. Cicero's expression is *perspexeratis*; the people "had seen them with their own eyes"; *perspicio* refers to direct observation or analogous actions (*TLL* 10.1.1739.63 "i. q. cernere, percipere, intueri sim.," 1739.70 "imprimis oculis"). The expression here is remarkable. No one in Cicero's audience had seen the persons he names alive: Cato (*cos.* 195), Laelius (*cos.* 140), Furius (*cos.* 136); Luscinus, (*cos.* 282, 278), Attilius Caiatinus, (*cos.* 258), Manlius Acidinus (*cos.* 179; this second set of three are also used as types of virtue elsewhere, cf. Cic. *Mur.* 3). The people before Cicero are, as with the centumviral court, which "they established" (*LA* 2.44, Table 4.4.D-p), the living embodiment of collective historical memory. It is as if someone were to say today of Washington's crossing of the Delaware, "You Americans have always favored the bold attack." Cf. ch. 4 n. 106 on civic memory.

54. So in the later legal tradition; cf. e.g. Ulp. *Dig.* 12.5.4.1 "Likewise if a thief gives [a stolen item] to prevent being reported, since both parties have made an illicit compact, the right to sue for recovery lapses"; *Dig.* 12.5.4.2; Berger *s.v. condicio turpis*. In *turpe iudicium* or *turpis actio* the meaning is not quite identical; the idea is that in such cases, which involved shameful conduct, the penalty was *infamia*.

populi Romani usually invokes the people's civic rights, especially when they are violated).[55] The idea is supported by invoking the meaning of a gesture—or rather, recasting it. Cicero calls Rullus "ragged and fierce" (*horridus et trux*—the only appearance of *trux* in Cicero's prose).[56] That is meant to recall the *propositio* of the speech, where Cicero describes the run-up to Rullus's *contio* to present the bill:

> Finally the tribunes of the plebs take up their offices. People can't wait for P. Rullus's assembly. Not only was he the driving force behind the agrarian bill but he had also been conducting himself more aggressively than the other tribunes. No sooner had he been elected than he affected a different appearance and speech and gait, his clothing worn, his form bedraggled and unkempt, his hair longer and beard thicker than before: all in all, he seemed, by the look of his eyes, to serve notice on everyone of the power of the office of tribune and to threaten the welfare of the state.

> *ineunt tandem magistratus tribuni plebis; contio exspectatur P. Rulli, quod et princeps erat agrariae legis et truculentius se gerebat quam ceteri. Iam designatus alio voltu, alio vocis sono, alio incessu esse meditabatur, vestitu obsoletiore, corpore inculto et horrido, capillatior quam ante barbaque maiore, ut oculis et aspectu denuntiare omnibus vim tribuniciam et minitari rei publicae videretur* (*LA* 2.13).

Rullus's appearance doubtless really did change: the very public nature of Roman politics, in which all the prominent personalities appeared before the people (an aspect of the "visibility" discussed earlier), discouraged inventing details out of whole cloth. The details here suggest mourning garb, a known gesture for eliciting

---

55. So of Verres's beating of Roman citizens (*Ver.* 2.5.144); of Clodius's politics by mob, which relies upon lower elements (*Dom.* 89) and threats of violence (*Red. Sen.* 7); and of the turbulent Antony, whose demise all *boni* hoped for, that the *libertas dignitasque populi Romani* might be restored (*Phil.* 3.19). The *dignitas populi Romani* would also be offended by imagining a Pompey who did not respect oaths, vitiating his vast accomplishments across the face of the earth (*Balb.* 13, with *excellens*), and by blocking the restoration of Cicero's house, when razed houses were a mark of especially heinous crimes (*Dom.* 102). The *nam superioribus capitibus dignitas populi Romani violabatur* of the senate speech, a recapitulatory passage (1.2), appears to refer to the electoral procedure (cf. Table 3.1.C-s).

56. In Cicero the word otherwise only appears in poetic quotes: *capite brevi, cervice anguina, aspectu truci* (Pac. 5W, cited in *Div.* 2.133), *e trucibusque oculis duo fervida lumina flagrant* (*N.D.* 2.107, a translation of Aratus). Is *horrido ac truce* a poetic quote, like *vegrandi macie torridum* (C31 in Appendix 2; discussion in ch. 9.2 Honestum, *fin.*)?

sympathy for a cause.[57] In a time of economic distress Rullus wanted to seem the voice of the poor. Perhaps Rullus thought the gesture a kind of clever historical rejoinder? In 133 the landholders who opposed the agrarian legislation of Tiberius Gracchus had donned mourning garb in protest[58] (and there was, perhaps, a kind of repertoire of remembered populist gestures, like Clodius shutting the *tabernae* in imitation of Tiberius's *iustitium*).[59] But Cicero, just as he did with Sulla's statue, inscribes a new meaning onto the gesture: Rullus had meant to roil the state all along. Shagginess was the sign not of a bleeding heart but, as it turns out, of a deranged mind, ready to trample the dignity of the people and abuse the powers of his office. He might have seemed "unkempt" (*horridus*); but he was really "savage" (also *horridus*), like a highway robber or a stormy sky.[60] If *stilus virum arguit* and *lex legislatorem*, so also *vultus animum*.

E also raises issues of procedure and guardianship and reinforces its point by allusion. In E, Cicero claims that the bill did not specify properties; he is surely right. That was impracticable and, by the bill's terms, impossible. The bill forbade purchases until all monies were gathered, making it unknown how much would be on hand (*LA* 2.71). Owners could not be forced to sell (*LA* 1.15, 2.67, 71), making it unknown which properties would be available. And prices were not fixed in advance (*LA* 1.14, 2.68, 72), making it unknown how much property could be bought. Still, the lack of specificity was potentially suspect: colonial and agrarian bills usually did name sites. Cicero makes the different process of this bill a deliberate act of concealment by Rullus: he refused to specify them by name (*non defini[t] neque nomina[t]*). That makes him a poor guardian: Rullus's vagary means that the people are dangling in blind hope (*obscura spe et caeca expectatione pendere*). That blindness is dramatized by an allusion. The chief question for the people was, is the land good or bad? Cicero represents that polarity with two places that are extreme opposites, the *mons Massicus* and the *Sila silva*. They are opposites in fertility: the *mons Massicus* had famously fine vineyards, but the *Sila*

---

57. Harvey 1972: 32–3; Bell 1997: 13–14. Hopwood 2007: 82 and n. 65 rightly sees Rullus's appearance as revolutionary but misses its semiotic significance in Roman culture, invoking physiognomy and the Cynic philosopher. Achard 1981: 223 groups *horridus* with vocabulary suggesting rusticity.

58. For the resistance of possessors, cf. Cic. *Sest.* 103; on their lamentation and garb, cf. App. *BC* 1.10; Plu. *TG* 10.5–7; for a view of their grounds for resentment, cf. Cic. *Off.* 2.78–79. On the gesture of changing clothing, see Dighton 2017.

59. For the incident, cf. Cic. *Dom.*, esp. 54 and 89; for this interpretation, see Russell 2016.

60. 'Unkempt': *TLL* 6.3.2992.17–49; 'savage' 6.3.2992.82–2993.22. Brigand: *trucem horridumque latronem* ([Quint.] *Decl.* 1.14); sky: *securus aspiciet fulminantis caeli trucem atque horridam faciem* (Sen. *Nat.* 6.32.4).

silva—its very name seems to mean simply 'The Forest'—was a woodland.[61] And they are opposites in accessibility, with all that that implies for exporting crops: the vineyards were on the south edge of Latium on the *via Appia*; the forest, in the "instep" of the Italian boot off the *via Popilia*. The stark difference—marked, with ironic acidity, by *quantulum*, lit. 'how very little' (a word that appears only twice elsewhere in Cicero's oratory)[62]—draws out the steep risk of unclarity. The *Sila silva* is an allusion to the memory of Sulla's colonies: some veterans complained that they had been "relegated to swamps and forests."[63] As Cicero turned the substance of complaints against Pompey into complaints against Rullus, here he turns complaints against Sulla's scheme into a defect of Rullus's plans. The allusion is not simple spitefulness. Some of the private land that Rullus's commission would buy would very likely have some from unprofitable land originally granted to Sulla's colonists.[64] On this count Rullus is (!) a new Sulla.

Cicero is by contrast a good guardian. In particular he alludes to—or rather virtually adopts—the role of a tribune. He is an aggressive defender of the people. That is the message of the shifting addressees. Cicero addresses the people (*Quirites*), then Rullus (*habes... possis... definis... tibi*), then the people (*deducamini*), then Rullus (*definis*), then once again the people (*inquit*), and once again Rullus (*emes*). This, rather like the auction in the popular speech or Rullus's letter to Pompey, is a script for playacting. Rullus was surely present and surely visible to Cicero. He harangues him in the fashion of the *contio*.[65] Cicero also understands the people's values. He is the defender of (here, a fairly conventional) *libertas*, an Unnamed Referent here. Thus he acknowledges the people's civic role: the plebs are to 'deliberate' (*deliberare*), a nod to (and an exaggeration of) open procedure.[66] (And that capacity is specially accented: *deliberare* is moved forward in the sentence (*ut saltem **deliberare***

---

61. *Sila* (*Sila silvam* is the conjecture of Müller 1892 *ad loc.* for the *italiam* of the MSS) probably meant simply 'the Forest' in the local Italic dialect (not standard Oscan, which preserves *-lw, cf. *selva*). Strabo (6.1.9) calls it "well-wooded and well-watered" (εὔδενδρός τε καὶ εὔυδρος). The forest was apparently, at least in points, open enough to allow grazing: cf. *pascitur in magna Sila formosa iuvenca*, Verg. G. 3.219; *A.* 2.715–19 imagines bulls fighting in that "vast" (*ingenti*) wood.

62. *Ver.* 3.3.231, *Div. Caec.* 57.

63. *Relegati in paludes et silvas*, Sal. *Or. Lep.* (*Hist.* 1.49M) 23 (an imagined speech of M. Aemilius Lepidus). Cf. Brunt 1971: 310–11. There is no doubt rhetorical exaggeration in the complaint; but some land surely was only partly drained or poorly drained (a "swamp") or in need of clearing work (a "forest").

64. For more detail on Sullan land, see ch. 7.3 The Voices of the (Un-)Tribune.

65. On the treatment of opponents by the convener of a *contio*, see Morstein-Marx 2004: 163–78.

66. *OLD s.v.* 1 'to engage in careful thought (usu. in consultation with others).' This is the only time the word appears in the agrarian speeches, except for *praesertim cum mihi deliberatum et*

plebes Romana possit); a complementary infinitive rarely precedes both subject and governing verb). He also acknowledges the people's constitutional authority: the final shape of the bill ought to reflect "how much power ... they think they should entrust [the decemvirs] with" (*quantum tibi ... committendum putet*). Last, he sympathizes with the people's values. *Intersit* and *expediat* ("what's in their interests" and "what suits their purposes"), paired only here in Cicero's oratory, are a kind of emphatic gloss on *commodum*, the watchword of populist politics.

These allusions to *libertas* are doubtless not much different from what other speakers did in popular contexts; *libertas* was the coin of that realm. But Cicero anchors his tribunician persona in a deeply suggestive gesture. He doesn't only complain about possible poor sites; he also lists possible good ones, naming one *ager* after another. But he names the *agri* in groups by direction, using city gates as markers. He must have gestured to each gate in turn, as I have suggested by the "blocking notes" in my translation. Cicero was thereby representing, with exactitude, the meaning of an agrarian bill: a magistrate sending citizens forth from the city gates to new, and clearly specified, colonies. Cicero surely had in mind the beginning of the formal ritual of colonization, where that is precisely what happened.[67] In short, Cicero acts out the role of a proper tribune. In that playlet there is also another mark of deference to, or at least cooperation with, the people. I take *audio* to mean that audience members (or claqueurs?),[68] having heard the names of districts lying to the south, responded by shouting out suitable territories to the north ("Yeah! Right! And what about ... ?"). On that view *audio* expresses Cicero's recognition and assent, just like English "I hear you" and like expressions, whence my rendering "Yes, yes, I know!" It is Cicero who truly hears the people's voices—figuratively and literally.

F continues the same tropes present in D and E. It questions the integrity of a measure of the bill. The language of the law permitted the purchase of uncultivated land (*qui possit arari aut coli*, lit. "that can be plowed or cultivated"). It may have been a regular, or at any rate precedented, practice to assign not cultivated but cultivable land. That would perforce have been the case whenever grazing land

---

constitutum sit ... from the *peroratio* of the senate speech (1.25; Cicero has "decided after careful consideration" that he will not accept a province or any other distinction a tribune is able to impede).

67. For the rituals of departing for a colony, cf. Gargola 2009: 67–70. On the management of colonization rituals, which may have normally included a consul, see Piña-Polo 2011: 180 with refs.

68. On claqueurs at assemblies, see Morstein-Marx 2004: 133–35; on the importance of shouting and other signs of approbation (or the reverse), see Bell 1997: 21 n. 149. *OLD s.v.* 12 takes *audio* as 'I am satisfied,' followed by Manuwald 2018: 331.

was converted to ploughland; and a law of Augustus apparently meant such land could be assigned.[69] But Cicero makes the clause, which might really have sparked legal disputes,[70] also into an act of deliberate deception. He puts the citation of the law into Rullus's mouth, thus making it his intentional design; and then he explicates his own ventriloquism (a neat trick). The explication depends on an ambiguity. The *possit* of the law meant 'is suitable for'; but it could mean 'is at all capable of.' The latter meaning is imposed on the law by Cicero's paraphrases, in which the law's *arari* 'plow' becomes *aratro perstringi* "scratch with a plow," with a word that means 'graze the surface,' and the law's *coli* 'tend' becomes *agricolarum cultus elabor[a]t* "eked out by the work of farmers," with a word that means 'take pains, secure by effort.' The effect is like restating English "that can be plowed" with "that *cáaàn* be plowed?" with a protracted vowel and rise-fall intonation.

The words of Rullus's law prove he is a huckster. As in the other two passages, Cicero anchors the idea by allusion. The otherwise unknown Veratius (or Neratius), it seems, cheerfully imagined where vineyards and olive groves might someday be, like the real estate agent whose "cozy fixer-upper" is a cramped and ramshackle cottage.[71] Cicero explains the joke, but doubtless some of the Forum crowd would have gotten it anyway. More important, they knew the kind of thing: the auction houses were just northwest of the Forum.[72] Perhaps Cicero gestured toward those houses as he did to the gates. As with the centumviral court, Cicero draws on his audience's familiarity with places and procedures. Rullus's gleaming promises, if you look at them close, are really venal exaggerations of the kind you can hear just

---

69. On this clause of Rullus's bill, see Havas 1976: 133, Ferrary 1988: 157–58. The title of Augustus's law was *qua falx et arater ierit* "Where the scythe and plough have gone" (Hyg. *limit.* 73.1, Hyg. Gr. *constit. limit.* p. 164.6, 166.10), which closely resembles the Rullan bill's *qui arari aut coli possit* (Ferrary 1988: 158). On the Augustan law, see Maganzani 2019, Brunt 1971: 296–97.

70. Hyginus notes of the Augustan law, "This law has a particular meaning: some people think it means solely cultivated land; in my opinion it means that usable land must be assigned, so that no one is assigned a parcel that is entirely woodland or pastureland" (*Haec lex habet suam interpretationem. Quidam putant tantum cultum nominari; ut mihi videtur, utile<m> ait agrum adsignare oportere. Hoc erit ne accipienti silvae universus modus adsignetur aut pascui, const. limit.*, 166.13–15).

71. Gel. 20.1.13 quotes Favorinus quoting Marcus Antistius Labeo referring to a Lucius Veratius who, "for a goof" (*pro delectamento*), would slap free men in the face and then immediately give them 25 *asses*—the fine for assault stipulated in the Twelve Tables (8.4). If that's our man, he enjoyed following the letter of the law and not the spirit. The form *Veratianae* adds to the effect; the adjective (*Veratianus*) serving for the genitive (*Veratii*) has a special home in commercial and legal relations; cf. Radford 1902.

72. The *Atria Licinia* were at the entrance to the *Macellum* or Marketplace (Cic. *Quinct.* 25; Serv. *Aen.* 1.726; Coarelli 1983: 32).

up the street. The name for the place that dogged farmers can scrape with their ploughs, *saxetum*, is perhaps also an allusion. The provenance of the word is rustic. The suffix *-etum* normally marks groves of trees and plants, like *querc-etum* 'oak forest,' *fic-etum* 'fig plantation,' *castan-etum* 'chestnut grove,' and must for obvious reasons have been common in country speech. Its tone here is probably also colloquial; that seems to be the tone when *-etum* is used with things other than plants.[73] That gives *saxetum* here a sense less like simply 'a rocky place' (the ordinary words for 'rocky' are *saxosus* or *scopulosus*)[74] than 'a field of rocks' or 'a grove of rocks.' But whatever the tone of *saxetum* precisely, its reference was specific. Cicero had pointed south, northwest, and east; now, I suggest, he pointed northeast. Out the *Porta Viminalis* was the *via Tiburtina* that led past the quarries in the Tiber valley, at the sites now called Salone and Grotta Oscura;[75] out the *Porta Collina* was the *via Salaria* that led to Fidenae some four miles away, on its scarped hill with neighboring stone pits.[76] Does *saxetum* even allude to a *Saxetum*, a proper name like *Argiletum*, of a now forgotten town?[77] Rullus does not have the spirit of a true tribune: he will not send you to Alba, or to Capena, or to Venafrum; he will send you to Rock Grove, just up the road there; you know the place.

The three addenda have a unifying theme: illicit sale (*turpissima*, D); buying and selling (*emendi et vendendi*, D; *in emendis et in vendendis rebus*, F); commerce (*mercaturam*, D); the mention of an auction house (F); the calculation of differing values (*quantulum interest*, E); unclear or misleading allegations about property (*non definis atque nominas*, E; *non definis locum*, F; *vero, inquit, 'qui . . .'* etc., F); assessing how much a certain sum will buy (*habes tantum pecuniam, qua . . .*, E); (probably) 'heaping things [onto a scale]' (*coacervare*, E)—even ventriloquizing Rullus (*'definio . . .'* E, *'vero' inquit*, F)—all this language is meant

---

73. Cooper 1895: 78 notes that "very rare and especially vulgar are the words formed by analogy from words other than names of trees, plants, etc.," citing *Argiletum* ('place of white clay,' a district in Rome), *olenticetum* ('stinking place' = a 'dungheap,' Apul. *Apol.* 8), and *busticetum* ('place of cremations,' Arn. *adv. nat.* 1.41, 7.15). For a survey of names in *-etum*, see Mayer 1954.

74. *L&S s.v.* render simply 'rocky place,' cf. *aspretum* 'rough place,' in the classical period only in Livy (9.24.6, 9.35.2, etc.) and Grattius (*Cyn.* 240); the *OLD* gives 'quarry.' The word is attested very rarely, otherwise only in Columella (*loca aprica, calculosa, glareosa, interdum et saxeta amat*, 5.10.9, of the fig tree), who also may have used *glabreta* 'bare places' (a variant reading at 2.9.9).

75. Heiken et al. 2013: 45–47; for the precise location of Grotta Oscura and Salone, see Russell 2013: 26, 50.

76. The quarries at Fidenae were the source of the stones in the Servian Wall. On the quarries, cf. Vitr. 2.7.1, Quilici and Quilici Gigli 1986.

77. Some 30 km southwest of Trieste as the crow flies, in what was Gallia Cisalpina, is the Slovenian town of Zazid < Ital. *Sasseto* < L. *Saxetum*.

to recall *emptio venditio*, the process of buying and selling, with its attendant legal obligations.[78] That is the Unnamed Referent here. It sets the roles of the principals: Cicero adopts the manner of a skeptical friend helping the people shop and ventriloquizes Rullus as a tricky seller praising his goods *plenius aequo*, to quote the Horace of the epigraph.[79] And the exchange recalls a particular obligation: the seller was liable for his allegations about the property (*dicta et promissa*) and was supposed to be acting in good faith (*bona fides*). But Rullus has a designed a law that lets him make false claims in bad faith—a corrupt law, that in effect, overrides the edicts of the *aediles curules* that governed the marketplace.[80] False promises break down trust. You know the kind of thing.

Home Sweet Home

The arguments which follow *LA* 2.67 = Table 5.3.1.F, what I described above as the third set (arguments G–L), appear in both speeches and are treated fully in Chapter 7.3. In them Cicero decries the perverse incentives of the bill: it compensates occupiers of public land, when they might have been simply ejected, and it allows possessors of infertile or swampy land to sell it to the resettlement project. In the popular speech the arguments are summarized and capped with an element that has no direct correspondent in the senate speech: a dramatization of the choice that now confronts the people. The amplification depends on the now familiar nexus between profit, process, and providers—but with some twists (Table 5.3.2).

Table 5.3.2. Part of the Rhetorical Structure of the Treatment of the Purchase of Land (*LA* 2.71)

---

ad populum

M. Staying in Rome (or not)

Vos vero, Quirites, si me audire voltis, retinete istam possessionem gratiae, libertatis, suffragiorum, dignitatis, urbis, fori, ludorum, festorum dierum, ceterorum omnium commodorum, nisi forte mavoltis relictis his rebus atque hac luce rei publicae in Sipontina siccitate aut in Salapinorum pestilentia{e finibus}Rullo duce conlocari.

(continued)

---

78. For a full account of *emptio venditio*, see Zimmerman 1990: 230–337; on the development of the legal theory of contract by Roman jurists, Fiori 2013: 40–75. For an example of the sale of defective property, used to illustrate the difference between *ius* and *aequitas*, cf. Cic. *Off.* 3.67.

79. On Roman law as manifest in the epigraph, see Carrasco García 2017.

80. On the aediles' edict and aedilician competencies, see Garofalo 1989.

Table 5.3.2. Continued

Aut dicat quos agros empturus sit; ostendat et quid et quibus daturus sit. Vt vero, cum omnis urbis, agros, vectigalia, regna vendiderit, tum harenam aliquam aut paludes emat, id vos potestis, quaeso, concedere?

The Choice to Remain. "But, fellow citizens! Please listen to me and preserve your *present* possession: influence [and] liberty, voting [and] stature; the city [and] the forum; the games [and] festival days, [and] all [your] other benefits. Or maybe you prefer leaving all these things and this light of the republic, to be planted, under the leadership of Rullus, in the midst of the deserts of Sipontum, or in the pestilence {districts} of the people of Salapia?"

The Choice to Leave. "The alternative is for Rullus to say which parcels he intends to purchase and show what he's handing out and to whom. But if his plan is to sell off every city and land and tax property and kingdom just to buy some sand pit or some swamp—tell me, how can you possibly allow him do so?"

Familiar elements appear. The procedures of the bill are deeply flawed: they allow too much money to be gathered (Rullus's having sold "every city," etc., refers to the fund-raising measures of the bill); they don't specify where the lands will be; the lands will be poor. As distinct from the rock groves and thick forests that the other clauses of the law (according to Cicero) guarantee, the Sullan possessors will sell off land that is barren or pestilential (*harenam aliquam aut paludes*). As with *saxetum* and *Sila silva*, Cicero makes the types of land memorable by names. The two named locations—both in Apulia, across the Apennines from Rome—symbolize the defects of aridity or swampiness. Sipontum lay at the edge of the north Apulian plain, which was dry in the summer.[81] Salapia was wet and swampy: the land lay near a coastal lagoon (the very name seems to mean 'Saltwater').[82] Colonies in those places had indeed struggled. The names reverse the ritual of colonization recalled in D. The Apulian toponyms must have sounded non-Latin to many in the audience (*Sip-ont-ina* ~ *Sip-ont-um* with the [Messapic?] *-untum* suffix of Apulian place names, e.g. *Butuntum, Hydruntum*;

---

81. *Pauper aquae Daunus*, Hor. *Carm.* 3.30.11; *siticulosae Apuliae*, *Epod.* 3.16. Also of note is the excellence of the Apulian onion, second only to the African (*post hos [bulbos] in Africa nati maxime laudantur, mox Apuli*, Plin. *Nat.* 19.95): onions do best in light and well-drained soil.

82. **Sal-ap-ia*, where **-ap-* may derive from the **h₂ep-* in Skt. *āpas* (**h₂óp-es*) 'waters,' Osc. *āpā* (**h₂ēp-eh₂*) 'water' or from the **h₂ékʷ-* in L. *aqu-a* with the Sabellic outcome of the labiovelar.

and *Salapia*, a southern-accented *Salaquia*). If Rullus is the one to lead you out the gates (*Rullo duce*), he will plant (*conlocari*) you out there somewhere, over the hills and far away—in the "Far'st" or "Okefenokee" or "Salt-woar."[83]

Thus is Rullus, yet again, a poor guardian. But there is also a change of accent in the idea. Here the people have it in their power to reject him: it is within their constitutional authority (*id vos potestis . . . concedere?*). Here the people are configured not as passive beneficiaries only but as active granters of power; *commodum* is linked to a thoughtful use of the constitutional or procedural branch of *libertas*. Cicero's posture of guardianship differs correspondingly. As before, he calls for clarity (*dicat . . . ostendat*); but now he is also only an advisor, and the people must choose to take his advice (*si me audire voltis*). That advice is to reject the deceptive lawcraft that leads to poor material results and embrace the established procedure that has already led—look around!—to fine results. That is the point of the list. The "piling up"—the figure is *congeries*[84]—is not a hodgepodge. The list ends with collective material pleasures (*ludorum, festorum dierum, ceterorum omnium commodorum*). And the list begins with political abstractions: *gratiae, libertatis; suffragiorum, dignitatis* "influence and liberty; voting and stature." The abstractions are probably meant to be alternating pairs, whence my punctuation and translations: individual choices (*gratia*, in the sense 'capacity to grant favors'; *suffragia*) and the collective possessions that make those choices possible (*libertas; dignitas* in the sense 'sovereignty').[85] This is exactly the same conception of the electoral calculus that underlies *LA* 2.16–17 and 2.21 (ch. 5.1): the abstractions represent the aggregate of individual calculations of maximal personal advantage;

---

83. The specific sites do not really support Cicero's argument. A colony at Sipontum had indeed failed; but it was refounded in 186 and was probably thereafter the site of further settlements—stable enough, it seems (Liv. 34.45.1–5, colony of 194; Liv. 39.23.3, refoundation in 186). Sipontum was important enough to be a point of contention between Antonius and Agrippa in 40 (D.C. 48.27.5–28.1). Strabo describes the Apulian plain as fertile (πάμφορός τε καὶ πολύφορος, 6.3.9 [p. 284]), and Varro owned transhumant sheep there, doubtless their winter pastures (Var. *R.* 2.1.6; Smith 1854: 164 col. 2 *s.v.* Apulia). The Salpini had indeed abandoned their town—but to resettle "in a healthful clime," they had only had to go some four miles inland (*itaque nunc Salpini quattuor milia passus progressi ab oppido veteri habitant in salubri loco*, Vitr. 1.4.12, Sallares 2002, 264–66; the date of abandonment is unknown). Cicero has in mind not the colonies but the general characteristics of Apulia and (in my view) the regional sound of the names.

84. συναθροισμός. Quint. *Inst.* 8.4.27 cites Cic. *Lig.* 9: *quid enim tuus ille, Tubero, destrictus in acie Pharsalica gladius agebat? cuius latus ille mucro petebat? qui sensus erat armorum tuorum? quae tua mens, oculi, manus, ardor animi? quid cupiebas? quid optabas?* ("And what was your drawn sword doing in the battleline at Pharsalus, Tubero? Whose flank was its point aiming for? What did your weapons feel? Your mind, your eyes, your hands, your fighting spirit—what were they? What did you want? What were you hoping for?").

85. Cf. Table 3.1 n. ii.

the material pleasures are the maximal communal advantage. But here there is no threat of division like that posed by Rullus's electoral mechanism; rather, the mechanisms the people already have—their influence and their votes and so on—lead to the results they already have (*istam*): games and feast days and the rest. All that is not so many properties (*possessiones*, plural) scattered hither and yon, but a single possession indivisible (*possessionem*, singular), better than so many plots of land.

And as in the other sections there is a powerful symbol for the idea: the "city" and "forum" (*urbis, fori*) themselves. They are the bridge between the two ends of the list and partake of the character of both: they are, in a sense, abstractions, the venues and metonyms of social and political life; but they are also material benefits, themselves impressive to see and experience. The symbols are aptly chosen. Cicero and the people were then in the very heart of the city, the Forum, where (parts of) public festivals and games took place and where (some) judicial, legislative, and electoral procedures were held. A metaphor enhances the idea. The whole *congeries* is summarized as "[all] these things and this light of the republic" (*his rebus et hac luce rei publicae*). *Lux* is not uncommon for the beauty of civic life.[86] *Lux* is also a favorite word of Cicero's for praising aspects of Roman life, and there are overtones of that use here, too.[87] But its use here is especially apt. The people oversee procedure: they are a light shining on it. And there are benefits to that role that they can see: it is a light for them. As Cicero pointed to the gates while he named possible settlements, he surely swept an arm across the scene as he spoke these words, encouraging the people to keep what they could see and all that it meant. Stock metaphors, like programmatic words, should also be examined for their resonances with the local context.

The polarity of the choice Cicero represents—"all this" versus "who knows what"—is of course specious. The opposite of "bad land" need not have been the "good city"; it could have been "good land" (and that is the promise of the *ager Campanus*, treated in ch. 9). And the city, with its crowding, irregular employment, and competition for resources, among other problems, was hardly an unqualified "good." But the polarity is meant to have a particular effect, which becomes clear in the light of this chapter and of Chapter 4. The passages analyzed in Chapter 4 developed the procedural side of *libertas*, in particular on the idea of the centrality of the popular assembly. In them the people were implicitly active,

---

86. *TLL* 7.2.1909.40–1920.5, cf. 7.2.1909.41-2 "in circumscribendo statu animantium vel rerum publico, aperto, libero sim. (immiscetur color gloriae . . .)."

87. *TLL* 7.2.1915.21–3 "pertinet ad quamlibet gloriam, salutem, felicitatem (adamat Cic[ero] in rebus Romanis celebrandis . . .)."

overseeing governance. The passages analyzed in this chapter evoke the practical side of *libertas*, that is, *commodum*, the expectation that public policy will yield personal gains. In them the people are largely passive, awaiting the delivery of benefits that they authorized. *LA* 2.71 represents a kind of blend of these strands. The people are here active, exercising sovereignty—but to reject, not to create. They are not voting something new into existence; they are voting it down. The action that Cicero enjoins on them is ultimately inaction; he rallies their populist energies to conservatism. That is why Cicero concentrates on pleasures like games and feast days, which were not simply spectacles but also featured banquets and largesse: those are exactly the places where *commodum* and the status quo already intersect; those—and even elections, which were a time for bribery[88]—are *commoda* that are already in hand, unlike the airy promises of the auction house, which turn out to be woodlands and swamps, the shams of a huckster and faithless guardian.

5.4. CONCLUSION

In short, Cicero's approach in the passages considered in this chapter plays against a materialist politics. His objective is to raise doubts about the *commoda* the bill will provide. There are more narrowly materialist doubts. What if Pompey gets less—won't I get less, too? What if the bill purchases poor land—is that what I will get, as it were on the edge of Atchafalaya or in the middle of Maine? What if I end up in Apulia—will it be endless toil in a desert with no festal days? And there are broader doubts. What if Pompey is hampered—will populist policies be stalled, too? What else will the intemperate powers behind the bill have a go at? Is hope foolish—isn't a bird in the hand worth two in the bush? Cicero will not have inspired each of those questions in each listener; but if he inspired enough of those questions in enough of them, then he created another current of resistance to the bill.

To raise those doubts Cicero probes certain measures of the bill from the perspective of procedure. He exploits a nexus already present in the minds of his audience, in which hopes and anxieties about personal gain were absorbed into questions of procedure and process, which thus became a proxy discourse for economics. The rhetorical exploitation of that discourse was, one might surmise, common enough, precisely because the nexus already existed in the minds of the audience; it was a button there to push, not a button that Cicero wired up. But Cicero refits and amplifies the idea. He appeals allusively to the semiotic charge

---

88. Yakobson 1992: 51; on *divisores*, see n. 14.

of various social practices and to known points of reference in order to highlight what are for him the key issues: authority, used well (himself, leading out colonies) or ill (Rullus, writing haughtily to Pompey and planting an auction platform on Pompey's turf); the untrustworthiness of the bill (with its exaggerated auctioneer's language and its sponsor, whose apparent display of tender-heartedness was really a threat hiding in plain sight); the thrum and flatness of the names of distant locales; and *commodum* (the beauties of the Forum itself, which symbolizes a fusion of political liberty and shared material pleasures). In most of those appeals Cicero comes off as the people's true protector. And that usurps the role that the sponsor of an agrarian bill might otherwise claim. Here, then, in the now familiar pattern, is another inversion. If the people, as Cicero would have it, were bathed in the light of their rights and their privileges, they could also see Cicero, enacting, by his very presence and by his treatment of them, the light of liberty—a *consul popularis*. That is, also at issue here is Cicero's ethos—one topic of Chapter 6.

6

Ideologies of Identity

CICERO AND RULLUS

6.1. INTRODUCTION

Secerni autem blandus amicus a vero et internosci tam potest adhibita diligentia quam omnia fucata et simulata a sinceris atque veris. Contio, quae ex imperitissimis constat, tamen iudicare solet quid intersit inter popularem, id est assentatorem et levem civem, et inter constantem et severum et gravem.

With careful attention, the false friend can be distinguished from the true just like everything faked and false can be told from the true and honest. A public assembly, which consists of the completely uneducated, can nonetheless tell the difference between a populist, which is to say a flatterer and fickle citizen, and a steady, serious, and authoritative one.

—Cicero, *de Amicitia* 95

Thus far I have concentrated mostly on Cicero's configurations of his audiences. But inevitably aspects of the personas of Rullus and Cicero have also emerged. This chapter examines those personas directly. Its first focus is the accounts of two elections: Cicero's, which is a major theme of the *exordium* (*LA* 2.1–10), and the decemvirs', which is the first topic of the body of the speech (*LA* 2.16–19). The import of those accounts can only now be made fully clear: they depend crucially on the techniques that previous chapters have revealed—in particular, allusion, inversion, and repurposing. Alertness to those techniques reveals the workings of their form: both accounts are, one might say, like a typical ode of Horace, which, by a kind of arc, begins in one place and by following implications and introducing modulations ends in quite another. From those modulations distinctive personas appear: Cicero, a *consul popularis*, who is bound to the people but not a partisan *popularis* (the famous phrase is not a one-off slogan but captures an idea deeply woven into fabric of the *exordium*); and his antitype Rullus, who is bound to a profiteering cabal—a *tribunus nobilis*, as it were, if *nobilis* has the unsavory connotations of populist rhetoric. Both types are, as it were, against type.[1] In those personas, in turn, appear the ideological categories of the late 60s and Cicero's struggles to negotiate them—to appear *constans* and *gravis* and not a *levis civis* and *assentator*.

6.2. (RE)READING CICERO'S ELECTION

in referenda autem gratia hoc vobis repromitto semperque praestabo, mihi neque in consiliis de re publica capiendis diligentiam neque in periculis a re publica propulsandis animum neque in sententia simpliciter ferenda fidem neque in hominum voluntatibus pro re publica laedendis libertatem nec in perferendo labore industriam nec in vestris commodis augendis grati animi benivolentiam defuturam.

In repaying my gratitude to you, I promise you in return my constant effort: careful attention in taking political positions; courage in repelling dangers from the state; trustworthiness in offering my honest opinion; a willingness to confront views not in the public interest; a strong work ethic; and, in my gratitude, a favorable disposition to policies that increase your advantages.

—Cicero, *Post Reditum ad Quirites* 24

At the very beginning of *de lege agraria* II, Cicero describes the kind of speech typically given by newly elected consuls—and the difficulties that those requirements pose in his own case, a man without noble forebears having to speak of himself; and he gives an account of his own remarkable election: he is a *novus homo*, the first member of his family to be elected consul;[2] he was elected *suo anno* "in his own year," that is, in the first year he could legally run; and he was returned virtually by acclamation, without the usual need to count ballots (Table 6.2.1).

---

1. Cf. Yakobson 2010: 200: "The populace had to choose which 'friend of the people' to believe: a consul acknowledging that he had no illustrious ancestors to recommend him (2.1) or a tribune of the plebs who took pride in being a noble (2.20)."

2. See n. 7.

Table 6.2.1. The *exordium* of *LA* 2 (§§1–4)

ad populum

A. The established practice

1. Est hoc in more positum, Quirites, institutoque maiorum, ut ei qui beneficio vestro imagines familiae suae consecuti sunt eam primam habeant contionem, qua gratiam benefici vestri cum suorum laude coniungant.

"The long-established practice of our forebears, fellow citizens, is that those who have achieved noble status for their family by your benefaction hold an assembly to express their gratitude to you even as they include praise of their own relations."

B. Cicero on his ancestors

Qua in oratione non nulli aliquando digni maiorum loco reperiuntur, plerique autem hoc perficiunt ut tantum maioribus eorum debitum esse videatur, unde etiam quod posteris solveretur redundaret. Mihi, Quirites, apud vos de meis maioribus dicendi facultas non datur, non quo non tales fuerint quales nos illorum sanguine creatos disciplinisque institutos videtis, sed quod laude populari atque honoris vestri luce caruerunt.

"Some people, in speeches of that kind, do sometimes appear worthy of their ancestors; but most end up showing instead that so much is owed to their ancestors that there was enough left over to pay to their descendants, too. For my part, fellow citizens, I do not have ancestors that I can speak about before you—not because there were never the kind of men that you see me to be, who am after all born of their blood and schooled in their ways; but rather because they lacked popular affirmation and the light that your honor provides."

C. Cicero on himself

2. De me autem ipso vereor ne adrogantis sit apud vos dicere, ingrati tacere. Nam et quibus studiis hanc dignitatem consecutus sim memet ipsum commemorare perquam grave est, et silere de tantis vestris beneficiis nullo modo possum. Qua re adhibebitur a me certa ratio moderatioque dicendi, ut quid a vobis acceperim commemorem, qua re dignus vestro summo honore singularique iudicio sim, ipse modice dicam, si necesse erit, vos eosdem existimaturos putem qui iudicavistis.

"Simply speaking about myself, on the other hand, would be arrogant—but then not doing so would be ungrateful. For me to recount myself the pursuits by which I achieved the dignity of this office would be disagreeable; at the same time to say nothing about your great benefactions is impossible. For that reason I will aim for a certain balance in my speech: what I have received from you, I will recount fully; but why I have proven worthy of the extraordinary judgment of the highest office you can bestow, I will explain with due modesty, confident that, if circumstances require, you, too—who after all made the judgment—will share the assessment."

(continued)

Table 6.2.1. Continued

D. *Novus homo*

3. Me perlongo intervallo prope memoriae temporumque nostrorum primum hominem novum consulem fecistis et eum locum quem nobilitas praesidiis firmatum atque omni ratione obvallatum tenebat me duce rescidistis virtutique in posterum patere voluistis.

"I stand here before you, the first 'new man' in a very long time—practically within living memory—that you have made consul; the bastion that the nobility had long kept under heavy guard and completely walled in you cut your way into under my leadership, intending that it lie forever open to candidates of talent."

E. Elected *suo anno*

Neque me tantum modo consulem, quod est ipsum per sese amplissimum, sed ita fecistis quo modo pauci nobiles in hac civitate consules facti sunt, novus ante me nemo. Nam profecto, si recordari volueritis de novis hominibus, reperietis eos qui sine repulsa consules facti sunt diuturno labore atque aliqua occasione esse factos, cum multis annis post petissent quam praetores fuissent, aliquanto serius quam per aetatem ac per leges liceret; qui autem anno suo petierint, sine repulsa non esse factos; me esse unum ex omnibus novis hominibus de quibus meminisse possimus, qui consulatum petierim cum primum licitum sit, consul factus sim cum primum petierim, ut vester honos ad mei temporis diem petitus, non ad alienae petitionis occasionem interceptus, nec diuturnis precibus efflagitatus, sed dignitate impetratus esse videatur.

"And not only have you made me consul, which is impressive in and of itself, but you did so in a way in which few nobles have ever been made consul in this state, and no new man until me. If you will take a moment to recall all the new men, this is what you will find: some became consul in their first campaign—but only after years of work and on the right slate (lit. "at some opportunity"), and in a run for office many years after their praetorships, and somewhat later than their age and the law allowed; those who ran the first year they could, on the other hand, never succeeded in their first campaign. I am the only new man in our history (lit. "that we can recall") who ran for consul as soon as it was legal and was elected consul the first time he ran. And that implies something about the honor you have bestowed upon me: that it was sought at the right moment in my life—not opportunistically tacked onto someone else's campaign; and that it was won, not by years of urgent entreaties, but in recognition of a justified request (*dignitate impetratus*)."

Table 6.2.1. Continued

F. Elected by acclamation

Est illud amplissimum quod paulo ante commemoravi, Quirites, quod hoc honore ex novis hominibus primum me multis post annis adfecistis, quod prima petitione, quod anno meo, sed tamen magnificentius atque ornatius esse illo nihil potest, quod meis comitiis non tabellam vindicem tacitae libertatis, sed vocem vivam prae vobis indicem vestrarum erga me voluntatum ac studiorum tulistis. Itaque me non extrema diribitio[ii] suffragiorum, sed primi illi vestri concursus, neque singulae voces praeconum, sed una vox universi populi Romani consulem declaravit.

"What I have just detailed—that I am the first new man in many years to whom you have granted this honor, in my first campaign, and in the first year I was allowed—is indeed very impressive, fellow citizens; but nothing can be more splendid and distinctive than this: when I was elected, you offered as a sign of your support and enthusiasm for me not the ballot, the silent champion of your liberty,[i] but your living voice. I was declared consul not by the final tally of votes, but by the first moments of your assembly—not by the voices of herald after herald, but by the single voice of the whole Roman people."

---

[i] Lit. "the champion or defender of your silent liberty." Quintus Cicero expresses a different view in *de Legibus*: "And the people shouldn't have been given a form of cover in which the ballot could conceal an incorrect vote and leave the good ignorant about who thought what" (*non latebra danda* [sc. *fuit*] *populo, in qua bonis ignorantibus quid quisque sentiret, tabella vitiosum occultaret suffragium, Leg.* 3.34). On the effects of the secret ballot, see Yakobson 1995 and cf. n. 67.

[ii] Richter's emendation; the manuscripts have *tribus* 'tribes,' which Manuwald 2018 obelizes.

The passage is not platitudes and flattery; rather, it is a distinctive combination and refitting of the ideological debates of Cicero's time, using the techniques and conceits that the previous analysis has revealed. Seeing them allows a passage like this, which has no direct comparandum (the beginning of the senate speech is lost), to be unpacked fully.

In both speeches the reconfiguration and inversion of critical concepts or shared points of reference—what I called the primacy of the local context—looms large, both on the smaller scale (*diligentia*, ch. 3.3; *licentia*, ch. 4.2) and on the broader, programmatic scale (signally *libertas* in ch. 4 and, as we will see in ch. 8, *dignitas*). *LA* 2.1–4 depend on such a reconfiguration. Cicero's handling of certain programmatic vocabulary is emblematic. *Dignitas* 'worthiness' and *virtus* 'valor; moral excellence' were, like *libertas*, polyvalent, if not outright contested, terms.³ Inasmuch as rank was inherited and family lines were trusted as repositories and guarantors of excellence ("The good man will do good deeds"—a matter of *ingenium*), then *dignitas* and *virtus* described inherited or inheritable qualities. But inasmuch as success and achievement demonstrated the possession of *dignitas* and *virtus* ("Good deeds make a good man"—a matter of *labor* and *industria*), then they were earned, or continually re-earned, qualities.

In short the terms lent themselves both to aristocratic and meritocratic understandings of status.⁴ Cicero here presses the terms in a meritocratic direction. He achieved the "dignity of this office" (*hanc dignitatem*, C) by his own "efforts" (*studiis*, C). (Is this *dignitatem* specially accented? Here, apparently for the first time in attested Latin, it is used metonymically for a magistracy, as are *honor* or τιμή).⁵ Cicero was granted office by the people *suo anno* because of his "worthiness" (*dignitas*, E; I have rendered the phrase *dignitate impetratus*, lit. "won by worthiness," as "in recognition of a justified request"), in a way hitherto denied not only to most *nobiles* (thus the aristocratic sense of the term is excluded) but also to every other new man before him (thus the meritocratic sense of the term is intensified). The citadel of the consulship, so jealously guarded by the aristocracy, the people have breached (D), that it may lie forever open to what I rendered "candidates of talent";⁶ Cicero's word is simply *virtuti* "virtue," which there plainly connotes accomplishment, or at least not inherited status. This accent on meritocracy is not self-praise; Cicero has in mind his own category shift. Election

---

3. Hellegouarc'h 1963: 388–415 provides a fine survey of the semantic applications of *dignitas*, describing with copious examples a semantic chain that, beginning from a core sense 'propriety' (~ *decet*), develops into 'doing what you should' (thus overlapping with *officium*) to 'the quality of someone who can be counted on to do what he should' (thus overlapping with *fides*) to 'suitability for performing the functions of an office' (thus overlapping with *virtus*) to 'the results of having won office' and thus both 'fame [for civic deeds]' (thus overlapping with *existimatio, fama, laus*) and the 'dignity of high office' itself (thus overlapping with *honos* and *auctoritas*), in particular a kind of right to exercise one's talents, a characteristic of the senate and the *nobiles*. That survey incidentally illustrates that many of the distinct individual senses existed at the same time, which is, *inter alia*, a clear mark of ideological contests.

4. On the tension between meritocracy and aristocracy implicit in this passage, see Gildenhard 2011: 52–58.

5. Or so suggests the *TLL* 5.1.1138.39. It becomes a Ciceronian usage thereafter.

6. Sallust's formulation of the situation is pungent: *Etiam tum alios magistratus plebs, consulatum nobilitas inter se per manus tradebat. Novos nemo tam clarus neque tam egregiis factis erat, quin indignus illo honore et <is> quasi pollutus haberetur* ("Even then the plebs [filled] other offices, [but] the nobility passed the consulship back and forth between themselves. There was no new man so distinguished or with deeds so fine that he did not seem unworthy of the rank, as if it had become polluted," *Jug.* 63.6–7).

to the consulship conferred nobility;[7] the group who resisted him (*nobilitas*, D) or whom he defeated (*nobiles*, E) was now his group, too. Cicero is reconfiguring the meaning of *nobilitas* through his own person. His labels for the aristocracy are the concretized use of words whose broader—and, for the Cicero of this passage, truer—meaning is the Unnamed Referent of the passage.

This stance, and its linguistic manifestations, are of course not wholly Cicero's invention: they draw from the anti-aristocratic strands of Roman politics. A signal recent example was Marius, the famous general, *novus homo*, and opponent of the arch-aristocrat Sulla—or at least Marius as the historian Sallust represented him: for instance, his Marius—in a *contio*—is made to say of the aristocracy, "So if they are right to look down on me, then they have to do the same to their ancestors, whose nobility, like mine, has its roots in acts of valor" (*quod si iure me despiciunt, faciant item maioribus suis, quibus, uti mihi, ex virtute nobilitas coepit, Jug.* 85.17).[8] But meritocracy is in one sense not really different from aristocracy, if it is just another path to the oligarchy. It is in the first instance to fend off such thoughts in (some of) his audience, I think—call it their dash of buyer's remorse—that Cicero develops the idea of meritocracy in a way that accents the role of the people as judges of merit. Thus in C Cicero professes no need to recall his merits in detail because the people themselves, who elected him in the first place, will, when they have to, arrive at the same opinion (*existimaturos*) as they already did (*iudicavistis*) when they found him worthy of "the extraordinary judgment of the highest office [they] can bestow" (*vestro summo honore singularique iudicio*). *Existimaturos* here recalls *existimatio*, the word for the 'reputation' or 'public standing' of a politician, sometimes not far from *dignitas*.[9] The act

---

7. The precise meanings of the terms *nobilis* and *novus homo* have been matters of debate (see Blom 2010: 35–60; Burckhardt 1990). On the view here endorsed, *nobilis* has the standard connotation of late Republican Latin, 'consular' (Shackleton Bailey 1986 after Gelzer 1912), and *novus homo* connotes not, narrowly, non-patrician (Brunt 1982) nor, broadly, a man with no senatorial ancestors (Wiseman 1971: 1) but, specifically, a man with no consular ancestors (Gelzer 1912: 25–29; Shackleton Bailey 1986). Shackleton Bailey's remark (1986: 260) is apt: "We must not forget that these terms are governed by usage, not by legal definition."

8. For the Marian and tribunician character of the *LA* 2.1–16, cf. Bell 1997: 20, Laser 1997: 147–9. On this speech of Marius in Sallust, see Blom 2010: 51–52, Earl 1961: 32–4. The remark of Steed 2017: 401 about the speeches of Sallust's *Histories* is *mutatis mutandis* applicable here: "Though Sallust wrote the speeches for a triumviral audience, he also preserved aspects of earlier political debate, and the speeches may be used with caution to understand politics in the politically charged environment of the 70s."

9. Hellegouarc'h 1963: 362–63; cf. 362: "Comme le mot l'indique par lui-même, *existimatio* désigne l'impression produite par l'homme politique sur ses concitoyens et l'opinion qu'ont ces derniers de sa personne et de ses actions." For an illustrative instance, cf. *hominem plurimorum studio atque omnium bona existimatione munitum* "a man enjoying widespread support and a

of election is described, as occasionally, by *iudicium*, here in a hendiadys (or so I take it) that links "highest office" to "judgment" and reinforced by *iudicavistis*.[10] The people have virtually "passed a decree" on Cicero.[11]

The allusions to people's judgment are supported by striking and memorable figures. The first, in the opening sentence of the speech (A), is another *pronominatio*. Newly installed consuls "achieved noble status for their family by your benefaction." What I have rendered "noble status" is literally *ius imaginum*, "the right to display the death masks" of ancestors. It was a cherished right of the nobility. The display of the masks, worn by actors, at a funeral of a family member highlighted the importance of a family to the community through the generations. Polybius describes the moving sight of "men famed for their excellence" (τῶν ἐπ' ἀρετῇ δεδοξασμένων ἀνδρῶν, 6.53), symbolically come back to life, as an inspiration to youth eager for glory and good. Sallust relates the same:

> I have oft heard that Quintus Maximus, Publius Scipio, and other distinguished men of our state besides were wont to say that, when they beheld the images of their elders, their hearts were set fiercely aflame for acts of valor (*virtus*); that it was not the waxen figures that had such force, but the memory of famous deeds lit a flame in the hearts of excellent men that cannot be put out until their own valor has won equal glory and fame. (*Jug.* 4.5–6)[12]

But in Cicero's *exordium* the *ius imaginum* becomes not a point of family pride (an aristocratic sensibility), nor again a spur to glory (a more meritocratic sensibility, in that real achievement is needed to live up to noble forebears), but the

---

universally good reputation" ([Q. Cic.] *Pet.* 28). For a broader summary of the range of *existimatio*, see Yavetz 1974: 36–40.

10. *OLD s.v.* 4.

11. For a similar use of *iudicium*, cf. "Who is the person about whom you—and that is a source of real authority—have made such great and distinguished judgments?" (*de quo homine vos—id quod maxime facit auctoritatem—tanta et tam praeclara iudicia fecistis?* Cic. *Man.* 43, referring to Pompey), and see *TLL* 7.2.609.47–610.3 "latius: 1 de decretis, praeceptis sim.: a hominum quorumlibet, maxime populi, senatus, principis."

12. *Nam saepe ego audivi Q. Maximum, P. Scipionem, praeterea civitatis nostrae praeclaros viros solitos ita dicere, quom maiorum imagines intuerentur, vehementissime sibi animum ad virtutem adcendi. Scilicet non ceram illam neque figuram tantam vim in sese habere, sed memoria rerum gestarum eam flammam egregiis viris in pectore crescere neque prius sedari, quam virtus eorum famam atque gloriam adaequaverit.* On this passage and the dialectical relation between history and memory the *Bellum Iugurthinum*, see Grethlein 2006. For a study of the history and didactic value of *imagines*, with their links to theatre in Roman culture more generally, see Montanari 2009, and cf. Plin. *Nat.* 35.6.

people's gift (for merit, no doubt—but still, theirs to grant, like the *honos singularis* of *LA* 2.46 = Table 2.1.I).

A metaphor makes the same point as the *pronominatio*. Cicero's forebears "lacked popular affirmation and the light that your honor provides" (*laude populari atque honoris vestri luce caruerunt*). *Honos*, as commonly, is used concretely for political office. But the phrase *honoris vestri lux* is unique in Cicero, and in it the dynamics of the metaphor of light are distinctive. *Lux* has a wide array of metaphorical meanings. It may mean the 'light of life.' That is one likely source of its use for the 'splendor' of common life or civic life, especially liberty.[13] It is as if light shines out from the state. An important actor may also 'bring' or 'restore' light to the state or the like by dispelling a threat or bringing back order— as it were, restoring life and thus light.[14] Those kinds of light follow a straight line: down upon the state or out from within it (analogous to the latter is the use of words for 'bright' like *clarus, illustris, splendidus* to mean 'distinguished' members of society; they "shine").[15] But in this instance the optical path is different. Cicero's relatives did not "appear" because the people did not "illuminate" them.[16] The path of that light is not straight; the "gleam" of the distinguished is reflected—a *nothum lumen*, in Catullus's memorable phrase for the light of the moon (34.15–16). And by extension, if Cicero—or, really, anybody else—is now *clarus* or *illustris*, it is with the people's light that they shine.

---

13. Civic life: *ut per se adflictum atque eversum propinquum suum non modo honeste partis bonis verum etiam communi luce privaret* (*Quinct.* 74, in reference to *deminutio capitis*), *vos obsecro, iudices, ut huic optimo viro, quo nemo melior umquam fuit, nomen equitis Romani et usuram huius lucis et vestrum conspectum ne eripiatis* (*Rab. Post.* 48, if Rabirius is convicted of *repetundae* and goes into exile), *lucem salutemque redditam sibi ac restitutam* (*Dom.* 75, of the *patria* welcoming Cicero's restoration). Liberty specifically: *quasi luce libertatis et odore aliquo legum recreatus* (*Ver.* 2.5.160), *iam pridem in hac re publica non solum tenebris vetustatis verum etiam luce libertatis oppressa sunt* (*Rab. Perd.* 13). Cf. ch. 5 nn. 86, 87.

14. Thus the accomplishments of Pompey defeating the pirates (*incredibilis ac divina virtus tam brevi tempore lucem adferre rei publicae potuit, Man.* 33); Plancus (*cuius memorabilis ac divina virtus lucem adfert rei publicae, Phil.* 13.44); Brutus (*ut, quocumque venisset Brutus, lux venisse quaedam et spes salutis videretur, Phil.* 10.12); Caesar (*lux liberalitatis et sapientiae tuae, Lig.* 6); and Cicero himself, suppressor of Catiline (*utrum me patria sic accepit ut lucem salutemque redditam sibi ac restitutam accipere debuit..., Dom.* 75).

15. For the range of the words, cf. Hellegouarc'h 1963: 227–229 (*clarus*), 458–461 (*splendor*, associated especially with equestrians), 461–462 (*illustris*, likewise for equestrians). On *clarus*, cf. also ch. 6 n. 63.

16. Another instance of the same phrase here used, *luce carere*, is exactly analogous: *[Isocrates] magnus orator et perfectus magister, quamquam forensi luce caruit intraque parietes aluit eam gloriam, quam nemo meo quidem iudicio est postea consecutus* (*Brut.* 32). Isocrates nursed his talents only in his schools and never won acclaim in the courts ("he lacked the light of the lawcourts"), where victory would have made him glow.

The idea of people as judges, thus developed by connotation, allusion, and figures, prepares the ground for the next move of the passage, where the idea informs a now familiar device. Process and procedure, as we have seen, are vital to Cicero's arguments in the second speech. Whether a measure respects the people and popular sovereignty can be read directly off its procedural forms; its means, rather than its ends, reveal its true nature. That is exactly the idea behind E and F. The details of the process of Cicero's election themselves—not his motives, not the context, not even really his career to that point, but simply the electoral procedure itself—are enlisted to suggest a perfect congruity between the people and Cicero. The implicit logic is: if they are the true judges of merit, and the process of his election was extraordinary, then that must mean that they and he have a special relationship.

E describes, fairly enough, the challenges of consular campaigns for "new men." Cicero overcame these handily, succeeding on his first try as soon as it was legally permissible. He inscribes a particular meaning onto that victory: it can only have been the people's willing and immediate recognition of his readiness for the supreme office—and they are skeptical judges, of nobility and new men alike, as the difficulties of all other candidates imply. Thus he did not need to beg for recognition endlessly (cf. *diuturnis precibus efflagitatus*; *efflagito* is 'ask for insistently or imperiously,' *OLD s.v.*) but had his request granted for the asking (cf. *impetratus*; *impetro* is 'obtain by request or entreaty,' *OLD s.v.*).[17] The account is selective, of course. Cicero's election was very much a matter of the right *occasio*: the slate and the tense economic and political situation of 64 were to his advantage.[18] Furthermore, he had spent the time since his praetorship not in a province, as many holders of *imperium* did, but in Rome, so as to be able cultivate support for his run—not *diuturnae preces*, perhaps, but a steady politicking that was not so different either.[19] But here, as in the other instances we have seen, Cicero elevates the narrow details of process and procedure over broader context.

---

17. Cf. "*efflagitare* significat vehementer et instanter postulare aut orare, i.q. *exposcere, exorare* sim." (*TLL* 5.2187.41), "latius in serm. communi i. q. alqd (sc. contendendo) *perficere, exsequi, obtinere* sim. (tam generatim de quavis perpetratione vel effectu . . . quam speciatim de exorando i. q. *precibus consequi* . . ." (*TLL* 7.1599.37–40).

18. Cf. ch. 2 n. 24.

19. In the summer of 65 Cicero purposes to find out the views of the aristocracy toward him (*Att.* 1.1.2); later that summer he asks Atticus's help in getting their support (*Att.* 1.2.2). Cicero's speech *in toga candida* (fragments F11–14 in Crawford 1994 = Asconius 69.4–69.26 Stangl) gives a picture of Catiline not deserving the support of the *principes civitatis, senatores*, the *equester ordo*, and the *plebs*—the groups that Cicero obviously knew he himself had to court.

Ideologies of Identity

F alludes to (most of) the process of a normal election.[20] Electoral units voted sequentially (fixed or determined by lot, according to the particular form of assembly); the ballots of each successive unit were cast and tallied; the winning tally of each was announced as it became known; when a candidate had reached a majority of units, victory was declared (even if some units had not voted yet). But so high was the people's opinion of Cicero that he was declared consul almost by acclamation, the one and only choice of the whole people.[21] The procedure that would ordinarily determine the people's choice wasn't even necessary; Cicero's procedure transcended procedure. This account, too, is not without certain elisions. The breaching of the aristocrats' citadel in D gives a distinctly populist color to Cicero's victory; but consuls were elected in the *comitia centuriata*, and the structure of that assembly, 196 "centuries" divided by income bracket, was weighted heavily in favor of the propertied, who voted first. The support of those classes was perforce critical to Cicero's victory. His election was not a matter of storming the manor house with torches and pitchforks.[22] But here, too, Cicero turns the process and procedure into a self-contained symbol of power relations.

In sum, the idea of the people as the chief, even sole, judges of true merit is supported by Cicero's account of the procedural details of his own election. He is truly the people's man: look no further than the way he was elected. That is a polemical complex of ideas, and it is anchored in a polemical allusion. If certain ideas have a Marian tinge, there is also a direct allusion to Marius. The image of the people as an offensive military force in D, vividly and correctly expressed,[23] is unique in the speech, and unique metaphors, as we have seen, repay close analysis. Military language used of a *novus homo* resisted by the aristocracy would certainly and ineluctably have recalled Marius—so much the more on Cicero's lips. Marius, like Cicero, was by birth an *eques*; and Marius, like Cicero, was an Italian townsman—and from the same town, Arpinum. Marius, in a typological reading

---

20. For a full survey of the mechanics of Roman elections, see Vishnia 2012.

21. On (the fiction and utility of) universal acclamation, see Bell 1997: 16–19.

22. Not that the *plebs* were without real influence; see Yakobson 1992: 32–52 and the references in ch. 1 n. 40.

23. The "barricading" of the consulship by the aristocracy is expressed by *obvallo*, 'stake all around *or* defensively' (a *vallus* is a palisade, or a rampart set with palisades), a rare, apparently poetic, word: before this passage it is attested only in Accius (*templum obvallatum ossibus*, 70W; cf. also *misera obvalla saxo sento* "wretched and enwalled with jagged rock" 71W, which, if correct, has *obvallus* as a byform of *obvallatus*) and thereafter not until Festus (186.31 Lindsay). Two other words are *voces propriae*. *Rescindere* is the right word for the military destruction of architectural features (cf. *L&S s.v.* I.), and *patere* is common for places laid open by force (cf. many of the examples in *TLL* 10.1.659.10–38).

of Roman history—and that is how Cicero himself read Marius[24]—prefigured Cicero, who has, as it were, now taken up the Arpinate's Burden.

If the *exordium* has an arc, *LA* 2.1–4 are its beginning: *nobilis* has been redefined meritocratically, and that has fused Cicero to the people. Cicero now moves forward along the arc: he sets that relationship in its wider political context. The chief problem, as in D, is the aristocracy. The consulship is hard enough, but the aristocracy will give Cicero no grace for any mistake and only grudging praise for any success; the *nobilitas* will offer him no trustworthy advice in times of doubt or sure help in times of struggle (element G, to continue the sequence of Table 6.2.1).[25] This is not sourness; there is a specific implication: they—named, again, with the reified *nobilitas*—will fail of their obligations. Cicero has certain values in mind. When they speak of him, they will show no *observantia*, due respect for Cicero's station; when Cicero speaks with them, they will show him no *fides*, the 'reliability' or 'sincerity' of an honest interlocutor.[26] That is, Cicero will have neither *amicitiae* 'friendships' nor a reliable *consilium* 'body of advisers'—the things that any Roman politician had to have. Such the price of his bond to the people. And for the people there is also a price; that is Cicero's next point (call it element H).[27] If Cicero fails, whether by poor planning or plain bad luck, certain men will blame the people as a body for preferring him to the aristocracy—named once more with the reified *nobilitas*. And that amounts to another failure of due

---

24. See Fuhrmann 1995: 16–18. On Cicero's use of historical *exempla* in his own self-fashioning, Blom 2010: 149–286; on Marius specifically, 182–83, 188–92, 204–208.

25. [For ease of cross-reference, the five continuous citations from the *exordium* over the next several notes will be lettered G–K, following on the sequence A–F of Table 6.2.1 and preceding the sequence LJ–S of Table 6.2.2.] G, Cicero and the aristocracy: *Hoc ego tam insigne, tam singulare vestrum beneficium, Quirites, cum ad animi mei fructum atque laetitiam duco esse permagnum, tum ad curam sollicitudinemque multo maius. Versantur enim, Quirites, in animo meo multae et graves cogitationes quae mihi nullam partem neque diurnae neque nocturnae quietis impertiunt, primum tuendi consulatus, quae cum omnibus est difficilis et magna ratio, tum vero mihi praeter ceteros, cuius errato nulla venia, recte facto exigua laus et ab invitis expressa proponitur; non dubitanti fidele consilium, non laboranti certum subsidium nobilitatis ostenditur* (*LA* 2.5).

26. Cf. "*observantia* is paying respect and deference to those who are our superiors in age, wisdom, honor, or another point of distinction" (*observantia est, per quam aetate aut sapientia aut honore aut aliqua dignitate antecedentes veremur et colimus*, Cic. *Inv.* 2.65, cf. 161); and "the fundament of justice is trustworthiness, that is, truthfulness and consistency in one's words and agreements" (*fundamentum . . . est iustitiae fides, id est dictorum conventorumque constantia et veritas*, Cic. *Off.* 1.23). For an assessment of Cicero's view of the cardinal virtues that draws out the importance of *fides* in civil society, see Atkins 1990.

27. H, the people and the aristocracy: *Quod si solus in discrimen aliquod adducerer, ferrem, Quirites, animo aequiore; sed mihi videntur certi homines, si qua in re me non modo consilio verum etiam casu lapsum esse arbitrabuntur, vos universos qui me antetuleritis nobilitati vituperaturi* (*LA* 2.6).

respect: begrudging the people their sovereign right to bestow *honores* and *beneficia*. The imagined failures thus allusively dramatize Cicero's redefinition: the *nobilitas* will abandon their political roles. That is a reworking of a standard trope of populist rhetoric, in which nobles exhibit *superbia* 'haughtiness' and *ignavia* 'worthlessness,'[28] but here those vices or their like are implied by the absence of the corresponding virtues.

But this bleak moral landscape will not discourage Cicero. That is his next point (I): there is nothing he will not willingly suffer in order to make sure that "what the people have done for [him] and thought of [him]" (*vestrum de me factum consiliumque*, §6) will be met with praise (*laudetur*).[29] Here, too, are allusions. *Factum* and *consilium* recall C, the people's election of Cicero and their *existimatio* of him, respectively (with *consilium* here in its sense 'considered conclusion').[30] And the idea of being inspired to praiseworthy deeds alludes to the very opening of the speech. Cicero has no *imagines* to gaze upon—but he can contemplate the people's assessment and choice of him. They are to him as noble forebears are to (proper) nobles: an inspiration to valor. And of that valor there are two proofs: they are Cicero's next topics (J and K). He describes two valorous acts, one in each of the chief venues of public life. In the senate house on January 1, says Cicero, he announced that the watchword of his magistracy would be *consul popularis*, something easy to say (*dictu facillimum*) from the Rostra but not so easy right in the middle of the senate (*in ipso senatu*). But Cicero, with the *imago* of the people in mind, as it were, could do no otherwise: "It is . . . quite impossible for me not to be *popularis* in this magistracy and in my general political attitude (*vita*), when I know that I was elected consul not through the support of powerful men, not through the good graces of the few, but by the judgment of the whole Roman people, in preference to men of high nobility, and that by no small measure" (K).[31]

---

28. Blom 2010: 51; Sall. *Jug.* 85.1.

29. I, Cicero's attitude: *Mihi autem, Quirites, omnia potius perpetienda esse duco quam non ita gerendum consulatum ut in omnibus meis factis atque consiliis vestrum de me factum consiliumque laudetur* (*LA* 2.6).

30. *TLL* 4.0.444.7 "decretum, consultum, sententia, iussum."

31. K, Cicero as *consul popularis*: *Ego autem non solum hoc in loco dicam, ubi est id dictu facillimum, sed in ipso senatu, in quo esse locus huic voci non videbatur, popularem me futurum esse consulem prima illa mea oratione Kalendis Ianuariis dixi. Neque enim ullo modo facere possum ut, cum me intellegam non hominum potentium studio, non excellentibus gratiis paucorum, sed universi populi Romani iudicio consulem ita factum ut nobilissimis hominibus longe praeponerer, non et in hoc magistratu et in omni vita essem popularis* (*LA* 2.6–7). For *omnis vita* as 'general political attitude' [*lit.* 'whole life'], cf. *OLD s.v.* 7 "manner or circumstances of life," which coincides with *mores* = 'consistent pattern of choices,' and cf. *Brut.* 108 *ut in vita sic in oratione*

The other chief venue of public life was, of course, the Forum and the Rostra. There, too, Cicero will be courageous (J). The typical late Republican *contio* aggressively rallied populist energies as a political tool.[32] Thus most consuls had come to avoid "public appearances here and the sight of you all" (*aditum huius loci conspectumque vestrum*).[33] But Cicero will appear: that will be the "guiding principle" (*lex et condicio*)[34] of his consulship—"major undertaking" (*summus labor*) and "ambitious plan" (*difficillima ratio*) though that be. The very *contio* at which Cicero made these remarks is a token of exactly that promise and prediction: thanks for a victory will shortly become an attack on a bill; a post-election address will become a *contio* of the political type—and a difficult one, opposed to populist proposal.[35] Here, too, a value is implicit: Cicero will not lack *constantia*—the virtue of those who faced their foes on the foes' turf.[36] That is exactly Cicero's brand of courage: in the senate house—just behind him—he is a *consul populáris*, accent on *populáris*; and in the Forum—just in front of him—he is a *cónsul popularis*, accent on *consul*. He is *constans*, *gravis*, and *severus* not just in a *contio* but in the *curia*.

The arc of the *exordium* has thus reached a kind of pivot point. Cicero, by a reading of the details of his own election, has developed the meaning of *nobilitas*, the chief unnamed referent of the passage, to the point that his own office of *consul*, that most lordly of offices—the "monarchic and kingly" (μοναρχικὸν ... καὶ βασιλικόν) element of the Roman constitution, as Polybius put it (6.12.9)—now merits, or so Cicero would have it, the most partisan of populist adjectives, *popularis*. The modulations of the *exordium* have let him lay claim to *popularis* by way

---

turbulentus, of P. Decius, tr. pl. 120, who brought L. Opimius to trial for having caused the murder of Gaius Gracchus and for having thrown citizens into prison without a judicial verdict; his "agitated" speech matched his "disruptive" politics.

32. See refs. in ch. 1 n. 23.

33. J, Cicero's guiding principle: *Accedit etiam ille mihi summus labor ac difficillima ratio consulatus gerendi, quod non eadem mihi qua superioribus consulibus lege et condicione utendum esse decrevi, qui aditum huius loci conspectumque vestrum partim magno opere fugerunt, partim non vehementer secuti sunt.* On the "transformation of the Rostra into a *locus popularis*" in the second century, see Vasaly 1993: 13–14; on the recovery of the Forum by tribunes after the restoration of the tribunate in 70 and the reapportionment of space, see Kondratieff 2009, esp. 337–47.

34. Lit. something like "terms and conditions," cf. e.g. *cum aequa lege et condicione venibant* "when [tithes] were sold on fair terms and conditions," *Ver.* 2.3.118; cf. *Ver.* 2.3.5, *Planc.* 41.

35. At the end of the speech (*LA* 2.101), Cicero takes pride in having overcome exactly that difficulty: cf. ch. 7.4.

36. On *constantia* in assemblies, see Morstein-Marx 2004: 166–69.

Ideologies of Identity 193

of its etymology: the truly *popul-aris* magistrate is one chosen by and bound to the *popul-us*, the people. It is easy to cry sophism: the pun is obvious; Cicero had occasionally made it before and would make it again.[37] But here, as the local context makes clear, the pun crystallizes the paradoxes of the *exordium* to this point.[38] That is, in effect, to call into question the real meaning not only of *nobilis* but of *popularis*, too.

And that is precisely Cicero's next step along the arc. As he implicitly challenged the meaning of *nobilis* by explicating his election, now he challenges the meaning of *popularis* by examining policy. Thus there is a shift of genre: he pivots from an *actio gratiarum* to deliberative oratory. But the chief intellectual trope, redefinition, does not shift: just as Cicero is truly *nobilis*, unlike some others, so he truly understands what makes *popularis* policies, unlike some others. Here Cicero's tactics in the *exordium* can be drawn out by comparison to a passage of the senate speech. Part of its *peroratio* makes the same points on the same template[39] (As usual in the text, Roman numerals in Table 6.2.2 indicate the order of elements, which varies slightly between the speeches; the sequence here follows that of the popular speech.)

Table 6.2.2. Rhetorical Structure of the Treatments of the State of Republic (*LA* 1.23, *LA* 2.8)

in senatu	*ad populum*
L. Simulated Populism	
(i.) Errastis, Rulle, vehementer et tu et non nulli conlegae tui qui sperastis vos contra consulem veritate, non ostentatione, popularem posse in evertenda re publica populares existimari.	(i.) Sed mihi ad huius <verbi> vim et interpretationem vehementer opus est vestra sapientia. Versatur enim magnus error propter insidiosas non nullorum simulationes qui, cum populi non solum commoda verum etiam salutem oppugnant et impediunt, oratione adsequi volunt ut populares esse videantur.

(continued)

---

37. For examples and discussion, see Seager 1972; Ferrary 1982: 728–30.

38. The pun also captures the stance of the speech: Cicero returns to the slogan at the speech's end, *LA* 2.101–3; cf. ch. 7.4.

39. On the role of this segment in the senate speech, cf. ch. 8.5.

Table 6.2.2. Continued

in senatu	*ad populum*
"You and certain of your colleagues, Rullus, hoped, even as you destroyed the government, to claim the mantle of *popularis* against a consul who is *popularis* in the true sense of the word, and not for show. And that was your mistake—a serious mistake."	"So, please, look very carefully at exactly what people mean when they use the <word> [sc. *popularis*]. There's a lot of confusion now because of the dangerous lies of certain persons, whose speeches give the impression that they are *popularis* even as they attack and undermine not just the people's advantages but indeed their very security."

M. State Beset with Worry

(iv.) Sollicitam mihi civitatem suspicione, suspensam metu, . . .	(ii.) Ego qualem Kalendis Ianuariis acceperim rem publicam, Quirites, intellego, plenam sollicitudinis, plenam timoris . . .
"[You've passed on] to me a state riven with suspicion, wracked with fear . . ."	"For my part, citizens, I see the kind of state I inherited on January 1: full of anxiety; full of worry; . . ."

N. Affected Groups

(vi.) . . . spem improbis ostendistis, timorem bonis iniecistis; . . .	(iii.) in qua nihil erat mali, nihil adversi quod non boni metuerent, improbi exspectarent;
". . . you've given hope to the wicked and struck fear into the good; . . ."	". . . a state where the good feared every kind of evil and every kind of reverse—and the wicked hoped for them."

O. Disruptive Plans

(v.) . . . perturbatam vestris legibus et contionibus et seditionibus tradidistis; . . .	(iv.) omnia turbulenta consilia contra hunc rei publicae statum et contra vestrum otium partim iniri, partim nobis consulibus designatis inita esse dicebantur;
". . . roiled by your laws and assemblies and disruptions; . . ."	"There was talk of all kinds of disruptive plans against the political structure of this state and your tranquility, some just being developed, others already underway when I was elected consul; . . ."

P. Financial Danger

(vii.) fidem de foro,	(v.) sublata erat de foro fides non ictu aliquo novae calamitatis, sed suspicione ac perturbatione iudiciorum, infirmatione rerum iudicatarum;

Table 6.2.2. Continued

in senatu	*ad populum*
"... you've [ruined] the credit market ..."	"... the credit market had collapsed, not because of some unexpected disaster but because of anxiety that the courts would be disarranged and settled legal judgments would be overturned; ..."

Q. Political Danger

(viii.) ... dignitatem de re publica sustulistis. "... and political stability as well!"	(vi.) novae dominationes, extraordinaria non imperia, sed regna quaeri putabantur. "... there was a feeling that the objective was new despotisms—irregular magistracies that were really kingships!"

R. Cicero willing to appear in *Contiones*

(ii.) Lacesso vos, in contionem voco, populo Romano disceptatore uti volo. "I challenge you to appear in a public assembly! I will convene it. I want the Roman people to judge between our positions."	(cf. J above, n. 33)

S. Peace the True Popular Ideal

(iii.) Etenim, ut circumspiciamus omnia quae populo grata atque iucunda sunt, nihil tam populare quam pacem, quam concordiam, quam otium reperiemus. "We can go through all the things the people value and cherish! But it won't matter: we will never find anything as popular as peace, and harmony, and tranquility."	(vii.) For S-p, see p. 196–97.

The two speeches offer the same basic analysis. Broadly it is a fair one. The Rullan bill probably could be represented as disruptive. The critique is sketched in P-p: the financial markets are under stress (*fides*, properly 'credit,' is, here as often elsewhere, metonymic for the banking system) because of interference in the judicial system. Cicero's references are not fully clear, but I take them to at least include the workings of the Rullan bill itself: the law-courts would be thrown into disarray with the loss of experienced judges to the decemviral commission (*suspicione ac perturbatione iudiciorum*),[40] and the creation of new titles by the commission would perforce sometimes include the undoing of apparently settled legal decisions (*infirmatione rerum iudicatarum*).[41] The speeches also share the idea of populist politics as disruptive.

But their underlying standards are different. The senate speech, as the template draws out, distills and elevates the legal concerns into a threat to "political stability" as a whole (Q-s)—so the evident connotations of *dignitas* here, probably with overtones of the aristocratic keyword. The popular speech, by contrast, invokes *libertas* without naming it. Thus in L-p. The people's *salus* is at risk (the word here, as often, means "security in respect of civil rights, freedom, etc."),[42] and their *commoda* are at risk. That is, both the constitutional and practical branches of *libertas* are referenced. The same pair is echoed in O-p. The populists' disruptive plans will affect the current condition of the state: there *hunc rei publicae statum* corresponds to *salus*. They will also affect the people's tranquility, where *vestrum otium* evidently takes the place of *commoda*. That is of course a reworking: *otium*, while it is a *commodum* of a sort, is not in any strict sense a material good. But that very reworking is the final conceptual modulation of the *exordium*:

> (S-p). Nor did I simply imagine all this; I saw it quite clearly: it was happening in plain sight. That is what prompted me to say in the senate that in

---

40. That accords with a sentence from the summary of the bill: "[The decemvirs are allowed] in the meantime to destroy the criminal courts; to make off with any members of the [advisory] panels (*consilia*, sc. those at Rome) they want" (*interea dissolvant iudicia publica, e consiliis abducant quos velint*, *LA* 2.34). The idea must be that the loss of expert consultants to the decemvirs would hobble legal processes at Rome; so perceptively Harvey 1972: 73–74.

41. Cf. Zumpt 1861: 35. For a full discussion of the possible referents here, see Drummond 1999 and discussion in Manuwald 2018: 206. On my view Cicero's language is adequately accounted for by the measures of the Rullan bill itself (not that other proposals cannot also fall under the same descriptions; it is to Cicero's purpose to paint with a broad brush). Talk of an agrarian bill might very well have had an effect on credit markets, inasmuch as land was the chief store of value (ironically, a problem the Rullan bill appears to have been designed to solve; cf. ch. 7.3 The Voices of the (Un-)Tribune) *init*.

42. *OLD s.v.* 4.

this magistracy I would be a consul for the people (*consul popularis*). After all, what is more for the people than peace (*pax*)? Peace, which, it seems to me, brings happiness not only to sentient beings but even to houses and fields. What is more for the people than liberty (*libertas*)? Liberty, which, as you know, not only men but even beasts seek to obtain and prefer to all things. What is more for the people than tranquility (*otium*)? Tranquility, which is so delightful that you, and your elders, and every brave (*fortissimus*) citizen, is willing to undertake great labors that they may at length enjoy it, especially if they are in positions of authority and high rank (*in imperio ac dignitate*)? This is, to be sure, all the more reason for us to give proper thanks and praise to our elders: it was their labor that lets us enjoy tranquility safely. And since I see that all of these things, Quirites—peace abroad, the liberty that belongs your nation and name, domestic tranquility—in a word, everything you hold important and valuable (*cara atque ampla*)—has been, as it were, deposited for protection into my consulship, how I could possibly not be "for the people"? (2.9)[43]

Otium becomes one member of a triplet beside *pax* and *libertas*. Each member of the triplet is metaphorized in broadly the same way. *Otium* is a precious inheritance, won by the toil and labor of the people and the elders and every virtuous citizen. *Libertas* is not a condition but a supreme natural good, the universal desire of all sentient creatures, veritably an Aristotlean sentiment about what is good.[44] *Pax* brings joy, not only to all and sundry, but "even to houses and fields," a phrase otherwise used of the chief targets of violent disorder.[45] That is,

---

43. *quae cum ego non solum suspicarer, sed plane cernerem—neque enim obscure gerebantur—dixi in senatu in hoc magistratu me popularem consulem futurum. Quid enim est tam populare quam pax? qua non modo ei quibus natura sensum dedit sed etiam tecta atque agri mihi laetari videntur. Quid tam populare quam libertas? quam non solum ab hominibus verum etiam a bestiis expeti atque omnibus rebus anteponi videtis. Quid tam populare quam otium? quod ita iucundum est ut et vos et maiores vestri et fortissimus quisque vir maximos labores suscipiendos putet, ut aliquando in otio possit esse, praesertim in imperio ac dignitate. Quin idcirco etiam maioribus nostris praecipuam laudem gratiamque debemus, quod eorum labore est factum uti impune in otio esse possemus. Qua re qui possum non esse popularis, cum videam haec omnia, Quirites, pacem externam, libertatem propriam generis ac nominis vestri, otium domesticum, denique omnia quae vobis cara atque ampla sunt in fidem et quodam modo in patrocinium mei consulatus esse conlata?*

44. "Let 'good' mean that which is chosen for its own sake or for the sake of which we choose something else; and that which is the aim of all things or of all things that have sense perception and cognitive capacity (or would be their aim if they had cognitive capacity)" (ἔστω δὴ ἀγαθὸν ὃ ἂν αὐτὸ ἑαυτοῦ ἕνεκα ᾖ αἱρετόν, καὶ οὗ ἕνεκα ἄλλο αἱρούμεθα, καὶ οὗ ἐφίεται πάντα, ἢ πάντα τὰ αἴσθησιν ἔχοντα ἢ νοῦν ἢ εἰ λάβοι νοῦν, *Rhet*. 1.18.2 = 1362a).

45. For all the apparent simplicity of the phrase, *tecta* and *agri* are joined only once elsewhere in Cicero: when Cicero's foes unleash upon his property (*meis omnibus tectis atque agris*) the

each member of the triplet is cast as a valuable possession or acquisition of some kind—a materialist cast that implicitly assimilates them to *commodum*. Cicero has here used the practical branch of *libertas* to subsume other meanings. Not only is peace thus advanced as the implicit antipode of populist politics, which, as also in the senate speech, is conflated with disruption and disorder, but that peace is distinctly conceptualized in terms of a materialist good. The *omnia quae populo grata atque iucunda sunt* of the senate speech (S-s) has a different cast. *Grata atque iucunda* is not a periphrasis for *commodum*; rather, if it has its usual connotation in Cicero, it refers to acts that restore political equilibrium.[46] In the senate speech Cicero is ready to debate Rullus not about "what the people want" but "what the people know will set things right."

The reconfiguring of *otium* is a paradox (yet another, in an *exordium* with so many).[47] The value sits ill with certain strands of *popularis* politics, which looked for reform and redistribution; in that way *otium*, inasmuch as it valorizes the status quo, is conservative. Indeed *otium* was associated especially with the *equites* (tranquility is good for business).[48] The reconfiguring thus reveals the last step of the arc Cicero has crafted. Having maneuvered himself into a place from which he can lay claim to *popularis*, he then converts the idea of *popularis* into sober and steady management (in the same way he converted *libertas* from popular sovereignty pure and simple into prudent cooperative governance).[49] The idea of sober management is supported by another political allusion. The *exordium* up to this point had nothing whatever to do with foreign policy; "peace" did not obviously

---

ruination and devastation they failed to bring to enemy cities or fend off from allies (*Har.* 3). In Livy the phrase is a merism for the targets of a scorched earth policy (*late populati sunt tecta agrosque*, 4.59.3; *vastandis agris urendisque tectis*, 10.11.6; *ad populandos finitimorum agros tectaque urenda*, 28.32.8; *populari agros et urere tecta*, 32.31.3).

46. That appears to be the collocational connotation of *populo gratum atque iucundum* or the like, if such connotation there is. Cicero uses the phrase of the Licinian and Aebutian laws (*LA* 2.21, treated in ch. 6.3); Verres's trial (*haec res, Ver.* 1.37; *haec causa, Ver.* 2.5.173); and a triumph which brought the satisfaction of seeing a feared enemy bound for punishment (*Ver.* 2.5.66). So also of Cicero's return from exile (with *dis immortalibus, senatui, populo Romano, cunctae Italiae, provinciis, exteris nationibus, vobismet ipsis* [= the college of priests], *Dom.* 147).

47. On *otium* generally see Jal 1961 and André 1966; for another view of the several shades of meaning of *otium* in these speeches, see also Vasaly 1988: 421–24.

48. Well, pre-"military-industrial complex" anyhow. On the *equites* and *otium*, cf. ch. 5 n. 3 and Thompson 1978: 134: "Although Cicero, as a *consul popularis*, claims to be the protector of the interests of the people, the goals which he says are *populare* (*pax, otium*, and *tranquillitas*) are, in fact, identical to the goals of the *optimates*."

49. Arena 2012: 231 explicates the logic of the *exordium* thus, an observation equally appropriate here: ". . . if Cicero is a genuine *popularis*, and nothing is so *popularis* as liberty, it follows that Cicero can only act according to the principles of liberty."

refer to "peace abroad," as in the last sentence of S-p. But that last modulation is deliberate: as *commodum* is turned into *otium*, which is joined to *pax*, now *pax* is turned into *pax externa*. And *pax externa*, like the *extraordinaria imperia* that appeared shortly before it (Q-p), is surely meant to recall Pompey: then still in the field, he had lately secured the whole eastern frontier and then some. The outlines of a polarity thus emerge: the current turmoil of domestic politics that ruins *otium* is a bad use of populist politics; but Pompey's accomplishments rest on a good use of the same. The *consul popularis* gestures to where *popularis* politics have succeeded. If the people look at things closely—with the *diligentia* of the chapter epigraph or the *sapientia* of L-p—they can see the difference.

In sum, whereas false *populares* have no regard for political structures and will not provide *commodum*, Cicero, whose election proves he is truly *popularis*, will provide *commodum* in the form of political stability. Thus the whole effect of the *exordium* becomes clear. On the level of genre, the *exordium* is a conventional act of thanks refracted through contemporary ideological polarities until it becomes a political manifesto. The epigraph of this section is closely comparable: the people's vote to bring Cicero back from exile he reinterprets as an endorsement of his own political perspectives even as he bows to popular sensibilities. On the level of politics, Cicero's refractions create a distinctive persona that transcends the polarities: the newly minted *nobilis*, obliquely but thoroughly, contests the meaning of *nobilitas* in a way that also lets him contest the meaning of *popularis* carefully and unmistakably.[50] None of the underlying ideas is particularly original but—to return again to the image of an ode of Horace—their recombination is distinctive. And on the level of technique, the *exordium* provides an example of the devices and approaches that inform the rest of the speech: known events are inscribed with new meanings; familiar concepts are extended and inverted; procedure is made the chief sign and symbol of power relations; key concepts

---

50. The observation of Yakobson 2010: 197–98 is to the point: "There is no reason to assume that the Roman populace was won over by Cicero because it mistook him for a *popularis* in some radical and subversive sense; moreover, by rhetorically asking for his hearers' assistance in defining this term, saying he is in need of their wisdom (2.7), Cicero tacitly conceded that his use of it was controversial. Manipulation—certainly, but hardly outright deception. One may question how far Cicero was really trying to mislead his audience as to where, fundamentally, he stood in contemporary politics—though he was certainly disingenuous in his treatment of the bill and of the issue of agrarian legislation in general, and manipulative in his 'co-optation' of the Gracchi (as 'good *populares*' of old, unlike Rullus). The degree of manipulation on Cicero's part involved in taking this line of argument at that particular point in his career was considerable—but hardly limitless. He did, after all, have a certain moderate Popular record when he was elected consul (*Com. Pet.* 53), and his optimate stance, adopted from then on, would be relatively moderate too. On a later occasion in 61, he would be willing, unlike the majority of the Senate, to accept a watered-down version of an agrarian bill (Cic. *Att.* 1.19.4)."

are captured in memorable images. The *exordium* of *de lege agraria* II thus neatly captures both topic and technique of the whole speech, the modulations, which come slowly to their point, conferring a certain delicacy that is entirely appropriate for proems, which are supposed to leave hearers in a receptive frame of mind.[51] Here, *mutatis mutandis*, is the same tact in taking an oppositional stance that Cicero displayed when arguing in 66 for Cornelius against noble opponents.[52]

6.3. (RE)READING THE DECEMVIRAL ELECTION

> *denique avarities et honorum caeca cupido,*
> *quae miseros homines cogunt transcendere fines*
> *iuris et interdum socios scelerum atque ministros*
> *noctes atque dies niti praestante labore*
> *ad summas emergere opes ...*
>
> And then the blind desire for office and greed,
> which drive the benighted to cross the bounds
> of law and now and again as allies and aides in crime
> to strive with utmost effort, night and day,
> to reach the peak of wealth ...
>
> —Lucretius, *de rerum natura* 3.59–63

As the details of the procedure of Cicero's election fix his relation to the people, so do the details of the decemviral election fix theirs—as it were in the opposite direction. The same complex of ideas and allusions that Cicero uses to create his own persona are used, in reverse, to create Rullus's; he is Cicero's antitype. Cicero's election and the decemviral election belong to formally distinct parts of the speech—the *exordium* and the first of the arguments, and with a kind of *propositio* between[53]—but the topics, concepts, and techniques of two treatments make them mirroring counterparts.

The Rullan bill specified its electoral mechanism in detail (*LA* 2.17–25). The commissioners would be elected by the *comitia tributa* or Tribal Assembly, the right body for commissionerships. But, as we have seen (chs. 1.4 Mechanisms, 5.1),

---

51. *exordium est oratio animum auditoris idonee comparans ad reliquam dictionem, quod eveniet, si eum benevolum, attentum, docilem fecerit* (Cic. *Inv.* 1.15).

52. On the trial of Cornelius, see ch. 1 nn. 16, 71; for Cicero's negotiation of its complex politics, see Ward 1970 with Crawford 1994: 67–72. Wiseman 1971: 175 calls Cicero's performance a "masterpiece of tact."

53. On the *propositio*, cf. ch. 4.1.

the voting mechanism itself was unusual. Seventeen of the thirty-five tribes, chosen by lot (*LA* 2.21), would be the electors (*LA* 2.16). This was the procedure used to elect the chief priest, which the law cited (*item eodemque modo ut comitiis pontificis maximi*, *LA* 2.18).[54] Rullus would preside at the election (*LA* 2.20), giving him the right to draw the lots for the electoral tribes on his own (*LA* 2.21) and to accept or reject candidacies (there was no independent certifying authority), including his own (*LA* 2.21, 2.22). Thus serving on the commission was not an innovation—annual magistrates hold land or colonial commissionerships both before and after the date of our speeches[55]—but, as Cicero points out, whether it was advisable, or even entirely legal, was questionable.[56] Caesar "agreed in advance" (προδιωμολογήσατο) not to serve on the commission for his later land law in order to avoid any imputation of personal advantage.[57] Last, as we have already seen, candidates had to declare in person (*LA* 2.24).

The measures had symbolic and practical value. The electoral mechanism, which gave the people a share in an elite privilege without violating religious scruples, had a populist cachet. So suggests its political history. Priestly colleges replenished their ranks by cooptation; that is, sitting members chose new members. But already by the third century, the *pontifex maximus* or chief priest was elected.[58] Tribunes tried to extend the procedure to the other priesthoods—C. Licinius Crassus unsuccessfully in 154 and Cn. Domitius Ahenobarbus successfully in 104.[59] The extension was abrogated by Sulla in 82 but partially restored

---

54. The phrasing *item eodemque modo*, which has parallels in legal idiom, suggests a direct quote; see Ferrary 1988: 147. An election held "likewise and in the same way" was not possible in the strictest sense, since tribunes did not preside at sacerdotal elections (a priest did; see Mommsen *RS*³ 2.1: 26).

55. For a list, see Mommsen *RS*³ 1.515 and nn. 2 and 3; Bauman 1979: 389–90. Thus, for example, three tribunes—the Gracchi brothers and M. Livius Drusus—had served, respectively, on the Gracchan commission and on the Livian commission of 91. Pompey served as grain commissioner in 52 during his third consulship.

56. Cicero (*LA* 2.21; p. 000) claims Rullus's candidature would violate a *lex Licinia* and a *lex Aebutia*, otherwise unknown old plebiscites, that forbade service on a commission to the proposer thereof, his colleagues, and his relatives by blood or marriage; cf. Rotondi 1912: 290. The date of the legislation is disputed; for different views, see Bauman 1979: 386–91 (pre-Gracchan), Zumpt 1861: 50 (post-Gracchan), Mommsen *RS*³ 3.1: 501 n.2 (inspired by the Gracchan movement).

57. D.C. 38.1.6–7. M. Livius Drusus (tr. 121) in 121 had done the same (Plut. *CG* 10.1).

58. Mommsen, *RS*³ 2.1: 27–32. The evidence is not perfectly clear. Livy 25.5.1 (212 BCE) records an election but 40.42.11 (181 BCE) refers to cooptation; Livy's epitomator (*per.* 18) records an election for 241 BCE (*Tib. Coruncan<i>us primus ex plebe pontifex maximus creatus est*, note *creatus*).

59. Licinius: Cic. *Amic.* 96; Laelius's opposition on that occasion: Cic. *Brut.* 83, *N.D.* 3.5; Domitius: *LA* 2.18, Vell. 2.12.3.

later in 63, the year of our speeches, by a law of Rullus's fellow tribune, Labienus, with Caesar's support.[60] The voting mechanism probably thus appealed to the people outright. That is probably why Cicero imagines that it wouldn't have troubled them at first blush: "The first section of the agrarian bill is designed in their minds to subtly probe your willingness to tolerate the curtailment of your liberty" (*primum caput est legis agrariae quo, ut illi putant, temptamini leviter quo animo libertatis vestrae deminutionem ferre possitis*, LA 2.16, ch. 5.1). All the measures together also had practical value. On a generous reading, they were meant to forestall any dirty tricks by opponents of the bill—for example, a bad-faith candidacy that, if victorious, could hamper the commission's work. But that purpose is not much different from trying to ensure that particular candidates be returned. A carefully vetted slate, or rigged lots, or targeted bribery to known electoral tribes, or some combination thereof could and would return the "right" candidates.[61]

The whole electoral procedure thus has the look of defensive measures readily convertible to, and perhaps in some cases meant to be, offensive weapons, too; it was already suspicious. To highlight those suspicions, Cicero views the components of the procedure as it were through the lens of his own election and the meaning he created out of it. The heart of the decemviral electoral mechanism, the election by a minority of tribes, we have already seen (ch. 5.1), where I linked it to the fear of exclusion. Now other details can be given their full weight. The failure of the *populares* to provide *commoda* continues a theme of the *exordium*: the anxiety of exclusion is the opposite of the rarefied *commodum*, in the form of *otium*, that Cicero will provide to all. The theme of the "whole Roman people" recurs: the body that elected Cicero (*vox universi populi Romani*, LA 2.4; *universi populi Romani iudicio*, LA 2.7) is the very body Rullus will strip of its vote (*populum Romanum universum privare suffragiis*), even though their sovereignty—as signally in Cicero's case—is the true source of all authority (*cum omnis potestates, imperia, curationes ab universo populo Romano proficisci convenit*). Last, the theme of the false *popularis* is continued, drawn out by using Rullus's title rather than his name: the unusual election mechanism was proposed *a populari tribuno plebis*; and a tribune of the plebs, of all people, had the idea of stripping the people of their vote.

Cicero next disposes of the parallel of the sacerdotal elections.

---

60. Abrogation (by the *lex Cornelia de sacerdotiis*): Liv. *per.* 89, D.C. 37.37.1; restoration: Pseudo-Ascon. *Div. Caec.* p. 102, ed. Orelli; D.C. *ibid*. For the details of Labienus's bill, cf. Taylor 1942.

61. See ch. 1.4 Mechanisms.

"The second section [of the law] reads, 'Likewise and in the same manner as in the elections for the chief priest.' Rullus has failed to realize that our ancestors were so devoted to the people that they wanted to seek the people's approval for the office of chief priest because of its importance, even though religious strictures forbade the people from electing priests. Cn. Domitius, tribune of the plebs and a most distinguished man, passed a law extending the same principle to the other priesthoods; since the people are religiously forbidden to confer priesthoods, he restricted the electoral tribes to a minority and required that the candidate they returned be adopted by the priestly college. Look at the difference between Domitius, a tribune of the plebs and a most noble man and Rullus, who, I'm sure, tried your patience when he claimed he was noble! Domitius, to the extent that it was possible, and was proper, and was permissible, developed a plan to give to the people a share in something that could not be handled by the religious rites of the people; whereas something that has always belonged to the people, that no one has ever pared back, that no one has ever altered—the requirement that those who will assign properties to the people first receive from them a benefit before they can give one in return—*that* is what Rullus has tried to deprive you of and rip completely out of your hands. Domitius found a way to give the people what was impossible to give them; Rullus here is trying to devise a means of ripping away what can never possibly be taken away" (*LA* 2.18–19).[62]

The full import of this passage, too, depends on the devices and themes of the *exordium*. The logic of the pun on *popularis* recurs: the ancestors, like Cicero, are true *populares* because they respected the people. The true meaning of *nobilis* reappears: Domitius, who proposed broadening the people's rights, is a *homo nobilissimus* (he is also *clarissimus*, which implies won achievement, not born

---

62. *'Item,'* inquit, *'eodemque modo,'* capite altero, *'ut comitiis pontificis maximi.'* Ne hoc quidem vidit, maiores nostros tam fuisse populares ut, quem per populum creari fas non erat propter religionem sacrorum, in eo tamen propter amplitudinem sacerdoti voluerint populo supplicari. Atque hoc idem de ceteris sacerdotiis Cn. Domitius, tribunus plebis, vir clarissimus, tulit, quod populus per religionem sacerdotia mandare non poterat, ut minor pars populi vocaretur; ab ea parte qui esset factus, is a conlegio cooptaretur. Videte quid intersit inter Cn. Domitium, tribunum plebis, hominem nobilissimum, et P. Rullum, qui temptavit, ut opinor, patientiam vestram, cum se nobilem esse diceret. Domitius, quod per caerimonias populi fieri non poterat, ratione adsecutus est, ut id, quoad posset, quoad fas esset, quoad liceret, populi ad partis daret; hic, quod populi semper proprium fuit, quod nemo imminuit, nemo mutavit quin ei qui populo agros essent adsignaturi ante acciperent a populo beneficium quam darent, id totum eripere vobis atque e manibus extorquere conatus est. Ille, quod dari populo nullo modo poterat, tamen quodam modo dedit; hic, quod adimi nullo pacto potest, tamen quadam ratione eripere conatur.

status);[63] but Rullus, who curtails the people's rights, tries their patience with his claims of nobility. That is a rewriting: If Rullus did claim he was noble, he meant it literally, invoking some relationship to a branch of the *gens Servilia*. His label for himself becomes an annoyance only because Cicero's speech has reconfigured its meaning. Last, the narrow focus on procedure, rather than purpose or broader context, also continues. Domitius is praiseworthy, and Rullus blameworthy, purely for the structure of their proposals. The means and methods of the bills, in and of themselves, precisely reflect the character of their proposers. *Lex legislatorem arguit*.

The *exordium* followed a kind of arc: the redefinition of *nobilis* was modulated into a redefinition of *popularis*. Cicero's treatment of the decemviral electoral mechanism follows a reverse and complementary arc: the false *popularis* is a *nobilis*—of a kind. The modulation begins to appear in the next measure treated:

> Someone might wonder what he has in mind with this utterly shameless insult. There is a plan, citizens—and what there absolutely isn't is good faith (*fides*) towards the Roman plebs and proper regard (*aequitas*) for you and your liberty! [The bill] orders the proposer of the law to hold the decemviral elections. Let me repeat that more clearly: Rullus—who is, of course, free of ambition and greed (*homo non cupidus neque appetens*)!—orders Rullus to hold the elections. Though that is not my objection here; I see there are precedents. But consider the effects of using only a minority of the people, for which there is *no* precedent: he will get to hold the elections; and he will be planning to announce [the elections of] those that this law is meant to give regal power (*regia potestas*) to. What about the whole people (*universo populo*)? He's not bringing [the matter] before them, and the authors of these designs don't think it *can* be brought to them, not successfully anyway. (*LA* 2.20)[64]

---

63. Hellegouarc'h 1963: 227–29; on Servilius, see ch. 8 n. 4. *Clarissimus* is elsewhere used in the popular speech of the Gracchi brothers (*venit enim mihi in mentem duos clarissimos, ingeniosissimos, amantissimos plebei Romanae viros, Ti. et C. Gracchos, plebem in agris publicis constituisse*, 2.10) and generals whose war spoils will be subject to decemviral assessment (*LA* 2.50; Table 8.2.A-p). For a somewhat different view of *clarus*, see Whitehead 2005, who, collecting all examples of *vir clarissimus*, argues that the phrase is virtually a technical term for consulars, also applied tendentiously to other high-achievers. Of *LA* 2.10 he remarks that Cicero is suggesting the Gracchi "should have been consulars or, in a *de facto* sense, were comparable" (170).

64. *Quaeret quispiam in tanta iniuria tantaque impudentia quid spectarit. Non defuit consilium; fides erga plebem Romanam, Quirites, aequitas in vos libertatemque vestram vehementer defuit. Iubet enim comitia decemviris habere creandis eum qui legem tulerit. Hoc dicam planius: iubet Rullus, homo non cupidus neque appetens, habere comitia Rullum. Nondum reprehendo; video fecisse alios; illud quod nemo fecit, de minore parte populi, quo pertineat videte. Habebit*

The familiar themes—warped procedure, trust in the people, or the lack thereof—appear yet again. But now another element makes its re-appearance. The Rullan bill, Cicero warned, had as its objects *regna* and *dominationes* (*LA* 2.8 = Table 6.2.2.Q-p): that threat is recalled here. It is overt in *regia potestas*. And it is implicit in *cupidus* and *appetens*: the latter commonly implies seeking unconstitutional power.[65] But that lust for power is given a particular inflection: it is not that Rullus himself would be king; it is, more particularly, that he would be the head of a junta—Theramenes or Critias, if you like, rather than Peisistratus. He is, in that sense, the reverse of Cicero: Cicero was elected "not through the great good graces of a few, but by the judgment of the whole Roman people" (*non excellentibus gratiis paucorum, sed universi populi Romani iudicio*, *LA* 2.7; n. 31); Rullus dodges the judgment of the "whole people" and fronts for the *pauci*. *Pauci*, which might otherwise have referred to *nobiles*, is applied to a cabal of *populares*.[66]

The imputation of a cabal underlies details of the next argument. Cicero now turns to the selection of the electoral tribes by lot. The imputation appears first in an allusion: "Lucky man that Rullus is, he will draw the names of the tribes he wants. And the men that the nine tribes, selected by Rullus himself, will choose as decemvirs will become our lords and masters in every respect, as I will presently show" (*homo felix educet quas volet tribus. Quos viiii tribus xviros fecerint ab eodem Rullo eductae, hos omnium rerum, ut iam ostendam, dominos habebimus, LA* 2.21). The sarcasm has a narrower point: just like a *novus homo* breaking into the consulship would have recalled Marius, a "lucky" man who creates "overlords" cannot have failed to recall Sulla. Sulla claimed *Felix* 'Lucky, Blessed' as a *cognomen* for himself—and notoriously enriched his powerful friends by sham procedure.[67] (Sallust makes a similar pun against *felix*: his Lepidus decries "your torpor, which makes plundering easy and lets a man seem as 'blessed' as he is brazen," *vostra socordia, qua raptum ire licet et quam audeat, tam videri felicem, Or. Lep.* (*Hist.* 1.49M) 20). There is another intimation. Rullus, by serving on his own commission, would

---

comitia: volet eos renuntiare quibus regia potestas hac lege quaeritur. Vniverso populo neque ipse committit neque illi horum consiliorum auctores committi recte putant posse.

65. The pairing is only in Cicero. On the resonances of *cupidus*, see Achard 1981: 328, 410–11. *Appetens* is the very word that will apply to the Roman people if they decide to annex Egypt; cf. Table 4.4.C-p and ch. 4 n. 133.

66. Achard 1981: 18 notes: "Les *pauci* des *De lege agraria* sont les quelques populaires qui veulent détruire le *status*, chez Salluste ce sont le plus nobles des nobles qui, à la fin du deuxième siècle et au début du premier, se passent de mains en mains les magistratures importantes."

67. He also alluded to the quality in naming his son *Faustus* 'Auspicious.' On Sulla's self-representation, cf. the references in ch. 4 n. 50.

be violating certain old laws—"and not consular laws either," adds Cicero, "if that makes any difference to you, but tribunician laws that deeply pleased and satisfied you and your ancestors" (*leges enim sunt veteres neque eae consulares, si quid interesse hoc arbitramini, sed tribuniciae vobis maioribusque vestris vehementer gratae atque iucundae*, 2.21).[68] Why *tribuniciae* is clear: Rullus is not true to his office. But why add *consulares*, as if such laws were somehow less binding? And why then dismiss the word, which only emphasizes it (not a full *praeteritio* but the same effect)? Cicero is invoking a loose understanding—call it a folk taxonomy—of types of law: that tribunician laws cut back aristocratic influence over the people (for example, by authorizing the secret ballot); but that consular laws policed the ruling class within itself (for example, by limiting electoral bribery).[69] Procedural adjustments by consuls were thus paradoxically a reminder of corruption. Chicago aldermen, as it were, sometimes go too far even for Chicago aldermen.

The intimations of a cabal have thus moved from a simple lust for power to a lust for money; that is, beside *honorum caeca cupido*, to recall the epigraph, *avarities* now appears:

> Thus, under this law, excellent laws are gotten rid of without any provisos: he's going to run for the office under his very own law; he's going to hold an election with the majority of the people disenfranchised; he's going to declare the election of the people he wants, himself first of all. And naturally he won't reject his colleagues, who are co-sponsors of the agrarian bill. They allowed him to appear at the head of the list in the summary notice of the law (*index*) and in its preamble (*praescriptione*)— but all the other profits (*fructus*) that this law promises are reserved, by signed mutual agreement (*communi cautione*), to be shared equally (*aequa ex parte*)! (*LA* 2.22)[70]

---

68. On the laws, cf. n. 56; on *gratus* and *iucundus*, n. 46.

69. The four laws that introduced secret balloting in various venues were all introduced by tribunes (the *lex Gabinia tabellaria*, 139 BCE; *lex Cassia tabellaria*, 137 BCE; *lex Papiria*, 131 BCE; *lex Coelia*, 107 BCE). Cf. Cic. *Leg*. 3.34–6 and see Rotondi 1912: 297, 302, 324. Marius as tribune also introduced a law which, according to Plutarch (*Mar.* 4.2), reduced the power of the nobles in the *comitia*: it narrowed the bridges (*pontes*) voters used to pass to the balloting site, reducing chances for coercion; see Bicknell 1969.

70. *Optimae leges igitur hac lege sine ulla exceptione tollentur: idem lege sibi sua curationem petet, idem maiore parte populi suffragiis spoliata comitia habebit, quos volet atque in eis se ipsum renuntiabit, et videlicet conlegas suos ascriptores legis agrariae non repudiabit, a quibus ei locus primus in indice et in praescriptione legis concessus est; ceteri fructus omnium rerum qui in spe legis huius positi sunt communi cautione atque aequa ex parte retinentur.* For *exceptione*, Naugerius' emendation, Manuwald retains the reading *suspicione* in the sense 'presentiment.'

The accusation is anchored by a now familiar technique: Cicero inscribes his own meaning on a known feature. The "notice" (*index*) of a law gave its name and a summary of its measures; the "preamble" (*praescriptio*) was beginning of the bill proper, which started with the proposer's name.[71] But Cicero reinterprets those formal details: the list of co-sponsors is here turned into a *cautio*. *Cautio* here has one of its legal meanings: a signed promise acknowledging a duty or debt.[72] Just as the list of properties becomes an auction lot (*LA* 2.46–9 = Table 3.1), the text of a law becomes a "promissory note" signed by cooperating parties. There is another legal allusion: the co-sponsors will divide the property *aequa ex parte* "in equal shares." Cicero has in mind a *societas*, a 'partnership' or 'joint venture' in which the proceeds and profits (NB *fructus*) are shared equally. But these *socii* are *socii scelerum*. Cicero's imposition of a new meaning on the stock formulas of the law is, as with Sulla's statue, also a convenient mnemonic for anyone who saw the text of the bill: by law a bill had to be displayed ("promulgated") for a fixed period before it was brought to the relevant *comitia*; the text of Rullus's bill might well have still have been posted.[73] As with the city gates or Sulla's statue, Cicero surely gestured toward where it was, or had recently been, hanging.

In sum, Cicero, who has claimed *popularis* in one form, denies that same sense of the concept to Rullus, in order to make him out to be a *nobilis* of a certain cut: loyal to his own small group and working the system to climb to the summit of wealth and power—*ad summas emergere opes*, as Lucretius put it. The last element of the electoral mechanism that Cicero treats anchors the conceptual complex in a memorable final flourish. According to Cicero, the bill required that candidates declare in person (*praesentem . . . profiteri iubet*, 2.24). That was, in fact, the usual expectation, though exemptions could be granted; probably, then, the bill barred them.[74] The idea was perhaps to prevent delays in seating

---

71. *Index*: *TLL* 7.1.1143.44–48, *OLD* s.v. 3a, Mommsen *RS*³ 2:315. *Praescriptio*: *TLL* 10.2831.58–69. See also Manuwald 2018: 239.

72. For the legal sense in Cicero, see Elmore 1913: 127–29. For the technical sense, see *TLL* s.v. 3.713.22–714.53; as a document, 714.9–53 and Roby 1902: 11. Cf. also Berger 1953 s.v. *cautio*: "*Cautio* is also used to indicate a written declaration of the debtor confirming his obligation and issued for the purpose of evidence."

73. By law, matters for *comitia* had to be displayed for a span of time covering three market days (*trinum nundinum* or *trinundinum*, cf. Cic. *Dom.* 41, *Phil.* 5.8); if that time had not yet passed, the text of the bill would still have been on display. Rullus's law was promulgated some time after December 10. On the *trinundinum*, cf. Lintott 1965.

74. "[S]ome scholars have argued that . . . Rullus' bill . . . forbade any exemptions (Balsdon 1962, 140–1, with further references), while others assume that a law forbidding candidature in absence was only passed after January 63 BCE (Mommsen, *RS*³ 1.503–4 n. 3; Gelzer 1983, 53 and n. 147)," Manuwald 2018: 243.

the commission (the bill has at least one other mark of haste).[75] Cicero does not attack the evident irregularity directly. Rather, he binds it to Pompey: he argues that the measure is meant specifically to prevent Pompey serving as a decemvir (*LA* 2.23–25). That may seem like a cheap gesture, trading on Pompey's popularity. And in the Rome of the late 60s, that popularity was at a high peak. Pompey had restored the tribunate as consul in 70. The plebiscites of 67 and 66 thus let him solve the problems of piracy and Mithridates (which, or so some might claim, the aristocracy couldn't or wouldn't). That had made him a popular hero. Any politician advancing himself in the 60s, it seems, had to claim to be advancing Pompey's interests.[76] The Rullan bill did that very thing—or at all events exempted Pompey by name from remitting war spoils, one of the bill's sources of funding (*LA* 1.13, 2.60). Cicero prefaces his claim that the sale of certain *vectigalia* was an attack on Pompey with an apology for mentioning him too often.[77]

But Cicero here handles the figure of Pompey in a way that brings the conceptual arc of *LA* 2.17–25 to completion, reinforcing the idea of a greedy cabal and recalling the key ideas of the *exordium*. The rhetorical form of the passage is designed for precisely that task: the idea of excluding Pompey is repeated five times five different ways—a miniature *commoratio*, if you like[78]—allowing different themes to be echoed each time. The first time recalls the people as true judges of virtue, as in the *exordium*: The "people behind these machinations" (*ei qui haec machinabantur*) foresaw that if the people could choose anyone they wanted for a job that required "trustworthiness, integrity, courage, and influence" (*fides, integritas, virtus, auctoritas*) they would choose Pompey first.[79] The second is a reminder of the people's successful use of sovereignty in *extraordinaria imperia*: these crafty framers oppose Pompey because they "realized" (*intellegebant*)

---

75. *LA* 1.4 = Table 3.1.E-s notes the auction is scheduled for January; it was January already. (Furthermore all the days after January 15 were comitial days, when the senate could not meet except by dispensation).

76. The *Commentariolum Petitionis* makes a relevant observation: "[Nobles are to be persuaded that] whatever populist pronouncements we might seem to make, we made them for the purpose of allying ourselves with Cn. Pompey, in order to have him with his considerable influence as a supporter, or at least not an opponent, in our own campaign" (*si quid locuti populariter videamur, id nos eo consilio fecisse ut nobis Cn. Pompeium adiungeremus, ut eum qui plurimum posset aut amicum in nostra petitione haberemus aut certe non adversarium*, 5.1).

77. *LA* 2.49 = Table 7.2.3.

78. In the *commoratio* (= ἐπιμονή) an orator dwells on the strong points of the case; cf. e.g. Longin. 12.2, Demetr. *Eloc.* 280, *Rhet. Her.* 4.58.

79. *Viderunt ei qui haec machinabantur, si vobis ex omni populo deligendi potestas esset data, quaecumque res esset in qua fides, integritas, virtus, auctoritas quaereretur, vos eam sine dubitatione ad Cn. Pompeium principem delaturos* (*LA* 2.23).

that Pompey was the best man for a position of trust (*fides*) and the right man for a high distinction (*honos*)—the people had, after all, put him in charge of wars everywhere on land and sea.[80] The third take on the idea depicts a Rullus who, as in the *praescriptio*, manipulates procedure to satisfy greed: he inserted the provision, which no other law ever had, to keep the people from assigning him in Pompey a colleague "to guard against and restrain [his] desires" (*custodem ac vindicem cupiditatum*).[81] The fourth version lays an accent on the greed of the few and *libertas* in its material aspect: it must be the case that the backers of the bill aim at tyranny (*regnum*); isn't it obvious that once this small cabal (*pauci homines*) cast their greedy eyes upon all of the people's property, their first move would be make sure Pompey would have no way to protect the people's liberty (*libertas*) and no office to secure their emoluments (*commoda*)?[82] The fifth permutation accents the idea of hidden designs, a theme of the brief *narratio*, and ultimately of sovereignty awry: the framers "saw then and see now" (*viderunt et vident*) that, even if through lack of foresight the people should pass the bill, once they realized its hidden designs (*cognitis insidiis*), they would want to elect Pompey as a bulwark (*praesidium*) against all its defects and crimes.[83] Thus does the idea of a greedy cabal, which emerges in the discussion of the election procedures and grows in importance over its course, eventually provide a script, augmented by many of the chief ideas of the speech thus far, into which Pompey, too, can be written. A grace note becomes a keynote becomes a template. To see Cicero as simply abusing Pompey's popularity would be to miss the point. Rather, that very popularity allows Cicero to make of Pompey a tool that is good to think with, a tool Cicero uses to expose, dramatize, and summarize the motivations and political thinking that, on his view, lie behind the Rullan bill. He inscribes a meaning onto Pompey, too.

---

80. *Etenim quem unum ex cunctis delegissetis ut eum omnibus omnium gentium bellis terra et mari praeponeretis, certe in decemviris faciendis sive fides haberetur sive honos, et committi huic optime et ornari hunc iustissime posse intellegebant* (*LA* 2.23).

81. *Praesentem enim profiteri iubet, quod nulla alia in lege umquam fuit, ne in eis quidem magistratibus quorum certus ordo est, ne, si accepta lex esset, illum sibi conlegam ascriberetis custodem ac vindicem cupiditatum* (*LA* 2.24).

82. *Hic, quoniam video vos hominis dignitate et contumelia legis esse commotos, renovabo illud quod initio dixi, regnum comparari, libertatem vestram hac lege funditus tolli. An vos aliter existimabatis? cum ad omnia vestra pauci homines cupiditatis oculos adiecissent, non eos in primis id acturos ut ex omni custodia vestrae libertatis, ex omni potestate, curatione, patrocinio vestrorum commodorum Cn. Pompeius depelleretur?* (*LA* 2.24–25).

83. *Viderunt et vident, si per imprudentiam vestram, neglegentiam meam legem incognitam acceperitis, fore uti postea cognitis insidiis, cum decemviros creetis, tum vitiis omnibus et sceleribus legis Cn. Pompei praesidium opponendum putetis* (*LA* 2.25).

6.4. CONCLUSION

To sum up: just as Cicero redefines *nobilis* in order to redefine *popularis*, so he denies the Rullan bill the label *popularis* in order to make Rullus out to be a *nobilis* of a certain cut. The genuine *nobilis* and true *popularis* is counterposed to a false *popularis* and a stereotypical *nobilis* and his ilk; and that band of corrupt aristocrats, in turn, is held up as a determined opponent of Pompey, who, like Cicero, is implicitly a true *popularis*. The modulations of the *exordium* and the first set of arguments adjust partisan slogans and stereotypes in order to create a map of contemporary ideological terrain onto which Cicero, Pompey, and Rullus are situated. The modulations and the ideas they bring to the fore lay the foundations for much of the argumentation we have seen in previous chapters. To name only some: a Cicero bound to the people is the Cicero who respects open procedure (ch. 4.2) and acts out a proper colonization (ch. 5.3 Bad Land). A people who are the true source of all authority are the people whose *libertas* enjoins upon them a duty of care and who must delegate their sovereignty prudently (ch. 4.1). The equating of *commodum* with *otium* prefigures Cicero's injunction to forego the slim chance of getting good land and keep instead the shared pleasures of feast days and games (ch. 5.3 Home Sweet Home). The reconfiguring of the ideology of *nobilis* lies behind the image of a respectful Sulla (ch. 4.2); the reconfiguring of the ideology of *popularis* lies behind the reversal of mood Cicero would effect (ch. 3.2 The Power of the Law) and the skepticism toward populist legislators he would foster (ch. 4.1). The idea of an elite cabal manipulating the levers of government for its own power and profit is echoed in the allegations of the bribery of Hiempsal and the Recentorici (ch. 4.3) and the planned seizure—or not—of Alexandria (ch. 4.4). A Rullus who is *cupidus* and *appetens* is one of a crew whose plans to sell property abroad amounts to *libido refrenanda* (ch. 4.2 *fin.*). The idea of a cabal ready to thwart Pompey lies behind Rullus's arrogant letter and impudent auction in front of his camp (ch. 5.2). A Rullus whose leading place in the *praescriptio* is ominous is the Rullus who is picked first, of all the decemvirs, to auction Pompey's territory (ch. 5.2). In short, no chief ideological rill of the main arguments does not find its expression, in some form, in the *exordium* and the treatment of the decemviral election.

The end of the arc has another effect. Obviously, in its final flourish, it assimilates Pompey to Cicero. Both of them become champions of the people resisted by a small, powerful, envious faction. But to my mind a more important effect runs in the reverse direction: the argument also assimilates Cicero to Pompey. If the people's support of Pompey over the last decade had proven a successful gambit, then, Cicero implies, so will their support of him—support which, in effect, he claims on his own terms by selectively interpreting the known procedural details of his election. He makes himself into a gauge by which to measure Pompey, and that claiming of Pompey makes Pompey into a gauge against which to measure Cicero. If Cicero were minting a coin, to use an image, as a promise and token of his coming consulship, the obverse would have an image of the Aventine Triad, dear to the plebs whose true voice he now is, and the reverse an image of Mithridates in chains, an illustration of sovereignty rightly used—and a reminder of plebiscite that he, who also chose rightly, had famously supported.[84] And if Cicero had not been an orator, he would have written an iambic diatribe in which Rullus paraded in mourning garb on the Rostra before wheeling off with a retinue of pretty boys to his posh estate at Formiae.

---

84. The so-called Aventine Triad, formed by Ceres, Liber, and Libera, was traditionally linked to the plebs; it is a kind of counterpart to the "Capitoline Triad" of Jupiter, Minerva, and Juno (replacing the older triad of Jupiter, Mars, and Quirinus).

7

Images of Identity

POMPEY, RULLUS, AND CICERO

7.1. INTRODUCTION

nec dubito quin multo locupletior in dicendo futurus sit, si quis omnium rerum atque artium rationem naturamque comprehenderit.

And I'm sure that someone who has mastered the principles and nature of reality and knowledge would be a much richer speaker for that.

—Cicero, *de Oratore* 1.80 (M. Antonius)

The ideological positioning of Cicero and Rullus established in the arc of the *exordium* and the first set of arguments sets their personas for the rest of the speech; their subsequent appearances can be viewed as so many glosses and expansions on that positioning. This chapter presents a selection of those instances that are especially noteworthy because of their imagery, the form of their argument, or their position or role in the speech. The several instances draw from many sources: legal debate, historical allusion, folk taxonomies, political stereotypes, even folk religion. Here, then, is another aspect of Cicero's technique: it is not only that his governing idea selects lexemes, figures, and images, but the governing idea adopts, adapts, and assimilates other modes of speech and other semiotic systems. The passages considered in this chapter, more than most, depend on Unnamed Referents.

That is testimony to the clarity and consistency of Cicero's creative vision. There are several implications which began to appear already in earlier chapters. Much of the force of Cicero's speeches derives not from persuasion in any strictly rational or logical sense but from deploying symbols and allusions and adducing (and remodeling) shared points of reference. He doesn't build an argument *for* his audiences; he builds an argument *out of* his audiences. That aspect of his technique presumes an audience sensitive to allusion and reference. Imagining such an audience is especially important for the passages considered in this chapter, where Cicero's confidence that he has awakened a point or frame of reference in his hearers' minds leaves clear marks even on the structure and sequence of the passages; he can depend on what he knows he made them remember. The first two agrarian speeches are, in that way, more like a Roman Ode of Horace than they are a *Tetralogy* of Antiphon. There is an implication, too, for Cicero's persona. He commands the relevant details of language that allow him to tap into the many rills and fields and zones of his audiences' psychic imaginary; he knows how to economically summon up frames of reference. This is not what the Antonius of the epigraph had in mind about wide education; but the effect is not different: a manner of speech that seems richer and deeper and truer. In these speeches, and in particular in the popular speech, that is not, I think, a mere rhetorical affect: rather it is a kind of parallel to Cicero's political message. For a politician whose overt claim is that he can transcend the limits of groups, a tone of voice that seems to be able to talk about everything and make it all fit together is entirely apt. The form is very much the content.

7.2. POMPEY'S EXEMPTION

Beneficia donari aut mali aut stulti putant.

Only the wicked or the stupid think favors are gifts.
—Publilius Syrus, *Sententiae* B37

The treatment of the decemviral electoral mechanism ends with a quintuple lament that Pompey will be excluded from service on the commission. That lament assimilated Pompey to Cicero: both are champions of the people resisted by a small, clever, envious faction. That persona is precisely the one Cicero puts to use at an important moment. Among the sources of funding for the Rullan bill were war spoils, which were technically public property. The bill attached spoils from both past and future wars (*LA* 1.11–13, 2.59).[1] Probably the bill had in mind mainly spoils from past campaigns, in particular the recent lucrative conquests of Lucullus, who was at the time of Cicero's speeches awaiting a triumph outside the city. Pompey was exempted by name from the requirement. That was a problem for Cicero. The exemption would have put Pompey in a superior position.

---

1. For a full treatment of those passages and more detail on the legal status of spoils, see ch. 8.3.

Many in the popular audience must have welcomed the idea, seeing it as a gesture of respect, and knowing it meant a richer triumph and a higher cash reward to Pompey's returning soldiers; it was both *honestum* and *utile*. Cicero's task, if he would resist the bill, was to reverse that perception as a selling point. Here, in effect, is an instance of the problem of the whole speech: undercutting a bill that to all appearances respected the people's authority and promised to provide material benefits.

Cicero attacks the exemption from the legal point of view. He views it through the lens of *beneficium*, which (among other meanings) is a favor granted by law (later, the term *privilegium* partly overlaps, but in Cicero's time *privilegium* means only unfavorable treatment).[2] The template of the introductions is identical (Table 7.2.1).

Table 7.2.1. Rhetorical Structure of the Treatment of Pompey's Exemption, Part 1 (*LA* 1.13, 2.60–1)

in senatu	ad populum
	A. Pompey Exempted
Hic tamen excipit Pompeium…	Hic tamen vir optimus eum quem amat excipit, Cn. Pompeium.
"However, he excepts Pompey…"	"But our excellent legislator at this point excepts his beloved Gnaeus Pompey."
	B. Parallel to or Context of the Exemption
…simillime, ut mihi videtur, atque ut illa lege qua peregrini Roma eiciuntur Glaucippus excipitur.	Vnde iste amor tam improvisus ac tam repentinus? Qui honore decemviratus excluditur prope nominatim, cuius iudicium legumque datio, captorum agrorum ipsius virtute cognitio tollitur, cuius non in provinciam, sed in ipsa castra decemviri cum imperio, infinita pecunia, maxima potestate et iudicio rerum omnium mittuntur, cui ius imperatorium, quod semper omnibus imperatoribus est conservatum, soli eripitur, is excipitur unus ne manubias referre debeat?

---

2. For this sense of *beneficium*, cf. *TLL* 2.0.1885.64–1886.7; on *privilegia* in the late Republic, see Greenidge 1901: 312–17.

Table 7.2.1. Continued

in senatu	*ad populum*
"... in exactly the same way, it seems to me, as Glaucippus is excepted from the law which banishes foreigners from Rome."	"Where does this unexpected and sudden love come from? The man who is excluded from the decemvirate virtually by name; who is stripped of his juridical, legislative, and jurisdictional rights over the territories captured by his own courage; into whose province—or rather into whose very camps!— decemvirs are sent, with *imperium*, limitless funds, and great power and judgment over everything; who is the only man ever to be stripped of his rights as commander, which have always been maintained for other commanders—this is the one man who is not required to turn in war spoils?"

C. Legal Character of the Exemption

Non enim hac exceptione unus adficitur beneficio, sed unus privatur iniuria.	Vtrum tandem hoc capite honos haberi homini, an invidia quaeri videtur? Remittit hoc Rullo Cn. Pompeius; beneficio isto legis, benignitate decemvirali nihil utitur.
"That is, the exemption doesn't grant a particular person a benefit; it spares a particular person an injury."	"What's this section of the law supposed to be doing? Giving the man an honor or stirring up ill-will against him? Gnaeus Pompey declines Rullus's offer; he wants no part of that kind of legal benefit or of decemviral liberality."

Both speeches argue that the exemption is legally unusual. But their reasoning differs. The senate version in B and C argues that the clause is not really a *beneficium* because it does not provide a benefit but instead spares an injury. A parallel is cited, the method of case law: an otherwise unknown Glaucippus was exempted by name from the effects of the *lex Papia de peregrinis* of 65.[3] The popular version, by contrast, allows that the measure *is* a *beneficium* (C-p)—it's just that Pompey rejects it. That version also adds another category, *benignitas*. This is not sarcasm or alliterative pleonasm. Rather, *benignitas* connotes an act of mercy that contravenes the law or, in dubious cases, chooses the more lenient option. That is the sense of *benignitas* in the later legal tradition,[4] and that must be its sense here (the

---

3. On the law, see Cic. *Off.* 3.47, *Arch.* 10; Rotondi 1912: 376; Husband 1916.

4. So in Gaius's famous formulation *semper in dubiis benigniora praeferenda sunt* (*Inst.* 50.17.56).

same sense appears in the senate speech, *LA* 1.10, Table 8.4.1.E-s). That is, Cicero is representing the exemption in two legally distinct ways: either it is a measure that grants a favor (*beneficio . . . legis*; that is a matter of the text, hence the word "law"), or it is a measure that spares someone a disability (*benignitate decemvirali*; that is a matter of an official's mercy, hence the relevant officials are named).

The two legal theories of the exemption underlie the two subsequent elements, which have no correspondents in the senate speech (Table 7.2.2).

Table 7.2.2. Rhetorical Structure of The Treatment of Pompey's Exemption, Part 2 (*LA* 2.61–62)

D. *Beneficium*

Nam si est aequum praedam ac manubias suas imperatores non in monumenta deorum immortalium neque in urbis ornamenta conferre, sed ad decemviros tamquam ad dominos reportare, nihil sibi appetit praecipue Pompeius, nihil; volt se in communi atque in eodem quo ceteri iure versari.

"If it is fair for commanders not to devote their loot and spoils to the monuments of the immortal gods or the enhancements of the city, but to turn it in to the decemvirs as if to their masters, Pompey wants no special consideration for himself—none! He prefers to be treated by the law in exactly the same way as everybody else."

E. *Benignitas*

Sin est iniquum, Quirites, si turpe, si intolerandum hos decemviros portitores omnibus omnium pecuniis constitui, qui non modo reges atque exterarum nationum homines sed etiam imperatores vestros excutiant, non mihi videntur honoris causa excipere Pompeium, sed metuere ne ille eandem contumeliam quam ceteri ferre non possit.

"But, citizens, if it is unfair, and disgraceful, and intolerable for these decemvirs to be posted like toll-gatherers over any money that anyone has—after all, they get to shake down not only kings and men of foreign nations but even *your* commanders!—then I don't think they are exempting Pompey to honor him: I think they are afraid that he will not accept an insult that others will."

F. Pompey's Attitude

Pompeius autem hoc animo est ut, quicquid vobis placeat, sibi ferendum putet; quod vos ferre non poteritis, id profecto perficiet ne diutius inviti ferre cogamini.

"But Pompey's attitude is that he thinks he should accept whatever you decide on; but if you are unable to accept something, he will make absolutely certain that you are not forced to keep doing so."

Cicero speaks for Pompey. The figure is not a *conformatio* in the strict sense, but the effect is an exact counterpart to Rullus's letter to Pompey: Cicero uses someone else's voice to create a symbol for power relations. The organizing motif of the dilemmatic structure (*si est aequum* ... , D; *sin est iniquum* ... , E) is *aequitas*.[5] Cicero's Pompey uses *aequitas* as the touchstone for assessing the measure. If surrendering spoils is fair, that means that the *ius* embodies *aequitas*, and Pompey is happy to be in same condition as everybody else (*volt se in communi atque in eodem quo ceteri iure versari*, D, NB *iure*), and he doesn't want any special deals—that is, *beneficia*. His principle is exactly that of Cic. *Top*. 23: "The guiding principle should be equity, which insists on identical rights in identical cases" (*valeat aequitas, quae paribus in causis paria iura desiderat*). If, on the other hand, surrendering spoils is unfair, that means that the *ius* does not embody *aequitas* (in fact the measure isn't even really a proper law, since it actually inflicts an injury, cf. *contumelia*, E). By that standard the decemvirs' remission becomes a would-be act of mercy—that is, *benignitas*. *Aequitas* is at issue here in another way, too. Were Pompey not excepted, he would be within his rights to strike back: just revenge is also a part of *aequitas* ("The natural law [aspect of *aequitas*] has two features: attributing to each his due and the right of revenge," *natura partes habet duas, tributionem sui cuique et ulciscendi ius*, Cic. *Top*. 90).[6]

The two legal views of the exemption thus make Pompey into a virtual personification of *aequitas*. They have two other effects. They set the terms for Pompey's attitude (F). He "must accept" whatever the people decide but will "make certain" they are coerced into nothing.[7] That is, *aequitas* has now been identified with the people's will: "accepting" refers to acquiescing in the just law described in D, and resisting the unjust law described in E. Pompey's *aequitas*—like Cicero's *dignitas* in the *exordium*—is rooted in the people's sovereignty. The different legal understandings also imply different motives for the decemvirs. If the law is equitable, then their *beneficium* sacrifices equity for political gain, no doubt in the hope of laying Pompey under obligation to them. Only fools think favors are free. But if the law is inequitable, then their *benignitas*, driven by fear, sacrifices consistency for financial gain, to extract cash from those less ready or

---

5. Cf. ch. 4 n. 67.

6. Cf. *Top*. 84 (*de aequo et iniquo: aequumne sit ulcisci a quocumque iniuriam acceperis*), *de Orat*. 3.116.

7. His stance here is exactly like that of Cicero in the *propositio*, ready to concede to the people's will or fight if needed (*LA* 2.16, n. 56).

able to defend themselves. The two kinds of exemption thus picture the decemvirs imagining themselves as above or below Pompey. Images crystallize those postures. The would-be granters of *beneficium* are *domini* "owners" or "lords" or "masters" (*domin[i]*, D-p). *Domini* regard generals not as agents of the state but as their own personal agents, who must "hand over" or "turn in" (*reportare*) their spoils like soldiers to their commander.[8] But the would-be exercisers of *benignitas* are instead "toll-takers" or "customs officials" (*portitores*, E-p). *Portitores* were notorious for their excess zeal;[9] hence *excutiant*, which denotes shaking garments so as to dislodge their contents.[10] Perhaps Cicero has in mind another legal issue here? War spoils were sometimes handled as if they were, in effect, private property, and the issue was a contentious one in Cicero's day.[11] The images damn the decemvirs either way: if booty is public, *domini* regard it as private; if it is private, *portitores* regard it as public. Be that as it may, it is now clear why, by way of preamble to this argument, Cicero recapitulates at length Pompey's alleged disabilities under the law (B-p). It might be that the decemvirs might have the right to demand remittance to the home office and opportunistically spare Pompey; or it might be that the decemvirs have the right to root through your luggage but wave Pompey timidly through; but either way, they are a greedy cabal who have crafted an authority they can licitly abuse, much like the other abuses they would inflict under their law.

One more feature of this passage deserves notice. Cicero makes bold to speak for Pompey in detail, as if he knew his thoughts. Another passage sheds light on that affect. As Cicero embarks on his allegation that the sale of Pompey's *vectigalia* is an insult, he apologizes for naming Pompey too often (Table 7.2.3; I provide the corresponding senate passage for comparison).

---

8. For *reportare* as 'bring home plunder from war,' cf. *OLD s.v.* 3.a. The soldiers' oath to return found property is preserved in Gellius 16.4.2.

9. Cf. "I came to understand how bitter the allies feel in the matter of *publicani* from citizens who recently complained about Italian port-dues—not so much that they had to pay them as about some unlawful conduct on the part of the toll-takers" (*illa causa publicanorum quantam acerbitatem afferat sociis, intelleximus ex civibus, qui nuper in portoriis Italiae tollendis non tam de portorio quam de nonnullis iniuriis portitorum querebantur*, Cic. *Q. fr.* 1.1.33). Plutarch observes, "We are annoyed and displeased with customs-officials, not when they pick up those articles which we are importing openly, but when in the search for concealed goods they pry into baggage and merchandise which are another's property. And yet the law allows them to do this and they would lose by not doing so" (*Curiosit.* 7 = *Mor.* 518E, tr. Helmbold).

10. 'Hitting [-*cutere*] so that things come out [*ex-*].' Classical examples for garments at *TLL* 5.2.1312.45–49.

11. See ch. 8.3.

Images of Identity

Table 7.2.3. Prior mentions of Pompey at the outset of the discussion of the proposed sale of his *vectigalia* (*LA* 1.5, 2.49–50)

in senatu	ad populum
Nam superiore parte legis quem ad modum Pompeium oppugnarent, a me indicati sunt . . .	Et mihi, quaeso, ignoscite, si appello talem virum saepius. Vos mihi praetori biennio ante, Quirites, hoc eodem in loco personam hanc imposuistis ut, quibuscumque rebus possem, illius absentis dignitatem vobiscum una tuerer. Feci adhuc quae potui, neque familiaritate illius adductus nec spe honoris atque amplissimae dignitatis, quam ego, etsi libente illo, tamen absente illo per vos consecutus sum.
"In the earlier part of the law I was the one who incriminated them for attacking Pompey . . ."	"And forgive me, I beg you, if I've been mentioning the man with some frequency. Two years ago in this very place, citizens, you imposed on me as praetor the role, together with yourselves, of protecting Pompey's dignity in his absence by whatever means I could. And thus far I have done what I could—and not because I know the man personally, or because I hoped for the distinction of high office (which I achieved through you in his absence, though to his pleasure)."

Cicero is referring to the favorable reception of his speech on the Manilian Law.[12] The echoes of the *exordium* are distinct. Here, too, Cicero and the people cooperate in a worthy purpose, just as they did in breaking open the fortified consulship. Here, too, the quality at issue is a *dignitas* implicitly determined by the people's favor; and here, too, Cicero is ultimately guided by the people's will (he remains true to "the role they imposed on him").[13] And with *hoc eodem in loco* "in this very place" Cicero virtually claims to have been a *praetor popularis* before he became a *consul popularis*, appearing in *contiones* in the people's

---

12. Scholars usually take that to be Cicero's reference; for an alternate view, see Rawson 1971.

13. Classen 1985: 323. *Persona* is occasional in the sense of 'role'; cf. *TLL* 10.1.1724.59–73 "spectat ad partes singulorum." For an example comparable to ours, cf. "I have always willingly played the part of leniency that nature herself has taught me, and I have never sought out the role of someone grave and stern—but I accepted it when the needs of the state thrust it upon me" (*has partis lenitatis . . . , quas me natura ipsa docuit, semper egi libenter, illam vero gravitatis severitatisque personam non appetivi, sed ab re publica mihi impositam sustinui, Mur.* 6). This sense is first found in Cicero, perhaps an extension or adaptation of the rhetorical sense of a 'role' or 'voice' (cf. *TLL* 10.1.1718.8–32) inspired by the comparable use of the Greek πρόσωπον.

interest. More important than themes, the passage recalls the *exordium* in its technique. As Cicero turns the details of his election into a symbol for his relationship with the people, so here he turns the favorable response to his speech on the Manilian Law into a kind of mandate from the people. That is a reverse: it was, after all, Cicero who delivered the oration; but Cicero highlights its reception—the vote, as it were, that confirms and supports a candidate's stump speech and thus imposes a duty on the candidate to be true to that speech. The apology for invoking Pompey too often thus explains precisely why Cicero can speak for him at all: Pompey, champion and servant of the people (F), is and must be defended and represented by Cicero, champion and servant of the people. Cicero's relationship with Pompey is not personal; it is ideological. They are, as it were, brothers in the same lodge, who know each other's ways because they share each other's beliefs. Claims to Pompey's authority must have been common in those days, but Cicero justifies his claim by assigning his own speech for Pompey a particular meaning. He is not claiming Pompey so much as asking the people to look into their memories, where they will already see him and Pompey standing side by side.

7.3. RULLUS

Laudes autem et vituperationes non separatim placet tractari,
sed in ipsis argumentationibus esse inplicatas.

Praise or blame, in my view, should not be handled as a separate
topic but integrated into the argumentation itself.

—Cicero, *de Inventione* 1.97

The details of the electoral mechanism depict Rullus and other supporters of the bill as a greedy cabal. This section discusses two symbolic images that support that idea—Rullus as a tyrant, and Rullus as a kind of un-tribune. Neither passage is invective in any strict sense; rather, the images and their imputations are worked into the fabric of other arguments.

Parades and Power

Having treated the electoral mechanism, Cicero turns to the decemvirs' powers: first, the character and symbols of thereof (*LA* 2.26–32 *potestatis*) and then to the specific modes of authority they will be allowed to exercise (*LA* 2.32 *formam*–35 *continentur*). The former treatment ends as follows (I include the very beginning of the latter to illustrate the transition):

Furthermore [Rullus] grants [the decemvirs] power that is nominally praetorian but effectively regal: he sets the term of office at five years, but makes it practically a lifetime (*sempiterna*) position, since it comes with so many powers and resources that no one could be stripped of it without his consent. And then he provides [them] with attendants, clerks, scribes, heralds, architects; and mules, too, and tents <and geldings (?)> and equipment; he drains resources out of the state treasury and supplements them from allies; he establishes a pool of two hundred surveyors of equestrian birth, twenty per decemvir, to serve as a bodyguard (*stipatores corporis*) and likewise the aides (*ministros*) and henchmen (*satellites*) of their power. There, fellow citizens, is the very look and feel of tyrants; and so far I've only shown you the emblems of power, not the power itself! Now someone might well say, "What do I care about a scribe, or a lictor, or a herald, or a chicken-keeper?" The nature of these things, citizens, is such that whoever would have them without your vote is either a magistrate with aspirations of kingship—or a private citizen that has lost his mind. But wait until you see the actual forms of power the decemvirs are granted! Then you will know that it's not the derangement of private persons but the insufferability of kings. First of all, then, their authority will include an unlimited power to acquire uncountable amounts of money ...."[14] (*LA* 2.32–33).

This passage has now-familiar touches: the accusation of kingship and a nod toward the importance of the popular vote. But there is much more here. The passage also has the look of simple list, but it instances several techniques we have

---

14. *Dat praeterea potestatem verbo praetoriam, re vera regiam; definit in quinquennium, facit sempiternam; tantis enim confirmat opibus et copiis ut invitis eripi nullo modo possit. Deinde ornat apparitoribus, scribis, librariis, praeconibus, architectis, praeterea mulis, tabernaculis,* †*centuriis*†*, supellectili; sumptum haurit ex aerario, suppeditat a sociis; finitores ex equestri loco ducentos, vicenos singulorum stipatores corporis constituit, eosdem ministros et satellites potestatis. Formam adhuc habetis, Quirites, et speciem ipsam tyrannorum; insignia videtis potestatis, nondum ipsam potestatem. Dixerit enim fortasse quispiam: "quid me ista laedunt, scriba, lictor, praeco, pullarius?" Omnia sunt haec huius modi, Quirites, ut, ea qui habeat sine vestris suffragiis, aut rex non ferundus aut privatus furiosus esse videatur. Perspicite quanta potestas permittatur; non privatorum insaniam, sed intolerantiam regum esse dicetis. Primum permittitur infinita potestas innumerabilis pecuniae conficiendae* .... After *tabernaculis,* the transmitted text has also *centuriis,* which has been obelized (Manuwald 2018) and emended variously to *tentoriis* ('tents,' Turnèbe [Turnebus]), *cantheriis* ('geldings,' Pacato [Panthagathus], and *centunculis* ('[patchwork *or* colored] saddlecloths,' Klotz; for other suggestions, see Nicolet 1970: 72-73 n. 2). *Centunculis* (from *cento* 'patchwork') is too specific (the word is not normal for 'saddlecloths,' but appears in that sense only as part of a stratagem described in Livy 7.14.7, cf. Fron. *Str.* 2.4.6). *Tentoriis* is redundant after the *tabernaculis* of the text (unless it is an intrusive gloss). *Cantheriis* makes good sense, if there were to be mules for carrying luggage but geldings for riding; cf. Cic. *Fam.* 9.18.4 (Paetus has sold a *cantherius* but still has a *mulus*).

seen: the creation of a symbol for power relations by reconfiguration, by allusion, and (probably) by invoking historical memory.

The passage intermingles distinct features of the bill, which fall broadly into two groups: what might be called constitutional features, like term and authority, and practical features, like support staff and equipment. The features generally were useful and even necessary. It was usual for colonial deputations to be supplied with mules, tents, and such equipment.[15] A five-year term would allow a decemvir to complete his work: establishing settlements with the attendant surveying took a long time.[16] *Praetoria potestas* would confer two useful powers: *imperium*, for establishing colonies and, entailed in *imperium*, *iurisdictio* or judicial authority in civil matters, for adjudicating property claims—the very two powers Cicero continually ascribes to the decemvirs.[17] *Praetoria potestas* as such, as opposed to simply *imperium*, was meant to allow establishing of the boundaries of public land outside of Italy[18] and, probably, to allow work in the bailiwick of provincial governors[19] and perhaps even in administrative districts not yet

---

15. Cf. Livy 42.1.7–11, Plu. *TG* 13, Gargola 2009: 67.

16. A three-man commission took three years to settle three or four hundred families in the 190s and in 183–181 in colonies at Vibo, Aquileia, and elsewhere (Brunt 1971: 79 with refs.). Likewise, Caesar's veterans began to be settled in 46, but the process was still not complete in March 44 (Brunt 1971: 296). The Rullan commission would have settled 5,000 settlers into the *ager Campanus* alone (*LA* 2.76, 96; C4 in Appendix 2), apart from its other business, which included sales in distant provinces and purchases from private owners scattered (one presumes) throughout Italy. Caesar's commission of 59, which concerned only the *ager Campanus*, had twenty commissioners: more hands for the survey work was another way of acknowledging its difficulty.

17. Various details also imply these powers. *Imperium* is implied by decemvirs with the bound rods or *fasces* (*LA* 1.9, 2.45) and lictors (*LA* 2.32), *pace* Lintott 1999: 144 n. 99 ("Cicero makes no allusion to the *decemviri* having lictors and *fasces*"). *Iurisdictio* is implied in decemvirs who can form *consilia* (*LA* 2.34) and delegate cases (*LA* 2.34). *Iurisdictio* is also implied by *poena sine provocatione, animadversio sine auxilio*, the decemvirs' alleged right to impose "penalty without appeal, and punishment without aid (= tribunician intercession, cf. *OLD s.v.* 2)." The phrases are inaccurate. *Poena* and *provocatio* concern chiefly criminal jurisdiction, not civil, like that of the decemvirs (see Harvey 1972: 72–73). But the decemvirs could change the status of land, which for those who lost possession would be *like* a criminal penalty, as Zumpt 1861: 67 n. 33 *fin.* astutely saw (*ademptio bonorum* 'seizure of goods' was one kind of *poena*). *Provocatio* here means, not protection from magisterial outrage (*pace* Manuwald 2018: 265), but the legal standing to appeal a property decision in a Roman court (so the *provocatio* proposed by Fulvius Flaccus for the Italians in 125; cf. V. Max. 9.5.1 and see Howarth 1999: 293–94); on that understanding of *provocatio*, the Rullan bill may not have permitted appeal of its decisions (reasonably, with an eye to stability). Cf. n. 75.

18. Praetorian rank was required to establish property boundaries; see Mommsen *RS*³ 2.1.435. Censors handled the issue inside the city.

19. Thus does Brennan 2000: 427 describe the Rullan bill as "another example of the phenomenon of interference in praetorian *provinciae*." For the location of the provincial territories, see

properly settled.[20] Surveyors would serve as assistant commissioners.[21] Support staff drawn from the civil service pool[22] would allow the decemvirs to work independently: the properties abroad were widely scattered, and the properties in Italy involved many complexities of title and assessment.[23] A guaranteed revenue stream would keep the commission from being starved of resources;[24] provided equipment would let it start work quickly.

The powers make sense for the task the bill was designed to accomplish. But many of them were also unusual. A fixed five-year term was an innovation in an agrarian bill—indeed, in any kind of command.[25] Cicero's remark that the appointment was effectively for life perhaps implies that the law also permitted extending the term of office in the way that provincial commands were prolonged (*prorogatio*). An agrarian and colonial commission with judicial authority and even *imperium* is not *per se* remarkable,[26] but *praetoria potestas* as such was not

---

ch. 8 n. 2. The only known governors in 63 are L. Manlius Torquatus (probably) in Macedonia; P. Servilius Globulus in Asia; and Pompey in Cilicia and Bithynia/Pontus (Brennan 2000: 711, 718, 721).

20. Some of the properties for sale under the bill (listed in full in ch. 8 n. 2) had been only very recently organized administratively, if at all. There is no evidence of *publicani* at work in Cyrene until 54; cf. Cic. *Planc.* 63 and Oost 1963: 14. The territories in south Asia Minor had been won by P. Servilius Vatia in his campaign against the Cilician pirates in 77–75. Servilius's successors as governors of Cilicia—L. Octavius Cn. f. (cos. 75), L. Licinius Lucullus (cos. 74), and Q. Marcius Rex (cos. 68)—seem to have done little for the organization of the district (Lucullus, in fact, was never there at all, spending his time in Bithynia, Pontus, Armenia, Syria, and Cappadocia; for his activity, see Magie 1950: 321–350).

21. Zumpt 1861: 66; Harvey 1972: 68, "expert surveyors, serving more as assistant land commissioners than as technicians."

22. *Scribae, librarii, praecones, architecti* (*LA* 2.32); *scriba, lictor, praeco, pullarius* (*LA* 2.32). These were civil servants, organized into *decuriae* or pools (evidence is lacking only for *decuriae architectorum*), that served the magistrates and promagistrates; on these grades, see Jones 1949.

23. The right to work independently appears in other laws: Mommsen believed the agrarian law of 111 allowed one of its *duumviri* to work in Africa and the other in Greece, which he called "ein Versuch durch die Teilung der Competenz die Collegialität illusorisch zu machen" (Mommsen *RS*³ 2.1.629 and n. 4); *contra* Johannsen 1971: 304–305. Caesar's bill of 59 had members of its twenty-man commission work individually to divide up the *ager Campanus*.

24. Cf ch. 1 n. 114.

25. See ch. 1 n. 105.

26. For example, a colonial commission of 194 had *imperium* (and thus *iurisdictio*); the Gracchan commission of 133 had both powers; the Appuleian commission of 90 had *iurisdictio*. The titles of the commissions show their powers: *triumviri agris **iudicandis** adsignandis* (the Gracchan commission in its original form, cf. Liv. *per.* 58 *ut idem triumviri **iudicarent** qua publicus ager, qua privatus esset*) and *xvir agris dandis attribuendis **iudicandis*** (the Appuleian commission).

demonstrably held by earlier commissions. Cicero's objections to the powers of the bill are thus historically and constitutionally fair or at least not unprincipled. He interweaves the powers to create a symbol of that (as he claims to see it) danger. The term of office, with its resources, is followed by list of staff and equipment. The latter concrete list becomes by juxtaposition a symbol of the former, abstract power. The force of that symbol depends on grammar and on semiotics. The list is asyndetic, which gives the effect of a parade passing by: group after group of persons ("attendants, clerks, scribes, heralds, architects"), and then animals and equipment laden with one thing ("tents") and then another ("equipment"). The "parade" must have recalled a magistrate with his lictors and the traveling retinue of a grandee on a road outside of town.[27] Cicero then replicates the maneuver; he speaks first abstractly, naming sources of revenue, and then gives a concrete image, the twenty surveyors. The latter glosses the former: the revenue means kingliness because the surveyors are like a bodyguard. "Bodyguards" of armed followers or mercenaries—ἐπίκουροι, among other words[28]—are a regular feature of the classical tyrant. For Aristotle the link was so obvious that asking for a bodyguard was inductive proof of tyrannical intention.[29] Some version of that idea was obviously current in the Rome of the Republic. Thence Cicero's labels for the surveyors. *Stipator*, lit. "one who presses in close," is usually linked to kings. *Satelles*, properly 'one of a bodyguard to a prince or despot,' is often derogatory; both senses are in play here.[30] (*Satelles* in the meaning '(violent) partisan, supporter'—which occurs later in the speeches—is a natural extension).[31] *Minister*,

---

27. Cf. Cicero's description of Milo's retinue: "As he was riding in a carriage with his wife, in his traveling cloak, accompanied with a large, heavily laden, effeminate, and gentle retinue of maid-servants and boys" (... *cum ... cum uxore veheretur in raeda, paenulatus, magno et impedito et muliebri ac delicato ancillarum puerorumque comitatu, Mil.* 28), followed by Milo's slaves (*Mil.* 29).

28. Hdt. 1.64.1, 6.39.2, Thuc. 6.55.3, 6.58.2.

29. *Rhet.* 1.2.19 = 1357b. Cypselus, who had no bodyguard, is the exception that proves the rule (Arist. *Pol.* 5.9.22 = 1315b).

30. *OLD s.vv. Stipator* is not common in Cicero; besides this passage, he uses it in speeches only of one L. Sergius, calling him "Catiline's arms-bearer, [Clodius's] bodyguard, standard-bearer of sedition" (*armiger Catilinae, stipator tui corporis, signifer seditionis, Dom.* 13) and of the bodyguard of temple slaves of Verres' protégé Apronius (*Ver.* 2.3.65). Cicero usually uses *satelles* metaphorically (thus with *cupiditatum, Ver.* 2.3.21; *audaciae, Catil.* 1.7; *scelerum, Prov.* 5); for a literal instance, like this one, cf. "But you see the magistrates, if you can call them that—well, you see the tyrant's loyal ministers holding office, you see his armies, you see his veterans lined up on our flank ... it's all a tinder-box" (*sed vides magistratus, si quidem illi magistratus, vides tamen tyranni satellites <in> imperiis, vides eiusdem exercitus, vides in latere veteranos, quae sunt* εὐρίπιστα *omnia, Att.* 14.4.2, written in April of 44).

31. *LA* 1.18, 2.84 = C36, C5 in Appendix 2.

too, often has the pejorative sense 'tool' or 'accomplice' rather than simply 'agent' or 'subordinate.'[32] If the decemvirs have the "look and feel of tyrants" (literally, "shape and appearance," *formam ... atque speciem*), that is a look Cicero has made them have: he has arranged the features of their authority to summon up a stereotype his audience recognized.

Perhaps that stereotype was supported by a specific reference—another decemvirate that empaneled extraordinary officers. According to Roman tradition, class conflict in the 450s led to the suspension of the consulship and the plebeian tribunate and the seating in 451 of a panel of ten, the so-called First Decemvirate, to govern the state and compile a body of laws. The decemvirate governed justly for that year. A second decemvirate was elected for 450 but quickly lapsed into tyranny.[33] The features of that decemvirate as Livy depicts it recall the picture Cicero paints here.[34] Those decemvirs, with a parade of 120 lictors (3.36.4), upset the populace, looking like ten kings (*decem regum species erat*, 3.36.5); they were rumored to have wanted power for life (3.36.9); they compiled a bodyguard of young patricians (*patriciis iuvenibus saesperant latera*, 3.37.6). And many of the features of the Second Decemvirate exactly parallel the features of the Rullan bill as Cicero depicts it elsewhere. Appius Claudius, the chief personality of both decemvirates, presided over a rigged election (3.35.9–10); so, Cicero claims, would Rullus (*LA* 2.21).[35] The Rullan bill was crafted in secret (*LA* 2.12); likewise the Second Decemvirate met without witnesses (*cotidie coibant remotis arbitris; consili[a] ... secreto ab aliis coquebant*, 3.36.2). Rullan commissioners would make private judicial decisions, like Rullus in Egypt (*LA* 2.43); so did the Second Decemvirate (*iudicia domi conflabant*, 3.36.8). To ensure conformity to its rulings, decisions of the decemvirates were not subject to *provocatio*, the cherished Roman right of appeal, but that provision was abused (3.36.6); likewise, according to Cicero, the Rullan bill would feature *poena sine provocatione, animadversio sine auxilio* "penalty without appeal, and punishment without aid" (*LA* 2.33, just after the above passage).[36] To what extent these particular

---

32. *TLL* 8.0.1003.60–1, 68–86 "i.q. adiutor ... in malam partem"; *OLD s.v.* 3b.

33. On the (legendary) tradition of the decemvirates, see Drummond 1989: 227–35, 718–25, Ogilvie 1965: 451–89.

34. The claim is first advanced by Harvey 1972: 33–34.

35. On the depiction of the Appii Claudii in Livy's account as stereotypical tyrants, see Vasaly 1987.

36. On these phrases, see n. 17. As noted there, they are constitutionally inaccurate—but their point is to assimilate the measures of the bill to the memory of the Second Decemvirate.

parallels suggested themselves to Cicero's audience—and to what extent Livy's later account represents the historical memory of a previous generation—is of course a complex question. But it is certain that the historical memory of Cicero's audience was richer and more detailed than some have supposed,[37] and I hope to have made it clear by this point that Cicero's rhetorical technique was more allusive than it has sometimes been regarded. And one feature of this passage suggests very strongly that Cicero has the Second Decemvirate in mind: his remark that anyone who would adopt the perquisites of office without due election is either an intolerable king or a private citizen gone mad (*aut rex non ferundus aut privatus furiosus esse videatur*). Why *privatus furiosus*? *Rex*, consonant with the speech's many accusations of kingly aspiration, was sufficient to make the point. The dichotomy implies a contrast between an official of some kind grossly overstepping his authority (that is, "king" is metonymic for a "magistrate with despotic aspirations") and an ordinary citizen arrogating authority (or trying to). The Second Decemvirate was both: when their term expired, the decemvirs laid aside neither their intention to rule nor their emblems of high office (*privati pro decemviris, neque animis ad imperium inhibendum imminutis neque ad speciem honoris insignibus prodeunt*, 3.38.1).[38] If the Second Decemvirate symbolized an institutional innovation that had begun with a populist veneer but become tyrannical, Cicero had a fine *exemplum* for his purposes. A ten-man kingship and feigned populism are exactly the points Cicero raises in the *propositio* (2.15).[39] The Second Decemvirate is the Unnamed Referent of these sections with their proud parade. Cicero's *vituperatio* is woven into the argument itself.

The Voices of the (Un-)Tribune

If Rullus is a king, he is also no tribune. That comes out strikingly in Cicero's handling of the provision for the purchase of land (*LA* 2.62–71). We have seen part of that section earlier (Table 5.3.1), where it is made to serve Cicero's claim that the bill will provide no *commodum*. A motif in the heart of that section, which is the focus here, supports that claim: the voice of the tribune. The tribune's voice partook of his own status as a kind of incarnation of the sovereignty of the people. He could, by a word (*veto!*), bar any magistrate's action; he could by the threat of that word bend or stay the political winds; he might call someone to appear before a public assembly to be harangued; he could not be interrupted

---

37. Cf. ch. 4 n. 106.

38. On the link of *insignia* to proper elections, see Mommsen *RS*³ 1:8.

39. Cf. ch. 1 n. 5.

Images of Identity 227

when he was speaking.[40] When Cicero describes the restoration of the tribunate in 70, he describes it specifically as a return to the Rostra of the tribune's voice (*locumque illum . . . a tribunicia voce desertum*).[41] The deviations and distortions of that voice in the mouth of Rullus show him to be the exact anti-type of a true Gracchan tribune. The semiotics of Rullus's voice don't match the ideal template of his office.

To see that, some detail about the agricultural economy is required. Sulla had established colonies throughout Italy for his retiring soldiers. Many grantees appear to have sold, transferred, or abandoned their land, some (much?) of which ended up in the hands of large landowners. That land commonly had two features. It was not always ideal: as we have seen, Sulla's colonists complained of being relegated to swamps and forests. And the land was illegally possessed: the original Sullan grants had forbidden alienation. The Rullan bill aimed to purchase (some of) this land for its colonial project. Many possessors of lesser-quality plots would likely have been willing to sell. For-profit agriculture depended heavily on slave labor,[42] and that labor was inefficient if the climate or soil was poor.[43] To free such possessors to sell, the Rullan bill created retroactive title, formally legitimating acquisitions (presumably only those made by purchase or deeded transfer).[44] Cicero in the third speech labels that legitimation shameless (*genus id agrorum certo capite legis impudentissime confirmari atque sanciri*, *LA* 3.3), but the whole plan was not a bad one, since it would, or could, improve yields from underproducing or even abandoned land and at the same time increase the liquidity of the financial markets, which depended on land as a store of value. But several arguments were open to opponents of the plan (not all of which will have applied to

---

40. Cf. V. Max. 9.5.2 (punishment of a consul who dared to interrupt a tribune conducting an assembly), Plin. *Ep.* 1.23.2 (*qui iubere posset tacere quemcumque* and *quem interfari nefas esset* "who may enjoin silence on anybody" and "whom it is strictly forbidden to interrupt," of a Republican tribune). For a summary of the tribune's powers, see Mommsen *RS*³ 2.1: 272–330.

41. *qui* [sc. L. Quinctius, tr. pl. 70] . . . *rostra iam diu vacua locumque illum post adventum L. Sullae a tribunicia voce desertum oppresserat, multitudinemque desuefactam iam a contionibus ad veteris consuetudinis similitudinem revocarat* (*Clu.* 110). On the restoration of the tribunate against the background of the politics of the time, see Santangelo 2014: 5–10.

42. For the role of slaves in the agricultural economy, see Rothe 2018: 16–18 with refs.

43. Varro noted that "noxious locales" (*gravia loca*), meaning swampy areas (for *gravis* as 'swampy, unwholesome,' cf. *TLL* 6.2.2296.10–60), are better worked not by slaves but by hired hands (*mercenarii*; such workers typically lived in and therefore knew the tricks of working the local area): *de quibus universis* [= kinds of persons employed in agriculture] *hoc dico, gravia loca utilius esse mercenariis colere quam servis, et in salubribus quoque locis opera rustica maiora, ut sunt in condendis fructibus vindemiae aut messis, R.* 1.17.3). Cf. Col. 1.7.3–4.

44. For a full legal analysis of the issue of title, see Drummond 2000.

every parcel). For example, one could argue that providing clear title to possessors after the fact might, in certain circumstances, relieve them of encumbrances that attached to the property: the Rullan bill was a windfall. One could also argue that secondary possessions were illegal and that the state was within its rights to simply reclaim the land rather than buying out possessors, which was like buying back stolen goods from the thief: Rullus's bill was a ransom payment. Last, one could argue that, in some cases, the land in question would be poor, among other things letting possessors profit from poor assets (which they shouldn't have acquired in the first place): Rullus's bill is a bill of goods.

Both speeches use only the "unjust compensation" and "poor land" arguments (and link them to each other).[45] To prepare for them, Cicero attacks a particular measure of the law: no one could be forced to sell; to use juristic language, there would be no *emptio ab invito*, roughly the "eminent domain" of common-law jurisdictions. Table 7.3.1 illustrates Cicero's two versions of that opening salvo (the letters here and in the next four tables continue the sequence begun in Table 5.3.1; Roman numerals indicate the different sequence of elements in each speech, and only the strictly corresponding elements of the senate speech appear).

Table 7.3.1. (*LA* 1.14, 2.67)

G. No Purchase from Unwilling Sellers

(i.) Cavet enim vir optimus ne emat ab invito. Quasi vero non intellegamus ab invito emere iniuriosum esse, ab non invito quaestuosum.	(i.) 67. . . . 'Idcirco,' inquit, 'agros nominare non possum quia tangam nullum ab invito.' Hoc, Quirites, multo est quaestuosius quam si ab invito sumeret; inibitur enim ratio quaestus de vestra pecunia, et tum denique ager emetur cum idem expediet emptori et venditori.
"Yes, because our excellent citizen stipulates that there be no purchase from an unwilling seller. As if we didn't know that there's injury in buying from an unwilling seller—but profit from a *not* unwilling one!"	"'The reason I can't name the fields specifically,' he says, 'is because I won't be seizing any property from an unwilling possessor.' Ah, but that, citizens, is much more profitable than if he did! That's because they'll be calculating how to profit with your money. Then and only then will the land be sold when the buyer and seller both agree on a price."

---

45. Cicero would make the "windfall" argument only after a *contio* of Rullus responding to *LA* 2; cf. *LA* 3.7–9, and see the chronology in ch. 1 n. 8.

G-p looks both backward and forward. Cicero had just alleged that Rullus's bill did not specify land in advance (Table 5.3.1.E–F); G-p represents Rullus's imagined rejoinder. Both speeches allege that the provision will mean higher prices, but G-p recalls the Cicero's allusions to *emptio venditio* (Ch. 5.3 Bad Land): hence *emptori* 'seller' and *venditori* 'buyer,' the names not of offices (*decemvir*, *quaesitor*)[46] or of legal status (*possessor*) but of purely economic functions. Cicero is again the skeptical friend in the marketplace, pointing out that the *commodum* at issue (that is the reference of *expediat* as in *LA* 2.66 = Table 5.3.1.E) is somebody else's, not the people who are buying into the deal with "their money." G-p also prepares for what follows. There is a sting in the words Cicero puts in Rullus's mouth. *Tangam*, literally 'touch,' has here its occasional sense 'take possession of'—usually implying an unjust seizure.[47] Rullus says "seize" where he might have said "reclaim." That suggests where his true sympathies lie: with possessors.

And that is Cicero's very next point, the "unjust compensation" argument (Table 7.3.2).

Table 7.3.2. (*LA* 1.14, 2.68)

H. Occupiers of Public Land Unjustly Compensated

(iii.) Facient idem ceteri libenter, ut possessionis invidiam pecunia commutent, accipiant quod cupiunt, dent quod retinere vix possunt.	(ii) 68. Sed videte vim legis agrariae. Ne ei quidem qui agros publicos possident decedent de possessione, nisi erunt deducti optima condicione et pecunia maxima. Conversa ratio. Antea cum erat a tribuno plebis mentio legis agrariae facta, continuo qui agros publicos aut qui possessiones invidiosas tenebant extimescebant; haec lex eos homines fortunis locupletat, invidia liberat. Quam multos enim, Quirites, existimatis esse qui latitudinem possessionum tueri, qui invidiam Sullanorum agrorum ferre non possint, qui vendere cupiant, emptorem non reperiant, perdere iam denique illos agros ratione aliqua velint? Qui paulo ante diem noctemque tribunicium nomen horrebant, vestram vim metuebant, mentionem legis agrariae pertimescebant, ei nunc etiam ultro rogabuntur atque orabuntur ut agros partim publicos, partim plenos invidiae, plenos periculi quanti ipsi velint decemviris tradant.

(continued)

---

46. The decemvirs were to have assistants called *quaesitores* (*LA* 2.34).

47. *OLD* s.v. 5b. For an example, cf. *de praeda mea praetor quaestores urbanos, id est populum Romanum, terruncium nec attigit nec tacturus est quisquam* "From my booty no one has

Table 7.3.2. Continued

"Others will be only too glad to do exactly the same thing with their possessions—convert ill-will into cash, get the deal they want, and give over the thing they didn't want to keep anyway!" [i]	"So do you see how this 'agrarian law' works? Not even people who are in possession of public lands are going to submit to ejection [ii] unless they get great deal of money and under the most favorable legal conditions. The whole system is backward. It used to be, when a tribune of the plebs mentioned an agrarian law, those who held public lands or resented properties would immediately start to worry; but those are the very people that this law restores to good graces [iii] and covers in wealth! Surely you realize, citizens, that there are many who can't maintain their extensive possessions; who can't endure the resentment of Sullan properties; who want to sell but can't find a buyer; and so want to just get rid of their holdings any way they can? The same people who not all that long ago used to dread the name of tribune night and day, who feared your authority, who quaked at the mention of an agrarian law, will now actually be sought out and asked—begged!—to set their own price when they sell the decemvirs land that's either [already] public or deeply resented and under weak title!" [iv]

[i] Lit. "what they are barely able to keep."
[ii] See Table 5.3.1 n. i.
[iii] Lit. "frees of ill-will [*sc.* from possessing Sullan properties]."
[iv] Lit. "full of envy, full of danger."

Both speeches have the same *inventio*: holders of ill-regarded land, who should be at a disadvantage, are instead favored, as their emotions show. In the senate speech the prospect of sale brings gladness: possessors will sell "gladly" (*libenter*) and receive "what they want." But in the popular speech the prospect of sale means relief from fear. It used to be a tribune's mere "mention" (*mentio*) of an agrarian law meant alarm (*extimescebant*); it used to be the "mention"

touched or will touch one thin dime except for the urban quaestors—which is to say, the Roman people" (Cic. *Fam.* 2.17.4).

(again *mentio*) of an agrarian law meant deep fear (*pertimescebant*); the tribune's very name (*nomen*) once meant dread (*metuebant*). The allusion is clearly to the Gracchi; and an unnamed—or rather half-named—referent of the passage is the power of a tribune's words and name. That underlies the image of speech at the segment's end. The chief power of tribunes was to intercede on a citizen's behalf—that is, to be begged. But here it is tribunes who supplicate: possessors will be "sought out and asked—begged!" (*etiam ultro rogabuntur atque orabuntur*). *Etiam ultro*, lit. "besides, furthermore," indicates that the action is unmotivated;[48] *rogabuntur atque orabuntur*, not far from "beg and plead," registers its intensity.[49] The tribune's voice of command has pointedly become a voice of entreaty—directed to those who should themselves be entreating. This tribune is no populist, as the electoral mechanism already showed, and his voice is no echo of the Gracchi. Hence Cicero's pungent phrase *conversa ratio*. The usual expression for "The situation is [now] reversed" seems to be *res conversa est*.[50] But here it's not a situation that's reversed; it's the whole way of operating: the whole "pattern" or "system" or "operating principle" (*ratio*) is backward.

Among the indulged possessors, according to Cicero, would be one Valgus—Rullus's own father-in-law.[51] Both speeches make the imputation (Table 7.3.3).

---

48. *Etiam ultro*, with *ultro* in the sense 'spontaneously' (cf. *OLD* s.v. 5), connotes the absence of an existing reciprocal obligation or prior expectation, e.g. *honoresque populi etiam ultro delatos repudiabit* "and he will reject public honors even if they are freely offered" (Cic. *Tusc.* 5.36). I have tried to draw out the sense by "will now actually be sought out" (cf. *OED* s.v. *actually* 5b "contrary to what one might think").

49. The phrase is otherwise only in early speeches (*Div. Caec.* 3, *Ver.* 2.1.72, 2.2.96, 2.2.103, 2.2.147, 2.3.69, *S. Rosc.* 144), some letters (*Att.* 16.16b.2, *Fam.* 2.7.4, 5.18.1, 13.66.2) and once in a dialogue (*Tusc.* 4.78). The first Verrine instance captures its flavor: *pertimuit iste ne Philodamus Neronis iudicio liberaretur; rogat et orat Dolabellam ut de sua provincia decedat, ad Neronem proficiscatur; se demonstrat incolumem esse non posse, si Philodamo vivere atque aliquando Romam venire licuisset* ("He panicked at the thought that Philodamus would be let go by Nero's decision. He begs and pleads with Dolabella to leave his province and go to Nero; he claims he cannot be safe, if Philodamus is allowed to live—and eventually find his way to Rome").

50. For the ordinary expression, cf. *et vide quam conversa res sit* (Cic. *Att.* 8.13.2), *domum ipsam tuam vi et rapinis funestam tibi ac tuis comparasti, videlicet ut nos commonefacias quam conversa res sit, cum in ea domo habitares, homo flagitiosissime, quae P. Crassi viri clarissimi fuit* ([Sal.] *Cic.* 3). Cf. also *et quaeso considerate quam convorsa rerum natura sit* (Sal. *Hist.* 1.77.13M). *Ratio conversa* vel sim. is otherwise only in Apuleius in a technical, astronomical sense (*Mun.* 13).

51. Or possibly *Valgius*; the name is attested only in *LA* 3.3 (*... non a vestrorum commodorum patrono, sed a Valgi genero esse conscriptam ...*). See Harvey 1972: 222–46, Manuwald 2018: 427.

Table 7.3.3. (*LA* 1.14, 2.68–9)

I. Rullus's Father-in-Law Unjustly Compensated

(ii.) Quantum tibi agri vendet, ut alios omittam, socer tuus, et, si ego eius aequitatem animi probe novi, vendet non invitus?	(iii.) Atque hoc carmen hic tribunus plebis non vobis sed sibi intus canit. 69. Habet socerum, virum optimum, qui tantum agri in illis rei publicae tenebris occupavit quantum concupivit. Huic subvenire volt succumbenti iam et oppresso, Sullanis oneribus gravi, sua lege, ut liceat illi invidiam deponere, pecuniam condere. Et vos non dubitatis quin vectigalia vestra vendatis plurimo maiorum vestrorum sanguine et sudore quaesita, ut Sullanos possessores divitiis augeatis, periculo liberetis?
"So your father-in-law—let's just talk about him—how much land will *he* sell you? And, if I'm any judge of his fortitude, will sell 'not unwillingly'?"	"And this song isn't one this tribune of the plebs is singing for you but for himself for his own purposes. His father-in-law—a 'respectable man'!—took control of all the land he pleased in the dark days of the republic. But now he's going under, now he's crushed, weighed down by Sullan burdens; and Rullus means to help him with his law so he can escape resentment and store up cash. And doesn't it bother you to sell off your tax properties, acquired by your elders with much sweat and blood, just to enrich Sullan possessors with wealth and free them from [legal] peril?"

Cicero's claim is plausible. Valgus had land near Casinum, where he had stitched together contiguous parcels into an estate,[52] and he also had vast holdings in *ager Hirpinus* in the south-central Appennines, where Sulla had seized territory.[53] Some, at least, of these possessions must have been illegally acquired, just as Cicero says, leaving them under weak title (cf. *habet incertos ac nullo iure possessos*, *LA* 3.14).[54] Familiar ideas are invoked to support the imputation: again

---

52. "The excellent, fruitful estates around Casinum which he linked together (he looked around him, imagined the many farms were a single estate, and proscribed neighboring properties until it matched the plan)" (*eos fundos quos in agro Casinati optimos fructuosissimosque continuavit cum usque eo vicinos proscriberet quoad oculis conformando ex multis praediis unam fundi regionem formamque perfecerit, LA* 3.14).

53. *totum enim possidet, LA* 3.8. Sulla sacked Aeculanum in that territory, which had refused to capitulate, and also took the nearby Bovianum by assault (App. *BC* 1.51). For a full list of textually attested *latifundia*, see White 1967.

54. See Harvey 1972: 222–46.

commodum and again the cabal. *Commodum* is invoked by raising the specter of lost tax properties. Their value is underscored by a populist argument, if not a populist slogan, *sanguine et sudore* "by blood and sweat": the benefits of land won by the toil of the many should not go to the few.[55] The image here recalls the *propositio* of the speech, where Cicero applies that same phrase, which is nowhere else in his oratory, to *libertas* itself:

> When I have laid out these points, citizens, if they seem wrong to you, I will bow to your authority and change my opinion; but if you come to believe sham generosity is actually a secret attack on your liberty, have no hesitation about defending, with a consul's help, the liberty which your ancestors bled and sweated so much to win (*plurimo sudore et sanguine . . . partam*) and you toiled not once to inherit." (*LA* 2.16)[56]

The other idea is that of the profiteering cabal, here in the form of nepotism, expressed memorably by *intus canit*, lit. "sings inward." *Carmen intus canere* was evidently to play a cithara only with the fingers of the left or inside hand, which might pluck chords, omitting the right or outside hand, which usually struck notes with a plectrum.[57] The posture appeared in an apparently famous

---

55. The idea is more commonly applied to victorious soldiers themselves: *milites, quorum sanguine Tarulae Scirtoque, pessumis servorum, divitiae partae sunt* ("the soldiers by whose blood riches were won for the worst of slaves, Tarula and Scirtus," Sal. *Or. Lep.* (*Hist.* 1.49M) 21, of two otherwise unknown minions of Sulla); *verum esse habere eos quorum sanguine ac sudore partus sit* ("It was right for those to have [land] by whose sweat and blood it was acquired," Liv. 2.48.2, a defense by the consul Caeso Fabius of an agrarian law in 479); *cur autem potius Campani agrum Italiae uberrimum, dignam agro urbem, qui nec se nec sua tutari possent, quam victor exercitus haberet qui suo sudore ac sanguine inde Samnites depulisset?* ("Why should the Campanians, who could not protect themselves or their things, possess the richest land in Italy, and a city befitting such land, rather than the victorious army who by its own sweat and blood dislodged the Samnites from it?" Liv. 7.38.6, the logic of soldiers posted in Campania planning a mutiny during the First Samnite War). More like Cicero's use is *Siciliamque et Sardiniam, benignissimas urbis nostrae nutrices, gradus <et> stabilimenta bellorum, tam multo sudore et sanguine in potestatem redactas . . . [senatus] dimisit* (V. Max. 7.6.1, of financial exigencies after Cannae). *Sanguen et sudor*, like "blood, sweat, and tears," was later used to describe other gains involving toil and sacrifice (Plin. *Ep.* 2.7.1, Sen. *Dial.* 7.25.8, *Ep.* 67.13).

56. *quae cum, Quirites, exposuero, si falsa vobis videbuntur esse, sequar auctoritatem vestram, mutabo meam sententiam; sin insidias fieri libertati vestrae simulatione largitionis intellegetis, nolitote dubitare plurimo sudore et sanguine maiorum vestrorum partam vobisque traditam libertatem nullo vestro labore consule adiutore defendere* (*LA* 2.16).

57. Ps.-Asc. ad Cic. *Ver.* 2.1.53, p. 237.1–4 Stangl: *cum canunt citharistae, utriusque manus funguntur officio. Dextra plectro utitur, et hoc est 'foris canere'; sinistrae digiti chordas carpunt, et*

statue,[58] and the phrase was proverbial both for thieves (the left hand was the thief's instrument)[59] and for those who consult their own advantage.[60] Here, too, then, is the idea of *commodum* derailed: Rullus sings for his father the same way "buyer" and "seller" work out their own deal *de vestra pecunia* (G-p). But Cicero also infuses the proverb with another idea. The elements of the proverbial turn are strung out: *atque hoc **carmen** hic tribunus plebis non vobis sed sibi **intus canit**.* That allows *carmen* 'song' to develop other resonances before it resolves into the proverb. And in this context the word would first have had tinges of its other, magical and religious, meanings: for Sullan possessors this tribune's words are a "[favorable] oracle" or an "inducement" (cf. *rogabuntur atque orabuntur*) or even a "magic charm" that banished their fear.[61] And his father-in-law, it turns out, benefits directly from that charmed speech.

And that is exactly the same kind of speech that shows up presently. Cicero, enlarging the "unjust compensation" argument and transitioning to the "poor land" argument, claims that the law has two kinds of properties in mind (Table 7.3.4).

---

hoc est 'intus canere.' Difficile est autem quod Aspendius citharista faciebat: ut non uteretur cantu utraque manu, sed omnia, id est universam cantionem, intus et sinistra tantum manu complecteretur. According to Anderson 1994: 176, the left hand only damped unwanted strings; but unless it had other, actively musical uses, the image makes little sense (and as Anderson there notes, left-hand plucking was "acoustically a disadvantageous procedure").

58. *Atque etiam illum Aspendium citharistam, de quo saepe audistis id quod est Graecis hominibus in proverbio, quem omnia intus canere dicebant, sustulit et in intimis suis aedibus posuit, ut etiam illum ipsum suo artificio superasse videatur* ("And he even made off with the famous statue of the Citharist of Aspendos—the one the Greeks used to say 'sang everything to himself,' in that saying that you have often heard—and he set up the statue in the farthest interior of his house. He's better at the statue's specialty than the statue!," *Ver.* 2.1.53).

59. Cf. *illa . . . furtifica laeva* (Pl. *Per.* 226), *nataeque ad furta sinistrae* (Ov. *Met.* 13.111). That is part of the effect in Catullus 12, where Marrucinus pinches a napkin with his left hand.

60. Ps.-Asc. ad Cic. *Verr.* 2.1.53, p. 237.5–7 Stangl: *unde omnes quotquot fures erant a Graecis Aspendii citharistae in proverbio dicebantur, quod, ut <ille> carminis, ita isti furtorum occultatores erant. valet hoc proverbium et in eos qui multum intestinis suis commodis consulunt praeter honestatem.* Cf. *Ver.* 2.1.53 in n. 58.

61. With overtones of 'solemn formula,' as of law (*TLL* 3.0.463.68–464.9, *OLD s.v.* 1e 'a legal formula or pronouncement; a ceremonial formula')? The *TLL* assigns this particular instance to the rare sense "de dicto (cogitatione) animum mulcente" (3.0.468.37). On *carmina* and witches, see Stratton 2007: 31–34; on *carmina* as ritualized speech, see Habinek 2005: 77–82.

Table 7.3.4. (*LA* 1.15, 2.70)

J. Law Has Two Kinds of Land in Mind

(v.) 15.... Spoliemus orbem terrarum, vendamus vectigalia, effundamus aerarium, ut locupletatis aut invidiae aut pestilentiae possessoribus agri tamen emantur.

"That way we can loot the whole world, sell off tax properties, and drain the treasury dry, so that possessors—of ill-will or of pestilence!—can get rich off selling their lands anyway."

[Cf. *invidiae* 'ill-will,' J.]

(iv.) 70. Nam ad hanc emptionem decemviralem duo genera agrorum spectant, Quirites. Eorum unum propter invidiam domini fugiunt, alterum propter vastitatem.

"But why do I say that? The decemvirs are looking to purchase two kinds of land, citizens. One kind is being abandoned by its owners because people resent it, and the other because it's desolate."

K. Resented Land

(v.) Sullanus ager a certis hominibus latissime continuatus tantam habet invidiam ut veri ac fortis tribuni plebis stridorem unum perferre non possit. Hic ager omnis, quoquo pretio coemptus erit, tamen ingenti pecunia nobis inducetur.

"The Sullan land that has been combined into large estates by certain parties is now so deeply resented that it could not endure a [simple] hiss from a tribune of the plebs—a brave and true one, anyway! But the enormous cost of all of that land is now going to be charged to our account, no matter how much was paid to buy it up."

J-p is not scaremongering. It really was true that some of the land that the decemvirs would purchase was former Sullan land or agriculturally mediocre (not mutually exclusive categories), exactly as the senate speech also says. The idea that a proper tribune could simply reclaim wrongly occupied land is expressed strikingly: he had merely to emit a *stridor* (K-p). *Stridor* is applied to variety of sounds like the 'whistle' of a hard wind, the 'whir' of slings, or, among animals, the 'squeak' of bats, the 'trumpeting' of an elephant, or the 'screech' of the *strix* or barn owl.[62] These sounds are mostly distinguished by having an apparent primary tone with a narrow range of (dissonant) under- or overtones (hence Catullus uses it for the Phyrgian pipes); and the dissonance (or irresolution) gives many of the sounds a tense and even unsettling quality (Seneca uses it for the equivalent of 'fingernails on a chalkboard').[63] Cicero's tribune is therefore probably not simply 'hissing.'[64] *Stridor* is rarely produced by humans—except for one kind: the witch. A witch in Tibullus holds sway over the dead by a *magicus stridor* (1.2.49). The awful voice of the Thessalian witch in Lucan includes "the shrieking and wailing of beasts" (*quod strident ululantque ferae*, 6.688). Some kind of shriek must have been used by witches—perhaps in imitation of the *strix*, a bird of bad omen.[65] Those are the overtones of the word here: the tribune's voice is compared to a witch's—a nod to Roman folk religion, where the witch is by no means a despicable character.[66] He and she can by a mere sound strike fear into hearts and drive the wicked and wickedness away. A *verus* and *fortis* tribune should be casting his *carmina*, as it were, on unjust possessors, thereby dissipating the imbalancing *invidia* aimed at them,[67] or perhaps purifying a tainted item—the very things that witches were hired to do.[68]

Last, Cicero turns to the other kind of "poor land," the agriculturally inferior (Table 7.3.5).

---

62. Wind: Acc. *trag.* 567R, 572W; whir: *B. Afr.* 83.2; bats: Ov. *Met.* 4.413; trumpeting: *B. Afr.* 72.4; screech: Ov. *Fast.* 6.139–40. For the identification of the *strix* with the barn owl, which does not "hoot" but does "screech," see Zarnott 2007: 328–29.

63. Phrygian pipes: *barbaraque horribili stridebat tibia cantu* ("and the foreign pipe sounded with its rough song," 64.264), from the depiction of a Bacchic revel and doubtless referring to the *tibiae impares*, lit. 'uneven pipes,' used in the worship of Cybele; their sound could be dark and raspy (cf. Bélis 1999: 25, 27), perhaps like an oboe. Cf. also *pectora rauco concita buxo*, Sen. *Ag.* 689 and West 1992: 91–92. Seneca: *feret iste aequo animo civile convicium et ingesta in contione curiave maledicta, cuius aures tracti subsellii stridor offendit?* ("How can he calmly endure the clamor of citizens and the curses poured out in an assembly or the senate house, if he is upset by the scraping of a bench being moved?" *de ira* 2.25.4).

64. Unless it was like the steam pipe hiss of Sam Sianis; see Royko 1982: 21.

65. Zarnott 2007: 328–29 cites Ov. *Am.* 1.12.19–20, Tib. 1.5.52, Luc. 6.688–89, Stat. *Theb.* 3.511–12; cf. Porphyrio's scholion on Hor. *Epod.* 5.19.

66. For a recovery of the witch and her valuable social functions from the invective often laid upon her in Roman literature, see Ripat 2016.

67. On witches and *invidia*, see Ripat 2016. For a suggestive use of *invidia* in connection to colonial resettlement, cf. *non equidem invideo, miror magis: undique totis | usque adeo turbatur agris* ("I feel not envy but rather wonder: every field everywhere is in a pitch of disruption"—the words of Meliboeus to Tityrus, the former ousted from his land, the latter settled on land, Verg. *Ecl.* 1.11–12).

68. For a typology of the names and functions of the Roman witch, see Paule 2014 with refs. On *sagae* for hire, cf. Col. 1.8.6. The usual use of spells in a rural context was, apparently, to

Table 7.3.5 (*LA* 2.70)

L. Infertile or Swampy Land.

[Cf. *pestilentiae* 'pestilence,' J. in Table 7.3.4]

(vi.) Alterum genus agrorum propter sterilitatem incultum, propter pestilentiam vastum atque desertum emetur ab eis qui eos vident sibi esse, si non vendiderint, relinquendos. Et nimirum illud est quod ab hoc tribuno plebis dictum est in senatu, urbanam plebem nimium in re publica posse: exhauriendam esse. Hoc enim est usus, quasi de aliqua sentina ac non de optimorum civium genere loqueretur.

"The other kind of land—too sterile to be cultivated [or] so unhealthy that it's desolate and deserted—will be purchased from owners who have realized that if they don't sell the land they will have to abandon it. Which is why what this tribune of the plebs said in the senate makes perfect sense! 'The urban plebs have too much influence in government; they need to be *drained off.*' Yes—that's the word he used! As if he were talking about some kind of bilge-water and not a class of excellent citizens."

Cicero's claim about land is broadly correct. For marshy land, at least, an interlocutor in Varro's *Res Rusticae* recommends the very strategy Cicero describes—sell or abandon.[69] The key to the passage is its apparent logical leap. There are two ideas in the passage: "The other kind of land is agriculturally poor" and "Rullus said the plebs had to be drained off like bilge-water." The ideas are not obviously connected. But they are linked by *et nimirum*, and that shows the logical connection. *Nimirum*, in origin something like "no wonder," sometimes functions as an inferential particle, marking a probable conclusion ("it must be the case that . . .") or offering corroborating evidence ("—of course, because . . ." or "and that makes sense,

---

entice away a neighbor's crops (cf. *qui fruges excantassit, Leg. XII* Tab. VIII.8a; Plin. *Nat.* 8.41). See also Cic. *Phil.* 13.25 (n. 70).

69. *Fundanius, quid potero, inquit, facere, si istius modi mi fundus hereditati obvenerit, quo minus pestilentia noceat? Istuc vel ego possum respondere, inquit Agrius; vendas, quot assibus possis, aut si nequeas, relinquas* ("Fundanius asked, 'What can I do to keep disease at bay, if I end up inheriting property of that kind [= near swamps]?' 'I can answer that question,' said Agrius; 'You can sell it, for the best price you can get—and if you can't sell, abandon it,' " 1.12.2).

because . . . ").[70] Here the word has the latter function (whence my translation): "it makes sense" that some of the land is swampy, because Rullus said the plebs have to be "drained off." Rullus's metaphor, unbeknown to himself, reveals the essence of his plan: the people are like wastewater, and the land is like a low-lying marsh where that water drains. Rullus was probably using a contemporary piece of political slang.[71] As populist *contiones* became more important in the first century, crowds "flowed down" into the Forum or the Campus Martius regularly—for some, so much "bilge-water" (the proper meaning of *sentina*) that had leaked in and needed to be "drained off." Rullus, if Cicero reports the truth, perhaps used the metaphor to seem oligarchic in an oligarchic venue, but Cicero exposes him—and not only that but, as with *eruo* in *LA* 3, reconfigures the metaphor by partly reliteralizing it. Of course he said "bilge-water"! He's buying you swamps! The idea is *similia similibus*, which, not accidentally in this context, is a principle of ancient magic.[72] Just as in the account of the decemviral election mechanism—and elsewhere—Rullus is no democrat and no true tribune. And again the idea manifests itself in his speech: Rullus's words won't make the rich leave for the poor; but the word he spoke in the senate will make the poor leave for poor land. The *ratio* of his tribunician voice is *conversa*.

7.4. THE PERORATIO OF THE POPULAR SPEECH

Pax est tranquilla libertas.

The real meaning of peace is liberty at rest.
—Cicero, *Philippic* 2.113

The conclusion of the popular speech revisits—and adjusts—the persona and principles Cicero developed in the *exordium* and thus makes a fitting end to this

---

70. Probable conclusion: *est illud quidem vel maximum animo ipso animum videre et nimirum hanc habet vim praeceptum Apollinis, quo monet ut se quisque noscat* ("The most important point is that the soul sees by way of its own self—that must be the meaning of the Delphic precept to 'Know thyself,'" *Tusc.* 1.52, cf. e.g. *Clu.* 143); Corroborating evidence *vel sim.*: *recesseris, undique omnes insequentur; manseris, haerebis. Nimirum recte veneficam appellas, a quo tibi praesentem pestem vides comparatam* ("Retreat, and everyone will attack from all sides; remain, and you're trapped. No wonder you call your opponent a *venefica*! You see he's readied your imminent destruction!" *Phil.* 13.25, with a pun on *venefica*, both 'poisoner' and 'witch'; cf. e.g. *Ver.* 2.4.57, *Brut.* 82).

71. On *sentina* as political insult, see Kühnert 1989. Cicero himself used the very metaphor in connection to an agrarian law: *qua constituta diligenter et sentinam urbis exhauriri et Italiae solitudinem frequentari posse arbitrabar* (*Att.* 1.19.4).

72. See e.g. Faraone 1991: 4–10, who uses the term "persuasive analogy."

chapter. The full *peroratio* has two halves. The first half (*LA* 2.98–99) is an *enumeratio* or "summation," in which "matters that have been discussed in different places over the course the speech are brought together in one place and arranged so as to be seen at a glance, thus refreshing the memory."[73] Thus the decemvirs, to name only some of the measures, will "loot our old tax-properties and scout out new ones" (*ut vetera vectigalia <nostr>a <expilaretis>, exploraretis nova*)—the sales of properties we saw in Chapter 3.[74] The decemvirs will "charge to the Roman people's account ill-regarded fields bought from Sullan possessors and abandoned and unhealthy fields bought from [their] relatives and [them]selves, at a price of [their] choosing" (*ut idem partim invidiosos agros a Sullanis possessoribus, partim desertos ac pestilentis a vestris necessariis et a vobismet ipsis emptos quanti velletis populo Romano induceretis*)—the poor land we saw in this chapter. The decemvirs aim to hamstring Pompey, as we saw in Chapter 5: "Cn. Pompey, by whose defense the state has very often been <protected> against bitter enemies and wicked citizens, they will be able to strip of his victorious <army> and the view of the people" (*ut ipsum Cn. Pompeium, quoius praesidio saepissime res publica contra acerrimos hostes et contra improbissimos civis <munita est, exercitu> victore atque horum conspectu privare possetis*). The decemvirs will have wide powers, as we saw in the *liberae legationes* passages of Chapter 2, able to "flit through every people and nation with supreme right of command, with unbound powers of judgment, and vast cash resources" (*ut volitaretis interea per gentis, per regna omnia cum imperio summo, cum iudicio infinito, cum omni pecunia*, with *volitare* that recalls the *vagabuntur* of *LA* 2.45 = Table 2.1.D-p). The sequence of clauses in the summary do not follow exactly the order in which Cicero treats them in the bill. He saves for last—and what comes last is always important—the immunities and legal privileges which were a part of the decemviral post: the decemvirs have arranged it that "no one can try [them] before the people, no one can bring [them] before the people, no one can compel [them] to appear in the senate, the consul cannot restrain [them] and the tribune of the people cannot restrain them" (*ut nemo ad populum Romanum vos adducere, nemo producere, nemo in senatum cogere, non consul coercere, non tribunus plebis retinere posset*). The decemvirs stand wholly outside the constitutional system; this is practically the *imperium maius* of emperors.[75]

---

73. *Conclusio est exitus et determinatio totius orationis. Haec habet partes tres: enumerationem, indignationem, conquestionem. Enumeratio est, per quam res disperse et diffuse dictae unum in locum coguntur et reminiscendi causa unum sub aspectum subiciuntur* (*Inv.* 1.98)

74. On the restoration, which is Clark's, see Manuwald 2018: 341.

75. Manuwald 2018: 408 stresses the failure of all ordinary checks and balances. But here some specific clauses of the law must be at issue, above and beyond the immunity from prosecution

The *peroratio* proper (*LA* 2.100–103) follows. It has three distinct parts. The first segment of the three revisits the themes of the first half of the *exordium*. In that passage, discussed in Chapter 6.2, Cicero reconfigures the meaning of *nobilis*; the letters here, which refer to the segments as labeled in the tables, discussion, and notes there, mark only some of the echoes:

> (*to the decemvirs*) I am not surprised that, in your foolishness and immoderation, you conceived all those desires; but I am very surprised that you thought you could achieve them when I was consul. (*to the people*) Every consul owes the state every effort of attentive care; but the burden falls most heavily on those who became consul not in their cradles but at the ballot-box. None of my ancestors vouched for me to the Roman people [B]; it was me you trusted. If you want what I owe, you have to find me and demand it from me alone.[76] When I was running for office, no family ancestors of mine recommended me to you; by the same token, if I ever fall short, no ancestral images are going to make excuses for me to you [B]. And that's why, so long as I have my life, which I with all [my] . . . to defend from their criminal attacks, I give you my word on this, fellow citizens: you have entrusted the state to someone watchful, unafraid, attentive, and <not idle>. Do I seem like the kind of consul who is afraid of a public assembly? [J] who shudders at a tribune of the plebs? who often stirs up trouble for no reason? who fears time in prison, if the tribune of the plebs chooses to arrest me? [Never!] Armed as I am with your weapons—equipped with *imperium* and authority, the most distinguished insignia [K]—I am not afraid to step up into this place [J] and, on your authority to resist a man's wickedness, and I do not fear that a state reinforced by such protections can be conquered or oppressed by people such as these. (*LA* 2.100–101)[77]

---

of an office holder during his term of office. I speculate that the Rullan bill contained language limiting nullification of its decisions (cf. n. 17), like the *lex agraria* of 111 had. That law (ll. 9–10) forbade subsequent senate decrees, judicial pronouncements, or laws that altered the right of ownership granted under the law. On this view, *LA* 2.99 exaggerates that ban on specific interference into a general personal right. Thus, no one could force a decemvir "into the senate" or "bring him to trial" on an issue of the law, because there would be no point.

76. The sense of *appellare* here is "*to address* in order to demand something, esp. the payment of money, *to dun*," *L&S s.v.* II.B.; "to apply to, call upon (to fulfil an obligation or pay a debt), dun; also, to demand the payment of," *OLD s.v.* 5.a.

77. *Haec ego vos concupisse pro vestra stultitia atque intemperantia non miror, sperasse me consule adsequi posse demiror. Nam cum omnium consulum gravis in re publica custodienda cura ac diligentia debet esse, tum eorum maxime qui non in cunabulis, sed in campo sunt consules facti. Nulli populo Romano pro me maiores mei spoponderunt; mihi creditum est; a me petere quod debeo, me*

Images of Identity

Here, as there, Cicero has no *imagines* (*LA* 2.1 = Table 6.2.1.B). Cicero's *insignia* are really the people's because here, as there, he is a *consul popularis* (*LA* 2.7 = K in ch. 6.2, n. 31). And here, as there, he is ready to stand in the hostile environs of a *contio* (J in ch. 6.2, n. 33). But the dynamics of the passage as a whole are not the same. In the imagery of the *exordium*, it was the people under Cicero's leadership breached the citadel of the consulship (Table 6.2.1.D); here, it is Cicero, armed with their authority, who is not afraid to march into a *contio* and join them in guarding the republic against a tribune. The populist oppositional discourse which underlay the *exordium* has now been fully reconfigured: its target now is not the jealous aristocracy but the people's own officer and his ilk. The steady denigration of Rullus over the course of the speech, which had at every turn made him out to be faithless to his charge, has allowed Cicero to redraw the terms of the polarity. Thus it is now not the wicked who are happy at the plans of the *populares*, as before (Table 6.2.2.N-p); rather, Rullus himself is wicked (cf. "a man's wickedness" = *improbitati hominis*), and his backers ("people such as these" = *istis*) must be defended against. The circle of the speech, one might say, is now complete. Cicero and the people breached the citadel of the aristocracy; Cicero and the people will now tame the disorder of the Forum. They broke the pride of the *curia*; now they will calm the storm of the *contio*.[78]

Thus does *LA* 2.100–101 recall and refit the chief themes of the *exordium* up through segment K. The next third of the *peroratio* corresponds to the next part of the *exordium*, where Cicero challenges the meaning of *popularis* (Table 6.2.2); again earlier themes are echoed.

> And even if I had been afraid before, I certainly would have no fear now—not after this assembly, not with an audience like this. Has there ever been an assembly where someone has argued so successfully for an agrarian bill as I have argued against one? If "arguing against" is even the right word and not "thwarting" and "overturning"! And that's what tells me, fellow citizens, that nothing is so important to the people as what I, the people's

---

ipsum appellare debetis. Quem ad modum, cum petebam, nulli me vobis auctores generis mei commendarunt, sic, si quid deliquero, nullae sunt imagines quae me a vobis deprecentur. Qua re, modo ut vita suppetat, quam ego summis <***> ab istorum scelere insidiisque defendere, polliceor hoc vobis, Quirites, bona fide: rem publicam vigilanti homini, non timido, diligenti, <non inerti,> commisistis. Ergo ego is consul <sim> qui contionem metuam, qui tribunum plebis perhorrescam, qui saepe et sine causa tumultuer, qui timeam ne mihi in carcere habitandum sit, si tribunus plebis duci iusserit? Ego cum vestris armis armatus sim <in>signi<bu>sque amplissimis exornatus, imperio, auctoritate, non horreo in hunc locum progredi {posse} vobisque auctoribus improbitati hominis resistere, nec vereor ne res publica tantis munita praesidiis ab istis vinci aut opprimi possit.

78. For the *contio* as a "storm" that must be calmed, cf. Morstein-Marx 2004: 62 n. 101 with refs.

consul, offer you for this year: peace, quiet, and tranquility [S]. Everything you feared might happen when I was still consul designate [M, O], by systematic planning I have taken care to prevent. Not only will you remain in tranquility, as you had always wanted [S], but I shall awaken a love for peace and tranquility even in those who detest it. They are the sort who turn to political disturbance and dissension to win honors and powers and riches; but you—whose influence depends on the right to vote, whose liberty depends on laws, whose opportunity for justice depends the courts and the fairness of the magistrates, whose property depends on peace—should maintain tranquility by all means possible [S]. Even the tranquility of idlers, though it comes to them from foul indolence, in and of itself brings them pleasure; how much luckier you will be, fellow citizens, if you can preserve your current condition, which is a possession you have not looked for out of laziness but won with your courage. By way of the harmony I have established with my colleague—to the disappointment of those who were going around saying our relationship as consuls was and would be contentious—I saw to everything: I provided for the grain supply,[79] I restored fiscal health [P], and I served notice on the tribunes of the people that they are not to undertake any disruptive schemes [O] while I am consul. (*LA* 2.101–3)[80]

---

79. Accepting Clark's 1909 conjecture *prospexi annonae* for the *prospexi sane* of the manuscripts (the latter printed by Manuwald 2018). *Prospexi sane* strikes me as colloquial, and I find no other quite comparable short sentence with *sane* in Cicero. I take the whole sentence (full text in n. 80) to refer, not to Cicero's planning generally, but specifically to the actions or imagined effects of the first speech (on the occasion when he announced his deal with Antonius, *LA* 1.26). On that view *providi omnibus* is a general claim: the speech "took care of all possible problems." Then follow three verbs referring to specific issues, corresponding exactly to categories of Table 6.2.2. There were political problems [Q]: in the first speech Cicero "served notice" (*denuntiavi*) on the tribunes (that captures the thrust of *LA* 1.27, discussed in ch. 8.5). There were fears of economic disruption [P]: in the first speech Cicero allayed them (if *fidem* is correctly restored). And there were disruptive plans (*turbulenta consilia* in the popular speech, O-p) that were somehow stayed by something that Cicero "saw to" (*prospexi*) in the first speech. *Annonae* makes excellent sense there: Cicero staved off the economic disruptions that (as he claims) would have followed colonizing the *ager Campanus*, which he calls *pulcherrimam populi Romani possessionem, subsidium annonae, horreum belli* (cf. C10 and C13 in Appendix 2).

80. *Si antea timuissem, tamen hac contione, hoc populo certe non vererer. Quis enim umquam tam secunda contione legem agrariam suasit quam ego dissuasi? si hoc dissuadere est ac non disturbare atque pervertere. Ex quo intellegi, Quirites, potest nihil esse tam populare quam id, quod ego vobis in hunc annum consul popularis adfero, pacem, tranquillitatem, otium. Quae nobis designatis timebatis, ea ne accidere possent, consilio meo ac ratione provisa sunt. Non modo vos eritis in otio qui semper esse volueratis, verum etiam istos quibus odio est otium quietissimos atque otiosissimos reddam. Etenim illis honores, potestates, divitiae ex tumultu atque ex dissensione civium comparari solent; vos, quorum gratia in suffragiis consistit, libertas in legibus, ius in iudiciis et*

Earlier themes are revisited. Cicero, again the people's consul (K), has now steadied a state that was troubled (M) by disruptive plans (O), which, among other things, damaged the economy (P). Themes, large and small, of other chapters are also echoed: the importance of voting (ch. 4.1) and of liberty (ch. 4.1) and of equitable magistrates (ch. 4.3).

But the passage is knit together chiefly by the idea of *otium*. That was the closing flourish of the *exordium* (ch. 6.2 *fin.*), where it took the place of *commodum*. Here the theme is enhanced all the more. It is not just that Cicero will provide *otium* to the people, as before: he more boldly claims that not only will he keep the peace for the peaceful—as, indeed, he had already done—but he will also pacify even the enemies of peace. Nor is it, as earlier, that the people, their elders, and every brave citizen is willing to undertake labors to win tranquility; rather, the people already have it, won by their courage and not sought after out of laziness, and they must maintain it. That is, there are two differences in the handling of the theme: the focus is on the present and on the people's (alleged) domestic opponents; and in the matter of *otium* the line between Cicero and the people is partly blurred. That is a distinct shift—perhaps the mark of an improvisation in the original delivery? Cicero had doubtless planned all along to advertise the harmony he had achieved with his consular colleague, M. Antonius Hybrida (and doubtless without quite saying how: he offered him the rich province of Macedonia for his proconsulship). The claim would have been unexpected; it was reasonable, just as Cicero says, to expect the consuls would not cooperate (the disreputable Antonius was an associate of Catiline, the future insurrectionist and Cicero's bitter opponent in the consular race for 63, and hoped to be elected to office with Catiline).[81] But circumstances presented Cicero with another chance to develop the idea of tranquility. His oratory, if the very beginning of this excerpt is any fair indication, had turned the mood of the assembly decisively against the bill; he had becalmed the "stormy" venue of the *contio*. Just as with his treatment of his own election, he reads a meaning into the action: "Your mood means you support me; I support a certain kind of *otium*; therefore you have boldly chosen to support that kind of *otium*; thus encouraged, I will suppress those that do

---

aequitate magistratuum, res familiaris in pace, omni ratione otium retinere debetis. Nam {et} si ii, qui propter desidiam in otio vivunt, tamen in sua turpi inertia capiunt voluptatem ex ipso otio, quam vos fortunati eritis, si hunc statum quem habetis vestra non ignavia quaesitum, sed virtute partum, {otium} tenueritis, Quirites! Ego ex concordia quam mihi constitui cum conlega, invitissimis iis hominibus qui nos in consulatu inimicos esse et fore iactabant, providi omnibus: prospexi annonae, revocavi fidem, tribunis plebis denuntiavi <ne> quid turbulenti me consule conflarent.

81. "Presumably people who supported Antonius and Catiline in the consular elections for 63 and assumed that Cicero and Antonius would not be able to cooperate (on the elections cf. Sall. *Cat.* 24.1; Asc. ad Cic. *Tog. cand.*, pp. 93–4 C.)," Manuwald 2018: 417.

not share our understanding." That is, the ending of the speech depends on precisely the same technique, assigning a particular meaning to the action of a public assembly, that the beginning did. The sovereignty of the people is folded into a particular policy. The real meaning of peace is liberty at rest.

The last third of the *peroratio* ends the speech thus:

> The best and firmest protection for the common weal, citizens, is that in the coming ("remaining") crises of the republic you display the same character that you have displayed to me today, in this great assembly, in defense of your own good. For my part (?) (*lit.* †for certain found†) I solemnly swear to you that I will make those who envied my election admit that in your collective choice of a consul you were very insightful indeed. (*LA* 2.103)

> *Summum et firmissimum est illud communibus fortunis praesidium, Quirites, ut, qualis vos hodierno die maxima contione mihi pro salute vestra praebuistis, talis reliquis temporibus rei publicae praebeatis. †Pro certo reperto†[82] polliceor hoc vobis atque confirmo me esse perfecturum ut iam tandem illi qui honori inviderunt meo tamen vos universos in consule deligendo plurimum vidisse fateantur.*

Elements, chiefly of the *exordium*, are again echoed and refitted (the letters again recalling the segments as labeled as in the tables and notes of ch. 6.2). Cicero was envied: so above the aristocracy would give him no sure aid (G). But the people were insightful: so above they saw and rewarded his *dignitas* (C, E). The whole body chose him: that refers to his election by acclamation (F). If the aristocracy once ringed a citadel that the people breached under Cicero (D), now the people under Cicero are the state's firmest guard. The Rullan bill was false populism (L), roiling the state (O), threatening tyranny (Q): here, having chosen to oppose it,

---

82. *Pro certo* is transmitted in all branches; *reperto* (or *repeto*) in only some. For the whole phrase *pro certo reperto* Clark 1909 prints *promitto recipio* (*recipio* being Müller's conjecture); Manuwald 2018, *pro certo {reperto}* (following Kasten's deletion of *reperto*). In my view *pro certo* is the problem. *Pro certo* in Cicero is not a simple adverbial phrase ('certainly') but always implies a change of category ('to consider *vel sim.* [something unsure or doubtful] for [a] sure [thing]'; that is the force of *pro*). With verbs for 'promising' and the like, *pro certo* would therefore mean something like "avow [something doubtful] as [if it were] certain" (exactly as in Livy's *quis enim rem tam veterem pro certo adfirmet?* "Who can possibly confirm that event so long past is certain?" 1.3.2). That sense does not suit the context. The whole phrase must conceal something like *pro mea parte,* describing Cicero's duty, corresponding to the duty just enjoined on the people: they must stand firm, and "for his part" he swears, etc. That accords with Cicero's proclamation in the *exordium* that he will do everything he can for the people (*omnia . . . perpetienda, LA* 2.6, segment I in ch. 6.2, n. 29).

the people understand that "their own good"—literally *salus* 'health,' in the sense of 'security of civil rights' or even 'liberty'—is at stake. And as before, Cicero inscribes a meaning upon an action: this *contio* was "very full" or even "crowded,"[83] and that here becomes a symbol of the will of the supermajority, an insulation against the divisive politics that Cicero (in the event, rightly) predicts are coming.

But the most important theme of the very end of the speech is, I submit, the idea of the oath. The idea of the *exordium*, that Cicero and the people are now bound to each other, here takes the form of swearing mutual fealty. Cicero solemnly swears to make his opponents regret their judgment of the people. *Polliceri et confirmare* are paired elsewhere to indicate solemn vows and, it seems, especially dramatic ones. A defendant throwing himself on the mercy of the court in Cicero's *de Inventione* is obligated to "solemnly swear" (*polliceri et confirmare*, lit. "promise and confirm") that he will henceforth keep to the straight and narrow.[84] In Caesar the Gaul Ambiorix, trying to lure a Roman garrison out of its winter quarters, "solemnly"—and lyingly—"swears an oath" (*polliceri et iure iurando confirmare*) that he will give them safe passage.[85] The language of oath is entirely appropriate on an inaugural occasion. And the idea of the oath is present in Cicero's words to the people, too. They aren't asked to swear an oath in so many words; but they are asked, as being the final bulwark of the common good, to maintain in the coming political storms the same unity which is manifest in their support for Cicero—which means, in effect, they are asked to continue to support him. That is the duty of the *populus* to a *consul popularis*. But there is something more here: Cicero also hints at the idea behind *tribunicia potestas*, the "authority of a tribune." The power of tribunes rested ultimately not on a law (a consul, for example, required a *lex curiata* to take office) but on an ancient oath of the plebs to defend their person.[86] The power of the tribune, which, as we have seen, Cicero consistently denies to Rullus and claims for himself, is the Unnamed Referent of the last sentences of the second agrarian speech. The people have, by their electoral action, created a *consul popularis* who is, in a sense, also a *tribunus consularis*. He owes his station to them, and to them he pledges his life and his sacred honor.

---

83. On the importance of crowd size at a *contio*, cf. Manuwald 2018: 461.

84. *postea polliceri et confirmare se et hoc peccato doctum et beneficio eorum, qui sibi ignoverint, confirmatum omni tempore a tali ratione afuturum; deinde spem ostendere aliquo se in loco magno iis, qui sibi concesserint, usui futurum* (2.106).

85. *BG* 5.27.10.

86. *tribunos vetere iure iurando plebis, cum primum eam potestatem creavit, sacrosanctos esse*, Liv. 3.55.10; Mommsen *RS*³ 2.1: 272–330.

8
Dignitas

8.1. INTRODUCTION

senatum rei publicae custodem, praesidem, propugnatorem conlocaverunt.

[Our ancestors] established the senate as the guardian and protector and defender of the state.

—Cicero, *pro Sestio* 137

The images of the *liberae legationes* (*LA* 1.8–9, 2.45–6, ch. 2), the wastrel (*LA* 1.3–4, ch. 3.3), and the auction (*LA* 1.3–4, 2.46–9, ch. 3.2) are tableaux meant to probe power relations. Together they position their listeners between anxiety and responsibility: the tableaux dramatize to each audience certain dangers inherent (in Cicero's view) in the bill's proposals, and they project onto each audience ideal roles and identities that (in Cicero's view) are checks on those perils. Thus, where the people are shown the dangers of the broad powers that only they can create but prompted to think through possible consequences, taking their sovereignty seriously, the senate are shown the dangers of an imbalanced competitive system (for example, the power of decemvirs abroad to extort) and at the same time prompted to exercise collective guidance, taking seriously the ideology of their high station (for example, as a council of elders hobbling a profligate).

This chapter deepens and sharpens the picture of the senate. Examining the popular speech has cleared the way. Two results of that analysis are relevant. Reading the *exordium* has shown how Cicero can manipulate ideological categories boldly and innovatively but at the same time obliquely and delicately. He does the same in the senate speech. Awareness of that technique is especially important for grasping its ideology, since most of its programmatic passages do not survive (its *exordium, propositio,* and *divisio* are lost; cf. Appendix 1). Second, analysis of the popular speech also showed that Cicero addressed two faces of *libertas*: popular sovereignty (ch. 4) and *commodum* (ch. 5). That is, in effect, to appeal to a heterogeneous audience with different "pet issues." The same is true of the senate speech. Some arguments seem to apply to the body as a whole, but others seem directed to particular groups. Some senators were supporters of Pompey or willing to use or countenance the populist movement for whatever reason. To them, I surmise, were chiefly directed certain arguments about the scope of the legislation. The old aristocracy needed no persuasion on that point. Some senators will have valued above all the traditional prerogatives of the senate or could be appealed to as if they did. To them, I think, are directed arguments that press for a collectivist, and not an individualist, model of *dignitas*. Hard-core populists will have been less interested in that point. Just as in the popular speech, then, there is a division between ideological and practical arguments—between *honestum* and *utile*. And just as in the popular speech, Cicero is the unifier who transcends categories. If in *de lege agraria* 2 he was a *consul popularis*, in *de lege agraria* 1 he is, one might say, a *consul senatorius*, interested in the real health and the proper role of the institution—which is to say, not a *consul equester*.

8.2. OUR GLORIES

Iure, lege, libertate, re publica communiter uti oportet; gloria atque honore, quomodo sibi quisque struxit.

Right, law, liberty, government should be enjoyed in common; glory and honor, according to what each man has managed to amass for himself.

—M. Porcius Cato, fragment 19

As we have seen (ch. 5.2), the Rullan bill proposed the sale of various public properties or their taxes from across the empire. Nested into the middle of Cicero's treatment of territories recovered from Mithridates by Pompey is his treatment of territories from Western Asia Minor, Greece, Spain, and Africa; that is, the treatment of Pompey's gains frames the list of other sales. That nested list merits separate treatment. In both speeches Cicero suggests that selling the *vectigalia*, which were conquered territories, offends against their conquerors. Sell off those parcels, he warns, and the achievements of the *maiores* who bequeathed them would be undone. But there are, so to speak, two sets of *maiores*: each speech links the allegedly offended conquerors to different ideals. The passages have the same template (Table 8.2, the boldface and italics will be explained presently).[1]

---

1. *LA* 1.5–6 and 2.50–55 are partially treated in two separate places, with some overlap—in ch. 5, in connection with *commodum*; and here, in connection with *dignitas*.

Table 8.2. Lists of Miscellaneous *Agri Vectigales* (*LA* 1.5–6, 2.50–51)

in senatu	*ad populum*
A. Territories in Western Asia Minor	
Iubent venire agros *Attalensium* atque *Olympenorum* quos populo Romano <P.> **Servili**, fortissimi viri, victoria adiunxit...	Iubet venire quae *Attalensium*, quae *Phaselitum*, quae *Olympenorum* fuerint, agrumque *Agerensem* et *Oroandicum* et *Gedusanum*. Haec **P. Servili** imperio et victoria, clarissimi viri, vestra facta sunt. Adiungit *agros Bithyniae regios*, quibus nunc publicani fruuntur...
"They order the sale of the territories of the *Attalenses* and the *Olympeni* which were annexed to the Roman people by the victory of **P. Servilius**, a very brave man..."	"[The bill *or* Rullus] orders the sale of what once belonged to the *Attalenses*, and to the *Phaselites*, and to the *Olympeni*, and of the territory of the *Agerenses* and *Oroandici* and *Gedusani*. All that became yours by the command and victory of **P. Servilius**, a most distinguished man. [The bill *or* Rullus] adds *the royal territories of Bithynia*, which the publicans now have use of..."
B. Mainland Greece and Vicinity	
deinde *agros in Macedonia regios* qui partim **T. Flaminini**, partim **L. Pauli** qui Persen vicit virtute parti sunt, deinde *agrum optimum et fructuosissimum Corinthium* qui **L. Mummi** imperio ac felicitate ad vectigalia populi Romani adiunctus est...	deinde *Attalicos agros in Cherroneso, in Macedonia* qui regis Philippi sive Persae fuerunt, qui item a censoribus locati sunt et certissimum vectigal <adferunt>. Ascribit <e>idem auctioni *Corinthios agros opimos et fertiles*, et *Cyrenenses* qui Apionis fuerunt...
"and [the sale of] *the royal territories in Macedonia* which were won partly by the courage of **T. Flamininus**, partly by that of **L. Paulus** who defeated Perses; and [they order the sale of] *the excellent and fruitful territory of Corinth* which was added to the tax properties of the Roman people by the command and good fortune of **L. Mummius**..."	"and the *Attalic territory in the Chersonese* and *in Macedonia* the territory which belonged to king Philip and Perses; they too have been farmed out by the censors and <bring> very reliable revenue. [The bill *or* Rullus] also puts up for sale in this auction *the territories of Corinth, rich and fertile*, and *those of Cyrene* which belonged to Apion..."

Table 8.2. Continued

in senatu	ad populum

C. Spanish and African Territories

post autem *agros in Hispania apud Carthaginem novam* **duorum Scipionum** eximia virtute possessos; tum *ipsam veterem Carthaginem* vendunt, quam **P. Africanus** nudatam tectis ac moenibus sive ad notandam Carthaginiensium calamitatem, sive ad testificandam nostram victoriam, sive oblata aliqua religione ad aeternam hominum memoriam consecravit.

et *agros in Hispania propter Carthaginem novam* et *in Africa ipsam veterem Carthaginem* vendit, quam videlicet **P. Africanus** non propter religionem sedum illarum ac vetustatis de consili sententia consecravit, nec ut ipse locus eorum qui cum hac urbe de imperio decertarunt vestigia calamitatis ostenderet, sed non fuit tam diligens quam est Rullus, aut fortasse emptorem ei loco reperire non potuit.

"[as well as the sale of] *the territories in Spain around New Carthage* occupied by the outstanding courage of the **two Scipios**; and they're even selling *old Carthage itself*, which, stripped of its roofs and walls, **P. Africanus** dedicated to the eternal memory of the world, whether to mark the Carthaginian disaster, or to bear witness to our victory, or in response to a religious scruple."

" . . . and sells off *territories in Spain near New Carthage* and *in Africa old Carthage itself*, which, to be sure, P. Africanus consecrated on the advice of his council not because of a religious scruple that attached to that site and its antiquity, or in order that the mother country of a people who struggled with this city for supremacy might display signs of the calamity [it suffered]; rather [Africanus] was not as diligent as Rullus is, or perhaps he couldn't find a buyer for that place!"

D. Mithridatic Territories (= Table 5.2.A)

His insignibus atque infulis imperi venditis, quibus ornatam nobis maiores nostri rem publicam tradiderunt, iubent eos agros venire quos rex Mithridates in *Paphlagonia, Ponto Cappadociaque* possederit (1.5–6).

verum inter hos agros captos veteribus bellis virtute summorum imperatorum adiungit *regios agros* Mithridatis, qui *in Paphlagonia*, qui *in Ponto*, qui *in Cappadocia* fuerunt, ut eos decemviri vendant

(continued)

Table 8.2. Continued

in senatu	ad populum
"Having sold off these symbols and garlands of empire that adorned the state that our elders passed on to us, they order the sale of the territories which king Mithridates possessed in *Paphlagonia, Pontus,* and *Cappadocia*."	"But among these territories captured in ancient wars by the courage of the highest commanders he adds *the former royal territories* of Mithridates—territory *in Paphlagonia* and *in Pontus* and *in Cappadocia*—with orders that the decemvirs sell them." (*etc.*)

In the popular speech the emphasis is on control of property. That speech, as the italics show, names more properties, mentioning thirteen to the senate's six (and with the plural *agri Corinthii* where the senate speech has *ager Corinthius*).[2] Expressions for gain and loss evoke a zero-sum economics. The Roman people are exploiting the territories now (*vestra facta sunt*, A-p; *quibus nunc publicani fruuntur*, A-p; *qui item a censoribus locati sunt et certissimum vectigal <adferunt>*, B-p),[3] and their former owners have lost them (*fuerint*, A-p; *fuerunt*, B-p *bis*).

Where the popular speech has more properties, the senate speech has more generals (in boldface). The generals are also described distinctly. In the popular version the accent is on accomplishment. Where Servilius is *fortissimus* before the senate, he is *clarissimus* "most distinguished" before the people (B-p). *Clarus* connoted achievement rather than inherent status; it is used nowhere in the senate speech.[4] The people's Servilius conquers *imperio ac victoria*. That unparalleled

---

2. Attalia in Pamphylia and Phaselis and Olympus in Lycia were taken by P. Servilius Isauricus (*RE* Servilius 93) during his operations on gulf of Adalia against Cilician pirates (Cic. *Ver.* 2.1.56, Liv. *per.* 90, Vell. 2.39.2). Of the other territories taken by Servilius, the *ager Agerensis*, the *ager Gedusanus*, and the *ager Oroandicus*, only the location of the last, in southeast Asia Minor, is known. For further details, cf. Manuwald 2018: 301–302 *s.vv.* (who obelizes *Agerensem*). The Macedonian territories were gained by T. Quinctius Flamininus (*RE* Quinctius 45) and L. Aemilius Paulus (*RE* Aemilius 114) after the battles of Cynoscephalae (197) and Pydna (168) respectively. The territory of Corinth was taken by L. Mummius (*RE* Mumminus 7a) in 146. The *agri Attalici* in the Thracian Chersonese (2.50) belonged to Attalus III and were ceded to Rome in 133 (Liv. *per.* 58). The *agri Cyreneses* were ceded to Rome in 96 by Ptolemy Apion, illegitimate son of Ptolemy VII Euergetes. The *agri Bithyniae regii* were ceded by Nicomedes IV to Rome in 75/74 (App. *Mith.* 71, *BC* 1.111).

3. Cf. Classen 1985: 324 and n. 63.

4. Cf. ch. 6 n. 63. Servilius was known as a fair administrator (Cic. *Ver.* 2.3.210, *Att.* 6.1.16), and honored by all (*florebat, in senatu princeps erat, amabatur a populo*, Schol. Gronov. 442 Or. = 322 Stangl). He also supported Manilius's bill (Cic. *Man.* 68) out of dislike for

phrase, apparently not a part of the regular honorific system, stresses accomplishment (*victoria*) rather than fortune. The accent in the senate speech, by contrast, is on inherent virtues. T. Flamininus (B-s) and L. Paulus (B-s), as well as the two older Scipios (C-s), possessed *virtus*. The *eximia virtus* "outstanding courage" of the Scipios is a regular phrase.[5] The person who possessed *virtus* was described as *fortis* (*virtuosus* is a late coinage);[6] that is the import of the *fortissimus* applied to P. Servilius Vatia (B-s). L. Mummius's victories (C-s) were secured not *imperio ac victoria* but *imperio ac felicitate*, where *felicitas* is the almost mystical 'good luck' of the most successful Roman generals.[7] An honorific inscription for L. Aemilius Regillus (fl. c. 190–189) recorded in Livy is similar: "Under his auspices, authority, good fortune, and command, the fleet of King Antiochus was scattered, wrecked, and routed" (*auspicio imperio felicitate ductuque eius . . . classis regis Antiochi . . . fusa contusa fugataque est*, 40.52.5–6).[8] The treatments of Carthage show a comparable distinction. In the popular speech Scipio dedicated the site (the *non . . . nec* is ironic) in order to record an existential struggle (the

---

Lucullus (*Prov.* 22). Later Servilius would be the first to vote for Cicero's return (*Red. Pop.* 17). Servilius is also styled *clarissimus* at *Ver.* 2.1.56, 2.3.210, *Red. Sen.* 25, *Dom.* 43, *Prov.* 1, and *Fam.* 13.68.3.

5. The phrase is common in Cicero (*S. Rosc.* 127, *Ver.* 2.1.56, 2.5.3, *Man.* 3 [with *singularis*], 36, *Clu.* 118, *Rab. Perd.* 26, *Red. Sen.* 13, *Dom.* 23, *Cael.* 43 [plu.], *Prov.* 32 [with *divina*], *Balb.* 40, *Phil.* 5.23, 47 [with *excellens*], *Fin.* 1.42 [plu. with *pulchrae*], *Fam.* 5.8.2 [with *pietas, gratia*], *Fam.* 5.17.5), Livy (2.45.16, 4.34.4, 30.14.6 [plu.], 30.30.13 [with *pietas*], 39.31.9), and elsewhere (*B. Hisp.* 23.3, 31.5, V. Max. 5.5.3 [plu.], [Quint.] *Decl. Min.* 278.13, Sen. *Ben.* 3.32.3, 3.33.3 [with *pietas*], 5.5.1). For military uses of the phrase with commemorative overtones comparable to our passage, cf. *Cn. Pompeius eximia virtute et felicitate in Hispania bellum gessit* "Cn. Pompey waged war in Spain with outstanding courage and good fortune" (Cic. *Font.* fr. 9); *prospero ductu parta victoria ob eximiam virtutem* "after a victory secured with successful command on account of outstanding courage" (Col. 1.3.10); Caes. *BC* 1.46.4.

6. "Il est évident toutefois que l'emploi de *fortis* n'a pas la même extension que celui de *bonus*: il reste avant tout le qualificatif de celui qui, d'une façon ou d'une autre, manifeste sa *virtus*, et non un terme générique comme l'est *bonus*," Hellegouarc'h 1963: 494. *Virtus* is like *voluptas* in that in the classical period it lacks a derived adjective (in the latter case after *volup(e)* became phrasal and then extinct; *iucundus, suavis*, and others fill the gap).

7. Cicero says the ideal commander requires knowledge of military science, courage, stature, and luck (*scientiam rei militaris, virtutem, auctoritatem, felicitatem, Man.* 28, cf. 47). On Caesar's claims to good fortune, see Murphy 1986.

8. The basic formula for a commanding general leading in the field was *ductu* and *auspicio (-is)*, which is widely attested (Liv. 3.1.4, 3.17.2, 5.46.6, 5.49.6, 6.12.6, 7.32.10, etc.). The two are, of course, potentially distinct, since field command did not always fall to the same party who had *ius auspiciorum*: hence *partim ductu, partim auspiciis suis* (Suet. *Aug.* 21.1). For more on these terms, see Levi 1938, Lemosse 1971.

Carthaginians "fought to the bitter end," *decertarunt*) and in order to respect a scruple that inhered in the ancient site. That is, Cicero foregrounds Scipio's practical concerns (and regard for process over pride: Scipio acted "on the advice of his counselors").[9] In the senate speech Scipio's particular reasons don't really matter (cf. *sive . . . sive . . . sive*); what matters is simply that he made the dedication *ad aeternam hominum memoriam*, a phrase Cicero otherwise uses to stress the physicality of monuments or the like.[10] Before the senate Cicero valorizes Scipio's dedicatory intent.

In short, Cicero's language in the senate speech evokes the theory and practice of commemoration. Commanders of outstanding virtue make dedications. That idea underlies the striking image which sums up the section (D-s): the conquered territories are *insignia atque infulae imperi* "symbols and garlands of empire" with which the republic was "adorned" (*ornatam*) by conquerors. Cicero has in mind triumphal rituals (five of the named commanders triumphed).[11] *Infulae*, used metaphorically in Cicero's speeches only here, must be triumphal adornments subsequently dedicated in a temple.[12] *Insignia*, 'decorations' (lit. "marks of distinction"), also refers to some kind of temple ornaments. In Tibullus there are *insignia* hanging on temple walls (*suspensa sacris insignia fanis*, 2.4.23), likely

---

9. *De consili sententia* applies to Scipio's consecration a regular phrase for a magistrate acting on the advice of his advisers. So of the famously deferential Tiberius: "He consulted his advisers on everything he did" (*nihil non de consilii sententia egit*, Suet. *Tib.* 18.1). For other examples, cf. Cic. *Balb.* 19, 38, *Brut.* 86, *Att.* 2.16.4, 4.2.5, 16.16c.2, 16.16f.2, Caes. *Civ.* 3.16, Liv. 45.26.12, and especially Cic. *Ver.* 2.45.54, where Verres apparently used the phrase as an excuse. Scipio did employ such a council: cf. App. *Lib.* 135.639–41.

10. Thus of the dedication of the *Mons Sacer* after the secession of the plebs (*ut . . . aeternae memoriae causa consecrarent*, Corn. 1 fr. 49.6) and of Catulus's restoration of the Capitolium (*tui nominis aeterna memoria*, *Ver.* 2.4.69); cf. *eaque exstructione quae sit ad memoriam aeternitatis ara Virtutis* (*Phil.* 14.34), of those who have gloriously died resisting Antony.

11. P. Servilius Vatia Isauricus (88); T. Flamininus (194/193); L. Aemilius Paulus (167/166); L. Mummius (142); P. Cornelius Scipio Africanus Aemilianus (147). P. and Cn. Cornelius Scipio died in battle.

12. *Infulae*, properly woolen fillets or bands worn on the forehead, symbolized religious consecration and were thus worn by priests (*TLL* 7.1.1499.6–25), suppliants (*TLL* 7.1.42) and sacrificial victims (*TLL* 7.1.1498.80–1499.6). The use of *infulae* on sacred places is claimed by Paul. Fest.: *infulae sunt filamenta lanea, quibus sacerdotes et hostiae templaque velantur* ("*Infulae* are the woolen cords used to wrap around priests, victims, and shrines," 100.7 Lindsay) but in attested passages the word for 'garlands' on places, like the altar, is *vitta* (cf. *OLD s.v. vitta*). Cf. Plu. *Aem.* 32.3 (garlands in temples), 33.2 (fillets and garlands on sacrificial oxen), Plin. *Nat.* 15.134, Sil. 15.119–120. (dedication of laurel wreath to Jupiter by triumphator). For the details of triumphs, see Beard 2007, Versnel 1970.

ex voto gifts.[13] *Insignia* were among the decorations in the house of C. Urbinus for a dinner honoring Metellus Pius, who had "returned triumphantly" (*regressus magna gloria*) from Spain; the house was "like a temple on festal day" (*in modum templi celeberrimi*).[14]

The imagery has three implications. One concerns the bill itself. Making captured properties into *infulae* makes them inviolable; that was what *infulae* connoted.[15] This is a grander version of a tactic we have seen before. Just as a legal sale might not be a respectable sale—*non omne quod licet honestum est*, the idea behind Cicero's invocation of *helluatio*—here, it might be said, the idea is *non omne quod licet fas est*. As before the senate was an advisory body reining in a wastrel, here it is the guardian of the civico-religious order against a proposal that is by implication impious. That leads to another implication, about the senate's preeminence. For the Cato of the epigraph the structure of the state was a common possession and glory a personal acquisition. Cicero's imagery implies a different relationship. Without *libertas* and the *res publica* there would be no *honor* and no *gloria*. That is, preeminence is a matter of achievement and recognition on a prescribed path. It is only accepted practices that even make glory possible; what gives meaning to individual accomplishments is the collective fabric. On my view that is a delicate blow against a strict culture of personal honor.[16] But in any case Cicero is, as we have so often seen, making use of the surrounding space. The senators were at that moment gathered in the very temple where triumphal processions ended, whose walls were adorned with the tokens of triumphal victory, in which Jupiter's statue was dressed as a triumphator.[17] Cicero anchors his argument in a feature of the temple of Jupiter Optimus Maximus just as he hung

---

13. For such gifts, cf. e.g. Hor. *C.* 3.26.3–4, V. *Aen.* 9.408, and the note of Murgatroyd 1994: 139–140.

14. *eum [= Metellum Pium] quaestor C. Vrbinus aliique cognita voluntate cum ad cenam invitaverunt, ultra Romanum ac mortalium etiam morem curabant exornatis aedibus per aulaea et insignia scenisque ad ostentationem histrionum fabricatis; simul croco sparsa humus et alia in modum templi celeberrimi* (Sal. *Hist.* fr. 2.70.3–8 M).

15. From their religious use *infulae* came to mean conditions that demanded respect (*TLL* 7.1.1499.56–1500.37 "translate de honore, dignitate"), like marks of high office (*praefecturae infulis ornatum* "distinguished with the honor of a prefecture," Spart. *Hadr.* 6.7, cf. *infulae imperiales, Cod. Just.* 7.37.3.5), and simply elevated status itself (*infularum loco sunt* "deserve respect," Sen. *Ep.* 14.11, cf. *Dial.* 12.13.6). Cicero's is the very first such metaphorical use; the idea is not an outward mark of distinction (so *L&S*) but inviolability (cf. Manuwald 2018: 133). Zumpt 1861: 6 n. 6 takes the state itself to be the priest ("infulae dicuntur res sacrae, quibus imperium quasi quibusdam infulis sacerdos ornatum est") and the reference to be chiefly to the *ager Carthaginiensis*, forbidden to cultivation.

16. On this aspect of the ancient Mediterranean personality, see Lebow 2008: 165–221.

17. Triumphator: Juv. 10.38.

his arguments about transparency on the nearby statue of Sulla.[18] He uses the environs to nuance the idea of inherent worth. The temple of Jupiter Optimus Maximus is the most frequently attested meeting place for the senate in the Republican period;[19] the decor of the temple itself, correctly read, itself tells the senate the exact meaning of its own privilege. All that leads to another implication. Pompey's conquests form the frame for this excerpt. The juxtaposition—or rather interpenetration—invites comparison of Pompey to the other generals. Dislike of the Rullan bill on traditionalist grounds is thus turned into respect for Pompey. The envy of the friends of Lucullus or others of like mind, whatever their reason, can have no place when fresh *infulae* are soon to be hung. Collectivism also means laying partisanship aside.

8.3. GOOD LAWS FOR ALL

Hard cases make bad law; bad law makes hard cases.
—Legal adage

A striking instance of how Cicero bends individualism, and even selfishness, toward the collective appears in the senate version of his discussion of military monies, the second major category of funds in the bill (*LA* 1.12–13, 2.59–61). One category was war spoils proper. They were of two kinds, *praeda* and *manubiae*. *Praeda* was the broadest category of 'loot';[20] legally public property,[21] it was to be liquidated and distributed to the army or remitted to the treasury.[22] Requiring the remittance of war spoils was not an innovation: that was the old law.[23] *Manubiae*, which probably originally meant something like *spolia* or 'spoils taken from a defeated enemy,'[24] came to be the name for spoils reserved for the

---

18. For another use of the temple as a symbol, cf. *LA* 1.18 in ch. 9.2 Honestum and C1 in Appendix 2.

19. Mommsen, *RS*³ 3.2: 928.

20. Excluding captives and precious metals: see Coudry 2009a: 25–27.

21. Coudry 2009a: 47–49; Churchill 1999: 94–95; Bona 1959: 349–51; Mommsen 1879: 449. Cf. Modestinus *dig.* 48.13.15 (*is qui praedam ab hostibus captam subripuit lege peculatus tenetur*).

22. The evidence for the procedures is gathered by Coudry 2009a.

23. Though not of course a consistent practice, as Cato's speech of 184, *uti praeda in publicum referatur*, alone suggests. For the obligation, cf. Polybius 10.16.6; for the soldiers' oath, cf. Gell. 16.4.2. For other primary passages, cf. Jonkers 1963: 29–30.

24. *Spolia quaesita de vivo hoste nobili per deditionem manubias veteres dicebant; et erat imperatorum haec praeda, ex qua quod vellent facerent* (Ps.-Asc. ad Cic. *Ver.* 2.1.157, p. 255.18–20 Stangl).

commander with *imperium*.²⁵ They, too, were public property, entrusted to the general but expected to be given over in due course for public purposes.²⁶ The bill also attached *aurum coronarium* 'gold for a crown, crown gold.' Once, allied and conquered cities had sent victors crowns of gold to be carried in their triumphs. At some point cash payments began to be made instead, still under the name *aurum coronarium*, and were even demanded by provincial governors who had not won a military victory.²⁷ If the gold was offered to a governor not in his own name but in the name of the Roman people,²⁸ then it was also public property held in trust, quite like *manubiae*, and hence fairly included in this measure of the bill. The measure apparently also included *pecuniae residuae*, lit. "remaining monies," that is, funds disbursed for a specific purpose but unspent. (That was considered a form of *peculatus* 'embezzlement'). As we have now so often seen, the bill had a keen nose for untapped sources of revenue and laid claim to such public properties as were available.

Both speeches attack the measure with the same image: it alters the judicial system, in effect creating a new standing jury-court (*quaestio*) with a wide writ over commanders' finances, partly subsuming the role of the already existing *quaestio perpetua peculatus*.²⁹ The order of ideas in the two passages is not quite the same; as usual, Roman numerals show the sequence of elements, which in this table is set by that of the senate speech.

---

25. Churchill 1999: 89–90. How that reservation worked and what precisely it meant have been disputed, chiefly due to conflicting definitions in the not always well-informed ancient sources, which in turn affect modern reference works (Gellius 13.25–26, for example, has *manubiae* only as the proceeds of the sale of booty kept by the general, the definition followed by the *OLD*; further examples in Shatzman 1972: 179–80). Tarpin 2009 regards *manubiae* as goods neither from the field of battle nor from pillage that have been converted to cash.

26. So Bona 1960 (with, however, the probably mistaken notion that *manubiae* were solely in the form of coin, a position refuted by Shatzman 1972). Since *manubiae* were public property, a general's heirs could be sued for *manubiae* still in his possession on his death (roughly the *actio in rem* or 'suit for the recovery of property' of private law). On Pompeius Strabo's death, for example, his son Pompey was sued for possessing nets and books won at Asculum in 89 (Plu. *Pomp.* 41 with Churchill 1999: 107). The Republican inscriptional attestations of *manubiae* are the dedications of consulars; in Livy *manubiae* are always held by ex-magistrates. By contrast, when tribunes dedicate, they do so *de praeda* (Churchill 1999: 89–90).

27. A law of Caesar in 59, the *lex Iulia repetundarum*, meant to stop that particular abuse (*Pis.* 90). On the crowns, see Östernberg 2009: 115–23, Coudry 2009b.

28. Zumpt 1861: 100: "Sed illud ex hoc ipso loco discimus, coronas populo Romano, qui sub imperatoris quasi persona triumpharet, dari consuesse: quare coronarium in aerarium publicum redigebatur, sed ita, ut imperatori eo ad monumenta i.e. aedificia condenda uti liceret."

29. On this court, see Gnoli 1979, esp. 84–91; *PW* 1.47 *s.v. quaestio*. Chairmen of the court are mentioned by Cicero (Orchivius in 66, *Clu.* 94 and 147; Servius Sulpicius Rufus in 65, *Mur.* 42), and the existence of the court seems to be implied by Plu. *Pomp.* 4.

Table 8.3.1. Rhetorical Structure of the Excerpts on Military Monies (*LA* 1.11–13, 2.59)

in senatu	*ad populum*
\multicolumn{2}{c}{A. Sources of Money in Bill Sufficient}
(i.) Num quisnam tam abstrusus usquam nummus videtur quem non architecti huiusce legis olfecerint? Provincias, civitates liberas, socios, amicos reges denique exhauriunt, admovent manus vectigalibus populi Romani. Non est satis.	(i.) Vix iam videtur locus esse qui tantos acervos pecuniae capiat; auget, addit, accumulat.
"Is it possible for any coin to be so well stashed that the masterminds behind this bill can't sniff out where it is? They drain provinces dry, and free states, allies, and even friend-kings… they lay their hands on the tax properties of the Roman people… but it's still not enough!"	"He's assembled such mounds of money by this point that there hardly seems a place to put it… [but] he adds, augments, accumulates [still more]!"
\multicolumn{2}{c}{B. Generals}
(ii.) Audite, audite vos qui amplissimo populi senatusque iudicio exercitus habuistis et bella gessistis:	(cf. *de clarissimis viris qui populi Romani bella gesserunt*, D-p)
"Listen, listen those of you who by the most honorable judgment of the people and the senate have commanded armies and waged wars!"	
\multicolumn{2}{c}{C. Spoils Must Be Declared}
(iii.) quod ad quemque pervenerit ex praeda, ex manubiis, ex auro coronario, quod neque consumptum in monumento neque in aerarium relatum sit, id ad decemviros referri iubet!	(ii.) 'Aurum, argentum ex praeda, ex manubiis, ex coronario ad quoscumque pervenit neque relatum est in publicum neque in monumento consumptum,' id profiteri apud decemviros et ad eos referre iubet.
"Whatever has come to each man from booty, from cash from spoils [or] from crown metal and has not been used in a monument or paid into the treasury the bill orders to be rendered to the decemvirs."	"The law orders that 'gold or silver that anyone has received from spoils, cash from spoils, or crown metal that has not been returned to the treasury or used in a monument' be declared before the decemvirs and submitted to them."

Dignitas

Table 8.3.1. Continued

in senatu	*ad populum*

D. *Quaestio* Established

(iv.) Hoc capite multa sperant; in omnis imperatores heredesque eorum quaestionem suo iudicio comparant...	(iii.) Hoc capite etiam quaestionem de clarissimis viris qui populi Romani bella gesserunt iudiciumque de pecuniis repetundis [i] ad decemviros translatum videtis.
"They have high hopes with this section [of the law]: they're readying a board of enquiry under their own jurisdiction against every commander and his heirs..."	"[You can see that] this section of the law also transfers to the decemvirs powers of inquiry into the most distinguished men who have waged the wars of the Roman people and judgment over cases of recovering money."

E. Scope of New *Quaestio*: Past Monies

(v.) ... sed maximam pecuniam se a Fausto ablaturos arbitrantur. Quam causam suscipere iurati iudices noluerunt, hanc isti decemviri susceperunt: idcirco a iudicibus fortasse praetermissam esse arbitrantur quod sit ipsis reservata.	(iv.) Horum erit nunc iudicium quantae cuiusque manubiae fuerint, quid relatum, quid residuum sit.
"... but they think they can extract the most money from Faustus [Sulla]. These decemvirs have taken up a cause that sworn judges refused to take up: perhaps they think the judges passed it by because it was reserved for them!"	"They will now have judgment on the quantity of everyone's cash from spoils, on what he submitted, on what was left over..."

F. Scope of New *Quaestio*: Future Spoils

(vi). Deinde etiam in reliquum tempus diligentissime sancit ut, quod quisque imperator habeat pecuniae, protinus ad decemviros deferat.	(v.) ... in posterum vero lex haec imperatoribus vestris constituitur, ut, quicumque de provincia decesserit, apud eosdem decemviros quantum habeat praedae, manubiarum, auri coronarii, profiteatur.

(continued)

Table 8.3.1. Continued

in senatu	*ad populum*
"Looking to the future, the law next decrees that whatever monies a commander possesses he shall submit forthwith to the decemvirs."	"...and for the future a law is being established for your commanders: whoever leaves a province will have to profess in front of these same decemvirs how much booty, cash from booty, and crown gold he has."

[i] Clark emended to *residuis*; *de pecuniis repetundis* suggests the criminal charge of extortion (*[res] repetundae*), already the competence of a jury-court. As Manuwald 2018: 318 points out, Cicero is "not referring specifically to the recovery of money extorted by Roman officials, frequently in the provinces, as a criminal offence, but to an investigation into the money potentially to be paid back to the treasury by Roman generals." Cicero, I think, uses *repetundis* in its literal sense ("reclaim") in order to recall the name of the court and thus memorably—and inaccurately—represent his view of decemviral overreach.

The keys to the passage are C and F (Table 8.3.1): C-p and F-p make the intention and structure of the law clear, and C-s and F-s are emblematic of the objective of the senate version. Where the senate speech appears to paraphrase the bill, the popular speech, as regards past gains at least, appears to quote it directly[30] (numerals indicate the order of elements; rows are lettered for ease of reference).

Table 8.3.2. (= Table 8.3.1.C expanded)

		in senatu			*ad populum*
			Past Gains		
a.		ø	i.		aurum, argentum
b.	ii.	ex praeda, ex manubiis	ii.		ex praeda, ex manubiis
c.	iii.	ex auro coronario	iii.		ex coronario
d.	i.	quod ad quemque pervenit	iv.		ad quoscumque pervenit
e.	v.	neque in aerarium relatum sit	v.		neque relatum est in publicum
f.	iv.	quod neque consumptum in monumento	vi.		neque in monumento consumptum
g.	vi.	id ad xviros referri iubet	vii.		id profiteri apud xviros et ad eos referri iubet

---

30. Ferrary 1988: 156.

Table 8.3.2. Continued

in senatu	ad populum
Future Gains	
h. *vii.* quod quisque imperator …	*viii.* quicumque de provincia decesserit
i. *viii.* … habeat pecuniae protinus ad xviros deferat.	*ix.* apud eosdem xviros quantum habeat praedae, manubiarum, auri coronarii, profiteatur.

The language of both versions illustrates the bill's care. Legitimate uses for *praeda, manubiae,* and *aurum coronarium* were not blocked. More important, the phrasing of the popular speech makes clear the bill's purpose. It did not target any and all unspent booty, as the senate speech implies, but specifically, and apparently only, gold and silver, presumably because it could be converted easily to coin. Of that, notably, there would be a shortage in 63.[31] The Rullan project could well do with hard currency to pay for the purchase of land.

But what spoils were targeted? Large commands were not on the horizon in 64. The East, thanks to Pompey, must have now seemed secure. The senate had been reluctant to annex Egypt, which might have required military intervention.[32] Caesar's lucrative, but dangerous, Gallic exploits can hardly have been foreseen. Most military operations since Sulla had been small, often waged by generals hunting for triumphs.[33] The bill probably imagined future campaigns would be on that scale (hence from them not just gold and silver, but all booty, was attached; cf. F-p). The chief target was surely larger, completed campaigns. Pompey had swept the Eastern Mediterranean and much of Asia Minor and would enrich the treasury spectacularly, but he was exempted by name (*LA* 1.13, 2.60). There were, however, other possible sources. At the time of Cicero's speeches, L. Licinius Lucullus and perhaps also Q. Caecilius Metellus (later Creticus) were outside the city, awaiting triumphs.[34] Lucullus had preceded Pompey in the East and returned to Rome

---

31. Thus Cicero as consul forbade the export of gold from Puteoli (*Vat.* 12, *Flac.* 67). The impetus for export was probably investment in the newly pacified East (so Gruen 1974: 427), although hoarding out of anxiety about Pompey's imminent return is also possible.

32. Cf. ch. 4 n. 85.

33. Thus, for example, the campaigns by M. Aemilius Lepidus against an Alpine tribe in Cisapline Gaul in 77; by C. Scribonius Curio against the Dardani and Moesi in Macedonia in 75–74; by M. Terentius Varro Lucullus against the Bessi in Macedonia in 72; and by M. Pupius Piso Frugi Calpurnianus in Farther Spain in 70–69.

34. Sal. *Cat.* 30.3–4 has Lucullus still outside the city in October 63.

with vast riches.³⁵ Metellus had subdued all of Crete.³⁶ A measure appropriating war spoils obviously had that wealth in mind—and might well have been content with only the gold and silver, especially during a shortage of coin.

But before the senate Cicero claims the bill's chief target is Faustus Sulla, son of the dictator. On the one hand, Faustus was indeed a possible target, if Cicero has described the measure correctly. There had been calls to prosecute him to recover funds that his father had appropriated from the treasury and from tax revenues (here the issue would be *pecuniae residuae*).³⁷ Under this measure Faustus could perhaps also be sued for the value of the properties of domestic opponents, whom by a legal fiction Sulla had styled enemies of the state, making their property *praeda* (here the issue would be spoils as such, turning Sulla's legal fiction against his son).³⁸ And possibly Faustus had inherited *manubiae* that his father ought to have spent. On the other hand, Faustus was also a difficult target. Much time had passed. Sulla's ledgers must have been complex. There were thorny legal questions (what was *praeda*? what is the relation of the decemvirate's jurisdiction to the *quaestio peculatus*, which already existed?).

The senate as a body knew all this perfectly well. And it is precisely this complexity, and even unclarity, that makes Faustus an attractive image for Cicero—and he is an image. Like Egypt in both speeches, Faustus was doubtless not the bill's immediate object; but he vividly symbolizes the possibility that the writ of the law could be expanded and manipulated. Would that happen? Who knew? That was a question of the intentions of the backers of the bill and more so of the eventual decemvirs. What and who would those be? Was Lucullus's wealth enough for their project—or, once they got a new tool, would they keep digging? Those are precisely the questions that the case of Faustus focalizes; the complexities of his situation capture exactly the difficulties of predicting how the law will be implemented. The point is not merely to appeal to the senate's own interests but to use those interests to make them ask certain sorts of questions.

---

35. πλοῦτος ... πολύς (Plu. *Luc.* 36.6). In his triumph in 63 there were eight mules with golden couches, fifty-six with ingots of silver, and a hundred and seven with around 2,700,000 pieces of silver coin (37.4).

36. He took the cities of Eleuthera, Lappa (D.C. 36.18.2), Knossos, Lyctus, Cydonia and "very many others" (Liv. *per.* 99).

37. Ascon. *Corn.* 64.26–65.8C gives the impression that there were frequent demands for the recovery of these monies; see Marshall 1984: 202–203. On the complications of the issue, see Gruen 1971: 56–57; 276. On Sulla's monies (presumably inherited by Faustus, as Marshall points out), see Shatzman 1975: 270–72, Barlow 1980: 211.

38. On the use of *praeda* in this sense, cf. Cic. *Ver.* 2.3.81; Sal. *Or. Lep.* (*Hist.* 1.49M) 17; on the sales, cf. Cic. *S. Rosc.* 124–8, Sal. *Hist.* 1.49 M, Vel. 2.28.4, Plu. *Sul.* 33.2.

And those are exactly the questions that other details of the passage prompt: they draw out issues of breadth and intention and design. In the popular speech we see only the means (the bill establishes a *quaestio*, D-p), but in the senate speech we see the breadth of the motive (the framers "hope for much," *multa sperant*, D-s). In the senate speech, as Table 8.3.2 shows, Cicero paraphrases the law to make its reach look broader. He begins not with the bill's true object, precious metals, as in the popular speech (*aurum argentum*, row **a**), but an expression that is as broad as possible, "whatever has come to each man" (*quod ad quemque pervenerit*, row **d**). Where the popular speech makes it clear than only precious metals were attached (row **a**), the senate speech makes it sound like all *praeda* is attached (row **b**). In the senate version future commanders must report not "booty, *manubiae*, and crown gold" but simply "any money they each have" (row **i**). What is more, in the senate speech Cicero makes the framer's efforts methodical, as if from the very beginning they had eventual broad use in mind. Whereas in the popular speech future commanders are simply subject to the law (*in posterum lex haec . . . constituitur*, F-p), in the senate speech a "stricture [on them] has been very carefully fixed for the foreseeable future" (*in reliquum tempus diligentissime sancit*, F-s), where *sancit* implies a tighter bind, and where *diligentissime*, like the faux *diligentia* of tallying up properties to sell them off, speaks to careful planning. The idea of careful planning also lies behind *architecti* (A-s), a metaphor only in the senate speech (and *architectus* is always pejorative in Cicero's oratory, unlike English 'architect' and more like 'mastermind').[39] The image sits ill with *olfecerint* 'sniffed out,' which recalls a scent hound; but that is the point. There is raw hunger—but there is also a plan, just as with the image of *cuniculis* 'tunneling' (*LA* 1.1 = Table 4.4.E) to Alexandria. Where the popular speech had a brazen night journey to Egypt, the senate speech had the steady work of organized, but voracious, sappers.

In short, Faustus is a kind of image, supporting the idea of the risk of a measure being pressed beyond its ostensible original purpose or at least into very unclear territory. The figure of Faustus has another effect. He had a kind of double identity. As heir of his father's sometimes ill-gotten gains, he was a natural target for anti-Sullans. Sulla's legacy remained a political football.[40] That was why jurors

---

39. Classen 1985: 327–28 n. 68. Besides this passage, *omnium architectum et machinatorem unum esse Chrysogonum* ("the mastermind and prime mover of everything was Chrysogonus," *S. Rosc.* 132); *ipsum principem atque architectum sceleris* ("the principal architect of the crime," *Clu.* 60); so also in Apuleius *Apol.* 74 (*omnium simulationum architectus, omnium malorum seminarium*).

40. See Marshall 1984.

had refused to convict Faustus on an earlier occasion, as Cicero notes here (E-s).[41] But Faustus was himself linked to Pompey. His abortive prosecution in 65 was apparently perceived as anti-Pompeian and prompted the retaliatory prosecution of M. Lucullus for his actions under Sulla.[42] Faustus was also, at that moment, serving under Pompey, and very creditably so,[43] and he would in a few years be engaged to Pompey's daughter. Faustus in that way focalized the problems of partisan politics. Cicero, I think, has a more particular point still. The measure about booty had a partisan cast. Lucullus and Metellus were indeed still outside the city—because their triumphs were being obstructed by Pompey's friends. The image of a Faustus prosecuted prompts the thought that a measure that would see Pompey's opponents discomfited might also see Pompey himself annoyed or embarrassed. If in Chapter 8.2 individualist aristocrats are encouraged to think collectively—and respect Pompey—then here populists who would curry Pompey's favor are encouraged to think systematically about how partisan measures can have unforeseen consequences. Bad politics, like bad laws, can hit more than their immediate target. What at first seems bold and creative may prove to have been risky and rash.

8.4. US

ὁμονοοῦσα δὲ ὀλιγαρχία οὐκ εὐδιάφθορος ἐξ αὑτῆς.

An oligarchy that is of one mind does not typically cause its own destruction.

—Aristotle, *Politics* 1306a

Our Morality

If Cicero thus calls certain subgroups of the senate to higher ground, he also projects an identity onto the whole senate, adapting aspects of their self-understandings in rather the same way as in the popular speech he turned *commodum* into *otium* and *libertas* into procedure. One passage concisely illustrates one such adaptation. Among the bill's sources of income was a tax on public lands

---

41. Cf. *Clu.* 94 and Cic. *Corn.* 1. fr. 34 Crawford = Asconius 73.1C; for more detail, see Crawford 1994: 67–148, Griffin 1973.

42. Cf. Plu. *Luc.* 37.1 and see Gruen 1971; 1974: 276–77; Marshall 1984: 203–205.

43. He would be the first to climb over the walls of Jerusalem later that year (Jos. *AJ* 14.69, *BJ* 1.149).

(*LA* 1.10, 2.56–7). In Italy itself the lands could only be taxed if they had become public property from 88 on, when Sulla and Q. Pompeius Rufus held the consulship, but outside of Italy there was no such restriction (in Table 8.4.1 numbers, as usual, indicate the slightly different sequence of elements).

Table 8.4.1. Rhetorical Structure of the Treatment of the Tax on Extra-Italian Lands (*LA* 1.10, 2.56–57)

in senatu	*ad populum*
A. Italian Lands	
(i.) etenim quod superiore parte legis praefinitum fuit, 'Sulla et Pompeio consulibus,'	(ii.) . . . non, ut antea, ab Sulla et Pompeio consulibus.
"After all, what was precisely limited in the earlier part of the bill—'[acquired] during the consulship of Sulla and Pompeius'—"	" . . . not, as before, beginning from the consulship of Sulla and Pompeius."
B. Extra-Italian Lands	
(ii.) . . . id rursus liberum infinitumque fecerunt.	(i.) Sequitur 'omnis agros extra Italiam' infinito ex tempore . . . ,
" . . . in this part of the bill they go back to having free and unlimited."	"The bill then mentions 'all properties outside of Italy,' with *no* time limitation . . ."
C. Imposition of Taxes	
(iii.) Iubet enim eosdem decemviros omnibus agris publicis pergrande vectigal imponere . . .	(iv.) . . . eique agro pergrande vectigal imponitur.
"The bill orders the decemvirs to impose an extremely large tax on all public lands—"	" . . . and an extremely large tax is imposed on the public property."
D. Power to Recense Lands	
(iv.) . . . ut idem possint et liberare agros quos commodum sit et quos ipsis libeat publicare.	(iii.) Cognitio decemvirum, privatus sit an publicus;

(*continued*)

Table 8.4.1. Continued

in senatu	*ad populum*
"…which means the same parties will be able to exempt the lands that suit them and appropriate the lands that please them."	"The right to determine whether a property is public or private [is granted] to the decemvirs…"

E. Critique of Scope of Power

in senatu	*ad populum*
(v.) Quo in iudicio perspici non potest utrum severitas acerbior an benignitas quaestuosior sit futura.	(v.) Hoc quantum iudicium, quam intolerandum, quam regium sit, quem praeterit, posse quibuscumque locis velint nulla disceptatione, nullo consilio privata publicare, publica liberare?
"In that kind of assessment it's hard to see what there will be more of: bitter cruelty or profitable kindness!"	"Who fails to see how broad, and intolerable, and lordly a power of assessment it is to be able, in whatever place they want, without any debate and without any advisory counsel, to appropriate private lands and exempt public lands?"

In the popular version the difference between lands inside and outside of Italy is simply described as such: *infinito ex tempore, non, ut antea* "with *no* time limitation—not, as before" etc. (B-p). The senate passage foregrounds the intention of the bill-writers: they "deliberately undid" (*rursus…fecerunt*, B-s) a previous restriction.[44] They meant to give themselves maximal freedom of choice: what had been carefully limited beforehand (*praefinitum*, A-s, a *vox propria* for circumscribing amounts and days)[45] they have rendered completely unlimited (*liberum infinitumque*, A-s,). As with *proscribit ~ perscribit* (*LA* 1.2 = Table 3.1.A–B-s), the point is anchored by using the same verb with different preverbs (*prae- ~ in-*), an occasional affect of the senate speech. And where the popular speech, as so often, implies a procedural violation—the power to recense is transferred to

---

44. *Rursus facere* is "to return into a previous state"; so of Antony's return to Caesar's good graces: *factus es ei rursus nescio quo modo familiaris* (*Phil.* 2.78). Cicero means that while land sales had a time restriction (for the date of 88, see ch. 4.4), other measures did not, and the tax is like them (cf. Manuwald 2018: 140–41).

45. "Days" are the first subcategory recognized by the *TLL* (10.2.641.50).

the decemvirs (*cognitio decemvirum*, D-p)— the senate version doubly and chiastically stresses the lack of limits: *et liberare agros* **quos commodum sit** *et* **quos ipsis libeat** *publicare* (D-s). Last, where the popular speech stresses procedural failure (*nulla disceptatione, nullo consilio*, E-p—a now familiar theme), the senate speech stresses attitudes, in a way perfectly consonant with the thrust of the passage: what will matter in each case is the attitude the decemvirs choose to take toward various property holders, "harshness" or "beneficence"—both postures of superiors, which is what the law makes them.[46]

Here, then, are the same themes that we saw in the senate version of Cicero's treatment of the free location of sale (ch. 4.2). There, as here, the decemvirs set themselves no limit; there, as here, there is an accent on whim: where the popular variant made darkness and desolation into symbols of violated procedure, the senate speech made them symbols of unrestricted choice (*in quibus* **commodum sit** *tenebris, ut in qua* **velint** *solitudine, LA* 1.7 = Table 4.2.E-s). That passage, as I suggested, was a kind of conceptual pun on the meanings of *licentia*, both 'legal permission' and '(moral) license.' It is now possible to support and sharpen that claim. The conceptual mechanism is one we now recognize: one idea modulated into another. Here the very same mechanism is in play: a legal concept is modulated into an ethical concept. *Praefinitum* ('prescribed [beforehand]') becomes *infinitum* ('indeterminate'), which implies 'boundless,' which is made to imply a lack of moral limits—in other words, legal *licentia* again means moral *licentia*. Neither of these passages is a particularly dramatic instance of that trope. But that is to be charged in the first instance to the damaged condition of the senate speech. Missing passages would undoubtedly also have argued that the bill's various legal "permissions" enabled and reflected moral "license." Several measures lent themselves to such treatment. For example, decemvirs could apparently visit any province at all (*omnis provincias obeundi . . . summa potestas datur, LA* 2.34). That was an old consular privilege, meant for a supreme authority.[47] *Imperium* was usually tied to the boundaries of a province, but this bill did not limit decemviral *imperium* formally (*iure*) or geographically (*regionibus . . . certis*).[48] That seems to be an adaptation of recent military commands (where the provision made sense for pursuing mobile and diffuse enemies).[49] The decemvirs would

---

46. For the likely connotation of *benignitas* here, cf. ch. 7.2.

47. Cic. *Att.* 8.15.3, *Phil.* 4.9.

48. *LA* 2.35; cf. ch. 1 n. 121.

49. *Infinitum*, applied by Cicero to M. Antonius's special command against the pirates in 74 (*Ver.* 2.2.8, 2.3.213), is, at least in part, literally meant ('un-bordered'); *contra* Brennan 2000: 427–28; Jameson 1970: 542.

have the effective rank of *praetor* (*praetoria potestas*, *LA* 2.32), creating an authority overlapping that of a provincial governor. That, too, was like recent military commands.[50] The decemvirs' term of office was five years (*LA* 2.32). Other agrarian commissions seem to have dissolved when their business was done; when fixed terms are attested, they are three years.[51] The popular speech treats all these features simply as marks of a lust for power. But it would have been clear to the senate—an audience that Cicero expects to recognize allusions to an interdict, to his expertise as past *praetor urbanus*, and to interference in the duties of quaestor, senate, and consul—that all the measures depended on expanding precedents, and those would have been perfect opportunities to play on the polyvalence of *licentia*. *LA* 1.7 and 1.10 are, I think, partial manifestations of themes and images that were developed more fully in lost parts of the senate speech.

Certainly the notion of *licentia* would have had a special resonance in 64 and 63. There is a paradox in the life of competitive political elites. A chief imperative for members of such an elite is maximizing their personal power. The corollary is limiting the power of other competitors. When the rules of competition are settled, the imperative and the corollary are in a kind of equilibrium. But proposed innovations in the rules—like an irregular quasi-magistracy or a different electoral mechanism—can disturb that equilibrium: the value assigned to the innovation will vary according to who seems likelier to benefit. Some, especially in times of uncertainty and stress, will think an innovation is worth the risk, to maximize personal power; others will think barring an innovation is prudent, to curb the sway of opponents. A new tool with a pleasant heft in your hand may seem menacing in your rival's. That is exactly the point Caesar makes about executing the Catilinarian conspirators: "Every bad precedent began with worthy objectives" (*omnia mala exempla ex rebus bonis orta sunt*, Sal. *Cat.* 51.27). Getting rid of the US Senate filibuster, to take a modern parallel, may seem like a very fine idea—until you find yourself in the minority party. By adopting and adapting traditional moral language and concepts, Cicero wants to make innovations that seemed attractive to some seem unattractive to all. That was ultimately the logic of the image of the interdict (ch. 3.3 The Wastrel, *fin.*), which configures senators as a unified body of moral guardians against one of their own not in his right mind. The strength of an oligarchy is in its unity of purpose.

---

50. The constitutional particulars are not always clear. For discussions of the precise relation of the *imperium* of Pompey's commands, *maius* or not, to that of governors, see Ehrenberg 1953; Jameson 1970.

51. See ch. 1 n. 105.

We See

In other passages the idea of a unified senate is put forward in another way: through the implication of shared perception. The bill attached the profits of any new *agri vectigales* from 63 on; Cicero treats the measure briefly at the end of the discussion of Pompey's exemption from remitting war spoils (Table 8.4.2).

Table 8.4.2. (*LA* 1.13, *LA* 2.62)

in senatu	*ad populum*
Sed cui manubias remittit, in huius vectigalia invadit. Iubet enim pecunia, si qua post nos consules ex novis vectigalibus recipiatur, hac uti decemviros. Quasi vero non intellegamus haec eos vectigalia quae Cn. Pompeius adiunxerit vendere cogitare.	Verum tamen cavet ut, si qua pecunia post nos consules ex novis vectigalibus recipiatur, ea decemviri utantur. Nova porro vectigalia videt ea fore quae Pompeius adiunxerit. Ita remissis manubiis vectigalibus eius virtute partis se frui putat oportere.
"So he lets him have his spoils—but he falls upon his tax contracts: if any money is earned from new tax contracts from this year forward, he orders the decemvirs to have use of it. As if we couldn't tell that they are planning to sell the tax contracts which Cn. Pompeius will have added!"	"But Rullus is very careful to ensure that if any money is earned from new tax contracts from this year forward, the decemvirs have use of it. And of course by new tax contracts he means the ones that Pompey will have added. In other words he thinks that if he lets Pompey keep his spoils, he should get to enjoy the tax contracts won by Pompey's courage."

The popular speech explains that Pompey's gains are the target (Rullus "sees what new *vectigalia* are coming") and strikes the now familiar note of unjust appropriation (*eius virtute partis*, "won by [Pompey's] courage," which recalls Rullus's letter to him). But the senate speech has senators seeing right through the idea ("as if we couldn't tell!"). We have seen that effect before: where the popular speech treats the exceptions of the Recentorici and Hiempsal separately (*LA* 1.10–11, Table 4.3.2), the senate speech treats them together—and imagines an incredulous senate: "Who did Rullus imagine would think that, in the whole wide world, he only managed to find *two* parties to spare—for free?" (*quem putet existimaturum duas causas in orbe terrarum repertas quibus gratis parceret? LA* 1.11, Table 4.3.1.J-s).

The senate also sees through the bill's colonial plan. The absence of named colonial sites leads Cicero to suggest in both speeches that a colony could even be founded right on the Janiculum hill, across the river from the Forum. The memorable claim is the penultimate argument of the speech, preparing for the subsequent dramatic treatment of the threat of a colonized Capua (a topic of ch. 9). The two treatments of the Janiculum draw from the same fund of ideas (the numbering here is from the full comparative table in Appendix 3; the Latin appears there). The senate version consistently accents the senate's perceptivity. Both speeches allege that Rullus wants to garrison Italy. In the popular speech it is a matter for accusation: "Is it your idea to occupy a place you deem suitable for your violence, fill it with a complement" etc. (J4-p). But in the senate speech, it is a trick that won't get past them: "Did you really think, Rullus, that we would hand over to you, and to your fellow plotters in this whole scheme, all of Italy, unarmed, so you could secure it with garrisons, occupy it with colonies, hold it bound fast with every kind of chain?" (J4-s). Likewise, both speeches claim Rullus's intention to garrison Italy is certain. In the popular speech, Cicero is the instructor: "And he really does plan to besiege and occupy all of Italy with his garrisons, Romans— pay heed to how, I ask you!" (J7-p). But the senate don't need to "heed"; they see the trick for themselves: "As to your desire to fill the whole of Italy with your colonies—did you think none of us would realize what was going on?" (J7-s).

The introduction to the Janiculum passage should be seen in this light (Table 8.4.3).

Table 8.4.3. (= J5 in Appendix 3) Failure of law to preclude colony on Janiculum (*LA* 1.16, 2.74)

in senatu	*ad populum*
Vbi enim cavetur ne in Ianiculo coloniam constituatis, ne urbem hanc urbe alia premere atque urgere possitis?	Quid igitur est causae quin coloniam in Ianiculum possint deducere et suum praesidium in capite atque cervicibus nostris conlocare?
"After all, where is the provision to prevent you from founding a colony right on the Janiculum—from pressing down on and in upon this city with another city?"	"Is there then any reason why they could not lead a colony out onto the Janiculum and establish their garrison on our heads and necks?"

The popular version, as so often, uses the surroundings, here to suggest division and inferiority: where the senate speech has the static "establish on the

Janiculum" (*in Ianiculo constitu[ere]*), the popular speech has the kinetic "lead out onto the Janiculum" (*in Ianiculum ... deducere*). That image, delivered to a crowd out of doors, must have suggested part peeling off, marching across the river, and swarming up the beetling hill in the near distance. That is another image of division, just as when only some tribes are favored after the election; and the image is suggestive. The Janiculum, still not much settled in Cicero's time, was a symbolic frontier: a red flag was flown on its summit when the *comitia centuriata* was meeting on the Campus Martius, to be lowered if an enemy approached (Dio 37.28). An "enemy" colony on that hill would convert it from symbolic frontier to hostile citadel—the very thing its annexation long ago was supposed to prevent.[52] And the Janiculum really still was a weak point in the city's defense: during the Civil Wars in 87, Marius and Cinna tried to seize it; during the Civil War of Lepidus in 70, Lutatius Catulus and Pompey secured it against his approach.[53] The senate version, by contrast, suggests a position of superiority: the risk there is not a boot on its neck; the risk is a rival center of authority, described in the language of strategic positioning (nothing will keep "them" from "pressing down on and in upon this city with another city," *urbem hanc urbe alia premere*). (Roughly the same language is used of Capua: *illam urbem huic urbi rursus opponere ... cogitant, LA* 1.18, C23 in Appendix 2). The people see the enemy up on the hill across the river; the senate "see the moves" on a chessboard or see a pin stuck in a map. And they can see the moves because they are astute readers: *cavetur ne* is a *vox propria* for designing legislation to avoid a particular result.[54] The senate can read between the lines and see that the bill "fails to close a loophole," one might say.

Treating the senate as if it were "us" who, positioned "up high," can "all see the moves" is obviously the projection of an identity: sage, perceptive, skeptical. But the things "they see" aren't necessarily certain. There were good reasons for exempting Hiempsal and the Recentorici.[55] Attaching future *vectigalia* would of course include Pompey's gains but the implication that he should have been named is not certain (a law might well simply specify a date). Whether a colony in the full, old military sense could really have been founded on the Janiculum is

---

52. *Ianiculum quoque adiectum, non inopia loci sed ne quando ea arx hostium esset* (Liv. 1.33.6).

53. Liv. *per*. 80; App. *BC* 1.67; Flor. 3.23.6.

54. Thus sarcastically of Rullus, *cavet enim vir optimus ne emat ab invito* (*LA* 1.14 = Table 7.3.1-5); seriously meant, *quid enim cavendum est in coloniis deducendis?* (*LA* 1.20 = C33 in Appendix 2). On this sense see *TLL* 3.638.66–639.83. *Caveo* is used in the popular speech to mean not 'observe proper limits' but 'look out for the interests of' (*regi amico cavet, LA* 2.58) or 'make sure' (*LA* 2.62 in Table 8.4.2).

55. Ch. 4 n. 55.

not certain, either: some of the language of the bill, quoted only in the senate version, speaks of leading *coloni* into *municipia*, which means that the bill envisioned (at least in part) viritane assignations into existing municipalities and colonies rather than the wholesale foundation of new colonies.[56] But Cicero's language makes skepticism into a token of shared identity. And he exercises that identity himself in another part of the Janiculum excerpt which has no correspondent in the popular version (Table 8.4.4).

Table 8.4.4. (= J6 in Appendix 3) Intention of Decemvirs not to build on Janiculum (*LA* 1.16)

in senatu	*ad populum*
'Non faciemus,' inquit. Primum nescio, deinde timeo, postremo non committam ut vestro beneficio potius quam nostro consilio salvi esse possimus.	ø
"'We wouldn't do that,' he says. For one thing, I'm not sure you won't; and for another, I'm worried you might; and above all, I don't intend to let you put us in a position where our safety depends on your good will as opposed to our own deliberation!"	ø

The passage, though brief, is richly suggestive. Cicero ventriloquizes a punch of Rullus in order to answer with a quick triplet of counterpunches. He thus evokes an *altercatio*, the "verbal exchange" that was a feature of certain debates.[57] It was an agonistic mode of speech and therefore apt for drawing sharp distinctions. Cicero evokes it to counterpose two models of interaction. There are personal favors (cf. *vestro beneficio*), and there is intelligent collective planning (cf. *nostro consilio*). The senate's political viability—that is the resonance here of *salvi*, lit. "safe, unharmed"—depends on recognizing that the models are, in this case, mutually exclusive. Self-interest, which might otherwise have allowed itself to

---

56. Cf. ch. 9 n. 4 with *LA* 1.17 and 2.74 (= J8 in Appendix 3).

57. For an instance of the practice, cf. "I crushed Clodius to his face in the senate in a set speech full of gravity but also in an exchange like this (and I only give you a small sample—the rest of it doesn't have the same force or wit out of the context of the fight to win—the *agôn*, as you Greeks say) (*Clodium praesentem fregi in senatu cum oratione perpetua plenissima gravitatis tum altercatione eius modi—ex qua licet pauca degustes; nam cetera non possunt habere eandem neque vim neque venustatem remoto illo studio contentionis quem* ἀγῶνα *vos appellatis*, Cic. *Att.* 1.16.8). For a description of the forensic version, see Quint. 6.3.4.

trust in hope of a favor or a reward, must in this case reject trust and prune back hopes; there is no room for "deals," only for collective plans. An oligarchy of one mind is a strong oligarchy.

The art of J6 is thus very precise: Cicero exploits the resonances of a known mode of speech to point to an ideal of common identity that looks past personal interests. The same is true of another passage where his own and the senate's sagacity are stressed. As we have seen, Pompey's recent gains in the east were subject to sale. The popular passage—ironically, of a military hero—uses military metaphors for the measure: it is a "thoroughly concealed ambush" (*penitus abstrusas insidias*, LA 2.49), and Rullus's law is like a battering ram meant to throw over Pompey's resources (*hanc fere legem ad illius opes evertendas tamquam machinam comparari*, LA 2.50, cf. ch. 5.2). The senate passage says simply: "Notice how now their intended goal is clearer than it was before. In the earlier part of the law I was the one who incriminated them for attacking Pompey; in this part of the law they incriminate themselves" (*videte nunc quo adfectent iter apertius quam antea. Nam superiore parte legis quem ad modum Pompeium oppugnarent, a me indicati sunt; nunc iam se ipsi indicabunt*, LA 1.5). The sentiment, with its accent on perspicacity, reflects the theme of this section. An idiom crystallizes it. *Adfectare viam* or *iter*, lit. "make for energetically,"[58] as a metaphor has a very particular connotation, referring to concealed, typically ambitious and destructive, plans, at the moment they are discovered.[59] The only other instance in late Republican Latin, also from Cicero, is closely comparable.[60] In the Republic the phrase, in its literal or metaphorical senses, is otherwise poetic, and that suggests that this is a literary quotation. (The line scans as an almost complete iambic

---

58. Thus *hi gladiatorio animo ad me adfectant viam* ("They're making for me with gangsterly intent!" Ter. *Ph.* 964), *victorque volentis | per populos dat iura viamque adfectat Olympo* (Verg. *G.* 4.561–2). *TLL* 1.1181 includes these instances with *viam* or *iter* under the general rubric "aggredi, adoriri, temptare."

59. Thus *scio quam rem agat: | ut me deponat vino, eam adfectat viam | post hoc quod habeo ut commutet coloniam* ("I see what he's up to—knocking me off balance with wine, that's his plan, and then making what I have here change residences," Pl. *Aul.* 574–6), *video quam rem agis. | quia commisi, ut me defrudes, ad eam rem adfectas viam* ("I see what you're up to! Because I've handed them over, you're putting your efforts into deceiving me!" Pl. *Men.* 685–6), *nam disciplinast isdem munerarier | ancillas primum ad dominas qui adfectant viam* ("Those who are trying to get to the mistresses regularly bribe the maids first," Ter. *Hau.* 300–1).

60. The *dominatio* of Sulla's cronies, Cicero alleges, "formerly operated in other spheres," but, as the prosecution of Roscius shows, "the road it's laying, the path it's taking" now aim at the very heart of the social contract: the integrity of the law courts, which are being abused for private ends (*quae quidem dominatio, iudices, in aliis rebus antea versabatur, nunc vero quam viam munitet et quod iter adfectet videtis, ad fidem, ad ius iurandum, ad iudicia vestra, ad id quod solum prope in civitate sincerum sanctumque restat*, S. *Rosc.* 140).

octonarius.)[61] If that is true, then the resonance is rich. Such quotes, which, like proverbs, step out of a moment and assimilate it to some broader template ("Here is an instance of a well-known pattern"), were often used to create distance, sometimes ironic, or to offer political handicapping, as when Deiotarus, hearing a rumor that Caesar was besieged in Africa but that Domitius had died in a shipwreck, remarked ἐρρέτω φίλος σὺν ἐχθρῷ "May friend die, if enemy die too."[62] But this quote begins the argument that Pompey is under attack, and that argument will be supported, in the passage we have seen, by alluding to the *infulae* on the temple walls. That is, Pompey's accomplishments will be linked to the whole symbolic system that represents and reinforces senatorial primacy. Thus the poetic quote, a token of shared intellectual culture, and expressing shared perspicacity, is preface to an argument about shared political culture. Here, too, then, is an inversion. As the culture of triumphs will be made a common possession, so here is the apt poetic quote a tool not of ironic detachment but of transcending partisanship. "We," with our perspicacity—and our taste—"can see" what is good for us all.

Dignitas

Common identity has another face. Two passages of the senate speech directly invoke a cardinal value of the upper class, *dignitas*. The appeal to a shared value is obvious—but it has a very particular point, which, just as with *libertas*, only the primacy of the local context reveals. At the end of the section on the settlement of colonies (*LA* 1.16–17, 2.73–75; cf. J8–9 in Appendix 3), Cicero imagines the loose language of the bill will mean an Italy filled with garrisons:

> It's clear from the text: "The decemvirs shall lead colonists of their choice into *municipia* and colonies of their choice and assign to them properties in locations of their choice"—which means that, once they've filled Italy

---

[61]. If Cicero omitted the first foot, then the line would have a caesura seven half-feet from the end, a common variant: ... | vĭdē|tĕ nūnc| qu(ō) ādfĕct|ēnt † ĭtĕr |ăpērt|ĭŭ(s) qu(am) ānt|ēā. Was Cicero quoting a messenger speech, which in tragedy often appear in this meter (see Moore 2012: 183)? The theme of "revelation" is appropriate for such a speech. Other scansions are possible (for example, the indirect question, if only that is the actual quote, scans as the end of a trochaic septenarius: ... qu(ō) ād|fĕctēnt || ĭtĕr ăp|ērtĭŭ(s) |qu(am) āntĕ|ā.

[62]. So, probably, the proverb he recited (*adesp*. 363 Nauck); Cicero renders it into Latin (*itaque cum esset ei nuntiatum Domitium naufragio perisse, te in castello circumsederi, de Domitio dixit versum Graecum eadem sententia, qua etiam nos habemus Latinum: 'pereant amici, dum inimici una intercidant,' Deiot*. 25).

full of their soldiers, not only will we have no hope remain of maintaining status (*dignitatis retinendae*)—we will have no hope of recovering liberty (*libertatis . . . recuperandae*)." (*LA* 1.17)

The corresponding segment of the popular speech cites *libertas*, resources, and *regnum*. The other passage concerns Capua. The Rullan bill planned to colonize the *ager Campanus*, whose leading city Capua was. In both speeches Cicero treats that measure in the last of the arguments, and in both speeches he imagines a Capua that has risen again among southern colonies now peopled with the decemvirs' thugs. The senate version ends thus—the very last sentence of the speech before the *peroratio*:

> (*to the senate*) What political options do you think you'll have, or what means to maintain your liberty (*libertas*) and stature (*dignitas*), once Rullus—and those whom you fear much more than Rullus—occupy Capua and the cities surrounding Capua with every available crew of the needy and unscrupulous, with every available resource, with all the silver and gold there is?
>
> *Quid enim existimatis integrum vobis in re publica fore aut in vestra libertate ac dignitate retinenda, cum Rullus atque ii quos multo magis quam Rullum timetis cum omni egentium atque improborum manu, cum omnibus copiis, cum omni argento et auro Capuam et urbis circa Capuam occuparint?* (*LA* 1.22)

The passages suggest the resonances of *dignitas* in this speech. It is a special status within a republican system. First, *dignitas* is linked to *libertas*, nested within it (*LA* 1.17) and standing above it (*LA* 1.22, where *ac* joins the more important member). Second, *dignitas* stands parallel to political opportunity (the connotation of *integrum in re publica* in 1.22).[63] This is something like the meaning of *integer* in the legal phrase *res integra* 'an unchanged legal situation' 'a still open matter' and recalls *salvi* from J6. These are expected features. *Dignitas* commonly connotes the superior status of aristocrats and their worthiness to govern.[64] But there is another element here—a contextual effect rather than a property of the word itself. The local context is vital. *Dignitas* is invoked only when rival

---

63. On the potentially problematic relationship between *dignitas* and *libertas*, see Wirszubski 1960: 15–17.

64. On the range of meanings of *dignitas*, see ch. 6 n. 3.

centers of authority appear; it is named when it is threatened ("Only he knows thy worth, who thee has lost," in Mickiewicz's phrase).[65] The threat is both real and metaphorical. There is a real threat. The image of dangerous colonies, which is also in the popular speech (cf. C23 in Appendix 2), should not be dismissed as exaggeration. Sullan colonies had been settled by unit, the better to be called back up if need be, and by the end of Cicero's consular year a band of disaffected veterans in Etruria would join Catiline's rebellion.[66] In 59 Caesar would settle the *ager Campanus* with his veterans, troops that both Antonius and Octavian tried to recall.[67] And Cicero's images surely put the senate in mind of Pompey's returning soldiers; in the event, Pompey would disband his army—but nobody yet knew that he would.

But the threat is also a kind of metaphor, which draws on certain other anxieties. Both speeches imagine the colonies will be staffed by violent men, clearly enough implying soldiers (cf. C5 in Appendix 2). But only here in the senate speech are the colonists described as "needy and unscrupulous" (*egent[es] et improb[i]*). And only the senate speech makes a dark allusion to "those whom you fear much more than Rullus"; when the popular speech hints at the backers of the bill without naming names, the issue is greed, not raw power.[68] The allusion to contemporary politics is clear. The "needy and unscrupulous" echoes a hostile view of the changed city population and above all the sometimes unruly *contiones* which had begun to dominate urban politics.[69] "Those whom you fear more than Rullus" are surely in part the *populares*, whose gathering energies were obvious to the senate (some of whom were themselves drivers of that energy). The ferment of contemporary politics was also a rival that needed to be guarded against. The armed camps to the south are a real geopolitical possibility but with distinct overtones of a political symbol.

---

65. Ile cię trzeba cenić, ten tylko się dowie | Kto cię stracił (*Pan Tadeusz*, 1.2–3, with reference to the poet's homeland).

66. *Catil.* 2.14, 20.

67. References in Manuwald 2007: 20.

68. "Go ahead then, citizens—entrust all these powers to the men that you suspect are angling for the decemvirate: you will discover some of them cannot acquire enough, and some cannot spend enough" (*committite vos nunc, Quirites, his hominibus haec omnia quos odorari hunc decemviratum suspicamini; reperietis partem esse eorum quibus ad habendum, partem quibus ad consumendum nihil satis esse videatur, LA* 2.65), a remark occasioned by Cicero's objection to buying land from private parties.

69. Morstein-Marx 2004:148–49. The characteristics of the colonists are not "ganz willkürlich" (Classen 1985: 337).

Guard against how? The vignettes and images of this and the previous chapters point the way. In the senate version of the sales of Italian and Sicilian properties, the image of the wastrel makes the senate into a panel of judges or family elders; and the military imagery makes them guardians of tradition (ch. 3.3). In the senate version of *liberae legationes*, the image of a perverted assize makes the senate into guardians of the constitutional and ethical order (ch. 2.4). Collective identity is a bulwark against disruption. Those appeals, like Cicero's appeals to *libertas*, though they may seem trite, push back against real difficulties. It was not illegal for a tribune to propose sales of public property. Nor was the writ of the decemvirs, given the complexity and purpose of their tasks abroad, simply unreasonable; and furthermore some senators doubtless coveted a decemviral position for themselves or their friends. Indeed, some senators might have seen the positions not as the opposite of *dignitas* but embodying it: the positions granted special privileges and offered political opportunities—the very features sometimes linked to and expressed by *dignitas*. Cicero's appeals to communal identity are to that extent revisionist and even contrarian. Preserving *dignitas* is not only a matter of resisting outside disruptions but also the enemy within. Some of those "whom [the senate] fear[ed] more than Rullus" were sitting in the temple of Jupiter Capitolinus at that very moment. Cicero's handling of *dignitas* in the senate speech is chiefly meant, not to glibly invoke the collective, but to challenge the thinking of those who understood the concept differently.

8.5. CONCLUSION

Is ordo vitio vacato, ceteris specimen esto.

The senate shall be free of moral fault and shall be to the other orders an example.

—Cicero, *de Legibus* 3.10

I have argued that in the popular speech Cicero does not simply invoke but reconfigures *libertas*, which runs through the popular speech mainly as an Unnamed Referent. He takes the element of sovereignty and narrows it chiefly to procedure, so as to find the Rullan bill wanting (and gesture to the ideal of the mixed constitution) (ch. 4); and he makes the element of *commodum* a lens through which to look at Pompey and settlement sites, disposing of any hope that the bill would help the one or provide the other (ch. 5). Cicero takes the standard slogans of the Republican *contio* and couples them to a narrower vision. It was Cicero's genius to see that his approach in the popular speech could be adapted to the senate speech. In that speech *dignitas* is the constant unnamed, and reconfigured, element. Cicero draws out two aspects of *dignitas* as touchstones for judging the Rullan bill unworthy. *Dignitas* meant political opportunity, and the Rullan bill offered such opportunities. But Cicero casts those opportunities as upsetting the competitive balance: that is one point of the senate version of the *liberae legationes* passage (ch. 2), and that is the point of conceptual pun on *licentia* (ch. 4). *Dignitas* meant high status, which the Rullan bill might, in its way, have reflected or augmented. But Cicero steadily recasts high status as meaning membership in a shared culture, like *patres* restraining a wastrel (ch. 3). In short, Cicero accents the collectivist, not the individualist, side of *dignitas*. He makes a largely implicit *dignitas* into the tie that binds.

That same reconfiguration is manifest in the passages considered in this chapter. Excesses must be clamped down on: the bill allows too much and presses precedent too far. A collective culture must be embraced: individual achievement is not possible without proper guardianship of the politico-religious system; and proper guardianship depends on exercising a shared perspicacity. But another aspect of that collectivist vision comes to the fore. The whole vision presupposes imbalance, tension, and competition. There is pressure from without: collective *dignitas* coalesces only in response to a threat. And there is pressure from within: the images of Faustus and Pompey's implied *infulae* are motivated by the complications of partisanship; and even Cicero's confident "we" elides some alternative possibilities. Cicero's use of *dignitas* and his invocation of unity are not superficial appeals, so much flag-waving, but an attempt to adjust an ostensibly shared, and certainly polyvalent, value to chart a path across the difficult terrain of contemporary politics.

It is precisely this complex understanding—a fragile communalism and a *dignitas* redefined—that underlies the *peroratio*.[70] That becomes clear if the *peroratio* is read like the *exordium* of the popular speech: with a sensitivity to the developing nuances of unnamed referents, even under the surface of apparent stock formulas. The *peroratio* falls into two halves, which, for reasons that will become clear, might be called agonistic and exhortative or protreptic respectively. Each half addresses first the tribunes, then the senate (Table 8.5).

---

70. For an assessment of the *peroratio* according to the terms of classical rhetoric, see Classen 1985: 343–44 and cf. "Da die Senatoren nicht an den Einzelheiten des Gesetzes, sondern nur an dessen allgemeinen politischen Aspekten und Konsquenzen interessiert sind, grieft Cicero hier über Rullus' Vorlage und die in der Rede erörterten Probleme hinaus und sucht seine Hörer mit ruhigen und beruhigenden Sätzen in ihrem Veranwortungsbewußtsein für den Staat anzusprechen" (344).

Table 8.5. The Structure of the *Peroratio* of *LA* 1

Agonistic	To the tribunes	1.23–5
	To the senate	1.26 (*–contemnere*)
Protreptic	To the tribunes	1.26–7 (*quam ob rem—perducat*)
	To the senate	1.27 (*quod si—videatur*)

The beginning of the agonistic half we have seen already (*LA* 1.23, Table 6.2.2): Cicero's analysis of the troubled state of the republic, which corresponds to the end of the *exordium* of the popular speech. The senate variant is sharply polemical. The parties responsible for the trouble, the tribunes, are accusingly named (*tu et non nulli conlegae*, K-s), as not in the popular speech (the corresponding phrase there is *non nullorum* "of certain persons," K-p). The tribunes' legislative and political activities are specified (*vestris legibus et contionibus et seditionibus*, P-s); the popular speech is vaguer (*omnia turbulenta consilia*, P-p). And the tribunes are the agents of disorder, "showing hope" to the wicked, "striking fear" into the good, and so on (*ostendistis, iniecistis*, O-s; *tradidistis*, P-s; *sustulistis*, R-s); the corresponding expressions in the popular speech avoid assigning agency to the tribunes.

The polemic is the first step to a redefinition of *dignitas*. The agonism is not meant only to draw a distinction between Cicero and the tribunes but also to draw out the importance of personal choice. That is the idea as the agonistic half of the *peroratio* continues. As the tribunes have—so far—chosen a certain path for their tribunate, so does Cicero have his own path chosen. He describes the topics of the coming second speech, and he declares the principles of his consulship (the sections will be lettered for convenience):

A. (*To the tribunes*) In the middle of all this turmoil (*hoc motu*) and upset (*hac perturbatione*) in people's minds and in the circumstances of society (*animorum atque rerum*), when the voice and authority of the consul suddenly shines out (*inluxerit*) in the great darkness, and shows that there is nothing to fear—no army, no [armed] band[s], no colonies; no sell-off of tax properties, no new form of authority, no kingdom of ten commissioners; no second Rome, no alternate seat of power; not while I am consul; and that there will be perfect tranquility, peace, and order—I suppose (*credo*) I shall have to worry (*verendum*) that that splendid agrarian law of yours will seem more "populist" [than all that]! And when I have made clear your plans, which are criminal; and the nature of the law, which is a fraud;[71] and the ambushes that are being laid against the Roman people by "populist" tribunes of the plebs—I suppose (*credo*) I shall have to be afraid (*pertimescam*) of opposing you [all] in a public assembly! Particularly since I have made it my firm purpose (*deliberatum et constitutum*) to conduct the consulship in the only way it can be freely and seriously (*graviter et libere*) conducted: by refusing to seek (*ut ... [non] appetiturus sum*) a province, or an office, or any distinction or benefit, or anything at all that could be vetoed by a tribune of the plebs. (*Turning to the senate*) [Let me repeat that:] the consul, before a full meeting of the senate, on his inaugural day, declares that, assuming that the government continues to operate as it now does, and that no situation arises that could not be respectably avoided, he will not assume governance of a province. That is how I intend to conduct myself in this consulship, conscript fathers: able to restrain a tribune of the plebs who takes his anger out on the state (*rei publicae iratum*) and to disregard one who takes his anger out on me (*mihi iratum*, *LA* 1.25–6).[72]

At the center of the passage are two parallel predictions, each marked by an ironic *credo* "I suppose": that when Cicero enumerates the measures of the law, he won't be afraid that the bill will seem more *popularis* than his own policy of *otium*; and that when he shows the falsehood and criminality of the law, he won't be afraid to appear against the tribunes in *contiones*. From the point of view of rhetorical theory, Cicero casts now familiar ideas about *otium* and the *contio* in terms of *pathos* and *ethos* respectively (the people will see the truth, and he will stand firm). From the point of view of political ideology, he sets up a distinction

---

71. On *fraus legis*, see ch. 4 n. 19.

72. *Hoc motu atque hac perturbatione animorum atque rerum, cum populo Romano vox et auctoritas consulis repente in tantis tenebris inluxerit, cum ostenderit nihil esse metuendum, nullum exercitum, nullam manum, nullas colonias, nullam venditionem vectigalium, nullum imperium novum, nullum regnum decemvirale, nullam alteram Romam neque aliam sedem imperi nobis consulibus futuram summamque tranquillitatem pacis atque oti, verendum, credo, nobis erit ne vestra ista praeclara lex agraria magis popularis esse videatur. Cum vero scelera consiliorum vestrorum fraudemque legis et insidias quae ipsi populo Romano a popularibus tribunis plebis fiant ostendero, pertimescam, credo, ne mihi non liceat contra vos in contione consistere, praesertim cum mihi deliberatum et constitutum sit ita gerere consulatum quo uno modo geri graviter et libere potest, ut neque provinciam neque honorem neque ornamentum aliquod aut commodum neque rem ullam quae a tribuno plebis impediri possit appetiturus sim. Dicit frequentissimo senatu consul Kalendis Ianuariis sese, si status hic rei publicae maneat neque aliquod negotium exstiterit quod honeste subterfugere non possit, in provinciam non iturum. Sic me in hoc magistratu geram, patres conscripti, ut possim tribunum plebis rei publicae iratum coercere, mihi iratum contemnere* (*LA* 1.25–6).

Dignitas

between person and policy. That polarity underlies the rest of the passage, transforming its polemical posture. First, it defines Cicero's character. In him person and policy are congruent: it is precisely his superior policy that gives him personal courage; he is able to be brave because he devotes himself to what is true. And that congruity, in turn, is exactly what explains his subsequent point: such a person by definition will not seek any personal benefit from his office. A distinct model of high stature has thus begun to appear: one that depends not on political posturing, personal connections, and self-seeking, consequences be damned, but on devotion to the common good. Polemics has been modulated into ideology. The polarity serves a second purpose: it sets the specific terms of Cicero's courage. He will resist a tribune's poor policy, and he will ignore a tribune's attacks on his own person. Polemics has been modulated into resolve.

All this amounts to a claim about political life: participating in politics depends on something like personal integrity. The imputation is deepened by a full set of allusions. The tribune's poor policy and personal hostility are both expressed by *iratus* 'angry,' as noted. The parallelism represents and evokes the polarity that organizes the passage. But the word itself also represents another affect of the passage: its philosophical cast. The language of emotions is prominent. The roil of the state is expressed by *hoc motu atque hac perturbatione animorum atque rerum*. *Perturb-* with *anim-* is occasional for an 'upsetting emotion,' especially fear, but most frequently Cicero uses the collocation in rhetorical and philosophical contexts to render πάθος in its sense of 'passion, irrational feeling, disturbance in the soul,'[73] so always when it is linked, as here, to *motus*.[74] Rullus is, twice, *iratus*, and *ira* 'anger' is a *perturbatio animi*.[75] His *ira* both parallels and effects the *perturbatio* of the state. And Cicero expresses his determination, twice, in terms of the absence of fear (*verendum, pertimescam*

---

73. For the general use of *perturbo*, see *TLL* 10.1.1825.40–1826.10; for the philosophical use, 1826.14–28. For illustrative examples of the collation as the opposite of rational: *quae motu animi et perturbatione sine ratione sunt* (*Part.* 2.43), *Off.* 1.93; as explicitly connected to πάθος: . . . *alterum quod idem* παθητικὸν *nominant, quo perturbantur animi et concitantur, in quo uno regnat oratio* (*Orat.* 128), *et progrediar quidem longius: non enim de aegritudine solum, quamquam id quidem primum, sed de omni animi, ut ego posui, perturbatione, morbo, ut Graeci volunt, explicabo* (*Tusc.* 3.13); as a rhetorical goal: *peroratio autem et alia quaedam habet et maxume amplificationem, cuius effectus hic debet esse, ut aut perturbentur animi aut tranquillentur, et si ita iam adfecti ante sint, ut aut augeat eorum motus aut sedet oratio* (*Top.* 98).

74. *Part.* 43, *Off.* 1.136, *Tusc.* 3.7, 3.23. *Att.* 8.11.1 (*quod me magno animi motu perturbatum putas, sum equidem, Att.* 8.11.1) goes on to quote Cicero's own *de Republica* about the standards of the ideal statesman.

75. Cf. e.g. *num reliquae quoque perturbationes animi, formidines libidines iracundiae?* (*Tusc.* 3.7), *quae perturbationibus animi, dolore cupiditate iracundia metu* (sc. *dicunt*), *quia necessitatis vim habent, adferunt auctoritatem et fidem* (*Top.* 74).

[ironically]): fear is also a *perturbatio animi*. His lack of *metus* both parallels and promises to effect the *summa tranquillitas pacis atque oti* that is his policy goal. This is not quite the ἀπάθεια 'freedom from emotions' of the Stoic sage,[76] but Cicero's willingness to buck the political winds and ignore personal attacks is a display of *constantia*—exactly the virtue of those who stood against their political enemies unruffled. The convener of a *contio* might call his opponent to the stage to hound him; but that was also a chance for the opponent to display his own steadiness under hostile fire.[77] And *constantia* is the opposite of *perturbatio animi*. As Cicero puts it in *de Officiis*, "The mind must be free of every passion—desire and fear, as well as grief [and pleasure] and anger—so as to achieve tranquility and security, which is what makes someone steadfast and respectable" (*vacandum autem omni est animi perturbatione cum cupiditate et metu tum etiam aegritudine [et voluptate] animi et iracundia ut tranquillitas animi et securitas adsit quae affert cum constantiam tum etiam dignitatem*, 1.69).[78] *Constantia* is the Unnamed Referent of this section, a tonic for the soul—and for the state. "As the leader of the state, so also those who dwell in it," as Ben Sira put it (καὶ κατὰ τὸν ἡγούμενον τῆς πόλεως πάντες οἱ κατοικοῦντες αὐτήν, 10:2).

Several other details of the passage develop its philosophical tinge and resonate with it. The passage begins from the metaphor of illumination. The image is meant to stand out. It sits somewhat ill with the preceding *perturbatio*, which is an image of motion, not of light; it uses not one of the ordinary words for light (*lux, lumen*, etc.) but *inluxerit*, from a verb which otherwise always has its subject the 'sun' or the 'day' or stands alone in the meaning 'begin to grow light, dawn';[79] and one subject of that *ilnuxerit* is *vox* 'voice,' a catachresis (voices don't "dawn"). Cicero has revitalized a common metaphor for bringing knowledge,[80] perhaps with philosophical enlightenment in mind.[81] Second, Cicero's denials are both ironic, marked with parenthetic *credo* (*verendum, credo, nobis*

---

76. On this feature of the sage, cf. Diogenes Laertius 7.117–118, Graver 2007: 35–60. For the figure and virtues of the sage, see Annas 2008, Kerferd 1990; on the Stoic version, Brouwer 2014.

77. See Morstein-Marx 2004: 166–69.

78. Cf. *fortis vero animi et constantis est non perturbari in rebus asperis nec tumultuantem de gradu deici ut dicitur sed praesenti animo uti et consilio nec a ratione discedere* (*Off.* 1.80).

79. *OLD s.v.* and *TLL* 7.1.388.9–13 list this use as the only instance of the figurative "shine out" / "translate: i. q. conspicuum fieri" until Velleius 1.5.1. There are some transitive uses in Plautus.

80. A single example: *vos denique in tantis tenebris erroris et inscientiae clarissimum lumen menti meae praetulistis* (*Sul.* 40)

81. On the opposition of light and dark in philosophical discourse, see Kenney 1971: 74 on Lucretius 3.1 *e tenebris tantis tam clarum extollere lumen* and cf. e.g. Sen. *Cl.* 1.1.4, *Ep.* 79.12, 102.28, 120.13, *Nat.* 1 *pr.* 2.

Dignitas

erit . . .; pertimescam, credo . . .). The tart sarcasm, in a philosophical context, is also philosophical: that is the manner of what modern scholarship often terms "the diatribe," an important mode of expression in ancient philosophical rhetoric.[82] Cicero is haranguing Rullus to higher ground out of the grip of his passions. And, last, Cicero's description of his own stance is consonant with that of a kind of sage. His posture is carefully and consciously chosen: it is *deliberatum* and *constitutum*, the only time he pairs those words. He will desire nothing of any kind: *appetiturus sum* recalls *appetitus*, Cicero's usual later translation for the ὁρμή of the Stoics.[83] His "possessive impulse" will not be directed toward any personal reward. His rejection of any external goods—he makes the expression as wide as possible—allows him to conduct his consulship *graviter et libere*, which recalls the *constantia* and self-sufficiency of the wise man.

Many in the senate would no doubt have recognized the tinge of this section (the famous Stoic Cato, who had probably been quaestor in 64, won't have been the only one). That coloring informs much of the remainder of the *peroratio*. Cicero turns from the senate back to the tribunes:

> **B.** And so—by the immortal gods!—compose yourselves, Tribunes of the Plebs, and abandon those who, unless you look ahead, shall shortly abandon you. Cooperate with us! Agree with the good! By shared effort and affection defend the republic we share!
>
> *Quam ob rem, per deos immortalis!* **conl**igite vos, tribuni plebis, deserite eos a quibus, nisi prospicitis, brevi tempore deseremini, **cons**pirate nobis**cum**, **cons**entite **cum** bonis, **comm**unem rem publicam **comm**uni studio atque amore defendite (LA 1.26).

The key to the excerpt is *conligite vos*. The expression depends on what came before. Its semantics draw on the philosophical cast of the first half of the *peroratio*. The tribunes are first of all to "compose themselves" or "come to their senses" or even "get a hold of themselves." The collation *se colligere* is often used of overcoming fear or confusion:[84] that is, the tribunes, like Rullus, are suffering from a *perturbatio animi*. The expression also continues the genre half-present in the first part of the *peroratio*. If A was mostly the excoriation and harangue typical of

---

82. On the genre (and problems of terminology), see Schenkeveld 1997: 230–47.

83. *TLL* 2.0.282.3–283.20; cf. *appetitum animi, quem* ὁρμὴν *Graeci vocant* (*Fin.* 5.17).

84. *TLL* 3.0.1614.52–3.0.1615.3. Cf. *quid est autem se ipsum colligere, nisi dissipatas animi partes rursum in suum locum cogere?* (Cic. *Tusc.* 4.78).

a diatribe, B is the exhortation; hectoring is followed by remedy. *Conligite vos* also expands on what came before. In A it was Cicero's *constantia* that stood against the tribunes' *perturbatio*; but now it is the unified front of all right-thinking citizens. That unity is strikingly manifest lexically, with seven occurrences of *cum/con-* in one form or another, as the boldface shows; Cicero's own stance in A has been universalized. Here is the forerunner of the ideas of the *concordia ordinum* and *consensus omnium bonorum* central to Cicero's later political ideology.

In short, a *peroratio* that began polemically and became an expression of resolve has now become an exhortation to a shared identity. But the communalism is fragile. Cicero directs his energy against the tribunes, but there are other faithless actors. Otherwise Cicero would not have warned the tribunes that they would soon be "deserted." There is trouble within. That is exactly Cicero's next point:

> **C.** Many are the hidden wounds of the body politic, many the destructive plans of wicked citizens; there is no external danger, no king, no race, no nation to fear—the ill lies within, internal and domestic. Each of us as he is able must remedy this ill and all of us should want to heal it.

> *Multa sunt occulta rei publicae volnera, multa nefariorum civium perniciosa consilia; nullum externum periculum est, non rex, non gens ulla, non natio pertimescenda est; inclusum malum, intestinum ac domesticum est. Huic pro se quisque nostrum mederi atque hoc omnes sanare velle debemus.* (*LA* 1.26)

This, I surmise, is not purely Cicero's invention but one version of a line of thought that must have been circulating at Rome (among alarmists and scolds, at the very least) since 66, when Pompey defeated Mithridates in the Battle of Lycus.[85] Almost the same idea recurs at the end of the second *Catilinarian* (2.11), where the idea of "external danger" (here, *nullum externum periculum est*) is overtly linked to Pompey: "Everything external, on land and sea, has been pacified by the courage of one man" (*omnia sunt externa unius virtute terra marique pacata*).[86] The inflection of the idea here is different: there, Cicero,

---

85. App. *Mith.* 100; Plu. *Pomp.* 32.1–7; DC 36.48–49.

86. *Nulla est enim natio, quam pertimescamus, nullus rex, qui bellum populo Romano facere possit. Omnia sunt externa unius virtute terra marique pacata: domesticum bellum manet, intus insidiae sunt, intus inclusum periculum est, intus est hostis. Cum luxuria nobis, cum amentia, cum scelere certandum est. Huic ego me bello ducem profiteor, Quirites; suscipio inimicitias hominum perditorum; quae sanari poterunt, quacumque ratione sanabo, quae resecanda erunt, non patiar ad perniciem civitatis manere* (*Catil.* 2.11).

as leader (*dux*), implicitly a civil equivalent to Pompey, will cure the disease as he is able and cut away what is past curing; but here it is everyone who must tend to the wounds, singly and collectively. Here, as not there, the wounds are hidden—the only "hidden wounds" in Cicero—which is a prompt to vigilance and skepticism—and even introspection? A trope that could have been turned into praise of Pompey, or praise of Cicero, is deployed as a call for collective responsibility.

But even so the idea of "peace abroad" doubtless put the senate in mind of Pompey, and thus of the pending effects of his return, both dangers and opportunities. And that meant thoughts of competition and feelings of division. Cicero knew his call to unity would prompt such feelings and thoughts, and his next claim addresses them:

> **D.** You're wrong, [tribunes], if you think that the senate agrees with what I'm saying but that the people have a different opinion. Everyone who wants to stay safe will follow the lead of a consul who is free of appetites, clear of misdeeds, careful in times of danger, without fear in times of strife.
>
> *Erratis, si senatum probare ea quae a me dicuntur putatis, populum autem esse in alia voluntate. Omnes qui se incolumis volent sequentur auctoritatem consulis soluti a cupiditatibus, liberi a delictis, cauti in periculis, non timidi in contentionibus.* (*LA* 1.27)

The passage, which begins with a form of *erro*, echoes the beginning of the *peroratio*, which begins the same way: *Errastis, Rulle, vehementer et tu et non nulli conlegae tui qui sperastis vos contra consulem veritate, non ostentatione popularem posse in evertenda re publica populares existimari* ("You and certain of your colleagues, Rullus, hoped, even as you destroyed the government, to claim the mantle of *popularis* against a consul who is *popularis* in the true sense of the word, and not for show. And that was your mistake—a serious mistake," Table 6.2.2.L-p). But in D the issue is not political personality conceived of in terms of offices and (let us call them) political parties (*consul popularis*); the issue is identity on a deeper level. It is conceived of in terms of the polarity of A. Cicero is personally ethical ("free of appetites, clear of misdeeds") and that affects his political path ("careful in times of danger, without fear in times of strife"). The idea of the sage again leaves its mark. He has no misguided appetites; and he is, not "bold" in times of strife, but "without fear" (*non timidi*), that is, he does not have *metus*, which is a *perturbatio animi*. Cicero again uses the polarity of A to suggest what kind of leadership can overcome the divisive temptations of partisanship and self-seeking.

If the *peroratio* thus moves from the agonistic to the protreptic, the protreptic itself now moves from exhortation to admonition:

> E. Accordingly if any of you is influenced by the hope that he can pump up his chances for political office by disruptive methods, first of all he should give up those hopes with me as consul, and second he should find my own case, in which he can see a consul of equestrian birth, instructive of the kind of life that most easily leads good men to political office and social prestige.

> *Quod si qui vestrum spe ducitur se posse turbulenta ratione honori velificari suo, primum me consule id sperare desistat, deinde habeat me ipsum sibi documento, quem equestri ortum loco consulem videt, quae vitae via facillime viros bonos ad honorem dignitatemque perducat.* (*LA* 1.27)

The admonition has two strands. There is prohibition: Cicero will block disruptiveness—an allusion to A, where he will "restrain" (*coercere*) tribunes that are "taking out their anger on the state." And there is exemplarity: Cicero is himself a model of the only correct path to *dignitas*, which, very much as in the *exordium* of the popular speech, is laid claim to on Cicero's terms. As there it was the people's recognition of his abilities, in this context it is Cicero's balanced soul and balanced politics.

The tribunes risk failing on both scores. They may be tempted by unbalanced politics: that is the point of *turbulentus* (which often connotes populist tactics).[87] And they may be tempted by selfishness: that is the point of the rare *velificari*. Literally 'spread sail, set sail' (the compounding of *vela facere* 'id.'),[88] the word is used figuratively with the dative to mean 'try to secure'; the nuance is probably 'spread sail in order to increase speed [in addition to the speed provided by rowing].'[89] In the late Republic the term is slightly pejorative political slang (hence my 'pump up his chances for'). Thus Marcus Caelius warns Cicero, then in Cilicia at a time when troubling news of Parthian activity was reaching Rome, to send a full report with all possible speed, lest someone say he "had puffed up

---

87. For *turbulentus* in anti-populist rhetoric, see Achard 1981: 81, 198, 285, 287; for the *contio* as a "storm" that must be calmed, see Morstein-Marx 2004: 60–67.

88. *OLD s.v. velum* 2b.

89. Cf. Eng. 'make sail' = 'to spread additional sails in order to increase a ship's speed,' *OED s.v.* 'make' 71b). The compound also may mean simply 'sail, journey' (*nauta per urbanas velificabat aquas*, Prop. 4.9.6), just as English 'make sail' may mean 'start on a voyage, set sail, sail' (*OED s.v.* 71a).

someone's sails or kept back something that should have been known" (*ne aut velificatus aliquoi dicaris aut aliquid quod referret scire reticuisse, Fam.* 8.10.2).[90] Letting rumors spread and worsen would make it easier for someone to angle for a Parthian command. The slang term is deliberate: it indexes a whole way of thinking and talking—self-interested, detached, calculating. It is the exact opposite of Cicero's idea of *dignitas* in *LA* 1.

The second half of the *peroratio* closes as did the first: Cicero turns from the tribunes back to the senate:

> **F.** Accordingly, conscript fathers, if you proclaim to me your willingness to defend the common dignity, I shall bring about something that the state sorely needs: the restoration of the authority of this order, after a long interval, to what it was in the days of our ancestors.

> *Quod si vos vestrum mihi studium, patres conscripti, ad communem dignitatem defendendam profitemini, perficiam profecto, id quod maxime res publica desiderat, ut huius ordinis auctoritas, quae apud maiores nostros fuit, eadem nunc longo intervallo rei publicae restituta esse videatur.* (*LA* 1.27)

This last sentence is the culmination of the ideas of the *peroratio*. There is a kind of admission of division: just as there were "hidden wounds" (C), so the senate is prompted to pledge its support—as if it needed to be. *Dignitas* is a common possession to be defended, just as the state was in B, and individualist meanings are thereby excluded, as implicitly in A (and the passages considered earlier in this chapter). The problems that the senate faces are, in that way, the very same as those that beset the tribunes, but handled here more delicately. The sentence also parallels ideas from the popular speech. There is a promise: as in its *peroratio* Cicero asks for the people's support and pledges them his own (ch. 7.4), so here he asks for the senate's support and promises them his own. There is Cicero's leadership: as in the *exordium* of the popular speech the people claim the consulship behind Cicero, so here the senate can reclaim their former authority behind Cicero. And there is a redefinition: as in the *exordium* of the popular speech Cicero redefines *nobilitas* (ch. 6.2), so here he redefines *dignitas*: does the "common dignity" mean the elevated status of the senate? or does it mean the

---

90. Tyrrell and Purser 1914: 123 nicely render 'wafted on his way' (Shackleton-Bailey's 'play into somebody's hands' misses the mark; that idiom implies unawareness of a larger scheme). Florus uses the word comparably of the first Brutus, who "angled for the favor of the citizens even at the price of disaster for his own clan and of parricide" (*favori civium etiam domus suae clade et parricidio velificatus est*, 1.9.5).

well-being of the commonwealth? Cicero means it to mean both: the dignity of the senate, which should be shared, is bound up with the dignity of the state, which is shared. To defend the senate is to be unified in defense of the health of the state. The senate shall be to the other orders an example.

This is precisely the vision that lies behind a dramatic gesture of Cicero's. He did not only speak of this vision; he also had it acted it out. After Cicero's first and second agrarian speeches, Rullus held a *contio* accusing him of being a shill for *Sullani possessores*. To that *contio* the brief third agrarian speech is a reply. The tribunes in response summoned the consuls to appear before the people. Plutarch describes the scene:

> Then, as soon as Antonius had been caught and was tractable,[91] Cicero opposed himself with more courage to the innovators. He denounced the proposed law in the senate at great length, and so terrified the very promoters of it that they had no reply to make to him.[92] And when they made a second attempt and after full preparation summoned the consuls to appear before the people, Cicero had not the slightest fear, but bidding the senate follow him and leading the way, he not only got the law rejected, but also induced the tribunes to desist from the rest of their measures, so overpowered were they by his eloquence. (*Cic.* 12.5–6)[93]

The stately parade of senators, arrayed behind Cicero to support him (cf. *si . . . vestrum mihi studium profitemini*, F)—as he held firm (*non timidi a contentionibus*, D); as he harangued the tribunes to his point of view (*conligite vos!* B); as he thus showed even the people could adopt a conservative line (*erratis si . . . populum . . . esse in alia voluntate [putatis]*, D); as the senate imitated his *constantia* so that their own *constantia* thereby steadied the state (cf. A)[94]—is a piece of performance art that acts out exactly the very particular idea of the role of the senate and Cicero constantly implicit in the speech and on clear display in the *peroratio*. It is a concise dramatization of the view of *dignitas* that informs and knits together the entire senate speech.

---

91. By being offered Cicero's province of Macedonia.

92. The second speech.

93. See Morstein-Marx 2004: 192 n. 130. The translation is mostly that of Perrin in the Loeb edition.

94. The reverse of the fearful, mealy-mouthed, and evasive senate brought to the Rostra after the death of Gaius Gracchus: cf. DS 34/35.33.7 and see Morstein-Marx 2004:170.

9

Two Views of Capua and the ager Campanus

9.1. INTRODUCTION

Ergo ut in oratore optimus quisque, sic in oratione firmissimum quodque sit primum.

Accordingly, just as the best orator for an occasion goes first, in a speech the strongest argument for the occasion should go first.

—Cicero, *de Oratore* 2.314

This chapter offers readings of the last and longest of the *argumenta* of the speeches—the colonization of the *ager Campanus* and the placement of a colony in Capua (*LA* 1.18–22 *occuparint*, 2.76–97). The chapter has two purposes. The first is to bring to light the deep coherence of Cicero's vision in these speeches. The core ideas revealed in previous chapters influence Cicero's choice of almost every detail and, as it is possible to see in these longer passages, also the arrangement and sequencing of elements. The second purpose is to reflect more broadly, though of necessity briefly, on some aspects of politics and rhetoric in the late Republic. Cicero's treatments of Capua and the *ager Campanus* are apt for that purpose: for many that settlement must have been the chief hope of the bill; Cicero makes the settlement into the chief danger. His treatments of Capua and the *ager Campanus* are emblematic of the creeping paralysis of late Republican politics, which rhetoric must have both reflected and deepened.

Rullus's bill planned to colonize two tracts of *ager publicus* (virtually the only *ager publicus* left in Italy).[1] The *ager Campanus*, the fertile southern district where

---

1. Cf. ch. 1 n. 102.

Capua was located (*LA* 1.18, 1.20 *fin*., 2.76), would be divided into plots of ten *iugera* (*LA* 2.78) for 5,000 settlers (*LA* 2.76, 77);[2] the nearby *ager Stella(ti)s* (*LA* 1.20, 2.86), into plots of twelve *iugera* (*LA* 2.86).[3] A colony would also be located in the chief city of the Campania, Capua (*LA* 1.18, 2.76).[4] Here it would not be a matter of purchasing land. The *ager Campanus* had been encroached on by private persons not long after its confiscation, and they had not been dislodged. Sulla had disrupted the arrangement, but in the following years large estate holders had probably resumed encroachments.[5] They, with their tenants, would have to be dispossessed.[6] In some (other?) cases the lands or title would probably be subdivided to accommodate new settlers.

The longest sections of each speech, and the last part of each oration before the *peroratio*—a prominent position—are Cicero's treatments of this proposal. Cicero's two discussions share almost all of the same topics. But they differ in four ways: some topics are not shared; and the shared topics are handled differently, appear in a different order, or appear a different number of times. The passages are too long, and the sequence of their shared ideas too varied, to allow the easy

---

2. The skepticism of Vasaly 1988: 412, that the *ager Campanus* was not really to be distributed, overlooks the fact that it was the last major piece of *ager publicus* available in Italy and an obvious target for redistribution, as in Caesar's second land bill of 49, which was based on the Rullan bill.

3. The district is called a *campus* rather than an *ager* by Suetonius (*Div. Jul.* 20.3). The nominative is not attested; some modern authorities prefer *Stellas*, others *Stellatis*.

4. Since Capua was already inhabited, these will have been viritane (*viritanus* < *viritim* 'man by man, individually') allotments into an existing municipality, rather than a fresh foundation, as the bill also imagined for other sites; cf. *LA* 1.17 = J8-s in Appendix 3; *LA* 2.75 = J7-s in Appendix 3. *LA* 1.17 uses the term *adsignent*, proper for viritane land assignments; cf. Harvey 1972: 103. For an overview of Capua in the Republican period, see Fredericksen 1959. For viritane assignments in Rullus's bill, see Gargola 2009: 179–80.

5. The senate recommended that L. Postumius, consul 173, undertake the task of removing private owners (Liv. 42.1.6), a task on which he spent a whole summer (42.9.7). In 165 P. Lentulus (*cos*. 162) was sent to purchase fields from private owners with state monies (Cic. *LA* 2.82, Licinianus 29–32 Criniti). Whatever arrangements resulted were disrupted during the civil conflicts of 83–82, when Campania suffered heavy damage (cf. e.g. Flor. 2.9.22, *Lamponius atque Telesinus, Samnitium duces, atrocius Pyrrho et Hannibale Campaniam Etruriamque populantur, et sub specie partium se vindicant*). Furthermore, a colony was established at Capua (*LA* 2.92, C31), which must have affected tenancies. The disruptions continued with the Third Servile War (73–71). Brunt 1971: 316 speculates that "it may be that especially since Sulla's time rich and powerful Romans had aggrandized their holdings of Campanian land once more, and that the aim of Rullus had not been (as Cicero suggests) to displace the 'optima plebs' in Campania but to distribute relatively large holdings in the hands of absentees, a plan that Caesar revived and carried out."

6. Cicero draws attention to the latter: "Those poor souls, born and raised in those fields, practiced in turning its loam, will have nowhere to go on such short notice" (*LA* 2.84, C18).

use of side-by-side presentation as in earlier chapters. A full comparison appears in Appendix 2; in this chapter and its notes, elements will be cited by the numbers of that appendix (C1, C2, etc.). Table 9.1, which lays out the themes in sequence, makes some chief differences clear. A dot indicates a theme unique to a speech; conversely the absence of a dot indicates a shared theme. Repeated themes are indicated with fractions that show which time of how many.

Table 9.1. The Sequence of Topics in the Treatment of Capua and the Ager Campanus (*LA* 1.18–21, 2.76–97)

in senatu

Honestum

1.18	•	C1	The backers of the bill hate Rome and the temple of IOM	
1.18		C2	A colony will be founded at Capua	
1.18		C23	Capua will be the chief city of a rival empire	1/3
1.18		C32	The rich environs of Capua induce arrogance	1/2
1.18		C5	The colonists will be thugs	
1.18		C36	Sudden wealth causes insolence	
1.19		C25	The elders destroyed the Capuan state	
1.19		C29	The elders' decision about Capua was not cruel	
1.19		C30	The elders' decision about Capua was wise	
1.19		C34	A recolonized Capua would be dangerous	
1.20		C33	The luxury of Capua corrupted even Hannibal	
1.20		C32	The rich environs of Capua induce arrogance	2/2
1.20		C23	Capua will be the chief city of a rival empire	2/3
1.20		C24	Capua was historically a threat	
1.20		C22	The cities around Capua will be colonized	

Vtile

1.20		C21	The *ager Stellas* is also slated for colonization	
1.21	•	C20	*Praeteritio*	1/3
1.21		C10	Epithets of the *ager Campanus (a.C.)*	
1.21		C17	The *a.C.* was not sold by Sulla or the Gracchi	
1.21	•	C20	*Praeteritio*	2/3
1.21		C11	The *a.C.* remained when other *vectigalia* were lost	
1.21		C13	The *a.C.* is reliable when other revenue is interrupted	
1.21		C15	The *a.C.* is productive [in peacetime]	
1.21		C12	The *a.C.* provides sustenance for armies	
1.21		C14	The *a.C.* is physically safe	
1.21	•	C20	*Praeteritio*	3/3

(*continued*)

Table 9.1. Continued

Honestum

1.22		C23	Capua will be the chief city of a rival empire	3/3

ad populum

2.76		C2	A colony will be founded at Capua	
2.76	•	C3	Cicero will speak of the people's dignity (*amplitudo*) and advantage (*commodum*)	

Vtile

2.76	•	C4	The bill proposes 5,000 colonists in Capua	
2.77		C5	The colonists will be thugs	1/3
2.78	•	C6	The colonists are straw men for would-be large landholders	1/2
2.79	•	C7	The distribution of plots will begin from the rural tribes	
2.79	•	C8	The *a.C.* is too small	
2.80	•	C9	The Roman people should keep their ancestral possessions	1/3
2.80		C10	Epithets of the *a.C.*	
2.80		C11	The *a.C.* remained when other *vectigalia* were lost	
2.80		C12	The *a.C.* provides sustenance for armies	
2.80		C13	The *a.C.* is reliable when other revenue is interrupted	1/2
2.81		C14	The *a.C.* is physically safe	
2.81		C15	The *a.C.* is productive [in peacetime]	1/2
2.81	•	C16	The *a.C.* was augmented by the elders	
2.81		C17	The *a.C.* was not sold by Sulla or the Gracchi	
2.81	•	C19	Communal possession of the *a.C.* is better than subdivision	1/2
2.81		C5	The colonists will be thugs	2/3
2.82	•	C6	The colonists are straw men for would-be large landholders	2/2
2.82	•	C9	The Roman people should keep their ancestral possessions	2/3
2.82		C15	The *a.C.* is productive [in peacetime]	1/2
2.83		C13	The *a.C.* is reliable when other revenue is interrupted	1/2
2.84	•	C18	The *a.C.* is currently occupied	
2.84		C5	The colonists will be thugs	3/3
2.84	•	C9	The Roman people should keep their ancestral possessions	3/3
2.85	•	C19	Communal possession of the *a.C.* is better than subdivision	2/2

Honestum

2.85		C21	The *ager Stellas* is also slated for colonization	
2.85–6		C22	The cities around Capua will be colonized	
2.86		C23	Capua will be the chief city of a rival empire	1/2
2.87		C24	Capua was historically a threat	
2.87–8		C25	The elders destroyed the Capuan state	
2.89		C23	Capua will be the chief city of a rival empire	2/2

Table 9.1. Continued

2.90	•	C26	The elders didn't destroy Capua completely because it was close enough to watch	
2.90	•	C27	Capua has subsequently been a reliable ally to Rome	
2.91	•	C28	A hobbled Capua has lost its political ambitions	
2.91		C29	The elders' decision about Capua was not cruel	
2.91		C30	The elders' decision about Capua was wise	1/2
2.92–4	•	C31	The arrogant colony of Brutus (90) illustrates the dangers of a resurgent Capua	
2.95		C30	The elders' decision about Capua was wise	2/2
2.95		C32	The rich environs of Capua induce arrogance	
2.95		C33	The luxury of Capua corrupted even Hannibal	
2.96		C34	A recolonized Capua would be dangerous	
2.96	•	C35	Rome and its environs are comparatively inferior	
2.97		C36	Sudden wealth causes insolence	

The key to the passages, reflected in the boldfaced headings, is the *divisio* that Cicero offers in the popular speech: "I shall speak first about *your* advantage, fellow citizens; then I shall return to the matter of honor and dignity" (*de commodo prius vestro dicam, Quirites; deinde ad amplitudinem et dignitatem revertar, LA* 2.76, C3). That reflects the classic philosophical and rhetorical division between *honestum* and *utile*, and it accounts for the handling of Capua and the *ager Campanus* in both speeches: a resurgent Capua is handled chiefly as a threat to Rome's *amplitudo* and *dignitas*, a matter of *honestum*, and the sale of the *ager Campanus* chiefly as economically undesirable, a matter of *utile*. That is, a resurgent Capua focalizes *honestum*; a lost *ager Campanus* focalizes *utile*. But, as the tables indicate, the themes are handled in opposite orders: the popular speech begins with the *ager Campanus* and *utile*; the senate speech, with Capua and *honestum*. Furthermore, the senate version deliberately brackets *utile*, nesting brief versions of the arguments in a *praeteritio* and promising fuller treatment in the popular speech.[7] The most frequently visited element of each version is exactly consonant with its cardinal value. In the senate that element is the threat

---

7. The *praeteritio* (*non queror ... pratermitto ... non dico ... praetermitto, LA* 1.21) enumerates in brief many of the points about the value of the *ager* that appear in the popular speech (C10–11, 15, 17). At the end of the enumeration Cicero says he will speak in the senate "[only] about the danger to safety and liberty" (*de periculo salutis ac libertatis loquor, LA* 1.21, C20)—a return to *honestum*.

posed by Capua (C23), which appears three times (and in that speech is also the final element of the argument); in the popular speech C5, the claim that the colonists will be thugs, and C9, the need to retain ancestral possessions, both appear three times (instances will be distinguished in the following discussion by superscripts). What Cicero thought *firmissimum* before each audience differed.

9.2. THE AGER CAMPANUS AND CAPUA IN LA 2

> *segnius irritant animos demissa per aurem*
> *quam quae sunt oculis subiecta fidelibus et quae*
> *ipse sibi tradit spectator.*
>
> What comes in by ear stirs the mind less well
> than what is laid before the faithful eyes,
> what a viewer relays to himself.
> —Horace, *Ars Poetica* 180–82

Vtile

The popular version, as the dots show, includes some dozen topics with no direct correspondent in the senate speech; two groups of them are the chief focus of this section. The run of arguments from 2.76–80 = C4–C9ᵃ is formed mostly of such topics. The run is aimed at a particular issue. Cicero's argument that the colonial scheme would fob off poor land on settlers did not apply to the *ager Campanus*: it was famously fertile and must have fired real hopes.[8] C4–C9ᵃ are designed to dampen them and suggest that retention is the better option. The mechanics of the arguments deserve notice. The various topics echo earlier themes; but the topics are also linked one to the next in a notable way: the successive arguments depend on Cicero's imagination of the audience's successive responses. That is, Cicero sets out an idea, which he knows will awaken another that he then builds on, thus awakening still another, which he builds on next, and so on. The several topics, despite appearances, are not so many bits flung at the problem to see what might stick; rather they form a complex of linked and overlapping ideas, modulated into and thus reinforcing each other. The complex might be represented as in Figure 9.2, beginning from "subdivision" and running clockwise.

---

[8]. "In der Volksversammlung . . . muß [Cicero] seine Hörer von ihrer Begeisterung für das Gesetz, das wenigstens einigen von ihnen das schönste Ackerland in Aussicht stellt, abzubringen und sie statt dessen durch Warnungen gegen Rullus' Pläne einzunehmen versuchen," Classen 1985: 342.

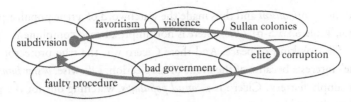

FIGURE 9.2. The Sequence of Ideas in *LA* 2.76–80

The run of arguments from C4 to C9ª is in that way a practical illustration of one of Cicero's techniques for creating and directing audience response.

C4 is the first of the topics proper, following the miniature *divisio* of C3. In form it is a bald statement: the bill proposed 5,000 colonists for a colony based in Capua. Just that statement might have been discouraging, if the number already seemed small to some (Sulla had settled perhaps 80,000).[9] To make it seem even smaller, Cicero subdivides it: *ad hunc numerum*, he adds, *quingenos sibi singuli sumunt* ("To make that total each decemvir gets to pick 500 men"). The subdivision plays against the fear of exclusion (the topic of ch. 5), and *sibi sumunt*, lit. "choose for themselves," plainly suggests some kind of favoritism. The prospect of favoritism and exclusion must have troubled some. But Cicero knows that others must have still held on to hope (someone has to get picked, after all). Hence the closing words of C4: "Take no comfort in that, I ask you; think about it—accurately and carefully!" (*quaeso, nolite vosmet ipsos consolari; vere et diligenter considerate*).

And hence the very next topic. The criterion for inclusion is very specific: the colonists will be thugs (C5ª). That idea appears twice more (but only once in the senate speech); its first appearance, here, is its fullest, amplified in two ways. First, Cicero prefaces the basic assertion ("Thugs will be picked") with a denial ("You won't be picked"): the people "can't possibly think that there's room in that number for you or men like you—upstanding, peaceful, and peaceable" (*num vobis aut vestri similibus integris, quietis, otiosis hominibus in hoc numero locum fore putatis?*). Second, Cicero avers that, though "the high office [the people] have granted him" (*vester honos*) demands constant vigilance, he is willing to connive at the scheme, if it really is in the people's interest (*si ita commodum vestrum fert*).[10] The amplifications echo the ideology of the *exordium*. There *otium* was

---

9. The number of veterans settled is a matter of debate. Appian puts the number at 120,000 (*BC* 1.104); Brunt 1971: 309, at 80,000; Schneider 1977: 127 estimates 70,000–120,000.

10. For other examples of this kind of reluctant deference to a dubious idea out of respect for the people, cf. *LA* 2.16 in ch. 7.3 Voices of the (Un-)Tribune and *LA* 2.62 (= Table 7.2.2.F, of Pompey).

folded into *commodum* and thus made the watchword of a true populist politics (*LA* 2.9, Table 6.2.2.S-p). *Otiosis* here is not simply a broad compliment: "peace" means Cicero's kind of peace. And there Cicero was the true protector of the people's interests because of the mode of his election. Likewise, *vester honos* here is not simply flattery: Cicero is a *consul popularis*, watching out for the people who have trusted him.

In short the amplifications evoke Cicero's vision of true populism. The allusion projects an identity onto the audience: behind him and at one with him. That wouldn't have disabled altogether the hope of those who wanted land. But it makes the terms clear: deciding what *commodum* means—material benefit or political stability. The deeper question is therefore what makes for a proper use of sovereignty. That is the notion Cicero turns to when he comes at last to the basic assertion. It is not just that there will be thugs; it's that the thugs will be paid for by the people's money: authorizing a Campanian colony, which will be formed of "men specially selected for violence, crime, and murder" (*ad vim, facinus, caedemque delecti*), means "allow[ing] . . . garrisons to be armed against you [etc.]—in your own name (*vestro nomine*)!" Just like the free legates who "abuse [the people's] name" (*vestro . . . nomine . . . abutuntur*, *LA* 2.45, Table 2.1.C-p), the colony will prove a poor—and in this case positively dangerous—use of sovereignty.

The use of the image of thugs involves a certain slippage. The opposite of *otium* earlier in the speech was instability: 'disorder' and 'disruption' in its various forms (*turbulenta consilia* and *perturbatio iudiciorum*, *LA* 2.8, Table 6.2.2.O- and P-p). But here the opposite of colonists who are *integri*, *quieti*, and *otiosi* will be experts in violence and murder. The slippage has a purpose. Cicero is drawing on the recent memory of Sullan colonies, settled by unit and studded like garrisons throughout Italy.[11] In one such colony, at Faesulae, revolution was apparently already brewing (had rumors reached Rome?),[12] and the indebted among the colonists were evidently a source of discontent.[13] In C5 Cicero fits the threat

---

11. "The allegations against Rullus were plausible, precisely because they corresponded with men's experience of the Sullan colonies," Brunt 1971: 301 n. 4; Harvey 1972: 25.

12. Sallust's language seems to imply that the arming of Faesulae and other places began not long after Cicero's election: *igitur comitiis habitis consules declarantur M. Tullius et C. Antonius, quod factum primo popularis coniurationis concusserat. Neque tamen Catilinae furor minuebatur, sed in dies plura agitare: arma per Italiam locis opportunis parare, pecuniam sua aut amicorum fide sumptam mutuam Faesulas ad Ma[l]lium quendam portare, qui postea princeps fuit belli faciundi* (*Cat.* 24.1–2).

13. *Tertium genus est aetate iam adfectum, sed tamen exercitatione robustum; quo ex genere iste est Manlius, cui nunc Catilina succedit. Hi sunt homines ex iis coloniis, quas Sulla constituit; quas ego universas civium esse optimorum et fortissimorum virorum sentio, sed tamen ii sunt coloni, qui*

of Sullan colonies redux into the ideological terms of the speech. That dramatizes and reifies the choice that Cicero has put before the people: there is Cicero's way, and there is the Sullan way. Thus does the prospect of favoritism become the prospect of violence. (Did that make some audience members redo the math—10 decemvirs −500 colonists = 5,000 men = the approximate strength of a legion?)

Cicero has thus put Sulla's colonies in his audience's mind. That allows him to move on to another feature of those colonies; the audience's own memory and knowledge lubricate the transition to the next "bubble" (see Figure 9.2). Some of the settlements, as we have seen, devolved from separate homesteads into large plantations under the control of magnates like Rullus's father-in-law. And that is Cicero's very next point: the same thing, he says, will happen in the *ager Campanus* (C6). The decemvirs themselves will hold the properties through their colonists (*deducent suos, quorum nomine ipsi teneant et fruantur*) and stitch together estates out of smaller contiguous parcels (*ista dena iugera continuabunt*). Thus the idea of dangerous colonists has now become the idea of elite corruption. That idea brought with it a whole host of stereotypes, and Cicero's amplifications in C6 depend on exactly those. The corrupt elite were wealthy. Cicero builds on that idea: the gobbled-up Campanian land will pay for the upkeep of their many slaves and their estates (*praedia*) at Cumae and Puteoli, famous resort towns and playgrounds of the rich and famous. The stereotype matches reality: though debt was high and credit tight, if the real estate market was depressed, then that was an incentive (for some, anyway—the long-sellers, as it were) to wait until prices rose again; and there was, if Cicero's second *Catilinarian* is a fair witness, just such a group of the wealthy.[14] And the corrupt elite also made secret and self-serving plans. Cicero builds on that idea, too. That is how C6-p closes: "So if [Rullus] really has your advantage in mind, let him come to me in person and argue about the division of the *ager Campanus!*" (*quod si vestrum commodum spectat, veniat et coram mecum de agri Campani divisione disputet*). By "coming to me," Cicero means that Rullus should face him in a *contio*: Cicero is ready to make good on his promise not to shun *contiones* (*LA* 2.6; ch. 6 n. 33). And Rullus, who has implicitly avoided clear explication, implicitly does not have the common good in mind. He is, once again, "singing a song to himself for his own purposes" (*LA* 2.68, Table 7.3.3.I-p), his promises of *commodum* a sham—an emblem of his dishonest style of governance.

se <*in*> insperatis ac repentinis pecuniis sumptuosius insolentiusque iactarunt (Cic. Catil. 2.20); and see Gruen 1970 esp. 239–40.

14. *Tu agris, tu aedificiis, tu argento, tu familia, tu rebus omnibus ornatus et copiosus sis et dubites de possessione detrahere, adquirere ad fidem?* (*Catil.* 2.18).

To sum up to this point: Cicero used *otium* to lead to the idea of violent thugs; violent thugs to suggest Sullan colonies; memories of colonies to draw out stereotypes of elite corruption; and now elite corruption to point to dishonest government. And in this speech bad government is often equated to deficient or manipulated procedure (ch. 4). That is exactly where the next element, C7, takes the line of thought. The distribution of land would begin from the first of the so-called rural tribes, the *Romilia* (the four urban tribes apparently stood at the head of the tribal order, when the order was not otherwise determined). Cicero paints the measure as failed process. The bill, arrogantly and injuriously, lops off part of the people and ignores the order of tribes (*quae est ista superbia et contumelia, ut populi pars amputetur, ordo tribuum neglegatur*). The counterpoint is open and fair procedure: if Rullus really does want to do right by everybody (*si . . . satis facere omnibus vobis cogitat*), then he should bring his plan forward (*proferat*), assigning specific lots to specific tribesmen of every tribe (*in iugera dena discribat, a Suburana usque ad Arniensem nomina vestra proponat*).

The implication is obvious: flawed procedures raise the chances of unfair results. That recalls exactly the unusual election mechanism (ch. 5.1), in which only seventeen of the thirty-five tribes would vote for the decemvirs. Here Cicero casts the problem in terms of tribal groups: why should the "rustics" who already have land get it but not urban tribes who don't? The argument is specious. Membership in a rural tribe no longer implied possession of rural land. By the 60s the rural tribes included citizens from (non-contiguous) geographical districts all over Italy, many of whom, for various reasons, had left their land in recent years.[15] The bill had good reason to target them: once the fertile Campanian parcels were subdivided, any poorer ground—and of that there would certainly be some— would require experienced hands.[16] If that is right, then the bill never had the aim of making city mice into country mice; it aimed to send the country mice back home.[17] Furthermore, whether the urban tribesmen, generally secure in their city privileges, were as a body hankering for the country life is open to doubt;[18] they might have been perfectly glad to see the urban population reduced—the less competition, the better.[19] But Cicero is not obfuscating or misleading here. Many

---

15. "Probably men registered in the urban tribes were predominantly freedmen, while peasants who had drifted into Rome remained in their old rural tribes; certainly, those who had migrated since the last census in 69 will have done so," Brunt 1971: 313.

16. So the agricultural writers; cf. ch. 7.3 and n. 43.

17. Cf. Thommen 1989: 51–52; Gruen 1974: 393–94.

18. Brunt 1988: 245, 251; *contra* Arena 2012: 230.

19. Cf. ch. 1.4 Sources of Land.

in his popular audience must have known all this perfectly well: they knew how the tribes worked; they knew who had come from where; they all rubbed shoulders with each other; they had heard Rullus's explanations. But Rullus, I surmise, had made excessively broad promises. Cicero pushes back, as so often, by turning the provisions of the law itself into an image for power relations. And here he makes those relations out to be a willingness to manipulate procedure to play favorites. If Rullus sang the praises of the yeoman farmer on a regreened countryside, Cicero points to practical problems.

Thus do the "inserts" of the popular speech return at length to the idea from which they set out: subdivision and exclusion. That is the very theme of the next topic, C8-p: the *ager Campanus* is insufficient. There isn't enough land for people to have 10 acres each, Cicero implies—and there's not even enough room to "cram" (*constipari*) "a crowd this big" (*tantum numerum hominum*) into the *ager*. The point is not literal (the *ager* was about 500 km^2) or not fully literal. Rather, Cicero—once again—takes advantage of the environs. *Constipo* is a rare word—in the Republic, otherwise used only once in Caesar, of troops "crammed together" under a rampart so tightly that the rear ranks could not receive the front ranks.[20] That also well describes the people: they were, at that very moment, standing shoulder to shoulder in the Forum, packed close to hear Cicero. And not even the whole of the people was there. The way they are now positioned is made into an analogue for the results of the colonial scheme. That gives a very specific point to the generalities that Cicero next voices: if they make the bill a law, the people, by their own act, would be allowing politics to fall into chaos, the dignity of the Roman people to be scorned, and themselves to be deluded, again, by a tribune of the plebs (*vexari rem publicam, contemni maiestatem populi Romani, deludi vosmet ipsos diutius a tribuno plebis patiemini?*). All the disruption needed to get the bill passed and all its high promises will nonetheless leave the people more or less as they are now—"crammed together." The viewers can see Cicero's meaning for themselves.

The idea of crowding has thus become the idea of shared civic identity (cf. *maiestatem populi Romani* "the dignity of the Roman people"). And that is ultimately the idea that caps the cycle of arguments from C4 to C9 and, so to speak, jumps out of the loop diagrammed in Figure 9.2: it is better, Cicero says, to retain ancestral possessions (C9^a). Cicero puts the idea briefly but strikingly: even if the field could be divided up, he asks, wouldn't the people prefer to keep it in their patrimony (*nonne . . . in patrimonio vestro remanere malletis*)? The punch lies in *patrimonium*. That is properly private property.[21] We have seen the metaphor

---

20. *ut se sub ipso vallo constipaverant recessumque primis ultimi non dabant* (*BG* 5.43.5).

21. See ch. 3 n. 67.

before: the senate were called to defend "the family wealth" from a drunken wastrel. Here the idea is broadly comparable: the *ager Campanus* is like an inheritance that would be difficult to divide up properly and fairly among all the family. There is a legal idea at play. *Coheredes* were within their rights to continue to hold a jointly inherited possession in common. And if the *coheredes* decided to divide but were unable to agree to terms, then each would become both plaintiff and defendant in a suit to distribute the property (the so-called *familiae (h)erciscundae actio*).[22] It is not just that it is better to keep the inheritance intact and have the benefit of its interest for all; it is that the prospect of division implies conflict and exclusion.

The popular version of the *utile* half of the argument ends as it begins: with topics mostly unique to itself (*LA* 2.84–85; C18, C5^c, C9^c, C19^b). Two powerful images frame the third appearances of themes we have seen. The first image is of an *ager Campanus* already occupied (C18). The land is not deserted of plebs (*agros desertos a plebe*); settling it will mean not establishing plebs but expelling them (*exturbari et expelli plebem ex agris*). The current occupants are "plebs" (*pleb[s]*) and "most excellent and virtuous plebs" at that (*pleb[s] optima et modestissima*); it is them the pleb-loving (*plebicola*) tribune of the plebs will expel, and "those poor souls" (*illi miseri*), born to those lands, expert in turning its clods, will have nowhere to go. The argument on its face is not strong: some, at least, of urban plebs would have been indifferent, so long as their competitors from rural tribes left; and some, at least, of the rural tribesmen would have been indifferent, so long as the current occupiers made way for them. But the force of the argument depends on recent history. The rural tribesmen now resident in the city had often abandoned their own farms: if their resettlement meant ousting occupants "born to those lands" who had "nowhere to go," then some, at least, of those occupants would drift into the city—taking the place of those who had left. One set of emigrants would replace another. The urban plebs will have regarded that as no particular bargain. That is why Cicero keeps repeating the word *plebs*: that links and melds the distinct groups and suggests reshuffling and not real resettlement. But resettlement might not have meant wholesale ouster. The Rullan commission might have subdivided the land further, as was sometimes done; the current colonists would have had their plots divided for the new colonists.[23] (Exactly that work is probably why each decemvir would have had twenty *finitores*). That might have taken the shine off the prospect of Campanian land for some: if nothing else, subdivision would take a long time. The rural tribesmen might well have

---

22. For a survey of the primary sources and discussion, see Audibert 1904.

23. Cf. ch. 1.4 Sources of Land and n. 103.

regarded that as no particular bargain. Cicero's apparent plea for sympathy is pitched in a way that also appeals to different kinds of self-interest.

Here, then, in a different guise, are issues we have seen: insufficiency and subdivision. The notion is reinforced with now familiar ideas. The current occupiers will be ousted for new colonists—but not for you. The land, warns Cicero, for the third time, will be peopled with thugs: full possession of the *ager Campanus* will be granted to "these hale, hearty, and bold henchmen of the decemvirs" (*his robustis et valentibus et audacibus decemvirum satellitibus*, C5ᶜ). (Is *his* "these I have mentioned"—or was Cicero using the shouts of Rullus's claqueurs against them?) "Henchmen" (*satellites*) recalls the dreaded Second Decemvirate (*LA* 2.32, ch. 7.3). *Robusti* 'strong'—or, if you like, 'in good shape'—alludes to Sullan colonists (Cicero in the second *Catilinarian* calls Sullan colonists *exercitatione robust[i]*, 2.20). And there is the idea of retention. The Roman people, advises Cicero, for the third time, should keep their ancestral possessions: "Whereas you declare of your forebears (*de vestris maioribus*), 'Our forebears (*maiores nostri*) bequeathed us this territory,' your descendants will declare of you, 'Our fathers (*patres nostri*) received this territory from their fathers (*a patribus suis*)—and lost it'" (C9³). *Praedico* is apt: it describes a public declaration,[24] and a public declaration of loss is all that will be left of once public property—like a marker where a historic building once stood. The repetition of *patres* and *maiores* adds to the effect: the long chain of tradition (*de maioribus . . . maiores*) risks being broken in a single generation (*patres nostri . . . a patribus suis*). Thus is the weight of communal possession laid on the shoulders of Cicero's audience.

The *utile* half of the argument ends with another powerful image (C19ᵇ). Its theme, that communal possession is better than subdivision is, in effect, the idea of C9, viewed synchronically rather than diachronically—not in terms of inheritance but of usufruct. That theme had already appeared earlier (C19ᵃ). There the audience, having been reminded that neither the Gracchi nor Sulla had included the *ager Campanus* in their settlement schemes, was asked, as in C9ᶜ, to imagine somebody else's view—not the disinherited future but current-day foreigners: a subdivided *ager Campanus* will mean that the Roman people passing by it can no longer boast that it is theirs and that foreigners journeying through it will no longer be told that it is the Roman people's; the people will lose property and will lose repute. C19ᵇ has a quite different tenor. Cicero builds an image from the *Campus Martius* or "Field of Mars," the district outside the city walls. If the whole Campus Martius could be divided into personal property, enough for each man to stand in a two-foot square (*cuique . . . bini pedes*), still, Cicero surmises,

---

24. Cf. *L&S* s.v. I.

the people would rather jointly hold the whole thing than each have only his own little bit; likewise, even if they could each have a small bit of the *ager Campanus*, it would be more respectable (*honestius*) for them to possess it collectively and not as individuals. The image obviously draws on previous ideas: it is an image of subdivision, like C4; and it recalls the ideas of being "jammed together" (*constipari*) of C8 and of shared inheritance of C9ᵃ. But, more important, the image exploits the significance of the *Campus Martius*. It was a symbol of sovereignty: electoral assemblies (the *comitia centuriata*, for consuls and praetors; the *comitia tributa*, for curule aediles and quaestors; and the *concilium plebis*, for tribunes) regularly met there.[25] It was a symbol of the risk of privatization: though formally public land since it was taken from the Tarquins, parcels had begun to be sold off during the time of Sulla, where private individuals had residences and gardens.[26] It was already a place where the Roman people could say, "This land belonged to our fathers but they gave it away." And last, the field had military resonances: it was literally the "Field of Mars," and the *comitia centuriata* was required to meet there because it was in origin a military assembly. In short, the Campus symbolized collective civic identity, rather as the Forum does (*LA* 2.71, Table 5.3.2.M). Perhaps the military resonances were the strongest. They certainly seem to underlie Cicero's next step. C19ᵇ closes with military imagery: if the people are being robbed to benefit others—another zero-sum image—should they not with all zeal defend their fields against this law as if it were an armed enemy (*nunc vero cum ad vos nihil pertineat, sed paretur aliis, eripiatur vobis, nonne acerrime, tamquam armato hosti, sic huic legi pro vestris agris resistetis*)? Thus is recalled not only one aspect of the semiotics of the field but the very beginning of the speech, where the people as an armed force breached the citadel of the aristocracy. Now, turned outward as it were, they must defend against an enemy coming after their fields. Now standing shoulder to shoulder means standing in their ranks, holding their position in the line of fire.

Honestum

That military imagery prepares for the next half of the argument, the blow to the *amplitudo* of the Roman people that a rival military power in Capua will represent. Cicero's *divisio* in the popular speech (*LA* 2.76, C3) had spoken of

---

25. Taylor 1966; 85; Lintott 1991: 46, 55.

26. Public land: Liv. 2.5.2 (the *ager* was *consecratus Marti*); sold off: Oros. 5.18.27. *Att.* 13.33a.1 (45) describes the *campus* as "being built over" (*coaedificari*). For further detail on the history of the district, see Coarelli 1997 and Davies 2017.

commodum and *amplitudo*, which, as I noted, are the equivalents of *utile* and *honestum*; *amplitudo* begins to be explored with *LA* 2.85, which imagines the colonial expansion of Capua, which, says Cicero, will become the chief city of a rival empire (C23). The discussion falls into two halves: a political history of Capua (*LA* 2.87–91) and ethical reflections on the connection between wealth and insolence (*LA* 2.92–97). As the dots in Table 9.1 show, each half of the discussion in the popular speech has topics unique to itself. This section draws attention to two sets of significant details from each of those halves that knit their arguments together.

One set of details involves the elders. The senate speech and the popular speech both express the essential points of Capua's history (Capua was a threat, C24, and therefore the Capuan state was debilitated by the elders, C25). And the speeches draw the same moral lesson (the elders' decision was not cruel, C29, but wise, C30). But the expression of the last idea is more frequent in the popular speech, where it is a minor motif attached to other themes. It appears in C25-p (the elders gutted the structures of Capua "in their wisdom," *homines sapientes*, *LA* 2.88); in C27-p (a gutted Capua was subsequently a reliable ally, as the elders, "with their godlike ability to think and plan," *homines divina mente et consilio praedit[i]*, rightly predicted, *LA* 2.90); and in C28-p (Capua lacks political ambitions because the elders "by their thoughtful plan," *ratione et consilio*, reduced it to torpid repose, *LA* 2.91). And that is the idea that in C30 caps off the discussion of Capua's political history: in leaving the city slack and weakened the elders "planned excellently for the future" (*multum in posterum providerunt*, *LA* 2.95). Appeal to the elders is an unsurprising feature in a Roman speech, of course.[27] But in these passages it is the culmination of a tactic in the second speech: the elders are held up as paragons of intelligent imperialism. That is how they appear in earlier *argumenta*. They understood how to keep peace abroad: they kept certain territories in Sicily "to anchor peace and commemorate war" (*vinculum pacis et monumentum belli*, *LA* 2.49, Table 3.1.E). The phrases, unparalleled in Cicero and rare in any event,[28] express clear-eyed political objectives: the retained territory (the singulars treat it as if it were indivisible) reminds the Sicilians of the process of their defeat and shackles their ambitions lest they lose still more. The elders also understood how to place settlements: discussing the looseness of the bill's language about colonial sites, Cicero recalls that the elders in their carefulness

---

27. For an analysis of the theme, see Kenty 2016.

28. The only other occurrence of *vinculum pacis* is in Seneca: *[Sexti Pompei] morte optime cohaerentis Romanae pacis vincula resoluta sunt* (*Dial.* 11.15.1). The only other occurrence of *monumentum belli* is in Silius Italicus, referring to representational scenes: *varia splendentia cernit | pictura belli patribus monumenta prioris | exhausti* (*Pun.* 6.654–56).

(*diligentia*) established colonies "as a guard against danger in such well-chosen places that they seemed to be, not towns of Italy, but the ramparts of empire" (*propugnacula imperi*, *LA* 2.73, cf. J2-p in Appendix 3). And the elders understood the long-term fiscal value of expansionism: the *agri vectigales* the Romans now possess were earned by the elders "with much [of their] sweat and blood" (*plurimo maiorum vestrorum sanguine et sudore quaesita*, *LA* 2.69, Table 7.3.3.I-p). The constant invocation of the elders in the Capua sections draws on this motif of geopolitically shrewdness and is meant to (try to) change the terms of the question: deciding about the *ager Campanus* is not only a decision about *commodum* (which *LA* 2.76–85 argue is illusory in any case); it is also a decision about intelligent geopolitics—which is what won for Rome the *amplitudo* it now enjoys. Cicero is not making a simple appeal to conservatism but a narrower appeal to responsible decision-making: if the people would change the current disposition of the *ager Campanus* and Capua, then they should also take into account the factors that led previous generations to create that disposition—which was no whim, but a matter of "long and frequent debate" (*de Capua multum est et diu consultatum*, *LA* 2.88, C25). The wisdom of the elders is notably the theme Cicero invokes as he transitions to the *peroratio*; that is one theme he wished the audience to remember: "It was this path of crime (*sceleris vestigia*) traced by M. Brutus that you chose to follow, P. Rullus, rather than [look to] the monuments of wisdom (*monumenta sapientiae*) established by our elders!" (*LA* 2.98, C37).

The ending of the popular version of the *honestum* argument is knit together by another theme: the physical space of Rome itself. That space—what the audience can see immediately around itself or knows intimately—provides a standard of judgment against which Rome is both stronger but potentially weaker. The popular version of C25 compares the destruction of Capua to that of Carthage and Corinth, the great rivals of Rome in centuries prior. Capua, however, was not razed to the ground; rather, buildings in the city were left standing. That was the elders' deliberate design, says Cicero, so that the city could serve as a manufacturing base for equipment needed in the fields and so that there would be a central point for gathering and storing produce (*comportandis condendisque fructibus*). His depiction of Capua would doubtless have made at least some of his audience think of the *Forum Holitorium*, the Vegetable Market, just outside the *Porta Carmentalis* in the Servian Wall and just to the west of the Forum where Cicero's audience then stood. Capua, some must have thought, is now a *forum holitorium* without a *Forum Campanum*. It is a farmer's market without a city. If any in Cicero's audience questioned his comparison—Corinth and Carthage were fully razed—it is perhaps chiefly to them that Cicero directs his next point: Capua was close enough so that, if any rebellion did arise, the senate and the Roman people could snuff it out before it gathered steam (C26). Capua was, at all events, a loyal ally thereafter in a whole series of wars (C27). Cicero lists them at length, beginning with Philip V of Macedon, defeated in 196, and ending with the Marsic War, which had ended in 87. The point is not amplification for its own sake. The point, in part, is to make people think now of military triumphs—which entered the city through the *Porta Carmentalis* or somewhere nearby.[29] And the point is also to make the audience think of the glories of the Roman military accomplishment, to which so many features of the Forum itself were monuments. The audience's mind, as it were, is conducted inside the walls in triumph, of which there is no like in Capua. Here, pitched not toward *commodum* but toward *amplitudo*, is a version of *LA* 2.71 = Table 5.3.2.M, which also appeals to the beauties of the city.

The physical space of Rome is used still more strikingly. The list of wars in which Capua was loyal has a sour note in the middle: the list includes "many civil disturbances ... which I won't go into here" (*multae ... seditiones domesticae quas praetermitto*), a clear reference to the civil wars and associated disruptions under Marius and Sulla. The Forum bore the memory of the murders and riots of those times, too. Cicero builds on that memory in the next section, C28. Ostensibly the passage is about Capua; stripped of senate and magistrates, it had been "reduced to a torpid and lazy repose" (*ad inertissimum ac desidiossimum otium perdu[cta]*). But the reasons deserve notice. Nobody had the right to address assemblies or make public policy; thus there was nobody to "roil the state with troublesome assemblies, disruptive senate decrees, unfair commands" (*qui malis contionibus, turbulentis senatus consultis, iniquis imperiis rem publicam miscerent*) in search of a pretext for revolution (*et rerum novarum causam aliquam quaererent*). There were no public offices (*honos*), and so nobody got carried away by the lust for glory (*non gloriae cupiditate efferebantur*). There was nothing left to fight about, and the lack of competition meant no discord (*non contentione, non ambitione discordes*). This is obviously less a real reflection on the federal politics of Capuans than it is a reflection of Cicero's view of the defects of recent and contemporary Roman politics. A hobbled Capua is half of an unexpressed analogy: if complete destruction has led to an undignified kind of leisure, then rebalance can lead to good leisure—the kind of leisure that, as we have seen, is a theme of the *exordium* and the *peroratio*.[30] Capua is both proof and object lesson to an audience that had, in the very place where they then stood, participated in *malae contiones* and heard *turbulenta senatus consulta* and seen the powerful *ambitione discordes*. The object lesson is therefore no cause for vaunting. There is work to do in Rome.

---

29. Beard 2007: 97–101.

30. For an account of Cicero's modulation of this 'bad' *otium* into the 'good' *otium* of the *peroratio*, see Vasaly 1993: 235–38.

The *honestum* part of the argument now turns to its second half, ethical reflections on the insolence caused by wealth. The idea was proverbial ("It is a lucky man who has both wealth and good sense," as Menander put it, μακάριος, ὅστις οὐσίαν καὶ νοῦν ἔχει, 114K), and the idea is the last topic of this half of the argument (C36). But it is illustrated first by a particular example (C31)—the colony of M. Iunius Brutus (father of the famous tyrannicide). As tribune for 83, he carried a bill to found a colony in Capua, which he must have done in the early months of 83—shortly before Sulla arrived to Campania and, apparently, dissolved the colony.[31] Cicero had evidently visited the colony in the brief period of its existence. He paints a (by his lights) shocking tableau. The two chief magistrates were not called *duumviri*, as in many towns, but *praetores*; their lictors carried not *bacilli* 'staffs' but *fasces* '[the] rods [of high office at Rome]'; the senate were addressed, as at Rome, as *patres conscripti*; a sacrifice was readied with *hostiae maiores* 'full-grown victims,' as at important public sacrifices in Rome. In short, the Capuan magistrates were imitating Roman consuls and constructing a rival Forum. The symbolic charge of the rituals would not have been lost on the audience. Here, too, physical space of Rome is thus the underlying theme. The question, ultimately, is power relations. To speak only of *fasces*, what do they represent? A grant of power or the will to power? Properly, the former, of course: as Cicero puts it of Verres, he "owed his *fasces* and axes to the benefice of the Roman people" (*qui beneficio populi Romani fascis et securis haberet*, *Ver.* 2.5.163). But the will to power inspired some to arrogate *fasces* to themselves without benefit of regular election. In 205 the seditious soldiers C. Albius and C. Atrius, "not content with tribunician symbols, dared lay claim to the insignia of ultimate power, *fasces* and axes" (*qui nequaquam tribuniciis contenti ornamentis, insignia etiam summi imperii, fasces securesque, attractare ausi*, Liv. 28.24.14). Later in 63 so would Catiline (*Catil.* 2.13, *Sul.* 17). This is exactly the problem imagined earlier in the speech, when Cicero lists the equipment of the decemvirs in a way that suggests the tyrannical Second Decemvirate (*LA* 2.32–33, ch. 7.3 Parades and Power). Brutus was, as Rullus would be, a kind of *privatus furiosus*—a non-curule magistrate acting as if he were one.

It was, by Cicero's lights, the riches of Capua that breathed into Brutus that lordly spirit. Cicero likens the arrogant Brutus to the Blossii and (probably) Cerrinus Vibellius Taurea: they had, respectively, rebelled against the Romans after Capua was conquered in 210 and worked against Rome during the Second Punic War.[32] The references, which are not explained, presuppose a deep

---

31. For full details, see Manuwald 2018: 380.

32. Liv. 23.8.5, 27.3.4–5; for further refs. and details, see Manuwald 2018: 392.

familiarity in Cicero's audience with historical names and their associations;[33] Brutus is here assimilated to a known template. But that, in the now familiar technique, is a rewriting. Brutus had participated in the revolt of Marcus Aemilius Lepidus against the Sullan constitution in 78 and taken the field against senatorial armies; he surrendered to Pompey, who apparently accepted his surrender but had him murdered.[34] His bad end had to do with his participation in armed revolt rather than Capua *per se*. But Cicero encourages the people to link Brutus's death, which they knew of, to the arrogance of Campania, which they believed in. (And he also puts the people in mind of a populist agitator who met his end at Pompey's hands. The image, in that way, enlists Pompey to Cicero's cause, as at the end of the *exordium*). Cicero reinforces his reconfiguration of Brutus by an appeal to another of the people's collective memories. He recalls his evidently memorable appearance: Brutus was "shrivel'd to thinness unmassive" (*vegrandi macie torridum*; or, if Housman's emendation is correct, *vegrandem ac retorridum* "hardly huge and wizen'd").[35] The unusual phrase suggests a poetic quote (hence my translations). It seems that Cicero is applying a well-known quote to Brutus's well-known appearance, or quoting those who already had. Brutus was a known object of mockery in a culture that mocked appearances.[36] That is an implicit *a fortiori* argument which builds on Cicero's use of the environs. If a mere *forum holitorium* was enough to make the dried-up tribune that we all remember from here in the Forum pick up *fasces* and sacrifice bulls, how much worse will it make the already bold?

The immediate environs are used in one more way in this part of the argument. Cicero's treatment of Capua presupposes, in the way of ancient ethnographic discourse, that the nature of a place makes its residents who they are.[37] That is the very idea to which he next turns after the "parable" of Brutus (C32): the rich Campania breeds arrogance. The senate speech also invokes the idea but only briefly, as one reason among others not to establish a colony at Capua; the popular

33. Morstein-Marx 2004: 72–77.

34. Cf. *Iunius RE* 52.

35. Housman 1913.

36. On the doubtlessly intended comic effect, cf. "Individuals corporally distinctive, be it through deformity or a more common departure from the ideals of attractiveness such as baldness, were ready targets for orators who sought to effect a sense of complicity with their audience in a gale of laughter," Bell 1997: 15. Cicero's Caesar recommends the practice (*de Orat.* 2.266; cf. 239).

37. On the ethnographic underpinnings of the passage, cf. Vasaly 1993: 148–51, 233 and n. 64. Gildenhard 2011:136 points out the contrast here to Cicero's frequent use elsewhere of the idea of "native stock."

version uses the idea to explain Brutus' colony. It provides the theory: people's habits are formed by their surroundings, not their bloodlines. And it provides examples: the Ligurians are hard people from a hard land; Carthiginians, from a port city in constant flux and flow, learn to lie; and Campanians in a lush land better than all others think that they are better than all others. Of course even Hannibal was corrupted (C33); of course a colonized Capua will be dangerous (C34). The senate speech has versions of C33 and C34, too; but the popular version adds an argument unique to itself, C35. Of course a revived Capua will be arrogant: she is laid out on an expansive plane (*planissimo in loco explicata*), sited splendidly (*praeclarissime sita*); but Rome is set on hills and valleys, "built up and piled high with upper stories, with not very good roads, [and] very narrow streets" (*in montibus positam et convallibus, cenaculis sublatam atque suspensam, non optimis viis, angustissimis semitis*). Capua is ringed by rich fields and rich towns like Naples, Pompeii, Cumae, and Puteoli; the fields around Rome, the *ager Vaticanus* and *Pupinia*, and the towns around Rome—Veii, Fidenae, Collatia; Lanuvium, Aricia, Tusculum—are no comparison.[38] But the realisms of the passage do not make it realistic—for example, what does the narrowness of a city's streets have to do with its martial efficacy? And the passage seems to sit ill with Cicero's praise of Roman urban life as a manifestation of *libertas* (*LA* 2.71 = Table 5.3.2.M). But the objective of the passage is not realism or even logical consistency. Its purpose is to vivify and concretize a particular view or idea of power relations, and its method is to draw on the people's own sense of place. Just as Cicero uses the crowding of the crowd to symbolize an *ager Campanus* subdivided, so he tries to stoke anxieties about a possible rival by drawing on the difficulties most Romans personally experienced—being jostled in the crowded streets, clambering up a hill or the ladders of apartment blocks, passing by modest or ruined nearby towns. If Capua is good to think with about Rome, the conditions of Rome and its environs are also good to think with about Capua.[39] Cicero is not the only one to have used the cramped conditions of the city to rhetorical effect. Gaius Gracchus

---

38. The *ager Vaticanus* and *Pupinia* were indeed infertile. For the poor climate of the *ager*, see Liverani 2016: 21; on *Pupinia*, Var. *R*. 1.9.5, Col. 1.4.3; other refs. in Manuwald 2018: 398. At Veii, destroyed in 396 (Liv. 5.1–22), only a small town survived, to become the *municipium Augustum Veiens*. Collatia and Fidenae were still small villages that had become private property (Strabo 5.3.2); little remained of either (Plin. *Nat.* 3.68; Hor. *Epist.* 1.11.7–8). The next three towns, rounding out the *a fortiori* argument ("These are better, but still unimpressive by comparison"), were more prosperous. Lanuvium, despite probably suffering during the Civil Wars of Marius and Sulla (App. *BC* 1.69), remained a viable community and would continue to flourish through the Empire. Aricia in the late Republic was a prosperous *municipium* (Cic. *Phil.* 3.15). Tusculum was a resort town with villas of the wealthy (Strabo 5.3.12).

39. On Campania in the Roman imagination, see Fielding and Newlands 2015.

had proposed a bill granting citizenship to allies; but that, argued C. Fannius, would mean cramped seating at the games.[40] The argument is not silly. Ultimately it is a zero-sum argument: somebody else's gain will mean our loss. And that, ultimately, is Cicero's idea here, too: a growing Capua means a shrinking Rome. Before the people an argument ostensibly about *amplitudo* sounds, in the end, like an argument about one face of *utile—commodum*. Look around: you can see the problem for yourselves.

9.3. CAPUA AND THE AGER CAMPANUS IN LA 1

> *respicere exemplar vitae morumque iubebo*
> *doctum imitatorem et vivas hinc ducere voces.*
>
> Life as it's lived should be the ideal
> of the representational art, there's the source
> of authentic characters—that's my advice.
>
> —Horace, *Ars Poetica* 318–19

Vtile

The senate version of the *utile* half of the argument is brief. Cicero frames it with *praeteritiones* (C20[a,c]), promising in the latter instance to treat the topic more fully in his *contio*. The version of the argument in the senate speech does indeed lack many of the arguments that the popular speech has. But the section is no the less striking for that. The order of elements in the senate speech is quite different from that in the popular speech. The treatment of *utile* proper begins with a series of epithets—the *laudes agri Campani*, as it were (C10)—which hang off the first *praeteritio*. The senate version of them is pitched to emphasize senate's responsible position, distinctly recalling earlier elements of the first speech. Where popular version calls the *ager* the "fundament of the tax-properties" (*fundamentum vectigalium*), the senate version has "a tax-property under the state's lock and seal" (*sub signo claustrisque rei publicae positum vectigal*). That recalls the senate's depiction as the family elders protecting the family wealth (ch. 3.3 The Wastrel): the storage rooms of a house—that is the metaphor here—might

---

40. "If you grant the Latins citizenship, do you really think you will [easily] find a place at an assembly the way you just have here or [be able to] take part in games and festal days? Don't you think they will fill everything up?" (*si Latinis civitatem dederitis, credo, existimatis vos ita, ut nunc constitisse, in contione habituros locum aut ludis et festis diebus interfuturos. nonne illos omnia occupaturos putatis? ORF* 32.3).

be locked with *claustra* and sealed with *signa*.[41] With *annonae* "of the grain supply" or "of the market price of grain," the public speech has the sympathetic word *solacium*, 'relief,' where the senate speech has the cooler *subsidium* 'aid'; so in Chapter 2 we saw a people close to suffering and a senate farther from it. Likewise with the image of a "granary" (*horreum*): in the popular speech it sustains legions (*legionum*); in the senate speech it subsidizes war (*belli*). The people see the troops; the senate sees the political problem. Where the people would be "letting [the *ager*] go to ruin" (*disperire patiemini*), a nod to their sovereignty, like the "tell me, how can you possibly allow him do so?" (*id vos potestis, quaeso, concedere?*) of *LA* 2.71 (Table 5.3.2.M), the senate will have been "unable to preserve" the *ager* (*servare non potuisse*), like the Cicero who fears that what the ancestors won could not even be kept on his watch (*ne retineri quidem potuisse iudicabuntur, LA* 1.4 = Table 3.1.D-s). After the *laudes* the next topic in the senate speech is C17: the *ager Campanus* was untouched by Sulla and the Gracchi. In both speeches Sulla's rule is a *dominatio*; but the program of the Gracchi differs: in the popular speech it is *benignitas* 'generosity'; in the senate speech it is *largitio*, a 'give-away,' the word used also in *LA* 1.4, where it is also linked to the idea of retention: the elders, Cicero says ironically there, won lands in courageous campaigns "in order that we could have something to sell to finance handouts!" (*ut esset quod nos largitionis causa venderemus*, Table 3.1.E-s).

The position of the senate is also registered in a more striking way. The remaining four topics of the treatment of *utile* in the senate speech, C12–C15, are each represented by a single brief clause, attached to another *praeteritio*. Cicero will "not mention [here] (C20[b]) that this is the only tax-property in the whole empire that is stable when others are lost (C11), that does not lapse when other [tax-properties] have been cut off (C13), that gleams in peacetime (C15), that does not lose value in war, that sustains the soldiery (C12), [and] that does not [have to] fear the enemy (C14)." The language is distinctive. "Gleams" is *niteat*, which, if it is meant here to suggest plant growth, is not otherwise unambiguously attested in that sense until Augustan poetry[42] (the related adjective *nitidus* is slightly earlier in that sense, already in Cicero).[43] The "soldiery" (*militem*), a collective singular of a type not common in prose until Livy,[44] may here be a propriety of military

---

41. Locked: *claves cum clostris in cellas II* (Cato *Agr.* 13.3, equipment for the *cella olearia*); sealed: *obsignate cellas* (Pl. *Cas.* 144, the order of the *domina* to her slaves).

42. *nitentia culta* (Verg. *G.* 1.153), *camposque nitentis | desuper ostentat* (Verg. *A.* 6.677–8); cf. *ubi aratro domefacta tellus nitet* (Petr. 99.3).

43. *Campos antea collisque nitidissimos viridissimosque* (Cic. *Ver.* 2.3.47).

44. On this word so used, cf. *L&S s.v.* II.A.

speech (and likewise *hostem* sg. for "the enemy").⁴⁵ Perhaps that is also one tone of *niteo*. *Eniteo* appears once as the functional opposite of *obsolesco* in a military context: *enituit aliquis in bello, sed obsolevit in pace* ("One shone in war but faded in peace," Plin. *Pan.* 4.5).

But more important than the lexicon is the overall form:

[quod] amíssis áliis |	remáneat,	|| intermíssis |	nòn conquiéscat,
in páce |	níteat,	|| in béllo |	nòn obsoléscat
mílitem |	susténtet,	|| hóstem |	nòn pertiméscat

As the formatting suggests, Cicero's *laudes agri Campani* have exactly the structure of a Saturnian verse: each line is divided into hemistichs, and each hemistich is divided into two cola; and most of those cola, as is typical for Saturnian verses, have one chief accent.⁴⁶ Furthermore, each line is linked across the caesura by some kind of verbal play, as is typical for archaic poetry: one a *figura etymologica* (*amissis* ~ *intermissis*), twice semantic opposites (*pace* ~ *bello*, *militem* ~ *hostem*). Each final colon has *non* followed by a quadrisyllable ending in *-escat*, not only giving vertical parallelism, but also producing end rhyme, an occasional affect of older poetry, as in Ennius's *haec omnia vidi inflammari,* | *Priamo vi vitam evitari,* | *Iovis aram sanguine turpari* "All this I saw afire, Priam by force unlifed of life, the altar of Jove by blood befouled" (95–108W, Cic. *Tusc.* 3.44–45). The whole effect might be captured thus:

Though others be lost, it stays; though others stop, it does not fail.
In peace it gleams; in war it does not fade.
The soldier it sustains; the foe it does not fear.

The senate could hardly have failed to miss these effects. Cicero is echoing the form and function of older *elogia*, songs of praise often composed in Saturnian meter. The resonances must have been suggestive. Just the form of the poem, quite apart from its content, reminds the audience of a common cultural inheritance from preceding generations, the authority of ancient voices; the spirit of the poem points back to the past and not outward to the present. Linked to the *ager Campanus*, it is a bow to the elders whose toils secured the Campania and whose policy established its current disposition. The wisdom of the elders, one might say, which appears five times in the popular speech, but only once in the

---

45. Leumann and Hofmann, 1928: 369–90, Hofmann and Szantyr 1965: 13–14.
46. For a full analysis of the Saturnian on accentual terms, see Mercado 2012.

senate speech, and that in the form of a single world (*consilio, LA* 20, C30), is, thanks to this poem, a more important theme than might at first glance appear. Are there other resonances? Had Cicero, who had just taken his oath of office, spoken prayers shortly before in the Saturnians often found in older formulas?[47] Is this praise poem thus another allusion to the environs, verbal rather than physical? And does this echo of an *elogium*, which often appears on tombstones, also echo that application, becoming a kind of tombstone from the future for a land that, if the bill is passed, will die, its name to survive only in song? The senate speech in its own way, like C9^c, imagines a loss looked back on from the future.

Honestum

The senate speech, like the popular speech, uses the colony at Capua itself to explore the idea of *honestum*: Capua represents a challenge to Rome's pre-eminence. The senate version, as the Table 9.1 shows, shares all but one of its ideas with the popular speech. The briefer treatments in the senate version have three distinct currents. There is a current of sarcasm. Like the popular speech, the senate version anticipates that the colonists will be thugs (C5). But the senate speech puts it sarcastically: Capua is where "'our' colonists, chosen for every kind of crime, will be settled" (*ibi nostri coloni delecti ad omne facinus . . . conlocabuntur*). *Nostri* has an edge to it: the colonists will be officially authorized, if the bill passes, so they're 'ours'—but not in any positive sense (the effect is more or less that of an ironic "our fine colonists"). The senate speech, like the popular speech, argues that sudden wealth causes arrogance (C36). Both versions use an *a fortiori* argument: the ancient Campanians, who were used to the wealth, were warped by it; how much worse will the colonists be! But the senate version is sarcastic about it: "I'm sure (*credo*) your minions," says Cicero, "will do a fine job keeping their insolence in check in the same city where people born to its former wealth and glory were unable to live in that affluence soberly!" Both speeches argue that a recolonized Capua would be dangerous (C34). The popular version is mathemetical: it asks what will happen in a colony of 5,000 once it appoints 100 decurions, 10 augurs, and 6 priests. The senate version is sarcastic: "I'm sure you can't see how dangerous all of this is—except you can, because want to overthrow the government and establish a new tyranny for yourselves" (*vos haec, nisi evertere rem publicam cuperetis ac vobis novam dominationem comparare, credo, quam perniciosa essent non videretis*).

A second current in the senate treatment might be called "strategic positioning." As we have seen (ch. 8.4), the risk of a colony on the Janiculum in the senate

---

47. For the rituals of consular accession, see Mommsen *SR*³ 1: 615–17.

speech is not a boot on the neck but a rival center of authority (*urbem hanc urbe alia premere,* LA 1.16, with the colony elevated to a "city"). The senate version looks at the situation as if at a map. The same kind of language is used when Capua is imagined as a rival center of the authority. The decemvirs' plan is to "set *that* city up against *this* one again, to ferry their resources and carry the name of empire there" (*illam urbem huic urbi rursus opponere, illuc opes suas deferre et imperi nomen transferre,* LA 1.18, C23ᵃ). Capua is a city that isn't being set up to defend Rome (*praeponitur* 'is put in front of') but to attack it (*opponitur* 'is set up against,' LA 1.20, C23ᵇ). The idea is anchored with a pun, as in C23ᵃ (*deferre ~ transferre*). The structure in which C23ᵇ is embedded can also be assigned to the language of strategic positioning. What, Cicero asks, should be avoided in establishing colonies (*quid cavendum est in coloniis deducendis,* C33)? If it's luxury (*luxuries*), then Capua has the wealth that corrupted Hannibal (C33); if it's haughtiness, the rich Campania is the birthplace of that (C32); and if it's a hostile outpost, then Capua is being set up to attack (C23ᵇ). Points that are made at length in the popular speech, without much connection between them, are brought together in short scope under a clear *divisio*, as if the senate, back at headquarters, were thinking through sites for colonies.

There is a third current, which might be called the "symbolic." When the elders hobbled the Capuan state (C25), the popular version has them "stripp[ing] that city of its magistrates, senate, and public council . . . and [leaving] no semblance of an independent government" (*si magistratus, senatum, publicum ex illa urbe consilium sustulissent, imaginem rei publicae nullam reliquissent*). The senate version, by contrast, has them "stripp[ing] Capua of its magistrates, its senate, its common council—in short, all the marks of [independent] government" (*magistratus, senatum, consilium commune, omnia denique insignia rei publicae sustulerunt*). The senate version has *insignia* 'mark, emblem,' where the popular version has *imago* 'likeness, semblance.' The proper meaning of *insigne* is an external mark of rank or status—a crown or a medal or a scepter or a striped toga. The metaphor of *insignia* makes a state into a distinguished person. That is the same metaphor as before, when the sale of certain *agri vectigales* would strip Rome of her *insignia* and *infulae*, like a triumphator stripped of his marks of honor (*LA* 1.6 = Table 8.2.D). The "symbolic" current appears most strongly as the section begins—the only element that is unique to the senate version of *honestum*: "To this point," says Cicero, "my argument has depended on suspicions and inference. But the next provision of the bill will absolutely do away with any possibility that anyone could misunderstand. The next provision will show plainly that the name of this republic (*nomen rei publicae*), the heart of the imperial city (*sedem urbis atque imperi,* lit. "seat of city and empire"), indeed even this very temple (*hoc denique templum*) of Jupiter Optimus Maximus—this, the citadel of all nations (*hanc arcem omnium gentium*)—they despise" (*LA* 1.18, C1). The accumulated parallel phrases (a *synathroismos*, Quint. 8.4.26) nest the temple among Roman political ideas and ideals:

nomen huius rei publicae	Rome as a form of political practice
sedem urbis atque imperi	The Capitoline hill
hoc ... templum	The temple of IOM
hanc arcem omnium gentium	The Capitoline as the foundation of world order

Nomen rei publicae is elsewhere used of the "form" of a government.[48] *Sedem urbis atque imperi* must refer specifically to the Capitoline, with *sedes* in its sense "abode," a sense proper to gods, but here extended to *urbis atque imperi*.[49] *Arx* with *gentium* is attested of the city,[50] but there the sense must be the metaphorical 'bulwark'; here the literal sense 'citadel' is more appropriate with reference to the Capitoline.[51] The chief nouns of each phrase, like the temple itself, connote identity and stability ('name,' 'seat,' 'citadel'). The temple is thus raised to its fullest significance—a symbol of the Roman order. The "name of empire" that the decemvirs would make an object of world-wide scorn (*LA* 1.2, Table 3.1.C) and the threat they pose to "this city" with "another city" (*ne urbem hanc urbe alia premere*) are focalized onto the temple. The preservation of that order is laid on the shoulders of the senate, who in the Republican period met in that temple more frequently than anywhere else.[52]

---

48. For this sense, cf. Cic. *Rep.* 3.45 *non video qui ... in multitudinis dominatu rei publicae nomen appareat* ("I don't see how it's possible to claim that the form of government is republican when there is mob rule").

49. The city itself is sometimes described as a *sedes* (*numquam haec urbs summo imperio domicilium sedem praebuisset*, *Prov.* 34; *urbem hanc ... sedem omnium nostrum*, *Sul.* 33; *alter eiusdem imperii domicilium sedesque servaret*, *Catil.* 3.26), but *sedem urbis* excludes that meaning. The idea is the "chief residence," or in English metaphor "the heart," of the political life of the city and empire. Was *hanc* lost before or after *sedem*? It is the only member of the *synathroismos* without a demonstrative. For other instances of *urbis atque imperi* in Cicero, cf. *testimonium huius u. a. i.*, *dom.* 132; *quem Statorem huius u. a. i. vere nominamus*, *Catil.* 1.33; *interitum huius u. a. i.*, *Catil.* 3.9; *totius u. a. i. occasum*, *Catil.* 3.19; *contra salutem urbis atque imperi*, *Catil.* 3.20; *in maximis periculis huius u. a. i*, *Flac.* 1; *custodes et conservatores huius u. a. i.*, *Sest.* 53).

50. Cf. *hanc urbem, lucem orbis terrarum atque arcem omnium gentium* (Cic. *Catil.* 4.11); *urbem hanc denique, sedem omnium nostrum, arcem regum ac nationum exterarum, lumen gentium, domicilium imperi* (Cic. *Sul.* 33).

51. Cf. *dignum Capitolio atque ista arce omnium nationum* (Cic. *Ver.* 2.5.184).

52. Mommsen, *RS*³ 3.2: 928; cf. ch. 8.2 *fin*. Achard 1981: 308 n. 46 sets this instance in the context of *impietas*, a charge against the *improbi*, the *bêtes noires* of optimate rhetoric (306–11).

These modes of speech—the sarcastic, the strategic, and the symbolic—might be put in terms of their broader congeners: the invective, the deliberative, and the sacral (in that peculiarly Roman version of the concept, if sacral is the right word for it, in which central politico-religious ideas are given expression—fetishized, even—in pregnant symbols and rituals). Cicero has observed the *vitam moresque* of the senate and drawn thence "authentic voices." His subtle but distinct polyphony is a very precise expression of the senate's proper functions: to censure the corrupt in its ranks, to soberly determine the best course of action, and to superintend religious matters—to exercise its duties toward itself, toward the state, and toward the gods. That is how a Roman senator should think about *honestum*; Cicero's modes of voice enact the ideal functioning of the body whose idealizing it is one object of the first speech to effect. If, in the *exordium* of the popular speech, Cicero turns himself into a symbol and servant of the people—an idealized people—here, in the last of the arguments of the senate speech, as probably in the lost *exordium*, he turns himself, in what he says and how he says it, into a symbol and servant of the senate—an idealized senate. That gives heft to the final words of the section: a warning that the Rullan bill will leave the senate no political options "to maintain their liberty and stature" (*in vestra libertate ac dignitate retinenda*, LA 1.22, ch. 8.4 Dignitas).

9.4. CODA: RHETORIC AND POLITICS

Die Grenzen meiner Sprache bedeuten die Grenzen meiner Welt.
—Ludwig Wittengenstein

The arguments about Capua are fine illustrations of the techniques and objectives of the whole speech. There is a reason for that. Like the *liberae legationes* passages from which this study began, which memorably symbolize authority gone awry, Capua and the *ager Campanus* memorably symbolize the (as Cicero sees it) empty promise of the bill. Both sets of passages engage directly with a central feature of the Rullan proposal: its formal mechanism and its hoped-for result. But the Capua passages make an appropriate ending to this study for another reason. The dangers to which Cicero draws attention were, at root, real; they are not in origin fervid or bilious rhetorical fantasies. Colonies really could be a danger. Faesulae, where settled Sullan colonists were soon to take up arms, was showing the danger of military colonies (and Cicero must be imagining that some of the colonies would be settled by Pompey's returning soldiers). Caesar would in a few years force a version of the Rullan bill through and settle troops in Capua—whom Pompey, Antonius, and Octavian all recalled, or tried to.[53] Despite Cicero's claims of a pacified Campania, Capua remained a source of resistance and opposition to Roman hegemony.[54] His listeners, or many of them, surely knew as much.

The manipulation of the popular assembly could also be a danger. That would be illustrated shortly by P. Clodius Pulcher, who exploited the theoretically full sovereignty of the people to weaponize the public assembly and widely expand the effective powers of the tribunate.[55] A colony on the Janiculum and decemvirs lording it in Egypt are not only (as I have thus far chiefly argued) symbols of power relations but also fair forecasts: Marius and Cinna had actually tried to seize the Janiculum; Caesar really would profit from the situation in Egypt. In light of all this Cicero's strategy in these speeches can be viewed as principled. He tries to appeal to a core value of each group of hearers in a way that encourages them to transcend its more selfish version: the people are encouraged to embrace *libertas* in a way that cannot be reduced simply to *commodum* but that includes responsible governance and cooperation with right-minded magistrates; the senate are encouraged to live up to a *dignitas* that means not personal pre-eminence but a collective responsibility without which pre-eminence is not even possible. Cicero himself was not always principled in that way; but it is also wrong to think that because he was sometimes unprincipled he was incapable of the articulation of genuine ideals.

But that also does not mean Cicero's approach is without its difficulties. The tactics of the speeches show up a problem of rhetoric itself. The dominance of Cicero's works in the history of Republican rhetoric makes it difficult to construct a full picture of the relation of rhetoric and politics in the late Republic; he is a splendid outlier. But there is a suggestive trace in Sallust. He represents the speech of Caesar in the debate whether to put the Catilinarian conspirators to death:

> Most of those who have given their opinions before me have lamented the fall of the republic in grand and polished fashion. They detailed what the savagery of war would be, what would befall the vanquished: girls and boys raped, children snatched from the arms of their parents, matrons

---

53. For Antony and Octavian, see the references gathered in Manuwald 2007: 20. Pompey: Caes. *BC* 1.14.

54. On the unrest in Italy in 63–60, of which Capua was a part, see Stewart 1995 and cf. Sal. *Cat.* 30.2 (*alii conventus fieri, arma portari, Capuae atque in Apulia servile bellum moveri* [sc. *nuntiabant*]).

55. On Clodius's political persona(e!), see Tatum 1999, esp. 150–75; Lintott 1967. On Clodius's mastery of the dynamics of public politics, see Tan 2013; Łoposzko and Kowalski 1990.

subject to every lust of the conqueror, shrines and homes looted, murder and arson—everywhere weapons, bodies, blood, and grief. But, ye gods, what was the purpose of such speech? To rouse your anger against the conspiracy? As if speech could fire someone whom such an awful and savage thing did not rouse! (*Cat.* 51.9–10)[56]

Caesar's (or, it may be, Sallust's) point is not merely that previous speakers exaggerated the horrors of war. His point is more specific: on his analysis they have lost sight of the political issues because they were distracted into clichés. The destruction of a city is—literally—the textbook example of the grand style in the *Rhetorica ad Herennium* (4.13). There, too, the free-born is violated (*violassent ingenuum*) and the matron defiled (*matremfamilias constuprassent*); there, too, temples are looted (*deum templis spoliatis*); there, too, are murder and fire.[57] That is, according to Caesar, previous speakers assimilated the situation to a known template and expatiated accordingly; in effect, they declaimed.[58] Caesar thus has a particular danger in mind: the widely taught and widely used templates of rhetoric could become, not tools to focus on a problem, but an inhibition to seeing and describing, and therefore intelligently addressing, a situation. The counterargument to Caesar's position is obvious: in this case the template has some fair correspondence to reality. The conspirators had, after all, colluded with the Allobroges, a disaffected foreign tribe;[59] rebellious troops were assembling up north; Catiline was dangerous. The dramatic image of a captured city made the stakes clear. The countercounterargument is that the template, by invoking the idea of war, carries with it an implicit solution to the problem: "destroy the (putative) enemy" (which Cato urged in the debate) rather than "be chary of setting precedent" (a point Caesar makes).[60]

---

56. *Plerique eorum, qui ante me sententias dixerunt, conposite atque magnifice casum rei publicae miserati sunt. Quae belli saevitia esset, quae victis adciderent, enumeravere: rapi virgines, pueros, divelli liberos a parentum complexu, matres familiarum pati, quae victoribus conlubuissent, fana atque domos spoliari, caedem, incendia fieri, postremo armis, cadaveribus, cruore atque luctu omnia conpleri. Sed per deos inmortalis, quo illa oratio pertinuit? An uti vos infestos coniurationi faceret? Scilicet, quem res tanta et tam atrox non permovit, eum oratio adcendet.*

57. For earlier parallels to the images in Caesar's speech, see Skard 1956: 23–24; Dunkle 1971: 15–16 notes "the commonplaces of tyrannical behavior."

58. Not inapposite are Juvenal's remarks: *declamare doces? o ferrea pectora Vetti | cum perimit saevos classis numerosa tyrannos* ("Or do you teach declamation? An iron breast thou hast, O Vettius, to hear the sing-song crowd kill, once more, the 'tyrants'—'savage,' of course," 1.150–1).

59. Cic. *Catil.* 3.4, Sal. *Cat.* 40.

60. Cato: Sal. *Cat.* 52; precedent: 51.25–42.

The underlying issue, in short, is the relationship between rhetoric and political reality. That was, of course, precisely the issue that Sallust's model for this scene, the Mytilenian debate in Thucydides, had in mind. His Diodotus, whose model of rhetoric is deliberative, asks what would be advantageous and wishes to spare the rebels; his Cleon, whose model of rhetoric is dicanic, asks what is just and wishes to execute the rebels.[61] The rhetorical model which each chooses affects his perception of the problem and his proposed solution. Does the Cicero of these speeches understand that issue? It is possible to argue that he does. He is not confined to, still less seduced by, the clichés of the popular address ("*Libertas* before all!") or of senatorial identity ("*Dignitas* before all!"), and he tries, by probing and redefining those same values, to call each audience to a better version of itself and to take the ideology of Roman governance seriously. But it is also possible to argue the opposite. Cicero sharply dramatizes the choice for or against the Rullan bill: Rullus and the decemvirs become tyrants, or Sulla reborn, or wayward youth, or the Second Decemvirate, or brutal governors, or the corrupt and greedy rich, and so on. Cicero uses clichés to escape clichés. And if Cicero wants to produce unity, he produces it by polarization, thereby deepening the problem that was a bar to unity in the first place.

That is to say, Cicero replicates the very problem he is trying to solve. I mentioned at the outset of this study the "crisis without alternative" of the late Republic, in the memorable phrase of Christian Meier: crises could not be solved without a boldness that bent the system—and thereby generated crises.[62] Solving problems caused problems. Cicero's first two agrarian speeches can be seen as the rhetorical reflection of exactly that problem. And they also reflect that problem in a subtler but, in my opinion, more important way. In both speeches Cicero offers himself, in the fashion of Roman culture, where the *exemplum* was a parable, as living proof of the ideals that he puts forward. He is a *consul popularis*, embodying the will of the people: in the *peroratio* of the popular speech, as in the *exordium*, he sets himself up as the embodiment and instrument—and guide—of the people's will. And if in the senate speech he is a *consul senatorius*, interested in the real health of the institution, by the end of the speech he is also a kind of *eques consularis*, whose *virtus* and *industria* have brought him to the highest office in the land and allowed him to offer himself to the tribunes as an example of the only true path to success. It is easy—and wrong—to ascribe all that to Cicero's vanity. He was, after all, a supreme official in an authoritarian state in a fractious time, and one might even say it was his duty to be all things to all people (that was certainly

---

61. Thuc. 3.36–49; MacKay 1962: 193.

62. Ch. 1.3 *fin*.

his view in retrospect).[63] And in a rhetorically overwrought environment, where commonplace could be met by commonplace could be met by commonplace, the example of Cicero's own life really did provide—on one reading—a token of the authenticity and veracity of his own arguments. Last, Cicero's later political ideology appears here distinctly. The Catilinarian conspiracy near the end of Cicero's consular year prompted Cicero's articulation of the ideal of the *consensus omnium bonorum*, "agreement among all the good." Such *consensus* required social groups to step outside of their own interests to consider the common good. Cicero in these speeches is offering himself as the instrument and symbol of harmony, a self-presentation that prefigures his later professed ideals.

But in so doing he does not step outside of the politics of personality. He does not cope with the structural inefficiencies or economic inequities of the Roman state (as did the Gracchi, or Caesar, or even the authors of the Rullan bill, who had plainly thought through the problems of the political economy very hard). Cicero folds the solution to the tensions of his time into a single individual. Furthermore, not only does he offer himself as a political role model and symbol; his allusions to so many other practices and institutions, and, as we have so often seen, especially places and their resonances, make him, as he doubtless intended, a kind of voice and embodiment of Roman culture: the tribune, the praetor, the annalist, the court reporter—even the Saturnian poet. He uses *himself* to think with. And that is exactly the problem. In order to champion communalism, Cicero elevates himself. In order to champion unity, he advertises his own distinctiveness. In order to stave off a bid for excess power (as he saw it), Cicero comes close to the kind of personalist rhetoric that autocrats use to justify themselves ("Only I can save you!"). Cicero's first two agrarian speeches are, in that sense—and when their language and its resonances are closely examined—a very precise record, not only of a difficult political moment, nor only of how a skilled practitioner of rhetoric negotiated that moment, but also of the limitations of late Republican political debate itself.[64]

---

63. "In the conduct of my consulship I did nothing without the advice of the senate and nothing without the approval of the people; I defended the senate-house on the Rostra and the people in the senate; I joined the commons with the leading men and the equestrian order with the senate" (*atque ita est a me consulatus peractus ut nihil sine consilio senatus, nihil non approbante populo Romano egerim, ut semper in rostris curiam, in senatu populum defenderim, ut multitudinem cum principibus, equestrem ordinem cum senatu coniunxerim, Pis. 7*).

64. On the "domestication of domination," see Ando 2011: 82–114.

APPENDIX I

Table of Major Divisions

This table illustrates the major divisions of the two speeches and notes chapters where the main treatments of various sections appear.

in senatu (LA 1)	*ad populum (LA 2)*
	INTRODUCTORY MATTERS
	EXORDIVM
[not extant]	1–10 *existimandi sunt*
	• 1–9: ch. 6.2 (Re)reading Cicero's Election
	PROPOSITIO
[not extant]	10 *nam vere dicam*–16 *defendere*
	• 13: ch. 5.3 Bad Land
	PROCEDURE
	The election of the decemvirs by 17 tribes
[not extant]	16 *primum*–19
	• 16–17: ch. 45.1
	• 18–19: ch. 6.3
	Rullus presides at *comitia*
[not extant]	20–22
	• 20–22: ch. 6.3
	• 21: ch. 5.1
	Pompey excepted from service as decemvir
[not extant]	23–25
	Power of decemvirs to be confirmed by a *lex curiata*
[not extant]	26–30

in senatu (LA 1)	ad populum (LA 2)
	Rights and privileges of decemvirs
[not extant]	31–32 *potestatis*
	Summary of powers of decemvirs
[not extant]	32 *formam*–35 *continentur*
	• 32–33: ch. 7.3 Parades and Power
	SALE OF PROPERTIES
	Sale of property recensed by the senate after 81
[not extant]	35 *datur*–37
	• 35: ch. 1 n. 121
	Sale of public property outside of Italy after 88
1	38–44
• 1: ch. 4.4	• 41–44: ch. 4.4
	Comparandum of *liberae legationes*
	45–46 *surripiatur*
	• 45–46: ch. 2, ch. 4.1
	Sale of *vectigalia* within Italy and without
2–6	46 *intellexistis*–55 *cogitarent*
• 2–4: ch. 3	• 47–49: ch. 3
• 6: ch. 5.2	• 50: ch. 5.2
	• 51–55: ch. 5.2
	Attack on Pompey
5 *videte*–*indicabunt*	49 *hic*–50 *possitis*
• 5: ch. 7.2	• 49–50: ch. 7.2
	Eastern possessions
5 *iubent*–*tradiderunt*	50 *iubet*–51 *potuit*
• 5–6: ch. 8.2	• 50–51: ch. 8.2
	Recent gains of Pompey
6	51 *verum*–55 *cogitarent*
• 6: ch. 5.2	• 51–55: ch. 5.2
	Free location of sale
7	55 *atque*–56 *vendent*
• 7: ch. 1.2 *Logos*	• 56: ch. 1.2 *Logos*
• 7: ch. 4.2	• 55–56: ch. 4.2
Comparandum of *liberae legationes*	
8–9	
• 8–9: ch. 2	

in senatu (LA 1)	*ad populum (LA 2)*

OTHER SOURCES OF CASH
Imposition of taxes on public lands gained after 88

10 *init.-futura*	56 *sequitur*–57 *liberare*
• 10: ch. 8.4 Our Morality	• 56–57: ch. 8.4 Our Morality

The *ager Recentoricus* and the possessions of Hiempsal in Africa excepted

10 *excipit enim*–11 *olfecerint*	57 *excipitur*–59 *capillatus*
• 10–11: ch. 4.3	• 57–59: ch. 4.3

All war spoils are to be surrendered to the decemvirs . . .

11 *provincias*–13 *deferat*	59 *vix iam-fin.*
• 11–13: ch. 8.3	• 59: ch. 8.3

. . . Pompey excepted

13 *hic*–13 *cogitare*	60–62 *oportere*
• 13: ch. 7.2, ch. 8.4 We See	• 60–62: ch. 7.2, ch. 8.4 We See

ACQUISTION AND DISTRIBUTION OF LAND
The purchase of land

14–15	62 *parta*–72
• 14–15: ch. 7.3 The Voices of the (Un)Tribune	• 65–67: ch. 5.3 Bad Land
	• 67–70: ch. 7.3 The Voices of the (Un)Tribune

The settlement of colonies

16–17	73–75
• 16–17: ch. 8.4	• 71: ch. 5.3 Home Sweet Home
• 16–17: App. 3	• 74–75, ch. 8.4 We See: App. 3

The settlement of a colony in Capua

18–22 *occuparint*	76–97
• 18–22: ch. 9.3 (cf. App. 2)	• 76–97: ch. 9.2 (cf. App. 2)

PERORATIO

22 *his ego rebus*–27	98–99 (a summary of the law)
• 23: ch. 6.2 (Re)reading Cicero's Election	• 98–99: ch. 7.4
	100–103 (*peroratio* proper)
• 26–27: ch. 8.5	• 100–103: ch. 7.4

APPENDIX 2

The Rhetorical Structure of the Treatments of Capua and the ager Campanus

The treatments of Capua in the two speeches draw from the same fund of ideas, but their expression and sequence varies. This chart is arranged to show what ideas are and are not shared or repeated. The sequence of elements is set by the first appearance of each in the fuller popular version. Some special notations are required:

C3	Thematic sections (C = Capua)
87	Standard text sections of the *OCT* et al.
i.	Sequential position of excerpt
(*prec.* i:C2), (*seq.* iii:C4)	Location of preceding and subsequent excerpts ("The immediately preceding excerpt, i, can be found in thematic section C2"; "The immediately subsequent excerpt, iii, can be found in thematic section C4")
⌊ ⌋	Phrase also cited in another thematic section ("The phrase *statuerunt homines sapientes* represents the theme of section C30")
e.g. . . . sunt senatus consulta complura ⌊statuerunt homines sapientes (C30)⌋, si agrum Campanis ademissent . . .	

[]
e.g. [cf. 87. statuerunt homines sapientes (xxxi:C24)]

Context of phrase cited in a given thematic section ("The phrase *statuerunt homines sapientes*, which comes from *OCT* section 87, represents the theme of the section in which it is here listed, but the excerpt from which it comes, xxxi, overall represents the theme of C24, and the phrase in context can be found there")

C1. The backers of the bill hate Rome and the temple of I.O.M.

(*incipit*) i. 18. Atque haec a me suspicionibus et coniectura coarguuntur. Iam omnis omnium tolletur error, iam aperte ostendent sibi nomen huius rei publicae, sedem urbis atque imperi, denique hoc templum Iovis Optimi Maximi atque hanc arcem omnium gentium displicere.¹ (*seq.* ii:C2)

∅

C2. A colony will be founded at Capua

(*prec.* i:C1) ii. 18. Capuam deduci colonos volunt...² (*seq.* iii:C23)

(*incipit*) i. 76. At enim ager Campanus hac lege dividetur ⌊orbi terrae pulcherrimus (C10)⌋ et Capuam colonia deducetur, urbem amplissimam atque ornatissimam.³ (*seq.* ii:C3)

---

1. "To this point my argument has depended on suspicions and inference. But now there can be absolutely no way anyone could misunderstand. Now they will show plainly that the name of this republic, the heart of the imperial city, indeed even this very temple of Jupiter Optimus Maximus—this, the citadel of all nations!—they despise."

2. "They wish to take colonists to *Capua*..."

3. "But what the law calls for is the division of the *ager Campanus*, the finest in the world, and the establishment of a colony in the exceedingly rich and lovely city of Capua."

C3. *Divisio*: Cicero will speak of the people's honor and advantage

∅   (*prec.* i:C2) ii. 76. Quid ad haec possumus dicere? De commodo prius vestro dicam, Quirites; deinde ad amplitudinem et dignitatem revertar, ut, si quis agri aut oppidi bonitate delectetur, ne quid exspectet, si quem rei indignitas commovet, ut huic simulatae largitioni resistat. Ac primum de oppido dicam, si quis est forte quem Capua magis quam Roma delectet.[4] (*seq.* iii:C4)

C4. The bill proposes 5,000 colonists in Capua

∅   (*prec.* ii:C3) iii. 76. V milia colonorum Capuam scribi iubet; ad hunc numerum quingenos sibi singuli sumunt.[5] (*seq.* iv:C5)
[cf. 96. huc isti xviri cum I∞ colonorum (xlii:C34)]

C5. The colonists will be thugs

(*prec.* iv:C32) v. 18. . . . ibi nostri coloni delecti ad omne facinus a decemviris conlocabuntur . . .,[6] (*seq.* vi:C36)

(*prec.* iii:C4) iv. 77. Quaeso, nolite vosmet ipsos consolari; vere et diligenter considerate. Num vobis aut vestri similibus integris, quietis, otiosis hominibus in hoc numero locum fore putatis? Si est omnibus vobis maiori<ve> vestrum parti, <quam>quam me vester honos vigilare dies atque noctes et intentis oculis omnis rei publicae partis intueri iubet, tamen paulisper, si ita commodum vestrum fert, conivebo. Sed si v hominum milibus ad vim, facinus caedemque delectis ⌊locus atque urbs quae bellum facere atque instruere possit (C24)⌋ quaeritur, tamenne patiemini vestro nomine contra vos firmari opes, armari praesidia, urbis, agros, copias comparari?[7] (*seq.* v:C6)

---

4. "What can we say to that? I shall speak first about *your* advantage, fellow citizens; then I shall return to the matter of honor and dignity, in a way that will keep anyone who is attracted by the richness of the territory or the town from entertaining hopes for them and in a way that encourages anyone troubled by the impropriety of the proposal to resist this feigned largesse. And in case there is anyone who finds Capua more attractive than Rome, I will speak first about the town."

5. "The law calls for 5,000 colonists to be enrolled for Capua; to make that total each decemvir gets to pick 500 men.

6. "That's where 'our' colonists, chosen for every kind of crime, will be settled by the decemvirs . . . ."

7. "Take no comfort in that, I ask you; think about it—accurately and carefully! You can't possibly think that there's room in that number for you or men like you—upstanding, peaceful, and peaceable? If there is room for all of you, or the better part of you, even though the high office you have granted me demands that I stay alert night and day and keep watch, eyes wide open, over every aspect of the government, still, if a plan like that [really] is to your advantage, I shall avert my gaze for a brief while. But what if the bill is designed to provide a base and a city, capable of supplying and engaging in a war, for 5,000 men specially selected for

Appendix 2

(*prec.* **xvii:C19**) **xviii.** 81. At qui homines possidebunt? 82. Primo quidem acres, ad vim prompti, ad seditionem parati qui, simul ac decemviri concrepuerint, armati in civis et expediti ad caedem esse possint;[8] (*seq.* **xix:C6**)

(*prec.* **xxiii:C18**) **xxiv.** 84. his robustis et valentibus et audacibus decemvirum satellitibus agri Campani possessio tota tradetur,[9] (*seq.* **xxv:C9**)

C6. The colonists are straw men for would-be large landholders

ø   (*prec.* **iv:C5**) **v.** 78. Nam agrum quidem Campanum quem vobis ostentant ipsi concupiverunt; deducent suos, quorum nomine ipsi teneant et fruantur; coement praeterea; ista dena iugera continuabunt. Nam si dicent per legem id non licere, ne per Corneliam quidem licet; at videmus, ut longinqua mittamus, agrum Praenestinum a paucis possideri. Neque istorum pecuniis quicquam aliud deesse video nisi eius modi fundos quorum subsidio familiarum magnitudines et Cumanorum ac Puteolanorum praediorum sumptus sustentare possint. Quod si vestrum commodum spectat, veniat et coram mecum de agri Campani divisione disputet.[10] (*seq.* **vi:C7**)

(*prec.* **xviii:C5**) **xix.** 82. deinde ad paucos opibus et copiis adfluentis totum agrum Campanum perferri videbitis.[11] (*seq.* **xx:C9**)

---

violence, crime, and murder? Will you still allow forces to be amassed against you? Garrisons to be armed [against you]? Cities and fields and troops to be assembled [against you]? All in your own name?"

8. "And what kind of people will take up possession? At first they will be hot-tempered, prone to violence, primed to revolt—ready, willing, and able to take up arms against [their fellow] citizens and commit murder as soon as the decemvirs snap their fingers."

9. "Possession of the whole *ager Campanus* will be granted to these hale, hearty, and bold henchmen of the decemvirs."

10. "They hold out to you the promise of *ager Campanus*—but that's what they covet themselves; they will lead out their picked colonists, but only so that they can possess and profit from the land in their names! They'll buy up more on top of that; they'll link together the individual 10-acre parcels. Now, they may counter that that is illegal, but it is also illegal even under Sulla's legislation, and—to look no farther afield—we all know how the *ager Praenestinus* is now in the hands of a few. And I don't see where they are short of funds except for [needing] plantations they can use to meet the costs of large slave families and estates in Cumae and Puteoli! So if Rullus really has your advantage in mind, let him come to me in person and argue about the division of the *ager Campanus*!"

11. "Then you will see the whole *ager Campanus* pass into the hands of a few [who are already] awash in wealth and resources."

C7. The distribution of plots will begin from the rural tribes

ø   (*prec.* v:C6). **vi**. 79. Quaesivi ex eo Kalendis Ianuariis quibus hominibus et quem ad modum illum agrum esset distributurus. Respondit a Romilia tribu se initium esse facturum. Primum quae est ista superbia et contumelia, ut populi pars amputetur, ordo tribuum neglegatur, ante rusticis detur ager, qui habent, quam urbanis, quibus ista agri spes et iucunditas ostenditur? Aut, si hoc ab se dictum negat et satis facere omnibus vobis cogitat, proferat; {in} iugera dena discribat, a Suburana usque ad Arniensem nomina vestra proponat.[12] (*seq.* vii:C8)

C8. The *ager Campanus* is too small

ø   (*prec.* vi:C7). **vii**. 79. Si non modo dena iugera dari vobis sed ne constipari quidem tantum numerum hominum posse in agrum Campanum intellegetis, tamenne vexari rem publicam, contemni maiestatem populi Romani, deludi vosmet ipsos diutius a tribuno plebis patiemini?[13] (*seq.* viii:C9)

C9. The Roman people should keep their ancestral possessions

ø   (*prec.* vii:C8) **viii**. 80. Quod si posset ager iste ad vos pervenire, nonne eum tamen in patrimonio vestro remanere malletis?[14] (*seq.* ix:C10)

---

12. "I asked him on January 1 to which parties and in what manner he intended to distribute the territory. He replied that he would begin from the Romilian tribe. First of all, what kind of haughty insult is that? Part of the people is lopped off, the order of tribes is disregarded, and the rural tribes, who have land, get it before the urban tribes? And the urban tribes are the ones hearing all these promises of the joy of land ownership! But maybe he says that isn't what he said and he plans to do right by all of you. Well then let's see his plan—let's see how he carves out 10-acre parcels, let's see which of you he signs up—from the Suburan tribe to the Tribe of the Arno!"

13. "But if it's clear to you that not only can you not be given 10 acres a piece but that a crowd that big can't even be crammed into the *ager Campanus*, will you still let [all this go on?]—politics falling into chaos? the dignity of the Roman people scorned? you yourselves deluded by a tribune of the plebs even longer?"

14. "And even if that district could come into your [individual] possession, wouldn't you prefer that it remain a part of your patrimony?"

(*prec.* xix:C6) xx. 82. Vobis interea, qui illas a maioribus pulcherrimas vectigalium sedis armis captas accepistis, gleba nulla de paternis atque avitis possessionibus relinquetur.[15] (*seq.* xxi:C15)

(*prec.* xxiv:C5) xxv. 84. et, ut vos nunc de vestris maioribus praedicatis, 'hunc agrum nobis maiores nostri reliquerunt,' sic vestri posteri de vobis praedicabunt, 'hunc agrum patres nostri acceptum a patribus suis perdiderunt.'[16] (*seq.* xxvi:C19)

C10. Epithets of the *ager Campanus*[17]

(*prec.* xvii:C20) xviii. 21.
b. pulcherrimam populi Romani possessionem,
a. nos caput patrimoni publici,

d. horreum belli [cf. C12],
e. sub signo claustrisque rei publicae positum vectigal [cf. C11],
c. subsidium annonae [cf. C13],
f. servare non potuisse, . . . (*seq.* xix:C17)

(*prec.* vii:C9) ix. 80.
a. Vnumne fundum pulcherrimum populi Romani, [cf. 76 orbi terrae pulcherrimus, i:C2]
b. caput vestrae pecuniae,
c. pacis ornamentum,
d. subsidium belli, *f.* horreum legionum [cf. C12],
e. fundamentum vectigalium [cf. C11],

g. solacium annonae [cf. C13],

h. disperire patiemini? (*seq.* x:C11)

---

15. "But you, whose ancestors captured by arms these rich, rich sources ('seats') of tax revenue and passed them to you, will be left with not a single clod of your fathers' and grandfathers' possessions."

16. "Whereas you declare of your forebears, 'Our forebears bequeathed us this territory,' your descendants will declare of you, 'Our fathers received this territory from their fathers—and lost it.'"

17. Senate version: "... [that this chief] source of the public patrimony, the most beautiful possession of the Roman people, an aid to the grain supply, a granary in wartime, a tax-property under the state's lock and seal we were unable to preserve"; popular version: "[This] single most beautiful estate of the Roman people, a [chief] source of your money, an ornament to peace, an aid in war, the fundament of the tax-properties, the granary of the legions, a relief to the grain supply—are you going to allow it to be utterly ruined?"

C11. The *ager Campanus* remained when other *vectigalia* were lost

(*prec.* xx:C20) xxi. 2 ... solum hoc in re publica vectigal esse quod amissis aliis remaneat,[18] (*seq.* xxii:C13)

(*prec.* ix:C10) x. 80. An obliti estis Italico bello amissis ceteris vectigalibus ...[19] (*seq.* xi:C12)

C12. The *ager Campanus* provides sustenance for armies

(*prec.* xxiii:C15) xxiv. 21. in bello non obsolescat, militem sustentet,[20] (*seq.* xxv:C14) [cf. 21 horreum belli (xviii:C10)]

(*prec.* x:C11) xi. 80. ... quantos agri Campani fructibus exercitus alueritis?[21] (*seq.* xii:C13) [cf. 21 subsidium belli, horreum legionum (xviii:C10)] [cf. 83 Cetera vectigalia belli difficultatibus adfliguntur; hoc vectigali etiam belli difficultates sustentantur (xxii:C13)]

C13. The *ager Campanus* is reliable when other revenue is interrupted

(*prec.* xxi:C11) xxii. 21. [*sc.* aliis] intermissis non conquiescat,[22] (*seq.* xxiii:C15) [cf. 21 subsidium annonae (xviii:C10)]

(*prec.* ii:C12) xii. 80. an ignoratis cetera illa magnifica populi Romani vectigalia perlevi saepe momento fortunae inclinatione temporis pendere? Quid nos Asiae portus, quid Syriae ora,[23] quid omnia transmarina vectigalia iuvabunt tenuissima suspicione praedonum aut hostium iniecta?[24] (*seq.* xiii:C14)

---

18. "[I do not say] that this is the only tax-property in the whole empire that is stable when others are lost...."

19. "Or have you forgotten that in the Italian war, when other tax properties were lost...,"

20. "... that does not lose value in war, that sustains the soldiery ... "

21. "... how big were the armies you nourished with the fruits of the *ager Campanus* [alone]?"

22. "... that does not lapse when other [tax properties] have been cut off...."

23. Manuwald 2018: 79 *ad loc.* prints † *syriae cura* †.

24. "Or don't you know that the other valuable tax-properties of the Roman people are liable to change at any time with the smallest shift of circumstances ('fortune')? Raise the slightest suspicion of brigands or enemy forces, and the ports of Asia, the coast of Syria, and all the overseas tax-properties will do us no good at all."

330   *Appendix 2*

                (*prec.* xxi:C15) xxii. 83. Itane vero? privatum haec causa commovit; populum Romanum ne agrum Campanum privatis gratis Rullo rogante tradat non commovebit? At idem populus Romanus de hoc vectigali potest dicere quod ille de suo fundo dixisse dicitur. Asia multos annos vobis fructum Mithridatico bello non tulit, Hispaniarum vectigal temporibus Sertorianis nullum fuit, Siciliae civitatibus bello fugitivorum M'. Aquilius etiam mutuum frumentum dedit; at ex hoc vectigali numquam malus nuntius auditus est. ⌊Cetera vectigalia belli difficultatibus adfliguntur; hoc vectigali etiam belli difficultates sustentantur (C12)⌋.[25] (*seq.* xxiii:C18)
                [cf. 21 solacium annonae (xviii:C10)]

C14. The *ager Campanus* is physically safe

(*prec.* xxiv:C12) xxvv. 21.   (*prec.* xii:C13) xiii. 81. At vero hoc agri Campani vectigal,
  hostem non pertimescat;[26]   Quirites, eius modi est ut cum domi sit et omnibus
  (*seq.* xvi:C20)   praesidiis oppidorum tegatur, tum neque bellis
                             infestum...[27] (*seq.* xiv:C15)

C15. The *ager Campanus* is productive [in peacetime]

(*prec.* xxii:C13) xxiii. 21. in   (*prec.* xiii:C14) xiv. 81. ... nec fructibus varium nec caelo ac loco
  pace niteat[28] (*seq.* xxiv:C12)   calamitosum esse soleat.[29] (*seq.* xv:C16)
  [cf. 18. ubertatem agrorum
  (iv:C32)]

---

25. "Really now? This situation upset a private citizen; but the Roman people won't be upset enough not to hand over the *ager Campanus* to private citizens for free under Rullus's bill? After all the Roman people can say the same thing about this tax property as [the private citizen] reportedly said about his estate. Asia bore you no fruit for many years because of the war with Mithridates; there was no tax revenue from the Spains during the crisis with Sertorius; during the slave war M'. Aquilius actually had to supply grain to Sicilian communities; but about this tax property there was never one bad report. Other tax properties are staggered by the difficulties of war; but this tax property underwrites the difficulties of war."

26. "... that does not [have to] fear the enemy;"

27. "But the chief characteristics of the tax revenue from the *ager Campanus*, fellow citizens, are these: it is located in Italy ('at home') and protected by defensive lines of towns; nor is it exposed to warfare...."

28. "... that gleams in peacetime..."

29. "... and its yields are regular, and its weather and locale are not subject to storms."

(*prec.* **xx:C9**) **xxi.** 82. At quantum intererit inter vestram et privatorum diligentiam! Quid? Cum a maioribus nostris P. Lentulus, qui princeps senatus <fuit>, in ea loca missus esset ut privatos agros qui in publicum Campanum incurrebant pecunia publica coemeret, dicitur renuntiasse nulla se pecunia fundum cuiusdam emere potuisse, eumque qui nollet vendere ideo negasse se adduci posse uti venderet quod, cum pluris fundos haberet, ex illo solo fundo numquam malum nuntium audisset.[30] (*seq.* **xxii:C13**)

[95 bonitate agrorum et fructuum magnitudine (xl:C32)]

C16. The *ager Campanus* was augmented by the elders

ø (*prec.* **xiv:C15**) **xv.** 81. Maiores nostri non solum id quod <de> Campanis ceperant non imminuerunt verum etiam quod ei tenebant quibus adimi iure non poterat coemerunt.[31] (*seq.* **xvi:C17**)

C17. The *ager Campanus* was not sold by Sulla or the Gracchi

(*prec.* **xviii:C10**) **xix.** 21. eum denique nos agrum P. Rullo concessisse, qui ager ipse per sese et Sullanae dominationi et Gracchorum largitioni restitisset;[32] (*seq.* **xx:C20**)

(*prec.* **xv:C16**) **xvi.** 81. Qua de causa nec duo Gracchi, qui de plebis Romanae commodis plurimum cogitaverunt, nec L. Sulla, qui omnia sine ulla religione quibus voluit est dilargitus, agrum Campanum attingere ausus est; Rullus exstitit qui ex ea possessione rem publicam demoveret ex qua nec Gracchorum benignitas eam nec Sullae dominatio deiecisset.[33] (*seq.* **xvii:C19**)

---

30. "And you will end up looking like much less careful managers than private citizens! Here's what I mean. Our ancestors sent P. Lentulus, chief of the senate, to that territory with public funds to purchase private holdings that encroached on Campanian public land. They say he reported back that, no matter the money [he offered], he was unable to buy back the farm from one particular person who simply refused to sell. And he could not be convinced to do so, he said, for this reason: while he had many farms, that was the only farm that had never given a bad report."

31. "Our ancestors not only did not reduce what they took from the Campanians, but even purchased [land] that was held by persons from whom it could not be rightfully taken."

32. "... that, in short, *we* turned over to P. Rullus a district that on its own managed to survive Sulla's dominion and the Gracchi's give-away."

33. "And that's why neither the two Gracchi, who thought a great deal about the advantages of the Roman plebs, nor L. Sulla, who handed out everything to whoever he wanted with no scruples whatever, ever laid a finger on the *ager Campanus*; it's Rullus who's [suddenly] appeared to cast the republic out of a possession from which neither the generosity of the Gracchi nor the tyranny of Sulla had ejected it."

C18. The *ager Campanus* is currently occupied

ø   (*prec.* xxii:C13) xxiii. 84. Deinde in hac adsignatione agrorum ne illud quidem dici potest quod in ceteris, agros desertos a plebe atque a cultura hominum liberorum esse non oportere. Sic enim dico, si Campanus ager dividatur, exturbari et expelli plebem ex agris, non constitui et conlocari. Totus enim ager Campanus colitur et possidetur a plebe, et a plebe optima et modestissima; quod genus hominum optime moratum, optimorum et aratorum et militum, ab hoc plebicola tribuno plebis funditus eicitur. Atque illi miseri nati in illis agris et educati, glebis subigendis exercitati, quo se subito conferant non habebunt...[34] (*seq.* xxiv:C5)

C19. The communal possession of the *ager Campanus* is better than subdivision

ø   (*prec.* xvi:C17) xvii. 81. Quem agrum nunc praetereuntes vestrum esse dicitis et quem per iter qui faciunt, externi homines, vestrum esse audiunt, is, cum erit divisus, <neque erit vester> neque vester esse dicetur.[35] (*seq.* xviii:C5)

(*prec.* xxv:C9) xxvi. 85. Equidem existimo: si iam campus Martius dividatur et uni cuique vestrum ubi consistat bini pedes adsignentur, tamen promiscue toto quam proprie parva frui parte malitis. Qua re etiam si ad vos esset singulos aliquid ex hoc agro perventurum qui vobis ostenditur, aliis comparatur, tamen honestius eum vos universi quam singuli possideretis. Nunc vero cum ad vos nihil pertineat, sed paretur aliis, eripiatur vobis, nonne acerrime, tamquam armato hosti, sic huic legi pro vestris agris resistetis?[36] (*seq.* xxvii:C21)

---

34. "Furthermore, in the promised distribution of parcels the usual principle can't even be said to apply: that plots of land should not lie empty of the plebs and the cultivation of free men. Let me be clear on that point: if the *ager Campanus* is divided up, plebs will not be settled down and set up there—they'll be driven off and cast out. The whole *ager Campanus* is [already] cultivated and possessed by plebs—and by excellent and unassuming plebs. That is the sort of people, of excellent character, excellent farmers and soldiers both, that will be ripped up root and branch by this 'pleb-loving' tribune of the plebs. Those poor souls, born and raised in those fields, practiced in turning its clods, will have nowhere to go on such short notice..."

35. "Now as you pass by the territory you say it is yours; when foreign men travel through it they are told it is yours; but once it is divided up <it will no longer be yours> and no one will say it is yours." *Neque erit* is a supplement of the *editio Hervagiana*; Clark 1909 added *vester*.

36. "This is my opinion [on all of this]: if the Campus Martius were divided up and each of you was assigned two feet of space where he could stand, you'd still rather have joint use of the

C20. *Praeteritio*

(*prec.* xvi:C21) xvii. 21. Non queror deminutionem vectigalium, non flagitium huius iacturae atque damni, praetermitto illa quae nemo est quin gravissime et verissime conqueri possit...[37] (*seq.* xviii:C10)

(*prec.* xix:C17) xx. non dico...[38] (*seq.* xxi:C11)

(*prec.* xxv:C14) xxvi. 21. praetermitto omnem hanc orationem et contioni reservo;[39] (*seq.* xxvii:C23)

∅

C21. The *ager Stellas* is also slated for colonization

(*prec.* xv:C22). xvi. 20. Atque his colonis agrum Campanum et Stellatem campum dividi iubet.[40] (*seq.* xvii:C20)

(*prec.* xxvi:C19). xxvii. 85. Adiungit Stellatem campum agro Campano et in eo duodena discribit in singulos homines iugera. Quasi vero paulum differat ager Campanus a Stellati;[41] (*seq.* xxviii:C22)

---

whole area than your own small private piece. In the same way even if some piece of this field were going to come to some of you individually ([which it isn't, because] it's only being shown to you, but it's really being prepared for others)—still it would be more respectable for you to possess it collectively and not as individuals. And since nothing actually *is* coming to you, but something is being taken away from you to ready it for others, shouldn't you resist this law in fierce defense of your fields like it was an armed enemy?"

37. "I will not complain about the reduction of tax revenues, or about this disgraceful and destructive loss, I will pass over topics that everybody can complain about in all truth and with all seriousness [, namely]..."

38. "I do not say..."

39. "I am going to skip that part of the oration here and save it for the public assembly."

40. "And he orders the *ager Campanus* and *ager Stellas* to be divided up for these colonists."

41. "To the *ager Campanus* he joins the *ager Stellas* and divides it up into parcels, twelve acres to a man. What is this manufactured distinction between the *ager Campanus* and the *ager Stellas?*"

C22. The cities around Capua will be colonized

(*prec.* xiv:C24). xv. 20. nunc omnes urbes quae circum Capuam sunt a colonis per eosdem decemviros occupabuntur; hanc enim ob causam permittit ipsa lex, in omnia quae velint oppida colonos ut decemviri deducant quos velint.[42] (*seq.* xvi:C21)

[cf. 22. urbis circa Capuam (xxvii: C23)]

(*prec.* xxvii:C21) xxviii. 86. Sed multitudo, Quirites, quaeritur qua illa omnia oppida compleantur. Nam dixi antea lege permitti ut quae velint municipia, quas velint veteres colonias colonis suis occupent. Calenum municipium complebunt, Teanum oppriment, Atellam, Cumas, Neapolim, Pompeios, Nuceriam suis praesidiis devincient, Puteolos vero qui nunc in sua potestate sunt, suo iure libertateque utuntur, totos novo populo atque adventiciis copiis occupabunt.[43] (*seq.* xxix:C23)

C23. Capua will be the chief city of a rival empire

(*prec.* ii:C2). iii. 18. illam urbem huic urbi rursus opponere, illuc opes suas deferre et imperi nomen transferre cogitant.[44] (*seq.* iv:C32)

---

42. "[But] now all the cities that surround Capua will be occupied by colonists under the direction of the same decemvirs—that is exactly why the law itself allows the decemvirs to take colonists 'of their choice' into all the towns 'of their choice.'" The same idea is expressed in fragment 2 of the senate speech: *Capuam colonis deductis occupabunt, Atellam praesidio communient, Nuceriam, Cumas multitudine suorum obtinebunt, cetera oppida praesidiis devincient* "They'll lead out colonists and occupy Capua with them, they'll fortify Atella with a garrison, they'll hold Cumae with their horde, they'll bind up the rest of the towns with garrisons" (Aquila, *Rhet. Lat. Min.* 43 Halm). The fragment must come from a *propositio* where Cicero summarized the features of the bill (the equivalent feature in the popular speech comes at *LA* 2.98–99 just before the *peroratio* proper, cf. ch. 7.4 *init.*).

43. "The real point, fellow citizens, is that they are looking for a high number to fill up all those towns. I've already mentioned that the law permits them to occupy with their colonists the *municipia* of their choice and old colonies of their choice. They'll fill up the *municipium* of Calenum, they'll oppress Teanum, they'll use their outposts to hem in Atella, Cumae, Naples, Pompeii, and Nuceria—and Puteoli, which is now an independent municipality, with its own laws and civil government ('liberty'), they will completely occupy with a new people and forces from outside."

44. "Their plan is to set *that* city up against this one once again, to ferry their resources and carry the name of empire *there*."

(*prec.* xii:C32). xiii. 20. si praesidium, non praeponitur huic urbi ista colonia, sed opponitur.⁴⁵ (*seq.* xiv:C24)
(*prec.* xxvi:C20). xxvii. 22. de periculo salutis ac libertatis loquor. Quid enim existimatis integrum vobis in re publica fore aut in vestra libertate ac dignitate retinenda, cum Rullus atque ei quos multo magis quam Rullum timetis cum omni egentium atque improborum manu, cum omnibus copiis, cum omni argento et auro Capuam et ⌊urbes circa Capuam (C22)⌋ occuparint?⁴⁶ (*seq.* xxviii:C37)
[cf. 20. urbem ipsam imperio domicilium praebere posse (ix:C30)]

(*prec.* xxviii:C22) xxix. 86.Tunc illud vexillum Campanae coloniae vehementer huic imperio timendum Capuam a decemviris inferetur, tunc contra hanc Romam, communem patriam omnium nostrum, illa altera Roma quaeretur.⁴⁷ (*seq.* xxx:C24)
(*prec.* xxxi:C25) xxxii. 89. Videte quantum intervallum sit interiectum ⌊inter maiorum nostrorum consilia et inter istorum hominum dementiam (C30)⌋. Illi Capuam receptaculum aratorum, nundinas rusticorum, cellam atque horreum Campani agri esse voluerunt, hi expulsis aratoribus, effusis ac dissipatis fructibus vestris eandem Capuam sedem novae rei publicae constituunt, molem contra veterem rem publicam comparant. Quod si maiores nostri existimassent quemquam in tam inlustri imperio et tam praeclara populi Romani disciplina <M.> Bruti aut P. Rulli similem futurum —hos enim nos duos adhuc vidimus qui hanc rem publicam Capuam totam transferre vellent—profecto nomen illius urbis non reliquissent.⁴⁸ (*seq.* xxxiii:C26)

45. "If it's a [hostile] outpost [that is to be avoided in founding a colony], that colony is not being set up not to defend this city but to attack it."

46. "[Here] I will speak [only] about the danger to safety and liberty. What kind of real political options or ways to maintain your liberty and standing do you think you'll have open to you, once Rullus—and those whom you fear much more than Rullus—occupy Capua and the cities surrounding Capua with every available crew of the needy and unscrupulous, with every available resource, with all the available silver and gold?"

47. "Then the banner of a Campanian colony, which is something this government should genuinely fear, will be carried into Capua by the decemvirs; then a second Rome will be sought [to pit] against this Rome, the common fatherland of us all."

48. "Look at the yawning gap between the [careful] plans of our ancestors and the derangement of these men. Our elders wanted Capua to be a place of refuge for ploughmen, a market-town for peasants, a silo and granary for the *ager Campanus*. [But] these men, [by contrast,] driving out the ploughmen, squandering and scattering your profits ('fruits'), [want to] establish that very same Capua as the base for a new state, [and] to prepare a massive offensive line ('bulk') against [their] old state. If our elders had ever thought that such a glorious empire and such a distinguished culture as the Roman people's could produce people like <M.> Brutus and P. Rullus—the only two people we have ever seen who want to transfer the whole seat of this government to Capua—they would certainly not have even let the name of that city survive."

C24. Capua was historically a threat

(*prec.* xii:C23) xiv. 20. At quem ad modum armatur, di immortales! Nam bello Punico quicquid potuit Capua, potuit ipsa per sese...⁴⁹ (*seq.* xv:C22)

(*prec.* xxix:C23) xxx. 87. In id oppidum homines nefarii rem publicam vestram transferre conantur, quo in oppido maiores nostri nullam omnino rem publicam esse voluerunt, qui tris solum urbis in terris omnibus, Carthaginem, Corinthum, Capuam, statuerunt posse imperi gravitatem ac nomen sustinere.⁵⁰ (*seq.* xxxi:C25)

[77. locus atque urbs quae bellum facere atque instruere possit (iv:C5)]

C25. The elders destroyed the Capuan state

(*prec.* vi:C36). vii. 19. Maiores nostri Capua magistratus, senatum, consilium commune, omnia denique insignia rei publicae sustulerunt, neque aliud quicquam in urbe nisi inane nomen Capuae reliquerunt...⁵¹ (*seq.* viii:C29)

(*prec.* xxx:C24) xxxi. 87. Deleta Carthago est, quod cum hominum copiis, tum ipsa natura ac loco, succincta portibus, armata muris, excurrere ex Africa, imminere iam duabus fructuosissimis insulis populi Romani videbatur. Corinthi vestigium vix relictum est. Erat enim posita in angustiis atque in faucibus Graeciae sic ut terra claustra locorum teneret et duo maria maxime navigationi diversa paene coniungeret, cum pertenui discrimine separentur. Haec quae procul erant a conspectu imperi non solum adflixerunt sed etiam, ne quando recreata exsurgere atque erigere se possent, funditus, ut dixi, sustulerunt. 88. De Capua multum est et diu consultatum; exstant litterae, Quirites, publicae, sunt senatus consulta complura. ⌐Statuerunt homines sapientes (C30)¬, si agrum Campanis ademissent, magistratus, senatum, publicum ex illa urbe consilium sustulissent, imaginem rei publicae nullam reliquissent, nihil fore quod Capuam timeremus. Itaque hoc

---

49. "But, ye gods, the [re-]arming! In the Punic War Capua accomplished what it did on the strength of its own resources..."

50. "The design of these wicked men is to transfer [control of] your government to a town that our elders wanted to have no government of its own at all—who believed that in the whole world only three cities were important enough and strong enough to be imperial capitals: Carthage, Corinth, and Capua.

51. "Our ancestors stripped Capua of its magistrates, its senate, its common council—in short, all the marks of [independent] government, and they left the city nothing but the bare name of 'Capua.'"

perscriptum in monumentis veteribus reperietis, ut esset urbs quae res eas quibus ager Campanus coleretur suppeditare posset, ut esset locus comportandis condendisque fructibus, ut aratores cultu agrorum defessi urbis domiciliis uterentur, idcirco illa aedificia non esse deleta.[52] (*seq.* xxxii:C23)

C26. The elders didn't destroy Capua completely because it was close enough to watch

ø (*prec.* xxxii:C23) xxxiii. 90. Verum arbitrabantur Corinthi et Carthagini, etiam si senatum et magistratus sustulissent agrumque civibus ademissent, tamen non defore qui illa restituerent atque qui ante omnia commutarent quam nos audire possemus; hic vero in oculis senatus populique Romani nihil posse exsistere quod non ante exstingui atque opprimi posset quam plane exortum <esset> ac natum.[53] (*seq.* xxxiv:C27)

52. "Carthage was destroyed: its abundant population and even the nature of the place—girt with ports, armed with walls—made it seem like it was rushing out of Africa and ready to threaten the two most fertile islands of Roman people. Of Corinth scarcely a trace was left. Its position on a narrow causeway of Greek peninsula made it a kind of choke point on land but a near-link between very different seaways, at the point where two bodies of water almost meet. Those cities, far as they were from the view of [our] empire, they struck down—indeed, they reduced them to nothing, as I said, lest they ever regain their former strength and rise again. As for Capua, it was the subject of frequent and long debate; there are many public records on the issue, citizens, and very many senate decrees. And this is what our elders in their wisdom decided: that if they took away the Campanians' territory from them, if they stripped that city of its magistrates, senate, and public council, if they left no semblance of an [independent] government, there would be no reason for us to fear Capua. And so if you look at old records you will find the reason the buildings there were not razed was only so that there would be a city that could be a supply-point for what was needed to keep the *ager Campanus* under cultivation; that there could be a central location for gathering and storing its produce; and that ploughmen after a hard day of farm work could have homes in a city."

53. "But [they had a different opinion] about Corinth and Carthage: there, they thought, even if they got rid of the senate and the magistrates, and stripped the people of their territory, there would always be someone who would try to restore them and be able to completely upset the order of things before we could even get wind of it. Here [in Italy], by contrast, in full view of the senate and Roman people, no [trouble] could arise that could not be snuffed out and put down as soon as it was obvious it had come into existence."

C27. Capua has subsequently been a reliable ally to Rome

ø   (*prec.* xxxiii:C26) xxxiv. 90. ⌊Neque vero ea res fefellit homines divina mente et consilio praeditos (C30).⌋ Nam post Q. Fulvium Q. Fabium consules, quibus consulibus Capua devicta atque capta est, nihil est in illa urbe contra hanc rem publicam non dico factum, sed nihil omnino est cogitatum. Multa postea bella gesta cum regibus, Philippo, Antiocho, Persa, Pseudophilippo, Aristonico, Mithridate et ceteris; multa praeterea bella gravia, Carthaginiense iii, Corinthium, Numantinum; multae in hac re publica seditiones domesticae quas praetermitto; bella cum sociis, Fregellanum, Marsicum; quibus omnibus domesticis externisque bellis Capua non modo non obfuit sed opportunissimam se nobis praebuit et ad bellum instruendum et ad exercitus ornandos et tectis ac sedibus suis recipiendos.[54] (*seq.* xxxv:C28)

C28. A hobbled Capua has lost its political ambitions

ø   (*prec.* xxiv:C27) xxxv. 91. Homines non inerant in urbe qui malis contionibus, turbulentis senatus consultis, iniquis imperiis rem publicam miscerent et rerum novarum causam aliquam quaererent. Neque enim contionandi potestas erat cuiquam nec consili capiendi publici; non gloriae cupiditate efferebantur, propterea quod, ubi honos publice non est, ibi gloriae cupiditas esse non potest; non contentione, non ambitione discordes. Nihil enim supererat de quo certarent, nihil quod contra peterent, nihil ubi dissiderent. Itaque ⌊illam

---

54. "Those men, with their godlike ability to think and plan, were absolutely right. After the consulship of Q. Fulvius and Q. Fabius, which was the year when Capua was defeated and captured, nothing happened in that city that was against the interests of this government—indeed, nothing was even thought of. There were many wars against kings in subsequent years—Philip, Antiochus, Perses, Pseudophilip, Aristonicus, Mithridates, and others; there were many serious wars besides—the third Punic war, the Corinthian war, the Numantine war; there were many civil disturbances in this state which I won't go into here; there were wars against our allies, the Fregellani [and] the Marsi; and in all those wars, foreign and domestic, Capua was not only not a hindrance but showed herself to be extraordinarily useful to us for supplying the war effort, for equipping our armies, and for housing them in her houses and buildings."

Campanam adrogantiam atque intolerandam ferociam (C33)⌋ ⌊ratione et consilio (C30)⌋ maiores nostri ad inertissimum ac desidiosissimum otium perduxerunt.⁵⁵ (*seq.* xxxvi:C29)

C29. The elders' decision about Capua was not cruel

(*prec.* vii:C25). viii. 19.... non crudelitate—quid enim illis fuit clementius qui etiam externis hostibus victis sua saepissime reddiderunt?—⁵⁶ (*seq.* ix:C30)

(*prec.* xxxv:C28) xxxvi. 91. Sic et crudelitatis infamiam effugerunt quod urbem ex Italia pulcherrimam non sustulerunt...⁵⁷ (*seq.* xxxvii:C30)

C30. The elders' decision about Capua was wise

(*prec.* viii:C29). ix. 20.... sed consilio, quod videbant, si quod rei publicae vestigium illis moenibus contineretur, ⌊urbem ipsam imperio domicilium praebere posse (C23)⌋;⁵⁸ (*seq.* x:C34)

(*prec.* xxxvi:C29) xxxvii. 91.... et multum in posterum providerunt quod nervis urbis omnibus exsectis urbem ipsam solutam ac debilitatam reliquerunt.⁵⁹ (*seq.* xxxviii:C31)

(*prec.* xxxviii:C31) xxxix. 95. Haec qui prospexerunt, maiores nostros dico, Quirites, non eos in deorum immortalium numero venerandos a nobis et colendos putatis? Quid enim viderunt? Hoc quod nunc vos, quaeso, perspicite atque cognoscite.⁶⁰ (*seq.* xl:C32)

---

55. "There wasn't anybody left in the city to roil the government with troublesome assemblies, disruptive senate decrees, unfair commands, looking for some pretext for revolution. That was because nobody had the right to call an assembly or propose policy; nobody was swept away by the desire for glory, for the simple reason that when there are no public offices, there can't be any desire for glory; there was no discord because of competition or ambition. [Why would there have been?] There was nothing left to fight over, no alternative to work for, no point to disagree on. And that is how our elders by their thoughtful plan reduced the fabled arrogance and insufferable fierceness of the Campania to a torpid and lazy repose."

56. "... not out of cruelty—has there ever been anyone on earth more merciful than they were, who very often returned property even to foreign foes they had defeated?"

57. "That is how they escaped a reputation for cruelty that destroying one of the most beautiful cities in Italy might have given them ..."

58. "... but by design, because they saw that, if a vestige of [independent] government remained within those walls, the city could offer a foundation for imperial aspirations (lit. 'dwelling place for empire')."

59. "... and [also] planned excellently for the future in cutting every sinew of that city and leaving it slack and weakened."

60. "And the men who foresaw all this—I mean our ancestors, fellow citizens—don't you think we should revere and honor them in the ranks of the immortal gods? For what did they see? The same thing that I would ask you to see and understand now."

[cf. 87. statuerunt homines sapientes (xxxi:C24)]

[cf. 90. inter maiorum nostrorum consilia et inter istorum hominum dementiam (xxxii:C23)].

[cf. 90. Neque vero ea res fefellit homines divina mente et consilio praeditos (xxxiv:C27)]

[cf. 91 ratione et consilio (xxxv:C28)]

C31. The arrogant colony of Brutus (90 BCE) illustrates the dangers of a resurgent Capua

ø (*prec.* xxxvii:C30) xxxviii. 92. Haec consilia maiorum M. Bruto, ut antea dixi, reprehendenda {et P. Rullo} visa sunt; neque te, P. Rulle, omina illa M. Bruti atque auspicia a simili furore deterrent. Nam et ipse qui deduxit, et qui magistratum Capuae illo creante ceperunt, et qui aliquam partem illius deductionis, honoris, muneris attigerunt, omnis acerbissimas impiorum poenas pertulerunt. Et quoniam <M.> Bruti atque illius temporis feci mentionem, commemorabo id quod egomet vidi, cum venissem Capuam colonia m<odo> deducta{m} L. Considio et Sex. Saltio, quem ad modum ipsi loquebantur, 'praetoribus,' ⌊ut intellegatis quantam locus ipse adferat superbiam (C32)⌋, quae paucis diebus quibus illo colonia deducta est perspici atque intellegi potuit. 93. Nam primum, id quod dixi, cum ceteris in coloniis duumviri appellentur, hi se praetores appellari volebant. Quibus primus annus hanc cupiditatem attulisset, nonne arbitramini paucis annis fuisse consulum nomen appetituros? Deinde anteibant lictores non cum bacillis, sed, ut hic praetoribus urbanis anteeunt, cum fascibus bini. Erant hostiae maiores in foro constitutae, quae ab his praetoribus de tribunali, sicut a nobis consulibus, de consili sententia probatae ad praeconem et ad tibicinem immolabantur. Deinde 'patres conscripti' vocabantur. Iam vero voltum Considi videre ferendum vix erat. Quem hominem 'vegrandi macie torridum' Romae contemptum, abiectum videbamus, hunc Capuae Campano fastidio ac regio spiritu cum videremus, Blossios mihi videbar illos videre ac Vibellios. 94. Iam vero qui metus erat tunicatorum illorum! et in Albana et Seplasia quae concursatio percontantium quid praetor edixisset, ubi cenaret, quo

Capua and the ager Campanus

C32. The rich environs of Capua induce arrogance

(*prec.* iii:C23). iv. 18. Qui locus propter Lubertatem agrorum (C15)⌋ abundantiamque rerum omnium superbiam et crudelitatem genuisse dicitur...[62] (*seq.* v:C5)

(*prec.* xi:C32). xii. 20. si superbia, nata inibi esse haec ex Campanorum fastidio videtur.[63] (*seq.* xiii: C23)

denuntiasset! Nos autem, hinc Roma qui veneramus, iam non hospites, sed peregrini atque advenae nominabamur.[61] (*seq.* xxxix:C30)

(*prec.* xxxix *in* 31). xl. 95. Non ingenerantur hominibus mores tam a stirpe generis ac seminis quam ex eis rebus quae ab ipsa natura nobis ad vitae consuetudinem suppeditantur, quibus alimur et vivimus. Carthaginienses fraudulenti et mendaces non genere, sed natura loci, quod propter portus suos multis et variis mercatorum et advenarum sermonibus ad studium fallendi studio quaestus vocabantur. Ligures duri atque agrestes; docuit ager ipse nihil ferendo nisi multa cultura et magno labore quaesitum. Campani semper superbi ⌊bonitate agrorum et fructuum magnitudine (C15)⌋, ⌊urbis salubritate,

---

61. "[But] these plans of [our] ancestors seemed worthless to M. Brutus, as I've said—{and to P. Rullus}. The ill omens and signs that M. Brutus provided have not deterred you from a similar madness, P. Rullus. The man who led out the colony; the men who were elected magistrates at Capua under his superintendence; the men who played any role at all, whether in the colonizing, in holding public office, or performing some other function—they all paid the bitterest penalties, as the unpatriotic do. But since I've mentioned <M.> Brutus and the events of those days, let me recall what I myself saw when I went to Capua just after the colony was founded, at the time when L. Considius and Sex. Saltius were 'praetors' (their word for it). [My recollections] will show you the kind of arrogance that that place inspires, which started to show up clearly and distinctly within only a few days after the foundation of the colony. First of all, as I've just said, they wanted themselves to be called 'praetors'; in other colonies the same office is called 'duumvir.' If that's the kind of ambition that appeared in just the first year, don't you think a few years after that they would have aspired to the name of 'consuls'? Furthermore, they were preceded not by lictors with staffs but by pairs of lictors with *fasces*, just like the urban praetors here. In the forum full-grown sacrificial animals had been readied; when they were approved from the tribunal by these 'praetors,' just as we consuls do, on the advice of an advisory council, they were sacrificed to the voice of the herald and the sound of the trumpeter. Then 'the conscript fathers' were summoned. And by that point the look on Considius's face—it was practically intolerable. When we saw him in Capua full of Campanian haughtiness and kingly pride—the reviled and rejected man that we used to see around Rome 'shrivel'd to thinness unmassive,' I thought that I was looking at the infamous Blossius or Vibellius. How awed the poor ('tunic-clad') people were of them! And what a crowd there was in Albana and Seplasia, asking what the praetor had decreed, where he was having dinner, where he had sent summons! And those of who had come from Rome here weren't called 'guests' but 'foreigners' and 'aliens.'"

62. "The place whose rich fields and universal abundance are said to have spawned haughtiness and cruelty..."

63. "If it's haughtiness [*sc.* that should be avoided in founding colonies], that's the very thing that seems to have sprung up in that very place from the excess pride of the Campanians."

descriptione, pulchritudine⌐ (C35). Ex hac copia atque omnium rerum adfluentia primum illa nata est adrogantia quae a maioribus nostris alterum Capua consulem postulavit...[64] *(seq. xli:C33)*

[cf. 91. illam Campanam adrogantiam atque intolerandam ferociam (xxxiv:C28)]

[cf. 92 ut intellegatis quantam locus ipse adferat superbiam (xxxviii:C31)]

C33. The luxury of Capua corrupted even Hannibal

(prec. x:C34) xi. 20. Quid enim cavendum est in coloniis deducendis? Si luxuries, Hannibalem ipsum Capua corrupit...[65] *(seq. xii:C32)*

(prec. xl:C32) xli. 95. deinde ea luxuries quae ipsum Hannibalem armis etiam tunc invictum voluptate vicit.[66] *(seq. xlii:C34)*

C34. A recolonized Capua would be dangerous

(prec. ix:C30). x. 19. vos haec, nisi evertere rem publicam cuperetis ac vobis novam dominationem comparare, credo, quam perniciosa essent non videretis.[67] *(seq. xi:C33).*

(prec. xli:C33) xlii. 96. Huc ⌐isti decemviri cum I∞ colonorum (C4)⌐ ex lege Rulli deduxerint, c decuriones, x augures, vi pontifices constituerint, quos illorum animos, quos impetus, quam ferociam fore putatis?[68] *(seq. xliii:C35)*

---

64. "People's characters are not so much bred into them from their family's seed and stock as from the way of life that nature herself supplies to us, which we take in and live by. The Carthaginians are cheats and liars not because of their race but because of the nature of the place: they were drawn by love of gain to the art of deception on account of the many different interactions they had with merchants and foreigners who came through their ports. If Ligurians are tough rustics, their land taught them to be: it gives nothing that has not been won by hard work and constant tilling. And the Campanians have always been haughty thanks to the richness of their fields and the abundance of the crops and their city with its beauty, fine climate, and [excellent] layout. From that vast richness and abundance was first born the arrogance that demanded from our elders that every other consul be from Capua."

65. "After all, what should be avoided in founding colonies? If it's excess, Capua corrupted Hannibal himself..."

66. "Furthermore that excess conquered Hannibal himself, who up to then had been unconquered by pleasure."

67. (*to Rullus et al.*) "And I'm sure that you wouldn't be able to see how dangerous all of this is, if you did not want to overthrow the government and establish a new tyranny for yourselves." (Rendered less literally in ch. 9.2).

68. "When that's the place where these decemvirs will take their 500 colonists under the law of Rullus and set up a hundred decurions and ten augurs and six priests, how confident do you think they'll be? how ready for violence? how fierce?"

C35. Rome and its environs are comparatively inferior

(*prec.* **xlii:C34**) **xliii. 96.** Romam in montibus positam et convallibus, cenaculis sublatam atque suspensam, non optimis viis, angustissimis semitis, prae sua Capua planissimo in loco explicata ac praeclarissime sita inridebunt atque contemnent; agros vero Vaticanum et Pupiniam cum suis optimis atque uberibus campis conferendos scilicet non putabunt. Oppidorum autem finitimorum illam copiam cum hac per risum ac iocum contendent; Veios, Fidenas, Collatiam, ipsum hercle Lanuvium, Ariciam, Tusculum cum Calibus, Teano, Neapoli, Puteolis, Cumis, Pompeiis, Nuceria comparabunt.[69]
(*seq.* **xliv:C36**)

[cf. 95 urbis salubritate, descriptione, pulchritudine, xl:C35]

C36. Sudden wealth causes insolence

(*prec.* **v:C5**) **vi. 18.** et, credo, qua in urbe homines in vetere dignitate fortunaque nati copiam rerum moderate ferre non potuerunt, in ea isti vestri satellites modeste insolentiam suam continebunt.[70] (*seq.* **vii:C25**)

(*prec.* **xliii:C35**) **xliv. 97.** Quibus illi rebus elati et inflati fortasse non continuo, sed certe, si paulum adsumpserint vetustatis ac roboris, non continebuntur; progredientur, cuncta secum ferent. Singularis homo privatus, nisi magna sapientia praeditus, vix cancellis et regionibus offici magnis in fortunis et copiis continetur, nedum isti ab Rullo et Rulli similibus conquisiti atque electi coloni Capuae in domicilio superbiae atque in sedibus luxuriosis conlocati non statim conquisituri sint aliquid sceleris et flagiti, immo vero etiam hoc magis quam illi veteres germanique Campani, quod in vetere fortuna illos natos et educatos nimiae tamen rerum omnium copiae depravabant, hi ex summa egestate in eandem

---

69. "In comparison with their Capua, laid out on an expansive plain and splendidly situated, they will jeer at Rome and denounce it, set as it is on hills and valleys, built up and piled high with upper stories, with not very good roads, very narrow streets. The Vatican or Pupinian districts they will think of no account compared to their own fine and fertile fields. Contrasting their rich supply of neighboring towns with ours they will laugh aloud: they'll be comparing Veii, Fidenae, and Collatia—or even Lanuvium, Aricia and Tusculum!—with Cales, Teanum, Naples, Puteoli, Cumae, Pompeii, and Nuceria!" *Praeclarissima sita* is Baiter's conjecture; Manuwald 2018: 96 *ad loc.* prints †*prae illis semitis*†.

70. "And I'm sure your minions will do a fine job keeping their insolence in check in the same city whose affluence in the days of its wealth and glory bested the self-discipline of its own natives."

(*prec.* xxvii:C23). xxviii.
22. his ego rebus, patres conscripti, resistam vehementer atque acriter neque patiar homines ea me consule expromere quae contra rem publicam iam diu cogitarint.[72] (*fin.*)

rerum abundantiam traducti non solum copia verum etiam insolentia commovebuntur.[71] (*seq.* xlv:C37)

C37. Segue to *peroratio*

(*prec.* xliv:C36) 98. Haec tu, P. Rulle, M. Bruti sceleris vestigia quam monumenta maiorum sapientiae sequi maluisti, haec tu cum istis tuis auctoribus excogitasti, ut ... *etc.*[73] (*fin.*)

---

71. "Haughty and puffed up as a result, there will be no containing them—perhaps not immediately, but definitely, once they've been there long enough to gain some strength. They will come forth, carrying everything before themselves. In the midst of great fortune and riches, one single private citizen cannot, unless endowed with great wisdom, keep himself within the boundaries and borders of duty—so how is it possible that colonists sought out and picked by Rullus and the likes of Rullus will not immediately seek out some criminal outrage when they are settled in the domicile of haughtiness and in luxuriant abodes? And they'll be even likelier to do so than the ancient native Campanians. Even though they were born in long-standing good fortune, still an excess of everything warped them. But [the decemvirs], brought over to that kind of abundance from the depths of poverty, will be affected not only by the wealth but also by its unfamiliarity!"

72. "These are the designs, conscript fathers, that I intend to oppose, fiercely and energetically, and so long as I am consul, I will not allow [these] people to put into action their long-standing designs against the commonwealth."

73. "It was this path of crime traced by M. Brutus that you chose to follow, P. Rullus, rather than [look to] the monuments of wisdom established by our elders. Here are the designs that you and your fellow instigators have thought up...." (A summary of the bill follows, the beginning of the *peroratio*; cf. ch. 7.4 *init.*).

APPENDIX 3

The Rhetorical Structure of the Treatment of the Placement of Colonies

in senatu	*ad populum*
J1. Proposal	
(i.) 16. Quid tum? quae erit in istos agros deductio, quae totius rei ratio atque descriptio? 'Deducentur,' inquit, 'coloniae.'	(i.) 73. Atque in hos agros qui hac lege empti sint colonias ab his decemviris deduci iubet.
"And then what? How will the transfer into those territories work, what are the principles and details of the master plan? 'Colonies will be led out,' he says."	"He orders colonies to be led by these decemvirs in to those territories that have been purchased under this law."
J2. Need to consider placement of colonies	
[cf. J3 *in quae loca* etc.]	(ii.) Quid? omnisne locus eius modi est ut nihil intersit rei publicae, colonia deducatur in eum locum necne, an est locus qui coloniam postulet, est \<qui\> plane recuset? Quo in genere sicut in ceteris rei publicae partibus est operae pretium diligentiam maiorum recordari, qui colonias sic idoneis in locis contra suspicionem periculi conlocarunt ut esse non oppida Italiae, sed propugnacula imperi viderentur. Hi deducent colonias in eos agros quos emerint; etiamne si rei publicae non expediat?

in senatu	*ad populum*
	"How's that? Is every place equally suitable for the establishment of a colony from the point of view of public policy, or are there some places that demand colonies and others that plainly do not? In this kind of thing—as in all other areas public policy—it is well to remember the carefulness of our ancestors, who established colonies as a guard against possible danger in such well-chosen places that they seemed to be, not towns of Italy, but the ramparts of empire. So these men are to lead colonies out to the fields they've purchased—even if it's not advantageous to the state?"

J3. Absence of details of colonies

(ii.) Quo\<t\>? quorum hominum? in quae loca? Quis enim non videt in coloniis esse haec omnia consideranda? "How many? With which men? Into what places? Everyone knows that these are all important issues with colonies!"	(v.) Tu non definias quo\<t\> colonias, in quae loca, quo numero colonorum deduci velis . . . "How dare you not define how many colonies you intend to establish and into what places and with what number of colonists!"

J4. Surrender of Italy to Rullus to garrison

(iii.) Tibi nos, Rulle, et istis tuis harum omnium rerum machinatoribus totam Italiam inermem tradituros existimasti, quam praesidiis confirmaretis, coloniis occuparetis, omnibus vinclis devinctam et constrictam teneretis? "Did you really think, Rullus, that we would hand over to you, and to your fellow plotters in this whole scheme, all of Italy, unarmed, so you could secure it with garrisons, occupy it with colonies, hold it bound fast with every kind of chain?"	(vi.) . . . tu occupes locum quem idoneum ad vim tuam iudicaris, compleas numero, confirmes praesidio quo velis, populi Romani vectigalibus atque omnibus copiis ipsum populum Romanum coerceas, opprimas, redigas in istam decemviralem dicionem ac potestatem? "Is your idea to occupy a place you deem suitable for your violence, fill it with a complement, secure it with a garrison of your choosing, and then, using the tax properties and all the resources of the Roman people, bind, repress, and reduce the Roman people into the decemvirs' power and control?"

in senatu	*ad populum*

J5. Failure of law to preclude colony on Janiculum

(iv.) Vbi enim cavetur ne in Ianiculo coloniam constituatis, ne urbem hanc urbe alia premere atque urgere possitis?

"After all, where is the provision to prevent you from founding a colony right on the Janiculum—from pressing down on and in upon this city with another city?"

(iv.) Quid igitur est causae quin coloniam in Ianiculum possint deducere et suum praesidium in capite atque cervicibus nostris conlocare?

"Is there then any reason why they could not lead a colony out onto the Janiculum and establish their garrison on our heads and necks?"

J6. Intention of Decemvirs not to build on Janiculum

(v.) 'Non faciemus,' inquit. Primum nescio, deinde timeo, postremo non committam ut vestro beneficio potius quam nostro consilio salvi esse possimus.

" 'We wouldn't do that,' he says. First, I'm not so sure; and for another, I'm worried you might; and above all, I don't intend to let you put us in a position where our safety depends on your good will as opposed to our own deliberation!"

ø

J7. Certainty of intention to garrison Italy

(vi.) 17. Quod vero totam Italiam vestris coloni{i}s complere voluistis, id cuius modi esset neminemne nostrum intellecturum existimavistis?

"As to your desire to fill the whole of Italy with your colonies, did you think none of us would realize what was going on?"

(vii.) 75. Vt vero totam Italiam suis praesidiis obsidere atque occupare cogitet, quaeso, Quirites, cognoscite. Permittit decemviris ut in omnia municipia, in omnis colonias totius Italiae colonos deducant quos velint, eisque colonis agros dari iubet.

"And he really does plan to besiege and occupy all of Italy with his garrisons, citizens—pay heed to how, I ask you. He allows the decemvirs to lead into towns and colonies anywhere in Italy colonists of their choosing and he orders lands to be given to those colonists."

in senatu	*ad populum*

J8. Citation/Paraphrase of of Law

(vii.) Scriptum est enim: 'Quae in municipia quasque in colonias decemviri velint, deducant colonos quos velint et eis agros adsignent quibus in locis velint,' ...	(iii.) 74. 'Et in quae loca praeterea videbitur.'
"It's clear from the text: 'The decemvirs shall lead colonists of their choice into *municipia* and colonies of their choice and assign to them properties in locations of their choice'..."	[The law reads,] "'And to whatever other places seems suitable.'"

J9. Impossibility of recovering liberty in a garrisoned Italy

(viii.) ... ut, cum totam Italiam militibus suis occuparint, nobis non modo dignitatis retinendae, verum ne libertatis quidem recuperandae spes relinquatur. (1.16–17)	(viii.) Num obscure maiores opes quam libertas vestra pati potest, et maiora praesidia quaeruntur, num obscure regnum constituitur, num obscure libertas vestra tollitur? Nam cum idem omnem pecuniam, maximam multitudinem <***>, idem totam Italiam suis opibus obsidebunt, idem vestram libertatem suis praesidiis et coloniis interclusam tenebunt, quae spes tandem, quae facultas recuperandae vestrae libertatis relinquetur? (2.73–75)
"... which means that, once they've filled Italy full of their soldiers, not only will we have no hope remain of maintaining status—we will have no hope of recovering liberty."	"Is this not plainly an attempt to gain greater resources than your liberty can endure, and greater garrisons? Is this not plainly an attempt to establish a kingdom? Is this not plainly the ruin of your liberty? When the same people <will have control *vel sim.*> of every [source of] money and of a great multitude and will have your liberty hemmed in by their garrisons and colonies, what hope—what possibility— of recovering your liberty will remain?"

Works Cited

Achard, Guy. 1981. *Pratique rhétorique et idéologie politique dans les discours 'optimates' de Cicéron*. Leiden.
Adams, J.N. 1978. "Conventions of Naming in Cicero." *The Classical Quarterly, New Series*, 28.1: 145–166.
Afzelius, A. l940. "Das Ackerverteilungsgesetz des P. Servilius Rullus." *Classica et Medievalia* 3: 214–235.
Agnes, Leopoldo. 1943. "Intorno alla 'Rogatio Servilia.'" *Rivista di filologia e di istruzione classica*, 43: 35–45.
Albrecht, Michael von. 2003. *Cicero's Style. A Synopsis*. Mnemosyne Supplement 245. Leiden/Boston.
Alexander, M. C. 1990. *Trials in the Late Roman Republic, 149 BC to 50 BC*. Toronto.
Anderson, Warren. 1994. *Music and Musicians in Ancient Greece*. Ithaca, New York.
Ando, Clifford. 2011. *Law, Language, and Empire in the Roman Tradition*. Philadelphia.
André, J.M. 1966. *L'otium dans la vie morale et intellectuelle romaine des origines à l'époque augustéenne*. Paris.
Annas, Julia. 2008. "The Sage in Ancient Philosophy," in Alesse, Francesca et al. (eds.), *Anthrophine Sophia: studi di filologia e storiografia filosofica in memoria di Gabriele Giannantoni*, Naples: 11–27.
Arena, V. 2012. *Libertas and the Practice of Politics in the Late Roman Republic*. Cambridge, UK.
Atkins, E.M. 1990. "'Domina et Regina Virtutum': Justice and Societas in De Officiis." *Phoenix* 35.3: 258–289.
Audibert, Adrien. 1904. "Nouvelle étude sur la formule des actions *familiæ erciscundæ et communi dividundo*." *Nouvelle revue historique de droit français et étranger* 28: 649–697.
Axer, Jerzy. 1980. "The Style and Composition of Cicero's Speech *Pro Roscio Comoedo*, Origin and Function" (= *Studia Antiqua*, 3). Warsaw.
Aymard, André. 1947. "Les capitalistes romains et la viticulture italienne." *Annales: Histoire, Sciences Sociales* 2.3: 257–265.
Badian, Ernst. 1959. "The Early Career of A. Gabinius (cos. 58 B.C.)." *Philologus* 103: 87–99.

Badian, Ernst. 1962. Review of Taylor 1960. *The Journal of Roman Studies* 52: 200–210.
Badian, Ernst. 1965. "M. Porcius Cato and the Annexation and Early Administration of Cyprus." *The Journal of Roman Studies* 55: 110–121.
Badian, Ernst. 1967. "The Testament of Ptolemy Alexander." *Rheinisches Museum für Philologie* 110: 178–192.
Badian, Ernst. 1968. *Roman Imperialism in the Late Republic*. Ithaca, New York.
Badian, Ernst. 1984. *Foreign Clientelae*. Oxford.
Badian, Ernst. 1990. "The Consuls, 179–49 BC." *Chiron* 20: 371–413.
Baldson, J.P.V.D. 1939. "Consular Provinces under the Late Republic, I. General Considerations." *The Journal of Roman Studies* 29.1: 57–73.
Baldson, J.P.V.D. 1962. "Roman History, 65–50 B.C.: Five Problems." *The Journal of Roman Studies* 52: 134–141.
Baldson, J.P.V.D. 1963. "The *Commentariolum Petitionis*." *The Classical Quarterly* 13.2: 242–250.
Barlow, C.T. 1980. "The Roman Government and the Roman Economy, 92–80 B.C." *American Journal of Philology* 101: 202–219.
Bauman, R.A. 1979. "The Gracchan Agrarian Commission: Four Questions." *Historia: Zeitschrift für Alte Geschichte* 28.4: 385–408.
Beard, Mary. 2007. *The Roman Triumph*. Cambridge MA/London.
Belis, Annie. 1986. "L' aulos phrygien." *Revue Archéologique* 1 n.s.: 21–40.
Bell, A.J.E. 1997. "Cicero and the Spectacle of Power." *The Journal of Roman Studies* 87: 1–22.
Berger, Adolf. 1953. *Encyclopedic Dictionary of Roman Law*. Philadelphia.
Bicknell, P. 1969. "Marius, the Metelli, and the *lex Maria Tabellaria*." *Latomus* 28.2: 327–348.
Blänsdorf, J. 2002. "Cicero erklärt dem Volk die Agrarpolitik (*De leg agr*. II)," in Defosse, P. (ed.), *Hommages à Carl Deroux. II—Prose et linguistique, Médecine* (Collection Latomus 267), Brussels: 40–56.
Blom, Henriette van der. 2010. *Cicero's Role Models: the Political Strategy of a Newcomer*. Oxford.
Boak, A.E.R. 1918. "The Extraordinary Commands from 80 to 48 B. C.: A Study in the Origins of the Principate." *The American Historical Review* 24.1: 1–25.
Bona, F. 1959. "Preda di guerrae occupazione privata di 'res hostium'." *Studia et Documenta Historiae et Iuris* 25: 309–370.
Bona, F. 1960. "Sul concetto di 'Manubiae' e sulla responsabilità del magistrato in ordine alla preda," *Studia et Documenta Historiae et Iuris* 26: 105–175.
Boren, H. C. 1961. "Tiberius Gracchus: The Opposition View." *American Journal of Philology* 82.4: 368–369.
Brennan, T.C. 2000. *The Praetorship in the Roman Republic*, 2 vol. Oxford.
Broughton, T.R.S. 1934. "Roman Landholding in Asia Minor." *Transactions and Proceedings of the American Philological Association* 65: 207–239.

Broughton, T.R.S. 1952. *Magistrates of the Roman Republic, Vol. 2: 99 BC–39 BC.* New York.

Broughton, T.R.S. 1986. *Magistrates of the Roman Republic, Vol. 3: Supplement.* New York.

Brouwer, René. 2014. *The Stoic Sage: The Early Stoics on Wisdom, Sagehood and Socrates.* Cambridge, UK.

Brunt, P.A. 1971. *Italian Manpower 225 B.C.–A.D. 14.* Oxford.

Brunt, P.A. 1974. *Social Conflicts in the Roman Republic.* London.

Brunt, P.A. 1982. "*Nobilitas* and *Novitas*." *The Journal of Roman Studies* 72: 1–17.

Brunt, P.A. 1988. *The Fall of Roman Republic and Related Essays.* Oxford.

Buchheit, V. 1975. "Ciceros Kritik an Sulla in der Rede für Roscius aus Ameria." *Historia* 24: 570–591.

Burckhardt, Leonhard A. 1990. "The Political Elite of the Roman Republic: Comments on Recent Discussion of the Concepts 'Nobilitas' and 'Homo Novus'." *Historia: Zeitschrift für Alte Geschichte* 39.1: 77–99.

Butler, Shane. 2002. *The Hand of Cicero.* New York/London.

Calboli, G. (ed.) 1969. *Cornifici: Rhetorica ad Herennium. Introduzione, testo critico e commento.* Bologna.

Canter, H.V. 1936. "Irony in the Orations of Cicero." *The American Journal of Philology* 57.4: 457–464.

Caplan, Harry. 1954. Cicero, *Rhetorica Ad Herennium*, with translation. Loeb Classical Library. Cambridge.

Carcopino, J. 2013 [1935]. *Jules César.* Édition revue et augmentée avec la collaboration de P. Grimal. Préface de J.-L. Brunaux. Paris.

Carrasco García, Consuelo. 2017. "Vicios y virtudes de la amistad. Metáforas jurídicas en Horacio (*epist.* 2.2/ *sat.* 1.3). *Revue historique de droit français et étranger* 95.2: 161–188.

Churchill, J.B. 1999. "*Ex qua quod vellent facerent*: Roman Magistrates' Authority over *Praeda* and *Manubiae*." *Transactions of the American Philological Association* 129: 85–116.

Ciaceri, E. 1939 [1926]. *Cicerone e i suoi tempi.* Vol I. *Dalla nascita al consolato (a. 106–63 a. C.),* 2nd ed. Milano/Genova/Roma/Napoli.

Clark, A.C. 1909. *M. Tulli Ciceronis orationes*, vol. IV. Oxford.

Classen, C.J. 1965. "Die Königszeit im Spiegel der Literatur der römischen Republik (Ein Beitrag zum Selbstverständnis der Römer)." *Historia: Zeitschrift für Alte Geschichte* 14: 385–403.

Classen, C.J. 1985. *Recht—Rhetorik—Politik. Untersuchungen zu Ciceros rhetorischer Strategie.* Darmstadt.

Coarelli, Filippo. 1983. *Il Foro Romano*, vol. 1. Rome.

Coarelli, Filippo. 1997. *Il Campo Marzio: Dalle origini alla fine della Repubblica.* Rome.

Comber, Michael, and Cataline Balmaceda. 2009. *Sallust: the War against Jugurtha.* Oxford.

Cooper, F.T. 1895. *Word Formation in the Roman* Sermo Plebeius. Boston/London.

Coudry, M. 2009a. "Partage et gestion du butin dans la Rome républicaine: procédures et enjeux," in Coudry, Marianne and Michael Humm (eds.), Praeda: *Butin de guerre et société dans la Rome républicaine/Kriegsbeute und Gesellschaft im republikanischen Rom*, Stuttgart: 21–79.

Coudry, M. 2009b. "Les origines républicaines de l'or coronaire," in Coudry, Marianne and Michael Humm (eds.), Praeda: *Butin de guerre et société dans la Rome républicaine/Kriegsbeute und Gesellschaft im republikanischen Rom*, Stuttgart: 153–185.

Craig, Christopher P. 1993. *Form as Argument in Cicero's Speeches: A Study of Dilemma*. American Classical Studies 37. Atlanta, GA.

Crawford, J.W. 1994. *M. Tullius Cicero: The Fragmentary Speeches. An Edition with Commentary*, 2nd ed. American Classical Studies 37. Atlanta, GA.

Crawford, M.H. 1974. *Roman Republican Coinage*. Cambridge, UK.

Crook, J.A. 1967. *Law and Life in Rome*. London.

Crook, J.A, A.W. Lintott, and E. Rawson, eds. 1994. The Cambridge Ancient History, 2nd ed., vol. 9. Cambridge, UK.

D'Amore, L. 1967. *M. Tullio Cicerone. De lege agraria oratio secunda. Introduzione e Commento*. Milano.

Davies, Penelope J.E. 2017. *Architecture and Politics in Republican Rome*. Cambridge, UK.

De Ligt, L. 2001. "Studies in Legal and Agrarian History IV: Roman Africa in 111 B.C." *Mnemosyne* ser. 4, 54.2: 182–217.

Deniaux, E. 1993. *Clientèles et pouvoir à l'époque de Cicéron*. Rome.

Devine, A.M., and Stephens, Laurence D. 2006. *Latin Word Order: Structured Meaning and Information*. Oxford.

Dighton, Aerynn. 2017. "Clothing and Political Protest in the Late Roman Republic." *Phoenix* 71, no. 3/4: 345–369.

Dowling, Melissa Barden. 2000. "The Clemency of Sulla." *Historia: Zeitschrift für Alte Geschichte* 49.3: 303–340.

Drogula, F.K. 2007. "*Imperium, Potestas*, and the *Pomerium* in the Roman Republic." *Historia: Zeitschrift für Alte Geschichte* 56:4: 419–452.

Drogula, F.K. 2011. "The *Lex Porcia* and the Development of Legal Restraints on Roman Governors." *Chiron* 41: 91–124.

Drummond, A. 1989. *Cambridge Ancient History* VII/2, 2nd edn. Cambridge, UK.

Drummond, A. 1999. "Tribunes and Tribunician Programmes in 63 B.C." *Athenaeum* 87: 121–67.

Drummond, A. 2000. "Rullus and the Sullan *possessores*." *Klio* 82: 126–53.

Dunkle, J. Roger. 1967. "The Greek Tyrant and Roman Political Invective of the Late Republic." *Transactions and Proceedings of the American Philological Association*, 98: 151–171.

Dunkle, J.R. 1971. "The Rhetorical Tyrant in Roman Historiography: Sallust, Livy and Tacitus." *The Classical World* 65.1: 12–20.

Dyck, Andrew R. 1997. *A Commentary on Cicero*, De Officiis. Ann Arbor.

Dyck, Andrew R. 2004. *A Commentary on Cicero, De Legibus*. Ann Arbor.
Earl, D.C. 1961. *The political thought of Sallust*. Cambridge, UK.
Earl, D.C. 1967. *The Moral and Political Tradition of Rome*. Ithaca, New York.
Ehrenberg, Victor. 1953. "*Imperium Maius* in the Roman Republic." *The American Journal of Philology*, 74.2: 113–136.
Ellis, Robinson. 1876. *A Commentary on Catullus*. Oxford.
Elmore, Jefferson. 1913. "The Greek *Cautio* in Cicero, *Fam*. VII, 18, I." *Transactions and Proceedings of the American Philological Association* 44: 127–131.
Ernout, Alfred, and Antoine Meillet. 2001 [1959]. *Dictionnaire étymologique de la langue latine: histoire des mots*. Retirage de la 4e éd. augmentée d'additions et de corrections. Paris.
Erskine, Andrew. 1991. "Hellenistic Monarchy and Roman Political Invective." *The Classical Quarterly* 41.1: 106–113.
Fairclough, Norman. 1992. *Discourse and Social Change*. Cambridge.
Fairclough, Norman. 1995. *Critical Discourse Analysis*. Boston.
Fairclough, Norman. 2010. *Critical Discourse Analysis Language*, 2nd ed. New York.
Faraone, C. A. 1991. "The Agonistic Context of Early Greek Binding Spells," in Faraone, C.A. and D. Obbink (eds.), *Magika Hiera: Ancient Greek Magic and Religion*, Oxford and New York: 3–32.
Ferrary, J.-L. 1977. "Recherches sur la legislation de Saturninus et de Glaucia." *Mélanges de l'École française de Rome* 89.2: 619–660.
Ferrary, J.-L. 1982. "Le idee politiche a Roma nell' epoca repubblicana," in Firpo, L. (ed.), *Storia delle idee politiche, economiche e sociali*, vol. 1, Turin: 724–804.
Ferrary, J.-L. 1988. "Rogatio Servilia agraria." *Athenaeum* 66: 141–64.
Ferrenbach, V. 1895. *Die amici populi Romani republikanischer Zeit*. PhD diss. Straßburg.
Fielding, Ian, and Carole E. Newlands. 2015. "Introduction: Campania: Poetics, Location, and Identity." *Illinois Classical Studies* 40.1: 85–90.
Fiori, Roberto. 2013. "The Roman Conception of Contract," in McGinn, Thomas A.J. (ed.), *Roman Law: Past, Present, and Future*, Ann Arbor: 40–75.
Fitzgerald, W. 1995. *Catullan Provocations*. Berkeley.
Flach, Deiter. 1990. *Römische Agrargeschichte*. München.
Fletcher, William G. 1939. "The Pontic Cities of Pompey the Great." *Transactions and Proceedings of the American Philological Association* 70: 17–29.
Fotheringham, Lynn S. 2013. *Persuasive Language in Cicero's* Pro Milone: *A close reading and commentary*. London.
Frank, Tenney. 1933. *An Economic Survey of Ancient Rome*, Vol. I. Baltimore.
Frederiksen, M.W. 1959. "Republican Capua: A Social and Economic Study." *Papers of the British School at Rome* 27: 80–130.
Frederiksen, M.W. 1966. "Caesar, Cicero and the Problem of Debt." *The Journal of Roman Studies* 56.1 and 2: 128–141.

Freese, J.H. 1930. *Cicero. The Speeches. With an English Translation. Pro Publio Quinctio—Pro Sexto Roscio Amerino—Pro Quinto Roscio comoedo—De lege agraria I., II., III.* Loeb Classical Library. London/Cambridge.

Frolov, Roman M. 2013. "Public meetings in ancient Rome: definitions of the *contiones* in the sources." *Graeco-Latina Brunensia* 18.1: 75–84.

Fuhrmann, M. 1995. *Cicero and the Roman Republic.* Oxford. (Translation of *Cicero und die römische Republik.* München, 1990).

Gabba, Emilio. 1950. "The 'lex Plotia agraria.'" *La Parola del Passato* 5.13: 66–8.

Gabba, Emilio. 1966. "Nota sulla *Rogatio Agraria* di P. Servilio Rullo," in Chevallier, R. (ed.), *Mélanges d'archéologie et d'histoire offerts à André Piganiol*, Paris: 769–775.

García Morcillo, M. 2008. "Staging Power and Authority at Roman Auctions." *Ancient Society* 38: 185–213.

García Morcillo, M. 2016. "Placing the *hasta* in the Forum: Cicero and the Topographic Symbolism of Patrimonial Sales," in García Morcillo, M., J. H. Richardson, and F. Santangelo (eds.), *Ruin or Renewal? Places and the Transformation of Memory in the City of Rome*, Rome: 113–133.

Gargola, Daniel J. 2009. *Lands, Laws, and Gods Magistrates and Ceremony in the Regulation of Public Lands in Republican Rome*, 2nd ed. Chapel Hill.

Garofolo, Luigi. 1989. *Il processo edilizio. Contributo allo studio dei* iudicia populi. [Padua].

Geffcken, K.A. 1973. *Comedy in the "Pro Caelio."* Mnemosyne Supplement 30. Leiden/Boston.

Gell, W. 1846. *The Topography of Rome and Its Vicinity.* London.

Gelzer, Matthias. 1912. *Die Nobilität der römischen Republik.* Leipzig/Berlin.

Gelzer, Matthias. 1968. *Caesar: Politician and Statesman.* Cambridge, MA.

Gelzer, Matthias. 2008 [1983]. *Cicero: ein biographischer Versuch.* Stuttgart.

Gildenhard, Ingo. 2011. *Creative Eloquence: the Construction of Reality in Cicero's Speeches.* Oxford.

Gnoli, F. 1979. *Ricerche sul crimen* peculatus. Milan.

Goethe, Johann Wolfgang. 1791. *Der Zauberlehrling.* Germany.

Gotoff, Harold C. 2002. "Cicero's Caesarian Speeches," in May, J.M. (ed.), *Brill's Companion to Cicero. Oratory and Rhetoric*, Leiden/Boston/Köln: 219–271.

Graver, Margaret. 2007. *Stoicism and Emotion.* Chicago.

Greenidge, A.H.J. 1901. *The Legal Procedure of Cicero's Time.* Oxford.

Greenwood, L.H.G. 1935. *Cicero: The Verrine Orations.* Vol. II. *Against Verres, Part 2, Books 3–5.* Cambridge, MA.

Grethlein, J. 2006. "Nam Quid Ea Memorem: *The Dialectical Relation of* Res Gestae *and* Memoria Rerum Gestarum *in Sallust's* Bellum Jugurthinum." *The Classical Quarterly*, n.s. 56.1: 135–148.

Griffin, Miriam T. 1973. "The Tribune C. Cornelius." *The Journal of Roman Studies* 63: 196–213.

Griffin, Miriam T. 2003. "*De Beneficiis* and Roman Society." *The Journal of Roman Studies* 93: 92–113.
Gruen, Erich. 1968. *Roman Politics and the Criminal Courts*. Cambridge, MA.
Gruen, Erich. 1970. "Veteres hostes, novi amici." *Phoenix* 24: 237–43.
Gruen, Erich. 1971. "Some Criminal Trials of the Late Republic: Political and Prosopographical Problems." *Athenaeum* 49: 54–80.
Gruen, Erich. 1974. *The Last Generation of the Roman Republic*. Berkeley.
Gruter, Wilhelm, and Gronovius. 1618. *Marci Tullii Ciceronis Opera Quae Extant Omnia ex MSS, Codicibus emendata, Studio atque industria Jani Gulielmii et Jani Gruteri, additis eorum notis integris: nunc denuo recognita ab Jacobo Gronovio*. Hamburg.
Gsell, S. 1928. *Histoire ancienne de l'Afrique du nord*, vol. 4. Paris.
Habinek, Thomas. 2005. *The World of Roman Song: From Ritualized Speech to Social Order*. Baltimore.
Hall, E.T. 1963. "A System for the Notation of Proxemic Behaviour." *American Anthropologist* 65.5: 1003–1026.
Hall, E.T. 1969. *The Hidden Dimension*. Garden City, N.Y.
Hall, J. 2009. *Politeness and Politics in Cicero's Letters*. Oxford.
Halliday, M.A.K. 2002. *Linguistic Studies of Text and Discourse*. London/New York.
Happ, Heinz. 1986. *Luxurius; Text, Untersuchungen, Kommentar, Band II: Kommentar*. Stuttgart.
Hardy, E.G. 1913. "The Policy of the Rullan Proposal in 63 B.C." *Journal of Philology* 32: 228–60.
Hardy, E.G. 1924. "The Agrarian Proposal of Rullus in 63 B.C," in Hardy, E.G., *Some Problems in Roman History: Ten Essays Bearing on the Administrative and Legislative Work of Julius Caesar*, Oxford: 68–98.
Harries, Jill. 2006. *Cicero and the Jurists: From Citizens' Law to the Lawful State*. London.
Harrison, Ian. 2008. "Catiline, Clodius, and Popular Politics at Rome during the 60s and 50s BCE." *Bulletin of the Institute of Classical Studies* 51: 95–118.
Harvey, Paul. 1972. *Cicero's Orations 'de lege agraria': Studies and Essays, with a Commentary on the Third Oration*. Diss. Penn.
Harvey, Paul. 1982. "Cicero, Consius, and Capua: II. Cicero and M. Brutus' Colony." *Athenaeum* 60: 145–71.
Havas, László. 1976. "La *rogatio Servilia*: contribution a l'étude de la propriété terrienne a l'époque du déclin de la république romaine." *Oikumene* 1: 131–156.
Heiken, G., R. Funciello, and D. de Rita. 2013. *The Seven Hills of Rome: A Geological Tour of the Eternal City*. Princeton.
Hellegouarc'h, J. 1963. *Le vocabulaire latin des relations et des partis politiques sous la république*. Paris.
Heller, John L. 1962. "Nepos σκορπιστής and Philoxenus." *Transactions and Proceedings of the American Philological Association* 93: 61–89.

Henderson, M.I. 1950. "*De commentariolo petitionis*." *The Journal of Roman Studies* 40.1–2: 8–21.

Hinard, F. 1985. *Les Proscriptions de la Rome républicaine*. Rome.

Hofmann, J.B., and A. Szantyr. 1965. *Lateinische Syntax und Stilistik*. München.

Hölkeskamp, K.J. 1995. "*Oratoris maxima scaena*: Reden vor dem Volk in der politischen Kultur der Republik," in Jehne, M. (ed.), *Demokratie in Rom? Die Rolle des Volkes in der Politik der römischen Republik (Historia*, Einzelschriften 96), Stuttgart: 11–49.

Hölkeskamp, K.J. 2000. "The Roman Republic: Government of the People, by the People, for the People?" *Scripta classica Israelica* 19: 203–33.

Hölkeskamp, K.J. 2006. "History and Collective Memory in the Middle Republic," in Rosenstein, N. and R. Morstein-Marx (eds.), *A Companion to the Roman Republic*, Malden, MA: 478–95.

Hölkeskamp, K.J. 2010. *Reconstructing the Roman Republic: An Ancient Political Culture and Modern Research*. Princeton, NJ, and Oxford.

Hölkeskamp, K.J. 2011. "The Roman Republic as Theatre of Power," in Beck, H., A. Duplá, M. Jehne, and F. Piña-Polo (eds.), *Consuls and* Res Publica: *Holding High Office in the Roman Republic*, Cambridge, UK: 161–181.

Hopwood, K. 2007. "Smear and Spin: Ciceronian Tactics in *De Lege Agraria II*," in Booth, J. (ed.), *Cicero on the Attack: Invective and Subversion in the Orations and Beyond*, Swansea: 71–103.

Housman, A.E. 1913. "Ciceroniana." *Journal of Philology* 32.64: 261–269.

Howarth, R.S. 1999. "Rome, Italians, and the Land." *Historia: Zeitschrift für Alte Geschichte* 48.3: 282–300.

Husband, Richard W. 1916. "On the Expulsion of Foreigners from Rome." *Classical Philology* 11.3: 315–333.

Jal, P. 1961. "Pax civilis—concordia." *Revue des études latines* 39: 210–31.

Jameson, Shelach. 1970. "Pompey's Imperium in 67: Some Constitutional Fictions." *Historia: Zeitschrift für Alte Geschichte* 19.5: 539–560.

Johannsen, K. 1971. *Die Lex Agraria des Jahres III v. Chr.*, Text und Commentar. Munich.

Jolowicz, H.F., and Barry Nicholas. 1972. *Historical Introduction to the Study of Roman Law*, 3rd ed. Cambridge.

Jones, A.H.M. 1949. "The Roman Civil Service (Clerical and Sub-Clerical Grades)." *The Journal of Roman Studies* 39: 38–55.

Jonkers, E.J. 1963. *Social and Economic Commentary on Cicero's "de lege agraria orationes tres."* Leyden.

Kaster, R. 2006. *Cicero: Speech on behalf of Publius Sestius*. Oxford.

Keaveney, A. 1982a. "Sulla and Italy." *Critica Storica* 19.4: 499–544.

Keaveney, A. 1982b. *Sulla: the Last Republican*. London; Dover, N.H.

Keil, Matthew A. 2017. "From Ὁμόνοια to *Concordia*: The Journey of a Greek Political Ideal to Rome through Southern Italy," in Reid, H.L, Susi Kimbell, and Davide

Tanasi (eds.), *Politics and Performance in Western Greece: Essays on the Hellenic Heritage of Sicily and Southern Italy*, Parnassus Press: 331–344.

Kelly, J.M. 1976. *Studies in the Civil Judicature of the Roman Republic*. Oxford.

Kenney, E.J. 1971. *Lucretius: De Rerum Natura Book III*. Cambridge, UK.

Kenty, Joanna. 2016. "Congenital Virtue: *Mos Maiorum* in Cicero's Orations." *The Classical Journal* 111.4: 429–462.

Kerferd, George B. 1990. "The Sage in Hellenistic Philosophical Literature (399 B.C.E.–199 C.E.)," in Gammie, John G., and Leo G. Perdue, *The Sage in Israel and the Ancient Near East*. Winona Lake, IN: 319–28.

Kinsey, T.E. 1971. *Pro P. Quinctio Oratio, Edited with Text, Introduction and Commentary*. Sydney.

Kondratieff, Eric J. 2009. "Reading Rome's Evolving Civic Landscape in Context: Tribunes of the Plebs and the Praetor's Tribunal." *Phoenix* 64.3/4: 322–360.

Kroll, W. 1923. *C. Valerius Catullus, herausgegeben und erklärt von Wilhelm Kroll*. Leipzig/Berlin.

Krostenko, B. 2004a. "Binary Phrases and the Middle Style as Social Code: *Rhetorica ad Herennium* 4.13 and 4.15." *Harvard Studies in Classical Philology* 102: 237–274.

Krostenko, B. 2004b. "Text and Context in the Roman Forum: The Case of Cicero's First Catilinarian," in Yost, W. and Wendy Olmsted (eds.), *A Companion to Rhetoric and Rhetorical Criticism*, Blackwell Companions to Literature and Culture, Malden, MA: 38–57.

Krostenko, B. 2004c. "Style and Ideology in the *pro Marcello*," in Welch, K. and T.W. Hillard (eds.), *Roman Crossings: Theory and Practice in the Roman Republic*, Swansea: 279–312.

Krostenko, B. 2017–2018. "Dancing, Declamation, and Deipnosophistry in the *Deiotariana*." *Palamedes* 12: 61–92.

Kühnert, B. 1989. "*Populus Romanus* und *sentina urbis*: zur Terminologie der *plebs urbana* der späten Republik bei Cicero." *Klio* 71: 432–41.

Kühnert, B. 1991. *Die plebs urbana der späten römischen Republik. Ihre ökonomische Situation und soziale Struktur* (Abhandlungen der sächsichen Akademie der Wissenschaften zu Leipzig, Philologisch-historische Klasse 73.3). Berlin.

Kumaniecki, Kazimierz. 1970. "Les discours égarés de Cicéron pro C. Cornelio." *Mededelingen van de koninklyke Vlaamse Academie voor Wetenschappen, Letteren en Schone Kunsten van Belgie* 32: 3–36.

Kunkel, W., and R. Wittmann. 1995. *Staatsordnung und Staatspraxis der römischen Republik. Zweiter Abschnitt. Die Magistratur*. München.

Lakoff, G. 1987. *Women, Fire, and Dangerous Things: What Categories Reveal About the Mind*. Chicago.

Landgraf, Gustav. 1914. *Kommentar zu Ciceros Rede pro Sexto Roscio Amerino*, 2nd ed. Leipzig.

Langacker, R. 1987. *Foundations of Cognitive Grammar*. Stanford.

Langlands, R. 2013. "Roman Exemplarity: Mediating between General and Particular," in Lowrie, Michelle, and Suzanne Lüdermann (eds.), *Exemplarity and Singularity: Thinking through Particulars in Philosophy, Literature, and Law*, London: 68–80.
Laser, G. 1997. Populo et scaenae serviendum est: *die Bedeutung der städtischen Masse in der späten Römischen Republik*. Trier.
Laughton, E. 1964. *The Participle in Cicero*. Oxford.
Lebow, Richard Ned. 2008. *A Cultural Theory of International Relations*. Cambridge, UK.
Leigh, Matthew. 2004. "The *pro Caelio* and Comedy." *Classical Philology* 99.4: 300–335.
Lemosse, Maxime. 1971. "A propos de 'ductu.'" *Irish Jurist* 6.1: 142–46.
Leonhardt, Jürgen. 1998–9. "Senat und Volk in Cicero's Reden '*De lege agraria*.'" *Acta classica Universitatis Scientiarum Debreceniensis* 34-5: 279–92.
Leumann, M., and J.B. Hofmann. 1928. *Lateinische Grammatik*. 5th ed. München.
Levi, M.A. 1938. "Auspicio imperio ductu felicitate." *Rendiconti—Istituto lombardo, Accademia di scienze e lettere* 71: 101–118.
Lewis, R.G. (ed.) 2006. *Asconius: Commentaries on Speeches of Cicero*, translated with commentary. Oxford.
Lintott, A.W. 1967. "P. Clodius Pulcher- 'Felix Catilina?'" *Greece & Rome* 14.2: 157–169.
Lintott, A.W. 1977. *The Classical Quarterly* 27.1: 184–186.
Lintott, A.W. 1965. "Trinundinum." *The Classical Quarterly* 15 no. 2: 281–285.
Lintott, A.W. 1990. "Electoral Bribery in the Roman Republic." *The Journal of Roman Studies* 80: 1–16.
Lintott, A.W. 1992. *Judicial Reform and Land Reform in the Roman Republic*. Cambridge, UK.
Lintott, A.W. 1993. *Imperium Romanum. Politics and administration*. London/New York.
Lintott, A.W. 1999. *The Constitution of the Roman Republic*. Oxford, New York.
Liverani, Paolo. 2016. "Un destino di marginalità: storia e topografia dell'area vaticana nell'antichità," in Presicce, Claudio Pariri and Laura Petacco (eds.), *Trasformazioni urbane e memoria collettiva: l'area vaticana, la Spina e Via della Conciliazione. La Spina: dall'Agro vaticano a Via della Conciliazione*, Rome: 21–29.
Lobur, J. 2008. Consensus, Concordia, *and the Formation of Roman Imperial Ideology*. New York and London.
Long, George. 1875. "Bonorum Emtio," in Smith, William (ed.), *A Dictionary of Greek and Roman Antiquities*, London: 208.
Łoposzko, T., and H. Kowalski. 1990. "Catalina und Clodius—Analogien und Differenzen." *Klio* 72: 199–210.
Lübtow, Ulrich von. 1932. *Der Ediktstitel* "Quod metus causa gestum erit." Bamberg.
Mack, D. 1937. *Senatsreden und Volksreden bei Cicero*. Würzburg.
Mackay, Christopher. 1995. "Lintott, Judicial Reform and Land Reform." *Bryn Mawr Classical Review. 1995.04.15*, Stable URL: https://bmcr.brynmawr.edu/1995/1995.04.15.

Mackay, Christopher. 2000. "Sulla and the Monuments: Studies in His Public Persona." *Historia: Zeitschrift für Alte Geschichte* 49.2: 161–210.

MacKay, L.A. 1962. "Sallust's 'Catiline': Date and Purpose." *Phoenix* 16.3: 181–94.

Mackie, N. 1992. "*Popularis* Ideology and Popular Politics at Rome in the First Century B.C." *Rheinisches Museum für Philologie* 135: 49–73.

Maganzani, Lauretta. 2019. "La cadastration et la réorganisation administrative de l'Italie à l'époque d'Auguste." *Revue historique de droit français et étranger* 97.3: 263–276.

Magdelain, André. 1978. *La loi à Rome: histoire d'un concept*. Paris.

Magie, David. 1950. *Roman rule in Asia Minor, to the end of the third century after Christ*. 2 vol. Princeton.

Malcovati, E. 1976–1979. *Oratorum Romanorum Fragmenta Liberae Rei Publicae*. 2 vol. Turin.

Manuwald, Gesine. 2007. *Cicero: Philippics 3–9. Texte und Kommentare*, 30. Berlin/New York.

Manuwald, Gesine. 2018. *Cicero: Agrarian Speeches: Introduction, Text, Translation, and Commentary*. Oxford.

Marek, V. 1983. *Marcus Tullius Cicero. Scripta quae manserunt omnia*. Fasc. 16. *Orationes de lege agraria, oratio pro C. Rabirio perduellionis reo*. Leipzig.

Marek, V. 1997. "Ager Recentoricus in Sicilia." *Graecolatina Pragensia* 15: 105–111.

Marouzeau, J. 1959. "Sur deux aspects de la langue du droit," in Lévy-Bruhl, Mélanges and his collaborators (eds.), *Droits de l'Antiquité et sociologie juridique: Mélanges Lévy-Bruhl*, Paris: 435–444.

Marshall, A.J. 1984. "Symbols and Showmanship in Roman Public Life: The *Fasces*." *Phoenix* 38: 120–141.

Marshall, B.A. 1972. "The *Lex Plotia Agraria*." *Antichthon* 6: 43–52.

Marshall, B.A. 1976. *Crassus: A Political Biography*. Amsterdam.

Marshall, B.A. 1984. "Faustus Sulla and Political Labels in the 60's and 50's B.C." *Historia: Zeitschrift für Alte Geschichte* 33.2: 199–219.

Mattingly, Harold B. 1969. "Saturninus' Corn Bill and the Circumstances of His Fall." *The Classical Review* 19.3: 267–270.

Mayer, Anton. 1954. *Die lat. Ortsbezeichnungen auf -ētum. Glotta* 33.3/4: 227–238.

Mazurek, Lindsey A. 2022. *Isis in a Global Empire: Greek Identity through Egyptian Religion in Roman Greece*. Cambridge, UK.

McGushin, P. 1992–1994. Sallust, *Historiae*, translated with introduction and commentary, 2 vol. Oxford.

Meier, Christian. 1980. *Res Publica Amissa*, 2nd ed. Wiesbaden.

Mercado, Angelo. 2012. *Italic Verse: A Study of the Poetic Remains of Old Latin, Faliscan, and Sabellic*. Innsbruck.

Miles, Josephine. 1976. "Values in Language; Or, Where Have 'Goodness, Truth' and 'Beauty' Gone?" *Critical Inquiry* 3.1 (Autumn 1976): 1–13.

Millar, Fergus. 1984. "The Political Character of the Classical Roman Republic, 200–151 B.C." *The Journal of Roman Studies* 74: 1–19.

Millar, Fergus. 1986. "Politics, Persuasion and the People before the Social War (150–90 B.C.)." *The Journal of Roman Studies* 76: 1–11.
Millar, Fergus. 1998. *The Crowd in Rome in the Late Republic*. Ann Arbor.
Millar, Fergus. 2002. *The Roman Republic in Political Thought*. Hanover.
Mitchell, T.N. 1979. *Cicero: The Ascending Years*. New Haven.
Mommsen, T. 1879. *Römische Forschungen*, 2 vol. Berlin.
Mommsen, T. 1887–1888. *Römisches Staatsrecht*, 3rd ed., 3 vol. Leipzig.
Montanari, E. 2009. Fumosae imagines: *Identità e memoria nell'aristocrazia repubblicana*. Rome.
Moore, Timothy J. 2012. *Music in Roman Comedy*. Cambridge, UK.
Morgan, M. Gwyn and John A. Walsh. 1978. "Ti. Gracchus (tr. p. 133 B.C.), The Numantine Affair, and the Deposition of M. Octavius." *Classical Philology* 73.3: 200–210.
Morstein-Marx, R. 1998. "Publicity, Popularity and Patronage in the *Commentariolum Petitionis*." *Classical Antiquity* 17.2: 259–288.
Morstein-Marx, R. 2004. *Mass Oratory and Political Power in the Late Roman Republic*. Cambridge, UK.
Morstein-Marx, R. 2013. "'Cultural Hegemony' and the Communicative Power of the Roman Elite," in Steel, Catherine and Henrietta van der Blom (eds.), *Community and Communication: Oratory and Politics in Republican Rome*, Oxford: 29–48.
Mouritsen, Henrik. 2001. *Plebs and Politics in the Late Roman Republic*. Cambridge, UK.
Mouritsen, Henrik. 2017. *Politics in the Roman Republic*. Cambridge, UK.
Müller, C.F.W. (ed.) 1892. *M. Tulli Ciceronis scripta quae manserunt omnia*, pars 2. Vol. 2. Leipzig.
Murgatroyd, Paul. 1994. *Tibullus: Elegies II, edited with introduction and commentary*. Oxford.
Murphy, Paul R. 1986. "Caesar's Continuators and Caesar's 'Felicitas.'" *The Classical World* 79.5: 307–317.
Murphy, Paul R. 1991. "On Questions Introduced by *Non* and *Nonne*." *The Classical Journal*, 86.3: 226–232.
Nicolet, Claude. 1970. "Les *finitores ex equestri loco* de la loi Servilia de 63 av. J.C." *Latomus* 29: 72–103.
Nisbet, R.G.M. 1970. "*The Commentariolum Petitionis*: Some Arguments Against Authenticity." *The Journal of Roman Studies* 19.3: 384–385.
North, J.A. 1990. "Democratic Politics in Republican Rome." *Past & Present* 126: 3–21.
Ober, Josiah. 1989. *Mass and Elite in Democratic Athens: Rhetoric, Ideology, and the Power of the People*. Princeton, NJ.
Ogilvie, R.M. 1965. *A Commentary on Livy, Books 1–5*. Oxford.
Oost, S.I. 1963. "Cyrene, 96–74 B.C." *Classical Philology* 58: 11–25.
Opelt, I. 1965. *Die lateinischen Schimpfwörter und verwandte sprachliche Erscheinungen: eine Typologie*. Heidelberg.

Östernberg, Ida. 2009. *Staging the World: Spoils, Captives, and Representations in the Roman Triumphal Procession*. Oxford.

Palmer, G. 1996. *Toward a theory of cultural linguistics*. Austin, TX.

Paul, G.M. 1984. *A Historical Commentary on Sallust's* Bellum Iugurthinum. Liverpool.

Paule, Maxwell T. 2014. "*Quae saga, quis magus*: On the Vocabulary of the Roman Witch." *The Classical Quarterly*, n.s. 64.2: 745–757.

Petersen, Walter. 1938. "The Greek Masculines in Circumflexed -ας." *Classical Philology* 32.2: 121–130.

Petersen, Walter. 1937. "Greek Place Names in -(ε)ών, Genitive -(ε)ῶνος." *Classical Philology* 32.4: 305–328.

Piña-Polo, F. 1996. *Contra arma verbis. Der Redner vor dem Volk in der späten römischen Republik* (translated from the Spanish by E. Liess). Stuttgart.

Piña-Polo, F. 2011. *The Consul at Rome: The Civil Functions of the Consuls in the Roman Republic*. Cambridge, UK.

Platner, Samuel Ball, and Thomas Ashby. 1929. *A Topographical Dictionary of Ancient Rome*. London.

Powell, J.G.F. 2010. "Hyperbaton and register in Cicero," in Dickey, Eleanor and Anna Chahoud (eds.), *Colloquial and Literary Latin*, Cambridge, UK: 163–85.

Quilici, L., and S. Quilici Gigli. 1986. *Fidenae* (Latium *Vetus* 5). Rome.

Quinn, Kenneth. 1973. Catullus: *The Poems*. Edited with introduction, revised text, and commentary. London.

Radford, R.S. 1902. *Use of the suffixes* -anus *and* -inus *in forming possessive adjectives from names of persons*. Baltimore.

Radin, M. 1911. "Literary References in Cicero's Orations." *Classical Journal* 6: 209–17.

Ramage, E.S. 1991. "Sulla's propaganda." *Klio* 73: 93–121.

Ramsey, J.T. 2007. "Roman Senatorial Oratory," in Dominik W. and J. Hall (eds.), *A Companion to Roman Rhetoric*, Oxford: 122–35.

Rauh, Nicholas K. 1989. "Finance and Estate Sales in Republican Rome." *Aevum* 63 fasc. 1: 45–76.

Rawson, B. 1971. "*De Lege Agraria* 2. 49." *Classical Philology* 66.1: 26–29.

Rawson, E. 1975. *Cicero: A Portrait*. (repr. with corr. 1983, 1994). London.

Richardson, J. 2008. *The Language of Empire: Rome and the Idea of Empire from the Third Century BC to the Second Century AD*. Cambridge, UK.

Richardson, John S. 1971. "The 'Commentariolum Petitionis.'" *Historia: Zeitschrift für Alte Geschichte* 20.4: 436–442.

Ripat, Pauline. 2016. "Roman Women, Wise Women, and Witches." *Phoenix* 70.1/2: 104–128.

Riggsby, Andrew M. 1999. *Crime and Community in Ciceronian Rome*. Austin, TX.

Robb, M.A. 2010. *Beyond Populares and Optimates: Political Language in the Late Republic*. Historia Einzelschriften 213. Stuttgart.

Robbins, Mary Ann. 1972. "Livy's Brutus." *Studies in Philology* 69.1: 1–20.

Roby, H. 1902. *Roman Private Law in the Time of Cicero and the Antonines*, vol. 2. Cambridge, UK.

Rosch, E. 1983. "Prototype Classification and Logical Classification: The Two Systems," in Scholnick, E.K. (ed.), 1983, *New Trends in Conceptual Representation: Challenges to Piaget's Theory?* Hillsdale: 73–86.

Roselaar, S.T. 2010. *Public Land in the Roman Republic. A Social and Economic History of Ager Publicus in Italy, 396–89 BC*. Oxford Studies in Roman Society and Law. Oxford.

Roselaar, S.T. 2012. "The Concept of *Commercium* in the Roman Republic." *Phoenix* 66.3/4: 381–413.

Rosenstein, N. 1995. "Sorting out the Lot in Republican Rome." *The American Journal of Philology* 116.1: 43–75.

Rothe, Ursula. 2018. "The Roman Villa: Definitions and Variations," in Marzano, Annalisa, and Guy P. R. Métraux (eds.), *The Roman Villa in the Mediterranean Basin: Late Republic to Late Antiquity*, Cambridge, UK: 42–58.

Rotondi, Giovanni. 1912. *Leges Publicae populi Romani*. Milan.

Royko, Mike. 1982. *Sez Who? Sez Me*. New York.

Russell, Amy. 2016. "Why did Clodius shut the shops? The rhetoric of mobilizing a crowd in the Late Republic." *Historia: Zeitschrift für Alte Geschichte* 65.2: 186–210.

Russell, B. 2013. *Gazetteer of Stone Quarries in the Roman World*. Data set/database, http://oxrep.classics.ox.ac.uk/databases/stone_quarries_database.

Sacchi, Osvaldo. 2005. "La nozione di *ager publicus populi romani* nella lex agraria del 111 a.C. come espressione dell'ideologia del suo tempo." *The Legal History Review* 1: 19–42.

Sage, Evan T. 1921. "Cicero and the Agrarian Proposals of 63 B.C." *Classical Journal* 16.4: 230–36.

Sallares, R. 2002. *Malaria and Rome. A History of Malaria in Ancient Italy*. Oxford.

Salmon, E.T. 1969. *Roman Colonisation under the Republic*. London.

Sandberg, K. 2001. *Magistrates and Assemblies: A Study of Legislative Practices in Republican Rome*. Rome.

Santangelo, Federico. 2007. *Sulla, the Elites and the Empire. A Study of Roman Politics in Italy and the Greek East*. Impact of Empire 8. Leiden/Boston.

Santangelo, Federico. 2014. "Roman Politics in the 70s B.C.: a Story of Realignments?" *The Journal of Roman Studies* 104: 1–27.

Schatzman, Israel. 1972. "The Roman General's Authority Over Booty." *Historia: Zeitschrift für Alte Geschichte* 21.2: 177–205.

Schenkeveld, D.M. 1997. "Philosophical Prose," in Porter, S.E. (ed.), *Handbook of Classical Rhetoric in the Hellenistic Period: 330 BC–AD 400*, Leiden: 195–264.

Schiller, A. Arthur. 1978. *Roman Law: The Mechanisms of its Development*. The Hague.

Schneider, H.-C. 1977. *Das Problem der Veteranenversorgung in der späteren Republik*. Bonn.

Schofield, Malcolm. 2021. *Cicero: Political Philosophy*. Oxford.
Scullard, H.H. 1960. "Scipio Aemilianus and Roman Politics." *The Journal of Roman Studies* 50: 73–74.
Scullard, H.H. 1982 [1959]. *From the Gracchi to Nero: A History of Rome from 133 B.C. to A.D. 68*. London.
Seager, R. 1969. "The Tribunate of C. Cornelius: Some Ramifications," in Bibauw, J. (ed.), *Hommages à M. Renard 2* (Collection Latomus 102), Brussels: 680–686.
Seager, R. 1972. "Cicero and the Word *Popularis*." *The Classical Quarterly* 22.2: 328–338.
Seager, R. 2002 (1979). *Pompey: a Political Biography*. Oxford.
Searle, John R. 1975. "A Taxonomy of Illocutionary Acts," in Günderson, K. (ed.), *Language, Mind, and Knowledge*, vol. 7, Minneapolis: 344–369.
Shackleton Bailey, D.R. 1965. *Cicero's Letters to Atticus. Vol. 1. 68–59 BC. 1–45 (Books I and II)*, Cambridge Classical Texts and Commentaries 3. Cambridge, UK.
Shackleton Bailey, D.R. 1968. *Cicero's Letters to Atticus. Vol. 3. 51–50 BC. 94–132 (V–VII.9)*, Cambridge Classical Texts and Commentaries 5. Cambridge, UK.
Shackleton Bailey, D.R. 1980. *Cicero: Epistulae ad Quintum fratrem et M. Brutum*, Cambridge Classical Texts and Commentaries 22. Cambridge, UK/London.
Shackleton Bailey, D.R. 1986. "*Nobiles* and *Novi* Reconsidered." *American Journal of Philology* 107.2: 255–260.
Shatzman, I. 1972. "The Roman General's Authority over Booty." *Historia: Zeitschrift für Alte Geschichte* 21.2: 177–205.
Shatzman, I. 1975. *Senatorial Wealth and Roman Politics*. Brussels.
Shaw, Brent D. 1975. "Debt in Sallust." *Latomus* 34.1: 187–196.
Sherk, R.K. 1969. *Roman Documents from the Greek East. Senatus Consulta and Epistulae to the Age of Augustus*. Baltimore.
Silver, Morris. 2016. "Public Slaves in the Roman Army: An Exploratory Study." *Ancient Society* 46: 203–240.
Skard, Eiliv. 1956. *Sallust und seine Vorganger: eine sprachliche Untersuchung*. Oslo.
Skinner, Q. 1980. "Language and Social Change," in Michaels, L. and C. Ricks (eds.), *The State of the Language*, Berkeley: 562–578.
Smith, R.E. 1957. "The *Lex Plotia Agraria* and Pompey's Spanish Veterans." *The Classical Quarterly* 7: 82–5.
Smith, William. 1854. *Dictionary of Greek and Roman Geography*. London.
Sohm, Rudolph. 1901. *The Institutes: A Text-book of the History and System of Roman Private Law*, 2nd ed., translated by James Crawford Ledlie. London/New York.
Solazzi, Siro. 1901. *Ancora Del Diritto Dei Creditori Separatisti: Sul Patrimonio Dell' Erede*. Roma.
Steel, Catherine, and Henriette van der Blom. 2013. *Community and Communication: Oratory and Politics in Republican Rome*. Oxford.
Steed, Kathryn S. 2017. "The Speeches of Sallust's *Histories* and the Legacy of Sulla." *Historia: Zeitschrift für Alte Geschichte* 66.4: 401–441.

Steel, Catherine. 2014. "The Roman Senate and the Post-Sullan *Res Publica.*" *Historia: Zeitschrift für Alte Geschichte* 63.3: 323–339.

Steinbock, B. 2013. *Social Memory in Athenian Public Discourse. Uses and Meanings of the Past.* Ann Arbor.

Stewart, Roberta. 1995. "Catiline and the Crisis of 63–60 B.C.: the Italian Perspective." *Latomus* 54.1: 62–78.

Stockton, David. 1962. "Cicero on Praetors Who Failed to Abide by Their Edicts." *Transactions and Proceedings of the American Philological Association* 93: 471–489.

Strasburger, H. 1956. *Concordia Ordinum. Eine Untersuchung zur Politik Ciceros,* Amsterdam.

Stratton, Kimberley. 2007. *Naming the Witch: Magic, Ideology, and Stereotype in Ancient World.* New York.

Strong, D.E. 1968. "The Administration of Public Building in Rome during the Late Republic and Early Empire." *Bulletin of the Institute of Classical Studies* 15: 97–109.

Sumi, Geoffrey S. 2002. "Spectacles and Sulla's Public Image." *Historia: Zeitschrift für Alte Geschichte* 51.4: 414–432.

Sumner, G.V. 1966. "Cicero, Pompeius, and Rullus." *Transactions and Proceedings of the American Philological Association* 97: 569–582.

Suolahti, J. 1963. *The Roman Censors: A Study on Social Structure.* Helsinki.

Syme, Ronald. 1938. "The Allegiance of Labienus." *The Journal of Roman Studies* 28: 113–25.

Tan, James. 2013. "Publius Clodius and the *Contio,*" in Steel, Catherine and Henrietta van der Blom (eds.), *Community and Communication: Oratory and Politics in Republican Rome,* Oxford: 117–132.

Tan, James. 2008. "*Contiones* in the Time of Cicero." *Classical Antiquity* 27.1: 163–201.

Tarpin, Michel. 2009. "Les *manubiae* dans la procédure d'appropriation du butin," in Coudry, Marianne and Michael Humm (eds.), Praeda: *Butin de guerre et société dans la Rome républicaine/Kriegsbeute und Gesellschaft im republikanischen Rom,* Stuttgart:81–102.

Tatum, W.J. 1999. *The Patrician Tribune.* Chapel Hill.

Taylor, Lily Ross. 1942. "The Election of the Pontifex Maximus in the Late Republic." *Classical Philology* 37.4: 421–4.

Taylor, Lily Ross. 1966. *Roman Voting Assemblies. From the Hannibalic War to the Dictatorship of Caesar.* Jerome Lectures 8, repr. 1990. Ann Arbor.

Taylor, Lily Ross. 2013 [1960]. *The Voting Districts of the Roman Republic. The Thirty-Five Urban and Rural Tribes* (Papers and Monographs of the American Academy in Rome 20) Rome, with updated material by J. Linderski (Papers and Monographs of the American Academy in Rome 34), Ann Arbor.

Thein, A.G. 2005. "The *via Latina,* the *via Labicana,* and the Location of *ad Pictas.*" *Papers of the British School at Rome* 73: 131–155.

Thielmann, Georg. 1961. *Die römische Privatauktion: zugleich ein Beitrag zum römischen Bankierrecht*. Berlin.

Thommen, L. 1989. *Das Volkstribunat der späten römischen Republik*. Stuttgart.

Thompson, C.E. 1978. "To the Senate and to the People: Adaptation to the Senatorial and Popular Audiences in the Parallel Speeches of Cicero." PhD diss., Ohio State University.

Thomson, D.F.S. 1997. *Catullus: edited with a textual and interpretative commentary*. Toronto/Buffalo, NY.

Timpe, Dieter. 1962. "Herrschaftsidee und Klientelstaatenpolitik in Sallusts *bellum Jugurthinum*." *Hermes* 90.3: 334–375.

Tracy, Catherine. 2008-2009. "The People's Consul: The Significance of Cicero's Use of the Term 'Popularis.'" *Illinois Classical Studies* 33–34: 181–199.

Tyrrell, William Blake. 1978. *A legal and historical commentary to Cicero's* Oratio pro C. Rabirio perduellionis reo. Amsterdam.

Tyrrell, R.Y., and L.C. Purser. 1914. *The Correspondence of M. Tullius Cicero*, 2nd ed., vol. 3. Dublin and London.

Vaan, Michiel Arnoud Cor de. 2008. *Etymological Dictionary of Latin and the Other Italic Languages*. Leiden /Boston.

Vanderbroeck, Paul J.J. 1987. *Popular Leadership and Collective Behavior in the Late Roman Republic (ca. 80–50 BC)*. Amsterdam.

Vasaly, Ann. 1987. "Personality and Power: Livy's Depiction of the Appii Claudii in the First Pentad." *Transactions of the American Philological Association* 117: 203–226.

Vasaly, Ann. 1988. "*Ars dispositionis*: Cicero's Second Agrarian Speech." *Hermes* 116: 409–27.

Vasaly, Ann. 1993. *Representations: Images of the World in Ciceronian Oratory*. Berkeley.

Versnel, H.S. 1970. *Triumphus: An Inquiry into the Origin, Development and Meaning of the Roman Triumph*. Leiden.

Veyne, Paul. 1964. Review of Jonkers 1963. *Latomus* 23: 573–574.

Vishina, R.F. 2012. *Roman Elections in the Age of Cicero: Society, Government, and Voting*. New York; London.

Walde, Alois, and Hofmann, J.B. 1938. *Lateinisches etymologisches Wörterbuch*. 3, neubearb. aufl. Heidelberg.

Wallace-Hadrill, A. (ed.) 1989. *Patronage in Ancient Society*. London, New York.

Ward, A.M. 1970. "Politics in the Trials of Manilius and Cornelius." *Transactions and Proceedings of the American Philological Association* 101: 545–556.

Ward, A.M. 1972. "Cicero's Fight against Crassus and Caesar in 65 and 63 B.C." *Historia* 21: 244–58.

Ward, A.M. 1977. *Marcus Crassus and the Late Roman Republic*. Columbia/London.

Waters, K.H. 1970. "Cicero, Sallust and Catiline." *Historia: Zeitschrift für Alte Geschichte*, 2: 195–215.

Watson, A. 1968. *The Law of Property in the Later Roman Republic*. Oxford.

Webster, Jonathan (ed.) 2015. *The Bloomsbury Companion to M.A.K. Halliday*. London/New York.

West, M.L. 1992. *Ancient Greek Music*. Oxford.

Wet, B.X. de. 1981. "Aspects of Plutarch's Portrayal of Pompey." *Acta Classica* 24: 119–32.

White, K.D. 1967. *Bulletin of the Institute of Classical Studies* 14: 62–79.

Whitehead, Simon. 2005. "Cicero's *vir clarissimus*," in Welch, Kathryn and T.W. Hillard (eds.), *Roman Crossings: Theory and practice in the Roman Republic*, Swansea/Oakville, CT: 141–208.

Williamson, C. 2005. *The Laws of the Roman people: Public Law in the Expansion and Decline of the Roman Republic*. Ann Arbor.

Wirszubski, C. 1960. *Libertas as a Political Idea at Rome During the Late Republic and Early Principate*. Cambridge.

Wiseman, T.P. 1969. "The Census in the First Century BC." *The Journal of Roman Studies* 59.1/2: 59–75.

Wiseman, T.P. 1971. *New Men in the Roman Senate. 139 B.C.–A.D. 14*. Oxford Classical and Philosophical Monographs. Oxford.

Wiseman, T.P. 1994. "The Senate and the *populares*, 69–60 B.C.," in Crook, J.A., A. A. Lintott, and E. Rawson (eds.), *The Cambridge Ancient History. Second Edition. Volume IX. The Last Age of the Roman Republic, 146–43 B.C.*, Cambridge: 327–67.

Wiseman, T.P. 2009. *Remembering the Roman People: Essays on Later Republican Politics and Literature*. Oxford.

Wiseman, T.P. 2014. "Popular Memory," in Galinsky, Karl (ed.), *MEMORIA ROMANA: Memory in Rome and Rome in Memory* (Memoirs of the American Academy in Rome, Supplementary Volume 10), Rome: 43–62.

Wissowa, G. 1912. *Religion und Kultus d. Römer*. 2nd ed. Munich.

Wood, Neal. 1983. "The Economic Dimension of Cicero's Political Thought: Property and State." *Canadian Journal of Political Science / Revue canadienne de science politique* 16.4: 739–756.

Wood, Neal. 1983. 1988. *Cicero's Social and Political Thought*. Berkeley/Los Angeles/London.

Yakobson, A. 1992. "*Petitio et Largitio*: Popular Participation in the Centuriate Assembly of the Late Republic." *The Journal of Roman Studies* 82: 32–52.

Yakobson, A. 1995. "Secret ballot and its effects in the late Roman Republic." *Hermes* 123: 426–442.

Yakobson, A. 1999. *Elections and Electioneering in Rome*. Stuttgart.

Yakobson, A. 2010. "Traditional Political Culture and the People's Role in the Roman Republic." *Historia: Zeitschrift für Alte Geschichte* 59.3: 282–302.

Yavetz, Zvi. 1974. "*Existimatio, Fama*, and the Ides of March." *Harvard Studies in Classical Philology* 78: 35–65.

Yonge, C. D. 1912. *Select Orations of Marcus Tullius Cicero; Literally Translated with Explanatory Notes*. Chicago.

Zarnott, W. Geoffrey. 2007. *Birds in the Ancient World from A to Z*. New York.

Zielinski, T. 1904. *Das Clauselgesetz in Ciceros Reden. Grundzüge einer oratorischen Rhythmik*. Leipzig.

Zimmerman, Reinhard. 1990. *The Law of Obligations: Roman Foundations of the Civilian Tradition*. Oxford.

Zumpt, A.W. 1861. *M. Tullii Ciceronis orationes tres de lege agraria*. Berlin.

Index

For the benefit of digital users, indexed terms that span two pages (e.g., 52–53) may, on occasion, appear on only one of those pages.
Tables and figures are indicated by *t* and *f* following the page number.

Argument, Techniques of
 argumentum a fortiori, 40, 56–57,
  91–93, 105, 108–9, 110–11, 135,
  304–5, 306n.38, 310
 inversions and
  reconfigurations, 96–97
 of *dignitas*, 246–86 *passim*
 of *diligentia*, 82
 of Gabinian and Manilian
  laws, 103–4 (*see also under*
  Legal Concepts:
  lex Manilia)
 of *index* of a law, 207
 of *libertas*, 98–140 *passim*
 of list of properties into auction
  lot, 71–79
 of *nobilitas*, 184–86, 203–4
 of *otium*, 196–99, 243–44, 293–
  95, 296
 of *patres conscripti* into *patres*
  familiarum, 85
 of personal appearance,
  Brutus, 304–5
 of personal appearance,
  Rullus, 167–68
 of rhetoric against
  Pompey, 160–61
 of staff and equipment of
  decemvirs, 223–25
 of Sulla's statue, 112–13, 139,
  140, 253–54
 Local Context, 14–15
  and *dignitas*, 246–86 *passim*
  and *libertas*, 98–140 *passim*
  and *popularis*, 192–93
  and Roman civic life, 175–76
 Projected Significance, 13–14,
  18, 49–50
 Projected Identity, 17–18
  of Cicero
   chairman of *repetundae* court,
    53–54, 85
   constans, 279–80
   consul popularis, 180–200, 245
   '*consul senatorius*,' 246–47
   friend in the
    marketplace, 172–73
   good guardian, 169–70, 175–76
   of but above his audiences, 7
   magister auctionis, 72–73, 85
  onto the people, 11, 17–18, 56–58,
   59–60, 84–85, 103–4, 120,
   139–40, 294, 297–98
  onto Pompey, 208–9, 217–20

Argument, Techniques of (*cont.*)
  onto the senate, 11, 17, 56–57, 58–59, 60–61, 85, 122–23, 269–70, 271–72, 275, 307–8
  onto Rullus
    arrogant noble, 124–25, 207–10
    disordered soul, 279–80
    head of cabal, 205
    helluo, 79–80
    hungry dog or pig, 82–84
    nepos, 71, 80–81
    nepotist, 231–38
    poor guardian, 168–69, 175–76, 237–38
    regal overlord, 134–35, 205, 220–26
Places and place names, use of semiotics of
  Campus Martius (crowding), 299–300
  Cappadocia (darkness), 124, 135–36
  Capua, layout of (expansive), 305–7
  Carthage (dedication), 250–52
  centumviral court (transparency), 135–36
  Egypt (corrupting kingdom), 131–32
  Forum Holitorium (compared to Capua), 302–3
  Forum Romanum (communal life), 175–76
  Janiculum (enemy colony), 268–69
  marketplaces (fair transactions), 172–73
  mons Massicus (good wine), 168–69
  Paphlagonia (darkness), 124, 135–36
  Pompey's camp (proxemics), 156
  Rome, city gates of (colonial ritual), 170, 176
  Rome, streets and buildings of (crowded), 305–7
  Salapia (poor land), 174–75
  Saxetum (?) (poor land), 171–72

  Sila silva (distant forestland), 168–69
  silva Scantia (state possession), 86–89
  Sipontum (poor land), 174–75
  Sulla, statue of (respect for sovereignty), 112–13, 140
  Temple of Jupiter Capitolinus (symbol of Roman order), 91, 253–54, 312
Unnamed Referent, 14, 65
  bonorum venditio, 74–75
  coheredes, 297–98
  colonization ritual, 170
  constantia, 279–80
  dignitas, 39, 61–62
  emptio vendito, 172–73
  fides, 190–91
  Forum Holitorium, 302–3
  libertas, 39, 61–62, 104, 139, 169–70
  licentia, 108–10, 265–66
  nobilitas, 184–85, 192–93, 199–200
  observantia, 190–91
  philosophical discourse, 279–80
  Pompey, 282–83
  potestas tribunicia, 230–31, 245
  provincial governor, 61–64, 157–58
  Second Decemvirate, 225–26

Figures of Speech and Thought
  amplificatio, 12–13, 71, 122–23
  commoratio, 208–9
  complexio, 114, 115*t*, 118, 118*t*, 120–21, 131–32, 136–37
  congeries, 175–76
  demonstratio, 55–56, 156n.33
  exsuperatio, 95–96
  figura etymologica, 54–55, 61–62, 90, 309
  interpretatio, 80–81
  pronominatio, 51–52, 79–80

προσωποποιία, 154
transgressio, 80–81

Latin words and phrases
adfectare viam, 271–72
adferre, referre, 87–88
appetens, 133
appetitus, 280–81
armis et virtute, 91–92
auctio, 71
calamitas, 49
carmen, 233–34
clarus, 203–4, 250–52
claustrum, 307–8
coacervare, 164t n.vi
committere, 57
concursatio, 54, 61–62
condonare, 57
constipare, 297
consulere, 144–45
credere, 278–79
cuniculi, 137–38
deducere, 55–56, 163t n.i
deliberare, 169–70
dignitas 'magistracy', 184–85
disperdere, 80–81, 84–85
divendere, 10–11, 13–14, 109–10
efflagito, 188
egredi, 56–57
(e)nitere, 308–9
eruere, 82–84
-etum, 171–72
ex ordine, 72–73
excutere, 217–18
eximia virtus, 250–52
existimatio, 185–86
felicitas, felix, 205–6, 250–52
formosus, 63, 157–58
fortis, 92–93
helluo, 79–80
immittere, 45, 47
impetrare, 188

indagare, 82–84
iners, 92–93
inlucesco, 280–81
insignia, 252–53, 311–12
intus canere, 233–34
ira, 279–80
iudicium et potestas, 54–55, 152–54
lex et condicio, 192
libido, 111–12
luctus, 74–75
lux, 176, 187
mea, sua lege, 11n.38, 154
metus, 46–47, 54, 60–61, 78–79, 279–80, 283
miles (collective singular), 308–9
minister, 223–25
miser, 47
nequissimi homines, 108–9
nervi, 75
nimirum, 237–38
nonne, 48–49
nummatus, 123–24
opes evertere, 159–60
pacatus, 91
pecunia, praesens and certa, 82–84
penes, 152–54
permittere ut possint, 10–11, 108
perturbatio, perturbatio animi, 277–78, 279–82, 283
polliceri et confirmare, 245
posse, 170–71
praedicare, 72–73, 299
praesto, 155
privatus, 47–48
proscribere, 90
recitare, 72
robustus, 299
sanctus, 58–59, 62
satelles, 223–25, 299
sedes antiqua(e), 123–24
sedes hospitalis, 55–56
stipator, 223–25

Latin words and phrases (*cont.*)
  stridor, 235–36
  tamen . . . sane, 87–88
  tangere, 229
  terror, 46–47, 60–61
  unctus, 82–84
  vagari, 45, 47
  vectigal ('exaction'), 124–25
  velificari, 284–85
  vinculum pacis et monumentum belli, 301–2

Legal Concepts, Features, and Mechanisms

aequa ex parte (see *societas*)
aequitas, 87–88, 120–21
  and agrarian laws, 5n.19
  and Egypt, 133
  and Pompey's spoils, 217–18
  as a quality of magistrates, 241–42
  and the *Recentorici*, 120–21, 122–23
  and the sale of Italian properties, 87–88
ager publicus, 27–28
  and agrarian law, 161–62
  ager Recentoricus as a special type of, 113n.51
  boundaries established by holder of *imperium*, 222–23
  reclaimed abroad, 55–56
  source of funds for the Rullan bill
    by sale, 39, 76, 126
    by tax, 262–63
  source of settlement sites, 27–28, 161–62, 166n.52, 173, 287–88, 299–300
ager vectigalis
  established by the elders, 301–2
  source of funds for the Rullan bill, 66, 75, 88–89, 105, 113–14, 147–48, 238–39, 247, 267, 311–12

amplitudo, 122–23, 291–92, 300–3, 305–7
auctio
  of Italian and Sicilian properties, 66t, 72–75, 77, 89, 90
  of Pompey's gains, 156, 158
aurum coronarium, 254–55, 259
bona fides, 172–73
bonorum emtio (see *bonorum venditio*)
bonorum venditio, 73–75, 112–13
  as symbol of impersonal power of law, 77
cautio, 206–7
clientela, 144–45, 146
colonial foundation, 170
contio (see under Social and Political Concepts and Practices)
dicta et promissa, 172–73
emptio venditio, 172–73, 229
familiae (h)erciscundae actio, 297–98
imperium
  of Cicero, 240
  of commanders, 152–54, 250–52, 254–55
  of *liberi legati*, 56–57
  of magistrates, 132–33
  of provincial governors, 62
  of Rullan decemvirs, 3–4, 45–46n.11, 52–53, 62–63, 158, 222–25, 265–66
lex Gabinia, 22, 57, 59–60, 63–64, 102, 103–4
index (of a law), 207
iudicium et potestas, 54–55, 152–54
lex Manilia, 22, 57, 59–60, 63–64, 102, 103–4, 142n.4, 160–61, 166–67, 219–20
libera legatio, liberi legati, 39–40, 47–48, 49, 56–57, 60–61
manubiae, 157–58, 254–55, 259, 260, 261 (see also *praeda*)
notio, 119–21

pascua censorum, 86–89
patrimonium, 85, 297–98
pecuniae residuae, 254–55, 260
pontifex maximus, electoral
    mechanism for, 34–36, 201–2
  used in Rullan bill, 142–44
praeda, 254–55, 259, 260, 261 (see also
    manubiae)
  from Sulla's proscriptions, 110–11
praescriptio (of a law), 207
privilegium, 214
quaestio
  de maiestate, 103–4
  new one allegedly established by
    Rullan bill, 255, 261
  peculatus, 255, 260
  de sicariis et veneficis, 55n.36
  de repetundis, 53–54
relictae possessiones, 86–89
societas, 207
tax property (see *ager vectigalis*)
vectigalia (see *ager vectigalis*)

Persons
  Aemilianus, Scipio (P. Cornelius
    Scipio Africanus
    Aemilianus), 121–22
  Caesar, C. Julius
    decries inflammatory rhetoric
      (in Sallust), 314–15
    and Egypt, 127, 136n.101, 314
    elected *pontifex maximus* by
      bribery, 34–36
    exacerbates debt on return, 26–27
    land law of, 19n.63, 30n.113, 34–36,
      96, 200–1, 223n.23, 288n.2,
      313–14, 317
    prosecutes killers of
      proscribed, 23–24
    re-erects Sulla's statue, 112n.49
    settles veterans in *ager*
      Campanus, 273–74
    supports popular election of
      pontifex maximus, 201–2
  Catiline (L. Sergius Catilina), 3–4, 24,
    49–50, 51n.24, 146–47, 243–
    44, 304
  Clodius (P. Clodius Pulcher), 86n.68,
    96, 167–68, 314
  Cotta, Gaius Aurelius, 113–14n.52, 121–22
  Crassus (M. Licinius Crassus)
    attempts to gain control of
      Egypt, 127–32
    finances Caesar's election as *pontifex*
      maximus, 34–36
    hopes to gain from the Rullan
      bill, 51–52
  Gracchi, Tiberius and Gaius
    Sempronii, 23–24, 199n.50,
    204n.63, 230–31, 299–300,
    307–8, 317
    Gaius, 17, 23–24, 105, 123n.71, 305–6
    Tiberius, 23–24, 100–1,
      134n.95, 167–68
  Hiempsal, 113–14, 121–22, 123–24,
    139, 269–70
  Juba, 123–24
  Lucullus (L. Licinius Lucullus)
    replaced by Pompey, 22, 33n.120,
      59–60, 153n.21, 160–61
    spoils targeted by Rullan bill, 160–
      61, 213–14, 259–60
  Marius, Gaius, as symbol of
    meritocracy, 185–86, 189–
    90, 205–6
  Pompey (Cn. Pompeius)
    Brutus killed because of, 304–5
    created peace, 198–99, 259–
      60, 282–83
    and Faustus Sulla, 261–62
    lawful possessor of Mithridatic
      territories, 154, 156
    lex Manilia an act of trust to, 57,
      59–60, 102

Persons (cont.)
    likened to triumphing generals,
        253–54, 271–72
    and Lucullus, 160–61
    and popular self-assertion, 147
    prospect of return, 26–27, 283
    Rullan bill benefits, 4, 30–32,
        51–52, 113–14, 267,
        313–14
    Rullan bill diminishes, 157–61,
        238–39, 267, 271–72
    Rullus' letter to, 155–56
    symbol of sovereignty, 207–11
  Rullus, Publius Servilius
    agrarian law, features of
        (*see* Rullan bill)
    career of, 2n.3
    as configured in *LA* 1 and 2
        (*see under* Argument:
        Projected Identity)
  Servilius, Publius (P. Servilius Vatia
    Isauricus), 250–52
  Sulla (Lucius Cornelius Sulla)
    abrogates electoral mechanism for
        pontifex maximus, 201–2
    auctions of, 110–11
    colonies of, 24–26, 168–69, 174–75,
        227–28, 235–36, 238–39,
        273–74, 286, 293f, 294–96,
        299, 313–14
    dissolves Capuan colony, 304
    Egyptian policies, 127, 136–37
    Felix, 205–6
    legacy, 261–62
    proscriptions, 21–22, 112–13, 260
    seized land, 126, 232–33, 299–300
    statue
        reconfigured, 112–13, 139,
            140, 253–54
        re-erected by Caesar, 112n.49
  Sulla, Faustus, 260, 261–62

**Rullan bill (*rogatio Servilia*),
    features of**
  appeal of decisions not permitted,
    222n.17, 239–40n.75
  candidates declare in person, 207–8
  colonial sites not specified, 31
  compared to *lex Gabinia* and *lex
    Manilia*, 63–64
  electoral mechanism
    (*see under* Legal
    Concepts: *pontifex
    maximus*, electoral
    mechanism for)
  funds, sources of
    sale of lands (*see also* Legal
        Concepts: *ager vectigalis*)
    Italy and Sicily, properties
        in, 32–33, 76
    properties recensed by the senate in
        81, 105
    public properties acquired
        after 88, 126
    spoils of war, 31–32
        Pompey exempted, 4, 207–8,
            267
    tax, 113–14
  imperium, 33–34, 39 (*see also* Legal
    Concepts: *imperium*)
    not confirmed by *lex curiata*, 34–36
  land for settlement, sources
    of, 28–29
    colonies in *Ager Campanus* and
        Ager Stella(ti)s, 28–29, 273
    Sullan colonies, 227–28
  land, type of for colonies, 170–71
  permitted local sales, 105
  praetoria potestas, 32–33, 222–25
  resettled Italians (?), 30–31
  title, granting of to new
    possessors, 29–30
  travel at state expense, 39